How To Use This Book

This book starts where most C tutorials leave off—just before you get into the really cool stuff! Fear not. If you are looking to take your programming knowledge to the next level, you've made the right purchase. This book provides useful tips and hands-on examples for developing your own application with the C programming language. You get a deeper understanding of several important C concepts, such as memory allocation and complex data types, then you learn application development through the design of a personal database.

Specific features that you'll see throughout the book are:

Do/Don't boxes: These give you specific guidance on what to do and what to avoid doing when programming in C.

 Notes: These provide essential background information so that you not only learn how to do things with C, but have a good understanding of what you're doing and why.

 Review Tips: It would be nice to remember everything you've previously learned, but that's just about impossible. If there is important C material that you have to know, these tips will remind you.

Expert Tips: Here's where the authors share their insight and experience as professional programmers—common bugs they've faced, time-saving coding techniques they've used, and pitfalls they've fallen into. Learn from their experiences.

Who Should Read This Book

Anyone who knows some C—through a primer book or an introductory class—but wants to learn more will benefit by reading this book. You spend several days covering advanced topics, yet a majority of this book is dedicated to helping you apply the C language to real applications. It is this hands-on knowledge of the C language that sets this book apart from others. In addition to helping you develop an appplication, you learn the concepts involved in development. As an added bonus during the development process, you will create a library of functions that you are sure to find useful.

Conventions

C listings are broken into three sections:

 The type icon denotes a new program for you to enter into your editor.

 The output icon highlights the results of compiling and executing the program.

 Analysis of the programs reveals insights and information about several key lines of the listing.

Throughout this book, the emphasis has been on providing useful information in a way that is fast, easy, and fun.

Teach
Yourself
Advanced C

in 21 Days

Teach Yourself
Advanced C
in 21 Days

Bradley L. Jones
Gregory L. Guntle

SAMS
PUBLISHING

A Division of Prentice Hall Computer Publishing
201 West 103rd Street, Indianapolis, Indiana 46290

This book is dedicated to all the people who have counted the stars at Beaubien, walked in the snows of Mt. Baldy in July, or gazed at the eagles hovering over Ponil. Like learning a programming language, going to such places takes hard work and dedication. But once they are reached, the value of the hard work is realized. To these people, this book is dedicated.

About the Authors

Bradley Jones

Bradley Jones is a professional programmer specializing in C development. He has helped in the development of systems for several national and international corporations. As an active member of the Indianapolis Computer Society, he heads the teaching of C and C++ as a leader of the C/C++ SIG. Bradley's other writings include co-authoring the bestseller, *Teach Yourself C in 21 Days* and *Even You Can Soup Up and Fix PCs*. He is the Chairman of the *INDY PC News* magazine, and is also a regular writer on topics ranging from C programming to virtual reality.

Gregory Guntle

Gregory Guntle has been working with microcomputers for 15 years. He has been doing technical editing for nine years. Formerly, he was manager of PC programming at RCI; he now supervises the installation and use of PCs in the company.

Overview

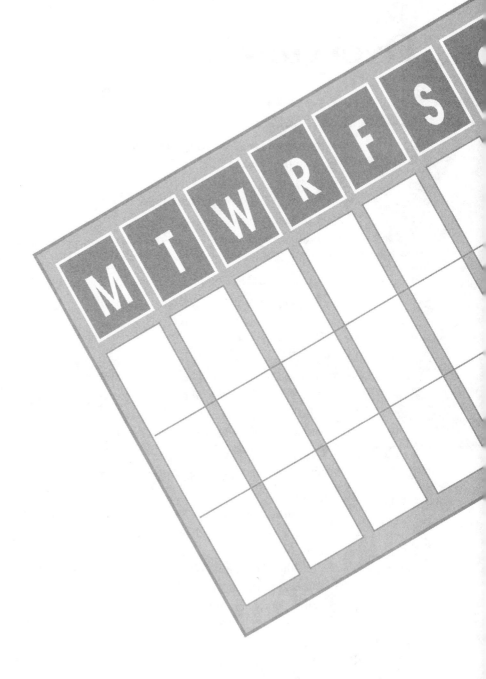

Contents

Acknowledgments

Pulling together a book takes a great deal of effort. Many people are involved in the process both directly and indirectly. Many of the people who were involved are listed in the book, several are not.

I would like to thank many of my coworkers for their support and encouragement in my writing of this book. It is helpful to have the support of such people as Connie, Dee, Mike, Paul, Dawn R., and the others.

I would like to thank Fran Hatton. Fran was the production editor who had the task of reading the book and guiding it to its completion. Fran, along with Mitzi Foster Gianakos, offered many good suggestions that helped to make this a better book. In addition, Dean Miller should be given credit for ensuring that I turned the chapters in on time. Greg Croy deserves thanks for thinking of me when this book was proposed.

I would like to especially thank Greg Guntle whose name also appears on this book. With the help of his technical expertise, we were able to bring a new level to this book. His background helped to create many of the functions that you will find extremely useful in your programming endeavors.

I would also like to thank Ray Werner. Ray provided Greg and me the means of communicating back and forth. Ray's Bulletin Board, The Electronic Editor, was a critical factor in the quick completion of this book. I greatly appreciate Ray's help in providing the board. Ray, who is also an author of many computer books, has truly been a valuable friend.

A special thanks goes to you, the reader, for purchasing this book. It is my hope that from this book you will be able to take a basic understanding of C and learn to apply it to developing applications that can be used at a professional level.

A final thanks goes to my wife, Melissa. Because of the short time frames allowed for writing a book, most of my free time has been spent at the computer. Her support in my writing has always been a critical factor in the success of this and my other books.

Introduction

Welcome to *Teach Yourself Advanced C in 21 Days*! This introduction begins the journey into many topics on C. In this introduction, you will learn:

☐ Who this book is intended for.

☐ Why you should use **this** C book.

☐ How the book has been layed out.

Why Advanced C and Why 21 Days?

By picking up this book, you have shown that you are interested in the C programming language. This book has been created to begin teaching where most C books stop. Because the basics of the C language are not covered, this book has been deemed advanced.

This book works through 21 days of material. Why 21 days? Twenty-one days is enough time to cover a great deal of material without taking so long that you, the reader, lose interest. While this book may seem thick, you will find that most chapters will take from one to three hours. The time each chapter will require depends on you. If you simply read the chapter, you will only need about an hour. If you type in the code (although all of it is included on the disk) and if you work the exercises that are provided to help your understanding, then the amount of time needed will increase.

The Assumptions About the Reader

In writing this book, I have made a few assumptions. I have assumed that you are already familiar with the basics of the C language. If you are not, then this book is not for you—at least not yet. As stated before, this book picks up where most C books stop. This book does not teach the basics of C. Nearly any other C book will suffice for providing you beginning knowledge. The book, *Teach Yourself C in 21 Days*, would be a good starting point; however, any beginning level C book will suffice.

The second assumption that I have made is that you don't want to just know the C language, but that you also want to know how to apply it. While you will spend several days covering advanced topics, a majority of this book is dedicated to helping you apply the C language to real applications. It is this application of the C language that helps to differ this book from others. In addition to helping you develop an application, you will learn the concepts involved in development. As an added bonus, during the development process you will create a library of functions that you will find useful.

What This Book Is About

This book starts by building on many of the topics presented in most beginning book. Day 1 jumps right into the material by presenting memory allocation concepts. This is followed by several additional days of advanced topics ranging from linked lists to using system resources.

Warning: The first few days will present concepts that are covered in some beginning C books. The information will differ from what is presented in beginning books in that it will not start at the beginning level. Instead, I have assumed that you already have a basic understanding of the concepts. In addition, they will not stop where most beginning books stop—they will go much farther. You will see how many of the beginning concepts that you already know can become complex.

Farther into the book, you will begin learning development techniques. This will include topics such as tips for writing portable code, creating and using libraries, writing structured computer applications, debugging, and much more.

This book has been designed to aid in your full understanding of using the C language and in applying it to real world applications. You will develop a multitude of functions. You will want to use many of these functions in your C programs.

By working through the developement of a real application, you will understand how to develop your own. In fact, you will easily be able to take what you learn from this book, along with the coding examples, and create your own applications. You could be doing this in just a few weeks.

What You Will Gain from This Book

When you complete this book, you will have a library of useful functions. In addition, you will have an application that you will be able to modify to your own uses. With this application, you will also have the knowledge to develop full-fledged applications on your own.

Hopefully, you are ready to begin your first week of learning advanced C. In this first week, you cover a lot of ground. Each day will present you with a different topic. Although it is suggested that you cover each topic in order, it is not necessary to do so during this first week.

On Day 1, you learn about allocating memory dynamically. Allocating memory dynamically is presented first because of its importance. Although you may not have used dynamic memory up to this point, as you develop larger programs, it will be quite useful.

On Day 2, you move into complex data types. Complex data types are extensions of the data types presented in most C books. In fact, you are probably already familiar with some of them. Complex data types include arrays of structures, function pointers, and variable length structures.

You move into one of the most confusing areas for C programmers on Day 3—linked lists. This is a topic that many C programmers manage to avoid; however, there are times when linked lists can be the perfect solution to a problem.

On Day 4, you have the most fun in the first week (later days will be even more fun). It is on Day 4 that you are shown some of the basic ways of tapping into the system resources of your computer. A couple of the things you will be doing on Day 4 include displaying colorful text on your screen and placing the cursor anywhere you want it.

Day 5 moves into a topic that is important if you plan to move or port your C programs to different computers or different compilers. Portablity is one of the key features of the C language, and Day 5 will help you understand how to keep your code portable. In addition, you will obtain an overview of how to write efficient code.

On Day 6, you will be introduced to a topic that is often hidden in the back of most programming books. The computer works with numbers while people work with text. This chapter helps you bridge the gap so that you can understand how the computer's numbers and your text are related.

The final day of the week is extremely important. This is an introduction to libraries. You may not have known it, but every C program you have written has used at least one library! Every compiler comes with its own libraries. In addition to these provided libraries, you can also create your own. On Day 7, you will create and use your own library.

The second and third weeks will diverge from the first week. You will begin the second week by developing a multitude of library functions. As the second week progresses, you will learn about developing applications. Not only will you learn the coding aspects of application development, you will also learn issues surrounding design and planning. By the end of the second week, you will be well into developing and coding a full-fledged C application.

The third week is dedicated mostly to continuing the development of the application started in the second week. Reporting, incorporating help, testing, and more will all be presented. At the end of the third week, you will have a complete understanding of all aspects of application development.

This is where you're headed. For now you should take things one day at a time. A good place to start is Day 1.

Storage Space: Working with Memory

How you use memory can make or break a program. As you write bigger and more dynamic programs, you need a better understanding of how your C programs use memory. Today will you learn:

☐ Why first understanding memory is important.

☐ What kind of storage different C variable types require.

☐ What dynamic memory allocation is.

☐ How to dynamically allocate memory with `malloc()`.

☐ What other memory functions will be of use.

It is important that you understand the complexities involved with memory. Starting with Day 2, "Complex Data Types," you will be writing programs that may require dynamically allocating memory.

Why Start the 21 Days with Memory Usage?

It is assumed that you have a basic understanding of the C language. In most beginning C books and beginning C classes, the overall objective is to teach C. The approach most often taken is to present the C keywords and explain what they can do. In addition, many of the common functions, such as `printf()`, that come with C compilers are presented along with what they can do. In presenting these basic concepts, relatively small programs are used, making memory conservation irrelevant.

As you begin to write bigger programs, you will find memory management to be of vital importance. You will find that to avoid running out of memory, your programs will be required to manage the memory needed. This book will quickly get into topics where it will be best to only use the memory you need. In addition, you may not always know how much memory you need until you run the program. This is definitely the case when you work with variable length structures on Day 2. You will find that understanding memory usage is almost mandatory when working with some complex data types and advanced C topics.

Variable Storage Requirements

Everything in C uses memory in one way or another. Listing 1.1 is an expanded version of a program that can be found in virtually all beginning C books. This

program displays the amount of storage space (memory) needed for different variable types and other C constructs.

 Listing 1.1. C variable sizes.

```
1:   /* Filename:  LIST0101.c
2:    * Author  :  Bradley L. Jones
3:    * Purpose :  This program prints the size of various C
4:    *            variable types and constructs.
5:    *=========================================================*/
6:
7:   #include <stdio.h>
8:
9:   void main(void)
10:  {
11:     char   *char_ptr;
12:     int    *int_ptr;
13:     long   *long_ptr;
14:     short  *short_ptr;
15:     float  *float_ptr;
16:     double *double_ptr;
17:     char   far *far_char_ptr;
18:
19:     struct test_tag {
20:        char a;
21:        int  b;
22:        }test_struct;
23:
24:     printf( "\n Type              Size " );
25:     printf( "\n===========================" );
26:     printf( "\n character         %d ", sizeof( char  ));
27:     printf( "\n integer           %d ", sizeof( int   ));
28:     printf( "\n short             %d ", sizeof( short ));
29:     printf( "\n long              %d ", sizeof( long  ));
30:     printf( "\n float             %d ", sizeof( float ));
31:     printf( "\n double            %d ", sizeof( double));
32:     printf( "\n char pointer      %d ", sizeof( char_ptr   ));
33:     printf( "\n int pointer       %d ", sizeof( int_ptr    ));
34:     printf( "\n short pointer     %d ", sizeof( short_ptr  ));
35:     printf( "\n long pointer      %d ", sizeof( long_ptr   ));
36:     printf( "\n float pointer     %d ", sizeof( float_ptr  ));
37:     printf( "\n double pointer    %d ", sizeof( double_ptr));
38:     printf( "\n far char pointer  %d ", sizeof( far_char_ptr));
39:     printf( "\n test_structure    %d ", sizeof( test_struct));
40:     printf( "\n===========================");
41:  }
```

```
Type            Size
===========================
character       1
integer         2
short           2
long            4
float           4
double          8
char pointer    2
int pointer     2
short pointer   2
long pointer    2
float pointer   2
double pointer  2
far char pointer 4
test_structure  4
===========================
```

As you can see from the output, different variable types are different sizes. This program simply uses the `sizeof` operator in conjunction with `printf()` to display the sizes of different variable types. Lines 26 through 31 print the standard C variable types. To make the program clearer, lines 11 to 17 declare pointer variables to be used in the `printf()` calls in lines 32 to 38. In line 39, a `test_struct` structure is printed. This structure was declared in lines 19 to 22. Depending on your compiler's settings, this may be off by 1 byte in size due to byte alignment. When the output was compiled, byte alignment was on. Byte alignment is covered on Day 2.

Review Tip: Remember, `sizeof` is a C keyword used to determine the size of any item in C.

Depending on what size machine you are using, your output—the sizes printed—may be different. For example, a mainframe C compiler may interpret an integer as being 4 bytes long instead of two. For virtually all IBM PC-compatible compilers, the sizes should match those given in the preceding output, with a possible exception being the structure—if byte alignment is off, it may be three instead of four.

Allocating at Compile Time

In Listing 1.1, the storage space required for all the variables was determined at the time the program was compiled. For a program to compile and later run, enough memory will have to be available for the program and all its variable allocations. In a

small program such as Listing 1.1, this is not a concern because there should always be more than enough available memory for the few variables being allocated.

Consider the case of having the following declaration in your program:

```
char buffer[1000];
```

When the program is compiled, a requirement of 1000 bytes of memory will be added to the memory requirements of the rest of the program. If the total of the program's memory requirements is not available, the program will not run. When the program runs, 1000 bytes of memory will be set aside to be used as the buffer character array. If buffer is never used to store information that is 1000 bytes long, memory space is wasted.

Consider a second example such as the following array:

```
char user_name[???];
```

If user_name is going to store my first name, "Bradley," it needs to be 8 characters long. Of course, I am assuming that only my first name is going to be stored, but what if my last name is supposed to be included also? If user_name is 8 characters long, there isn't room for my full name. In addition, if user_name is going to be used to store other names, it will need to be big enough to hold the largest.

Review Tip: Don't forget that "Bradley" takes 8 bytes to store—the eighth byte is for the Null terminator.

A name is a simplistic example because the number of bytes are minimal; however, it easily illustrates the point. Most programmers will set a certain size for a name field and allow the space to be wasted. What if you have an array of names? Listing 1.2 demonstrates how memory can be wasted.

Listing 1.2. A program showing wasted memory.

```
1:   /* Filename:  LIST0102.c
2:    * Author   :  Bradley L. Jones
3:    * Purpose  :  This provides an example of allocating memory
4:    *             for an array.
5:    *=========================================================*/
6:
7:   #include <stdio.h>
8:
```

continues

Listing 1.2. continued

```
 9:   #define MAX 100
10:
11:   void main(void)
12:   {
13:       char student_name[MAX][35];
14:
15:       long x;
16:
17:       printf("\nEnter student names, a blank line will end\n");
18:
19:       for( x = 0; x < MAX; x++ )
20:       {
21:           printf("Enter student %5.5d: ", x+1);
22:           gets(student_name[x]);
23:
24:           if( student_name[x][0] == '\0')
25:               x = MAX;
26:       }
27:
28:       printf("\n\nYou entered the following:\n");
29:
30:       for ( x = 0; student_name[x][0] != '\0' && x < MAX; x++ )
31:       {
32:           printf("\nStudent %5.5d:", x+1);
33:           printf(" %s", student_name[x]);
34:       }
35:
36:   }
```

Output

```
Enter student names, a blank line will end
Enter student 00001: Connie Crank
Enter student 00002: Deanna Alexander
Enter student 00003: Dawn Johnson
Enter student 00004: Bruce Crouch
Enter student 00005: Sherman Denman
Enter student 00006:


You entered the following:

Student 00001: Connie Crank
Student 00002: Deanna Alexander
Student 00003: Dawn Johnson
Student 00004: Bruce Crouch
Student 00005: Sherman Denman
```

 Analysis This program allows you to enter up to MAX number of students. In this case, MAX is defined as 100 in line 9. If you are entering only the number of students in a single class, you may only need 20 to 30, but what if you are entering the names of all the students in the United States? In this case, you are going to need more than 100 students. To increase the value of MAX from 100, you have to modify the code and recompile. This means the program, at present, is only useful to people wanting to enter 100 or fewer names.

There is another problem that can be illustrated with this listing. Change line 9 to define MAX as 100,000. This is not large enough to enter all the students in the United States, but it should handle all the students in a large city. Recompile the program. You may find that you can't recompile! You will probably get an error similar to the following:

```
Error LIST0102.C ##: Array size too large
```

The compiler knows that you are trying to use too much memory. Because of the way the computer addresses memory, you are limited to 64K of memory for data. Later today, you will see how to get around this limitation.

Dynamic Memory Allocation

One way to avoid trying to second guess the number of variables or the amount of memory you require is to dynamically allocate memory. Dynamic allocation of memory means that memory is requested when it is needed. Instead of determining memory requirements at the time the program is compiled, memory is requested as the program is running. This means that if your program doesn't need the memory, the memory is left available. In addition, the program will only need to request the memory it requires. If you are collecting the names of only 352 students, you only reserve memory for the 352 students.

There are several general functions that are used when allocating memory dynamically. To be effective in your use of dynamically allocated memory, you should understand the purpose of each of these. These include:

- ☐ malloc()
- ☐ free()
- ☐ realloc()
- ☐ calloc()

9

The *malloc()* Function

Among the more popular functions to allocate memory is `malloc()`. The `malloc()` function enables you to set aside a specified number of bytes of memory. The function prototype for `malloc()` is

```
void *malloc(size_t size);
```

This prototype is found in the STDLIB.H header file of most compilers. This memory allocation function sets aside *size* bytes of memory and returns a pointer to the starting byte of the newly allocated memory. This pointer can then be used as a reference to the allocated memory. If there is not enough memory available, then NULL is returned. Listing 1.3 presents an example of `malloc()`'s use.

Type **Listing 1.3. Using the `malloc()` function.**

```
 1:  /* Filename:  LIST0103.c
 2:   * Author  :  Bradley L. Jones
 3:   * Purpose :  This provides an example of allocating memory
 4:   *            for an array dynamically.
 5:   *=========================================================*/
 6:
 7:  #include <stdio.h>
 8:  #include <stdlib.h>
 9:
10:  void main(void)
11:  {
12:     long nbr_students = 0;
13:     long ctr;
14:
15:     char *student_name;
16:     char trash[80];      /* to clear keyboard buffer */
17:
18:     while( nbr_students < 1 ¦¦ nbr_students > 2000000000 )
19:     {
20:        printf("\nHow many students will be entered? ==> ");
21:        scanf("%ld", &nbr_students);
22:        gets(trash);         /* clear out keyboard buffer */
23:     }
24:
25:     student_name = (char *) malloc( 35*nbr_students);
26:
27:     if( student_name == NULL )    /* verify malloc() was successful */
28:     {
29:        printf( "\nError in line %3.3d: Could not allocate memory.",
30:                __LINE__ );
31:        exit(1);
32:     }
```

```
33:
34:        for( ctr = 0; ctr < nbr_students; ctr++ )
35:        {
36:            printf("\nEnter student %5.5d: ", ctr+1);
37:            gets(student_name+(ctr*35));
38:        }
39:
40:        printf("\n\nYou entered the following:\n");
41:
42:        for ( ctr = 0; ctr < nbr_students; ctr++ )
43:        {
44:            printf("\nStudent %5.5d:", ctr+1);
45:            printf(" %s", student_name+(ctr*35));
46:        }
47:
48:        /* this program does not release allocated memory! */
49:    }
```

How many students will be entered? ==> 5

Enter student 00001: Connie Crank

Enter student 00002: Deanna Alexander

Enter student 00003: Dawn Johnson

Enter student 00004: Bruce Crouch

Enter student 00005: Sherman Denman

You entered the following:

Student 00001: Connie Crank
Student 00002: Deanna Alexander
Student 00003: Dawn Johnson
Student 00004: Bruce Crouch
Student 00005: Sherman Denman

This program differs from Listing 1.2 in that it leaves it to the person running the program to determine how many names are going to be entered. You don't have to guess how many student names there will be. Lines 20 and 21 prompt the user for the number of names that are going to be entered. Line 25 attempts to use malloc() to dynamically allocate the memory. Notice that the program allocates the specific amount requested. If there is not enough memory available, an error message is displayed in line 29; otherwise, the user is allowed to enter the names in lines 34 to 38.

Some other items in this program deserve mentioning. Line 16 declares a character array, or string, called trash. This string also could have been dynamically allocated using the malloc() function. The trash string is used in line 22 to remove any remaining keystrokes that may still be in the keyboard buffer.

Another point worth mentioning is the defined constant in line 30. The __LINE__ constant is replaced by the compiler with the current line number. You may be wondering why __LINE__ was used in line 30 instead of the number 30. The answer is simple: If the program is changed and recompiled, the line number for the parameter to the printf() may change. By using __LINE__, the programmer does not need to worry about making a change. If 30 had been used, the line number would need to be manually changed any time the program changed.

> **Review Tip:** The __LINE__ preprocessor directive is a defined constant. When the program is compiled, it is replaced with the current line number. Another popular preprocessor directive is __FILE__. This constant is replaced by the current source file's name.

The *free()* Function

Allocating memory allows memory to be set aside for when it is needed; however, to complete the cycle, the memory should be deallocated, or freed, when it is no longer needed. When a program ends, the operating system is generally able to clean up memory; however, many programs will want to deallocate the memory so that other parts of the program can use it. Listing 1.4 shows what can happen when memory allocations are not cleaned up.

> **Warning:** The following listing may cause your machine to lock up.

Listing 1.4. Allocating memory without freeing it.

```
1:  /* Filename:  LIST0104.c
2:   * Author  :  Bradley L. Jones
3:   * Purpose :  This program shows what happens when dynamically
4:   *            allocated memory is not released.
5:
```

```
   *=================================================================*/
6:
7:    #include <stdio.h>
8:    #include <stdlib.h>
9:
10:   int do_a_book_page( long );
11:
12:   void main(void)
13:   {
14:      int rv;
15:      unsigned long nbr_pages = 0;
16:      unsigned long page = 0;
17:
18:      printf("\n\nEnter number of pages to do ==> ");
19:      scanf( "%d", &nbr_pages );
20:
21:      for( page = 1; page <= nbr_pages; page++)
22:      {
23:         rv = do_a_book_page( page );
24:
25:         if (rv == 99)
26:         {
27:            printf("\nAllocation error, exiting...");
28:            exit(1);
29:         }
30:      }
31:
32:      printf( "\n\nDid all the pages!\n" );
33:   }
34:
35:   int do_a_book_page( long page_nbr )
36:   {
37:      char *book_page;            /* pointer to assign allocation to */
38:
39:      book_page = (char *) malloc( 1000 );
40:
41:      if( book_page == NULL )
42:      {
43:         printf( "\nError in line %3.3d: Could not allocate memory.",
44:                  __LINE__);
45:         return(99);
46:      }
47:      else
48:      {
49:         printf( "\nAllocation for book page %d is ready to use...",
50:                  page_nbr);
51:      }
52:
53:      /***********************************************************
```

continues

Listing 1.4. continued

```
54:        * code to get information and assign it at the location  *
55:        * that was previously obtained with malloc().            *
56:        * Code might then write the page to disk or something.    *
57:        ********************************************************/
58:
59:        /*** WARNING: This function does not release allocated memory! ***/
60:
61:        return(0);
62:  }
```

```
Enter number of pages to do ==> 4

Allocation for book page 1 is ready to use...
Allocation for book page 2 is ready to use...
Allocation for book page 3 is ready to use...
Allocation for book page 4 is ready to use...


Did all the pages!
```

Second run:

```
Enter number of pages to do ==> 1000

Allocation for book page 1 is ready to use...
Allocation for book page 2 is ready to use...
Allocation for book page 3 is ready to use...
Allocation for book page 4 is ready to use...
Allocation for book page 5 is ready to use...
Allocation for book page 6 is ready to use...
Allocation for book page 7 is ready to use...
Allocation for book page 8 is ready to use...


                         . . .


Allocation for book page 46 is ready to use...
Allocation for book page 47 is ready to use...
Allocation for book page 48 is ready to use...
Allocation for book page 49 is ready to use...
Allocation for book page 50 is ready to use...
Error in line 044: Could not allocate memory.
Allocation error, exiting...
```

Notice that after a certain number of allocations, the program stops. In addition, you may find your entire machine locks up. Now replace the comment in line 59 with the following:

```
free( book_page );
```

When you rerun the program, you should no longer run out of memory to allocate for the book page. When you enter a number such as 1000, the output displays all the way to page 1000.

Notice that there was not a memory allocation error. The free() function releases the memory so that it can be reused.

> **Note:** It is good programming practice to always deallocate any memory that is dynamically allocated. Memory allocation errors can be very hard to find in large programs.

DO	DON'T

DO check the return value from malloc() to ensure that memory was allocated.

DO avoid using malloc() for allocating small amounts of memory. Each memory allocation made with malloc() contains some overhead—typically 16 bytes or more.

DON'T forget to free allocated memory with the free() function. If you don't free the memory, and the pointer to it goes out of scope, the memory will be unavailable during the execution of the rest of the program.

The *realloc()* Function

In addition to being able to allocate blocks of memory, you may also want to change the size of the memory block. The function realloc() was developed for this specific reason. realloc() increases or decreases the size of an allocated block of memory. The prototype for realloc() as described in the STDLIB.H header file will be similar to the following:

```
void *realloc(void *originalblock, size_t size);
```

The size parameter for the realloc() function is just like the one in the malloc() function—it is the number of bytes that is being requested. The originalblock parameter is the pointer to the block of memory that had previously been allocated.

15

Once the reallocation of memory is completed, the *originalblock* pointer may or may not exist. If the allocation fails, which would occur in the case of a request for a larger block of memory that is unavailable, the pointer will be retained. In this failed case, the realloc() function will return a NULL pointer. If the allocation is completed successfully, the *originalblock* pointer could be gone. The reason for this is that the reallocation may not be in the same location. If necessary, realloc() will move the allocated memory to another location. Listing 1.5 presents an example of realloc().

 Listing 1.5. The use of realloc().

```
1:   /* Filename:  LIST0105.c
2:    * Author   :  Bradley L. Jones
3:    * Purpose  :  This provides an example of using realloc() to
4:    *             get additional dynamic memory as needed
5:
*=====================================================================*/
6:
7:   #include <stdio.h>
8:   #include <stdlib.h>
9:
10:  #define NAME_SIZE   35
11:
12:  void main(void)
13:  {
14:     long student_ctr = 0;
15:     long ctr;
16:     char *student_name = NULL;
17:     while( (student_name =
18:            realloc( student_name,
                       (NAME_SIZE * (student_ctr+1)))) != NULL )
19:     {
20:        printf("\nEnter student %5.5d: ", student_ctr+1);
21:        gets(student_name+( student_ctr * NAME_SIZE));
22:        if( student_name[student_ctr * NAME_SIZE] == NULL )
23:        {
24:
25:           break;
26:        }
27:        else
28:        {
29:           student_ctr++;
30:        }
31:     }
32:
33:     printf("\n\nYou entered the following:\n");
34:
35:     for ( ctr = 0; ctr < student_ctr; ctr++ )
36:     {
37:        printf("\nStudent %5.5d:", ctr+1);
```

```
38:          printf(" %s", student_name+(ctr*NAME_SIZE));
39:      }
40:
41:      free(student_name);
42:  }
```

Enter student 00001: Mario Andretti

Enter student 00002: A. J. Foyt

Enter student 00003: Rick Mears

Enter student 00004: Michael Andretti

Enter student 00005: Al Unser, Jr.

Enter student 00006:

You entered the following:

Student 00001: Mario Andretti
Student 00002: A. J. Foyt
Student 00003: Rick Mears
Student 00004: Michael Andretti
Student 00005: Al Unser, Jr.

This program follows the flow of some of the previous listings, except that it reallocates the storage space for the names. Each time there is a new name, a call to realloc() (line 18) attempts to increase the size of the student_name. Users will be able to enter names until there is not enough memory left to allocate, or until they choose not to enter a name. Notice that realloc() is used to allocate the first instance of student_name. The first time that line 18 is reached, student_name is NULL. Passing a NULL string as the first parameter of realloc() is equivalent to calling malloc().

The *calloc()* Function

The calloc() function is quite similar to malloc(). There are two differences. The first difference is in the initialization of the allocated memory. When malloc() allocates memory, it does not initialize, or clear, the newly allocated memory; whatever was previously stored at the allocated memory location will still be there. With a call to calloc(), the allocated memory is cleared by initializing the block with zeros.

The second difference is that `calloc()` allows for an additional parameter. The prototype for `calloc()`, which is in the STDLIB.H header file, should be similar to the following:

```
void *calloc( size_t number_items, size_t block_size );
```

The *block_size* parameter is the same as the size value passed to the `malloc()` function. It is the number of bytes that you want allocated in your memory block. The *number_items* parameter is the number of blocks you want allocated. For example, if you did the following call, the `calloc()` would try to allocate 10 blocks of 100 bytes of memory, or 1000 bytes in total:

```
pointer = calloc( 10, 100 )
```

This would have the same result as a `malloc( 1000 )` in regard to the amount of space allocated. The following two calls would attempt to allocate the same amount of memory. The difference would be that `calloc()` would also initialize the memory to zeros.

```
pointer = malloc( 1000 );
pointer = calloc( 1, 1000);
```

You might be asking why you need the extra parameter. Up to this point, you have been dealing with character data only. With character data, typically, each character requires 1 byte, so it is easy to see from the `malloc()` call how many characters are going to be stored. If you were going to store integers, calling `malloc()` with 1000 does not make it clear that only 500 integers are going to be allocated. In addition, this is making an assumption that an integer will be 2 bytes. Listing 1.6 is an example of how `calloc()` is used:

 Listing 1.6. Using `calloc()`.

```
 1:  /* Filename:  LIST0106.c
 2:   * Author  :  Bradley L. Jones
 3:   * Purpose :  This provides an example of allocating memory for an
 4:   *            array dynamically with the calloc function.
 5:   * Descript:  Program allows grades to be entered before printing
 6:   *            an average.
 7:   *===============================================================*/
 8:
 9:  #include <stdio.h>
10:  #include <stdlib.h>
11:
12:  void main( void )
13:  {
14:      int  nbr_grades = 0;
```

```
15:     int   total = 0;
16:     int   ctr;
17:     int   *student_grades;
18:     char trash[80];                /* to clear keyboard buffer */
19:
20:     while( nbr_grades < 1 || nbr_grades >= 10000 )
21:     {
22:        printf("\nHow many grades will be entered? ==> ");
23:        scanf("%ld", &nbr_grades);
24:        gets(trash);                /* clear out keyboard buffer */
25:     }
26:
27:     student_grades = (int *) calloc( nbr_grades, sizeof(int));
28:
29:     if( student_grades == NULL )
30:     {
31:        printf( "\nError in line %3.3d: Could not allocate memory.",
32:                __LINE__);
33:        exit(1);
34:     }
35:
36:     for( ctr = 0; ctr < nbr_grades; ctr++ )
37:     {
38:        printf("\nEnter grade %4.4d: ", ctr+1);
39:        scanf("%d", student_grades+ctr);
40:     }
41:
42:     printf("\n\nYou entered the following:\n");
43:
44:     for ( ctr = 0; ctr < nbr_grades; ctr++ )
45:     {
46:        printf("\nGrade %4.4d:", ctr+1);
47:        printf(" %d", *(student_grades+ctr));
48:
49:        total += *(student_grades+ctr);
50:     }
51:
52:     printf("\n\nThe average grade is: %d\n\n", (total/nbr_grades));
53:
54:     /* Free allocated memory */
55:
56:     free(student_grades);
57: }
```

```
How many grades will be entered? ==> 5

Enter grade 0001: 100

Enter grade 0002: 80
```

```
Enter grade 0003: 85

Enter grade 0004: 90

Enter grade 0005: 95


You entered the following:

Grade 0001: 100
Grade 0002: 80
Grade 0003: 85
Grade 0004: 90
Grade 0005: 95
The average grade is: 90
```

This program allows a number of grades to be entered and printed, along with an average grade. This program uses `calloc()` in line 27 in a way that makes the program portable from one computer type to another. The objective of line 27 is to allocate 5 integers. Regardless of what computer this program is compiled on, there will be enough room for the 5 integers. This is accomplished by using the `sizeof` operator to determine the size of an integer. Granted, `malloc()` could be used to do the same thing, but the `calloc()` is clearer. The following is a function call that uses `malloc()` to accomplish the same task:

```
ptr = malloc( sizeof(int) * 5 );
```

Listing 1.6 follows the same flow as the other programs presented so far. Lines 20 through 25 prompt the user for how many grades will be entered. Line 23 uses the `scanf()` function to accept a number. Line 24 clears any remaining information that may be in the keyboard buffer, including the carriage return the user typed when entering the grades in line 23. The `while` statement keeps reprompting the user for the number of grades as long as the number that is entered is less than 1 or greater than 10,000. Line 27 then allocates the space for the grades to be stored.

As should be done with any call to a dynamic memory allocation function, line 29 ensures the space was indeed allocated. If not, an error message is displayed and, in line 33, the program exits. Lines 36 to 40 use a `for` loop to prompt the user to enter the previously specified number of grades. Because the counter is started at 0, when prompting the user (in line 38), 1 is added. A user will be more familiar with the first grade being 1 instead of 0. Line 39 actually gets the grade using `scanf()`. Notice that the grade is placed at a position within the memory previously allocated. The offset into this memory is based on the `ctr` value.

Once all the grades are entered, the program uses an additional `for` loop (lines 44 to 50) to print the grades. As the `for` loop prints each grade, line 49 adds the grade to the total. Notice that in lines 47 and 49 the array is being dereferenced with the asterisk (*) to actually obtain the values. (If this dereferencing is confusing, a quick review of pointers, which will be covered on Day 2, should help.) Line 56 is one of the most important lines in the program. Notice that this is where the `student_grade` array is deallocated. At this point, all the memory that was allocated dynamically is released back.

Expert Tip: It does not matter whether you use `malloc()` or `calloc()` to allocate memory dynamically. If you are allocating a single area, then `malloc()` is easiest to use. If you are allocating several items of the same size, then `calloc()` is a better choice.

DO   DON'T

DO use the `sizeof` operator when allocating memory to help make your programs portable, that is, `malloc( sizeof(int) * value)`.

DON'T assume that a dynamic allocation function always works. You should always check the return value to ensure the memory was obtained.

DON'T assume that a call to `realloc()` will allocate memory in the same location. If there is not enough memory at the original location, `realloc()` may move the original block to a different location.

Allocating More than 64K

All the functions described so far have a maximum allocation capability. They cannot allocate more than 64K of memory. You saw this in Listing 1.4, which lacked a `free()` statement. The program always stopped before it allocated more than 64 times (64,000 bytes, 1,000 bytes at a time). The way around this limitation is to use functions that allow additional memory to be allocated. This additional memory is termed *far memory*.

Unlike the general memory allocation functions, the far memory allocation functions are not ANSI standard. This means that each compiler may have different functions that perform these allocations. For the Borland compilers, these functions are:

☐ `farmalloc()`

Prototype:

```
void far *farmalloc( unsigned long size);
```

☐ `farcalloc()`

Prototype:

```
void far *farcalloc( unsigned long nbr_units, unsigned long size);
```

☐ `farrealloc()`

Prototype:

```
void far *farrealloc( void far *old_block_ptr, unsigned long size);
```

☐ `farfree()`

Prototype:

```
void far *farfree( void far*block_ptr);
```

For the Microsoft compiler, the available far functions are:

☐ `_fmalloc()`

Prototype:

```
void __far *fmalloc( size_t size);
```

☐ `_fcalloc()`

Prototype:

```
void __far *_fcalloc( size_t nbr_units, size_t size);
```

☐ `_frealloc()`

Prototype:

```
void __far *_frealloc( void __far *old_block_ptr, size_t size);
```

☐ `_ffree()`

Prototype:

```
void __far *_ffree( void __far*block_ptr);
```

These functions work nearly identically to the general memory allocation functions; however, there are a few exceptions. First, you must include a different header file. If you are using a Microsoft compiler, you must include the malloc.h header. If you are using a Borland compiler, you include the alloc.h header file. For other compilers, you should consult the library reference section of the manuals. In addition, a difference in the Borland functions is that instead of taking an unsigned integer parameter (size_t), they take an unsigned long parameter.

Listing 1.7 is a rewrite of Listing 1.4 using the farmalloc() function. Notice that the other listings in this chapter could be similarly modified to use the far functions. For specific usage of your compiler's far memory allocation functions, you should consult your compiler's library reference manual.

 Warning: The ability to use the far memory allocations is dependent upon which memory model you are using to compile your programs. Tiny model programs cannot use the far functions. In compact, large, and huge memory models, the far functions are similar to their counterparts, except they take unsigned long parameters. In addition, memory allocated with far functions require that the pointers used to access them be declared as far.

 Listing 1.7. Use of far memory allocation functions.

```
1:   /* Filename:  LIST0107.c
2:    * Author  :  Bradley L. Jones
3:    * Purpose :  This program shows what happens when memory allocated
4:    *            dynamically with farmalloc() is not released.
5:    *=================================================================*/
6:   #include <alloc.h>
7:   #include <stdio.h>
8:   #include <stdlib.h>
9:
10:  int do_a_book_page( long );
11:
12:  void main()
13:  {
14:     int rv;
15:     unsigned long nbr_pages = 0;
16:     unsigned long page = 0;
17:
18:     printf("\n\nEnter number of pages to do ==> ");
```

continues

Listing 1.7. continued

```
19:     scanf( "%d", &nbr_pages );
20:
21:     for( page = 1; page <= nbr_pages; page++)
22:     {
23:         rv = do_a_book_page( page );
24:
25:         if (rv == 99)
26:         {
27:             printf("\nAllocation error, exiting...");
28:             exit(1);
29:         }
30:     }
31:
32:     printf( "\n\nDid all the pages!\n" );
33: }
34:
35: int do_a_book_page( long page_nbr )
36: {
37:     char far * book_page;       /* pointer to assign allocation to */
38:
39:     book_page = (char *) farmalloc( 1000 );
40:
41:     if( book_page == NULL )
42:     {
43:         printf( "\nError in line %3.3d: Could not allocate memory.",
44:                 __LINE__ );
45:         return(99);
46:     }
47:     else
48:     {
49:         printf( "\nAllocation for book page %ld is ready to use...",
50:                 page_nbr);
51:     }
52:
53:     /***********************************************************
54:      * code to get information and assign it at the location   *
55:      * that was previously obtained with malloc().             *
56:      * Code might then write the page to disk or something.    *
57:      ***********************************************************/
58:
59: /*** WARNING: This function does not release allocated memory! ***/
60:
61:     return(0);
62: }
```

For Microsoft compilers, replace the following lines:

```
6:      #include <malloc.h>
39:     book_page = (char *) _fmalloc( 1000 );
```

Enter number of pages to do ==> 4

Allocation for book page 1 is ready to use...
Allocation for book page 2 is ready to use...
Allocation for book page 3 is ready to use...
Allocation for book page 4 is ready to use...

Did all the pages!

Second run:

Enter number of pages to do ==> 10000

Allocation for book page 1 is ready to use...
Allocation for book page 2 is ready to use...
Allocation for book page 3 is ready to use...
Allocation for book page 4 is ready to use...
Allocation for book page 5 is ready to use...
Allocation for book page 6 is ready to use...
Allocation for book page 7 is ready to use...
Allocation for book page 8 is ready to use...

            . . .

Allocation for book page 9995 is ready to use...
Allocation for book page 9996 is ready to use...
Allocation for book page 9997 is ready to use...
Allocation for book page 9998 is ready to use...
Allocation for book page 9999 is ready to use...
Allocation for book page 10000 is ready to use...

Did all the pages!

This program has just a few changes from Listing 1.4. In line 6, a new include file was added for the far allocation function. In line 37, the addition of the far keyword for the book_page variable enables it to be used to address far memory. The final change is in line 39, where the appropriate far memory allocation function has replaced the malloc() function in Listing 1.4.

As with Listing 1.4, after a certain number of allocations, the program stops. As before, you may find that your entire machine locks up. However, as you will see, this program does not run out of memory as quickly as Listing 1.4. With the farmalloc() or _fmalloc() statement, you have access to much more of the computer's available RAM.

In using the far version of the malloc() statement, you had to also make one additional change. In line 6, an additional header file needed to be included. Depending on your

25

compiler, this may have been either alloc.h or malloc.h.

In Listing 1.4, you replaced the comment that was in line 59 with the following:

```
free( book_page );
```

Because you are using a far memory allocation function, you want to use the appropriate far function in Listing 1.7. For Microsoft compilers, this is `_ffree()`; for Borland compilers, use the `farfree()` function instead.

DO	DON'T

DON'T forget that the far memory allocation functions are not ANSI standard functions. This means they may not be portable from one compiler to another.

DO use the far free function to allocate memory that was allocated with a far function.

Summary

Today you learned about the dynamic memory allocation functions. These functions enable you to allocate specific amounts of memory at runtime rather than at compile time. The capability to dynamically allocate memory can help to make more versatile programs. Not only were the general, ANSI standard allocation functions presented, but so were several additional non-ANSI standard functions. The non-ANSI standard functions are used to allocate larger chunks of memory than are allowed by the general functions, such as `malloc()`.

Q&A

Q Why is a topic such as memory allocation covered on Day 1?

A As you begin to write bigger programs and develop more advanced programs, you will find that memory management is of vital importance. As early as Day 2, you will see several advanced concepts that require memory to be allocated dynamically. These include variable length structures and linked lists.

Q What are memory models?

A Memory models deal with the amount of space that is available for a program and its data. When compiling a C program, you must specify to the compiler which memory model is being used. Typically this value—either tiny, small, compact, medium, large, or huge—is set to a default value. Appendix A contains a detailed explanation of the differences among the memory models.

Q Should I be worried if I did not understand everything in this chapter?

A No! Although programs as early as Day 2 will be using the dynamic memory functions, these programs will explain what they are doing at the time. As you work on these new programs, the function presented becomes clearer.

Q What are common reasons for using dynamic memory allocation functions?

A There are two major uses for dynamic memory allocation functions. The first is to keep a program's initial memory requirements (or allocation) as small as possible. This allows the program to load and execute even if it is under another program's control. Secondly, a major reason for using dynamic memory allocation functions is to assure the memory can be released when it is no longer needed.

Workshop

The Workshop consists of quiz questions to help you solidify your understanding of the material covered and exercises to provide you with experience in using what you've learned.

Quiz

1. Why is understanding memory important?
2. What is dynamically allocated memory?
3. What is the most memory you can dynamically allocate?
4. How do you release memory that has been dynamically allocated?
5. What is the difference between `malloc()` and `calloc()`?
6. What is the difference between `malloc()` and `farmalloc()`?

Exercises

1. Write a code fragment that dynamically allocates memory to hold 10 integers using the `malloc()` command.

2. Rewrite your answer in Exercise 1 using the `calloc()` function.

3. Write a function to allocate enough memory to hold 20,000 `long` values. This function should return a pointer to the array, or `NULL` if the memory could not be allocated.

4. **BUG BUSTER:** Is there anything wrong with the following code fragment?

```
#include <stdlib.h>
#include <stdio.h>
#define MAX  100
void main(void)
{
    string = malloc( MAX );
    printf( "Enter something: " );
    gets( string );
    puts( string );          /* do something like printing */
    free( string );
}
```

5. **BUG BUSTER:** Is there anything wrong with the following function?

```
/* Day 1: Exercise 5 */
#include <stdlib.h>
#include <stdio.h>

void main(void)
{
    long *long_array;
    long  total = 0;
    int   ctr;

    long_array = calloc( sizeof(long), 10 );
    printf( "Enter 10 numbers: " );
    for( ctr = 0; ctr < 10; ctr++ )
    {
        scanf( "%ld", long_array+ctr );
```

```
        total += *(long_array+ctr);
    }

    printf( "\n\nTotal of numbers is: %ld", total );
}
```

6. **ON YOUR OWN:** Write a program that declares a structure containing a first name, last name, and middle initial. Do not limit the number of names the user is able to enter. Print the names after the user is done entering them. Use a dynamic memory function.

> **Note:** Answers are not provided for the ON YOUR OWN exercises. You are on your own!

> **Tip:** ON YOUR OWN programs typically require rewriting listings presented within the day's materials.

7. **ON YOUR OWN:** Write a function that allocates a given amount of memory and initializes the memory to a specified value. Following is an example prototype and an example call:

Prototype:

```
void * initialize_memory( void * pointer, size_t size, char
initializer);
```

Calling the function:

```
char *name;
/* initialize name to Xs */
name = (char *) initialize_memory( (char *)name, 35, 'X');
```

Complex
Data Types

The basic building blocks of a program are variables. Variables are created with data types. The basic data types are presented in every beginning C book. Today you will go beyond these basic data types. Today you learn:

☐ What are considered the basic data types.

☐ How to use single and multiple dimensioned arrays.

☐ How to use pointers in complex situations, including:

    ☐ A review of pointers.

    ☐ Using pointers with other pointers.

    ☐ Using pointers with functions.

    ☐ Using pointers with structures.

☐ What complex data types can be created with structures and unions.

☐ What dynamic or variable-length structures are.

What Are Data Types?

There are many basic data types in C. These are presented in virtually every C book. Several of these data types were used in the listings in Day 1. In addition, virtually every C program will use data types to declare variables. The basic data types are presented in Table 2.1.

Table 2.1. The basic data types.

Data Type	Description
char	character
int	integers
short	short integers
long	long integers
float	decimal numbers
double	larger decimal numbers

The basic data types are used in creating variables, which in turn store information for your programs to use. The data type you use when declaring the variable determines the type of information that can be stored as specified by the description in Table 2.1.

Note: A *variable* is a name given to a location in memory. The data type used when naming, or creating, the variable determines how much space is reserved.

2

The Values of the Basic Data Types

You should be familiar with the basic data types and the modifiers that can be applied to them from your previous experience with C. Most important are the `signed` and `unsigned` modifiers. Table 2.2 shows the minimum and maximum values that each of the basic data types can hold and their typical memory size in bytes.

Table 2.2. Maximum and minimum values of basic data types.

Variable Type	Size	Minimum	Maximum
signed character	1 byte	−128	128
unsigned character	1 byte	0	255
signed integer	2 bytes	−32,768	32,767
unsigned integer	2 bytes	0	65,535
signed short integer	2 bytes	−32,758	32.767
unsigned short integer	2 bytes	0	65,535
signed long integer	4 bytes	−2,147,483,648	2,147,483,647
unsigned long integer	4 bytes	0	4,294,967,295
float	4 bytes	3.4E-38	3.4E38
double	8 bytes	1.7E-308	1.7E308

Creating Your Own Data Types

C provides a command that enables you to create your own data types. Actually, you don't create them; you simply rename the existing types using the `typedef` keyword. The following presents the `typedef`'s use:

```
typedef existing_type new_type_name;
```

For example:

```
typedef float decimal_number;
```

When the previous type definition is declared, `decimal_number` can be used just like any of the other variable types. For example,

```
char   x;
int    y;
decimal_number z;
```

By using the `typedef` keyword, you can increase the readability of your code. In addition, as you work with the more intricate types, using type definitions can make the code seem a little less complex.

Several new types are generally created using type definitions. The following are some of the type definitions that have been included with a wide variety of compilers:

```
typedef int             BOOL;
typedef unsigned char   BYTE;
typedef unsigned short  WORD;
typedef unsigned int    UINT;
typedef signed long     LONG;
typedef unsigned long   DWORD;
typedef char far*       LPSTR;
typedef const char far* LPCSTR;
typedef int             HFILE;
typedef signed short int SHORT;
```

You should notice that the types that have been created here are in all uppercase letters. This is so you don't confuse them with variables. If you have the Microsoft or Borland compilers, you'll find the preceding type definitions in the VER.H file and several other files.

Expert Tip: You should be aware of the preceding type definitions; many advanced programs use them.

Advanced Data Usage: Grouping Data

By using the basic data types, you can create complex or advanced data types. You create new ways of associating and accessing data when you group basic data types. There are three basic groupings of data types that are commonly used in C programs. Because these groups are common, their usage is detailed in most basic C books. They will be briefly reviewed here. The three types of groupings are:

☐ Arrays

☐ Structures

☐ Unions

Arrays

An *array* allows a group of similar data to be accessed using a single variable. This data is all of the same data type. The data type can be one of the basic data types presented earlier, or it can be any of the complex data types presented in this chapter. This even includes other arrays. Listing 2.1 shows how basic arrays can be accessed.

Listing 2.1. Accessing arrays and their data.

```
1:   /* Program:  array.c
2:    * Author:   Bradley L. Jones
3:    * Purpose:  Demonstration of accessing arrays and their
4:    *           data.
5:    *=========================================================*/
6:
7:   #include <stdio.h>
8:
9:   char text[15] = {'B','R','A','D','L','E','Y',' ',
10:                    'J','O','N','E','S', 0, 'X' };
11:
12:  int number_array[7] = { 66, 82, 65, 68,
13:                          76, 69, 89 };
14:
15:  void main( void )
16:  {
17:     int ctr;
18:
19:     printf( "\n\nPrint Character array...\n\n");
20:
21:     for (ctr = 0; ctr < 15; ctr++)
```

continues

Listing 2.1. continued

```
22:      {
23:          printf( "%c", text[ctr] );
24:      }
25:
26:      printf( "\n\nReprint text with offsets...\n\n");
27:
28:      for (ctr = 0; ctr < 15; ctr++)
29:      {
30:          printf( "%c", *(text+ctr));
31:      }
32:
33:      printf( "\n\nReprint using string function...\n\n");
34:      printf( "%s", text );
35:
36:      printf( "\n\nPrint number array...\n\n");
37:
38:      for (ctr = 0; ctr < 7; ctr++)
39:      {
40:          printf( "%d ", number_array[ctr] );
41:      }
42:  }
```

Print Character array...

BRADLEY JONES X

Reprint text with offsets...

BRADLEY JONES X

Reprint using string function...

BRADLEY JONES

Print number array...

66 82 65 68 76 69 89

This program shows how single dimension arrays can be defined, preinitialized, and displayed. When an array is created, each element is similar to an individual variable. The difference between individual variables and the array elements is that the array elements have the same name. In addition, array elements are stored one after the other in memory, whereas individual variables could be stored anywhere. Figure 2.1 shows what memory might look like for the text character array in Listing 2.1.

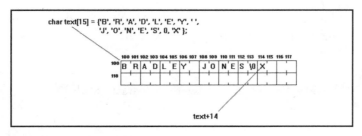

Figure 2.1. *The* text *character array in memory.*

Listing 2.1 should be review. Lines 9 and 10 declare a character array called text and initialize it. Lines 12 and 13 declare and initialize a numeric array, number_array. These two arrays are then used in the program. Lines 21 through 24 use a for loop to print each value of the text character array using a subscript. As you can see, the subscripts in C start with 0 not 1. Other languages, such as BASIC, use 1 as the first subscript.

 Review Tip: C uses 0 (not 1!) as the first subscript.

Lines 28 through 31 offer a different method for printing the same character array. Rather than subscripts, a memory offset (pointer) is used. The value of text by itself is the address of the first element of the text array. By using the dereference operator (*), the value at the address stored in text (or stated in computerese, *pointed to* by text) can be printed. Using Figure 2.1 as a reference, you can see the value of text might be 100. The first time line 30 is reached, the value of text + ctr is equal to text, or 100, because ctr is zero. Looking at the printf(), you see that the character at address 100 is printed. In the case of text, this character is B. The next time through the for loop, the value pointed to at text + ctr—or at 100 + 1—is printed. The value at 101 is R. This continues through the end of the for loop. If these concepts are new to you, or if you are unsure of what dereferencing is, read the pointer review section that follows later today. If it is still confusing, you may want to consult a beginning C book for a review on pointer basics. *Teach Yourself C in 21 Days* has two chapters on pointers and their use.

Line 34 prints the text character array a third way. This time the character array is printed as a string. You should understand the difference between a character array and a string—the difference is sometimes subtle. A *string* is basically a null-terminated character array, which means it ends at the first null character. When line 34 prints, it stops printing at the 15th character—the X is not printed. This is because the end of the string is considered to be the null in position 14.

> **Review Tip:** A null character is a character with a numeric value of 0.

The numeric array, `numeric_array`, is printed in lines 38 through 41. As you can see, this is just like the character array only numbers, rather than characters, are being printed.

Structures

Unlike arrays, which allow data of the same type to be grouped together, *structures* allow data of different types to be stored. The following is an example of a structure delcaration.

```
struct date_tag {
    int month;
    char breaker1;
    int day;
    char breaker2;
    int year;
};
```

By grouping different data types, you can see that it's easy to create new types. With the preceding structure, you can declare a structure variable that will hold a date. This single variable will contain a month, day, year, and two breakers. Each of these parts of the declared variable can then be accessed. Listing 2.2 shows the use of a structure.

 Listing 2.2. Use of the date structure.

```
 1:  /* Program:   STRUCT.C
 2:   * Author:    Bradley L. Jones
 3:   * Purpose:   Program to use a date structure
 4:   *=================================================*/
 5:
 6:  #include <stdio.h>
 7:
 8:  struct date_tag {
 9:     int  month;
10:     char breaker1;
11:     int  day;
12:     char breaker2;
13:     int  year;
14:  } date1;
15:
```

```
16:   void main(void)
17:   {
18:     struct date_tag date2 = { 1, '/', 1, '/', 1998 };
19:
20:     printf("\n\nEnter information for date 1: ");
21:     printf("\n\nEnter month: ");
22:     scanf("%d", &date1.month);
23:     printf("\nEnter day: ");
24:     scanf("%d", &date1.day);
25:     printf("\nEnter year: ");
26:     scanf("%d", &date1.year);
27:
28:     date1.breaker1 = '-';
29:     date1.breaker2 = '-';
30:
31:     printf("\n\n\nYour dates are:\n\n");
32:     printf("Date 1: %d%c%d%c%d\n\n", date1.month,
33:                                      date1.breaker1,
34:                                      date1.day,
35:                                      date1.breaker2,
36:                                      date1.year );
37:
38:     printf("Date 2: %d%c%d%c%d\n\n", date2.month,
39:                                      date2.breaker1,
40:                                      date2.day,
41:                                      date2.breaker2,
42:                                      date2.year );
43:
44:     printf("\n\n\nSize of date_tag structure: %d",
45:     sizeof(date1));
46:   }
```

Output

```
Enter information for date 1:

Enter month: 12

Enter day: 25

Enter year: 1994


Your dates are:

Date 1: 12-25-1994

Date 2: 1/1/1998


Size of date_tag structure: 8
```

This listing should also provide a review. Later today, you will see advanced use of structures—structures with variable lengths. You can see in lines 8 through 14 that the date structure has been defined. In fact, you can see that a variable, date1, has been declared. In line 18, another variable, date2, is declared using the struct keyword along with the previously defined structure's tag, date_tag. At the time of date2's declaration, each of its elements is also initialized.

Lines 20 through 26 enable the user to enter the information for date1. Using printf(), the user is prompted for each of the numeric elements of the structure. Lines 28 and 29 set the breaker values to dashes. These could have been slashes or any other values. Lines 32 through 42 print the values from the individual dates.

Word Alignment

In Listing 2.2, lines 44 and 45 were added to help demonstrate word alignment. How big is the date structure? Typically, the size of the structure is the size of its elements added together. In the case of the date structure, this would consist of three integers (each two bytes) and two characters (each a single byte). This adds up to a total of eight as the preceding output presented. Figure 2.2 demonstrates the memory placement of each of the date structure's elements.

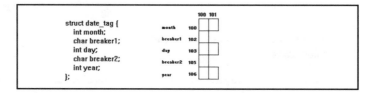

Figure 2.2. *The date structure in memory with word alignment off.*

You may have gotten the answer of 10 instead of 8 in the output for Listing 2.2. If you did, you compiled with the word-alignment option on. Word alignment is an option that can be set when compiling. If this alignment is on, each element of a structure is stored starting at the beginning of a byte. The exception to this is character elements following other characters. In this case, they can start on an odd byte. A word is the same as an unsigned short—two bytes. Check your compiler's compile options to see how to compile the listing with word alignment on and off. Run Listing 2.2 again after compiling each way. Figure 2.3 shows the memory placement for each of the date structure's elements with word alignment on.

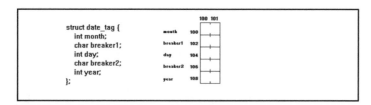

Figure 2.3. *The date structure in memory with word alignment.*

DO capitalize the new types you create with type definitions so that you don't confuse them with variables.

DO understand word alignment. At some point, your data won't seem to be what you think it is. This could be because you are dealing with data that has been aligned differently from how you are accessing it.

DO review a beginning C book, such as *Teach Yourself C in 21 Days*, if you don't understand structures and arrays.

Unions

Unions are a special kind of structure. Instead of storing the individual items one after the other, each element is stored in the same location of memory. The following is an example of a union declaration for a date string and the previously declared date structure.

```
union union_date_tag {
    char str_date[8+1];
    struct date_tag struct_date;
} birthdate;
```

Figure 2.4 shows what this looks like in memory.

Each of the values in the union can be accessed; however, only one can be accessed at a time. This is not a concern in the case of the birthdate union, but consider a union that has mixed values, as in the following:

```
union mix_tag {
    int number;
    char string[10];
    char float;
}values;
```

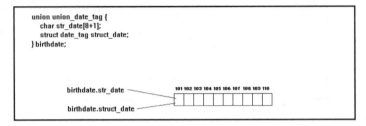

Figure 2.4. *The birthdate union.*

This union contains values that require different amounts of storage space. Only one of these values can be used at a time. If you have an integer value stored in number, you cannot have a value stored in the string or the float variables. This is because these values share a location in memory. Each of the variables is independent. Listing 2.3 helps to demonstrate the independence of these variables.

Type

Listing 2.3. Unions in memory.

```
1:   /* Program:   UNION.C
2:    * Author:    Bradley L. Jones
3:    * Purpose:   Demonstrate a Union
4:    *=====================================================*/
5:
6:   #include <stdio.h>
7:
8:      struct date_struct_tag {
9:          int   month;
10:         char separater1;
11:         int   day;
12:         char separater2;
13:         int   year;
14:     };
15:
16:  union date_tag {
17:     char full_date[8+1];
18:     struct date_struct_tag date;
19:  };
20:
21:  void main(void)
22:  {
23:
24:    union date_tag date1;
25:    union date_tag date2;
26:
27:    printf("\n\nEnter string date (1) (Format: MM/DD/YY): ");
28:    gets(date1.full_date);
29:
```

```
30:     printf("\n\nEnter information for structure date 2: ");
31:     printf("\n\nEnter month: ");
32:     scanf("%d", &date2.date.month);
33:     printf("\nEnter day: ");
34:     scanf("%d", &date2.date.day);
35:     printf("\n\nEnter year: ");
36:     scanf("%d", &date2.date.year);
37:
38:     date2.date.separater1 = '-';
39:     date2.date.separater2 = '-';
40:
41:     printf("\n\n\nYour dates are:\n\n");
42:
43:     printf("String - Date 1: %s\n\n", date1.full_date);
44:
45:     printf("Structure - Date 2: %0d%c%0d%c%d\n\n",
46:                                     date2.date.month,
47:                                     date2.date.separater1,
48:                                     date2.date.day,
49:                                     date2.date.separater2,
50:                                     date2.date.year );
51:
52:
53:     printf("String - Date 1"
            "(printed as a Structure): %0d%c%0d%c%d\n\n",
54:                                     date1.date.month,
55:                                     date1.date.separater1,
56:                                     date1.date.day,
57:                                     date1.date.separater2,
58:                                     date1.date.year );
59:
60:     printf("Structure - Date 2 (printed as String): %s\n\n",
61:                                     date2.full_date);
62: }
```

```
Enter string date (1) (Format: MM/DD/YY): 12/15/63


Enter information for structure date 2:

Enter month: 01

Enter day: 21


Enter year: 1998
```

```
Your dates are:

String - Date 1: 12/15/63

Structure - Date 2: 1-21-1998

String - Date 1 (printed as a Structure): 12849/13617/13110

Structure - Date 2 (printed as a String): J_
```

Analysis The UNION.C program enables you to store a date as either a string date or a date composed of a structure. It uses a union to enable you to store them in the same area of memory.

The structure that is to be used in the union is defined in lines 8 through 14. This structure contains three integer values and two character values. Lines 16 through 19 actually define the union. The character string portion of the union will be called full_date. The structure will be called date. Notice that this is just a definition of the union. The union is not actually declared until lines 24 and 25. Two unions are declared, date1 and date2. Lines 27 and 28 fill in the first date union, date1, with a string value. Lines 30 through 39 fill in the second union, date2, by prompting for three integers and then filling in the separators with dashes.

Lines 43 through 50 print the values of date1 and date2 so that you can see them. More importantly, lines 53 through 61 reprint the values, but this time the opposite part of the union is used. date1 was entered as the string part of the date union. Lines 53 through 58 print this string date using the structure portion of the union. Notice that the output doesn't appear to be correct. This is because a string is stored differently than numeric values.

Pointers in Review

Pointers were mentioned previously when talking about printing the character arrays. Because understanding pointers is required for a solid understanding of C, every beginning C book covers them in some detail. A pointer is a special kind of variable. A pointer is a numeric variable used to hold a memory address. When you declare a pointer, you specify the type of variable that is located at the address stored in the pointer variable. The following are the declarations for three different pointers.

 **Review Tip:** A pointer is a numeric variable that is used to hold a memory address. For example:

```
char *char_ptr;
int *int_ptr
struct date_tag *date_ptr;
```

As you can see, pointers are declared like other variables with the exception of the asterisk. `char_ptr` is defined as a pointer to a character, `int_ptr` is a pointer to an integer, and `date_ptr` is a pointer to a `date_tag` structure. You know these are declared as pointers by the asterisks preceding them. (An asterisk in a declaration always means the variable is a pointer.)

As already stated, `char_ptr` is a pointer to a character. The `char_ptr` variable does not hold a character. Instead, it will hold a number, and more exactly `char_ptr` will hold the number of a memory address used to store a character. Figure 2.5 shows a pointer and its variable in memory.

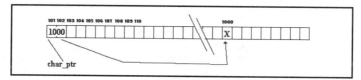

Figure 2.5. *A pointer in memory.*

Finding the Address of a Variable

If a pointer is used to hold a memory address, then it's important to be able to find addresses. In Figures 2.1 through 2.5, you saw how different variables were stored in memory. In most of the examples, the starting memory address was 100. These are simple examples. When variables are actually stored in memory, they can be stored in a variety of locations. In addition, the locations may vary each time the program is run. To truly know where a variable is stored, you need to find its address. C provides, an "address of" operator, which is an ampersand (&), to enable you to determine the address of any variable. Listing 2.4 demonstrates using both a pointer and the "address of" operator.

  Listing 2.4. A pointer review.

```c
1:  /* Program:  Pointer.c
2:   * Author:   Bradley L. Jones
3:   * Purpose:  To show the basics of pointers
4:   *=================================================*/
5:
6:  #include <stdio.h>
7:
8:  void main(void)
9:  {
10:     int a_number;
11:     int *ptr_to_a_number;
12:     int **ptr_to_ptr_to_a_number;
13:
14:     a_number = 500;
15:
16:     ptr_to_a_number = &a_number;
17:
18:     ptr_to_ptr_to_a_number = &ptr_to_a_number;
19:
20:
21:     printf("\n\nThe number is: %d", a_number);
22:     printf("\nThe value of the address of the number is %ld",
23:             &a_number);
24:     printf("\n\nThe value of the pointer to a number is %ld",
25:             ptr_to_a_number);
26:     printf("\nThe value of the address of the ptr to a nbr is %ld",
27:             &ptr_to_a_number);
28:     printf("\n\nThe value of the ptr to a ptr to a nbr is %ld",
29:             ptr_to_ptr_to_a_number);
30:
31:     printf("\n\n\nThe indirect value of the ptr to a nbr is %d",
32:             *ptr_to_a_number);
33:     printf("\nThe indirect value of the ptr to a ptr to a nbr is %ld",
34:             *ptr_to_ptr_to_a_number);
35:     printf("\nThe double indirect value of the ptr to a ptr to a nbr"
                "is %d",
36:             **ptr_to_ptr_to_a_number);
37:  }
```

Output

```
The number is: 500
The value of the address of the number is 78053364

The value of the pointer to a number is 78053364
The value of the address of the ptr to a nbr is 78053362
```

```
The value of the ptr to a ptr to a nbr is 78053362


The indirect value of the ptr to a nbr is 500
The indirect value of the ptr to a ptr to a nbr is 78053364
The double indirect value of the ptr to a ptr to a nbr is 500
```

 Listing 2.4 declares three variables. Line 10 declares an integer variable, a_number, which is assigned the value of 500 in line 14. Line 11 declares a pointer to an integer called ptr_to_a_number. This is assigned a value in line 16. As you can see, it is assigned the address of (&) the previously declared number, a_number. The third declared variable, ptr_to_ptr_to_a_number, is a pointer to a pointer. This pointer is assigned the address of the pointer, ptr_to_a_number (line 18).

Lines 21 through 36 print the values of the previously declared and initialized variables. Line 21 prints the value of the initial integer value, a_number. Line 22 prints the address of a_number as a long value. Since line 16 assigned this value to ptr_to_a_number, it should equal the value printed in line 24. Line 26 prints the address of the pointer, ptr_to_a_number. This helps to demonstrate that a pointer is just another variable that is located at an address in memory and contains an individual value. Line 31 prints the indirect value of ptr_to_a_number. The indirect value of a pointer is the value at the location stored in the pointer variable. In this case, the value will be 500.

DO	**DON'T**

DON'T confuse a pointer's address with its stored value.

Pointers to Pointers

A pointer to another pointer was declared in Listing 2.4. Because a pointer is itself a variable, there is no reason why you can't declare one pointer to hold the address of another pointer. As shown in Listing 2.4, you can declare multiple layers of pointers by simply stacking the asterisks in the declaration. Figure 2.6 shows a variable, var, declared in memory with a value of 500. It also shows a pointer, ptr1, to this variable. Additionally, the figure shows a pointer, ptr2ptr, that points to ptr1, which actually makes it a pointer to a pointer. Listing 2.4 presented an example of this using slightly different variable names.

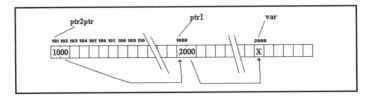

Figure 2.6. *Representation of pointers.*

Pointers to Functions

You can create pointers to functions because they are stored in memory also. These pointers must be declared differently than variable pointers. A declaration for a pointer to a function would be declared as:

```
return_type (*func_pointer)(parameter_list);
```

where `func_pointer` is the name of the function pointer. `parameter_list` is the parameters that are to be passed to the function being pointed to. `return_type` is the data type that the function will return. Listing 2.5 presents a simple example of using a function pointer.

Type **Listing 2.5. Using a function pointer.**

```
1:   /* Program:   list0205.c
2:    * Author:    Bradley L. Jones
3:    * Purpose:   Demonstrate a function pointer
4:    *=================================================*/
5:
6:   #include <stdio.h>
7:
8:   void main(void)
9:   {
10:      int (*func_ptr)();
11:
12:      func_ptr = printf;
13:
14:      (*func_ptr)("\n\nHello World!\n\n");
15:   }
```

```
Hello World!
```

Analysis Line 10 is the declaration for the function pointer, `func_ptr`. Notice that the parentheses are around the asterisk and the pointer's name, `func_ptr`. If you leave these parentheses off, you get different results:

```
int *func_ptr();
```

This is the same declaration without the parentheses. Instead of being a prototype for a pointer to a function, it is a prototype for a function that returns a pointer to an integer.

You can see in line 12, `printf` was assigned to `func_ptr`. When this assignment was made, the parentheses were left off the `printf`. This was so the address of the `printf` would be passed to `func_ptr` and not the return value a call to `printf()`. Although not necessary, this could also have been done by using the "address of" operator as follows:

```
func_ptr = &printf;
```

Line 14 is the call to the function. Notice that once again the asterisk is used to dereference the function. Because the parentheses to the right have a higher precedence, you need to include an extra set of parentheses around the function name and asterisk. Line 14 is equivalent to calling `printf()`.

The Practical Use of a Function Pointer

There are several occasions when you'll want to pass a function pointer to another function. The `qsort()` function is a prime example of such an instance. The ANSI C function, `qsort()`, expects a pointer to a function to be passed to it. The `qsort()` function sorts the entries in a table by calling a user-defined function. Following is the prototype for `qsort()`:

```
void qsort( void *base, size_t nelem, size_t width,
            int (*fcmp)(const void *, const void *));
```

Notice that the third parameter in this prototype, `fcmp`, is a pointer to a function. Listing 2.6 shows how different functions can be passed in this third parameter.

Type **Listing 2.6. Passing pointers to functions.**

```
1:   /* Program:  sort.c
2:    * Author:   Bradley L. Jones
3:    * Purpose:  Demonstrate a function pointer being
4:    *           passed as an argument
5:    *=================================================*/
6:
7:   #include <stdio.h>
```

continues

Listing 2.6. continued

```
8:    #include <stdlib.h>
9:    #include <string.h>
10:
11:   int sort_a_to_z(const void *first, const void *second);
12:   int sort_z_to_a(const void *first, const void *second);
13:
14:   void main(void)
15:   {
16:      int  ctr = 0;
17:      int  total;
18:      char list[10][256];
19:
20:      printf("\n\nPress <Enter> after each word. Enter QUIT to
                end\n");
21:
22:      gets(list[ctr]);
23:
24:      while( stricmp(list[ctr], "QUIT") != NULL )
25:      {
26:         ctr++;
27:         if(ctr == 10)
28:           break;
29:
30:         gets(list[ctr]);
31:      }
32:      total = ctr;
33:
34:      qsort((void *) list, total, sizeof(list[0]), sort_a_to_z);
35:
36:      printf("\nThe items sorted A to Z\n");
37:      for(ctr = 0; ctr < total; ctr++ )
38:      {
39:         printf("\n%s", list[ctr]);
40:      }
41:
42:      qsort((void *) list, total, sizeof(list[0]), sort_z_to_a);
43:
44:      printf("\n\nThe items sorted Z to A\n");
45:      for(ctr = 0; ctr < total; ctr++ )
46:      {
47:         printf("\n%s", list[ctr]);
48:      }
49:   }
50:
51:   int sort_a_to_z( const void *first, const void *second)
52:   {
53:      return( strcmp((char*)first, (char *)second) );
54:   }
55:
```

```
56:  int sort_z_to_a( const void *first, const void *second)
57:  {
58:      return( strcmp((char*)second, (char *)first) );
59:  }
```

Press <Enter> after each word. Enter QUIT to end
Mississippi
Illinois
Indiana
Montana
Colorado
South Dakota
Florida
California
Alaska
Georgia

The items sorted A to Z

Alaska
California
Colorado
Florida
Georgia
Illinois
Indiana
Mississippi
Montana
South Dakota

The items sorted Z to A

South Dakota
Montana
Mississippi
Indiana
Illinois
Georgia
Florida
Colorado
California
Alaska

 This program enables the user to enter up to ten words or phrases. It then sorts the words into ascending and descending orders using qsort(). As you saw in the preceding prototype, qsort() takes a pointer to a function as the third parameter. A function name without the parentheses is the address of the function. Two different functions are passed in the SORT.C listing. In line 34, qsort() is called

with `sort_a_to_z` as the third parameter. In line 42, `sort_z_to_a` is passed. Notice that these functions were prototyped in lines 11 and 12. It was necessary to prototype them before using them.

The rest of this program shouldn't present anything new. In line 20, the user is given a prompt to enter words. In lines 22 through 31, the program gets the information from the user. Line 32 assigns the counter, `ctr`, to `total`. `ctr`, and now `total`, contains the number of items that were entered. This is necessary for knowing how many items are to be sorted and printed. Lines 36 through 40 and 44 through 48 print the sorted values in the `list` array after each call to `qsort()`.

Complex Data Types (or Complex Data Combinations)

Virtually all of the basic data types presented so far today can be combined. When you combine the data types, you create what could be termed complex data types. These data types aren't really any more complex than the basic types. It's just that you have to be aware of what combinitations you have made. Some of the more common combinations of data types are:

☐ Pointers to structures.

☐ Arrays of structures.

☐ Variable-length structures.

Pointers to Structures

There are two commonly used ways to pass information from one function to another. The first and most common way is *passing by value* in which a value is passed to the called function. The second way, known as *passing by reference*, is to pass a pointer that references the data being passed. When you pass a pointer to a function, the new function has the capability to modify the original data. In addition, less computer resources are used in passing a pointer (reference) than in passing a copy (value). In the case of structures and other large data constructs, this can become important. The amount of space available to pass information is limited. In addition, there are a variety of instances where you'll want to modify the original data and not a copy of the data. Because of this, pointers to data and pointers to structures can be very important. Listing 2.7 presents an example of a pointer to a structure.

>
> **Note:** An additional use of pointers to structures is in linked lists, which are covered in Day 3.

Type **Listing 2.7. Using a pointer to a structure.**

```
1:  /* Program:  list0207.C
2:   * Author:   Bradley L. Jones
3:   * Purpose:  Program to demonstrate a pointer to a
4:   *             structure
5:   *=================================================*/
6:
7:  #include <stdio.h>
8:  #include <stdlib.h>
9:  #include <string.h>
10:
11: struct name_tag {
12:    char last[25+1];
13:    char first[15+1];
14:    char middle;
15: };
16:
17: char *format_name( struct name_tag *name );
18:
19: void main(void)
20: {
21:   struct name_tag name;
22:
23:   char input_string[256];
24:   char *full_name;
25:
26:   printf("\nEnter name:");
27:   printf("\n\nFirst name    ==> ");
28:   gets(input_string);
29:   strncpy(name.first, input_string, 15);
30:   name.first[15] = NULL;
31:
32:   printf("\nMiddle initial ==> ");
33:   gets(input_string);
34:   name.middle = input_string[0];
35:
36:   printf("\nLast name     ==> ");
37:   gets(input_string);
38:   strncpy(name.last, input_string, 25);
39:   name.last[25] = NULL;
40:
```

continues

Listing 2.7. continued

```
41:    full_name = format_name( &name );
42:
43:    printf("\n\nThe name you entered: %s", full_name);
44:    free(full_name);
45: }
46:
47: char *format_name( struct name_tag *name )
48: {
49:     char *full_name;
50:     char tmp_str[3];
51:
52:     full_name = malloc( 45 * sizeof(char) );
53:
54:     if( full_name != NULL )
55:     {
56:        strcpy( full_name, name->first );
57:        strcat( full_name, " " );
58:
59:        tmp_str[0] = name->middle;
60:        tmp_str[1] = '.';
61:        tmp_str[2] = NULL;
62:
63:        strcat( full_name, tmp_str);
64:        if(name->middle != NULL)
65:           strcat( full_name, " ");
66:
67:        strcat( full_name, name->last );
68:     }
69:
70:     return(full_name);
71: }
```

Output

```
Enter name:

First name      ==> Bradley

Middle initial ==> Lee

Last name       ==> Jones


The name you entered: Bradley L. Jones
```

This program enables you to enter information into a name structure. The structure, `name_tag`, holds a first, middle, and last name. This structure is declared in lines 11 through 15. Once the name is entered in lines 26 to 39, the name is then formatted into the `full_name` variable. The function, `format_name()`, is used to do the formatting. This function was prototyped in line 17. `format_name()` receives a pointer to a structure as its only parameter and returns a character pointer for the name string. Once the name is formatted, line 43 prints it. Line 44 concludes the program by freeing the space that was allocated for the name by `format_name()`.

Lines 47 through 71 contain the `format_name()` function. This function formats the name into the format of first name, space, middle initial, period, space, last name. Line 52 allocates memory with the `malloc()` command. (This should be familiar from Day 1.) Line 54 verifies that memory was allocated for the full name. If it was, the members of the name structure are formatted. Notice that this function uses the indirect membership operator (`->`). This function could have used indirection. The following would be an equivalent to line 59:

```
tmp_str[0] = (*name).middle;
```

Notice that there are parentheses around the structure pointer. This is because the member operator (`.`) has a higher precedence than the indirection operator (`*`).

Arrays of Structures

Arrays of structures are also commonly used. An array of structures operates just like an array of any other data type. Listing 2.8 is an expansion of Listing 2.7. This listing allows multiple names to be entered and placed into an array of name structures.

Listing 2.8. Using an array of structures.

```
 1:    /* Program:   list0208.C
 2:     * Author:    Bradley L. Jones
 3:     * Purpose:   Program to demonstrate an array of
 4:     *            structures
 5:     *=================================================*/
 6:
 7:    #include <stdio.h>
 8:    #include <stdlib.h>
 9:    #include <string.h>
10:
11:    #define NAMES  2
12:
```

continues

Listing 2.8. continued

```
13:   struct name_tag {
14:      char last[25+1];
15:      char first[15+1];
16:      char middle;
17:   };
18:
19:   char *format_name( struct name_tag *name );
20:
21:   void main(void)
22:   {
23:     struct name_tag names[NAMES];
24:
25:     int   ctr = 0;
26:     char input_string[256];
27:     char *full_name;
28:
29:     printf("\n\nThis program allows you to enter %d names.", NAMES);
30:     for( ctr = 0; ctr < NAMES; ctr++)
31:     {
32:        printf("\nEnter name %d.", ctr+1);
33:        printf("\n\nFirst name    ==> ");
34:        gets(input_string);
35:        strncpy(names[ctr].first, input_string, 15);
36:        names[ctr].first[15] = NULL;
37:
38:        printf("\nMiddle initial ==> ");
39:        gets(input_string);
40:        names[ctr].middle = input_string[0];
41:
42:        printf("\nLast name     ==> ");
43:        gets(input_string);
44:        strncpy(names[ctr].last, input_string, 25);
45:        names[ctr].last[25] = NULL;
46:     }
47:
48:     printf("\n\nThe names: \n");
49:
50:     for( ctr = 0; ctr < NAMES; ctr++ )
51:     {
52:        full_name = format_name( &names[ctr] );
53:        printf("\nName %d: %s", ctr+1, full_name);
54:        free(full_name);
55:     }
56:   }
57:
58:   char *format_name( struct name_tag *name )
59:   {
60:      char *full_name;
61:      char tmp_str[3];
62:
```

```
63:        full_name = malloc( 45 * sizeof(char) );
64:
65:        if( full_name != NULL )
66:        {
67:           strcpy( full_name, name->first );
68:           strcat( full_name, " " );
69:
70:           tmp_str[0] = name->middle;
71:           tmp_str[1] = '.';
72:           tmp_str[2] = NULL;
73:
74:           strcat( full_name, tmp_str);
75:           if(name->middle != NULL)
76:              strcat( full_name, " ");
77:
78:           strcat( full_name, name->last );
79:        }
80:
81:        return(full_name);
82:    }
```

Output

```
This program allows you to enter 2 names.
Enter name 1.

First name      ==> Boris

Middle initial ==>

Last name       ==> Yeltsin

Enter name 2.

First name      ==> Bill

Middle initial ==> E

Last name       ==> Clinton


The names:

Name 1: Boris Yeltsin
Name 2: Bill E. Clinton
```

Analysis

As stated before, this listing is quite similar to Listing 2.7. The listing allows names to be entered into an array. When all the names are entered, they are formatted and printed.

The difference in this listing should be easy to follow. In line 11, a defined constant, NAMES, is declared. This constant contains the number of names that will be entered. By using a defined constant, it becomes easy to change the number of names to be entered. Line 23 is also different. Instead of just declaring a name structure, an array is being declared. Lines 30 and 50 contain for loops that are used to get the multiple occurrences of names.

Like regular arrays, structure arrays will also use subscripts to access each element. This can first be seen in line 35. Notice that the subscript goes on the structure name, names, not the member name. Other than adding the subscript, this program will operate similar to Listing 2.7.

Variable-Length Structures

Variable-length structures are simply structures that can vary in size. In a normal structure, such as the following, you can determine the size:

```
struct employee_kids_tag{
    char first_name[15+1];
    char last_name [19+1];
    char child1_name[19+1];
    char child2_name[19+1];
};
```

You should be able to determine that variables declared with the employee_kids_tag will be 76 characters long. This is calculated by adding the sizes of the individual elements, plus any byte alignment that may occur. The employee_kids_tag structure would work well for all the employees who have two children or fewer, but what if John Smith has 12 kids? You wouldn't be able to store all his kids' names in a single structure. There are several solutions to get around this. The first is to modify the structure to declare 12 names for the children rather than 2. The following code shows this being done with an array instead of individual child name variables:

```
struct employee_kids_tag{
    char first_name[15+1];
    char last_name [19+1];
    char children_names[19+1][12];
};
```

This structure enables you to store the first and last name of the employee along with up to 12 children's names. As long as the array size is big enough to hold the most children that any employee has, this structure works; however, this is typically not an optimal solution. Figure 2.7 shows what the memory usage of this structure would be

when a variable is declared. Notice that there is a great deal of memory allocated. If most of the employees have only one or two kids, the majority of this allocated space will never be used.

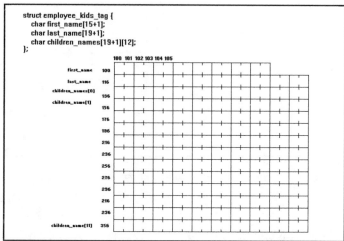

Figure 2.7. *The* `employee_kid_tag` *structure for 12 kids—potentially a lot of wasted space.*

Variable-length structures offer a solution to this type of problem by enabling you to change the number of elements in the array. If employee Sherman Smith has two kids, you declare the array with two elements. If Dawn Johnson has six kids, you declare the structure with six elements. Figure 2.8 shows how the memory usage should be.

As you can see in Figure 2.8, memory isn't completely conserved because we have the spaces at the end of each name; however, we did save space by only storing names when we have to.

Declaring the structure so that there can be different numbers of children would be done as follows:

```
struct employee_kids_tag{
    char first_name[15+1];
    char last_name [19+1];
    int  number_of_children;
    char child_name[];
};
```

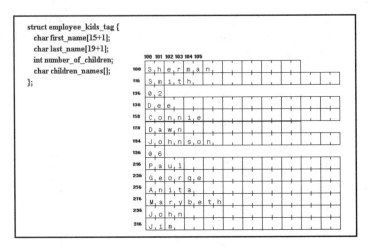

Figure 2.8. *Variable-length structures—conserving memory usage.*

Notice that two things have changed. First, we added an integer, `number_of_children`, stating how many children there are. Without this, we would have a much harder time knowing how many kids there are, and thus how big the structure is. The second change is in the `child_name` array. There isn't a number in the array! This signals that it is a variable-length array. It will be up to you to determine how big it is. (Hence the previously mentioned `number_of_children`.)

Warning. Some compilers won't allow you to declare an array without a value. In these cases, you should leave the last member, `child_name[]`, out of the structure.

When Are Variable-Length Structures Used?

You might be thinking that it would be much easier to use a consistent number of array elements. As long as you selected a size that meets a majority of your needs, you could be happy. While this may suffice, there are many instances that you may find that you need to use the variable-length structures. Although small or simple programs can afford the luxury of wasting space, more complex programs cannot. In addition, many programs that work with disk files require that you work with variable-length structures.

There are several examples of programs that use variable-length structures. Calendar programs, programs that modify executable (EXE) files, programs that work with bit-mapped graphics files, and word processor programs are just a few.

A Variable-Length Structure Example

The best way to understand the usage of variable-length files is to use them. The following example will use a variable-length structure to create a journal entry. The format of the journal entry will be as follows:

```
struct journal_entry_tag {
    int text_size;
    char text_entry[];
}
```

As you can see, this is a relatively simple structure. The first member of the structure is an integer that tells the size of the following character array, text_entry. Listing 2.9 uses this structure.

Listing 2.9. Program using variable-length structure.

```
1:  /*  Program: list0209.c
2:   *  Author:   Bradley L. Jones
3:   *  Purpose: Demonstrates a variable length file.
4:   *=================================================*/
5:
6:  #include <stdio.h>
7:  #include <stdlib.h>
8:  #include <string.h>
9:
10: typedef struct {
11:     int text_size;
12:     char text_entry[];
13: } JOURNAL_ENTRY;
14:
15: void main( void )
16: {
17:     JOURNAL_ENTRY entry[10];
18:
19:     char  buffer[256];
20:     int   ctr;
21:
22:     FILE *out_file;
23:
24:     if(( out_file = fopen( "TMP_FILE.TXT", "w+")) == NULL )
25:     {
26:         printf("\n\nError opening file.");
```

continues

Listing 2.9. continued

```
27:          exit(99);
28:      }
29:
30:      printf("\n\nYou will be prompted to enter 10 strings.\n");
31:
32:      for( ctr = 0; ctr < 10; ctr++ )
33:      {
34:          printf("\nEnter string %d:\n", ctr+1);
35:          gets(buffer);
36:          entry[ctr].text_size = strlen(buffer);
37:          fwrite( &entry[ctr].text_size, 1, sizeof( int), out_file);
38:          fwrite( buffer, 1, entry[ctr].text_size, out_file);
39:      }
40:
41:      printf("\n\nTo view your file, type the following:");
42:      printf("\n\n   TYPE TMP_FILE.TXT");
43:
44:      fclose(out_file);
45:  }
```

You will be prompted to enter 10 strings.

Enter string 1:
aaaa

Enter string 2:
BBBBBBBBBBBB

Enter string 3:
CCCCCCCCCCCCCCCCCCCCCCCCCCCCCCCCCCCCCCCCC

Enter string 4:
DDDDDDDDDDDDDDDDDDDDDDDDDDDDDDDDDDDDDDDDDDDDDDDDDDDDDDDDDDDDDDDDDDDDDDDDDDDDDDD

Enter string 5:
EEE

Enter string 6:
FFFFFFFFFFFFFFFFFFFFFF

Enter string 7:
GGGGGGGGGGGGGGGGGGGGGGGGGGGGGGGGGGGGGGGGGGG

Enter string 8:
HHHHHHHH

```
Enter string 9:
IIIIIIIIIIIIIIIIIIIIIIIIIIIIIIIIIIIIIIIIIIIIIIIIIIIIIIIIIIIIIIIIIIIIII

Enter string 10:
JJJJJJJJJJJJJJJJJJJJJJJJJJJJJJJJJJ


To view your file, type the following:

    TYPE TMP_FILE.TXT
```

Typing the TMP_FILE.TXT file displays the following:

```
__aaaa__BBBBBBBBBBBB__CCCCCCCCCCCCCCCCCCCCCCCCCCCCCCCCCCCCCCCCCCCC__
DDDDDDDDDDDDDDDDDDDDDDDDDDDDDDDDDDDDDDDDDDDDDDDDDDDDDDDDDDDDDDDDDDDDDDDD
__EEE__FFFFFFFFFFFFFFFFFFFFFF__GGGGGGGGGGGGGGGGGGGGGGGGGGGGGGGGGGGGGG__
HHHHHHH__IIIIIIIIIIIIIIIIIIIIIIIIIIIIIIIIIIIIIIIIIIIIIIIIIIIIIIIIIIIII__
JJJJJJJJJJJJJJJJJJJJJJJJJJJJJJJJJJ
```

You should note that the underscores in the output from typing TMP_FILE.TXT are actually numeric values. These will appear as unusual symbols on your screen. This listing isn't exactly clear on using the variable-length structure. To accurately demonstrate variable-length structures will take several pages of code. Later in this book, several variable-length structures will be used. The previous output demonstrates how a file can be created that applies to a simplistic variable-length structure. You could easily reverse this program so that it reads the file that was created. You could read each of these into the JOURNAL_ENTRY structures. You would need to dynamically allocate space for the character array within the structure.

This program presents some interesting items. In line 22, a file pointer is declared. This pointer is used in line 24 to point to the TMP_FILE.TXT file. This is the file for the variable-length journal entries. Lines 37 and 38 write the information out to the file. In line 37, the portions of the structure that are constant in size are written. In this case, it is a single field. In line 38, the variable length portion is written out. An exercise at the end of this chapter asks you to write a program that reads this file and prints out the information.

Summary

Although a lot of what was presented today should have been familiar, some of the material might have been new to you. Today began with a review of the basic data types, the definition of the typedef statement and its use, followed by advanced data types (or advanced groupings of data types). This included working with arrays, structures, and unions. A review of pointers was also provided—simple pointers, pointers to pointers, pointers to functions, and pointers to structures. The day moved to arrays of structures before concluding with variable-length structures.

Q&A

Q Can you program in C without fully understanding pointers?

A Yes; however, you'll be extremely limited in what you'll be able to do. Pointers are found in virtually every real-world application.

Q How many dimensions can an array have?

A The number of levels an array can have is compiler-dependent. It becomes more confusing to use multidimensional arrays the more levels you use. Most applications rarely need more than three levels.

Q How many levels of indirection can you have with pointers?

A As with arrays, you don't want too many levels of indirection. You rarely go more than three levels deep with pointers (pointer to a pointer to a pointer). Although going two levels deep is not unusual (pointer to pointer), anything more should be avoided if possible.

Workshop

The Workshop provides quiz questions to help you solidify your understanding of the material covered and exercises to provide you with experience in using what you've learned.

Quiz

1. What are considered the basic data types?

2. What C keyword can be used to help increase the readability of your code?

3. What is the data type of a variable declared as a DWORD?

4. What are three ways of grouping data?

5. What is the value of NULL or the Null character?

6. Why is it important to know about word alignment?

7. What is a pointer?

8. How do you determine the address of a variable?

9. What is the difference between the following two prototypes?

```
return_type (*name)(parameter_list);

return_type *(name)(parameter_list);
```

10. What is a benefit of using variable-length structures?

Exercises

1. Write the code for the data type necessary to store a social security number of the format 999-99-9999. Don't use a simple string (character array).

2. Write the code for the data type necessary to store a type long variable called number in the same area of memory as a string variable called string. The length of string should be four characters.

3. Write a program that declares a pointer variable. The pointer variable should be assigned its own address.

4. Write a program that declares and initializes a double-dimensioned array. The program should also print the array to the screen.

5. How would you create a data element that could hold 10 social security numbers (from Exercise 1)?

6. Modify Listing 2.1 to print the numeric array as characters. What is printed?

7. **ON YOUR OWN:** Write a program that reads the information in the TMP_FILE.TXT created by Listing 2.9.

8. **ON YOUR OWN:** Write a program that sorts the TMP_FILE.TXT text entries and writes them back out.

9. **ON YOUR OWN:** If you are using a Windows compiler, consult your documentation for information on the Microsoft Windows file formats. Most of the file formats used by Microsoft Windows employ variable-length structures similar to those presented today. Another good reference book would be Tom Swan's book, *Inside Windows File Formats* from SAMS Publishing.

Lists and Trees

Linked lists and their associated data types are considered advanced topics in C. Most beginning C books touch lightly on the topic of linked lists and leave it to the programmer to figure them out when they are needed. There are several classes of linked lists. Single-linked lists are the most commonly used. There are also double-linked lists, binary trees, and more. Today you will learn:

☐ What linked lists are.

☐ How to use single-linked lists.

☐ About double-linked lists.

☐ How to use stacks and queues.

☐ How to use binary trees.

Linked Structures

Linked list is a general classification for several methods of storing information in which the data stored is connected, or linked, together. As you should be able to guess, this linking takes place with the use of pointers.

> **Expert Tip:** Linked lists are not used a great deal. There are instances where linked lists are a perfect solution. On Day 17 and Day 18, you will use both single-linked and double-linked lists, so it is important that you understand the concepts involved in using them.

There are two types of linked lists that are commonly used: single- and double-linked lists. The specific type of linked list is determined by how the data groups are connected. A *single-linked list* has a single connection between each group of information. A *double-linked list* has two connections between each data group.

> **Note:** Single-linked lists are generally referred to as "linked lists" or "linear linked lists."

Using a Single-Linked List

Single-linked lists, and linked lists in general, are used for several reasons. The main reason is speed. When working with sorted disk files, it can be time consuming to add in a new element. If you add a new element to the beginning of a disk file, each of the following elements must be shifted. With a linked list, you work in memory. Because memory is much faster than disk access, you can manipulate the data in the list faster. In addition, sorted disk files are generally stored in sorted order. With a linked list, pointers are used to keep the elements sorted. If a new element is to be added, it can be placed anywhere. Only the links need to be adjusted. This again increases the speed.

Linked lists involve using a structure that contains a pointer member. The pointer member, however, is special. In the structure

```
struct element {
    int data;
    struct element *next;
};
```

the pointer contains the address of another structure. In fact, it's a pointer to a structure of its own type. The pointer in the structure, called next in this case, points to another element structure. This means that each structure, or link, can point to another structure at the same time. Figure 3.1 illustrates a single link using the preceding element structure. Figure 3.2 illustrates using a linked list of such structures.

Figure 3.1. *An element link.*

Figure 3.2. *Links in a linked list.*

Notice that in Figure 3.2, each element points to the next. The last element doesn't point to anything. To help show that the last element doesn't point to an additional link, the pointer is assigned the value of NULL. In C, NULL is equal to zero.

The last link in a single-linked list always points to NULL; however, how do you locate the other links? To prevent the loss of links, you must set up an additional pointer. This pointer is commonly referred to as a head pointer. The *head pointer* always points

to the first element in the link. If you know where the first pointer is, you can access its pointer to the second element. The second element's pointer can then be accessed to get to the third. This can continue until you reach a NULL pointer, which would signify the end of the list. It's possible that the head pointer could be NULL, which would mean the list is empty. Figure 3.3 illustrates the head pointer along with a linked list.

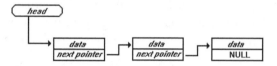

Figure 3.3. *The head pointer.*

Note: The head pointer is a pointer to the first element in a linked list. The head pointer is sometimes referred to the "first element pointer" or "top pointer."

Listing 3.1 presents a program that isn't very practical. It creates a three element linked list. Each of the elements is used by going through the original element. The purpose of this program is to illustrate the relationship between elements. In the following sections, you'll see more practical ways of creating and using linked lists.

Type   **Listing 3.1. A first look at a linked list.**

```
 1:  /* Program:   list0301.c
 2:   * Author:    Bradley L. Jones
 3:   * Purpose:   Demonstrate the relations in a linked list
 4:   * Note:      Program assumes that malloc() is successful.
 5:   *            You should not make this assumption!
 6:   *=========================================================*/
 7:
 8:  #include <stdio.h>
 9:  #include <stdlib.h>
10:
11:  #define NULL 0
12:
13:  struct list
14:  {
15:     char    ch;
16:     struct list *next;
```

```
17:  };
18:
19:  typedef struct list LIST;
20:
21:  typedef LIST *LISTLINK;
22:
23:  int main( void )
24:  {
25:     LISTLINK  first;                  /* same as a head pointer */
26:
27:     first = (LISTLINK) malloc( sizeof(LIST) );
28:
29:     first->ch = 'a';
30:     first->next = (LISTLINK) malloc( sizeof(LIST) );
31:
32:     first->next->ch = 'b';
33:     first->next->next = (LISTLINK) malloc( sizeof(LIST) );
34:
35:     first->next->next->ch = 'c';
36:     first->next->next->next = NULL;
37:
38:     printf("\n\nPrint the character values...");
39:
40:     printf("\n\nValues from the first link:");
41:     printf("\n   ch is %c", first->ch );
42:     printf("\n   next is %d", first->next );
43:
44:     printf("\n\nValues from the second link:");
45:     printf("\n   ch is %c", first->next->ch );
46:     printf("\n   next is %d", first->next->next );
47:
48:     printf("\n\nValues from the third link:");
49:     printf("\n   ch is %c", first->next->next->ch );
50:     printf("\n   next is %d", first->next->next->next );
51:
52:     free( first->next->next );
53:     free( first->next );
54:     free( first );
55:
56:     return(0);
57:  }
```

```
Print the character values...

Values from the first link:
    ch is a
    next is 1618

Values from the second link:
    ch is b
    next is 1626
```

3

```
Values from the third link:
   ch is c
   next is 0
```

As stated before, Listing 3.1 isn't the most practical listing; however, it demonstrates many important points regarding linked lists. First, in reviewing the listing you should notice that the linked list's structure is declared in lines 13 through 17. In addition, lines 19 and 21 use the `typedef` command to create two constants. The first is `LIST`, which will be a new data type for declaring a structure of type `list`. The second defined constant, in line 21, is a pointer to a `LIST` data type called `LISTLINK`. This data type, `LISTLINK`, will be used to create the links to the different `LIST` elements in the linked list.

The main part of the program actually starts in line 25 where a pointer to the list structure is declared using the `LISTLINK` constant. This pointer, called `first`, will be used to indicate the beginning of the linked list that is being created. Line 27 allocates the first element in the link. Using `malloc()`, enough space is allocated for one `LIST` element. A pointer is returned by `malloc()` and is stored in `first`. Notice that the program doesn't check to ensure that `malloc()` was successful. This is a poor assumption on the program's part. It's a good programming practice to always check the return value of a memory allocation function.

Line 29 assigns a value to the character variable, `ch`, in the structure. If the linked list element contained other data, it could also be filled in at this point. Line 30 contains the pointer called `next`, that links this element with the next element in the list. If this were the only element in the list, the value of NULL, or zero, could be assigned to the `next` pointer as follows:

```
first->next = NULL;
```

Because an additional link is being added to the list, the `next` pointer is used. In this case, another `malloc()` statement is called to allocate memory for the following element of the list. Upon completion of the allocation, line 32 assigns a value of 'b' to the data item, `ch`. Line 33 repeats the process of allocating memory for a third element. Because the third element is the last being assigned, line 36 caps off the linked list by assigning the value of NULL to the `next` pointer.

Lines 40 through 50 print the values of the elements to the screen so that you can observe the output. The values printed for `next` may vary. Lines 52 through 54 release the memory allocated for the elements in reverse order that they were allocated in.

This program accesses each element by starting with the first element in the list. As you can see, this could be impractical if you have a large number of links. This program is only effective for providing an example, but it's impractical for actually using linked lists.

Using a Linked List

Linked lists are used similar to disk files. Elements or links can be added, deleted, or modified. Modifying an element presents no real challenge; however, adding and deleting an element may. As stated earlier, elements in a list are connected with pointers. When a new element is added, the pointers must be adjusted. Where the new element is added affects how pointers are modified. Elements can be added to the beginning, middle, or end of a linked list. In addition, if the element is the first to be added to the list, the process is a little different.

Adding the First Link

You'll know you are adding the first element to a linked list if the head pointer is NULL. The head pointer should be changed to point to the new element. In addition, because the element being added is the only element, the "next" pointer should be set to NULL. Figure 3.4 illustrates the final result.

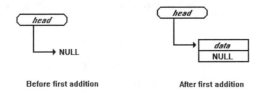

Before first addition   After first addition

Figure 3.4. *Adding the first element to a linked list.*

The following code fragment includes the element structure defined previously along with two type definitions:

```
struct _element {
    int data;
    struct _element *next;
};

typedef struct _element ELEMENT;
typedef ELEMENT *LINK;
```

The _element structure will be used by means of the two type definitions. When an instance of _element needs to be declared, ELEMENT will be used. ELEMENT is a defined data type for the _element structure. The second defined data type, LINK, is a pointer to an _element structure. These defined constants will be used in later examples. The following code fragment illustrates adding an initial element to a linked list:

```
LINK first = NULL;
LINK new = NULL;

/* enter a new item */
new = (LINK) malloc( sizeof(ELEMENT) );
scanf("%d", &(next->data));

if (first == NULL)
{
    new->next = NULL;
    first = new;
}
```

This fragment starts by including two declarations for pointers to an _element structure using the LINK typedef. Because these are pointer values, they are initialized to NULL. The first LINK pointer, called first, will be used as a head pointer. The second LINK, called new, will contain the link that will be added to the list. The link is created and then data for the link is retrieved. The addition of the new element to the list occurs in the last five lines. If the first pointer—which is the head pointer—is equal to NULL, then you know the list is empty. You can set the pointer in the new element to NULL because there isn't another one to point to. You can then set the head pointer, first, to the new element. At this point, the element is linked in.

Notice that malloc() is used to allocate the memory for the new element. As each new element is added, only the memory needed for it is allocated. The calloc() function could also be used. You should be aware of the difference between these two functions. The main difference is that calloc() will clear out the new element; the malloc() function won't.

Warning: The malloc() in the preceding code fragment didn't ensure that the memory was allocated. You should always check the return value of a memory allocation function.

Tip: When possible, initialize pointers to NULL when you declare them.

Adding to the Beginning

Adding an element to the beginning of a linked list is similar to adding an element to a new list. When an element is added to the beginning, two steps are involved. First, the "next" pointer of the new element must be set to the original first element of the list. This can be done by setting the new element's "next" pointer equal to the head pointer. Once this is done, the head pointer must be reset to point to the new element that now begins the list. Figure 3.5 illustrates this process.

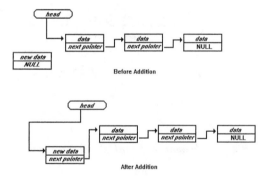

Figure 3.5. *Adding an element to the beginning of a linked list.*

Again using the element structure, the following code fragment illustrates the process of adding an element to the beginning of a linked list:

```
/* adding an element to the beginning of a list */
{
    new->next = first;
    first = new;
}
```

The next pointer in the new element is set to point to the value of the head pointer, first. Once this is set, the head pointer is reset to point to the new element.

> **Warning:** It is important to take these two steps in the correct order. If you reassign the head pointer first, you will lose the list!

Adding to the Middle

Adding an element to the middle of a list is a little more complicated, yet this process is still relatively easy. Once the location for the new element is determined, you'll adjust the pointers on several elements. Figure 3.6 illustrates the process of adding an element to the middle of a linked list.

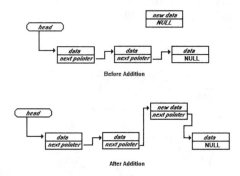

Figure 3.6. *Adding an element to the middle of a linked list.*

As you can see from Figure 3.6, when a new element is added to the middle, two pointers have to be adjusted. The "next" pointer of the previous element has to be adjusted to point to the new element. In addition, the "next" pointer of the new element needs to be set to the original value of the "next" pointer in the previous element. Once these pointers are readjusted, the new element is a part of the list. The following code fragment illustrates this addition:

```
/* adding an element to the middle */
insert_link( LINK prev_link, LINK new_link )
{
    new_link->next = prev_link->next;
    prev_link->next = new_link;
}
```

This fragment presents a function that moves the previous link's next pointer to the new link's next pointer. It then sets the previous link's next pointer to point to the new element.

Adding to the End

The final location to which you can add a link is the end of a list. Adding an element to the end is identical to adding a link to the middle. This case is mentioned separately because the value of the previous element's "next" pointer is NULL (or zero). Figure 3.7 illustrates adding an element to the end of a linked list.

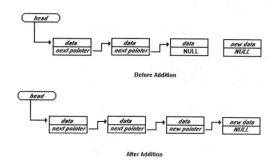

Figure 3.7. *Adding an element to the end of a linked list.*

Implementing a Linked List

Now that you've seen the ways to add links to a list, it's time to see them in action. Listing 3.2 presents a program that uses a linked list to hold a set of characters. The characters are stored in memory by using a linked list.

Type

Listing 3.2. Adding to a linked list of characters.

```
 1:  /* Program:   list0302.c
 2:   * Author:    Bradley L. Jones
 3:   *            Gregory L. Guntle
 4:   * Purpose:   Inserts a char in a list
 5:   *            Used on a single link list
 6:   *=======================================================*/
 7:
 8:  #include <stdio.h>
 9:  #include <stdlib.h>
10:
11:
12:  #ifndef NULL
13:  #define NULL 0
14:  #endif
15:
16:  struct list
17:  {
```

continues

Listing 3.2. continued

```
18:     char    ch;
19:     struct list *next_rec;
20:  };
21:
22:  typedef struct list LIST;
23:  typedef LIST *LISTPTR;              /* Pointer to the structure list */
24:
25:  LISTPTR add_to_list( char, LISTPTR );   /* Function to add new item
                                                                to list */
26:  void show_list(void);
27:  void free_memory_list(void);
28:  void insert_list( char, LISTPTR );
29:
30:  LISTPTR first = NULL;                   /* same as a head pointer */
31:
32:
33:  int main( void )
34:  {
35:     LISTPTR rec_addr;
36:     int i=0;
37:
38:     rec_addr = add_to_list( 'A', (LISTPTR)NULL );  /* Add 1st char */
39:     first = rec_addr;                              /* Start of our
                                                            list */
40:
41:     /*  Build initial list */
42:     printf("Before insertion\n");
43:     while ( i++<5 )
44:        rec_addr = add_to_list( 'A'+i, rec_addr );
45:     show_list();                        /* Dumps the entire list - BEFORE */
46:
47:     printf("\n\nAfter insertion\n");
48:     /*  Now insert two chars into current list */
49:     i=0;
50:     rec_addr = first;        /* Start at beginning */
51:     while( i<2 )             /* Travel chain to 3rd position */
52:     {
53:        rec_addr = rec_addr->next_rec;
54:        i++;
55:     }
56:     insert_list( 'Z', rec_addr );
57:     show_list();                        /* Dumps the entire list - AFTER */
58:
59:     free_memory_list();                       /* Release all memory */
60:
61:     return(0);
62:  }
63:
64:  /* Function: add_to_list
65:   * Purpose : Inserts new record at end of the list
```

```
66:     *
67:     * Entry    : char ch = character to store
68:     *            LISTPTR prev_rec = address to previous data record
69:     *
70:     * Returns : Address to this new record
71:     *========================================================*/
72:
73:    LISTPTR add_to_list( char ch, LISTPTR prev_rec )
74:    {
75:        LISTPTR new_rec=NULL;                 /* Holds address of new rec */
76:
77:        new_rec = (LISTPTR)malloc(sizeof(LIST)); /* Get memory location */
78:        if (!new_rec)                            /* Unable to get memory */
79:        {
80:            printf("\nUnable to allocate memory!\n");
81:            exit(1);
82:        }
83:
84:        new_rec->ch = ch;          /* Store character into new location */
85:        new_rec->next_rec = NULL;  /* Last record always pts to NULL */
86:
87:        if (prev_rec)                 /* If not at first record */
88:          prev_rec->next_rec = new_rec; /* Adjust pointer of previous rec
89:                                           to pt to this new one */
90:        return(new_rec);          /* return address of this new record */
91:    }
92:
93:    /* Function: insert_list
94:     * Purpose : Inserts new record anywhere in list
95:     * Entry    : char ch = character to store
96:     *            LISTPTR prev_rec = address to previous data record
97:     *
98:     * Returns : Address to this new record
99:     *========================================================*/
100:
101:   void insert_list( char ch, LISTPTR prev_link )
102:   {
103:       LISTPTR new_rec=NULL;                 /* Holds address of new rec */
104:
105:       new_rec = (LISTPTR)malloc(sizeof(LIST)); /* Get memory location */
106:       if (!new_rec)                            /* Unable to get memory */
107:       {
108:           printf("Unable to allocate memory!\n");
109:           exit(1);
110:       }
111:
112:       new_rec->ch = ch;
113:       new_rec->next_rec = prev_link->next_rec;
```

3

continues

Listing 3.2. continued

```
114:     prev_link->next_rec = new_rec;
115: }
116:
117:
118: /* Function: show_list
119:  * Purpose : Displays the information current in the list
120:  * Entry   : N/A
121:  * Returns : N/A
122:  *=======================================================*/
123:
124: void show_list()
125: {
126:     LISTPTR cur_ptr;
127:     int counter = 1;
128:
129:     printf("Rec addr  Position  Data  Next Rec addr\n");
130:     printf("========  ========  ====  =============\n");
131:     cur_ptr = first;
132:     while (cur_ptr)
133:     {
134:         printf("  %X    ", cur_ptr );   /* Address of this record */
135:         printf("     %2i       %c", counter++, cur_ptr->ch);
136:         printf("      %X   \n",cur_ptr->next_rec);  /* Address of
                                                        next rec */
137:         cur_ptr = cur_ptr->next_rec;
138:     }
139: }
140:
141: /* Function: free_memory_list
142:  * Purpose : Frees up all the memory collected for list
143:  * Entry   : N/A
144:  * Returns : N/A
145:  *=======================================================*/
146:
147: void free_memory_list()
148: {
149:     LISTPTR cur_ptr, next_rec;
150:     cur_ptr = first;          /* Start at beginning */
151:     while (cur_ptr)           /* Go until hit end of list = NULL */
152:     {
153:         next_rec = cur_ptr->next_rec; /* Get address of next record */
154:         free(cur_ptr);                /* Free current record */
155:         cur_ptr = next_rec;           /* Adjust current */
156:     }
157: }
```

```
Before insertion
Rec addr  Position  Data  Next Rec addr
========  ========  ====  =============
  654        1       A        65C
  65C        2       B        664
  664        3       C        66C
  66C        4       D        674
  674        5       E        67C
  67C        6       F         0


After insertion
Rec addr  Position  Data  Next Rec addr
========  ========  ====  =============
  654        1       A        65C
  65C        2       B        664
  664        3       C        684
  684        4       Z        66C
  66C        5       D        674
  674        6       E        67C
  67C        7       F         0
```

This listing demonstrates several times when a link can be added. In line 37, the first link is added to an empty list. In line 43, a function is called to add a link to the current position at the end of the list. Finally, in line 55, a function is called to add a link at a position in the middle of the list.

This listing uses a structure in lines 15 through 19 that defines the link that will be used. The list will contain a character, ch, and a pointer to the next link, next_rec. Lines 21 and 22 create type definitions for the link structure called LIST. In addition, in line 22, a constant for a pointer to the structure is declared as LISTPTR. These constants make the declarations later in the listing easier to follow.

In line 29, the head pointer, first, is declared and initialized to NULL. The first pointer is declared with the pointer previously defined as LISTPTR. The first pointer will be used to always point to the beginning of the linked list. Additional variables are declared in main().

Line 37 uses a function called add_to_list() to add the first link. This link will contain the character 'A.' Lines 63 through 90 contain the add_to_list() function. This function takes the new character to be added and the previous link's address, and it returns the new link's address. Line 76 allocates memory for the new link. Line 77 ensures the allocation was successful. If it wasn't, then an error message is printed and the program exits. Line 83 assigns the new character to the newly allocated link. The

next pointer assigns NULL to the next pointer. If this isn't the first link, the previous link's next_rec pointer is assigned to this new link, which effectively places the new link at the end of the list. Line 89 returns the address of the new link. This function adds links in a manner similar to what was shown in Figure 3.7.

Back in main(), lines 42 and 43 loop through adding five more links. Line 44 then prints the list to the screen using show_list() in lines 117 through 138. The show_list() function prints headings and then, starting with the first link, navigates through the list. This is done by accessing the next link through the next_rec pointer (line 136).

In lines 48 through 53, the program starts at the beginning of the list and loops through two links. Line 55 then uses the insert_list() function to insert a link in the middle of the list. The insert_list() function, in lines 92 through 114, declares a temporary link called new_rec. Lines 104 through 109 allocate and verify the new_rec link. Line 111 assigns the character to the new link. Line 112 assigns the value from the previous link's next_rec pointer to the new link's next_rec pointer. The previous link's next_rec pointer is then assigned the value of the new link. This places the link into the list in a fashion similar to what was presented in Figure 3.6.

Deleting from a Linked List

The ability to add information to a linked list is good; however, there are times when you'll want to remove information too. Deleting links, or elements, is similar to adding them. You can delete links from the beginning, middle, and end of linked lists. In addition, you can delete the last link in the list. In each case, the appropriate pointers need to be moved. Also, the memory used by the deleted link needs to be freed.

Note: Don't forget to free memory when deleting links!

DO   **DON'T**

DON'T forget to free any memory allocated for links when deleting them.

DO understand the difference between calloc() and malloc(). Most importantly, remember that malloc() doesn't initialize allocated memory—calloc() does.

Stacks

A *stack* is a special linked list. A stack differs from the normal linked list in that it's always accessed from its top. This means new elements are always added at the top, and if an element is to be removed, it's taken from the top. This gives the stack a *Last In First Out*, or LIFO, order. It's this LIFO nature that makes a stack what it is by nature. For comparison, consider dishes; you stack them on a shelf one at a time. To remove the first dish that you placed on the shelf—the one on the bottom—you must remove each of the dishes that you placed on top of it. The first dish placed on the shelf is the last dish you can remove. Figure 3.8 illustrates a stack.

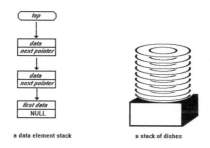

a data element stack   a stack of dishes

Figure 3.8. *Two sketches of stacks; elements in a linked list and dishes on a shelf.*

Using a stack basically requires the use of four functions. These functions check whether the stack is empty, return the value of the top item on the stack, push a new item onto the stack, and pop an old item off of the stack. Each of these functions is necessary for the completion of a program using a stack. Listing 3.3 illustrates the use of these four functions.

Type Listing 3.3. STACK.C. Using a stack.

```
1:  /* Program:   stack.c
2:   * Author:    Bradley L. Jones
3:   * Purpose:   Demonstration of a stack.  (LIFO)
4:   * Note:      Program assumes that malloc() is successful.
5:   *            You should not make this assumption!
6:   *=========================================================*/
7:
8:  #include <stdio.h>
9:  #include <stdlib.h>
```

continues

Listing 3.3. continued

```
10:
11:   #define NULL 0
12:
13:   struct stack
14:   {
15:     int    value;
16:     struct stack *next;
17:   };
18:
19:   typedef struct stack LINK;
20:
21:   typedef LINK *LINK_PTR;
22:
23:   /*** prototypes ***/
24:   void push_stack( LINK_PTR *link1, int val );
25:   void pop_stack( LINK_PTR *link1, int *val );
26:   int is_stack_empty( LINK_PTR link1 );
27:   int get_stack_data( LINK_PTR link );
28:
29:
30:   int main( void )
31:   {
32:     LINK_PTR first = NULL;
33:
34:     int ctr,
35:         nbrs[10];
36:
37:     for( ctr = 0; ctr < 10; ctr ++ )
38:     {
39:       nbrs[ctr] = ctr;
40:       printf("\nPush # %d, nbrs[ctr] = %d", ctr, nbrs[ctr]);
41:       push_stack(&first, nbrs[ctr]);
42:     }
43:
44:     printf("\n-----------");
45:
46:     for( ctr = 0; ctr < 10; ctr ++ )
47:     {
48:       pop_stack(&first, &nbrs[ctr]);
49:       printf("\nPop # %d, nbrs[ctr] = %d", ctr, nbrs[ctr]);
50:     }
51:
52:     return(0);
53:   }
54:
55:   /*---------------------------*
56:    * Name:    push_stack()
57:    * Purpose: Places a value into a new link on the stack.
58:    *          Returns the value of the data stored.
59:    * Params:  link = the next field from the previous link
```

```
60:    *            val   = value being placed on the stack.
61:    * Return:  None
62:    *--------------------------*/
63:
64:   void push_stack( LINK_PTR *link1, int val )
65:   {
66:     LINK_PTR tmp_link;
67:
68:     tmp_link = (LINK_PTR) malloc( sizeof(LINK) );
69:     tmp_link->value = val;
70:     tmp_link->next  = *link1;
71:     *link1 = tmp_link;
72:   }
73:
74:   /*--------------------------*
75:    * Name:     pop_stack()
76:    * Purpose: Removes a link from the stack.
77:    *           Returns the value of the data stored.
78:    * Params:  link = the current link that is to be removed.
79:    *           val  = value of the removed link
80:    * Return:  None
81:    *--------------------------*/
82:
83:   void pop_stack( LINK_PTR *link1, int *val )
84:   {
85:     LINK_PTR first = *link1;
86:
87:     if ( is_stack_empty(first) == 0 )   /* if not empty */
88:     {
89:       *val   = first->value;
90:       *link1 = first->next;
91:       free( first );
92:     }
93:     else
94:     {
95:       printf("\n\nStack is empty");
96:     }
97:   }
98:
99:   /*--------------------------*
100:   * Name:      is_stack_empty()
101:   * Purpose:  Checks to see if a link exists.
102:   * Params:   link1 = pointer to links
103:   * Return:   0 if the stack is not empty
104:   *            1 if the stack is empty
105:   *--------------------------*/
106:
107:  int is_stack_empty( LINK_PTR link1 )
108:  {
109:    int rv = 0;
```

continues

Listing 3.3. continued

```
110:
111:   if( link1 == NULL )
112:      rv = 1;
113:
114:   return( rv );
115: }
116:
117: /*-----------------------------*
118:  * Name:      get_stack_data()
119:  * Purpose:   Gets the value for a link on the stack
120:  * Params:    link = pointer to a link
121:  * Return:    value of the integer stored in link
122:  *-----------------------------*/
123:
124: int get_stack_data( LINK_PTR link )
125: {
126:    return( link->value );
127: }
```

```
Push # 0, nbrs[ctr] = 0
Push # 1, nbrs[ctr] = 1
Push # 2, nbrs[ctr] = 2
Push # 3, nbrs[ctr] = 3
Push # 4, nbrs[ctr] = 4
Push # 5, nbrs[ctr] = 5
Push # 6, nbrs[ctr] = 6
Push # 7, nbrs[ctr] = 7
Push # 8, nbrs[ctr] = 8
Push # 9, nbrs[ctr] = 9
---------------------
Pop # 0, nbrs[ctr] = 9
Pop # 1, nbrs[ctr] = 8
Pop # 2, nbrs[ctr] = 7
Pop # 3, nbrs[ctr] = 6
Pop # 4, nbrs[ctr] = 5
Pop # 5, nbrs[ctr] = 4
Pop # 6, nbrs[ctr] = 3
Pop # 7, nbrs[ctr] = 2
Pop # 8, nbrs[ctr] = 1
Pop # 9, nbrs[ctr] = 0
```

This listing may seem complex at first glance; however, a large portion of it should be easily discernible. Line 11 defines the constant, NULL, to the value of zero. Lines 13 through 21 define the structure, stack, that will be used for the linked list to create the actual stack. Lines 24 through 27 present prototypes for the four functions that are typically needed when using stacks. After the prototypes, the program is ready to begin in line 30.

This program pushes several numbers onto a stack and then pops them off. The numbers are pushed on within a for loop in lines 37 through 42. Line 41 calls push_stack() to place the number. Because the numbers are always added to the top, the first structure in the linked list is passed to the push_stack() function. The value being pushed is stored in nbrs[ctr]. This happens to be the same value as the counter variable, ctr (see line 39). Line 48 takes each value off of the stack. Each value is placed in the nbrs array as it is taken off. The value is then printed in line 49. Once all ten values are popped off of the stack, the program ends.

The push_stack() function is relatively simple. Line 66 declares a LINK_PTR pointer called tmp_link that is used to hold the value of the new link being passed to the function. Lines 68 through 71 then perform the necessary steps to copy a link to the beginning of a list. Notice that the return value of malloc() is never checked to ensure that it succeeded. You should always check the return values of memory allocation functions.

The pop_stack() function accepts a pointer to the first link in the list along with a pointer to the value being placed on the stack. Line 85, like line 66, creates a new LINK_PTR pointer and copies the first pointer in the linked list to it. Line 87 calls the is_stack_empty() function. This function simply checks to ensure the first link is equal to NULL (line 111). If it is, there is no reason to pop any more links because the stack is empty. If the stack isn't empty, then the value of the first link is assigned to the parameter, val. The first pointer that was passed in is passed to the next pointer so it can be removed without losing the pointer to the beginning of the string. Finally, line 91 releases the memory used by the original beginning link back to the system using a call to free().

The fourth function commonly used isn't used by this program. The function is get_stack_data(). If the link was more complex than a simple single data type, you would want a function that could manipulate and return the data in a link. This function could have been used if there was a need to see a data value without actually removing it from the stack.

Queues

Queues, like stacks, are special forms of linked lists. A queue is similar to a stack in that it's accessed in consistent ways. However, where a stack was LIFO (Last In First Out), a queue is *First In First Out* (FIFO). That is, instead of being accessed only from the top like a stack, it's accessed from both the top and the bottom. A queue has new items added only to the top. When an element is removed, it's always taken from the bottom. A queue can be compared to a ticket line. The person who gets in line first is served first. In addition, people must always enter at the end of the line. Figure 3.9 illustrates a queue.

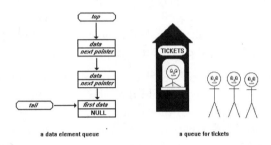

a data element queue   a queue for tickets

Figure 3.9. *Queues.*

A queue can be used with the same basic functions used to access a stack. You'll want the ability to see whether the queue is empty, to add an item to the top (or beginning) of the queue, to get an element from the bottom (or end) of the queue, and to see what is next in the queue. Each of these functions helps to complete a queue program.

A queue could be accomplished with a single-linked list; however, working with a queue becomes much easier with a double-linked list.

Double-Linked List

Single-linked lists enable the user to move between the elements starting at the top and working toward the bottom (or end). Sometimes it's advantageous to be able to work back toward the top. A queue would be one example of many such instances. You can traverse a list from both ends by adding a second set of links (pointers) between the elements. The double set of pointers causes the list to be double-linked. Figure 3.10 illustrates a double-linked list.

In Figure 3.10, you should notice that all the components of a single-linked list are present. In addition, a head pointer and a tail pointer are both present. As with a single-linked list, the head pointer will always point at the top or first element of the list. The tail pointer will always point at the last. If there are no elements in the list, the head and the tail pointers will both be NULL. If there is only one element, then the two pointers will be equal to the first—and only—element.

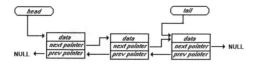

Figure 3.10. *A double-linked list.*

 Note: A double-linked list must have a tail pointer in addition to its head pointer. With the exception of queues, single-linked lists don't have to have tail pointers; they are only required in double-linked lists.

A structure for an element in a double-linked list is different from that of a single-linked list in that it contains an additional pointer. The format of a structure for a double-linked list would be similar to the following:

```
struct element {
    <data>
    struct element *next;
    struct element *previous;
};
```

The <data> can be whatever data you are storing in your linked list. The next pointer points to the following element in the list. If the element is the last in the list, then next will contain the NULL value. The previous pointer contains the address of the previous element in the list. In the case of the first element—where there isn't a previous element, the value of previous will be NULL.

Binary Trees

A *binary tree* is a special double-linked list. It is also a special type of data tree. A *data tree* is a set of data elements that are all linked together into a hierarchical structure. Each element in a tree is called a *node*. Like a linked list that starts at its head pointer, a tree starts with what is its *root*. The root then has *sub-nodes* that are each connected to it. Sub-nodes can have even more sub-nodes below them. The bottom nodes, those that do not have any additional sub-nodes, are called *leaf nodes*. Figure 3.11 illustrates a tree structure.

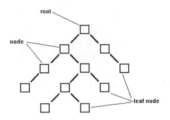

Figure 3.11. *A tree structure.*

A binary tree differs from a general tree in that each node can have a maximum of two sub-nodes. In a binary tree, the sub-nodes are commonly referred to as the left node and right node. Figure 3.11 could be considered a binary tree because none of the nodes have more than two sub-nodes.

As with linked lists, nodes in a tree are connected by using pointers to the element structures. For a binary tree, the structure contains two pointers—one for the left node and one for the right. Following is a generic structure for a binary tree node:

```
struct node {
    <data>
    struct node *left;
    struct node *right;
};
```

The <data> can be any data that is to be joined together in the binary tree. The node pointer, left, points to the sub-node to the left. The node pointer, right, points to the sub-node to the right.

Using a Binary Tree

A binary tree offers faster access time over a regular linked list. To find a single element in a linked list, you must access each element from one end of the list until you find the appropriate element. With a binary tree, a logarithmic number of checks can be made to determine where a specific link is.

Consider the order in which a binary tree's nodes are accessed. There are three general orders for accessing the elements in a linked list. You can access them *in order*, starting with the left sub-node working toward the root and then down the right sub-node. *Pre-order* access is to access the root first, and then the left sub-node, followed by the right sub-node. The third way to access a binary tree is in *post-order*. This is accessing the left sub-node first, and then the right sub-node, followed by the root. Figure 3.12 illustrates the order that the nodes would be accessed in each of these methods.

> **Expert Tip:** Binary trees are used to sort information. You should use a binary tree instead of a single-linked list or double-linked list when you need to access a single element in the fewest steps.

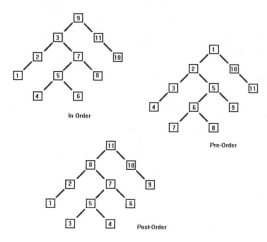

Figure 3.12. *Binary tree access orders.*

Listing 3.4 illustrates the three orders of accessing a linked list. This program enables you to enter a number of names. Each name is added to the tree based on where it fits. The values are added in order. Once all the values are entered, the program enables you to print them in each of the three orders described previously.

Type   Listing 3.4. Using a binary tree.

```
1:  /* Program:  list0304.c
2:   * Author:   Bradley L. Jones
3:   *           Gregory L. Guntle
4:   * Purpose:  Demonstrate binary tree
5:   *=======================================================*/
6:
7:  #include <stdio.h>
8:  #include <stdlib.h>
9:  #include <string.h>
10: #include <conio.h>
11: #include <ctype.h>
12:
13: #ifndef NULL
```

continues

91

Listing 3.4. continued

```
14:  #define NULL 0
15:  #endif
16:
17:  #define FALSE 0
18:  #define TRUE  1
19:
20:  typedef struct  name_addr NAME;
21:  typedef NAME      *NAMEPTR;
22:  typedef NAMEPTR *REFtoNAMEPTR;
23:
24:  struct name_addr
25:  {
26:    char last_name[20];
27:    char first_name[10];
28:    struct name_addr *left_rec;
29:    struct name_addr *right_rec;
30:  };
31:
32:  NAMEPTR root;                    /* root of tree */
33:
34:  void get_names(NAME);
35:  void display_menu(void);
36:  void display_header(char *);
37:  void search_list(NAME, REFtoNAMEPTR);
38:  void dump_postorder(NAMEPTR);
39:  void dump_preorder(NAMEPTR);
40:  void dump_in_order(NAMEPTR);
41:  NAMEPTR get_space(void);
42:
43:  int main( void )
44:  {
45:    NAME hold_name;
46:    int menu_sel;
47:
48:    do
49:    {
50:      printf("\n\n");
51:      printf("\tBinary Tree List\n");
52:      printf("\t    Main Menu\n");
53:      printf("\t=================\n\n");
54:      printf("\tA  Add name to list\n");
55:      printf("\tD  Display list\n");
56:      printf("\tX  eXit\n");
57:      printf("\n\t    Enter selection: ");
58:      menu_sel = getche();
59:      menu_sel = toupper( menu_sel );
60:      switch( menu_sel )
61:      {
62:          case 'A':   get_names(hold_name);
63:                      break;
```

```
64:          case 'D':   display_menu();
65:                      break;
66:          case 'X':
67:                      break;
68:          default :   break;
69:      }
70:
71:    } while( menu_sel != 'X' );
72:
73:    return 0;
74: }
75:
76: /*==========================================================*
77:  * Function: get_names                                      *
78:  * Purpose : Accepts name into the list                     *
79:  * Returns : N/A                                            *
80:  *==========================================================*/
81:
82: void get_names(NAME name_rec)
83: {
84:    int finished = FALSE;
85:
86:    printf("\n\n\tAdding New Names\n");
87:    while (!finished)
88:    {
89:       printf("Last name   (enter only to exit): ");
90:       gets(name_rec.last_name);
91:       if (strlen(name_rec.last_name))     /* Is there a name */
92:       {
93:         printf("First name: ");
94:         gets(name_rec.first_name);
95:         search_list(name_rec, &root);     /* Add info to tree */
96:         printf("\n%s has been added to the list.\n",
name_rec.last_name);
97:       }
98:       else
99:         finished = TRUE;
100:   }
101: }
102:
103: /*==========================================================*
104:  * Function: display_menu                                   *
105:  * Purpose : Menu for dumping the data from the list        *
106:  * Returns : N/A                                            *
107:  *==========================================================*/
108:
109: void display_menu()
110: {
111:    int menu_sel;
112:
```

continues

Listing 3.4. continued

```
113:    do
114:    {
115:      printf("\n\n");
116:      printf("\tDisplay Names Menu\n");
117:      printf("\t==================\n\n");
118:      printf("\tI   In Order\n");
119:      printf("\tP   PreOrder\n");
120:      printf("\tO   PostOrder\n");
121:      printf("\tQ   Quit back to Main Menu");
122:      printf("\n\n\t   Enter selection: ");
123:      menu_sel = getche();
124:      menu_sel = toupper( menu_sel );
125:      switch( menu_sel )
126:      {
127:          case 'I':   display_header("In ORDER");
128:                      dump_in_order(root);
129:                      break;
130:
131:          case 'P':   display_header("Pre-ORDER");
132:                      dump_preorder(root);
133:                      break;
134:
135:          case 'O':   display_header("Post-ORDER");
136:                      dump_postorder(root);
137:                      break;
138:
139:          case 'Q':
140:          default :   break;
141:      }
142:    } while(menu_sel != 'Q');
143: }
144:
145: /*========================================================*
146:  * Function: display_header                              *
147:  * Purpose : Displays a header for the report            *
148:  * Returns :                                             *
149:  *========================================================*/
150:
151: void display_header(char *title)
152: {
153:    printf("\n\n\tDUMP OF DATA IN LIST - %s\n", title);
154:    printf("Addr Last Name          First Name ");
155:    printf(" Left Right\n");
156:    printf("==== =========          ========== ");
157:    printf(" ==== ====\n");
158: }
159:
160: /*========================================================*
161:  * Function: get_space                                   *
162:  * Purpose : Gets memory for new record                  *
```

```
163:    * Returns : Address to free memory                          *
164:    *=========================================================*/
165:
166:  NAMEPTR get_space()
167:  {
168:      NAMEPTR memspace;
169:
170:      /* Get memory location */
171:      memspace = (NAMEPTR)malloc(sizeof(NAME));
172:
173:      if (!memspace)                /* If unable to get memory */
174:      {
175:          printf("Unable to allocate memory!\n");
176:          exit(1);
177:      }
178:      return(memspace);
179:  }
180:
181:  /*=========================================================*
182:   * Function: search_tree                                    *
183:   * Purpose : Displays the information current in the list   *
184:   * Entry   : N/A                                            *
185:   * Returns : N/A                                            *
186:   *=========================================================*/
187:
188:  void search_list(NAME new_name, REFtoNAMEPTR record)
189:  {
190:      int result;                   /* Holds result of comparison */
191:      NAMEPTR newrec;               /* Holds addr of prev rec-for */
192:                                    /* storing later             */
193:
194:      if ( *record == NULL )     /* The place for new name? */
195:      {
196:          newrec = get_space();   /* get space for holding data */
197:              /* store information */
198:          strcpy(newrec->last_name, new_name.last_name);
199:          strcpy(newrec->first_name, new_name.first_name);
200:          newrec->left_rec = NULL;
201:          newrec->right_rec = NULL;
202:          *record = newrec;        /* Place this new rec addr into
203:                                      last rec's appropriate pointer */
204:      }
205:      else
206:      {
207:          newrec = *record;   /* Get address of record past - will
208:                               * be used to link to new record - at
209:                               * this point this variable holds
210:                               * either the left or right branch
211:                               * address.
212:                               */
```

continues

Listing 3.4. continued

```
213:
214:        /* Compare new name against this rec */
215:        result = strcmp(new_name.last_name, newrec->last_name);
216:
217:        if (result < 0)         /* Send addr not content */
218:           search_list(new_name, &newrec->left_rec);
219:        else
220:           search_list(new_name, &newrec->right_rec);
221:    }
222: }
223:
224: /*========================================================*
225:  * Function: dump_postorder                              *
226:  * Purpose : Displays the contents of the list in POST   *
227:  *           ORDER                                       *
228:  * Entry   : root of tree                                *
229:  * Returns : N/A                                         *
230:  *========================================================*/
231:
232: void dump_postorder(NAMEPTR data)
233: {
234:    if (data)     /* If there is data to print */
235:    {
236:         /* keep going left until hit end */
237:        dump_postorder(data->left_rec);
238:         /* Now process right side */
239:        dump_postorder(data->right_rec);
240:        printf("%4X %-20s %-10s  %4X  %4X\n", data,
241:                     data->last_name, data->first_name,
242:                     data->left_rec,  data->right_rec);
243:    }
244: }
245:
246: /*========================================================*
247:  * Function: dump_preorder                               *
248:  * Purpose : Displays the contents of the list PREORDER  *
249:  * Entry   : root of tree                                *
250:  * Returns : N/A                                         *
251:  *========================================================*/
252:
253: void dump_preorder(NAMEPTR data)
254: {
255:    if (data)                  /* If there is data to print */
256:    {
257:        printf("%4X %-20s %-10s  %4X  %4X\n", data,
258:                 data->last_name, data->first_name,
259:                 data->left_rec,  data->right_rec);
260:         /* Now process left side */
261:        dump_preorder(data->left_rec);
262:         /* then right */
```

```
263:      dump_preorder(data->right_rec);
264:   }
265: }
266:
267: /*========================================================*
268:  * Function: dump_in_order                               *
269:  * Purpose : Displays the contents of the list in order  *
270:  * Entry   : root of tree                                *
271:  * Returns : N/A                                         *
272:  *========================================================*/
273:
274: void dump_in_order(NAMEPTR data)
275: {
276:   if (data)            /* If there is data to print */
277:   {
278:        /* keep going left until hit end */
279:      dump_in_order(data->left_rec);
280:      printf("%4X %-20s %-10s  %4X  %4X\n", data,
281:             data->last_name, data->first_name,
282:             data->left_rec,  data->right_rec);
283:      dump_in_order(data->right_rec);
284:   }
285: }
```

```
Binary Tree List
   Main Menu
==================

A  Add name to list
D  Display list
X  eXit

    Enter selection: A

    Adding New Names
Last name  (enter only to exit): Jones
First name: Bradley

Jones has been added to the list.
Last name  (enter only to exit): Guntle
First name: Gregory

Guntle has been added to the list.
Last name  (enter only to exit): Johnson
First name: Jerry

Johnson has been added to the list.
Last name  (enter only to exit): Zacharia
First name: Zelda
```

```
Zacharia has been added to the list.
Last name  (enter only to exit):
```

In order:

```
          DUMP OF DATA IN LIST - In ORDER
Addr Last Name             First Name    Left Right
==== =========            ==========    ==== =====
 94E Guntle                Gregory          0  974
 974 Johnson               Jerry            0    0
 928 Jones                 Bradley        94E  99A
 99A Zacharia              Zelda            0    0
```

Pre-order:

```
          DUMP OF DATA IN LIST - Pre-ORDER
Addr Last Name             First Name    Left Right
==== =========            ==========    ==== =====
 928 Jones                 Bradley        94E  99A
 94E Guntle                Gregory          0  974
 974 Johnson               Jerry            0    0
 99A Zacharia              Zelda            0    0
```

Post-order:

```
          DUMP OF DATA IN LIST - Post-ORDER
Addr Last Name             First Name    Left Right
==== =========            ==========    ==== =====
 974 Johnson               Jerry            0    0
 94E Guntle                Gregory          0  974
 99A Zacharia              Zelda            0    0
 928 Jones                 Bradley        94E  99A
```

This is a long listing that deserves a detailed explanation; however, I am only going to provide an overview. You'll find that until you need to actually use a linked list, understanding the low-level details isn't extremely important. However, it is important to understand the concepts involved.

Lines 34 through 41 prototype the functions that are used in this listing. These functions include get_names(), which is presented in lines 76 through 101. This function simply prompts the user for names and adds them to the binary tree. The next function prototyped is display_menu(). In lines 103 through 143, this function uses printf() to display a reporting menu on the screen. The getche() function is used to get the user's input.

The third function prototyped is display_header(). In lines 145 through 158, the display_header() function is used by each of the three reporting functions to print headers on the report. The three reports are also prototyped. The reports are each in their own functions, dump_postorder(), dump_preorder(), and dump_inorder().

Each of these functions operates similarly. They read the tree and print each node. The difference is in the order that the nodes are navigated.

Two additional functions, search_list() and get_space(), have been prototyped. The search_list() function, which appears in lines 181 through 222, works to navigate through the list for inserting new records. The get_space() function, which appears in lines 160 through 179, simply allocates space for new links in the tree.

All of these functions combined with the main() function provide a menuing program that enables you to create a binary tree. While somewhat long, this program uses some of the same logic provided in the single-linked list and the stack that were presented earlier today.

DO	**DON'T**

DO use a double-linked list when you must be able to go forward and backward in a linked list.

DO use a binary tree when access time is critical.

Summary

Today, procedures were presented for enabling data to be used in sorted orders. These procedures included linked lists and trees. These constructs are generally used when speed is important. Because these constructs work in memory, access time is extremely fast. In addition, pointers are used to always keep the elements in order. Two special linked lists, stacks and queues, were presented. Stacks use a LIFO, or Last In First Out, order of access. Queues use a FIFO, or First In First Out, order of access. Double-linked lists enable both the preceding and following elements to be accessed. This is different from a single-linked list that can only be traversed from beginning to end. Binary trees are another form of linked data. Binary trees have even quicker retrieval time at the cost of storing additional linkage information.

Q&A

Q What is the difference between a single-linked list, a linear linked list, and a single linked list?

A There is no difference. These are three terms for the same thing. In addition, a double-linked list is the same thing as a double linked list. These are all different ways of saying the same thing.

Q Are any additional pointers, other than the tail pointer and head pointer, used with a linked list?

A A third pointer that is external to the elements in a linked list may be used. This is a "current" pointer. This additional pointer may be used if it's important to know where you are currently working in a list.

Q What is the advantage of a binary tree over a linked list?

A A binary tree allows for quicker searching of the element saved. The cost of the quicker search is the need to store additional pointer information.

Q Are there other trees than just binary trees?

A Yes. Binary trees are a special form of tree. They are easier to understand than general trees. A general tree involves much more complex manipulations than were presented with the binary trees.

Workshop

The Workshop provides quiz questions to help you solidify your understanding of the material covered and exercises to provide you with experience in using what you've learned.

Quiz

1. What does NULL equal?

2. What does it mean if the head pointer is equal to NULL?

3. How are single-linked lists connected?

4. How does a stack differ from a normal linked list?

5. How does a queue differ from a normal linked list?

6. What is a tail pointer? What is a top pointer?

7. Is a tail pointer needed in a single-linked list?

8. What is the advantage of a double-linked list over a single-linked list?

9. What is the benefit of using `calloc()` over `malloc()` when allocating memory for new list elements?

10. What is the advantage of using a binary tree over a single-linked list?

Exercises

1. Write a structure that is to be used in a single-linked list. The structure should hold the name of a Disney character and the year the character was first introduced.

2. Write a structure that is to be used in a double-linked list. The structure is to hold the name of a fruit or vegetable.

3. Write a structure that is to be used with a binary tree. The structure is to hold the first name and ages of all the people in your family.

4. **ON YOUR OWN:** Write a function that will count the number of elements in the tree created in Listing 3.4. Add this to the program's menu.

5. **BUG BUSTER:** What is wrong with the following linked list structure?

```
struct customer {
    char lastname[20+1];
    char firstname[15+1];
    char middle_init;
    struct customer next;
};
```

6. In what order will the nodes in the following figure be accessed when using in order access? (Consider a single sub-node as being a left node even though the figure may show it going right.)

7. In what order will the nodes be accessed if using pre-order?

8. In what order will the nodes be accessed if using post-order?

9. **ON YOUR OWN:** Rewrite Listing 3.6 to sort the linked list elements in zip code order.

Tapping into System Resources

Today you will be introduced to many concepts that are not in most beginning C books. Several of today's topics will help bring your C programs to a new level. In addition, after today's lessons, you will have several useful functions. Today you will learn:

- [ ] The downside of tapping into system resources.
- [ ] The various methods for taking advantage of system resources.
- [ ] How to use the ANSI driver to control the screen.
- [ ] How to change colors, key values, and the cursor's position.
- [ ] What direct video memory updating is.
- [ ] What BIOS is and how it differs from the ANSI functions.

What Are System Resources?

System resources are resources provided by your computer system that add functionality. Such resources help you accomplish many tasks that would otherwise be nearly impossible. These tasks could include working with the video display, loading fonts, accessing disk drives, determining memory size, accessing the keyboard, reading a joystick, and much more.

System resources can't be used without any concerns. The cost of using system resources can vary. The largest concern with using system resources should be with portability. Depending on which system resources you access, you could greatly limit the portability of your programs. The resources that will be presented today can be found on most IBM-compatible machines running MS/DOS or an operating system that supports MS/DOS. A different computer platform, such as a Macintosh, may not be able to run the programs presented.

Working with the Display

One of the characteristics of C is its flexibility. Typically, there are several ways to accomplish similar tasks. Each method has its own pros and cons. This is especially true when working with system resources. There are various system resources that can be used to work with information on a display. Three areas will be examined along with some of their individual pros and cons. These areas are:

☐ Using ANSI functions

☐ Using direct memory access

☐ Using BIOS

The first two areas will be covered today, and the third will be covered in detail on Day 8, "Tapping System Resources via BIOS."

Using ANSI Functions

ANSI stands for American National Standards Institute. ANSI sets standards for more than just computer languages. ANSI is often mentioned in describing the standards set for the C language. The ANSI standards go beyond just the C programming language. The ANSI committee is devoted to developing standards for any area that will promote the productivity and international competiveness of American enterprises.

The ANSI terminal standards can be used on an IBM-compatible computer that has loaded the ANSI.SYS system driver. The ANSI.SYS driver comes with Microsoft and PC DOS. Once installed, the ANSI system driver enables the computer to use functions that allow for cursor movement, display extended graphics, and redefine key values. To install the ANSI.SYS driver, consult the manuals that came with your computer's operation system.

The Pros and Cons of Using the ANSI Functions

There are pros and cons to using the ANSI functions. The most obvious benefit is that using the ANSI functions is relatively simple. Once the driver has been installed, the functions are easily called. Later today, you'll see how easy this is. Another benefit is that the ANSI functions are well documented. Since the ANSI driver generally comes with the computer's operating system, there is usually an abundance of documentation. The commands that you learn later today can be used in your C programs. They can also be used in other languages, or in native operation system commands such as PROMPT.

Using ANSI functions isn't without a downside. The biggest problem comes from running on a system that doesn't support the ANSI functions. If the program doesn't support the ANSI functions, or if the ANSI.SYS driver has not been loaded, then gibberish may be displayed on the screen. It's this reliance on the ANSI.SYS driver that causes most programmers to avoid the ANSI functions. That not all operating systems support the ANSI terminal functions should be a factor when considering whether to use them.

In the following sections, several tables list ANSI controls and functions. These functions all require the ANSI.SYS driver to be loaded on your computer to operate properly. Following is an example of the line in a CONFIG.SYS file that loads the ANSI driver.

```
DEVICE=C:\DOS\ANSI.SYS
```

You should consult your computer's operating system manuals before modifying the CONFIG.SYS.

The ANSI Functions

The ANSI functions aren't really functions. Instead they are really escape sequences to control the system's video screen and keyboard. An *escape sequence* is a series of ASCII characters. A complete table of the individual ASCII characters is presented in Appendix B.

The first ASCII character in the escape sequence is either the escape character (value 27 or 1Bh) or the left-bracket character. The characters following the escape or left-bracket character determine what process occurs. The escape sequence may be upper- or lowercase letters depending on what the escape sequence does. This will be demonstrated later.

Note: A variety of functions will be created that use the ANSI functions. Later today and in later days, you'll learn other ways to accomplish the same task using better methods.

Escape Sequences

Several tables follow that contain the codes that will be used in the ANSI escape sequences. Tables 4.1 and 4.2 present the ANSI color codes.

Table 4.1. ANSI foreground colors.

Code	Color
30	Black
31	Red
32	Green

Code	Color
33	Yellow
34	Blue
35	Magenta
36	Cyan
37	White

Table 4.2. ANSI background colors.

Code	Color
40	Black
41	Red
42	Green
43	Yellow
44	Blue
45	Magenta
46	Cyan
47	White

By themselves, the values presented in these tables don't make a great deal of sense; however, later you'll see how to use these codes. Table 4.3 presents the ANSI text control characters that can also be used. These can be used in conjunction with the ANSI colors. Table 4.4 provides video mode controls that can be used to change the width or type of the video mode.

Table 4.3. The ANSI text controls.

Code	Control
0	All attributes off
1	Bold on

continues

Table 4.3. continued

Code	Control
4	Underscore
5	Blink on
7	Reverse video on
8	Concealed on

Table 4.4. Setting video mode.

Control	Resolution	Type
0	40×148×25	monochrome text
1	40×148×25	color text
2	80×148×25	monochrome text
3	80×148×25	color text
4	320×148×200	4-color graphics
5	320×148×200	monochrome graphics
6	640×148×200	monochrome graphics
7	(enables line wrapping)	
13	320×148×200	color graphics
14	640×148×200	color 16-color graphics
15	640×148×350	monochrome 2-color graphics
16	640×148×350	color 16-color graphics
17	640×148×480	monochrome 2-color graphics
18	640×148×480	color 16-color graphics
19	320×148×200	color 256-color graphics

Table 4.5 presents the ANSI character values that can be used.

Table 4.5. ANSI character values.

Key	Code	SHIFT +code	CTRL +code	ALT +code
F1	0;59	0;84	0;94	0;104
F2	0;60	0;85	0;95	0;105
F3	0;61	0;86	0;96	0;106
F4	0;62	0;87	0;97	0;107
F5	0;63	0;88	0;98	0;108
F6	0;64	0;89	0;99	0;109
F7	0;65	0;90	0;100	0;110
F8	0;66	0;91	0;101	0;111
F9	0;67	0;92	0;102	0;112
F10	0;68	0;93	0;103	0;113
F11	0;133	0;135	0;137	0;139
F12	0;134	0;136	0;138	0;140
HOME (num keypad)	0;71	55	0;119	—
UP ARROW (num keypad)	0;72	56	(0;141)	—
PAGE UP (num keypad)	0;73	57	0;132	—
LEFT ARROW (num keypad)	0;75	52	0;115	—
RIGHT ARROW (num keypad)	0;77	54	0;116	—
END (num keypad)	0;79	49	0;117	—
DOWN ARROW (num keypad)	0;80	50	(0;145)	—
PAGE DOWN (num keypad)	0;81	51	0;118	—
INSERT (num keypad)	0;82	48	(0;146)	—
DELETE (num keypad)	0;83	46	(0;147)	—
HOME	(224;71)	(224;71)	(224;119)	(224;151)
UP ARROW	(224;72)	(224;72)	(224;141)	(224;152)

continues

Table 4.5. continued

Key	Code	SHIFT +code	CTRL +code	ALT +code
PAGE UP	(224;73)	(224;73)	(224;132)	(224;153)
LEFT ARROW	(224;75)	(224;75)	(224;115)	(224;155)
RIGHT ARROW	(224;77)	(224;77)	(224;116)	(224;157)
END	(224;79)	(224;79)	(224;117)	(224;159)
DOWN ARROW	(224;80)	(224;80)	(224;145)	(224;154)
PAGE DOWN	(224;81)	(224;81)	(224;118)	(224;161)
INSERT	(224;82)	(224;82)	(224;146)	(224;162)
DELETE	(224;83)	(224;83)	(224;147)	(224;163)
PRINT SCREEN	—	—	0;114	—
PAUSE/BREAK	—	—	0;0	—
BACKSPACE	8	8	127	(0)
ENTER	13	—	10	(0
TAB	9	0;15	(0;148)	(0;165)
NULL	0;3	—	—	—
A	97	65	1	0;30
B	98	66	2	0;48
C	99	66	3	0;46
D	100	68	4	0;32
E	101	69	5	0;18
F	102	70	6	0;33
G	103	71	7	0;34
H	104	72	8	0;35
I	105	73	9	0;23
J	106	74	10	0;36
K	107	75	11	0;37

Key	Code	SHIFT +code	CTRL +code	ALT +code
L	108	76	12	0;38
M	109	77	13	0;50
N	110	78	14	0;49
O	111	79	15	0;24
P	112	80	16	0;25
Q	113	81	17	0;16
R	114	82	18	0;19
S	115	83	19	0;31
T	116	84	20	0;20
U	117	85	21	0;22
V	118	86	22	0;47
W	119	87	23	0;17
X	120	88	24	0;45
Y	121	89	25	0;21
Z	122	90	26	0;44
1	49	33	—	0;120
2	50	64	0	0;121
3	51	35	—	0;122
4	52	36	—	0;123
5	53	37	—	0;124
6	54	94	30	0;125
7	55	38	—	0;126
8	56	42	—	0;126
9	57	40	—	0;127
0	48	41	—	0;129

4

continues

Table 4.5. continued

Key	Code	SHIFT +code	CTRL +code	ALT +code
-	45	95	31	0;130
=	61	43	—	0;131
[	91	123	27	0;26
]	93	125	29	0;27
\	92	124	28	0;43
;	59	58	—	0;39
'	39	34	—	0;40
,	44	60	—	0;51
.	46	62	—	0;52
/	47	63	—	0;53
`	96	126	—	(0;41)
ENTER (keypad)	13	—	10	(0;166)
/ (keypad)	47	47	(0;142)	(0;74)
* (keypad)	42	(0;144)	(0;78)	—
- (keypad)	45	45	(0;149)	(0;164)
+ (keypad)	43	43	(0;150)	(0;55)
5 (keypad)	(0;76)	53	(0;143)	—

**Table is from Microsoft DOS manual.

Types of ANSI Sequences

Using the values in the previous tables, you can accomplish a multitude of tasks. Each task, or function, uses a different sequence of characters. For example:

```
1B[r;cH
```

where r = a row on the screen

where c = a column on the screen

This escape sequence can be used to move the cursor position. The 1B is the value for ESCAPE, hence the phrase escape sequence. The left bracket begins the sequence and the rest of the sequence determines the specific functionality. To use the escape sequence, you simply print it to the screen. This can be done with the `printf()` function. Consider the following C functions in Listing 4.1.

 Listing 4.1. CPUT.C. Place the cursor on the screen.

```c
void put_cursor( int row, int col )
{
    printf( "\x1B[%d;%dH", row, col );
}
```

4

This function moves the cursor to the position on the screen specified by `row` and `col`. The value printed in the `printf()` function is the ANSI escape sequence for moving the cursor. If the escape sequence was used without a row and column value, then the cursor would move to the top, left position (home) on the screen.

Moving the Cursor

Several escape sequences are available to move the cursor. For example, the escape sequence

```
1B[xA
```

moves the cursor up, toward the top of the screen. The cursor moves the number of lines specified by x. If the cursor is already at the top, or if the number is larger than the number of lines available to move, then the cursor stops at the top line. You can easily put this sequence into a more usable C function, as shown in Listing 4.2.

 Listing 4.2. CUP.C. Move the cursor up.

```c
void move_cursor_up( int nbr_rows )
{
    printf( "\x1B[%dA", nbr_rows );
}
```

Following is an escape sequence that moves the cursor down:

```
1B[xB
```

This operates in the same manner as moving the cursor up. Listing 4.3 shows a function that makes use of this escape sequence.

Type **Listing 4.3. CDOWN.C. Move the cursor down.**

```
void move_cursor_down( int nbr_rows )
{
    printf( "\x1B[%dB", nbr_rows );
}
```

In addition to moving the cursor up and down, you may also want to move the cursor forward and backward. The escape sequence to move the cursor forward is:

```
1B[xC
```

The sequence to move the cursor backward is:

```
1B[xD
```

Each of these sequences attempts to move the cursor. Like the previous functions, if the function attempts to move the cursor beyond the edge of the screen, the cursor stops at the edge. Listings 4.4 and 4.5 provide two C functions that are more usable.

Type **Listing 4.4. CRIGHT.C. Move the cursor right.**

```
void move_cursor_right( int nbr_col )
{
    printf( "\x1B[%dC", nbr_col );
}
```

Type **Listing 4.5. CLEFT.C. Move the cursor left.**

```
void move_cursor_left( int nbr_col )
{
    printf( "\x1B[%dD", nbr_col );
}
```

With these five functions, you have everything you need to control the movement of the cursor. There are two additional cursor functions that may be useful. These are functions to save and restore the cursor.

Use the escape sequence

1B[s

to save the current cursor position. Only the last position can be saved. If you call on this function more than once, only the last position will be remembered.

You can restore the saved cursor position by using the following escape sequence:

1B[u

This puts the cursor back to the position saved. Listing 4.6 and Listing 4.7 contain two C functions that make using these escape sequences easier.

 Listing 4.6. SAVECURS.C. Save the current cursor position.

```
void save_cursor_position( void )
{
    printf("\x1B[s");
}
```

 Listing 4.7. RSTRCURS.C. Restore the saved cursor position.

```
void restore_cursor_position( void )
{
    printf("\x1B[u");
}
```

Erasing the Screen

Several escape sequences are available for erasing either part or all of the screen. The types of functions and the escape sequences available to accomplish them follow.

To erase the entire screen:

1B[2J

This escape sequence clears the entire screen. When completed, the cursor is placed in the top, left position on the screen. Listing 4.8 shows a function for using this escape sequence.

Listing 4.8. CLRSCRN.C. Clear the screen.

```
void clear_screen( void )
{
    printf("\x1B[2J");
}
```

The `clear_screen()` function clears the entire screen. Sometimes there is a need to clear only portions of the screen. The following escape sequence clears the characters on a line starting at the position of the cursor:

```
1B[K
```

The following function in Listing 4.9 uses this escape sequence to clear to the end of the line. You should note that the character at the location of the cursor is also cleared.

 Listing 4.9. CLEAREOL.C. Clear to the end of the line.

```
void clear_eol( void )
{
    printf( "\x1B[K" );
}
```

All of these cursor functions are easily used. Listings 4.1 and 4.2 pull these functions into files called A_CURSOR.C and A_CURSOR.H respectively. These files contain all the functions shown up to this point. By compiling the A_CURSOR.C file along with the A_CURSOR.H file, you can use them in all of your programs without retyping them. Listing 4.3 is a program that illustrates the use of several of these functions. Notice that this program doesn't include the code for each of the functions used. Instead, it includes the header file with the prototypes, A_CURSOR.H. When you compile Listing 4.3, you'll want to also compile A_CURSOR.C. This can be done as follows:

```
TCC LIST0403.C A_CURSOR.C
```

You should replace TCC with the appropriate compile command for your compiler. If you are using an integrated development environment, you should have both files open.

> **Note:** If you decide to use the ANSI functions in many of your programs, you may want to create a library containing all of them. Instructions on creation and use of a library are provided on Day 7, "Using Libraries."

Type

Listing 4.10. A_CURSOR.C. The ANSI cursor functions.

```
1:   /* Program: A_CURSOR.c
2:    * Author:  Bradley L. Jones
3:    * Purpose: Source file for a multitude of ANSI cursor
4:    *          functions.
5:    *=====================================================*/
6:
7:   #include "a_cursor.h"
8:   #include <stdio.h>
9:
10:   /*----------------------------*
11:    *           The Functions    *
12:    *----------------------------*/
13:  /*** put the cursor on the screen ***/
14:  void put_cursor( int row, int col )
15:  {
16:      printf( "\x1B[%d;%dH", row, col );
17:  }
18:
19:  /*** move the cursor up ***/
20:  void move_cursor_up( int nbr_rows )
21:  {
22:      printf( "\x1B[%dA", nbr_rows );
23:  }
24:
25:  /*** move the cursor down ***/
26:  void move_cursor_down( int nbr_rows )
27:  {
28:      printf( "\x1B[%dB", nbr_rows );
29:  }
30:
31:  /*** move cursor to the right ***/
32:  void move_cursor_right( int nbr_col )
33:  {
34:      printf( "\x1B[%dC", nbr_col );
35:  }
36:
37:  /*** move the cursor to the left ***/
38:  void move_cursor_left( int nbr_col )
39:  {
40:      printf( "\x1B[%dD", nbr_col );
41:  }
42:
43:  /*** Save the cursor's position ***/
44:  void save_cursor_position( void )
45:  {
46:      printf("\x1B[s");
47:  }
48:
```

continues

Listing 4.10. continued

```
49:  /*** Restore the cursor's position ***/
50:  void restore_cursor_position( void )
51:  {
52:      printf("\x1B[u");
53:  }
54:
55:  /*** clear the screen ***/
56:  void clear_screen( void )
57:  {
58:      printf("\x1B[2J");
59:  }
60:
61:  /*** clear to end of line ***/
62:  void clear_eol( void )
63:  {
64:      printf( "\x1B[K" );
65:  }
```

Listing 4.11. A_CURSOR.H. The ANSI cursor functions header file.

```
1:   /* Program: A_CURSOR.H
2:    * Author:  Bradley L. Jones
3:    * Purpose: Header file for the multitude of ANSI cursor
4:    *          functions.
5:    *=======================================================*/
6:
7:   /*----------------------*
8:    *   Function prototypes   *
9:    *----------------------*/
10:
11:  void put_cursor( int row, int col );
12:  void move_cursor_up( int nbr_rows );
13:  void move_cursor_down( int nbr_rows );
14:  void move_cursor_right( int nbr_col );
15:  void move_cursor_left( int nbr_col );
16:  void save_cursor_position( void );
17:  void restore_cursor_position( void );
18:  void clear_screen( void );
19:  void clear_eol( void );
20:
21:  /*---------- end of file ----------*/
```

Listing 4.12. LIST0403.C. Using the ANSI cursor functions.

```
1:  /* Program: LIST0403.c
2:   * Author:  Bradley L. Jones
3:   * Purpose: Demonstrates ANSI cursor escape sequences.
4:   *=========================================================*/
5:
6:  #include <stdio.h>
7:  #include "a_cursor.h"
8:
9:  /*** Function prototypes ***/
10: void box( int ul_row, int ul_col, int lr_row, int lr_col,
11:           unsigned char ch );
12: void main(void)
13: {
14:    int row,
15:        column,
16:        x,
17:        y;
18:
19:    save_cursor_position();
20:    clear_screen();
21:
22:    box( 1, 18, 3, 61, '*' );
23:
24:    put_cursor( 2, 21 );
25:    printf( "   THIS IS AT THE TOP OF THE SCREEN   " );
26:
27:    box( 15, 20, 19, 60, 1 );
28:    box( 16, 24, 18, 56, 2 );
29:
30:    restore_cursor_position();
31: }
32:
33: void box( int ul_row, int ul_col, int lr_row, int lr_col,
34:           unsigned char ch )
34: {
35:    int x, y;
36:
37:    if( (ul_row > lr_row) || (ul_col > lr_col) )
38:    {
39:        printf( "Error calling box." );
40:    }
41:    else
42:    {
43:      for( x = ul_row; x <= lr_row; x++ )
44:      {
45:          put_cursor( x, ul_col);
```

continues

119

Listing 4.12. continued

```
46:
47:            for( y = ul_col; y <= lr_col; y++ )
48:            {
49:                printf( "%c", ch );
50:            }
51:        }
52:    }
53: }
```

Note: As stated earlier, to use the ANSI functions, the ANSI.SYS driver must be loaded, otherwise, you won't get the expected results.

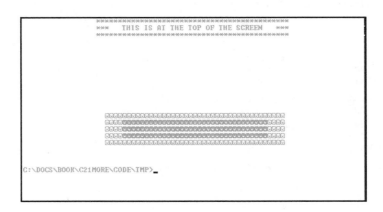

 As you can see, working with the ANSI functions gives you a great deal of control over the output. Listing 4.1 is a listing that you'll want to build on as you learn more ANSI functions later today. This listing, A_CURSOR.C, contains all of the ANSI cursor functions. Line 7 includes a header file called A_CURSOR.H which is presented in Listing 4.2. The A_CURSOR.H header file contains function prototypes for all of the functions in Listing 4.1. You'll want to include the A_CURSOR.H header file in any programs that include the ANSI cursor functions. Listing 4.3 is an example of one such program.

Listing 4.3 is a fun program. It uses the ANSI function that you have learned to create a new function called box(). Line 10 contains the prototype for the box() function. As you can see, it takes several parameters. The parameters tell you where the box is to be located. The upper-left row (ul_row), the upper-left column (ul_col), the

lower-right row (lr_row), and the lower-right column (lr_col) are all passed along with the character that the box is to be made with.

The box() function is defined in lines 33 to 53. This function used two for loops to create the box. Each line of the box is drawn one at a time. The cursor is placed at the beginning of each line using the put_cursor() functions. A printf() call then places each character on the line. Later today, this function will be enhanced to also include color.

There are a few other notables in this program. Line 19 uses the save_cursor_position() function to save the cursor position. Line 30 restores the position just before the program ends. Line 20 clears the screen using the clear_screen() function. Line 22 calls the box() function which creates a box centered in the top of the screen. Line 24 places the cursor in the box using the put_cursor() function so line 25 can type a header into the middle of the box. Lines 27 and 28 call the box function two more times. The character with a decimal value of 1, a clear smiley face, is printed in the first call to box(). The second call to box() prints solid smiley faces in the middle of the original box.

ANSI and Color

You can use the ANSI driver to manipulate the screens colors also. Changing colors is a little more difficult than the functions shown before. Table 4.1 presented the foreground colors that can be used. Foreground colors are used on the information that is presented on the screen. This includes all the text. Table 4.2 presented the background colors that are available through the ANSI driver. This is the color that will be put on the screen behind the text.

Foreground and background colors are often used in conjunction with each other. Typically, you'll want to state what color is in the foreground and what color is in the background. When you use the ANSI colors, once you set them, they apply from that point on.

The ANSI command to set the color is as follows:

```
1B[a;b;...;nm
```

For this escape sequence, you can stack several commands at once. The parameters, *a*, *b*,...,*n* are each replaced with a command from Tables 4.1, 4.2, and/or 4.3. If conflicting commands are given, the final command is used. For instance calling for the foreground color black (30) followed by the foreground color red (31) would result in red. After all, you can't use two foreground colors at once. Don't be confused, you can have more than one foreground color on your screen, but you can't try to write a single character in both black and red at the same time. Listings 4.4 and 4.5

demonstrate the use of the ANSI color attributes. Listing 4.4 is a header file that is included in Listing 4.5. You'll need to remember to use the A_CURSOR source file that was used with Listing 4.3 since a few of the earlier ANSI functions are also used.

Type **Listing 4.13. ANSICLRS.H. The ANSI colors.**

```
 1:  /* Program: ANSICLRS.h
 2:   * Author:  Bradley L. Jones
 3:   * Purpose: Header file for ANSI colors
 4:   *=======================================================*/
 5:
 6:  /*------------------------*
 7:   *     Foreground colors     *
 8:   *------------------------*/
 9:
10:  #define F_BLACK    30
11:  #define F_RED      31
12:  #define F_GREEN    32
13:  #define F_YELLOW   33
14:  #define F_BLUE     34
15:  #define F_MAGENTA 35
16:  #define F_CYAN     36
17:  #define F_WHITE    37
18:
19:  /*------------------------*
20:   *     Background colors     *
21:   *------------------------*/
22:
23:  #define B_BLACK    40
24:  #define B_RED      41
25:  #define B_GREEN    42
26:  #define B_YELLOW   43
27:  #define B_BLUE     44
28:  #define B_MAGENTA 45
29:  #define B_CYAN     46
30:  #define B_WHITE    47
31:
32:  /*------------------------*
33:   *        Attributes        *
34:   *------------------------*/
35:
36:  #define  BOLD       1
37:  #define  UNDERSCORE 4
38:  #define  BLINK      5
39:  #define  REVERSE    7
40:  #define  CONCEAL    8
41:
42:  /*---------- end of file ----------*/
```

Listing 4.14. LIST0405.C. Using the ANSI colors.

```
 1:   /* Program: LIST0405.c
 2:    * Author:  Bradley L. Jones
 3:    * Purpose: Demonstrates ANSI colors.
 4:    *=======================================================*/
 5:
 6:   #include <stdio.h>
 7:   #include "a_cursor.h"
 8:   #include "ansiclrs.h"
 9:
10:   /*** Function prototypes ***/
11:
12:   void box( int ul_row, int ul_col,
13:             int lr_row, int lr_col,
14:             unsigned char ch,
15:             int fcolor, int bcolor );
16:
17:   void color_string( char *string, int fcolor, int bcolor );
18:   void set_color( int fore, int back );
19:
20:   void main(void)
21:   {
22:      int row,
23:          column,
24:          x,
25:          y;
26:
27:      set_color( F_WHITE, B_MAGENTA );
28:
29:      clear_screen();
30:
31:      box( 3, 19, 5, 62, ' ', F_BLACK, B_BLACK);   /* shadow */
32:      box( 2, 18, 4, 61, '*', F_YELLOW, B_BLUE );
33:
34:      put_cursor( 3, 21 );
35:      color_string( "    THIS IS AT THE TOP OF THE SCREEN    ",
36:                    F_RED, B_BLUE );
37:
38:      box( 16, 21, 21, 61, ' ', F_BLACK, B_BLACK ); /* shadow */
39:      box( 15, 20, 20, 60, '*', F_RED, B_GREEN );
40:
41:      set_color( F_WHITE, B_BLACK );
42:      put_cursor( 23, 0);
43:   }
44:
45:   void box( int ul_row, int ul_col,
46:             int lr_row, int lr_col,
47:             unsigned char ch,
48:             int fcolor, int bcolor )
```

continues

123

Listing 4.14. continued

```
49:  {
50:     int x, y;
51:
52:     if( (ul_row > lr_row) || (ul_col > lr_col) )
53:     {
54:         printf( "Error calling box." );
55:     }
56:     else
57:     {
58:        set_color( fcolor, bcolor);
59:
60:        for( x = ul_row; x <= lr_row; x++ )
61:        {
62:            put_cursor( x, ul_col);
63:
64:            for( y = ul_col; y <= lr_col; y++ )
65:            {
66:                printf( "%c", ch );
67:            }
68:        }
69:     }
70:  }
71:
72:  void color_string( char *string, int fcolor, int bcolor )
73:  {
74:    set_color( fcolor, bcolor );
75:    printf( string );
76:  }
77:
78:  void set_color( int fore, int back )
79:  {
80:     printf("\x1B[%d;%dm", fore, back );
81:  }
```

Note: Since this isn't a full-color book, the output printed here isn't in color. On your monitor (if it is colored), this output should appear in color.

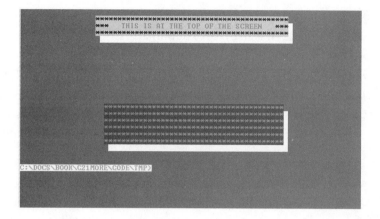

```
***********************************************
*** THIS IS AT THE TOP OF THE SCREEN     ***
***********************************************
```

```
******************************************
******************************************
******************************************
******************************************
```

```
C:\DOCS\BOOK\C21MORE\CODE\TMP>
```

The set color function could be added to the A_CURSOR.C program. In addition, the header file, A_CURSOR.H, could be set up to include the prototypes for the extra functions, box(), set_color(), and color_string(). You should combine all the ANSI functions together so that they are easily accessible. You may want to consider a better name for the files since there would be more than just cursor functions when the new function is added.

Listing 4.5 is similar to Listing 4.3. The main difference is color has been added to the output. Line 8 includes the ANSICLRS.H header file that is presented in Listing 4.4. This header file contains defined constants for each of the colors and other text attributes. By using defined constants such as these, your programs are much easier to read. It's not always intuitive to know that 31 means foreground red.

Several of the functions in Listing 4.5 are slightly modified from Listing 4.3. The box() function has two additional parameters, fcolor and bcolor. These are used to set the color of the box. Lines 31 and 32 demonstrate the use of the box function with the additional parameters. Lines 31 and 32 also illustrate a programming trick. Line 31 creates a black box. Line 32 then overwrites the black box with a colored box. The original black box becomes a shadow for the second box. This is how most shadows are created.

There is a second trick that has been used. Line 27 sets the color to white on magenta using the new function set_color(). Line 29 then calls the clear_screen(). You should notice that the screen is cleared to the last background color set, in this case magenta. The last color set also carries on after the program ends. For this reason, line 41 sets the color to something usable—white on black.

Most of the code presented should be easy to follow. The difficult areas were covered when Listing 4.3 was analyzed. The only actual new code is the `set_color()` function in lines 78 through 81. As you can see, the foreground and background colors are passed to a `printf()` statement. As before, an escape sequence is used.

In addition to color and cursor placement, you can change the mode of the monitor also. Table 4.4 displayed the monitor modes that can be used. Be careful using these modes; there is no guarantee that every monitor will support all modes.

Other ANSI Functions

The ANSI functions also give you the ability to redefine the keys on the keyboard. Table 4.5 can be used to accomplish this. There are several reasons to redefine characters. One is to re-map your keyboard to a different keyboard layout. Another reason might be to re-map keys a game uses. You might map the 'A' key to be the same as a right arrow, the 'D' to be a left arrow, the 'S' to be a down arrow, and the 'W' to be an up arrow. This would allow a game player an option of which keys to use, the letters—which would be easier for a left-handed person—or the actual arrows.

Listing 4.15. Illustrates re-mapping of keys using the ANSI escape sequences.

```
1:  /* Program: LIST0406.c
2:   * Author:   Bradley L. Jones
3:   * Purpose:  Demonstrates ANSI keyboard values.
4:   * Note:     Running this program will set the F1 key to
5:   *           display "Bradley". It will set the F2 key to
6:   *           display "Jones". Running the program with an
7:   *           extra command line parameter will reset the
8:   *           F1 and F2 keys.
9:   *=======================================================*/
10:
11: #include <stdio.h>
12:
13: #define F1   "0;59"
14: #define F2   "0;60"
15:
16: int main(int argc)
17: {
18:     if( argc < 2 )
19:     {
20:         printf("\x1B[%s;66;114;97;100;108;101;121p",F1);
21:         printf("\x1B[%s;74;111;110;101;115p",F2);
22:     }
23:     else
24:     {
25:         printf("\x1B[%s;%sp",F1, F1);
```

```
26:        printf("\x1B[%s;%sp",F2, F2);
27:      }
28:
29:      return;
30:  }
```

After this program runs, there is no output.

This program appears to do nothing when executed because there isn't any output. However, after the program runs, the F1 and F2 keys will function differently. Run the program and then press the F1 and F2 keys. Your program has now changed their functionality to print "Bradley" and "Jones" instead of performing their normal functions. If you re-execute the program and pass a parameter as follows:

LIST0406 X

then the program will reset the F1 and F2 keys to their original functions.

As shown in the listing, this isn't a complex program. Lines 13 and 14 define the F1 and F2 keys to make them easier to work with. Line 16 begins the main() function. Since we are going to use a command line parameter to toggle the key values, we need to receive the argc variable. The argc variable contains the number of items on the command line including the program currently running. If a program runs without any command line parameters, then the argc variable will contain 1. Line 18 checks the value. If it is 1—less than 2—then the values of F1 and F2 are re-mapped (lines 20 and 21). The re-mapped values are stacked following the original value to be reassigned. In this case, there are several values being assigned to the F1 and F2 keys. The reassignment values stop when the letter 'p' is reached. Lines 25 and 26 are executed when there is an additional value on the command line. In these cases, the values of F1 and F2 are mapped to themselves. This, in effect, resets them to their original values.

In today's exercises, you'll be asked to write a program similar to this one. Instead of having the function keys print text such as your name, you'll assign DOS commands to them.

The Extended ASCII Characters

The ANSI functions are often combined with the extended ASCII character set. The extended character set is considered to be the characters from 128 to 255. These characters include special type characters, line characters, and block characters. Many

of these characters are used to create boxes and grids that can be used on the screen. Appendix A contains an ASCII chart that shows all of the different characters available. Later in the book, you'll develop an application that uses many of the extended characters to create a user-friendly screen.

Using Direct Memory Access

Memory is set aside for use by the video display. This memory can be accessed directly to manipulate the graphics or characters that are on the screen. Because this is memory that is directly mapped to the video display, a change can be seen instantly. By updating the video display's memory directly, you can gain the fastest screen updates.

This speed comes at the cost of portability. The memory reserved for the video display isn't always in the same location. In an IBM-compatible computer system, a part of the memory between 640K and 1M is reserved for the video display. Portability is lost because the area reserved isn't always guaranteed to be the same from computer system to system. To use this direct video memory, the system must be 100-percent IBM-compatible with an IBM PC's hardware. It's safe to assume that the same brand of computer with the same type of hardware will have video memory stored in the same location. It's not safe to assume that all other computers will use the same location. In addition, memory for using a CGA monitor isn't always allocated in the same area that memory for a VGA monitor would be.

Note: Borland includes a variable called `directvideo`. If this variable contains a value of 1, then a program's video display activities go directly to the video memory. If the `directvideo` variable contains the value of 0, then BIOS is used. BIOS is converted in the next section. The default for `directvideo` is 1.

Because BIOS functions are more portable, they will be covered in this book. Direct video programming is beyond the scope of this book. If you are interested in direct video programming, consult a graphics book that has been written for your specific compiler.

What Is BIOS?

BIOS stands for Basic Input/Output System. Every MS/PC DOS computer operates with some form of BIOS. The BIOS is a set of service routines that are activated by software interrupts. A *software interrupt* is an interruption that causes the operating system (DOS) to respond. By going through these service routines, and therefore BIOS, you avoid interacting directly with the computer's hardware. This eliminates concerns, such as the possibility of different locations for video memory, because the BIOS determines where and what you need based on the interrupt you cause.

There are BIOS services for a multitude of different input and output activities. This includes being able to manipulate the screen, keyboard, printers, disks, mouse, and more. In addition, there are services available to manipulate the system date and time. On Day 8, tables will be presented that detail many of the available interrupts. For now, it is more important to know that these functions exist.

It's better to use BIOS instead of direct memory video access or the ANSI functions. Direct memory access has a downside that has already been described—you don't know for sure where the video memory will be located. The downside of the ANSI functions is the external device driver; ANSI.SYS must be loaded for the functions to work. If you run Listing 4.3 without the device driver, you get the following result:

```
[s [2J
[1;18H*********************************************_[2;18H**************
**************************_[3;18H*******************************************
--[2;21H--THIS IS AT THE TOP OF THE SCREEN--[15;20H-----------
---------------[16;20H----------------------------[17;20H---
-----------------------------------[18;20H----------------------
---[19;20H----------------------------------[16;24H-----------
---------- [17;24H---------------------------[18;24H--------
----------------[u--------------------------------------------
```

This isn't the desired result. By going through the BIOS, you don't need external device drivers, nor do you have to determine where video memory is located. The BIOS takes care of that for you.

While all of this makes the BIOS calls sound like the perfect answer, there is a downside to using BIOS also. The speed of going through BIOS isn't going to be as good as accessing video memory directly. You should note that these speeds are both extremely fast. In addition, using the BIOS isn't going to be as easy as using the ANSI functions. Neither of these negatives outweighs the additional portability that you gain by using the BIOS functions.

Summary

Today, you were provided with a great deal of information that can be fun. You were shown how to use the ANSI.SYS driver to manipulate the screen. This included learning how to place the cursor, clear the screen, change the colors, and re-map keyboard values. In addition, you were given an overview of writing directly to video memory. The day ended with a high-level discussion on BIOS, which will resume on Day 8. On Day 8, you'll be presented with many examples, along with a list of the many BIOS interrupt functions that are available.

Q&A

Q Are the functions learned today portable to other computer systems?

A The functions covered in today's materials are portable to some computers. The ANSI functions are portable to any computer system that supports the ANSI terminal standards. The BIOS functions are portable to computers that are 100-percent compatible with IBM BIOS. In addition, older versions of BIOS may not support all of the functions. You can consult your DOS manuals and system documentation to determine what interrupts your computer supports.

Q ANSI functions are simple to use. Why are they not recommended?

A If you ran today's ANSI functions without the ANSI.SYS driver loaded, then you already know the answer to this question. By using the ANSI functions, you are reliant upon an external factor—the ANSI driver.

Q What is meant by BIOS functions being portable?

A The portability of BIOS functions isn't necessarily the same as the portability that will be discussed later in this book. The calls to BIOS functions aren't necessarily portable C code—each compiler may call interrupts slightly differently. What is meant by portability is that an executable program (.EXE or .COM) will have a better chance of running on many different computer configurations than if you use ANSI functions or direct memory writes. BIOS function calls are only portable to IBM-compatible machines; however, they can have a multitude of different video monitors, modems, printers, and so on.

Workshop

The Workshop provides quiz questions to help you solidify your understanding of the material covered and exercises to provide you with experience in using what you've learned.

Quiz

1. What does ANSI stand for?

2. Why is it important to know what ANSI is?

3. What is a reason for using ANSI functions?

4. What is a reason not to use ANSI functions?

5. What is the value of red?

6. What is the difference between a foreground color and a background color?

7. When does an ANSI color quit being applied?

8. What is the benefit of using direct video memory updates?

9. What is the downside of using direct video memory updates?

10. What does BIOS stand for?

Exercises

1. What does the following do?

   ```
   "\x1B[5A"
   ```

2. What are the values of the following color sets?

   Black on White

   White on Black

   Yellow on Blue

   Yellow on Red

3. What is the escape sequence for the following colors?

   Yellow on Blue

   Bright Yellow on Red

4. **BUG BUSTER:** What, if anything, is wrong with the following?

```
/* ANSI escape sequence to set the color */

printf("\x1B[31;37m");
```

5. **BUG BUSTER:** What, if anything, is wrong with the following?

```
void clear_entire_line( int row, int fcolor, int bcolor)
{
    put_cursor( row, 1);
    set_color( fcolor, bcolor );
    clear_eol();
}
```

6. Write a function called `put_color_string()` that takes screen coordinates, a foreground color, a background color, and a string as parameters. The function should print the string at the provided coordinates in the given colors.

7. Write a program that re-maps the Shifted function keys. The values you assign should be the most common DOS commands that you use. This makes using these DOS commands just a little easier. (See Listing 4.6 if you need help.)

Following are some examples of values you might use:

Shift F1 HELP
Shift F2 DIR
Shift F3 CLS
Shift F4 CHKDSK
Shift F5 CD C:\ID\T7G
   Or whatever game you most often run.

8. **ON YOUR OWN:** Write a function that creates a box using the extended characters in the ASCII Table.

9. **ON YOUR OWN:** Write a function that centers a string on a line.

10. **ON YOUR OWN:** Write a function that enables the user to enter values that are then assigned to function keys. (Similar to Exercise 7, only interactive with the user.)

Efficiency and Porting

When writing programs, it's easy to use everything the compiler provides. With a language such as C, it's easy to write code that can be used on different computers including PC compatibles, Macintoshes, mini-computers, and mainframes. Because of C's flexibility, you need to know in advance the direction in which you are headed. Today you learn:

☐ What is meant by efficiency and porting.

☐ The difference between efficiency and maintainability.

☐ What types of applications are most likely to be nonportable.

☐ How to ensure portability with the ANSI standard.

What Are Efficiency and Portability?

If you were to take a course in computer programming, two topics would inevitably be mentioned: efficiency and portability. These topics can be especially important when programming in C.

Efficiency

When efficiency is mentioned, it is typically in reference to writing the least amount of code to gain the most functionality. An efficient program is one that only uses system resources when needed. In addition, it is coded to use as little redundant or unnecessary code as possible.

Compilers, Computers, and Efficiency

In days past, if you wanted the most efficient code, you wrote it in assembler. By writing at such a low level, you could weed out any non-essential commands. Today's compilers and computers are much better equipped than those of yesteryear. If you talk to programmers of the early 1980s, you'll hear tales of writing small programs that use minimal resources. Today's computers allow a larger amount of leeway.

Efficiency Versus Maintainability

Although writing efficient code is important, the greatest cost of creating programs is the amount of time spent programming code. It is best to design the code to

minimize the amount of time that must be spent on it. Because writing efficient code can often be time-intensive, the quicker it is written, the less efficient the code may be.

Programming time can be broken down to two phases. The first is the initial time spent developing and coding a program. The amount time for this phase depends on the approach taken. (In Day 12, you'll be shown different ways to approach the initial development of a program.) The second phase is maintaining the program. This maintenance can involve either fixing problems or adding enhancements. Such maintenance can quickly add up to much more time than what was initially spent developing the program.

Coding a program for efficiency can also lead to code that is harder to maintain. When efficiency is the most important factor, coding tricks may be employed. These tricks may make sense to the person who programmed them; however, they seldom are clear to the person who maintains the code. For this reason, the efficiency gained by the coding tricks may be lost in the time and effort spent maintaining them.

 Expert Tip: Coding for maintainability is usually more important than coding for the ultimate efficiency.

White Space

Many super-techie programmers try to write compact code. These programmers, along with many others, believe that compact code is more efficient. The next two listings each contain the same code; however, one contains more spacing.

 Listing 5.1. Code with spacing.

```
1:   /* Program: list0501.c
2:    * Author:  Bradley L. Jones
3:    * Purpose: This program and list0502.c demonstrate the
4:    *          differences made by white space in a listing.
5:    *=======================================================*/
6:
7:   int main(void)
8:   {
9:      int ctr, ctr2;
10:
11:     printf( "\n\nA program with useless output" );
12:
```

 is a small graphic. *(Note: the SAMS Learning Center tab)*

continues

5

135

Listing 5.1. continued

```
13:     printf( "\n" );
14:
15:     for( ctr = 0; ctr < 26; ctr++ )
16:     {
17:         printf( "\n" );
18:
19:         for( ctr2 = 0; ctr2 <= ctr; ctr2++ )
20:         {
21:             printf( "%c", ('A' + ctr ));
22:         }
23:     }
24:
25:     return;
26: }
```

A program with useless output

```
A
BB
CCC
DDDD
EEEEE
FFFFFF
GGGGGGG
HHHHHHHH
IIIIIIIII
JJJJJJJJJJ
KKKKKKKKKKK
LLLLLLLLLLLL
MMMMMMMMMMMMM
NNNNNNNNNNNNNN
OOOOOOOOOOOOOOO
PPPPPPPPPPPPPPPP
QQQQQQQQQQQQQQQQQ
RRRRRRRRRRRRRRRRRR
SSSSSSSSSSSSSSSSSSS
TTTTTTTTTTTTTTTTTTTT
UUUUUUUUUUUUUUUUUUUUU
VVVVVVVVVVVVVVVVVVVVVV
WWWWWWWWWWWWWWWWWWWWWWW
XXXXXXXXXXXXXXXXXXXXXXXX
YYYYYYYYYYYYYYYYYYYYYYYYY
ZZZZZZZZZZZZZZZZZZZZZZZZZZ
```

Listing 5.2. Compact code.

```
1:  /* Program: list0502.c
2:   * Author:  Bradley L. Jones
```

```
3:    * Purpose: This program and list0501.c demonstrate the
4:    *          differences made by white space in a listing.
5:    *=========================================================*/
6:    int main(void){
7:    int ctr,ctr2;
8:    printf("\n\nA program with useless output");
9:    printf("\n");
10:   for(ctr=0;ctr<26;ctr++){
11:   printf("\n");
12:   for(ctr2=0;ctr2<=ctr;ctr2++){printf("%c",('A'+ctr));}}
13:   return;}
```

```
A program with useless output

A
BB
CCC
DDDD
EEEEE
FFFFFF
GGGGGGG
HHHHHHHH
IIIIIIIII
JJJJJJJJJJ
KKKKKKKKKKK
LLLLLLLLLLLL
MMMMMMMMMMMMM
NNNNNNNNNNNNNN
OOOOOOOOOOOOOOO
PPPPPPPPPPPPPPPP
QQQQQQQQQQQQQQQQQ
RRRRRRRRRRRRRRRRRR
SSSSSSSSSSSSSSSSSSS
TTTTTTTTTTTTTTTTTTTT
UUUUUUUUUUUUUUUUUUUUU
VVVVVVVVVVVVVVVVVVVVVV
WWWWWWWWWWWWWWWWWWWWWWW
XXXXXXXXXXXXXXXXXXXXXXXX
YYYYYYYYYYYYYYYYYYYYYYYYY
ZZZZZZZZZZZZZZZZZZZZZZZZZZ
```

These programs simply print each of the characters of the alphabet. Each consecutive letter is printed one more time than the previous. The letter A is printed once, the letter B twice, up to the letter Z, which is printed 26 times. The output demonstrates that by changing the white space, you don't change the way the program operates.

If you look at the size of the two object files and the two executable files created, you'll find that they are the same. Table 5.1 contains all the associated files and their sizes. The source files are different sizes because of the white space, which is removed by the compiler. However, white space doesn't make the code less efficient. In fact, while white space makes the source file a little bigger, it doesn't detract from a program's efficiency.

Table 5.1. The file sizes of the two listings.

Filename	Size
LIST0501.C	527
LIST0502.C	431
LIST0501.EXE	6536
LIST0502.EXE	6536
LIST0501.OBJ	383
LIST0502.OBJ	383

If you look at Listings 5.1 and 5.2 again, you'll see that Listing 5.1 is much easier to read and understand. The code in Listing 5.1 is also easier—and quicker—for others to maintain.

 Review Tip: Use white space to make your programs more readable.

DO   **DON'T**

DO use white space to make your programs more readable.

DO consider maintainability over efficiency when coding your programs.

Portability

One of the major reasons people choose C as their programming language is its portability. C is one of the most portable languages. A program written in a portable

language can be moved from one compiler to another, or from one computer system to another. When moved, the program can be recompiled without any coding modifications. These two areas—hardware portability and compiler portability—are what characterize a portable language. C programs can be written to be portable across both. A C program is truly portable if it can be recompiled on any type of machine with any C compiler.

The ANSI Standard

Portability doesn't happen by accident. It occurs by adhering to a set of standards adhered to by the programmer and your compiler. If you use a compiler that doesn't adhere to the portability standards, you'll be unable to write usable portable code. For this reason, it is wise to choose a compiler that follows the standards for C programming set by the American National Standards Institute (ANSI). The ANSI committee also sets standards for many areas including other programming languages. The ANSI standards are predominantly accepted and used by programmers and compilers.

Standards aren't always good. Too many standards can limit your ability to create effective programs. Because C is a powerful language, it could be detrimental to implement too many standards. The ANSI standards leave a lot of undefined areas to prevent this power limitation. The downside to undefined areas is each compiler can create its own implementations. There are several such areas that will be detailed later today.

The ANSI Keywords

The C language contains relatively few keywords. A *keyword* is a word that is reserved for a program command. The ANSI C keywords are listed in Table 5.2.

Table 5.2. The ANSI C keywords.

asm	auto	break	case	char
const	continue	default	do	double
else	enum	extern	float	for
goto	if	int	long	register
return	short	signed	sizeof	static
struct	switch	typedef	union	unsigned
void	volatile	while		

Most compilers provide other keywords. Examples of compiler-specific keywords are near and huge. Although several compilers might use the same compiler-specific keywords, there is no guarantee that they will be portable to every ANSI standard compiler.

Case Sensitivity

Case sensitivity is an important issue in programming languages. Unlike some languages that ignore case, C is case-sensitive. This means that a variable named x is different than a variable named X. Listing 5.3 illustrates this.

 Listing 5.3. Case sensitivity.

```
 1:  /* Program: list0505.c
 2:   * Author:   Bradley L. Jones
 3:   * Purpose: This program demonstrates case sensitivity
 4:   *=======================================================*/
 5:
 6:  int main(void)
 7:  {
 8:     int    var1 = 1,
 9:            var2 = 2;
10:     char   VAR1 = 'A',
11:            VAR2 = 'B';
12:     float  Var1 = 3.3,
13:            Var2 = 4.4;
14:     int    xyz  = 100,
15:            XYZ  = 500;
16:
17:     printf( "\n\nPrint the values of the variables...\n" );
18:
19:     printf( "\nThe integer values:   var1 = %d, var2 = %d",
20:             var1, var2 );
21:     printf( "\nThe character values: VAR1 = %c, VAR2 = %c",
22:             VAR1, VAR2 );
23:     printf( "\nThe float values:     Var1 = %f, Var2 = %f",
24:             Var1, Var2 );
25:     printf( "\nThe other integers:   xyz = %d, XYZ = %d",
26:             xyz, XYZ );
27:
28:     printf( "\n\nDone printing the values!" );
29:
30:     return;
31:  }
```

```
Print the values of the variables...

The integer values:   var1 = 1, var2 = 2
The character values: VAR1 = A, VAR2 = B
The float values:     Var1 = 3.300000, Var2 = 4.400000
The other integers:   xyz = 100, XYZ = 500

Done printing the values!
```

This program uses several variables with the same names. In lines 8 and 9, var1 and var2 are defined as integer values. In lines 10 and 11, the same variable names are used with different cases. This time VAR1 and VAR2 are in all uppercase. In lines 12 and 13, a third set of declarations is made with the same names, but a different case. This time Var1 and Var2 are declared as float values. In each of these three sets of declarations, values are placed in the variables so that they can later be printed. The printing for these three sets of declarations occurs in lines 19 to 24. As you can see, the values placed in the variables are retained, and each is printed.

Lines 14 and 15 declare two variables of the same type—integers—and the same names. The only difference between these two variables is that one is uppercase and the other is not. Each of these variables has its own value, which is printed in lines 25 and 26.

Although it's possible to use only case to differentiate variables, this isn't a practice to enter into lightly. Not all computer systems that have C compilers available are case sensitive. Because of this, code may not be portable if only case is used to differentiate variables. For portable code, you should always ensure that variables are differentiated by something other than only the case of the variable name.

Case sensitivity can cause problems in more than just the compiler. It can also cause problems with the linker. The compiler may be able to differentiate between variables with only case differences, but the linker may not. Case sensitivity can affect the workings of both the compiler and the linker.

Most compilers and linkers enable you to set a flag to cause case to be ignored. You should check your compiler to determine the flag that needs to be set. When you recompile a listing with variables differentiated by case only, you should get an error similar to the following:

```
list05xx.c:
Error list05xx.c 15: Multiple declaration for 'var1' in function main
*** 1 errors in Compile ***
```

Of course, var1 would be whatever variable you are using.

5

Portable Characters

Characters within the computer are represented as numbers. On an IBM PC or compatible, the letter *A* is represented by the number 6, and the letter *a* is represented by the number 97. These numbers come from an ASCII table.

If you're writing portable programs, you cannot assume that the ASCII table is the character translation table being used. A different table may be used on a different computer system. On a mainframe, character 65 may not be *A*.

> **Warning:** You must be careful when using character numerics. Character numerics may not be portable.

There are two general rules about how a character set is to be defined. The first restriction is that the size of a character's value can't be larger than the size of the char type. In an 8-bit system, 255 is the maximum value that can be stored in a single char variable. Because of this, you wouldn't have a character with a value greater than 255. If you were working on a machine with a 16-bit character, 65,535 is the maximum value for a character.

The second rule restricting the character set is that each character must be represented by a positive number. The portable characters within the ASCII character set are those from 1 to 127. The values from 128 to 255 are not guaranteed to be portable. These extended characters can't be guaranteed because a signed character has only 127 positive values.

Guaranteeing ANSI Compatibility

The predefined constant `__STDC__` is used to help guarantee ANSI compatability. When the listing is compiled with ANSI compatibility set on, this constant is defined—generally as 1. It is undefined when ANSI compatibility isn't on.

Virtually every compiler gives you the option to compile with ANSI enforced. This is usually done by either setting a switch within the IDE (Integrated Programming Environment) or by passing an additional parameter on the command line when compiling. By setting the ANSI on, you help ensure that the program will be portable to other compilers and platforms.

To compile a program using Borland's Turbo C, you would enter the following on the command line:

```
TCC -A program.c
```

If you are compiling with a Microsoft compiler, you would enter:

```
CL /Ze program.c
```

The compiler then provides additional error checking to ensure that ANSI rules are met. In some cases, there are errors and warnings that are no longer checked. An example is prototype checking. Most compilers display warnings if a function isn't prototyped before it is used; however, the ANSI standards don't require this. Because ANSI doesn't require the prototypes, you may not receive the required prototype warnings.

There are several reasons why you wouldn't want to compile your program with ANSI compatibility on. The most common reason involves taking advantage of your compiler's added features. Many features, such as special screen handling functions, aren't ANSI standard, or they are compiler-specific. If you decide to use these compiler-specific features, you won't want the ANSI flag set. In addition, if you use these compiler-specific features, you may eliminate the portability of your program. Later today, you'll see a way around this limitation.

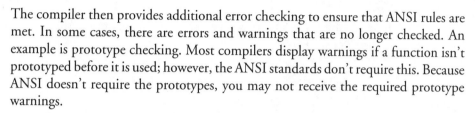

DO use more than just case to differentiate variable names.

DON'T assume numeric values for characters.

Using Portable Numeric Variables

The numeric values that can be stored in a specific variable type may not be consistent across compilers. There are only a few rules that are defined within the ANSI standard in regards to the numeric values that can be stored in each variable type. On Day 2, Table 2.1 presented the values that are typically stored in IBM-compatible PCs. These values, however, aren't guaranteed.

The following rules can be observed about variable types:

☐ A character (char) is the smallest data type. A character variable (type char) will be 1 byte.

☐ A short variable (type short) will be smaller than or equal to an integer variable (type int).

☐ An integer variable (type int) will be smaller than or equal to the size of a long variable (type long).

☐ An unsigned integer variable (type unsigned) is equal to the size of a signed integer variable (type int).

☐ A float variable (type float) will be less than or equal to the size of a double variable (type double).

Listing 5.4 is commonly used to print the size of the variables on the machine that the program is compiled on.

Listing 5.4. The size of the data types.

```
1:  /* Program: list0506.c
2:   * Author:  Bradley L. Jones
3:   * Purpose: This program prints the sizes of the variable
4:   *          types of the machine the program is compiled on.
5:   *=========================================================*/
6:
7:  int main(void)
8:  {
9:    printf( "\nVariable Type Sizes" );
10:   printf( "\n=========================" );
11:   printf( "\nchar             %d", sizeof(char) );
12:   printf( "\nshort            %d", sizeof(short) );
13:   printf( "\nint              %d", sizeof(int) );
14:   printf( "\nfloat            %d", sizeof(float) );
15:   printf( "\ndouble           %d", sizeof(double) );
16:
17:   printf( "\n\nunsigned char    %d", sizeof(unsigned char) );
18:   printf( "\nunsigned short   %d", sizeof(unsigned short) );
19:   printf( "\nunsigned int     %d", sizeof(unsigned int) );
20:
21:   return;
22: }
```

```
Variable Type Sizes
=========================
char             1
short            2
int              2
float            4
double           8

unsigned char    1
unsigned short   2
unsigned int     2
```

 As you can see, the `sizeof()` operator is used to print the size in bytes of each variable type. The output shown is based on being compiled on a 16-bit IBM-compatible PC with a 16-bit compiler. If compiled on a different machine or with a different compiler, the sizes may be different. For example, a 32-bit compiler on a 32-bit machine may yield 4 bytes for the size of an integer rather than 2.

Maximum and Minimum Values

If different machines have variable types that are different sizes, how can you know what values can be stored? It depends on the number of bytes that make up the data type, and whether the variable is signed or unsigned. Table 5.3 shows the different values that can be stored based on the number of bytes. The maximum and minimum values that can be stored for integral types, such as integers, are based on the bits. For floating values such as floats and doubles, larger values can be stored at the cost of precision. Table 5.3 shows both integral variable and floating decimal values.

Table 5.3. Possible values based on byte size.

Number of Bytes	Unsigned Maximum	Signed Minimum	Signed Maximum
Integral Types			
1	255	-128	127
2	65,535	-32,768	32,767
4	4,294,967,295	-2,147,483,648	2,147,438,647
8		1.844674 x E19	
Floating Decimal Sizes			
4*		3.4 E-38	3.4 E38
8**		1.7 E-308	1.7 E308
10***		3.4 E-4932	1.1 E4932

*Precision taken to 7 digits

**Precision taken to 15 digits

***Precision taken to 19 digits

Knowing the maximum value based on the number of bytes and variable type is good; however, as seen earlier, you don't always know the number of bytes in a portable program. In addition, you can't be completely sure of the level of precision used in floating-point numbers. Because of this, you have to be careful about what number you assign to variables. For example, assigning the value of 3,000 to an integer variable is a safe assignment, but what about assigning 100,000? If it's an unsigned integer on a 16-bit machine, you'll get unusual results because the maximum value is 65,535. If a 4-byte integer is being used, then assigning 100,000 would be okay.

 **Warning:** You aren't guaranteed that the values in Table 5.3 are the same for every compiler. Each compiler may choose a slightly different number. This is especially true with the floating-point numbers which may have different levels of precision. Tables 5.4 and 5.5 provide a compatible way of using these numbers.

ANSI has standardized a set of defined constants that are to be included in the header files LIMITS.H and FLOAT.H. These constants define the number of bits within a variable type. In addition, they define the minimum and maximum values. Table 5.4 lists the values defined in LIMITS.H. These values apply to the integral data types. The values in FLOAT.H contain the values for the floating-point types.

Table 5.4. The ANSI-defined constants within LIMITS.H.

Constant	Value
CHAR_BIT	Character variable's number of bits.
CHAR_MIN	Character variable's minimum value (signed).
CHAR_MAX	Character variable's maximum value (signed).
SCHAR_MIN	Signed character variable's minimum value.
SCHAR_MAX	Signed character variable's maximum value.
UCHAR_MAX	Unsigned character's maximum value.
SHRT_MIN	Short variable's minimum value.
SHRT_MAX	Short variable's maximum value.
USHRT_MAX	Unsigned short variable's maximum value.

Constant	Value
INT_MIN	Integer variable's minimum value.
INT_MAX	Integer variable's maximum value.
UINT_MAX	Unsigned integer variable's maximum value.
LONG_MIN	Long variable's minimum value.
LONG_MAX	Long variable's maximum value.
ULONG_MAX	Unsigned long variable's maximum value.

Table 5.5. The ANSI-defined constants within FLOAT.H.

Constant	Value
FLT_DIG	Precision digits in a variable of type float.
DBL_DIG	Precision digits in a variable of type double.
LDBL_DIG	Precision digits in a variable of type long double.
FLT_MAX	Float variable's maximum value.
FLT_MAX_10_EXP	Float variable's exponent maximum value (base 10).
FLT_MAX_EXP	Float variable's exponent maximum value (base 2).
FLT_MIN	Float variable's minimum value.
FLT_MIN_10_EXP	Float variable's exponent minimum value (base 10).
FLT_MIN_EXP	Float variable's exponent minimum value (base 2).
DBL_MAX	Double variable's maximum value.
DBL_MAX_10_EXP	Double variable's exponent maximum value (base 10).
DBL_MAX_EXP	Double variable's exponent maximum value (base 2).

5

continues

Table 5.5. continued

Constant	Value
DBL_MIN	Double variable's minimum value.
DBL_MIN_10_EXP	Double variable's exponent minimum value (base 10).
DBL_MIN_EXP	Double variable's exponent minimum value (base 2).
LDBL_MAX	Long double variable's maximum value.
LDBL_MAX_10_DBL	Long double variable's exponent maximum value (base 10).
LDBL_MAX_EXP	Long double variable's exponent maximum value (base 2).
LDBL_MIN	Long double variable's minimum value.
LDBL_MIN_10_EXP	Long double variable's exponent minimum value (base 10).
LDBL_MIN_EXP	Long double variable's exponent minimum value (base 2).

The values in Tables 5.4 and 5.5 can be used when storing numbers. Ensuring that a number is above or equal to the minimum constant and less than or equal to the maximum constant will ensure that the listing will be portable. Listing 5.5 prints the values stored in the ANSI-defined constants and Listing 5.6 demonstrates the use of some of these constants. The output may be slightly different depending on the compiler used.

Listing 5.5. The values stored in the ANSI-defined constants.

```
1:  /* Program:  list0507.c
2:   * Author:   Bradley L. Jones
3:   * Purpose:  Display of defined constants.
4:   *=====================================================*/
5:
6:  #include <stdio.h>
7:  #include <float.h>
8:  #include <limits.h>
9:
```

```
10:   int main( void )
11:   {
12:       printf( "\n CHAR_BIT      %d ", CHAR_BIT );
13:       printf( "\n CHAR_MIN      %d ", CHAR_MIN );
14:       printf( "\n CHAR_MAX      %d ", CHAR_MAX );
15:       printf( "\n SCHAR_MIN     %d ", SCHAR_MIN );
16:       printf( "\n SCHAR_MAX     %d ", SCHAR_MAX );
17:       printf( "\n UCHAR_MAX     %d ", UCHAR_MAX );
18:       printf( "\n SHRT_MIN      %d ", SHRT_MIN );
19:       printf( "\n SHRT_MAX      %d ", SHRT_MAX );
20:       printf( "\n USHRT_MAX     %d ", USHRT_MAX );
21:       printf( "\n INT_MIN       %d ", INT_MIN );
22:       printf( "\n INT_MAX       %d ", INT_MAX );
23:       printf( "\n UINT_MAX      %ld ", UINT_MAX );
24:       printf( "\n LONG_MIN      %ld ", LONG_MIN );
25:       printf( "\n LONG_MAX      %ld ", LONG_MAX );
26:       printf( "\n ULONG_MAX     %e ", ULONG_MAX );
27:       printf( "\n FLT_DIG       %d ", FLT_DIG );
28:       printf( "\n DBL_DIG       %d ", DBL_DIG );
29:       printf( "\n LDBL_DIG      %d ", LDBL_DIG );
30:       printf( "\n FLT_MAX       %e ", FLT_MAX );
31:       printf( "\n FLT_MIN       %e ", FLT_MIN );
32:       printf( "\n DBL_MAX       %e ", DBL_MAX );
33:       printf( "\n DBL_MIN       %e ", DBL_MIN );
34:
35:       return(0);
36:   }
```

5

```
CHAR_BIT      8
CHAR_MIN      -128
CHAR_MAX      127
SCHAR_MIN     -128
SCHAR_MAX     127
UCHAR_MAX     255
SHRT_MIN      -32768
SHRT_MAX      32767
USHRT_MAX     -1
INT_MIN       -32768
INT_MAX       32767
UINT_MAX      65535
LONG_MIN      -2147483648
LONG_MAX      2147483647
ULONG_MAX     3.937208e-302
FLT_DIG       6
DBL_DIG       15
LDBL_DIG      19
FLT_MAX       3.402823e+38
FLT_MIN       1.175494e-38
DBL_MAX       1.797693e+308
DBL_MIN       2.225074e-308
```

This listing is straightforward. The program consists of `printf()` function calls. Each function call prints a different defined constant. You'll notice the conversion character used (that is, `%d`) depends on the type of value being printed. This listing provides a synopsis of what values your compiler used. You could also have looked in the FLOAT.H and LIMITS.H header files to see if these values had been defined. This program should make determining the constant values easier.

Type   **Listing 5.6. Using the ANSI-defined constants.**

```
1:  /* Program: list0508.c
2:   * Author:  Anon E. Mouse
3:   *
4:   * Purpose: To use maximum and minimum constants.
5:   *
6:   * Note:    Not all valid characters are displayable to the
7:   *          screen!
8:   *=========================================================*/
9:
10: #include <float.h>
11: #include <limits.h>
12: #include <stdio.h>
13:
14: int main( void )
15: {
16:     unsigned char ch;
17:     int  i;
18:
19:     printf( "Enter a numeric value.");
20:     printf( "\nThis value will be translated to a character.");
21:     printf( "\n\n==> " );
22:
23:     scanf("%d", &i);
24:
25:     while( i < 0 || i > UCHAR_MAX )
26:     {
27:        printf("\n\nNot a valid value for a character.");
28:        printf("\nEnter a value from 0 to %d ==> ", UCHAR_MAX);
29:
30:        scanf("%d", &i);
31:     }
32:     ch = (char) i;
33:
34:     printf("\n\n%d is character %c", ch, ch );
35:
36:     return;
37: }
```

Output

```
Enter a numeric value.
This value will be translated to a character.

==> 5000


Not a valid value for a character.
Enter a value from 0 to 255 ==> 69


69 is character E
```

Analysis

This listing shows the UCHAR_MAX constant in action. The first new item you should notice is the includes in lines 10 and 11. As stated earlier, these two include files contain the defined constants. If you are questioning the need for FLOAT.H to be included in line 10, then you're doing well. Because none of the decimal point constants are being used, the FLOAT.H header file is not needed. Line 11, however, is needed. This is the header file that contains the definition of UCHAR_MAX that is used later in the listing.

Lines 16 and 17 declare the variables that will be used by the listing. An unsigned character, ch, is used along with an integer variable, i. When the variables are declared, several print statements are issued to prompt the user for a number. Notice that this number is entered into an integer. Because an integer is usually capable of holding a larger number, it is used for the input. If a character variable were used, a number that was too large would wrap to a number that fits a character variable. This can easily be seen by changing the i in line 23 to ch.

Line 25 uses the defined constant to see if the entered number is greater than the maximum for an unsigned character. We are comparing to the maximum for an unsigned character rather than an integer because the program's purpose is to print a character, not an integer. If the entered value isn't valid for a character (and that is an unsigned character), then the user is told the proper values that can be entered (line 28) and is asked to enter a valid value.

Line 32 casts the integer to a character value. In a more complex program, you may find it's easier to switch to the character variable than to continue with the integer. This can help to prevent reallocating a value that isn't valid for a character into the integer variable. For this program, the line that prints the resulting character, line 34, could just as easily have used i rather than ch.

Classifying Numbers

There are several instances when you'll want to know information about a variable. For instance, you may want to know if the information is numeric, a control character,

5

an uppercase character, or any of nearly a dozen different classifications. There are two different ways to check some of these classifications. Consider Listing 5.7, which demonstrates one way of determining if a value stored in a character is a letter of the alphabet.

Type

Listing 5.7. Is the character an alphabetic letter?

```
1:   /* Program: list0509.c
2:    * Author:  Bradley L. Jones
3:    * Purpose: This program may not be portable due to the
4:    *          way it uses character values.
5:    *=========================================================*/
6:
7:   int main(void)
8:   {
9:      unsigned char x = 0;
10:     char trash[256];              /* used to remove extra keys */
11:     while( x != 'Q' && x != 'q' )
12:     {
13:        printf( "\n\nEnter a character (Q to quit) ==> " );
14:
15:        x = getchar();
16:
17:        if( x >= 'A' && x <= 'Z')
18:        {
19:           printf( "\n\n%c is a letter of the alphabet!", x );
20:           printf("\n%c is an uppercase letter!", x );
21:        }
22:        else
23:        {
24:           if( x >= 'a' && x <= 'z')
25:           {
26:              printf( "\n\n%c is a letter of the alphabet!", x );
27:              printf("\n%c is an lowercase letter!", x );
28:           }
29:           else
30:           {
31:              printf( "\n\n%c is not a letter of the alphabet!", x );
32:           }
33:        }
34:        gets(trash); /* eliminates enter key */
35:     }
36:     printf("\n\nThank you for playing!");
37:     return;
38:   }
```

```
Enter a character (Q to quit) ==> A

A is a letter of the alphabet!
A is an uppercase letter!

Enter a character (Q to quit) ==> g

g is a letter of the alphabet!
g is an lowercase letter!

Enter a character (Q to quit) ==> 1

1 is not a letter of the alphabet!

Enter a character (Q to quit) ==> *

* is not a letter of the alphabet!

Enter a character (Q to quit) ==> q

q is a letter of the alphabet!
q is an lowercase letter!

Thank you for playing!
```

This program checks to see if a letter is between the uppercase letter A and the uppercase letter Z. In addition, it checks to see if it is between the lowercase a and the lowercase z. If x is between one of these two ranges, then you would think you could assume that the letter is alphabetic. This is a bad assumption! There is not a standard for the order in which characters are stored. If you are using the ASCII character set, you can get away with using the character ranges; however, your program isn't guaranteed portability. To guarantee portability, you should use a character classification function.

There are several character classification functions. Each is listed in Table 5.6 with what it checks for. These functions will return a zero if the given character doesn't meet its check; otherwise it will return a value other than zero.

Table 5.6. The character classification functions.

Function	Purpose
isalnum()	Checks to see if the character is alphanumeric.
isalpha()	Checks to see if the character is alphabetic.
iscntrl()	Checks to see if the character is a control character.

continues

Table 5.6. continued

Function	Purpose
isdigit()	Checks to see if the character is a decimal digit.
isgraph()	Checks to see if the character is printable (space is an exception).
islower()	Checks to see if the character is lowercase.
isprint()	Checks to see if the character is printable.
ispunct()	Checks to see if the character is a punctuation character.
isspace()	Checks to see if the character is a whitespace character.
isupper()	Checks to see if the character is uppercase.
isxdigit()	Checks to see if the character is a hexadecimal digit.

With the exception of an equality check, you should never compare the values of two different characters. For example, you could check to see if the value of a character variable is equal to 'A', but you wouldn't want to check to see if the value of a character is greater than 'A'.

```
if( X > 'A' )      /* NOT PORTABLE!! */
...

if( X == 'A' )     /* PORTABLE */
...
```

Listing 5.8 is a rewrite of Listing 5.7. Instead of using range checks, the appropriate character classification values are used. Listing 5.8 is a much more portable program.

Type **Listing 5.8. Using character classification functions.**

```
1:  /* Program: list0510.c
2:   * Author:  Bradley L. Jones
3:   * Purpose: This program is an alternative approach to
4:   *          the same task accomplished in Listing 5.9.
5:   *          This program has a higher degree of portability!
6:   *=========================================================*/
7:
8:  #include <ctype.h>
9:
10: int main(void)
11: {
```

```
12:    unsigned char x = 0;
13:    char trash[256];                    /* use to flush extra keys */
14:    while( x != 'Q' && x != 'q' )
15:    {
16:       printf( "\n\nEnter a character (Q to quit) ==> " );
17:
18:       x = getchar();
19:
20:       if( isalpha(x) )
21:       {
22:          printf( "\n\n%c is a letter of the alphabet!", x );
23:          if( isupper(x) )
24:          {
25:             printf("\n%c is an uppercase letter!", x );
26:          }
27:          else
28:          {
29:             printf("\n%c is an lowercase letter!", x );
30:          }
31:       }
32:       else
33:       {
34:          printf( "\n\n%c is not a letter of the alphabet!", x );
35:       }
36:       gets(trash);    /* get extra keys */
37:    }
38:    printf("\n\nThank you for playing!");
39:    return;
40: }
```

```
Enter a character (Q to quit) ==> z

z is a letter of the alphabet!
z is an lowercase letter!

Enter a character (Q to quit) ==> T

T is a letter of the alphabet!
T is an uppercase letter!

Enter a character (Q to quit) ==> #

# is not a letter of the alphabet!

Enter a character (Q to quit) ==> 7

7 is not a letter of the alphabet!

Enter a character (Q to quit) ==> Q
```

5

```
Q is a letter of the alphabet!
Q is an uppercase letter!

Thank you for playing!
```

The outcome should look virtually identical to Listing 5.9—assuming that you ran the program with the same values. This time, instead of using range checks, the character classification functions were used. Notice that line 8 includes the CTYPE.H header file. When this is included, the classification functions are ready to go. Line 20 uses the isalpha() function to ensure that the character entered is a letter of the alphabet. If it is, a message is printed in line 22 stating as much. Line 23 then checks to see if the character is uppercase with the isupper() function. If x is an uppercase character, then a message is printed in line 25, otherwise the message in line 29 is printed. If the letter was not an alphabet letter, then a message is printed in line 35. Because the while loop starts in line 14, the program continues until Q or q is pressed. You might think line 14 detracts from the portability of this program, but that is incorrect. Remember that equality checks for characters are portable, and non-equality checks aren't portable. "Not equal to" and "equal to" are both equality checks.

DO	DON'T

DON'T use numeric values when determining maximums for variables. Use the defined constants if you are writing a portable program.

DON'T assume that the letter A comes before the letter B if you are writing a portable program.

DO use the character classification functions when possible.

DO remember that "!=" is considered an equality check.

Converting a Character's Case

A common practice in programming is to convert the case of a character. Many people write a function similar to the following:

```
char conv_to_upper( char x )
{
    if( x >= 'a' && x <= 'z' )
    {
        x -= 32;
    }
    return( x )
}
```

As you saw earlier, the `if` statement may not be portable. The following is an update function with the `if` statement updated to the portable functions presented in the previous section:

```
char conv_to_upper( char x )
{
    if( isalpha( x ) && islower( x ) )
    {
        x -= 32;
    }
    return( x )
}
```

This second example is better than the previous listing in terms of portability; however, it still isn't completely portable. This function makes the assumption that the uppercase letters are a numeric value that is 32 less than the lowercase letters. This is true if the ASCII character set is used. In the ASCII character set, `'A'` + 32 equals `'a'`; however, this is not necessarily true on every system. Particularly, it is untrue on non-ASCII character systems.

There are two ANSI standard functions that take care of switching the case of a character. The `toupper()` function converts a lowercase character to uppercase; the `lowercase()` function converts an uppercase character to lowercase. The previous function rewritten would look as follows:

```
toupper();
```

As you can see, this is a function that already exists. In addition, this function is defined by ANSI standards, so it should be portable.

Portable Structures and Unions

When using structures and unions, care must also be exercised if portability is a concern. Byte alignment and the order in which members are stored are two areas of incompatibility that can occur when working with these constructs.

Byte alignment, which was discussed on Day 2, is an important factor in the portability of a structure. A program can't assume that the byte alignment will be the same or that it will be on or off. The members could be aligned on every 2 bytes, 4 bytes, or 8 bytes. You cannot assume to know.

When reading or writing structures, you must be cautious. It's best to never use a literal constant for the size of a structure or union. If you are reading or writing structures to a file, the file probably won't be portable. This means you only need to concentrate

on making the program portable. The program would then need to read and write the data files specific to the machine compiled on. The following is an example of a read statement that would be portable:

```
fread( &the_struct, sizeof( the_struct ), 1, filepointer );
```

As you can see, the `sizeof` command is used instead of a literal. Regardless of whether byte alignment is on or off, the correct number of bytes will be read.

When you create a structure, you may assume that the members will be stored in the order in which they are listed. In fact, many of the figures of structures that were presented on Day 2 made this assumption. This assumption is not guaranteed. There isn't a standard that states that a certain order must be followed. Because of this, you can't make assumptions about the order of information within a structure. Listing 5.9 shows an incomplete program that makes such an assumption.

Listing 5.9. A program that may not be portable.

```
1:    /* Program: list0511.c
2:     * Author:  Bradley L. Jones
3:     * NOTE:    THIS IS AN INCOMPLETE PROGRAM
4:     * Purpose: Demonstrates potentially non-portable code!
5:     *=============================================================*/
6:
7:    struct date
8:    {
9:       int  year;   /* year in YYYY format */
10:      char month;  /* month in MM format  */
11:      char day;    /* day in DD format    */
12:    }
13:
14:    int main(void)
15:    {
16:       struct date today, birthday;
17:
18:       set_up_values(&today, &birthday);
19:
20:       if ( *(long *)&today == * (long *)&birthday )
21:       {
22:           do_birthday_function();
23:       }
24:    }
```

This program doesn't actually run. This program would accept two dates, one for today's date and one for a birthdate. It then compares the values of the two dates in line 20 to see if they are equal. If they are, the program completes the `do_birthday_function()`.

As you probably guessed, line 20 may not be portable because it takes the value stored in the today structure and compares it to the value stored in the birthday structure This is a tricky way to compare the two structures. Because the structure members are stored in the order in which they should be compared, it's easier to compare the complete values of the entire structure instead of manipulating each member. This makes the assumption that a date would be stored in year, month, day order as declared in the date structure. Two dates—such as 1991, 12, 25 and 1993, 08, 01— could be compared as 19911225 and 19930801.

Because the compiler isn't required to store the date structure in year, month, day order, this program wouldn't be guaranteed as portable. A second portability issue also exists. This program assumes that the total size of the structure (2 characters and an integer) is equal to the size of a long. This is not guaranteed.

Preprocessor Directives

There are several preprocessor directives that have been defined in the ANSI standards. You use two of these all the time. They are #include and #define. There are several other preprocessor directives that are in the ANSI standards. The additional preprocessor directives that are available under the ANSI guidelines are listed in Table 5.7.

Table 5.7. ANSI standard preprocessor directives.

#define	#if
#elif	#else
#endif	#error
#ifdef	#ifndef
#include	#pragma

Later today, you will see an example of using some of the preprocessor directives to create programs with compiler-specific code and still retain portability.

Using Predefined Constants

Every compiler comes with predefined constants. A majority of these are typically compiler specific. This means that there is a good chance that they won't be portable from one compiler to the next. There are, however, several predefined constants that are defined in the ANSI standards. Some of these constants are:

__DATE__	This is replaced by the date at the time the program is compiled. The date is in the form of a literal string (text enclosed in double quotes). The format is "Mmm DD, YYYY". For example, January 1, 1998 would be "Jan 1, 1998".
__FILE__	This is replaced with the name of the source file at the time of compilation. This will be in the form of a literal string.
__LINE__	This will be replaced with the number of the line on which __LINE__ appears in the source code. This will be a numeric decimal value.
__STDC__	This literal will be defined as 1 if the source file is compiled with the ANSI standard. If the source file wasn't compiled with the ANSI flag set, this value will be undefined.
__TIME__	This is replaced by the time that the program is compiled. This time is in the form of a literal string (text enclosed in double quotes). The format is "HH:MM:SS". An example would be "12:15:03".

Note: The following listing needs to be compiled with the ANSI compatibility flag on. This is usually set by passing an additional parameter when compiling. For example, with Borland's Turbo C, you would enter the following:

```
TCC -A LIST0512.C
```

The -A tells the compiler to compile as an ANSI-compatible source file. If you don't compile with the ANSI compatibility flag, you'll get an error similar to the following:

```
list0512.c:
Error list0512.c 24: Undefined symbol '__STDC__' in function
main
*** 1 errors in Compile ***
```

The best way to understand the predefined constants is to see them in action. Several of the predefined ANSI constants are presented in Listing 5.10.

Type **Listing 5.10. The predefined ANSI constants in action.**

```
1:  /* Program: list0510.c
2:   * Author:  Bradley L. Jones
3:   * Purpose: This program demonstrates the values printed
4:   *          by some of the pre-defined identifiers.
5:   * Note:    In order for this to compile, the ANSI standard
6:   *          compiler switch must be set.
7:   *=======================================================*/
8:
9:  #include <string.h>
10:
11: int main(void)
12: {
13:   printf("\n\nCurrently at line %d", __LINE__ );
14:
15:   printf("\n\nThe value of __DATE__ is: ");
16:   printf(__DATE__);
17:
18:   printf("\n\nThe value of __TIME__ is: ");
19:   printf(__TIME__);
20:
21:   printf("\n\nThe value of __LINE__ is: %d", __LINE__ );
22:
23:   printf("\n\nThe value of __STDC__ is 1 if ANSI compatibility
          is on");
24:   (__STDC__ == 1) ? printf("\nANSI on") : printf("\nANSI off");
25:
26:   printf("\n\nThe value of __FILE__ is: ");
27:   printf(__FILE__);
28:
29:   return;
30: }
```

Output

```
Currently at line 13

The value of __DATE__ is: Nov 27 1993

The value of __TIME__ is: 10:14:03

The value of __LINE__ is: 21

The value of __STDC__ is 1 if ANSI compatibility is on
ANSI on

The value of __FILE__ is: list0512.c
```

5

Listing 5.10 demonstrates the ANSI predefined constants by simply printing their values using printf() function calls. Line 13 prints the value of __LINE__. As you can see in the output, this is the value of 13. Line 16 prints the value of __DATE__. To show that this is a simple string, the __DATE__ constant is passed as the only parameter to printf(). Lines 15 and 16 could be printed as:

```
printf("\n\nThe value of __DATE__ is: %s", __DATE__);
```

Line 19 prints the __TIME__ constant. Like the date, this is printed as a separate string, but could have been combined with the previous printf() statement. Line 24 determines the value of __STDC__. This is not a good line because if __STDC__ is defined, ANSI is on. If it isn't defined, the compiler will give an error and the program won't compile.

Line 27 wraps up the listing by printing the filename it had when it was compiled. If you rename the executable, the value of __FILE__ will still be the original filename.

Using Non-ANSI Features in Portable Programs

A program can use non-ANSI-defined constants and other commands and still be portable. This is accomplished by ensuring the constants are used only if compiled with a compiler that supports the features used. Most compilers provide defined constants that can be used to identify themselves. By setting up areas of the code that are supportive for each of the compilers, you can create a portable program. Listing 5.11 demonstrates how this can be done.

Listing 5.11. A portable program with compiler specifics.

```
1:  /* Program: list0511.c
2:   * Author:  Bradley L. Jones
3:   * Purpose: This program demonstrates using defined
4:   *          constants for creating a portable program.
5:   * Note:    This program gets different results with
6:   *          different compilers.
7:   *=======================================================*/
8:
9:  #ifdef _WINDOWS
10:
11: #define STRING "DOING A WINDOWS PROGRAM!"
12:
13: #else
14:
15: #define STRING "NOT DOING A WINDOWS PROGRAM"
16:
17: #endif
18:
19: int main(void)
```

```
20:  {
21:      printf( "\n\n") ;
22:      printf( STRING );
23:
24:  #ifdef _MSC_VER
25:
26:      printf( "\n\nUsing a Microsoft compiler!" );
27:      printf( "\n   Your Compiler version is %s", _MSC_VER );
28:
29:  #endif
30:
31:  #ifdef __TURBOC__
32:
33:      printf( "\n\nUsing the Turbo C compiler!" );
34:      printf( "\n   Your compiler version is %x", __TURBOC__ );
35:
36:  #endif
37:
38:  #ifdef __BORLANDC__
39:
40:      printf( "\n\nUsing a Borland compiler!" );
41:
42:  #endif
43:
44:      return(0);
45:  }
```

Output

```
NOT DOING A WINDOWS PROGRAM

Using the Turbo C compiler!
   Your compiler version is 300

NOT DOING A WINDOWS PROGRAM

Using a Borland compiler!

NOT DOING A WINDOWS PROGRAM

Using a Microsoft compiler!
   Your compiler version is >>
```

Borland

5

Borland

Microsoft

Analysis

This listing takes advantage of defined constants to determine information about the compiler being used. In line 9, the ifdef preprocessor directive is used. This directive checks to see if the following constant has been defined. If the constant has been defined, the statements following the ifdef are executed until an endif preprocessor directive is reached. In the case of line 9, a determination of whether _WINDOWS has been defined is made. An appropriate message is applied to the constant STRING. Line 22 then prints this string, which states whether this listing has been compiled as a Windows program or not.

Line 24 checks to see if _MSC_VER has been defined. _MSC_VER is a constant that contains the version number of a Microsoft compiler. If a compiler other than a Microsoft compiler is used, this constant won't be defined. If a Microsoft compiler is used, this will be defined with the version number of the compiler. Line 27 will print this compiler version number after line 26 prints a message stating that a Microsoft compiler was used.

Lines 31 through 36 and lines 38 through 42 operate in similar manners. They check to see if Borland's Turbo C or Borland's professional compiler were used. The appropriate message is printed based on these constants.

As you can see, this program determines what compiler is being used by checking the defined constants. The object of the program is the same regardless of which compiler is used—print a message stating which compiler is being used. If you are aware of the systems that you will be porting, you can put compiler-specific commands into the code. If you do use compiler-specific commands, you should ensure that the appropriate code is provided for each compiler.

ANSI Standard Header Files

Several header files that can be included are set by the ANSI standards. It's good to know which header files are ANSI standard since these can be used in creating portable programs. Appendix E contains the ANSI header files along with a list of their functions.

Summary

Today, you were exposed to a great deal of material. This information centered around efficiency and portability. Efficiency needs to be weighed against maintainability. It's better to write code that can be easily maintained even if it operates a few nano-seconds slower. C is one of the most portable languages—if not the most portable language. Portability doesn't happen by accident. ANSI standards have been created to ensure that C programs can be ported from one compiler to another and from one computer system to another. There are several areas to consider when writing portable code. These areas include variable case, which character set to use, using portable numerics, ensuring variable sizes, comparing characters, using structures and unions, and using preprocessor directives and preprocessor constants. The day ended with a discussion of how to incorporate compiler specifics into a portable program.

Q&A

Q How do you write portable graphics programs?

A ANSI does not define any real standards for programming graphics. With graphics programming being more machine dependent than other programming areas, it can be somewhat difficult to write portable graphics programs.

Q Should you always worry about portability?

A No, it's not always necessary to consider portability. Some programs that you write will only be used by you on the system you are using. In addition, some programs won't be ported to a different computer system. Because of this, some nonportable functions, such as `system()`, can be used that wouldn't be used in portable programs.

Q Do comments make a program less efficient?

A Comments are stripped out by the compiler. Because of this, they don't hurt a program. If anything, comments add to the maintainability of a program. You should always use comments where they can make the code clearer.

Workshop

The Workshop provides quiz questions to help you solidify your understanding of the material covered and exercises to provide you with experience in using what you've learned.

Quiz

1. Which is more important—efficiency or maintainability?

2. What is the numeric value of the letter a?

3. What is guaranteed to be the largest unsigned character value on your system?

4. What does ANSI stand for?

5. Are the following variable names valid in the same C program?

```
int firstname,
    FIRSTNAME,
    FirstName,
    Firstname;
```

6. What does `isalpha()` do?

7. What does `isdigit()` do?

8. Why would you want to use functions such as `isalpha()` and `isdigit()`?

9. Can structures be written to disk without worrying about portability?

10. Can `__TIME__` be used in a `printf()` statement to print the current time in a program? For example:

    ```
    printf( "The Current Time is:  %s", __TIME__ );
    ```

Exercises

1. **BUG BUSTER:** What, if anything, is wrong with the following function?

   ```
   void Print_error( char *msg )
   {
       static int ctr = 0,
                   CTR = 0;
       printf("\n" );
       for( ctr = 0; ctr < 60; ctr++ )
       {
           printf("*");
       }
       printf( "\nError %d, %s - %d: %s.\n", CTR, __FILE__, __LINE__,
   msg );
       for( ctr = 0; ctr < 60; ctr++ )
       {
           printf("*");
       }
   }
   ```

2. Rewrite a listing in this chapter and remove all the unneeded spaces. Does the listing still work? Is it smaller than the original listing?

3. Write a function that verifies that a character is a vowel.

4. Write a function that returns 0 if it receives a character that isn't a letter of the alphabet, 1 if it is an uppercase letter, and 2 if it is a lowercase letter. Keep the function as portable as possible.

5. **ON YOUR OWN:** Understand your compiler. Determine what flags must be set to ignore variable case, allow for byte alignment, and guarantee ANSI compatibility.

6. Is the following code portable?

```
void list_a_file( char *file_name )
{
    system("TYPE " file_name );
}
```

7. Is the following code portable?

```
int to_upper( int x )
{
    if( x >= 'a' && x <= 'z' )
    {
        toupper( x );
    }
    return( x );
}
```

Number Systems

Understanding numbers and number systems may seem like a strange topic; however, these are very important for fully understanding the power of C. Today you will learn:

☐ Why number systems are so important.

☐ Which number systems are important.

☐ How to convert from one number system to another.

☐ How to work with the number systems.

The Importance of Number Systems

Numbers are the key to computer programming. This can become obvious within the C programming language. The reason they are important is because every element of a computer program breaks down into a numeric value. Even what appears to be letters and symbols are only numbers to the computer. To go one step further, every numeric value within the computer—and hence every letter or symbol—can be represented with the numbers zero and one. For example, to the computer, the letter A is:

```
01000001
```

Review Tip: Why does the computer represent everything with ones and zeros? Simply stated, ones and zeros are equated with on and off. A computer can store information in memory as magnetic charges that are either positive or negative. If a charge is positive, it is on. This can be equated to one. If a charge is negative, it is off. This negative charge can be equated to zero.

Deriving the Numbers the Computer Used

You may be asking, "How does the computer know what numbers to use?" Depending on the computer, the numbers used to represent various characters may be different. In the case of IBM-compatible computers, a set of number representations have been standardized. This set of numbers is represented within an ASCII

Character Table. ASCII stands for American Standard Code for Information Interchange. The ASCII Character Table contains every standard character and its numeric equivalent. Appendix B contains a complete ASCII Character Table.

Listing 6.1 presents a program that displays the values available in the ASCII Character Table. Nothing in this program should be new to you.

Listing 6.1. ASCII values.

```
1:   /* Program:   list0601.c
2:    * Author:    Bradley L. Jones
3:    * Purpose:   Print all the ASCII character values.
4:    *=========================================================*/
5:
6:   #include <stdio.h>
7:
8:   void main(void)
9:   {
10:      unsigned char ch;
11:      char trash[256];
12:
13:      printf("\n\nThe ASCII VALUES:" );
14:
15:      for( ch = 0; ch < 255; ch++ )
16:      {
17:         printf("\n%3.3d:  %c", ch, ch );
18:
19:         if( ((ch % 20) == 0) && (ch != 0) )
20:         {
21:            printf("\nPress <Enter> to continue");
22:            gets(trash);
23:         }
24:      }
25:      printf("\n%3.3d:  %c", ch, ch );
26:   }
```

6

```
The ASCII VALUES:
000:
001:  ☺
002:  ☻
003:  ♥
004:  ♦
005:  ♣
006:  ♠
007:
008:
009:
010:

011:  ♂
012:  ♀
013:
014:  ♫
015:  ☼
016:  ►
017:  ◄
018:  ↕
019:  ‼
020:  ¶
Press enter to continue
```

```
019:  !!
020:  ¶
Press enter to continue

021:  §
022:  ▬
023:  ↕
024:  ↑
025:  ↓
026:
027:
028:  ∟
029:  ↔
030:  ▲
031:  ▼
032:
033:  !
034:  "
035:  #
036:  $
037:  %
038:  &
039:  '
040:  <
Press enter to continue_
```

```
039:  '
040:  <
Press enter to continue

041:  >
042:  *
043:  +
044:  ,
045:  -
046:  .
047:  /
048:  0
049:  1
050:  2
051:  3
052:  4
053:  5
054:  6
055:  7
056:  8
057:  9
058:  :
059:  ;
060:  <
Press enter to continue_
```

```
059:  ;
060:  <
Press enter to continue

061:  =
062:  >
063:  ?
064:  @
065:  A
066:  B
067:  C
068:  D
069:  E
070:  F
071:  G
072:  H
073:  I
074:  J
075:  K
076:  L
077:  M
078:  N
079:  O
080:  P
Press enter to continue_
```

```
079:  O
080:  P
Press enter to continue

081:  Q
082:  R
083:  S
084:  T
085:  U
086:  V
087:  W
088:  X
089:  Y
090:  Z
091:  [
092:  \
093:  ]
094:  ^
095:  _
096:  `
097:  a
098:  b
099:  c
100:  d
Press enter to continue_
```

```
099:  c
100:  d
Press enter to continue

101:  e
102:  f
103:  g
104:  h
105:  i
106:  j
107:  k
108:  l
109:  m
110:  n
111:  o
112:  p
113:  q
114:  r
115:  s
116:  t
117:  u
118:  v
119:  w
120:  x
Press enter to continue_
```

```
119:  w
120:  x
Press enter to continue

121:  y
122:  z
123:  {
124:  |
125:  }
126:  ~
127:  ⌂
128:  Ç
129:  ü
130:  é
131:  â
132:  ä
133:  à
134:  å
135:  ç
136:  ê
137:  ë
138:  è
139:  ï
140:  î
Press enter to continue
```

```
139:  Ï
140:  î
Press enter to continue

141:  ì
142:  Ä
143:  Å
144:  É
145:  æ
146:  Æ
147:  ô
148:  ö
149:  ò
150:  û
151:  ù
152:  ÿ
153:  Ö
154:  Ü
155:  ¢
156:  £
157:  ¥
158:  ₧
159:  ƒ
160:  á
Press enter to continue
```

```
159:  ƒ
160:  á
Press enter to continue

161:  í
162:  ó
163:  ú
164:  ñ
165:  Ñ
166:  ª
167:  º
168:  ¿
169:  ⌐
170:  ¬
171:  ½
172:  ¼
173:  ¡
174:  «
175:  »
176:  ░
177:  ▒
178:  ▓
179:  │
180:  ┤
Press enter to continue
```

```
179:  │
180:  ┤
Press enter to continue

181:  ╡
182:  ╢
183:  ╖
184:  ╕
185:  ╣
186:  ║
187:  ╗
188:  ╝
189:  ╜
190:  ╛
191:  ┐
192:  └
193:  ┴
194:  ┬
195:  ├
196:  ─
197:  ┼
198:  ╞
199:  ╟
200:  ╚
Press enter to continue
```

```
199:  ‖
200:  
Press enter to continue

201:  
202:  ∏
203:  
204:  ∏
205:  =
206:  ╫
207:  ╪
208:  ╨
209:  ╤
210:  ∏
211:  ∏
212:  ╘
213:  F
214:  ∏
215:  ∏
216:  ╤
217:  ∫
218:  ┌
219:  █
220:  ■
Press enter to continue
```

```
219:  █
220:  ■
Press enter to continue

221:  ▌
222:  ▐
223:  ▀
224:  α
225:  β
226:  Γ
227:  π
228:  Σ
229:  σ
230:  µ
231:  τ
232:  Φ
233:  θ
234:  Ω
235:  δ
236:  ∞
237:  ø
238:  €
239:  ∩
240:  ≡
Press enter to continue
```

```
234:  Ω
235:  δ
236:  ∞
237:  ø
238:  €
239:  ∩
240:  ≡
Press enter to continue

241:  ±
242:  ≥
243:  ≤
244:  ⌠
245:  ⌡
246:  ÷
247:  ≈
248:  °
249:  ·
250:  ·
251:  √
252:  ⁿ
253:  ²
254:  ■
255:  
C:>
```

Analysis As stated earlier, nothing in this program should be new to you. Line 10 declares an unsigned character variable, ch, which will be used to print the values in the table. A character is the smallest variable type (excluding a bit—covered later). A character can store 256 different values—hence the number of values in the ASCII table. As you can see in line 15, these 256 values are printed starting with 0 and ending with 255. Line 17 does the actual printing. The numeric value is printed first followed by the character value. Both the numeric and character values are of the same variable, ch. This line shows that the two are, in essence, equivalent.

Line 19 contains an if statement that allows the program to automatically break after printing every 20 values. If your screen can display more lines, you can adjust this number. Line 22 uses the gets() function to simply get any information the user may enter on the screen. The variable trash was declared to be 256 bytes long because this is the maximum number of characters the keyboard buffer will allow before requiring the enter key to be pressed. Line 25 prints the final value of the table.

Note: If you are tempted to change line 15 in Listing 6.1 to the following so that you can remove line 25, beware! This won't work:

```
for( ch = 0; ch <= 255; ch++ )
```

The maximum value a character can hold is 255. When the variable increments to 256, it actually rolls around so 256 equals 0. Because 0 is less than 255, the loop starts all over!

A few of the values may not print to the screen. This is because values such as a beep (ASCII value 7) cannot be seen. If your computer has a speaker, then when character 7 is printed in the output, you will hear a beep. In addition, you may notice that number 10 of the output precedes a blank line. This value is translated to a line feed. When the line feed is printed by the program, it causes a line to be skipped.

Which Number Systems Are Important?

There are a multitude of number systems available. The number system you should be most familiar with is the decimal, or base 10, system. The decimal system is the number system that you learn in school. In addition to the decimal system, three other numbers systems are typically referred to when programming. These are binary, octal, and hexadecimal.

Listing 6.2 is a program that enables you to enter a character and then translates the character into its equivalent numeric values. The decimal, hexadecimal, octal, and binary values will all be displayed.

 Listing 6.2. A character translation program.

```
1:   /* Program:   list0602.c
2:    * Author:    Bradley L. Jones
3:    * Purpose:   Print numeric values of an entered character.
4:    *=========================================================*/
5:
6:   #include <stdio.h>
7:   #include <stdlib.h>
8:
9:   char *char_to_binary( int );
10:
11:  void main(void)
12:  {
13:     int ch;
14:     char *rv;
15:
16:     printf("\n\nEnter a character ==>" );
17:     ch = getchar();
18:
19:     printf("\n\nYour character:     %c", ch );
20:     printf("\n\n Decimal value:    %d", ch );
21:     printf("\n Octal value:       %o", ch);
22:     printf("\n Hexadecimal value: %x", ch );
23:
24:     rv = char_to_binary(ch);
25:
26:     printf("\n Binary value:      %s", rv);
27:     printf("\n\nYour character:     %c", ch );
28:  }
29:
30:  char *char_to_binary( int ch )
31:  {
32:    int  ctr;
33:    char *binary_string;
34:    int  bitstatus;
35:
36:    binary_string = (char*) malloc( 9 * sizeof(char) );
37:
38:    for( ctr = 0; ctr < 8; ctr++)
```

continues

177

Listing 6.2. continued

```
39:    {
40:        switch( ctr )
41:        {
42:          case 0:  bitstatus = ch & 128;
43:                   break;
44:          case 1:  bitstatus = ch & 64;
45:                   break;
46:          case 2:  bitstatus = ch & 32;
47:                   break;
48:          case 3:  bitstatus = ch & 16;
49:                   break;
50:          case 4:  bitstatus = ch & 8;
51:                   break;
52:          case 5:  bitstatus = ch & 4;
53:                   break;
54:          case 6:  bitstatus = ch & 2;
55:                   break;
56:          case 7:  bitstatus = ch & 1;
57:                   break;
58:        }
59:
60:        binary_string[ctr] = (bitstatus) ? '1' : '0';
61:
62: //     printf( "\nbitstatus = %d, ch = %d, binary_string[%d] = %c",
63: //              bitstatus, ch, ctr, binary_string[ctr]);
64:    }
65:
66:    binary_string[8] = 0;  /* Null Terminate */
67:
68:    return( binary_string );
69: }
```

```
Enter a character ==>A
Your character:    A

Decimal value:     65
Octal value:       101
Hexadecimal value: 41
Binary value:      01000001

Your character:    A
```

This program uses the conversion parameter within the `printf()` function's string to display the decimal, octal, and hexadecimal values. Lines 16 and 17 prompt the user for a character and store it in the integer variable, `ch`. This could also have been an unsigned character variable; however, when translating characters

to numbers as this program is doing, it is often easier to use an integer. Line 19 uses the %c conversion character in the printf() to directly print the character. Line 20 uses the %d conversion character, which translates the character to a numeric value. Lines 21 and 22 use the %o and %x conversion values to print the octal and hexadecimal values. Line 26 prints the binary value of the character. The main() function ends by once again printing the original character.

Line 24 calls a function to convert the character to its binary value. Some compilers will allow a %b conversion character to work. This program has its own conversion function, char_to_binary(), in lines 30 through 69. This function converts each digit of the binary number individually. Lines 62 and 63 have been commented out. These lines were added so that the programmer could see each digit being converted. Later today, you will see this conversion function again. At that time, each line will be explained.

DO	**DON'T**

DON'T be confused by all the number systems. The rest of today will describe and explain each number system in detail.

DO read the rest of today's material if you do not understand these number systems.

The Decimal Number System

As stated, the decimal system is the base 10 system that you started learning to count with in kindergarten. Once you realize how the decimal system actually works, the other number systems will be easy to understand.

There are two keys to understanding a number system. The first is to know what number system you are using. Second, you should know the number system's base. In the case of the decimal number system, the base is 10. In fact, the name of the number system will generally stand for the base number. Decimal stands for 10.

The base also states how many different numbers (or characters) are used when representing numbers. In addition, using the base, you can translate numbers from other number systems to the more familiar decimal system.

To aid in the understanding of the different number systems, consider the objects in Figure 6.1. How many objects are in the two pictures?

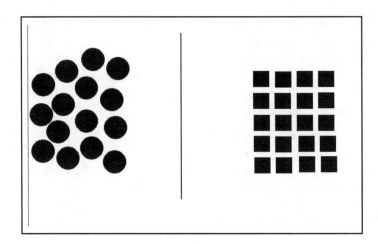

Figure 6.1. *Count the objects on each side.*

You should have answered 15 circles and 20 squares. These are decimal numbers. How did you determine that the answer to the first was a 1 followed by a 5 (fifteen)? You probably just counted and the answer was obvious. However, the logic you may have used to determine this is slightly more complex.

Remembering back, you should know that the right most digit, 5 in the first case, is the "ones" values. The 1 is the "tens" value. Bigger numbers may have "hundreds," "thousands," or more.

As already stated, the decimal number system is base 10. Also stated was that a base 10 system has only 10 digits to use, 0 through 9. The way a number is written is determined by its base. For each digit from right to left, the number is the base, 10 in the case of decimal, to an exponential power. This starts at the right side with the base to the power of 0, and increases by an additional power for each digit to the left. Table 6.1 illustrates this for the decimal number system.

Table 6.1. Decimal digits.

Digit	Base Decimal Value	Digit Equivalent	Name
First	$10^0 =$	1	Ones
Second	$10^1 =$	10	Tens

Digit	Base Decimal Value	Digit Equivalent	Name
Third	$10^2 =$	100	Hundreds
Fourth	$10^3 =$	1,000	Thousands
Fifth	$10^4 =$	10,000	Ten-Thousands
Sixth	$10^5 =$	100,000	Hundred-Thousands
Seventh	$10^6 =$	1,000,000	Millions

Data in Decimal

As stated earlier, all computer information is represented as numbers. It is possible to view this number in its decimal formats. Listing 6.3 takes a file as a parameter and displays each line in its decimal format instead of characters.

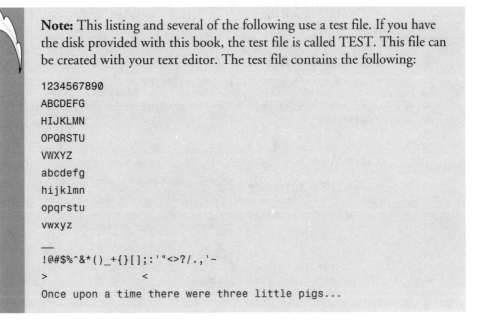

Note: This listing and several of the following use a test file. If you have the disk provided with this book, the test file is called TEST. This file can be created with your text editor. The test file contains the following:

```
1234567890
ABCDEFG
HIJKLMN
OPQRSTU
VWXYZ
abcdefg
hijklmn
opqrstu
vwxyz


!@#$%^&*()_+{}[];:'"<>?/.,'~
>              <
Once upon a time there were three little pigs...
```

6

Type Listing 6.3. Program to type a file in decimal.

```
1:  /* Program:   decdump.c
2:   * Author:    Bradley L. Jones
3:   * Purpose:   This program types out a file. It displays
4:   *            the decimal equivalent of each character.
5:   *=========================================================*/
6:
7:  #include <stdio.h>
8:  #include <string.h>
9:  #include <stdlib.h>
10:
11: main(int argv, char *argc[])
12: {
13:     int ch;
14:     unsigned int  line = 1;
15:
16:     FILE *fp;
17:
18:     if( argv != 2 )
19:     {
20:        printf("\n\nOops!  Proper usage is:");
21:        printf("\n\n%s in_file ", argc[0]);
22:        printf("\n\nOriginal file will be printed in decimal");
23:        return(1);
24:     }
25:
26:     /***  Open the file  ***/
27:     if (( fp = fopen( argc[1], "r" )) == NULL )
28:     {
29:        printf( "\n\nOops!  Error in opening file: %s\n\n", argc[1]);
30:        exit(99);
31:     }
32:
33:     printf("\n%5.5d:  ", line );
34:
35:     while( (ch = fgetc( fp )) != EOF )
36:     {
37:        printf("%d ", ch );
38:
39:        if(ch == '\n')
40:        {
41:           line++;
42:           printf("\n%5.5d:  ", line );
43:        }
44:     }
45:
46:     fclose( fp );
47:
48:     return(0);
49: }
```

```
D:\TYAC>DECDUMP TEST
00001:   49 50 51 52 53 54 55 56 57 48 10
00002:   65 66 67 68 69 70 71 10
00003:   72 73 74 75 76 77 78 10
00004:   79 80 81 82 83 84 85 10
00005:   86 87 88 89 90 10
00006:   97 98 99 100 101 102 103 10
00007:   104 105 106 107 108 109 110 10
00008:   111 112 113 114 115 116 117 10
00009:   118 119 120 121 122 10
00010:   1 2 10
00011:   33 64 35 36 37 94 38 42 40 41 95 43 123 125 91 93 59 58 39
         34 60 62 63 47 46 44 96 126 10
00012:   62 32 32 32 32 32 32 32 32 32 32 32 32 32 32 32 60 10
00013:   10
00014:   79 110 99 101 32 117 112 111 110 32 97 32 116 105 109 101 32
         116 104 101 114 101 32 119 101 114 101 32 116 104 114 101
         101 32 108 105 116 108 101 32 112 105 103 115 46 46 46 10
00015:   10
00016:
```

This program uses a command line argument. Line 18 checks to see if a single parameter was entered along with the program name at the time the user started the program. If not, error messages are printed and the program exits. Line 27 attempts to open the filename entered when the program was started. If the file cannot be opened for reading, an error message is printed and the program exits. The heart of this program is in lines 33 through 44. Line 33 does an initial print of the first line number. Line 35 then reads a character from the file. Line 37 prints the character as a decimal value using the %d within the printf() function. Line 39 then checks to see if the character is a carriage return. If the character is a carriage return, a new line number is printed. Once the end of the file is reached, the printing of the characters stops, and the file is closed before exiting the program.

This program prints line numbers followed by the data from the file. The output is from using the TEST file described earlier. You should notice that a few extra characters seem to get printed in the output. Most obvious should be the extra number 10 at the end of each line. This is the line feed or carriage return that you would not normally see in a text file. In addition, you should notice that in output line 00012 the spaces are printed as 32s. These values can be seen in the ASCII Character Table.

The Binary Number System

As you can see by the output in Listing 6.3, looking at the decimal representations of characters is not very readable. In addition, these values are really not very helpful. One

6

of the most descriptive number systems to use with computers is binary. Listing 6.4 is a rewrite of Listing 6.3, except that information is printed in binary.

Type **Listing 6.4. Program to type a file in binary.**

```
1:   /* Program:  bindump.c
2:    * Author:   Bradley L. Jones
3:    * Purpose:  This program types a file to the screen.
4:    *           It displays the binary equivalent of each
5:    *           character
6:    *=========================================================*/
7:
8:   #include <stdio.h>
9:   #include <string.h>
10:  #include <stdlib.h>
11:
12:  char *char_to_binary( int );
13:
14:  main(int argv, char *argc[])
15:  {
16:      int ch,
17:          letter = 0;
18:
19:      unsigned int line = 1;
20:
21:      FILE *fp;
22:
23:      if( argv != 2 )
24:      {
25:          printf("\n\nOops!  Proper usage is:");
26:          printf("\n\n%s in_file ", argc[0]);
27:          printf("\n\nOriginal file will be printed in Binary.");
28:          exit(1);
29:      }
30:
31:      /*** Open the file   ***/
32:      if (( fp = fopen( argc[1], "r" )) == NULL )
33:      {
34:          printf( "\n\nOops!  Error opening file: %s\n\n", argc[1]);
35:          exit(99);
36:      }
37:
38:      printf("\n%5.5d: ", line );
39:
40:      while( (ch = fgetc( fp )) != EOF )
41:      {
42:
43:          printf("%s ", char_to_binary(ch) );
44:
45:          if(ch == '\n')
```

```
46:        {
47:          line++;
48:          letter = 0;
49:          printf("\n%5.5d: ", line );
50:        }
51:        else
52:        if( ++letter >= 7 )              /* for formatting output */
53:        {
54:          printf("\n          ");
55:          letter = 0;
56:        }
57:
58:      }
59:
60:    fclose( fp );
61:
62:    return(0);
63:  }
64:
65:
66:
67:  char *char_to_binary( int ch )
68:  {
69:    int  ctr;
70:    char *binary_string;
71:    int  bitstatus;
72:
73:    binary_string = (char*) malloc( 9 * sizeof(char) );
74:
75:    for( ctr = 0; ctr < 8; ctr++)
76:    {
77:      switch( ctr )
78:      {
79:        case 0:  bitstatus = ch & 128;
80:                 break;
81:        case 1:  bitstatus = ch & 64;
82:                 break;
83:        case 2:  bitstatus = ch & 32;
84:                 break;
85:        case 3:  bitstatus = ch & 16;
86:                 break;
87:        case 4:  bitstatus = ch & 8;
88:                 break;
89:        case 5:  bitstatus = ch & 4;
90:                 break;
91:        case 6:  bitstatus = ch & 2;
92:                 break;
93:        case 7:  bitstatus = ch & 1;
94:                 break;
95:      }
```

continues

Listing 6.4. continued

```
96:
97:         binary_string[ctr] = (bitstatus) ? '1' : '0';
98:     }
99:
100:    binary_string[8] = 0;   /* Null Terminate */
101:
102:    return( binary_string );
103: }
```

```
D:\TYAC>bindump test

00001: 00110001 00110010 00110011 00110100 00110101 00110110
       00110111 00111000 00111001 00110000 00001010
00002: 01000001 01000010 01000011 01000100 01000101 01000110
       01000111 00001010
00003: 01001000 01001001 01001010 01001011 01001100 01001101
       01001110 00001010
00004: 01001111 01010000 01010001 01010010 01010011 01010100
       01010101 00001010
00005: 01010110 01010111 01011000 01011001 01011010 00001010
00006: 01100001 01100010 01100011 01100100 01100101 01100110
       01100111 00001010
00007: 01101000 01101001 01101010 01101011 01101100 01101101
       01101110 00001010
00008: 01101111 01110000 01110001 01110010 01110011 01110100
       01110101 00001010
00009: 01110110 01110111 01111000 01111001 01111010 00001010
00010: 00000001 00000010 00001010
00011: 00100001 01000000 00100011 00100100 00100101 01011110
       00100110 00101010 00101000 00101001 01011111 00101011
       01111011 01111101 01011011 01011101 00111011 00111010
       00100111 00100010 00111100 00111110 00111111 00101111
       00101110 00101100 01100000 01111110 00001010
00012: 00111110 00100000 00100000 00100000 00100000 00100000
       00100000 00100000 00100000 00100000 00100000 00100000
       00100000 00100000 00100000 00100000 00111100 00001010
00013: 00001010
00014: 01001111 01101110 01100011 01100101 00100000 01110101
       01110000 01101111 01101110 00100000 01100001 00100000
       01110100 01101001 01101101 01100101 00100000 01110100
       01101000 01100101 01110010 01100101 00100000 01110111
       01100101 01110010 01100101 00100000 01110100 01101000
       01110010 01100101 01100101 00100000 01101100 01101001
       01110100 01101100 01100101 00100000 01110000 01101001
       01100111 01110011 00101110 00101110 00101110 00001010
00015: 00001010
00016:
```

Analysis This output was also obtained by running the program with the TEST file that was described earlier in the chapter. Note that there is a lot more data printed out in the output. Because the information is in binary, it is the most accurate representation of what is truly stored.

Looking at the listing, you can see that it is very similar to the Listing 6.3. The `main()` function allows a command line argument to be received (line 14). Lines 23 through 29 verify that one and only one command line parameter was entered. If there were more, or less, then an error message is printed and the program exits. Line 32 attempts to open the file. If the open fails, line 34 prints an error message and exits.

The heart of the program is lines 38 through 63. Line 38 prints the first line number before jumping into a `while` loop. Line 40 begins the loop. Each character is gotten from the file using the `fgetc()` function. The `while` loop continues until the end of the file is reached (EOF). Line 43 prints the binary character using `printf()`. Notice that the string that is printed is the return value from the `char_to_binary()` function. This is the same function used in Listing 6.2 earlier. Line 45 checks to see if the character read—and just printed—was the newline character. If it is, line 47 increments the line number, line 48 resets the letter count, and line 49 prints the new line number on a new line. If the character read is not a newline character, then the `else` condition in lines 51 to 56 is executed. The `else` condition checks to see how many characters have been printed on the line. Because the binary representation of the file can get long, only 7 characters from the file being used are printed on each line. Line 52 checks to see if seven characters have already been printed. If seven characters have been printed, a new line is started that is indented over a few spaces (line 54). The letter count is reset to 0, and the next interaction of the `while` loop occurs.

The `char_to_binary()` function may not be as easy to follow as the rest of the program. Lines 69 to 71 declare three variables that will be used along with the `ch` integer that was passed in. `ch` contains the character that is to be converted. Each character will be translated into a single binary number. Since characters can be any number from 0 to 255, an 8-digit binary number will be needed.

Why eight digits? Consider Figure 6.1 again. This time look at it in the context of binary numbers. How many items are there in the pictures? Instead of the decimal 15 and 20 that you answered before, count the items using the binary system. The answers are 00001111 and 00010100. Just as you had "ones," "tens," "hundreds," and so on. in the decimal system, you have equivalent categories in the binary system. From the word binary you can deduce that there are two different digits that can be used. These are 0 and 1. One object would be 1, two (decimal) objects would be 10.

6

You should not read this as ten because it is two. The categories for the binary system can be determined using the base just as you did for the decimal system earlier. Table 6.2 illustrates the digit groupings for the binary system.

Table 6.2. Binary digits.

Digit	Base Value	Decimal Equivalent	Digit Name
First	$2^0 =$	1	Ones
Second	$2^1 =$	2	Twos
Third	$2^2 =$	4	Fours
Fourth	$2^3 =$	8	Eights
Fifth	$2^4 =$	16	Sixteens
Sixth	$2^5 =$	32	Thirty-twos
Seventh	$2^6 =$	64	Sixty-fours
Eighth	$2^7 =$	128	One-twenty-eights

Only the first eight digits are represented here. This is typically all you will need when converting characters. Eight bits make up a byte. A byte is the amount of space typically used to store a character. Consider the following binary numbers:

```
00000001 equals 1 in decimal
00000010 equals 2 in decimal
00000100 equals 4 in decimal
00000101 equals 4 + 1 or 5 in decimal
11111111 equals 128 + 64 + 32 + 16 + 8 + 4 + 2 + 1 or 255 in decimal.
```

To translate the binary numbers to decimal, you simply add the decimal values from Table 6.2 for the corresponding digits that are not zero.

Now look back at the char_to_binary() function in Listing 6.4. You can see that lines 79 through 94 have the decimal equivalent values that are listed in Table 6.2. Instead of converting from binary to decimal as the previous examples displayed, the program converts the decimal value to binary. Following the flow of this function, you can see how to convert from decimal to binary. We know that there are only eight digits in the binary number because a character can only be from 0 to 256. The program starts at the left of the eight-digit binary number and determines the value of each digit. Line 75 is a for statement that uses the ctr variable to keep track of which of the eight digits is being determined. Line 77 switches to a `case` statement that works with the individual digit. The first time through, the digit being worked on (`ctr`) will be 0. This `case`, in lines 79 and 81, does a binary math statement. The binary AND operator (`&`) is used to determine if the character contains a bit value for 128. This is done by using the binary AND operator with the number you are testing for, in this case 128. If the character does contain the bit for 128, then `bitstatus` will be set to a non-zero number. After doing this, the `switch` statement is left, and the conditional operator is used in line 97. If the value in `bitstatus` does equals zero, then the number did not contain a bit value for 128. If `bitstatus` does not equal zero, you know that the character's decimal value did contain a bit for 128. Because the value of a character cannot be greater than 255, you know that 128 will be divisible at most one time into `ch`. Using the `for` loop, you can then cycle through each bit value for the character's numeric value. This continues through to the eight digits.

Line 100 null-terminates the binary number which is now stored as a string. Line 102 returns this string. Notice that this string is actually a pointer to a character array. Line 73 used the `malloc()` function to allocate the nine characters needed to hold the binary number. This function allocates a string for holding the binary number. If this function were called often, the calling functions should free the binary strings. By not freeing the string, memory is being lost.

Review Tip: You can test if a bit is on or off by using the binary AND operator (`&`). For example, if you AND a character with the the value of 128, then all of the bits will be set to zeros (off) except for the bit in the 128 position. This bit will be left as it is. If it is on, it will remain on.

Note: Listing 6.2 uses the `char_to_binary` function also. It, however, included two extra lines:

```
printf( "\nbitstatus = %d, ch = %d, binary_string[%d] = %c",
        bitstatus, ch, ctr, binary_string[ctr]);
```

These two lines could be added to Listing 6.4 between lines 96 and 98. They print each step of the binary conversion.

6

The Hexadecimal Number System

As you could see by the previous program, displaying a file in its binary values may be more helpful than looking at its decimal values. However, it is also easy to see that looking at the binary values provides much more information than is really needed. What is needed is a number system that can represent each of the 256 different values of a character and still be easily converted to binary. Actually, using a base 256 number system would provide too many different characters to be useful. The number system that seems to provide the best representation is the hexadecimal, or base 16, system. It takes only two digits to represent all 256 character values.

Table 6.3. Hexadecimal digits.

Digit	Base Value	Decimal Equivalent	Digit Name
First	$16^0 =$	1	Ones
Second	$16^1 =$	16	Sixteens
Third	$16^2 =$	256	Two-hundred fifty-sixes

Looking at Table 6.3, you can see that by the time you get to the third digit of a hexadecimal number, you are already at a number equivalent to 256 in the decimal system. By including 0, you can represent all 256 characters with just two digits! If hexadecimal is new to you, you might be wondering how you can represent 16 characters. Remember the base determines the number of characters that are used in displaying the number. Table 6.4 illustrates the hexadecimal characters and the decimal equivalents.

Table 6.4. The hexadecimal digits.

Hexadecimal Digit	Decimal Equivalent	Binary Equivalent
0	0	0000
1	1	0001
2	2	0010
3	3	0011

Hexadecimal Digit	Decimal Equivalent	Binary Equivalent
4	4	0100
5	5	0101
6	6	0110
7	7	0111
8	8	1000
9	9	1001
A	10	1010
B	11	1011
C	12	1100
D	13	1101
E	14	1110
F	15	1111

The alpha characters in a hexadecimal number can be either upper- or lowercase.

Note: Hexadecimal numbers are generally followed with lowercase h to signify that they are hexadecimal. For example, 10h would be hexadecimal 10, not decimal 10. Its decimal equivalent would be 16.

6

There is a second reason why hexadecimal numbers are preferred by programmers. It is easy to convert a binary number to and from hexadecimal. Simply convert each of the two digits of the hexadecimal number individually and concatenate the result. Or, if converting from binary to hexadecimal, convert the left four digits to a single hexadecimal number and then convert the right four. Consider the following examples.

Converting from hexadecimal to binary:

☐ Hexadecimal value: F1h (or 241 decimal).

☐ Converting the first digit, F, to binary yields 1111.

☐ Converting the second digit, 1, to binary yields 0001.

☐ The total binary equivalent of F1 is 1111 0001 or 11110001.

Converting from binary to hexadecimal:

☐ Binary value: 10101001 (or 169 decimal).

☐ Converting the first four digits, 1010, yields A in hexadecimal.

☐ Converting the second four digits, 1001, yields 9 in hexadecimal.

☐ The total hexadecimal equivalent of 10101001 is A9h.

Listing 6.5, HEXDUMP.C, is a rewrite of the programs you have seen before. This program simply prints the hexadecimal values of a file.

 Listing 6.5. Program to type a file in hexadecimal.

```
1:   /* Program:   hexdump.c
2:    * Author:    Bradley L. Jones
3:    * Purpose:   This program types a file to the screen.
4:    *            It displays the hexadecimal equivalent of
5:    *            each character
6:    *======================================================*/
7:
8:   #include <stdio.h>
9:   #include <string.h>
10:  #include <stdlib.h>
11:
12:  main(int argv, char *argc[])
13:  {
14:     int ch;
15:     unsigned int line = 1;
16:
17:     FILE *fp;
18:
19:     if( argv != 2 )
20:     {
21:        printf("\n\nOops!  Proper usage is:");
22:        printf("\n\n%s in_file ", argc[0]);
23:        printf("\n\nOriginal file will be printed in HEX.");
24:        exit(1);
25:     }
26:
```

```
27:     /***  Open the file  ***/
28:     if (( fp = fopen( argc[1], "r" )) == NULL )
29:     {
30:        printf( "\n\nOops!  Error in opening file: %s\n\n",
31:                  argc[1]);
32:        exit(99);
33:     }
34:
35:     printf("\n%5.5d:  ", line );
36:
37:     while( (ch = fgetc( fp )) != EOF )
38:     {
39:        printf("%X ", ch );
40:
41:        if(ch == '\n')
42:        {
43:          line++;
44:          printf("\n%5.5d:  ", line );
45:        }
46:     }
47:
48:     fclose( fp );
49:
50:     return(0);
51:  }
```

Output

```
D:\TYAC>HEXDUMP TEST

00001:  31 32 33 34 35 36 37 38 39 30 A
00002:  41 42 43 44 45 46 47 A
00003:  48 49 4A 4B 4C 4D 4E A
00004:  4F 50 51 52 53 54 55 A
00005:  56 57 58 59 5A A
00006:  61 62 63 64 65 66 67 A
00007:  68 69 6A 6B 6C 6D 6E A
00008:  6F 70 71 72 73 74 75 A
00009:  76 77 78 79 7A A
00010:  1 2 A
00011:  21 40 23 24 25 5E 26 2A 28 29 5F 2B 7B 7D 5B 5D 3B 3A 27 22
        3C 3E 3F 2F
        2E 2C 60 7E A
00012:  3E 20 20 20 20 20 20 20 20 20 20 20 20 20 20 20 3C A
00013:  A
00014:  4F 6E 63 65 20 75 70 6F 6E 20 61 20 74 69 6D 65 20 74 68 65
        72 65 20 77
        65 72 65 20 74 68 72 65 65 20 6C 69 74 6C 65 20 70 69 67 73
        2E 2E 2E A
00015:  A
00016:
```

6

193

This program is similar to the binary and decimal dump programs that you have already seen. The big difference is in line 39. In order to print a hexadecimal value in C, you simply need to use the %X specifier. This will automatically print the hexadecimal value.

The Octal Number System

The octal number system is rarely used in C or by C programmers. It is often mentioned because it is easy to convert to using the printf() conversion character, %o. The octal number system is the base 8 number system. As you should conclude from this, there are 8 digits, 0 through 7.

 Listing 6.6. Program to type a file in octal.

```
 1:  /* Program:  octdump.c
 2:   * Author:   Bradley L. Jones
 3:   * Purpose:  This program types a file to the screen.
 4:   *           It displays the octal equivalent of each
 5:   *           character
 6:   *=====================================================*/
 7:
 8:  #include <stdio.h>
 9:  #include <string.h>
10:  #include <stdlib.h>
11:
12:  main(int argv, char *argc[])
13:  {
14:     int ch;
15:     unsigned int line = 1;
16:
17:     FILE *fp;
18:
19:     if( argv != 2 )
20:     {
21:        printf("\n\nOops!  Proper usage is:");
22:        printf("\n\n%s in_file ", argc[0]);
23:        printf("\n\nOriginal file will be printed in Octal.");
24:        exit(1);
25:     }
26:
27:     /*** Open the file ***/
28:     if (( fp = fopen( argc[1], "r" )) == NULL )
29:     {
30:        printf( "\n\nOops!  Error in opening file: %s\n\n",
31:                   argc[1]);
32:        exit(99);
33:     }
```

```
34:
35:        printf("\n%5.5d:   ", line );
36:
37:        while( (ch = fgetc( fp )) != EOF )
38:        {
39:            printf("%03o ", ch );
40:
41:            if(ch == '\n')
42:            {
43:              line++;
44:              printf("\n%5.5d:   ", line );
45:            }
46:        }
47:
48:        fclose( fp );
49:
50:        return(0);
51:    }
```

```
D:\TYAC>OCTDUMP TEST

00001:    061 062 063 064 065 066 067 070 071 060 012
00002:    101 102 103 104 105 106 107 012
00003:    110 111 112 113 114 115 116 012
00004:    117 120 121 122 123 124 125 012
00005:    126 127 130 131 132 012
00006:    141 142 143 144 145 146 147 012
00007:    150 151 152 153 154 155 156 012
00008:    157 160 161 162 163 164 165 012
00009:    166 167 170 171 172 012
00010:    001 002 012
00011:    041 100 043 044 045 136 046 052 050 051 137 053 173 175 133
          135 073 072
          047 042 074 076 077 057 056 054 140 176 012
00012:    076 040 040 040 040 040 040 040 040 040 040 040 040 040 040
          040 074 012
00013:    012
00014:    117 156 143 145 040 165 160 157 156 040 141 040 164 151 155
          145 040 164 150 145 162 145 040 167 145 162 145 040 164 150
          162 145 145 040 154 151 164 154 145 040 160 151 147 163 056
          056 056 012
00015:    012
00016:
```

Listing 6.6 is a rewrite of Listing 6.5. Notice that the only difference between these two programs, other than the comments, is the printf() conversion specifier in line 39. Instead of using %x for hexadecimal, %03o is used. The 03 zero pads the corresponding variable three characters. The o displays the octal value.

195

DO understand the number systems.

DON'T confuse different number systems. Generally the following rules are used in using numeric constants:

- ☐ Octal numbers start with 0, that is, 08 would be octal 8.

- ☐ Hexadecimal numbers generally start with x, that means x8 is hexadecimal 8.

  Warning, x08 would be octal!

- ☐ Decimal numbers do not start with 0 or x.

A Final Program

Oftentimes, you will find that you want to see a program in more than one format. The programs presented thus far have presented the data using only a single number system. Following is a program that you will find to be more useful. It does have one flaw. It does not print the last few characters of the file.

Listing 6.7. Program to type a file in hexadecimal with the character representations.

```
 1:  /* Program:   hex.c
 2:   * Author:    Bradley L. Jones
 3:   * Purpose:   This program types a file to the screen.
 4:   *            The information is presented in its regular
 5:   *            form and its hexadecimal equivalent.
 6:   * Notes:     This program has an imperfection. The last
 7:   *            23 or fewer characters in the file will not
 8:   *            be printed.
 9:   *=======================================================*/
10:
11:  #include <stdio.h>
12:  #include <string.h>
13:  #include <stdlib.h>
14:
15:  main(int argv, char *argc[])
16:  {
17:      int  ch,
18:           ctr;
```

```
19:      char buffer[24];
20:
21:      FILE *fp;
22:
23:      if( argv != 2 )
24:      {
25:          printf("\n\nOops!  Proper usage is:");
26:          printf("\n\n%s in_file ", argc[0]);
27:          printf("\n\nOriginal file will be printed in HEX.");
28:          return(1);
29:      }
30:
31:      /***  Open the file  ***/
32:      if (( fp = fopen( argc[1], "r" )) == NULL )
33:      {
34:          printf( "\n\nOops!  Error in opening file: %s\n\n",
35:                      argc[1]);
36:          exit(99);
37:      }
38:
39:      fread(buffer, 24, sizeof(char), fp );
40:
41:      while( !feof(fp))
42:      {
43:          for( ctr = 0; ctr < 24; ctr++ )
44:          {
45:              if( (ctr % 4) == 0 )
46:                  printf(" ");
47:              printf("%02X", buffer[ctr] );
48:          }
49:
50:          printf( " " );
51:
52:          for( ctr = 0; ctr < 24; ctr++ )
53:          {
54:              if( buffer[ctr] == '\n' )
55:                  buffer[ctr] = '.';
56:
57:              printf("%c", buffer[ctr] );
58:          }
59:
60:          printf("\n");
61:
62:          fread(buffer, 24, sizeof(char), fp );
63:      }
64:
65:      fclose( fp );
66:
67:      return(0);
68:  }
```

```
31323334 35363738 39300A41 42434445 46470A48 494A4B4C 1234567890.ABCDEFG.HIJKL
4D4E0A4F 50515253 54550A56 5758595A 0A616263 64656667 MN.OPQRSTU.VWXYZ.abcdefg
0A68696A 6B6C6D6E 0A6F7071 72737475 0A767778 797A0A01 .hijklmn.opqrstu.vwxyz._
020A2140 2324255E 262A2829 5F2B7B7D 5B5D3B3A 27223C3E _.!@#$%^&*()_+{}[];:'"<>
3F2F2E2C 607E0A3E 20202020 20202020 20202020 2020203C ?/.,'~.>              <
0A0A4F6E 63652075 706F6E20 61207469 6D652074 68657265 ..Once upon a time there
20776572 65207468 72656520 6C69746C 65207069 67732E2E  were three little pigs
```

As you can see, this program prints the hexadecimal values of the file entered along with the actual character representation. This makes it easy to see what values are actually stored in a file. You also should notice that the new lines and other special characters are printed as single characters with no special processing. This means that the output is an actual representation of what is in the file. The hexadecimal numbers in the output are grouped in sets of four. Every two characters is an individual hexadecimal number. The break between every four is simply for readability.

Summary

This chapter covered many of the number systems that are commonly referred to in programming. While you use the decimal number system every day, it is not the most practical number system to use when dealing with computer data. The binary number system, which consists of two digits, is the most accurate representative for showing the computer's view of data. The hexadecimal system can easily be converted to and from binary. This easy conversion, along with its capability to represent many numbers with just a few digits, makes it the better number system for working with computer data. The octal system is also mentioned since C provides ways of easily converting to it.

Q&A

Q Why would you want to convert characters to decimal values?

A Once you are comfortable with the other number systems, you typically will not use the decimal system. If you are not comfortable with the other number systems, it is easier to add and subtract using decimal. For example, to change an uppercase letter to lowercase, you add 32 (decimal) to it. This makes more sense to most people. If you are looking at a file to determine what is there, the hexadecimal representation is the easiest to read.

Q **Is the octal number system important?**

A Typically, the octal number system is not used. Most programmers opt to use the hexadecimal system. The binary system is used mainly when doing bit manipulations or when working with binary data files (hence the name binary). Octal is seldom used.

Q **What is the difference between the lowercase x specifier and the upper-case X conversion specifier in the `printf()` function?**

A The x, or X, specifier prints out the hexadecimal value. If the lowercase x is used, the alpha digits of any hexadecimal numbers will be in lowercase. If the uppercase X is used, then the alpha digits of any hexadecimal numbers will be in uppercase. The difference is simply in the presentation of the hexadeci-mal numbers.

Workshop

The Workshop provides quiz questions to help you solidify your understanding of the material covered and exercises to provide you with experience using what you've learned.

Quiz

1. Why are numbers important in computing?

2. What determines what numeric value a letter gets translated to?

3. What is meant by decimal value?

4. Why are binary numbers important?

5. Why would you want to use hexadecimal numbers?

6. Why might you want to look at the numeric values of your data?

7. What digits are used in the binary number system?

8. What digits are used in the decimal number system?

9. What digits are used in the octal number system?

10. What digits are used in the hexadecimal number system?

Exercises

1. What are the numeric equivalents of the letter B? Compute for binary, octal, decimal, and hexadecimal. (Don't use the programs from the chapter to answer this!)

2. What are the numeric equivalents of the following character: ☺

3. What are the decimal values of the following ASCII characters?

   a. X

   b. space

   c. x

   d. 1

   e. ♥

4. What characters do the following numbers represent?

   a. 65

   b. 63

   c. 5

   d. 125

   e. 57

5. Rewrite Listing 6.2 to accept a decimal number instead of a character. Have the program print each of the other numeric representations.

6. Write a function that takes advantage of the information provided in the ASCII Character Table. This function should convert a lowercase letter to an uppercase letter, or an uppercase letter to lowercase. Do not use library functions provided by the compiler! Name the function switch_case().

7. **BUG BUSTER:**

```
char x;
for ( x = 'a'; x < 'Z'; x++ )
{
    printf( "%c ", x);
}
```

8. **ON YOUR OWN:** Write a program that reads a file and counts the number of occurrences of each character. Remember to differentiate between characters that may appear the same such as the difference between a null (decimal value 0) and a space (decimal value 32).

Using Libraries

As you create more and more useful functions, it may seem to become harder and harder to get them all linked together. C offers a way of grouping all of your useful functions into libraries. Today you learn:

☐ How to work with multiple source files.

☐ How #include files operate.

☐ What libraries are.

☐ Why libraries are important.

☐ How to create a library.

☐ How to use the library you create.

☐ A note about libraries you are already using.

Review of Program Creation

At this point in your C learning experience, you may or may not have written programs using more than one C source file. A C source file is a file that contains programming instructions (code). As your programs get larger, you reach a point where it is best to use more than one source file.

> **Expert Tip:** It is up to each person to determine when code should be broken into multiple source files. When the code gets beyond 250 lines, as a rule, you may want to begin breaking it into separate files. It is best to have only related functions in a file. For an application, you may choose to put the screen functions in one file, the database functions in a second file, and the rest of the functions in a third file.

Using one or more source files that you create, you can begin the process of creating an executable file. Typically, these end with the extension of .C. Header files, which are included in the source files, typically have an extension of .H. Using the compiler, header files are converted to object files (.OBJ). The objects are then linked with library files (.LIB) to create executable files (either .EXE or .COM). Figure 7.1 shows this process.

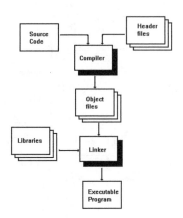

Figure 7.1. *The creation of an executable file.*

How To Work with Multiple Source Files

As you begin writing larger programs, or as you begin to write functions that may be reusable, you should start using multiple source files. There are several reasons for using separate source files. The first is size. Programs can get very large. Having multiple source files over 20K is not uncommon in "real-world" applications. In order to make maintaining files easier, most programmers break them into separate files that contain similar functions. For example, a programmer may set up three different source files for a large application. The programmer may put all of the screen functions in one file, all of the edit functions in another, and all the remaining code in a final source file. Figure 7.2 shows the creation of this executable file.

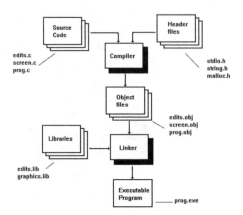

Figure 7.2. *The creation of an executable file with multiple source files.*

How To Include Header Files with *#include*

Header files are used in conjunction with the source files (.C). You have seen header files included in virtually every program in this book so far. These header files are generally included as follows:

```
#include <stdio.h>
```

In this example, stdio.h is the name of the header file. The #include is a preprocessor directive. This directive causes the following filename to be included in the current source file—hence the name. After the inclusion, the code in the header file becomes a part of the original source file. The following listings help to illustrate this point. These should all be in the same directory when you compile.

 Listing 7.1. Using include files.

```
1:    /* Program:    list0701.h
2:     * Author:     Bradley L. Jones
3:     * Purpose:    This is an include file with half a program.
4:     *=========================================================*/
5:
6:    #include <stdio.h>
7:
8:    int main( void )
9:    {
10:
```

```
11:    printf("\nHELLO ");
12:
13:
```

 Listing 7.2. A second header file.

```
1:    /* Program:   list0702.h
2:     * Author:    Bradley L. Jones
3:     * Purpose:   This is another include file with the second
4:     *            half of a program.
5:     *=========================================================*/
6:
7:
8:      printf("WORLD!\n");
9:
10:     return;
11:   }
```

 Listing 7.3. The source file.

```
1:    /* Program:   list0703.c
2:     * Author:    Bradley L. Jones
3:     * Purpose:   This is a program to demonstrate include
4:     *            files.
5:     *=========================================================*/
6:
7:    #include "list0701.h"
8:    #include "list0702.h"
9:
10:
```

> **Note:** To compile the previous listing, you need to only compile Listing 7.3 (LIST0703.C).

 HELLO WORLD!

 When LIST0703.C is compiled, the other two files are automatically included. This is obvious from the fact that the program runs! Listing 7.3 only contains the code for including the other two files. Listing 7.1 contains only the first half

of the code needed to produce the output. Line 11 of Listing 7.1 prints out the HELLO portion of the output. Listing 7.2 contains the code to print WORLD! Notice that Listing 7.3 does not appear to contain any relevant code at all. Lines 1 to 5 are simply comments and lines 7 and 8 are the includes.

The way the files in lines 7 and 8 of Listing 7.3 are included is slightly different than the way that you have been including files up until now. In addition, these lines are different than the include in line 6 of Listing 7.1. Instead of using <> around the file to be included, double quotes are used. Whether you use <>s or quotes makes a difference in what is included. Actually, the characters surrounding the included filename signal to the compiler where to look for the include file. Double quotes tell the compiler to look in the current directory for the include file first. The <> characters tell the compiler to start by looking in the include directory that was set up with the compiler.

Listing 7.4 is an equivalent listing to the previous three listings. This listing replaces the include statements in Listing 7.3 with the corresponding code listings. The pre-compiler would combine these listings into a listing similar to the following.

Type **Listing 7.4. Partially precompiled version of Listing 7.3.**

```
 1:  /* Program:   list0703.c
 2:   * Author:    Bradley L. Jones
 3:   * Purpose:   This is a program to demonstrate include
 4:   *            files.
 5:   *=========================================================*/
 6:
 7:  /* Program:   list0701.h
 8:   * Author:    Bradley L. Jones
 9:   * Purpose:   This is an include file with half a program.
10:   *=========================================================*/
11:
12:  #include <stdio.h>
13:
14:  int main( void )
15:  {
16:
17:    printf("\nHELLO ");
18:
19:
20:
21:  /* Program:   list0702.h
22:   * Author:    Bradley L. Jones
23:   * Purpose:   This is another include file with the second
24:   *            half of a program.
25:   *=========================================================*/
26:
```

```
27:
28:    printf("WORLD!\n");
29:
30:    return;
31: }
```

HELLO WORLD!

Lines 7 to 17 are an inserted copy of Listing 7.1. These lines of code replace the
#include directive in Listing 7.3. Lines 21 to 31 are Listing 7.2. Again these lines
have replaced the #include directive used in line 8 of Listing 7.3. This listing
does not accurately reflect how the preprocessor would change the includes in line 12
also. This header file, stdio.h, would also be expanded out with the code in that file.
This file is too long to add to this listing. In addition, each compiler comes with its
own version of this file.

> **Note:** The preceding listings were presented as a demonstration of how
> the #include directive works. The #include directories should not be
> used in the manner presented.

What Libraries Are

What is a library? A library is a set of functions that have been grouped together. A
library allows all of the functions to be grouped into a single file. Any subset of the
functions can be used by linking them with your programs.

Libraries enable you to share common functions. In fact, many—if not most—of the
functions that you use in your programs are in libraries that were provided with your
compiler. This includes functions such as printf(), scanf(), strcmp(), malloc(),
and more. Most compilers come with a library reference manual that describes the
usage of each function within the library. Notice that you don't need the source code
for these functions. In fact, you don't really have to know how the internals of these
functions work. What you do need to know is how to call them and what values they
return. For instance, when using a function such as puts(), you need to know that a
constant character pointer (a string) is passed to it. You also need to know that the
function returns an integer. It is also beneficial to know what values the integer can

be and what each value represents. Whether `puts()` is written with a `for` loop or using system calls is irrelevant to its use. You can use the function without knowing its internals.

Review Tip: It is not required that you use a return value from a function. Some functions, such as `scanf()`, are used without regard to their return value.

You are not limited to the libraries the compiler comes with. You can create your own libraries of useful functions. Several of the later chapters in this book will have you create libraries of functions that will be useful in many of your applications. In addition, once you have created a library, you can give it to others to link with their programs. It is not uncommon to create several of your own libraries. In addition, most major programming shops have several of their own libraries.

In addition to creating your own libraries or getting them from your friends, you can also purchase libraries. The phrase "don't reinvent the wheel" is true for C programmers. If you are looking to get a quick jump on developing large scale applications, then the decision to purchase libraries should be considered. There are libraries available to do a number of tasks ranging from accessing or creating standard database formats to doing high-resolution graphics.

Note: Although "reinventing the wheel" is not necessarily good, it is important for learning. Many of the topics covered in this book could be avoided by purchasing libraries. However, by covering these topics, you will better understand how many of the functions work.

Working with Libraries

Virtually every C compiler comes with the capability to create libraries. This is invariably done with a library program. You will need to consult your computer's manuals to determine its library program.

If you are using Microsoft, the program used to manipulate libraries is LIB.

If you are using a Borland compiler, your library program is TLIB.

This book will use LIB from this point on. If you are using the Borland compiler, you will simply need to type TLIB in place of LIB. If you are using a compiler other than Microsoft's or Borland's, then you will need to consult your manuals for compatibility. Other compilers should have library functions that operate in a similar manner.

There are several tasks that may be done to manipulate libraries. Some of the functions you can perform on libraries include:

☐ Create a new library.

☐ List functions in a library.

☐ Add a function to a library.

☐ Update or replace a function in a library.

☐ Remove a function from a library.

The next few sections will cover each of these. In doing so, the following listings will be used. Enter these four listings and save them under their corresponding names.

> **Note:** There is no output for each of the following listings. As you will see, these listings contain only individual functions. They are not complete "stand-alone" listings. They will be used in the following library manipulations.

 **Listing 7.5. A state edit.**

```
 1:  /* Program:  State.c
 2:   * Author:   Bradley L. Jones
 3:   * Purpose:  Validate a state abbreviation
 4:   * Note:     Valid states are:
 5:   *           AL, AK, AZ, CA, CO, CT, DE, FL, GA,
 6:   *           HI, IA, ID, IL, IN, KS, KY, LA, MA,
 7:   *           MD, ME, MI, MN, MO, MS, MT, NB, NC,
 8:   *           ND, NE, NH, NV, NY, OH, OK, OR, PA,
 9:   *           RI, SC, SD, TN, UT, VT, WS, WV, WY,
10:   * Return:   One of the following is returned:
11:   *           0 - Valid state
12:   *           1 - Invalid state
13:   *=====================================================*/
14:
```

continues

Listing 7.5. continued

```
15:    #include <string.h>
16:    #include <stdio.h>
17:
18:    int is_valid_state( char *state )
19:    {
20:       char all_states[101] = {"ALAKAZCACOCTDEFLGA"
21:                               "HIIAIDILINKSKYLAMA"
22:                               "MDMEMIMNMOMSMTNBNC"
23:                               "NDNENHNVNYOHOKORPA"
24:                               "RISCSDTNUTVTWSWVWY" };
25:       int ctr;
26:
27:       for(ctr = 0; ctr < 100; ctr+=2)
28:       {
29:          if (strncmp(all_states+ctr, state, 2)==0)
30:          {
31:             return(0);    /* found state */
32:          }
33:       }
34:       return(1);
35    }
```

 This function is an edit function. The comments in the first few lines of this function provide most of the details of what the function will do. As you see, the information in these comments completely documents the function's purpose and use. This function edits a string that is passed in to verify that it is a valid two-digit state abbreviation. A for loop starting in line 27 is used to move an offset through the all_states array. In line 29, each set of two characters of the all_states array is compared to the two characters passed to the function. If a match is found, the state is considered valid and the value of 0 is returned in line 31. If the state is not found, then the value of 1 is returned in line 34.

Like the state function there are several other edits that only allow for specific values. Listing 7.6 presents a function to verify the sex code.

Type **Listing 7.6. A sex code edit.**

```
1:    /* Program:   Sex.c
2:     * Author:    Bradley L. Jones
3:     * Purpose:   Validate a sex code
4:     * Note:      Valid sex code. Valid values are:
5:     *            M or m - Male
6:     *            F or f - Female
7:     *            U or u - Other
8:     * Return:    One of the following is returned:
```

```
9:    *              0 - Valid code
10:   *              1 - Invalid code
11:   *====================================================*/
12:
13:   int is_valid_sex( char sex_code )
14:   {
15:      int rv = 0;
16:
17:      switch( sex_code )
18:      {
19:         case 'F':
20:         case 'f':
21:         case 'M':
22:         case 'm':
23:         case 'U':
24:         case 'u': rv = 0;
25:                   break;
26:         default:  rv = 1;
27:      }
28:      return(rv);
29:   }
```

Analysis

This edit function verifies that the character received is a valid abbreviation for a sex code. The assumed valid values are M for male, F for female, and U for unknown. (This is the '90s!) This time a switch statement in line 17 is used to determine if the values are valid. If not, 1 is again returned. If the sex_code value is valid, then 0 is returned. You should notice that lines 20, 22, and 24 include the lowercase letters. This helps to make the edit more complete. Following in listing 7.7 is a more complex edit for a date.

Type

Listing 7.7. A date edit.

```
1:   /* Program:  date.c
2:    * Author:   Bradley L. Jones
3:    * Purpose:  Pseudo-validate a date
4:    * Note:     This is not a very complete date edit.
5:    * Return:   One of the following is returned:
6:    *              +0  - Valid date
7:    *              -1  - Invalid day
8:    *              -2  - Invalid month
9:    *              -3  - Invalid year
10:   *====================================================*/
11:
12:   int is_valid_date( int month, int day, int year )
13:   {
14:      int rv = 0;
```

continues

Listing 7.7. continued

```
15:
16:     if( day < 1 || day > 31 )
17:     {
18:        rv = -1;
19:     }
20:     else
21:     {
22:        if( month < 1 || month > 12 )
23:        {
24:           rv = -2;
25:        }
26:        else
27:        {
28:           if( year < 1 || year > 2200 )
29:           {
30:              rv = -3;
31:           }
32:        }
33:     }
34:     return( rv );
35:  }
```

 This is a third edit. As you can see, this is not as detailed as it could be. This edit validates a date. It receives three integers—month, day, and year in line 12. This edit does not fully edit the date. In line 16, it verifies that the day is 31 or less. In line 22, the edit checks to see if the month is from 1 to 12. In line 28, it checks to see that the year is a positive number less than 2200. Why 2200? Why not! It is just an arbitrary number that is higher than any date that would be used in any of my systems. You can use whatever cap you feel is adequate.

If the date values pass all of these checks, then 0 is returned to the calling function. If all the values don't pass, a negative number is returned signifying what was in error. Notice that three different negative numbers are being returned. A program calling the is_valid_date() function will be able to determine what was wrong. Listing 7.8 presents a function that uses the is_valid_date() function.

Type   **Listing 7.8. A birthdate edit.**

```
1:  /* Program:  bdate.c
2:   * Author:   Bradley L. Jones
3:   * Purpose:  Pseudo-validate a birthdate
4:   * Note:     This is not a very complete date edit.
5:   * Return:   One of the following is returned:
6:   *
7:   *              0  - Valid date
```

```
 8:    *              -1  - Invalid day
 9:    *              -2  - Invalid month
10:    *              -3  - Invalid year
11:    *              -4  - Invalid birthday (valid date > 1995 )
12:    *=======================================================*/
13:
14:   int is_valid_birthdate( int month, int day, int year )
15:   {
16:      int rv = 0;
17:
18:      rv = is_valid_date( month, day, year );
19:
20:      if( rv >= 0 )
21:      {
22:         if( year >= 1995 )
23:         {
24:            rv = -4;
25:         }
26:      }
27:      return( rv );
28:   }
```

Analysis This edit is a little more specific to applications. Like the date edit, it is not as complete as it could be. The reason for this simplicity is that this function is for use in describing library functions, not to emphasize editing values—although properly written edits are important.

The birthdate edit is a more specific version of the date edit. In fact, a part of the birthdate edit is to call the date edit (line 18). If the date edit in line 18 passes, then the birthdate edit verifies in line 22 that the date was before January 1, 1995. This is done by simply checking the year. If the year is equal to or greater than 1995, then the date is equal to or greater than January 1, 1995. A more appropriate check would be to verify that the date is before today's date. After all, you aren't born yet if your birthdate is tomorrow. Line 24 adds an additional error code to be returned if the date is valid but it is after January 1, 1995. If the date is invalid, the value returned from the date edit is returned. Notice that this edit requires the date edit to be complete.

How To Create a Library

Now that you have a set of edit functions, you will want to use them. The following program, presented in Listing 7.9 and Listing 7.10, uses the four edits that have been created. To create a program from multiple source files, you simply include them all when you compile. If you were using Borland's Turbo compiler, you could type:

```
TCC list0709.c state.c sex.c date.c bdate.c
```

The final outcome of this compilation would be an executable file called list0709.EXE.

 Listing 7.9. Using the edit functions.

```
 1:   /* Program:   list0709.c
 2:    * Author:    Bradley L. Jones
 3:    * Purpose:   This is a program to demonstrate the use of
 4:    *            the edit functions.
 5:    *=========================================================*/
 6:
 7:   #include <stdio.h>
 8:   #include "edits.h"
 9:
10:   void main(void)
11:   {
12:      int rv;
13:
14:      printf("\n\nUsing the edits:");
15:
16:      printf("\n\nUsing the state edit:");
17:      rv = is_valid_state("xx");
18:      printf("\n     State = xx, return value: %d", rv);
19:      rv = is_valid_state("IN");
20:      printf("\n     State = IN, return value: %d", rv);
21:
22:      printf("\n\nUsing the sex code edit:");
23:      rv = is_valid_sex('x');
24:      printf("\n     Sex code = x, return value: %d", rv);
25:      rv = is_valid_sex('F');
26:      printf("\n     Sex code = F, return value: %d", rv);
27:
28:      printf("\n\nUsing the date code edit:");
29:      rv = is_valid_date( 8, 11, 1812);
30:      printf("\n     Month: 8\n     Day:    11");
31:      printf("\n     Year:  1812, return value: %d", rv);
32:      rv = is_valid_date( 31, 11, 1812);
33:      printf("\n     Month: 31\n     Day:    11");
34:      printf("\n     Year:  1812, return value: %d", rv);
35:
36:      printf("\n\nUsing the birthdate code edit:");
37:      rv = is_valid_birthdate( 8, 11, 1999);
38:      printf("\n     Month: 8\n     Day:    11");
39:      printf("\n     Year:  1812, return value: %d", rv);
40:      rv = is_valid_date( 8, 11, 1812);
41:      printf("\n     Month: 31\n     Day:    11");
42:      printf("\n     Year:  1812, return value: %d", rv);
43:   }
```

Listing 7.10. A header file for the edit functions.

```
1:  /* edits.h
2:   * Prototypes for EDITS library
3:   *================================================*/
4:
5:  #if defined( __EDITS_H )
6:    /* this file has already been included */
7:  #else
8:  #define __EDITS_H
9:
10: int is_valid_state( char *state );
11: int is_valid_sex( char sex_code );
12: int is_valid_date( int month, int day, int year );
13: int is_valid_birthdate( int month, int day, int year );
14:
15: #endif
```

```
Using the edits:

Using the state edit:
    State = xx, return value: 0
    State = IN, return value: 1

Using the sex code edit:

    Sex code = x, return value: 0
    Sex code = F, return value: 1

Using the date code edit:
    Month:  8
    Day:    11
    Year:   1812, return value: 0
    Month:  31
    Day:    11
    Year:   1812, return value: -2

Using the birthdate code edit:
    Month:  8
    Day:    11
    Year:   1812, return value: -4
    Month:  31
    Day:    11
    Year:   1812, return value: 0
```

7

If additional listings are created that call these edit functions, you could include each of the appropriate edits during their compilations. This would be okay, but linking in a single library rather than a bunch of source files makes using the edits much easier.

Listing 7.9 should not offer any surprises. Line 8 includes a header file called edits.h. Notice that this is the same name as the library. This header file is presented in Listing 7.10. edits.h contains prototypes for each of the functions that are being included. It is good practice to create a file containing prototypes. Also notice the additional preprocessor directives in lines 5 to 8 and line 15 in Listing 7.10, edits.c. The `#if defined()` directive checks to see if the following value, `__EDITS_H`, has already been defined. If it has, then a comment is placed in the code stating that the file has already been included (line 6). If the value.it has not been defined, then line 8 defines the value. If `__EDITS_H` has been defined, then the code from lines 8 to 14 is skipped. This logic helps to prevent a header file from being included more than once.

> **Expert Tip:** Many programmers use the directives that are presented in Listing 7.10 in their own header files. This prevents the header files from being included more than once. Many programmers will create the defined name by adding two underscores to the name of the header file. Since periods cannot be part of a defined constant, the period is typically replaced with an additional underscore. This is how the define for Listing 7.10, `__EDITS_H`, was derived.

In the rest of the listing, each edit is called twice. In one case, an edit is called with valid data. In the second case, the edit is called with bad data.

Creating the library requires that each of the functions to be included be compiled into object files. Once you have the objects, you can create the library by using your compiler's library program. As stated earlier, Borland's library program is TLIB and Microsoft's is LIB. To create the library, you simply add each function to it.

DO   DON'T

DO understand the concepts behind libraries.

DON'T put different types of functions in the same library. A library should contain functions that have similarities. Examples of different libraries may be a graphics library, an edits library, a file management functions library, and a statistical library.

DO take advantage of the `#ifdef` preprocessor directive in your header files to prevent re-including the file.

Adding New Functions to a Library

Adding functions to a library is done with the addition operator (+). This is true for both Borland and Microsoft compilers. To add a function, use the following format for the library command:

```
LIB libname +function_filename
```

libname is the name that you want the library to have. This name should be descriptive of the functions that are stored in the library. This brings up a good point. All of the functions stored in an individual library should be related in some fashion. For instance, all of the functions being used in the examples are edit functions. It would be appropriate to group these functions into a single library. A good name for the library might be EDITS.

Expert Tip: Only related functions should be stored in a library together.

function_filename is the name of the object file that is going to be added into the library. It is optional whether you include the .OBJ extension on the function filename. If you don't, the library program will assume that the extension is .OBJ. It is also assumed that the *libname* will have a .LIB extension. To create a library called EDITS that contains the is_valid_state function, you would enter the following:

```
LIB EDITS +state.obj
```

Compiler Warning: LIB is used in all the examples from this point on. Most compilers use a different program when working with libraries. As stated earlier, Borland uses TLIB. If using the Microsoft compiler, you will use LIB; however, you will need to add a semicolon to the end of each LIB statement.

To add additional functions, also use the addition operator. There is not a real difference between adding a function versus creating a library. If the library name already exists, you are adding functions. If it does not, you are creating a library. If you wanted to add the other three functions to the EDITS library, you would enter the following:

7

```
LIB EDITS +sex.obj +date.obj +bdate.obj
```

This adds the is_valid_sex(), is_valid_date(), and is_valid_birthdate() functions to the library. You should note that although the .OBJ extensions were included, they were not necessary.

Separate Source Files

You should notice that the functions are put into separate source files. By doing so, maintenance of future changes is made easier. Each function is isolated so that future enhancements only affect a single source file. Files are added at the object file level. A single object file is created from a source file. You should make it a practice of putting library functions into their own source files.

 Expert Tip: You should make it a practice to put library functions into their own source files.

Using a Library

Once you have created a library, you can use it rather than each of the individual files that had been created. In fact, once the object files are stored in the library, you only need the original source file to make changes. You could give a library file to other users; they will be able to include any of its functions within their own programs. To use the library with Listing 7.9, you would enter the following at the command line:

```
CL list0709.c edits.lib
```

You should replace CL with the compile command that your compiler uses. Notice that the library file comes last. It should always be listed after all of the source files. This is equivalent to having included each of the files as shown previously.

Listing Information in a Library

Once you have created a library, you will probably want to know what functions are in it. Most library programs enable you to produce a listing that provides this information. To do this, you add the name of the list file to the command line as follows:

```
LIB libname ,listfile
```

In this case, *listfile* is the name of the file that the information on the library will be stored. A comma should be included on the command line before the list filename.

You could have included any operations in the command line after the library name and before the list filename. This includes the addition of functions as you have already seen, or any of the actions that follow.

Each compiler may produce a slightly different list file. If you use the Borland compiler, you would type the following to get a listing of the EDITS library stored in a file called INFO.LST:

```
TLIB EDITS ,INFO
```

If you are using the Borland compiler, you will notice that the .LST extension is the default extension that is added to the list file if an extension is not provided. Other compilers, such as the Microsoft compilers, may not add an extension to the list file automatically. As stated earlier, the .LIB extension is automatically added to a library file and therefore is not needed in the library name. If you typed the INFO.LST file, you would see the following:

```
Publics by module

BDATE      size = 46
    _is_valid_birthdate

DATE       size = 66
    _is_valid_date

SEX        size = 79
    _is_valid_sex

STATE      size = 203
    _is_valid_state
```

This provides you with information on both functions that are stored and the name of the file that the function is a part of. If you are using the Microsoft compiler, you would enter the following:

```
LIB EDITS ,LISTFILE.LST;
```

Printing the list file should provide output similar to the following:

```
_is_valid_birthdate..bdate        _is_valid_date....date
_is_valid_sex.....sex             _is_valid_state...state


state            Offset: 00000010H  Code and data size: cbH
  _is_valid_state

sex              Offset: 000002d0H  Code and data size: 4fH
  _is_valid_sex
```

```
date              Offset: 00000430H  Code and data size: 42H
  _is_valid_date

bdate             Offset: 00000560H  Code and data size: 2eH
  _is_valid_birthdate
```

While this is formatted a little different from the Borland output, the contents provide virtually the same information.

Removing Functions from a Library

In addition to adding functions to libraries, you can also remove functions that are no longer needed or that you don't want to distribute with a library. To remove a function, the subtraction operator (-) is used. The format is the same as adding functions.

```
LIB  libname -function_filename
```

As you can see, it is easy to remove a function. The following would remove the birthdate edit from the edit library:

```
LIB EDITS  -bdate.obj ,list
```

Notice that a list file called list is also being printed. Following is what would now be contained in the Borland and Microsoft list files after the subtraction:

```
_is_valid_date....date              _is_valid_sex.....sex
_is_valid_state...state

sex               Offset: 00000010H  Code and data size: 4fH
  _is_valid_sex

date              Offset: 00000160H  Code and data size: 42H
  _is_valid_date

state             Offset: 00000280H  Code and data size: afH
  _is_valid_state
```

```
Publics by module

DATE      size = 66
    _is_valid_date

SEX       size = 79
    _is_valid_sex

STATE     size = 175
    _is_valid_state
```

Updating Preexisting Functions in a Library

Updating a library is equivalent to deleting a function and then adding it again. The following could be used to update the is_valid_state() function:

```
LIB EDITS -state
```

```
LIB EDITS +state
```

Where LIB is your appropriate library program. You could also do this by combining the operations as such:

```
LIB EDITS -+state
```

This will remove the old state edit from the EDITS library and then add the new state function. This only works if the source filename is the same for both the old and the new function.

Extracting or Moving a Module from a Library

Not only can you put modules or object files into a library, but you can also copy them out of a library. To do this, you use the asterisk operator (*). The following pulls a copy of the STATE.OBJ file from the EDITS library where LIB is your appropriate library program:

```
LIB EDITS *state
```

Once you have keyed this, you will have made a copy of the state edit (within the STATE.OBJ file) that was in the EDITS library. This file will still be in the library also. The following will pull a copy of the STATE.OBJ file from the library and also remove it from the library:

```
LIB EDITS -*state
```

This will remove the state edit and create the object file.

What Libraries Are Available Already

As stated earlier, each compiler comes with its own set of libraries that have been created. In addition, most compilers come with Library Reference Manuals that detail each of the functions within the libraries. Generally, these standard libraries are automatically linked into your programs when you compile. If you use some of the more specific features of your compiler—such as graphics—then you may need to link in additional libraries.

A Final Example Using the Edits Library

Listing 7.11 is a listing that requires the EDITS.LIB file that you created earlier today. Notice that this is a completely different program from the one presented earlier. By including the library when compiling and linking, you can easily reuse the edit functions.

 Listing 7.11. Using the EDITS.LIB—again!

```
1:  /* Program:   list0711.c
2:   * Author:    Bradley L. Jones
3:   * Purpose:   This is a program to accept a valid birthday.
4:   * Note:      Requires EDITS.LIB to be linked
5:   *=========================================================*/
6:
7:  #include <stdio.h>
8:  #include "edits.h"
9:
10: void main(void)
11: {
12:     int rv;
13:     int month=0,
14:        day= 0,
15:        year=0;
16:
17:     printf("\n\nEnter your birthday (format: MM DD YY ):");
18:     scanf( "%d %d %d", &month, &day, &year );
19:
20:     rv = is_valid_birthdate(month, day, year);
21:
22:     while( rv < 0 )
23:     {
24:       printf("\n\nYou entered an invalid birthdate(%d-%d-%d)",
25:              month, day, year);
26:
27:       switch( rv )
28:       {
29:         case -1:  printf("\nError %d: BAD DAY", rv);
30:                   break;
31:         case -2:  printf("\nError %d: BAD MONTH", rv);
32:                   break;
33:         case -3:  printf("\nError %d: BAD YEAR", rv);
34:                   break;
35:         case -4:  printf("\nError %d: BAD BIRTHDATE", rv);
36:                   break;
37:         default:  printf("\nError %d: UNKNOWN ERROR", rv);
38:                   break;
```

```
39:        }
40:
41:        printf("\n\nRe-enter your birthday (format: MM DD YY):");
42:        scanf( "%d %d %d", &month, &day, &year );
43:
44:        rv = is_valid_birthdate(month, day, year);
45:    }
46:
47:    printf("\n\nYour birthdate is %d-%d-%d", month, day, year);
48: }
```

```
Enter your birthday (format: MM DD YY ):8 32 1965


You entered an invalid birthdate(8-32-1965)
Error -1: BAD DAY

Re-enter your birthday (format: MM DD YY):13 11 1965


You entered an invalid birthdate(13-11-1965)
Error -2: BAD MONTH

Re-enter your birthday (format: MM DD YY):8 11 -89


You entered an invalid birthdate(8-11—89)
Error -3: BAD YEAR

Re-enter your birthday (format: MM DD YY):8 11 1999


You entered an invalid birthdate(8-11-1999)
Error -4: BAD BIRTHDATE

Re-enter your birthday (format: MM DD YY):8 11 1965


Your birthdate is 8-11-1965
```

Analysis This program enables you to enter the birthdate of a person. The user is required to enter the information until it is correct. If invalid information is entered, then the user is required to re-enter the entire date. As you will quickly see, the is_valid_birthdate() function or more appropriately, the is_valid_date() function that the birthday calls is not entirely accurate. It will consider dates such as February 30th valid. One of today's exercises asks you to rewrite this function so that it is more accurate.

7

Summary

Today, you were presented with a quick review of using multiple source files. This was followed with an explanation of using include files with the `#include` directive. The difference between double quotes and the more familiar <> signs was explained. The day then progressed into a description of libraries—what they are and why they are important. The usage of libraries along with how to add functions to them, remove functions from them, or update functions within them was explained. In addition, information on listing out information about a library was covered.

Q&A

Q Do all the functions in a library link into a program, thus increasing the programs size with unused functions?

A No! Only the functions that are called are linked.

Q Why can't I put all the functions in a library in the same source file?

A By isolating the functions into separate source files, you make the code easier to maintain. Since you add, update, and remove functions at the source code level, you isolate functions and changes by having separate source files. If you make a change to a function, you don't want to risk changing other functions.

Q What happens if you add a function to a library that is already there?

A You should be careful not to re-add a function. Some libraries will accept a function more than one time. This corrupts your library since you will not be sure which function is being used.

Q Can more than one library be used at a time?

A Yes! You will invariably use the default libraries that come with your compiler. When you create or add your own, you are most often using these libraries in addition to the default libraries. Some compilers have limitations to the number of libraries you can link in; however, these limits are seldom reached. For example, the Microsoft limit is 32 libraries.

Q What other functions can be performed on libraries?

A Only the basics of library manipulation were presented today. Most library programs will do additional functions; however, the way these more advanced functions are performed is not as standard. You should consult your compiler's manuals for more information. Such functions may include combining libraries or expanding some of the compiler's default libraries.

Workshop

The Workshop provides quiz questions to help you solidify your understanding of the material covered and exercises to provide you with experience in using what you've learned.

Quiz

1. What is a library?

2. Where do libraries come from?

3. How do you add a function to a library?

4. How do you remove a function from a library?

5. How do you update a function in a library?

6. How do you list the information in a library?

7. How do you copy an object file from a library?

8. How do you extract or move an object out of a library into an object file?

9. What is the difference between including a file with quotes and with <>s?

10. Can source files be included in libraries?

Exercises

1. How would you create a library called STATES.LIB containing the modules RI.OBJ, IL.OBJ, IN.OBJ?

2. How would you get a listing from the STATES library?

3. How would you create the STATES library from Exercise 1 and get a listing at the same time?

4. How would you add KY.OBJ and FL.OBJ to the STATES library?

5. How would you remove the KY module from the STATES library?

6. How would you replace the FL module with a new one in the STATES library?

7. How would you get a copy of the IL object from the STATES library?

8. Create a function to verify that a string contains all uppercase alpha characters (A to Z). If the string does contain all uppercase characters, return 1; otherwise, return 0.

9. Add the previous function to your edits library.

10. **ON YOUR OWN:** Rewrite the date edit to be more accurate. It should take into consideration the number of days that a particular month has. You may also want to include leap years!

11. **ON YOUR OWN:** Update your edits library with your new birthdate function.

12. **BUG BUSTER:** What is wrong with the following?

    ```
    CL source1.c library.lib source2.obj
    ```

13. **ON YOUR OWN:** Create a listing file for some of the libraries that come with your compiler. These libraries are typically stored in a subdirectory called LIBRARY or LIB. You should notice many familiar functions.

2

At this point, you should have completed the first week. If you skimmed or skipped chapters in the first week, it will be okay to continue into Week Two. There is one exception: If you are not familiar with libraries, you should read Day 7.

On Day 8, you will begin using BIOS functions. BIOS functions are detailed along with what they can do. The functions presented on Day 8 will be the first that you will be able to add to your own library.

On Day 9, you replace several of the functions that you may have created on Day 4. These new functions will not only be more flexible, but they will also eliminate the need for external drivers such as ANSI.SYS. These text graphics functions will be used in later chapters for creating a full-fledged application.

On Days 10 and 11, you will create a multitude of functions. Many of these functions will be used in the application that will be developed starting on Day 12.

Functions included in these chapters will do such tasks as scrolling, clearing the screen, hiding the cursor, and more.

On Day 12, you will begin the process of developing applications. Before coding your application, you should begin with some preparation. Several methods of preparation exist. In addition to the preliminary steps, there are methods for the entire process of developing an application. Day 12 provides an overview of several different methodologies that can be employed in developing an application.

Day 13 begins the process of coding an application. This will most likely be the day that is the most fun of the second week. The concepts behind developing an entry and edit screen are covered. In addition, you will be presented with all the code necessary for creating an entry and edit screen. Many of the functions created in Days 8 through 11 will be used.

The week ends with menus and action bars being added to your application. Day 14 provides an overview of using menus and action bars. In addition, you are guided in adding menus to the front of your application. Action bars are also added to your entry and edit screen.

The third week is dedicated mostly to continuing the development of the application started in the second week. Reporting, incorporating help, testing, and more will all be presented. At the end of the third week, you will have a complete understanding of all aspects of application development.

This is where you're headed. For now, you should continue to take things one day at a time starting with Day 8.

 Warning: Although skipping days in Week One was okay, you cannot skip days in Week Two or Week Three.

Tapping into System Resources via BIOS

On Day 4, you learned how to take advantage of the ANSI functions. As you saw, the ANSI functions require the use of an external program to operate correctly. Today you'll learn a better way of manipulating the resources of your system by doing the following:

☐ Review what was covered on Day 4.

☐ Review what BIOS is.

☐ Learn what an interrupt is.

☐ Get an overview of the multitude of BIOS functions available.

☐ See how to use some of the interrupt services to work with your system.

System Resources in Review

System resources are resources provided by your computer system that enable you to gain functionality by calling on them. By using system resources, you can create programs that have much more use. In addition, some tasks would be nearly impossible without them. Tasks that can be accomplished include working with the video display, loading fonts, accessing disk drives, determining memory size, accessing the keyboard, reading a joystick, and much more.

As stated on Day 4, system resources can't be used without any concerns. The cost of using system resources can vary. On Day 4, you learned that the largest concern with using system resources should be portability. Depending on which systems resources you access, you could greatly limit the portability of your programs. The resources that will be presented today can be found on most IBM-compatible machines running MS/DOS or an operating system that supports MS/DOS. A different computer platform, such as a Macintosh, won't be able to run the programs presented today.

Working with the Display

On Day 4, you were told that one of the characteristics of C is that it is flexible. Typically, there are several ways to accomplish similar tasks. Each method that can be implemented has its own pros and cons. Also on Day 4, you were presented with three different methods of accessing or manipulating system resources. In particular, you were shown how to manipulate the computer's video monitor. The three areas that were presented were:

☐ The ANSI functions

☐ Direct memory access

☐ BIOS

A Review of Using ANSI Functions

ANSI stands for American National Standards Institute. There are several different areas of standards created by ANSI. The ANSI terminal standards can be used on an IBM-compatible computer that has loaded the ANSI.SYS system driver. The ANSI.SYS driver comes with Microsoft and PC DOS. Once installed, the ANSI system driver enables the computer to use functions that allow for cursor movement, display extended graphics, and redefining key values. Using the ANSI.SYS driver was presented in detail on Day 4.

As you learned on Day 4, there are both pros and cons to using the ANSI functions. The most obvious benefit is that using the ANSI functions is extremely simple. Once the ANSI.SYS driver has been installed, the functions are easily called. Another benefit of the ANSI functions is that they are well documented. Because the ANSI driver generally comes with the computer's operating system, there is usually an abundance of documentation.

As you may have seen, using ANSI functions isn't without its downside. The most negative impact is when you use an ANSI function on a system that doesn't support the ANSI terminal functions. If the program doesn't support the ANSI functions, or if the ANSI.SYS driver hasn't been loaded, then gibberish may be displayed on the screen. Because of this reliance on the ANSI.SYS driver, most programmers choose to avoid the ANSI functions. The fact that not all operating systems support the ANSI terminal emulation functions could also impact a decision to use ANSI functions.

A Review of Using Direct Memory Access

Direct memory access was also discussed on Day 4. Memory is set aside for use by the video display. This memory can be accessed directly to manipulate the graphics or characters that are on the screen. Because this is memory that is directly mapped to the video display, a change to the memory can be seen instantly on the screen. By updating the video display's memory directly, you can gain the fastest screen updates.

This fast speed comes at the cost of portability. The memory set aside for the video display isn't always in the same locations. While it's safe to assume that the memory will be set aside, it's not safe to assume where. Portability is lost because the area set aside is not always guaranteed to be the same from computer system to computer system. To use this direct video memory, the system must be 100-percent IBM-compatible with an IBM PC's hardware. It's safe to assume that the same brand of computer with the same type of hardware will have video memory stored in the same location. It isn't safe to assume that all other computers will use the same location—not even all IBM-compatible systems. In addition, memory for using a CGA monitor isn't always allocated in the same area that memory for a VGA monitor would be.

What Is BIOS?

The use of BIOS was also mentioned on Day 4 as the third alternative for manipulating system resources. BIOS stands for Basic Input/Output System. Every IBM-compatible MS/PC DOS computer operates with BIOS. *BIOS* is a set of service routines that are activated by software interrupts. A *software interrupt* is an interruption caused by the currently running program that causes the operating system (DOS) to respond. By going through these service routines, and therefore BIOS, you avoid interacting directly with the computer's hardware. This eliminates concerns, such as the possibility of different locations for video memory, because the BIOS determines where and what you need based on the interrupt you cause.

There are BIOS services for a multitude of different input and output activities. This includes being able to manipulate the screen, the keyboard, printers, disks, mouse, and more. In addition, there are services available to manipulate the system date and time. Tables will be presented that will detail many of the available interrupts. For now, it's more important to know how to use them and why.

It's better to use BIOS instead of direct memory video access or the ANSI functions. Direct memory access has a downside that has already been described—you don't know for sure where the video memory will be located. The downside of the ANSI functions is that the external device driver, ANSI.SYS, must be loaded for the functions to work.

By going through the BIOS, you don't need external device drivers, nor do you have to determine where video memory is located. The BIOS takes care of that for you.

While all of this makes the BIOS calls sound like the perfect answer, there is a downside to using BIOS also. The speed of going through BIOS isn't going to be as fast as accessing video memory directly. In addition, using the BIOS isn't going to be

as easy as using the ANSI functions. Neither of these negatives outweighs the additional portability that you gain by using the BIOS functions. The speed difference between BIOS and direct memory is negligible for most applications. In addition, once you create a BIOS function, you can store it in your own library and never have to worry about the underlying code. Another problem with BIOS is the portability of accessing the interrupts. Different compilers use different commands. The difference in these commands is minimal between most compilers.

DO	DON'T

DO understand the differences among ANSI, direct memory, and BIOS functions.

DON'T use BIOS functions if you plan to port your code to computers that are not IBM-compatible.

Using BIOS

To work with BIOS, you simply set up any needed information and then call the appropriate interrupts number. When you call an interrupt, you pass information within registers. Don't worry about registers at this time. In addition to passing interrupt numbers, you may also need to pass function numbers. *Function numbers* are more specific instructions to BIOS. Table 8.1, presented later today, lists some of the major interrupts and their functions. For instance, interrupt 16 (0x10h in hex) is an interrupt for video display functions. There are several different video display functions that can be used. Table 8.2, which is also presented later today, lists several of the specific functions. For instance, interrupt 0x10h (video display processes) used with function 0x02h will set the cursor position. In some cases, there are even lower breakdowns of functions into *subfunctions*. For example, the video interrupt 0x10h has a function to work with the color pallet (0x10h), which has several subfunctions. Subfunction 0x01h will set the screen's border color.

Using the interrupt calls requires setting up information first. Following are two structures that can be used to pass information to BIOS. These two structures are followed by a union that combines the structures into one. This set of structures and the related union are given as they appear in both the Borland and Microsoft compilers:

```
struct WORDREGS {
    unsigned int    ax, bx, cx, dx, si, di, cflag, flags;
};

struct BYTEREGS {
    unsigned char   al, ah, bl, bh, cl, ch, dl, dh;
};

union   REGS    {
    struct  WORDREGS x;
    struct  BYTEREGS h;
};
```

```
/* word registers */

struct _WORDREGS {
    unsigned int ax;
    unsigned int bx;
    unsigned int cx;
    unsigned int dx;
    unsigned int si;
    unsigned int di;
    unsigned int cflag;
    };

/* byte registers */

struct _BYTEREGS {
    unsigned char al, ah;
    unsigned char bl, bh;
    unsigned char cl, ch;
    unsigned char dl, dh;
    };

/* general purpose registers union -
 * overlays the corresponding word and byte registers.
 */

union _REGS {
    struct _WORDREGS x;
    struct _BYTEREGS h;
    };
```

As you can see, regardless of the compiler, these are set up in the same manner. Naming may be a little different so you will want to check your compiler for specific names to use. Within the examples presented in this book, the following code fragment will be included. Even if you have the Borland or Microsoft compilers, you can include the following, or if you wish, you can use the structures declared in your compiler.

8

Note: The structures shown previously are defined in the DOS.H header file in the include directory of the corresponding compiler. If your compiler is ANSI-compatible, it should have similar declarations in its DOS.H header file.

Listing 8.1. BIOSREGS.H.

```
1:  /* Header:  BIOSREGS.H
2:   * Purpose: Include generic structures for BIOS registers
3:   *------------------------------------------------------*/
4:  #ifdef __BIOSREGS_H
5:  #define __BIOSREGS_H 1
6:
7:  struct XREG
8:  {
9:      unsigned int ax;
10:     unsigned int bx;
11:     unsigned int cx;
12:     unsigned int dx;
13:     unsigned int si;
14:     unsigned int di;
15:     unsigned int cflag;
16: };
17:
18: struct HREG
19: {
20:     unsigned char al, ah;
21:     unsigned char bl, bh;
22:     unsigned char cl, ch;
23:     unsigned char dl, dh;
24: };
25:
26: union REGS
27: {
28:     struct XREG x;
29:     struct HREG h;
30: };
31:
32: #endif
```

This is just a header file so there isn't any output. As you can see, the XREG and HREG structures are virtually identical to what was presented from the Borland and Microsoft compilers earlier. This header file should be compatible with either of those compilers, along with any other DOS-based compiler. The REGS union

235

declared in lines 26 to 32 will be used when calling BIOS. You should be aware that XREG and HREG are used for different reasons. The use of these will be covered later. For now, remember that REGS is a union, which means that you can use XREG or HREG, but not both at the same time.

At this point, you may feel somewhat lost and confused. To help clear up what has been presented so far, here are a few examples. Listing 8.2 presents an example of using an interrupt to get the current date via an interrupt call to BIOS.

 Listing 8.2. LIST0802. Using BIOS interrupt call.

```
 1:  /* Program: LIST0802.c
 2:   * Author:  Bradley L. Jones
 3:   * Purpose: Demonstrates a BIOS function to get current
 4:   *          date.
 5:   *=========================================================*/
 6:
 7:  #include "biosregs.h"
 8:  #include <dos.h>
 9:  #include <stdio.h>
10:
11:  /*** Function prototypes ***/
12:  void current_date( int *month, int *day, int *year );
13:
14:  void main(void)
15:  {
16:    int month, day, year;
17:    printf("\nDetermining the current date...");
18:
19:    current_date( &month, &day, &year );
20:
21:    printf("\n\nThe current date is: %d/%d/%d.", month, day, year);
22:  }
23:
24:  void current_date( int *month, int *day, int *year)
25:  {
26:      union REGS inregs, outregs;
27:      inregs.h.ah = 0x2a;
28:
29:      int86(0x21, &inregs, &outregs);
30:
31:      *month = outregs.h.dh;
32:      *day   = outregs.h.dl;
33:      *year  = outregs.x.cx;
34:  }
```

> **Note:** Line 29 uses a non-ANSI-compatible function. This means that some compilers may use a different name for the int86() function. Microsoft documents the use of _int86(); however, int86() works. Borland uses int86(). Consult your function reference for specific information on your compiler. For the remainder of this book, the function name of int86() will be used; however, you should be able to replace it with your compiler's comparable command. In the case of the Microsoft compiler, simply add the underscore.

```
Determining the current date...

The current date is: 12/22/1993.
```

When you run this program, you should end up with the current date on your screen instead of 12/22/1993. The date is received via an interrupt call. In this program, two values are declared to be of type REGS. Remember that REGS is the union that holds the register values (see Listing 8.1). The inregs union is used to hold the values going into the interrupt call. The outregs variable is used to hold the values being returned.

To get the date, the function number 0x2Ah (33 decimal) is used with a call to BIOS. The function number goes into the ah register. The ah register is a part of the h structure of the inregs REGS union. The function 0x2Ah is a function within interrupt 0x21h. Line 27 sets this function number into the ah register. Line 29 calls the BIOS interrupt using int86(). If you are using a Microsoft compiler, remember that you may need to use _int86() instead.

The int86() function passes the interrupt, the registers that are going into and coming out from BIOS. Once called, the values in the outregs variable can be used. Lines 31, 32, and 33 get the values for the day, month, and year from these outregs registers.

As you progress through the rest of this book, several functions will be developed using BIOS interrupt calls. On Day 7, you learned to work with libraries. Many of the BIOS functions that you create will be useful in many of your programs. You should create a library of all of your BIOS functions.

BIOS and the Cursor

On Day 4, you learned to use the ANSI.SYS driver to place the cursor at different locations on the screen. Following are two functions that are similar to two ANSI

functions used on Day 4. These two functions are cursor() in Listing 8.3, which places the cursor, and get_cursor() in Listing 8.4, which gets the cursor's current location. In addition, Listing 8.5 demonstrates the use of these two functions.

 Listing 8.3. PCURSOR.C. Placing the cursor at screen coordinates.

```
 1:  /* Program: PCURSOR.C
 2:   * Author:   Bradley L. Jones
 3:   * Purpose: Demonstrates a BIOS function to position the
 4:   *          cursor on the screen.
 5:   * Note:    This function places the cursor at a given
 6:   *          location on the screen. The upper left position
 7:   *          of the screen is considered (0,0) not (1,1)
 8:   *=======================================================*/
 9:
10:  #include "biosregs.h"
11:  #include <dos.h>
12:
13:  void cursor(int row, int column);
14:
15:  void cursor( int row, int column)
16:  {
17:      union REGS inregs;
18:
19:      inregs.h.ah = 0x02;
20:      inregs.h.bh = 0;
21:      inregs.h.dh = row;
22:      inregs.h.dl = column;
23:
24:      int86(0x10, &inregs, &inregs);
25:  }
```

Listing 8.4. GCURSOR.C. Getting the coordinates of the cursor.

```
 1:  /* Program: GCURSOR.C
 2:   * Author:   Bradley L. Jones
 3:   * Purpose: Demonstrates a BIOS function to get the position
 4:   *          of the cursor on the screen.
 5:   * Note:    This function considers the upper left position
 6:   *          of the screen to be (0,0) not (1,1)
 7:   *=======================================================*/
 8:
 9:  #include "biosregs.h"
10:  #include <dos.h>
11:
```

```
12:   void get_cursor(int *row, int *column);
13:
14:   void get_cursor( int *row, int *column)
15:   {
16:       union REGS inregs;
17:
18:       inregs.h.ah = 0x03;
19:       inregs.h.bh = 0;
20:
21:       int86(0x10, &inregs, &inregs);
22:
23:       *row    = (int) inregs.h.dh;
24:       *column = (int) inregs.h.dl;
25:   }
```

Listing 8.5. LIST0805.C. Using the BIOS cursor functions.

```
1:    /* Program: LIST0805.c
2:     * Author:  Bradley L. Jones
3:     * Purpose: Demonstrates the use of the cursor() and
4:     *          get_cursor() functions.
5:     *=======================================================*/
6:
7:    #include <stdio.h>
8:
9:    /*---------------------------------*
10:   *       Function Prototypes        *
11:   *---------------------------------*/
12:
13:   void get_cursor(int *row, int *column);
14:   void cursor(int row, int column);
15:   void main(void);
16:
17:   void main(void)
18:   {
19:       int row, column;
20:
21:       get_cursor( &row, &column);
22:
23:       cursor( 10, 40 );
24:       printf("x(10,40)", 10, 40);
25:
26:       cursor( 0, 0 );
27:       printf( "x(0,0)");
28:
29:       cursor( 1, 1 );
30:       printf( "x(1,1)");
```

continues

Listing 8.5. continued

```
31:
32:    cursor( 24, 70 );
33:    printf( "x(24,70)");
34:
35:    cursor(row, column);
36:    printf("x(%d,%d)", row, column);
37:
38: }
```

```
x(0,0)
>x(1,1)05
x(2,0)
>




                                    x(10,40)






                                                    x(24,70)
```

To compile Listing 8.5, you need to include the PCURSOR.C and GCURSOR.C in your compile line. If you are compiling from the command line, this would require entering the following (TCC should be replaced with your compiler's command):

```
TCC LIST0805.C PCURSOR.C GCURSOR.C
```

An alternative to this is to create a library and link it with LIST0805 as shown on Day 7.

The output you receive from running this program may vary just a little. This program doesn't clear the screen before it starts, therefore, any information that was on the screen before the program is executed will remain. In the output shown here, you can see some of the remains of the command to run the program (second line of output).

Notice that the x marks where the cursor was placed. Listing 8.5 is extremely simple. Line 21 starts the program by getting the position of the cursor so that we can put it back when the program ends. Lines 23 to 36 call the cursor() function and then print the value of the location. The last call to cursor() positions the cursor back where it was when the program started.

The PCURSOR.C listing (Listing 8.3) contains the cursor() function. This function uses an interrupt to BIOS to place the cursor. Line 10 includes the registers that were presented earlier today. Line 11 includes the DOS.H header file that contains the function prototype for the interrupt function in line 24. Line 13 contains the prototype for the cursor function. If you are creating a library of these functions, you should create a header file that contains all of the function prototypes for all of the functions in your library. Line 19 sets the ah register to the function number 2. The bh register is set to 0. If you were working with multiple video pages, then this would be set to the number of the video page. Lines 21 and 22 contain dh and dl, which are set to the values passed to the cursor() function in the row and column variables. This is the actual row and column where the cursor will be placed. Line 24 wraps this function up by calling the int86() function. Interrupt 16 (0x10h) is called with the values that were set. This causes the cursor to be placed.

The get_cursor() function in Listing 8.4 is similar to the cursor() function. The big difference is that function 3 is placed in the ah register instead of function 2. The bh register is still set to the video page number. Because we're not doing video paging, this function sets the bh register to 0. The int86() function is then called in line 21 to finally set the cursor position. Once the BIOS function is called, the dh and dl registers contain the values for the row and column value of the cursor. These values are placed in the variables that are pointed to by row and column.

In addition to getting and putting the cursor, you can also change the cursor's shape. Listing 8.6 presents a function that allows you to manipulate the cursor. In addition, Listings 8.7 and 8.8 show this new function in action. Listings 8.7 and 8.8 should be compiled independently. Each should link in the cursor code.

Listing 8.6. set_cursor_size(), manipulating the cursor's shape.

```
1:   /* Program: SCURSOR.C
2:    * Authors: Bradley L. Jones
3:    *          Gregory L. Guntle
4:    * Purpose: BIOS function to set the cursor size.
5:    *=====================================================*/
6:
7:   #include <dos.h>
8:
9:   #define SET_CURSOR_SIZE   0x01
10:  #define BIOS_VIDEO        0x10
11:
12:  void set_cursor_size(int start, int end)
13:  {
```

continues

Listing 8.6. continued

```
14:     union REGS inregs;
15:
16:     inregs.h.ah = SET_CURSOR_SIZE;
17:     inregs.h.ch = start;
18:     inregs.h.cl = end;
19:     int86(BIOS_VIDEO, &inregs, &inregs);
20: }
```

Listing 8.7. BIGCURS.C. Using the `set_cursor_size()` function.

```
1:  /* Program: BIGCURS.c
2:   * Authors: Bradley L. Jones
3:   *          Gregory L. Guntle
4:   * Purpose: Changes the cursor to a big cursor.
5:   *=========================================================*/
6:
7:  /*** prototype ***/
8:  void set_cursor_size( int, int );
9:
10: int main(void)
11: {
12:    set_cursor_size( 1, 8 );
13:    return 0;
14: }
```

Listing 8.8. SMLCURS.C. Using the `set_cursor_size()` function.

```
1:  /* Program: SMLCURS.c
2:   * Authors: Bradley L. Jones
3:   *          Gregory L. Guntle
4:   * Purpose: Changes the cursor to a small cursor.
5:   *=========================================================*/
6:
7:  /*** prototype ***/
8:  void set_cursor_size( int, int );
9:
10: int main(void)
11: {
12:    set_cursor_size( 7, 8 );
13:    return 0;
14: }
```

Note: There is no output for these two programs. See the analysis.

 Listings 8.7 and 8.8 both use the `set_cursor_size()` function presented in Listing 8.6 to change the size of the cursor. Listing 8.7, BIGCURS.C, is a program that calls the `set_cursor_size()` function to change the cursor to a large block. After running BIGCURS.C, your cursor will be replaced with a large cursor. The SMLCURS.C program is similar, except that it sets the cursor to a small underscore.

Both of these programs operate by passing two values to the `set_cursor_size()` function. The `set_cursor_size()` function in Listing 8.6 is similar to the other BIOS functions. In line 16, the `ah` register is set with the function number that will be set. This listing differs in that a defined constant helps to make the setting of the function easier to understand. An additional defined constant, `BIOS_VIDEO`, also helps to make the program easier to read. Defined constants such as these can be placed in a header file and included in several of your functions.

The `set_cursor_size()` accepts two parameters, `start` and `end`. These values are used to change the size of the cursor. As you can see in BIGCURS.C, setting the `start` to 1 and the `end` to 8, you get a large cursor. Setting the `start` to 7 and the `end` to 8 provides a more traditionally sized cursor as shown in the SMLCURS.C listing.

 Tip: Put all of your related BIOS functions into a library. (This will be an exercise.)

 Expert Tip: As you should begin to see, BIOS functions are very powerful. You will be creating several BIOS functions over the next few days. You will see these functions in use during the development of an application in the second half of this book. Most of these functions will be useful long after you are done with this book.

Using BIOS for Other Functions

So far you have seen only a single date function and a few cursor functions. These functions barely scratch the surface of what functions are available by using interrupt routines. The multitude of different interrupts available is dependent upon your system and the systems that you're running the programs on. Table 8.1 lists the common interrupts and the areas they cover. Many of the interrupt functions that should be available using these interrupts are listed in Table 8.2.

Table 8.1. The ROM BIOS interrupts.

Interrupt	Function Types
16 (0x10h)	Video display functions
17 (0x11h)	Computer equipment function
18 (0x12h)	Conventional memory function
19 (0x13h)	Disk functions
20 (0x14h)	Serial communication port functions
21 (0x15h)	I/O subsystem functions
22 (0x16h)	Keyboard functions
23 (0x17h)	Parallel port functions
24 (0x18h)	ROM BASIC function
25 (0x19h)	System reboot function
26 (0x1Ah)	Clock driver functions
51 (0x33h)	Mouse functions

Table 8.2. The ROM BIOS interrupts.

Function (SubFunction)	Number (Hex)
Interrupt 16 (0x10h)	
Set video mode	0 (0x00h)
Set type of cursor	1 (0x01h)

Function (SubFunction)	Number (Hex)	
Set position of cursor	2 (0x02h)	
Get position of cursor	3 (0x03h)	
Get position of light pen	4 (0x04h)	
Set display page	5 (0x05h)	
Scroll window up	6 (0x06h)	
Scroll window down	7 (0x07h)	
Get char/attribute where cursor is located	8 (0x08h)	
Put char/attribute where cursor is located	9 (0x09h)	
Put character where cursor is located	10 (0x0Ah)	
Set background, border, and palette	11 (0x0Bh)	
Write a pixel	12 (0x0Ch)	
Read a pixel	13 (0x0Dh)	
Using teletype mode, write a character	14 (0x0Eh)	
Determine video mode	15 (0x0Fh)	
Set pallet	15	0 (0x00h)
Set border	15	1 (0x01h)
Set both, pallet and border	15	2 (0x02h)
Toggle bit for blink/intensity	15	3 (0x03h)
Determine video mode	15	
Set palette	16 (0x10h)	0 (0x00h)
Set color of border	16	1 (0x01h)
Set both, palette and border	16	2 (0x02h)
Toggle bit for blink/intensity	16	3 (0x03h)
Get palette	16	7 (0x07h)
Get color of border	16	8 (0x08h)

continues

Table 8.2. continued

Function (SubFunction)	Number (Hex)	
Get both, palette and border	16	9 (0x09h)
Set color register	16	16 (0x10h)
Set a block of color registers	16	18 (0x12h)
Set state of color page	16	19 (0x13h)
Get color register	16	21 (0x15h)
Get block of color registers	16	23 (0x17h)
Get state of color page	16	26 (0x1Ah)
Set gray-scale values	16	27 (0x1Bh)
Load a user font	17 (0x11h)	0 (0x00h)
Load ROM 8x14 font	17	1 (0x01h)
Load ROM 8x8 font	17	2 (0x02h)
Set block specifier	17	3 (0x03h)
Load ROM 8x16 font	17	4 (0x04h)
Load user font, reprogram controller	17	16 (0x10h)
Load ROM 8x14 font, reprogram controller	17	17 (0x11h)
Load ROM 8x8 font, reprogram controller	17	18 (0x12h)
Load ROM 8x16 font, reprogram controller	17	20 (0x14h)
Set Interrupt 31 (1Fh) pointer	17	32 (0x20h)
Set Interrupt 67 (43h) for a user's font	17	33 (0x21h)
Set Interrupt 67 (43h) for ROM 8x14 font	17	34 (0x22h)
Set Interrupt 67 (43h) for ROM 8x8 font	17	35 (0x23h)
Set Interrupt 67 (43h) for ROM 8x16 font	17	36 (0x24h)
Get information on font	17	18 (0x30h)
Get information on configuration	18 (0x12h)	16 (0x10h)
Select alternate print screen	18	32 (0x20h)

Function (SubFunction)	Number (Hex)	
Set scan lines	18	48 (0x30h)
Enable or disable loading palette	18	49 (0x31h)
Enable or disable the video	18	50 (0x32h)
Enable or disable gray-scale summing	18	51 (0x33h)
Enable or disable cursor emulation	18	52 (0x34h)
Switch active display	18	53 (0x35h)
Enable or disable screen refresh	18	54 (0x36h)
Write string in teletype mode	19 (0x13h)	
Determine or set display combination code	26 (0x1Ah)	
Get information on state/functionality	27 (0x1Bh)	
Save or restore the video state	28 (0x1Ch)	

Interrupt 17 (0x11h)

Get equipment configuration

Interrupt 18 (0x12h)

Get size of conventional memory

Interrupt 19 (0x13h)

(Disk drive functions)	
Reset the disk system	0 (0x00h)
Get status of disk system	1 (0x01h)
Read a sector	2 (0x02h)
Write a sector	3 (0x03h)
Verify a sector	4 (0x04h)
Format a track	5 (0x05h)
Format a bad track	6 (0x06h)
Format a drive	7 (0x07h)

continues

Table 8.2. continued

Function (SubFunction)	Number (Hex)
Get the drive parameters	8 (0x08h)
Initialize the fixed disk	9 (0x09h)
Read a long sector	10 (0x0Ah)
Write a long sector	11 (0x0Bh)
Do a seek	12 (0x0Ch)
Reset the fixed disk	13 (0x0Dh)
Read sector buffer	14 (0x0Eh)
Write sector buffer	15 (0x0Fh)
Get the drive status	16 (0x10h)
Recalibrate the drive	17 (0x11h)
Controller RAM diagnostic	18 (0x12h)
Controller drive diagnostic	19 (0x13h)
Controller internal diagnostic	20 (0x14h)
Get the type of disk	21 (0x15h)
Get status of disk change	22 (0x16h)
Set the disk type	23 (0x17h)
Set the media type for format	24 (0x18h)
Park drive heads	25 (0x19h)
Format drive (ESDI)	26 (0x1Ah)

Interrupt 20 (0x14h)

Initialize the serial port	0 (0x00h)
Write a character to the serial port	1 (0x01h)
Read a character from the serial port	2 (0x02h)
Determine serial port status	3 (0x03h)

Function (SubFunction)	Number (Hex)
Extended initialize serial port	4 (0x04h)
Extended serial port control	5 (0x05h)

Interrupt 21 (0x15h)

Turn cassette motor on	0 (0x00h)
Turn cassette motor off	1 (0x01h)
Read from cassette	2 (0x02h)
Write to cassette	3 (0x03h)
Intercept keyboard	79 (0x4Fh)
Event to wait	131 (0x83h)
Read from joystick	132 (0x84h)
SysReq key press	133 (0x85h)
Pause (delay)	134 (0x86h)
Move an extended memory block	135 (0x87h)
Determine extended memory size	136 (0x88h)
Start protected mode	137 (0x89h)
Have device wait	144 (0x90h)
Get the system environment	192 (0xC0h)
Determine the address of the extended BIOS data area	193 (0xC1h)
Pointing device functions	194 (0xC2h)

Interrupt 22 (0x16h)

(Keyboard functions)	
Read a character from the keyboard	0 (0x00h)
Get the status of the keyboard	1 (0x01h)
Get keyboard flags	2 (0x02h)

continues

Table 8.2. continued

Function (SubFunction)	Number (Hex)
Set rate for repeat	3 (0x03h)
Set the keyboard to click	4 (0x04h)
Push a character and scan code	5 (0x05h)
Read a character (enhanced keyboard)	16 (0x10h)
Get status of keyboard (enhanced keyboard)	17 (0x11h)
Get keyboard flags (enhanced keyboard)	18 (0x12h)

Interrupt 23 (0x17h)

(Parallel port functions)	
Write a character to the parallel port	0 (0x00h)
Initialize parallel port	1 (0x01h)
Get status of parallel (print) port	2 (0x02h)

Interrupt 24 (0x18h)

(ROM BASIC)

Interrupt 25 (0x19h)

Re-boot the computer system.

Interrupt 26 (0x1Ah)

(CMOS clock driver)	
Determine tick count	1 (0x00h)
Set tick count	2 (0x02h)
Determine the time	3 (0x03h)
Set the time	4 (0x04h)
Determine the date	5 (0x05h)
Set the date	6 (0x06h)
Set the alarm	7 (0x07h)

Function (SubFunction)	Number (Hex)
Reset the alarm	8 (0x08h)
Set the sound source	128 (0x80h)

Interrupt 51 (0x33h)

(Mouse functions)

Reset and get mouse status	0 (0x00h)
Display the mouse pointer	1 (0x01h)
Hide the mouse pointer	2 (0x02h)
Determine mouse position and button status	3 (0x03h)
Set the mouse pointer position	4 (0x04h)
Determine the button press information	5 (0x05h)
Determine the button release information	6 (0x06h)
Set the horizontal limits for the pointer	7 (0x07h)
Set the vertical limits for the pointer	8 (0x08h)
Set the shape of the pointer (graphics)	9 (0x09h)
Set the pointer type (text)	10 (0x0Ah)
Read the mouse motion	11 (0x0Bh)
Set a user-defined mouse event handler	12 (0x0Ch)
Light pen emulation on	13 (0x0Dh)
Light pen emulation off	14 (0x0Eh)
Set exclusion area for mouse pointer	16 (0x10h)
Set threshold for double speed	19 (0x13h)
Switch user-defined event handlers for mouse	20 (0x14h)
Determine save state buffer size for mouse	21 (0x15h)
Save the mouse's driver state	22 (0x16h)
Restore the mouse's driver state	23 (0x17h)

continues

Table 8.2. continued

Function (SubFunction)	Number (Hex)
Set an alternate mouse event handler	24 (0x18h)
Determine address of alternate event handler	25 (0x19h)
Set the mouse's sensitivity	26 (0x1Ah)
Get the mouse's sensitivity	27 (0x1Bh)
Set the mouse's interrupt rate	28 (0x1Ch)
Select a pointer page	29 (0x1Dh)
Determine the pointer page	30 (0x1Eh)
Disable the mouse driver	31 (0x1Fh)
Enable the mouse driver	32 (0x20h)
Reset the mouse driver	33 (0x21h)
Set the mouse driver message language	34 (0x22h)
Get the language number	35 (0x23h)
Get information on mouse	36 (0x24h)

It is beyond the scope of this book to provide detailed examples of using each and every interrupt, their functions, and all of their subfunctions. A few of these interrupts will be used in functions presented in the next section. In addition, many of the interrupts will be used as this book progresses.

Note: If you want more information on BIOS interrupts, there are several other books available that go into much more detail. A few to consider are Jack Purdum's *C Programmer's Toolkit* and *DOS Programmer's Reference* both published by Que Corporation. In addition, there is the *C Programmers Guide to NetBios, IPX, and SPX* by SAMS Publishing. Many books on assembly language also talk about the BIOS functions.

Examples of Using BIOS

This section contains a couple of additional BIOS functions that you may find useful. The first function, keyhit(), determines if a character has been entered into the keyboard. If a character has not been entered, the program continues on. The keyhit() function will be presented in Listing 8.9. The second function clears the keyboard and waits for a keyhit. This function, kbwait(), will be useful when you need to wait for a keystroke and you need to remove any characters that a user may have typed ahead. The kbwait() function is presented in Listing 8.10. As stated earlier, several additional functions will be presented throughout the rest of this book.

 Listing 8.9. keyhit( ). A function to determine if a keyboard character has been pressed.

```
 1:   /* Program: KEYHIT.C
 2:    * Authors: Bradley L. Jones
 3:    *          Gregory L. Guntle
 4:    * Purpose: BIOS function to determine if a key has been
 5:    *          hit.
 6:    * Return:  0 - key not hit
 7:    *          # - key that was hit.
 8:    *             If # > 0x100, then key is a scan code.
 9:    *=========================================================*/
10:
11:   #include <dos.h>
12:
13:   int keyhit( void )
14:   {
15:       int    flag;
16:       union REGS inregs;
17:
18:       inregs.h.ah = 0x06;
19:       inregs.h.dl = 0xFF;
20:       flag = int86(0x21, &inregs, &inregs);
21:
22:       if(( flag & 0x40 ) == 0 )
23:       {
24:          if( inregs.h.al == 0 )
25:          {
26:             /* extended character, get second half */
27:             inregs.h.ah = 0x06;
28:             inregs.h.dl = 0xFF;
29:             int86(0x21, &inregs, &inregs);
30:             return( inregs.h.al + 0x100 );
31:          }
32:          else
33:          {
```

continues

Listing 8.9. continued

```
34:              return inregs.h.al;  /* the key hit */
35:          }
36:      }
37:      else
38:      {
39:          return 0;  /* key not hit */
40:      }
41: }
```

Type

Listing 8.10. `kbwait( )`. A function to clear the keyboard buffer.

```
1:  /* Program: KBWAIT.C
2:   * Authors: Bradley L. Jones
3:   *          Gregory L. Guntle
4:   * Purpose: BIOS function to clear the keyboard buffer
5:   *          and wait for a key to be pressed.
6:   *=======================================================*/
7:
8:  #include <dos.h>
9:  #include <stdio.h>
10:
11: void kbwait( void )
12: {
13:     union REGS inregs;
14:
15:     inregs.h.ah = 0x0C;
16:     inregs.h.al = 0x08;
17:     int86(0x21, &inregs, &inregs);
18: }
```

Type

Listing 8.11. LIST0811. C. A program demonstrating the previous two functions.

```
1:  /* Program: list0811.c
2:   * Author:  Bradley L. Jones
3:   * Purpose: Demonstrates the use of the kbwait() and
4:   *          keyhit() functions.
5:   *=======================================================*/
6:
7:  #include <stdio.h>
8:
9:  /*------------------------------------------*
10:  *        Function Prototypes               *
11:  *------------------------------------------*/
```

```
12:
13:   int keyhit(void);
14:   void kbwait(void);
15:
16:   int main(void)
17:   {
18:      int ctr = 65;
19:      char buffer[256];
20:
21:      printf("\n\nClearing the keyboard buffer.");
22:      printf("\nPress any key to continue...");
23:
24:      kbwait();
25:
26:      printf("\nMoving on...");
27:
28:      while(!keyhit())
29:      {
30:        printf("%c", ctr );
31:
32:        if( ctr >= 90 )
33:           ctr = 65;
34:        else
35:           ctr++;
36:      }
37:
38:      printf("DONE");
39:
40:      return 0;
41:   }
```

Analysis This program displays a message and then asks you to press any key to continue. Once you continue, the program begins printing the letters of the alphabet. These letters are printed until a key is pressed. Using a while loop in line 28, allows the program to do what is contained in lines 29 to 36 until a key is hit (keyhit() returns a key value). After each placement of a letter, the keyhit() function is used to determine if a character has been pressed. If not, the program continues to the next letter. If a character has been pressed, then the program prints "Done" and ends. Because keyhit() returns the value of the key pressed, this program could be changed to check for a specific key before ending.

Creating Your Own Interrupts

Not all of the interrupts have functions behind them. Because of this, you can create your own interrupt events. This could be an event such as causing the speaker to beep,

or a memory resident program. Unfortunately, writing your own interrupt functions is beyond the scope of this book.

Compiler-Specific BIOS Functions

Many compilers come with several of their own functions that are already set up to perform specific BIOS interrupt tasks. Microsoft comes with several. These include:

`_bios_equiplist`	Uses interrupt 0x11h (17) to perform an equipment checklist.
`_bios_memsize`	Uses interrupt 0x12h (18) to provide information about available memory.
`_bios_disk`	Uses interrupt 0x13h (19) to issue service requests for hard and floppy disks.
`_bios_serialcom`	Uses interrupt 0x14h (20) to perform serial communications services.
`_bios_keybrd`	Uses interrupt 0x16h (22) to provide access to keyboard services.
`_bios_printer`	Uses interrupt 0x17h (23) to perform printer output services.
`_bios_timeofday`	Uses interrupt 0x1Ah (26) to access the system clock.

Note: When using the Microsoft or the Borland predefined BIOS functions, you need to include the BIOS.H header file.

The Borland compilers also have several preincluded BIOS interrupt functions. These include the following:

`biosequip`	Uses interrupt 0x11h (17) to check equipment list.
`_bios_equiplist`	Uses interrupt 0x11h (17) to check equipment list.
`biosmemory`	Uses interrupt 0x12h (18) to determine the size of memory.
`_bios_memsize`	Uses interrupt 0x12h (18) to determine the size of memory.
`biosdisk`	Uses interrupt 0x13h (19) to perform disk drive services.
`_bios_disk`	Uses interrupt 0x13h (19) to perform disk drive services.

bioscom	Uses interrupt 0x14h (20) to perform serial communications services.
_bios_serialcom	Uses interrupt 0x14h (20) to perform serial communication services.
bioskey	Uses interrupt 0x16h (23) to work with the keyboard interface.
_bios_keybrd	Uses interrupt 0x16h (23) to work with the keyboard interface.
biosprint	Uses interrupt 0x17h (24) to perform printer services.
_bios_printer	Uses interrupt 0x17h (24) to perform printer services.
biostime	Uses interrupt 0x1Ah (26) to read or set the system clock.
_bios_timeofday	Uses interrupt 0x1Ah (26) to read or set the system clock.

You may choose to use these functions, or you may decide to call the interrupts on your own using a more generic int86() type of function.

A Note on Compiler Functions Versus BIOS Functions

Now that you've gotten a glimpse of the many functions that can be created using BIOS and have reviewed some compiler-specific functions, it is important to consider why you would ever need to create a new function using BIOS—or any of the other methods presented. There are at least two major reasons for creating your own functions. The first is for the sake of learning. By creating you own functions, you better understand the underlying code. Once you create a function, you can put it into a library and use it everywhere. A second reason is flexibility. The compiler functions are what they are. You cannot change them or modify them to your specific needs. By writing your own functions, you can create them just the way you want them.

As this book continues, you will see several BIOS functions in action. In addition, you will also see several more complex functions that have BIOS functions in their underlying code.

Note: Remember, some compilers use int86() and some use _int86(). You will need to check your compiler's library reference manual to determine which function is correct for you.

Summary

Today, you were provided with the most powerful way of manipulating your computer system's resources. This was through the use of interrupt calls to BIOS. The acronym, BIOS, stands for Basic Input/Output System. You also were provided with information on why BIOS functions are better to use than ANSI escape sequences and direct memory access. In addition, you were presented with tables containing information on many of the system resources that BIOS can manipulate. This includes placing the cursor, clearing the screen, changing colors, remapping keyboard values, working with modems, reading joystick commands, and much, much more. A few examples of using BIOS functions were presented to give an overall idea of what using them requires. BIOS functions will be revisited off and on throughout the rest of this book.

Q&A

Q Is the BIOSREGS.H header file presented in Listing 8.1 necessary?

A You were shown the values presented by Microsoft and Borland compilers. If you include DOS.H, you may not need to include the BIOSREGS.H header file. Other compilers may or may not need the register structure. Most of the programs from this point on won't include the BIOSREGS.H header file. If your compiler doesn't have the register union and structures, you should include BIOSREGS.H.

Q Are the functions learned today portable to other computer systems?

A The functions covered in today's material are portable to some computers. The BIOS functions are portable to computers that are 100-percent compatible with IBM BIOS. In addition, older versions of BIOS may not support all of the functions. You should consult your DOS manuals and system documentation to determine what interrupts your computer supports.

Q What is meant by BIOS functions being portable?

A The portability of BIOS functions is not necessarily the same as the portability that will be discussed later in this book. The calls to BIOS functions are not necessarily portable C code—each compiler may call interrupts slightly differently. What is meant by portability is that an executable program (.EXE or .COM) will have a better chance of running on many different computer configurations than if you use ANSI functions or direct memory

8

writes. BIOS function calls are only portable to IBM-compatible machines; however, they can have a multitude of different video monitors, modems, printers, and so on.

Q Why might someone want to use direct video access instead of BIOS functions?

A If manipulating the video monitor at the highest speeds possible is imperative to an application, then direct video memory access may be the best solution. For graphics-intensive games, it's often necessary to directly manipulate the video memory to get the best results and the smoothest graphical movements.

Q Are all the interrupts presented today always available?

A No! Older versions of the DOS operating system may not support all of the interrupts presented. If you are using an extremely old version of DOS, such as 2.01, or even 3.0, then you may find that several of the functions are not supported. Your DOS manuals may contain a list of supported interrupts.

Workshop

The Workshop provides quiz questions to help you solidify your understanding of the material covered and exercises to provide you with experience in using what you've learned.

Quiz

1. What does BIOS stand for?

2. What are two reasons to use BIOS functions instead of ANSI functions?

3. What is a reason to use the BIOS function instead of direct memory access when updating the video display?

4. What is an interrupt number?

5. What is an interrupt function?

6. What is an interrupt subfunction?

7. What does interrupt 0x33h function do?

8. What does function 2 of interrupt 51 (0x33h) do?

9. What does interrupt 25 (0x19h) do?

10. Do all computers support all BIOS functions?

Exercises

1. Create a library containing all of the BIOS functions presented today. Call this library TYAC.LIB. This library can be used in future chapters. This library should contain the following functions:

```
current_date()
cursor()
get_cursor()
set_cursor_size()
keyhit()
kbwait()
```

Note: You should also create a header file with the same name as your library. This header file should contain the function prototypes for the functions in your library.

2. Create a function that enables you to scroll the screen up one line at a time. This function can be created via a BIOS interrupt. You should set the following registers:

```
ah = 0x07
al = 1
ch = 0
cl = 0
dh = 25
dl = col
bh = 0
```

The BIOS interrupt is 0x10.

3. Rewrite the function from Exercise 2. This time write the function generically so that it can be used to scroll the screen—or a portion of the screen— up or down:

ah should be set to interrupt 0x07 to scroll up or 0x06 to scroll down.

al should be set to the number of lines to scroll.

ch should be set to the number of the starting row on the screen area to be scrolled (0 is the first line on the screen).

cl should be set to the number of the starting column on the screen area to be scrolled (0 is the first column on the screen).

dh should be set to the width of the scrolling area. (This should be added to the row to only scroll the intended area.)

dl should be set to the height of the scrolling area. (This should be added to the column to only scroll the intended area.)

bh should be used for an attribute. In this case, always set bh to 0.

4. Write a program that uses the function from Exercise 3.

5. Add the previous function to your TYAC.LIB library. You should also add the prototype to the TYAC.H header file along with defined constants for SCROLL_UP and SCROLL_DOWN.

6. **BUG BUSTER:** What, if anything, is wrong with the following?

```
void current_date( int *month, int *day, int *year)
{
    union REGS inregs, outregs;
    inregs.h.ah = 0x2a;

    int86(0x21);

    *month = outregs.h.dh;
    *day   = outregs.h.dl;
    *year  = outregs.x.cx;
}
```

Text Graphics (Using BIOS)

On Day 8, you were introduced to BIOS functions, which will be useful in the programs you will develop. Day 8, however, barely scratched the surface of the functions you'll need when you create a full-scale application later in this book. Many of the functions you'll need relate to how you set up your screen and text graphics. Today you will learn:

☐ What is meant by text graphics versus non-text graphics.

☐ How to combine Day 8's functions in a more organized manner.

☐ How to enhance your cursor functions from Day 8.

☐ How to create several useful screen and text functions to add to your library.

☐ How to add several new functions to your TYAC library.

Different Levels of Graphics

The level of graphics that can be used on a computer vary. Generally, graphics are broken down according to their levels of complexity. The complexity of each level is directly proportional to the portability of the system created using them. The different levels include:

☐ Monochrome text

☐ Colored text

☐ Pixel graphics

☐ Character graphics

Monochrome text is the least graphical and the most portable. This uses the characters that are in the ASCII chart with values from 0 to 127 or a similar set of characters. Because color is not considered and no characters other than those in the table are used, this monochrome text is sometimes not considered graphical.

Colored text is a little more graphical and less portable because not all systems support color. Colored text still uses the same character set as the monochrome text; however, the text can be displayed in a variety of colors. Virtually all personal computer systems today support colored text. Even some monochrome (single-colored) monitors support colored text by using gray-scale. Monochrome monitors that support gray-scale display colors in different shades or intensities of a single color. Most monochrome notebook computers support gray-scales of 16, 64, or 256 colors. You should understand, however, that there are some monochrome monitors that only support a single color.

Pixel graphics use the individual pixels—or dots—within a computer monitor. Because they work at a pixel level, any character can be displayed. The resolution, or clarity, of a displayed character depends on the computer, number of pixels in the computer's screen, and the number of colors that the screen can support. This includes CGA, EGA, VGA, Super VGA and more. Because the level of graphics that can be done depends on the computer system, this is much less portable than the other graphics methods. What is gained is the displayed graphics are not limited to the ASCII character set. Instead, any picture or graphic can be displayed.

 Note: Most computer systems today support pixel graphics at VGA level resolutions (640×480 pixels).

 **Note:** If you run a program with a higher graphics resolution and a monitor that supports only a lower graphics resolution, you can get unpredictable results. For example, if a program that supports VGA-level pixel graphics is run on a monitor that only supports colored text, the outcome may be a blank screen. Worse, the output may be garbled colors on the screen.

Character Graphics

Character graphics are similar to the color text. However, instead of being limited to the ASCII characters 0 to 127, character graphics also include the characters from 128 to 255. These additional characters are referred to as the *extended character set.* This extended character set provides many additional characters that can help give an application a more graphical look and feel without losing the portability of going to full pixel graphics. Appendix B shows the entire ASCII character set. Those characters with the values from 128 to 255 are considered the extended ASCII character set.

By using many of the characters provided in the extended set, you can create lines, boxes, grids, and more. In addition, character graphics include color. The number of colors used is generally left at the same level as the lowest pixel graphics—CGA. Figure 9.1 shows some of the character graphics in use.

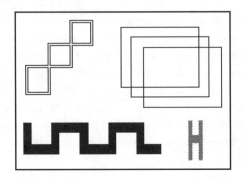

Figure 9.1. *Character graphics in use.*

> **Note:** Most DOS-based applications use character graphics. Packages that use character graphics are WordPerfect 5.2 for DOS, Paradox for DOS, DBASE IV, and Lotus 123 for DOS. Most of these packages also allow for some pixel graphics.

Organizing Your Functions

Starting on Day 12, this book will begin guiding you through the development of a complete application. In developing this application, you'll use several of the functions that you have developed on earlier days. In addition, you'll also use many new functions. Most of the functions will be developed over the next few days. Today, you'll develop several functions, including a line function and a box function, that use the character graphics.

Before learning new functions, you should ensure that your current functions are organized. In one of the exercises on Day 8, you created a library containing your functions and a header file. The header file should contain function prototypes for your functions along with any additional information that may be needed by your library's functions. Listing 9.1 is an updated version of the TYAC.H header file that you created on Day 8.

Type   **Listing 9.1. The enhanced TYAC.H header file.**

```
1:    /* Program: TYAC.H
2:    *           (Teach Yourself Advanced C)
```

```
3:     * Authors: Bradley L. Jones
4:     *          Gregory L. Guntle
5:     * Purpose: Header file for TYAC library functions
6:     *=========================================================*/
7:
8:     #ifndef _TYAC_H_
9:     #define _TYAC_H_
10:
11:    /* DOS and BIOS Interrupts */
12:    #define BIOS_VIDEO        0x10
13:    #define DOS_FUNCTION      0x21
14:
15:    /* BIOS function calls */
16:    #define SET_VIDEO         0x00
17:    #define SET_CURSOR_SIZE   0x01
18:    #define SET_CURSOR_POS    0x02
19:    #define GET_CURSOR_INFO   0x03
20:    #define WRITE_CHAR        0x09
21:    #define SET_COLOR         0x0B
22:    #define GET_VIDEO         0x0F
23:    #define WRITE_STRING      0x13
24:
25:    /*  Types of Boxes   */
26:    #define DOUBLE_BOX        2
27:    #define SINGLE_BOX        1
28:    #define BLANK_BOX         0
29:
30:    /*  Box fill flags   */
31:    #define BORDER_ONLY       0
32:    #define FILL_BOX          1
33:
34:    /* Colors */
35:    #define   BLACK           0
36:    #define   BLUE            1
37:    #define   GREEN           2
38:    #define   CYAN            3
39:    #define   RED             4
40:    #define   MAGENTA         5
41:    #define   BROWN           6
42:    #define   WHITE           7
43:    #define   GRAY            8
44:    #define   LIGHTBLUE       9
45:    #define   LIGHTGREEN      10
46:    #define   LIGHTCYAN       11
47:    #define   LIGHTRED        12
48:    #define   LIGHTMAGENTA    13
49:    #define   YELLOW          14
50:    #define   BRIGHTWHITE     15
51:
```

continues

Listing 9.1. continued

```
52:   /* used to set scrolling direction */
53:   #define SCROLL_UP     0x07
54:   #define SCROLL_DOWN   0x06
55:
56:   /*----------------------*
57:       Function Prototypes
58:    *----------------------*/
59:
60:       /* Gets the current date */
61:   void current_date(int *, int *, int *);
62:
63:       /* Positions the cursor to row/col */
64:   void cursor(int, int);
65:       /* Returns info about cursor */
66:   void get_cursor(int *, int *, int *, int *, int *);
67:       /* Sets the size of the cursor */
68:   void set_cursor_size(int, int);
69:
70:       /* clear the keyboard buffer */
71:   void kbclear( void );
72:       /* determine keyboard hit */
73:   int  kbhit( void );
74:
75:       /* scroll the screen */
76:   void scroll( int row,   int col,
77:                int width, int height,
78:                int nbr,   int direction);
79:
80:   #endif
```

Analysis

As you can see, this header file contains a function prototype in lines 58 to 74 for each of the functions that should be in your library. By including this header file in any of the programs you are using, you'll be sure to have all the prototypes that you need for the library functions. You'll also be able to keep any other information in this header file that is needed by your functions.

This version of the TYAC.H header file includes several other items. Lines 11 and 12 include defined constants for BIOS interrupt numbers. Lines 14 to 22 include defined constants for BIOS function numbers. These defined constants will be used in many of the functions created today. By using the defined constants instead of the actual numbers, your individual functions will be more readable.

Lines 28 to 30 declare a few additional defined constants, which will be used in creating a border on a box function later today. Lines 32 to 48 define the basic colors.

This is similar to the defined constants that were created for the ANSI functions on Day 4. A final set of defined constants are declared in lines 51 and 52. These were used in the control break function presented in the Day 8 exercises.

The TYAC.H header file will by dynamic. As you create each of your new functions, you should add the prototype into TYAC.H. By doing this and by adding each function to your TYAC.LIB library, you'll ensure that you'll have a complete library to use.

Tip: You should give your library the same name as the header file—TYAC. This will help you keep the two related together. (TYAC stands for Teach Yourself Advanced C.)

Note: The TYAC.LIB library and TYAC.H header file will be used from this point on. Each function you create on the following days should be added to your library. In addition, you should add the new function prototypes to TYAC.H.

Enhancing Your Cursor Functions

The cursor functions on Day 8 contained only the basic row and column parameters. The BIOS calls that work with the cursor will provide much more information than just the row and column of the cursor. While you may not always need the additional information, it's better to go ahead and make your functions a little more functional. The get_cursor() and cursor() functions presented originally in Listings 8.3 and 8.4 should be enhanced. Listings 9.2 and 9.3 contain new cursor functions.

Listing 9.2. PCURSOR.C. A function to put the cursor on screen.

```
1:  /* Program: PCURSOR.C
2:   * Authors: Bradley L. Jones
3:   *          Gregory L. Guntle
```

continues

269

Listing 9.2. continued

```
 4:    * Purpose: Demonstrates a BIOS function to position the
 5:    *            cursor on the screen.
 6:    * Note:    This function places the cursor at a given
 7:    *            location on the screen. The upper left position
 8:    *            of the screen is considered (0,0) not (1,1)
 9:    *=======================================================*/
10:
11:   #include <dos.h>
12:   #include "tyac.h"
13:
14:   void cursor(int row, int column)
15:   {
16:       union REGS inregs;
17:
18:       inregs.h.ah = SET_CURSOR_POS;
19:       inregs.h.bh = 0;
20:       inregs.h.dh = row;
21:       inregs.h.dl = column;
22:       int86(BIOS_VIDEO, &inregs, &inregs);
23:   }
```

Listing 9.3. GCURSOR.C. A function to get cursor from screen.

```
 1:   /* Program: GCURSOR.C
 2:    * Authors: Bradley L. Jones
 3:    *          Gregory L. Guntle
 4:    * Purpose: Demonstrates a BIOS function to get the position
 5:    *            of the cursor on the screen.
 6:    * Note:    This function considers the upper left position
 7:    *            of the screen to be (0,0) not (1,1)
 8:    *=======================================================*/
 9:
10:   #include <dos.h>
11:   #include "tyac.h"
12:
13:   void get_cursor(int *row, int *column, int *page, int *start,
                      int *end)
14:   {
15:       union REGS inregs, outregs;
16:
17:       inregs.h.ah = GET_CURSOR_INFO;
18:       inregs.h.bh = 0;
19:       int86(BIOS_VIDEO, &inregs, &outregs);
20:       *row    = (int) outregs.h.dh;
21:       *column = (int) outregs.h.dl;
```

```
22:        *page   = (int) outregs.h.bh;
23:        *start  = (int) outregs.h.ch;
24:        *end    = (int) outregs.h.cl;
25:  }
```

Analysis

The PCURSOR.C listing operates exactly as it did before. Only minor cosmetic changes have been made. Notice that in line 12, the TYAC.H header file is now being included. This enables you to use any of the defined constants in this function. In addition, it ensures that the function's prototype is included. In lines 18 and 22, two defined constants are used from the TYAC.H header file: GET_CURSOR_INFO and BIOS_VIDEO. This makes the cursor() function's code a little easier to read.

The GCURSOR function in Listing 9.3 is different from the function presented on Day 8. Like the cursor() function in Listing 9.2, the TYAC.H header file has been included, and the defined constants have been used. In line 13, you'll notice a much larger change. The get_cursor() function now has three additional parameters, page, start, and end. These three parameters give the function the capability to pass additional information back to the calling program. Now when you use get_cursor(), you won't only get the row and column location of the cursor, but you'll also get the video page that the cursor is on and the start and end scan lines that make up the cursor's shape. (See the set_cursor_size() in Day 8 for information on the cursor.) This additional information makes the function much more useful.

> **Warning:** When you change a function, you need to recompile it and update your library. If you change the parameters passed to a function, you need to change the prototype within the header file also. In addition, if you change a header file, you may need to recompile all the programs that use the header file to ensure that you don't cause problems in your other functions.

> **Note:** An explanation of a video page will be covered later today.

You might be wondering why Day 8 did not present the get_cursor() functions with the additional parameters. You'll generally write a function to serve a specific need.

As time goes on, you'll find that you need to update or enhance the function. The cursor functions are a prime example of such changes. You should update your library and header file with these newer versions.

DO	DON'T

DO continue to add your functions to (or update) your TYAC.LIB library.

DON'T forget to update your library and header file when you change a function.

DO use defined constants to make your programs and functions easier to read—and debug.

Creating New Functions

In the following sections, several new functions will be presented that will help you create applications. You'll learn a few functions that help in your use of text graphics and a function that enables you to pause until a key is entered.

Text Graphics Functions

Several text graphics functions will be presented. Many of these functions can be used with the functions you have created on previous days. These include the following:

- [ ] Setting the video mode.
- [ ] Getting the video mode.
- [ ] Setting the border color.
- [ ] Writing a character.
- [ ] Writing a character multiple times.
- [ ] Drawing a line.
- [ ] Drawing a box.
- [ ] Drawing a box with borders.

You'll want to add several of these functions to your TYAC library.

Working with the Video Mode

When you begin to work with character graphics and character graphic functions, you must have a little background information. Most computer monitors display 25 rows, each with 80 characters; however, you should never assume this. Two functions will be extremely useful when using character graphics. These are a function to set the video mode and to get the video mode (Listings 9.4 and 9.5).

Listing 9.4. GVIDEO.C gets the video mode.

```
1:   /* Program: GVIDEO.C
2:    * Authors: Bradley L. Jones
3:    *          Gregory L. Guntle
4:    * Purpose: Demonstrates a BIOS function which gets the
5:    *          current video mode.
6:    *========================================================
7:    *
8:    *   Display modes (partial list):
9:    *
10:   *      0   40 by 25 black and white text
11:   *      1   40 by 25 16-color text
12:   *      2   80 by 25 black and white text
13:   *      3   80 by 25 16-color
14:   *
15:   *      4   320 by 200 4-color
16:   *      5   320 by 200 4-color
17:   *      6   640 by 200 2 color
18:   *
19:   *      7   80 column  mono text
20:   *
21:   *     64   80 by 43 (EGA)
22:   *          80 by 50 (VGA)
23:   *========================================================*/
24:
25:   #include <dos.h>
26:   #include "tyac.h"
27:
28:   void get_video(int *columns, int *display_mode, int *display_page)
29:   {
30:       union REGS inregs, outregs;
31:
32:       inregs.h.ah = GET_VIDEO;
33:       int86(BIOS_VIDEO, &inregs, &outregs);
34:       *columns = (int) outregs.h.ah;
35:       *display_mode = (int) outregs.h.al;
36:       *display_page = (int) outregs.h.bh;
37:   }
```

 This program gets information on the video mode. This will fill in the values of three different variables that have pointers passed on to the `get_video()` function. The first parameter, `column`, will be filled in with the number of columns available. The second parameter, `display_mode`, will be filled in with a numeric value. The value will signal which mode the video is set to. The comments in lines 8 to 22 detail the different values that the video mode could be. The third parameter, `display_page`, will be filled with the display page number. There can be more than one video page; however, only one can be active at a time. *Video pages* are areas reserved to set up screen information; however, they are not visible until they are made active. Most programs ignore video paging and simply use the current page. As shown earlier, one of the additional parameters for the cursor functions was for the video page number.

Lines 30 to 36 contain the bulk of this program. As you can see, the `get_video()` function looks like many of the other BIOS functions. There has been one subtle change. Instead of using an interrupt and a function number, defined constants are used. The `GET_VIDEO` and `BIOS_VIDEO` constants should make this function easier to understand.

The ability to get the video mode is important; however, sometimes you'll want to set it. The `set_video()` function does just that.

Type

Listing 9.5. SVIDEO.C sets the video mode.

```
1:   /* Program: SVIDEO.C
2:    * Authors: Bradley L. Jones
3:    *          Gregory L. Guntle
4:    * Purpose: Demonstrates a BIOS function to set the video
5:    *          mode.
6:    *=====================================================*
7:    *
8:    *   Display modes (partial list):
9:    *
10:   *      0   40 by 25 black and white text
11:   *      1   40 by 25 16-color text
12:   *      2   80 by 25 black and white text
13:   *      3   80 by 25 16-color
14:   *
15:   *      4   320 by 200 4-color
16:   *      5   320 by 200 4-color
17:   *      6   640 by 200 2 color
18:   *
19:   *      7   80 column  mono text
20:   *
21:   *      64  80 by 43 (EGA)
```

```
22:    *           80 by 50 (VGA)
23:    *=========================================================*/
24:
25:    #include <dos.h>
26:    #include "tyac.h"
27:
28:    void set_video(int display_mode)
29:    {
30:        union REGS inregs;
31:
32:        inregs.h.ah = SET_VIDEO;
33:        inregs.h.al = display_mode;
34:        int86(BIOS_VIDEO, &inregs, &inregs);
35:    }
```

9

The set_video() function accepts a numeric parameter for the mode. These are the same numbers that are returned by the get_video() function. You should notice that this function attempts to set the mode even if an invalid mode is passed. By not editing the display mode that is to be set, this function will be capable of setting additional modes that may be supported in the future. You may want to consider adding logic to prevent any invalid display modes from being set. In an exercise at the end of the day, you'll be asked to use these functions to write a program.

Setting the Border Color

Once you are able to work with the video mode, you are ready to forge into text graphics and color functions. Most of the functions work on the screen; however, there is also a border to the screen that can be colored. Listing 9.6 contains a function to set the border color.

Listing 9.6. SBRDCLR.C sets the border color.

```
1:    /* Program: SBRDCLR.C
2:     * Authors: Bradley L. Jones
3:     *          Gregory L. Guntle
4:     * Purpose: Sets the border color.
5:     *=========================================================*/
6:
7:    #include <dos.h>
8:    #include "tyac.h"
9:
10:   void set_border_color(int color)
11:   {
12:       union REGS inregs;
13:
```

continues

Listing 9.6. continued

```
14:        inregs.h.ah = SET_COLOR;   /* Set Color Palette */
15:        inregs.h.bh = 0;           /* BL contains background and border
                                          color */
16:        inregs.h.bl = color;       /* New color */
17:        int86(BIOS_VIDEO, &inregs, &inregs);
18:    }
```

This listing contains the set_border_color() function, which sets the color of the border to the value passed in color. This color should be one of the values contained in TYAC.H that is included in line 8. As you can determine from this listing, the border color is set using the BIOS_VIDEO interrupt (0×10) and the SET_COLOR function (0×0B). In addition, the bh register needs to be set to 0. The actual color number is set in line 16 to the bl register.

> **Warning:** The set_border_color() function in Listing 9.5 does not contain any error trapping. You may wish to add edit checks limiting the acceptable values to this function. You should consider adding error trapping to all the functions that are presented.

Writing a Character in Color

While setting the border's color is fun, it's often not done. What is often done is writing a character to the screen. Although the ANSI putchar() function does a splendid job of putting a character on the screen, it doesn't do it in color. Listing 9.7 presents a new function for writing a character in color.

Listing 9.7. WRITECH.C. A function to write a character in color.

```
1:    /* Program: WRITECH.C
2:     * Authors: Bradley L. Jones
3:     *          Gregory L. Guntle
4:     * Purpose: Writes a character at a the current cursor
5:     *          location.
6:     *=======================================================*/
7:
8:    #include <dos.h>
9:    #include "tyac.h"
```

```
10:
11:    void write_char(char ch, int fcolor, int bcolor)
12:    {
13:        union REGS inregs;
14:
15:        inregs.h.ah = WRITE_CHAR;
16:        inregs.h.al = ch;                /* Character to write */
17:        inregs.h.bh = 0;                 /* Display page goes here */
18:        inregs.h.bl = (bcolor << 4 ) ¦ fcolor;
19:        inregs.x.cx = 1;
20:        int86(BIOS_VIDEO, &inregs, &inregs);
21:    }
```

Analysis
This function writes a character at the cursor's current location. For this reason, the function is good to use in conjunction with the cursor() function learned earlier. As you can see by line 11, the function takes three parameters. The first, ch, is the character to be printed. The second two are the foreground color, fcolor, and the background color, bcolor. These are used in line 18 to set the color of the character to be printed.

This setting of the color might seem confusing, but it works. Because the numbers for the colors are small, they don't require an entire byte for each of the background and foreground colors. Instead, the background color is placed in the high order bits of an individual character (the top half). The foreground colors are stored in the lower bits (or the bottom half). To accomplish this, the background color, bcolor, is shifted four positions and then "OR"ed into the same register as the foreground color. This isn't an uncommon practice for setting a foreground/background color combination into a single field.

A few other registers are also set in this function. The first is the ah register, which is set to function WRITE_CHAR (0×09 defined in your TYAC.H header file). The x.cx register is set to 1, the bh register to 0, and the al register to ch, which is the character that is going to be printed. (The cx register will be covered in the next section.) The bh register is set to the video page number. We are assuming zero here; however, if you decide to work with video paging, this function can be modified to assign the video page to the bh register. In line 20, writing the character is accomplished by passing these register values with an interrupt 0×10—the defined value of BIOS_VIDEO in your TYAC.H file.

 Note: The TYAC.H header file presented in Listing 9.1 contained the colors that are available. The foreground colors can be any one of the 16 colors presented. The background colors are only the first eight.

Repeating a Character

Often you'll want to print a character several times. For example, to draw a line of asterisks, you could call the write_char() several times in a row. Or alternatively, you could create a function to do this for you. Listing 9.8 shows a function that you may think accomplishes the task of printing a character a given number of times.

 Listing 9.8. Using a for loop to repeat a character.

```
1:   /* Program: LIST0907.C
2:    * Authors: Bradley L. Jones
3:    *          Gregory L. Guntle
4:    * Purpose: Writes a character several times.
5:    *=======================================================*/
6:
7:   #include "tyac.h"
8:
9:   void repeat_char(char ch, int howmany, int fcolor, int bcolor)
10:  {
11:      int ctr;
12:
13:      for( ctr = 0; ctr < howmany; ctr++ )
14:      {
15:        write_char( ch, fcolor, bcolor );
16:      }
17:  }
```

Analysis As you can see, this is a straightforward function. It simply calls the write_char() function the number of times requested. This function doesn't work the way you might expect. It writes the character the number of times stated in howmany; however, it will write them on top of each other! The write_char() function has no control of the cursor. You have to move the cursor yourself. Each time you write a character, you need to move the cursor over one column. In addition, you have to determine where the cursor originally was to know the values to increment.

While you could get a function like this to work, there is an easier—and better—alternative. Listing 9.9 presents a function that looks virtually identical to the write_char() function presented in Listing 9.8; however, there are a few subtle differences.

Listing 9.9. REPEATCH.C. A better repeating character function.

```
 1:   /* Program: REPEATCH.C
 2:    * Authors: Bradley L. Jones
 3:    *          Gregory L. Guntle
 4:    * Purpose: Repeats a character starting at a the current
 5:    *          cursor location.
 6:    *========================================================*/
 7:
 8:   #include <dos.h>
 9:   #include "tyac.h"
10:
11:   void repeat_char(char ch, int howmany, int fcolor, int bcolor)
12:   {
13:       union REGS inregs;
14:
15:       inregs.h.ah = WRITE_CHAR;
16:       inregs.h.al = ch;                /* Character to write */
17:       inregs.h.bh = 0;                 /* Display page goes here */
18:       inregs.h.bl = (bcolor << 4 ) ¦ fcolor;
19:       inregs.x.cx = howmany;           /* Nbr of times to display */
20:       int86(BIOS_VIDEO, &inregs, &inregs);
21:   }
```

Analysis

The first difference you'll notice is that the function is called repeat_char() instead of write_char(). In line 11, you can see that an additional parameter is passed to the function. This parameter, howmany, specifies the number of times the character is to be repeated. In line 19, the value in howmany is assigned to the x.cx register. For the write_char() function, the number 1 was assigned to the cx register. This is because when you write a character, you are only repeating the character one time.

With these minor differences, the repeat_char() function is complete. You may be wondering why the write_char() function isn't eliminated and the repeat_char() function always used. If you call repeat_char() and pass the value of 1 in the howmany field, then you are essentially accomplishing the write_char() function. The basic reasons for having separate functions are readability and usability. When you write a character in color, generally you don't think of repeating it.

Drawing a Line

You already know how to draw a line with character graphics even though you may not be aware of it. A line is simply a set of repeated line characters. There are several line characters in the extended ASCII character set. These include characters 179 and 186 for drawing vertical lines and characters, and 196 and 204 for drawing horizontal lines. Listing 9.10 demonstrates the use of the `repeat_char()` function to print not only a line of asterisks, but also text lines using some of the extended ASCII characters.

> **Note:** When you compile this program, you should link in your TYAC library. You should add each new function you learn to your TYAC library. Many of the remaining programs (listings that create executable files) assume that you are linking the TYAC library. In addition, they assume that you have updated it with any new functions.

Listing 9.10. Using the `repeat_char()` function and drawing lines.

```
1:   /* Program: LIST0909.C
2:    * Authors: Bradley L. Jones
3:    *          Gregory L. Guntle
4:    * Purpose: Use the repeat_char() function.
5:    *=======================================================*/
6:
7:   #include <stdio.h>
8:   #include "tyac.h"
9:
10:  void pause(char *message);
11:
12:  int main(void)
13:  {
14:     int fcolor, bcolor;
15:
16:     for( bcolor = 0; bcolor < 8;  bcolor++ )
17:     {
18:        for( fcolor = 0; fcolor < 16; fcolor++ )
19:        {
20:           cursor( fcolor+2 , 0 );
21:           repeat_char( 205, 70, fcolor, bcolor );
22:        }
23:        pause("Press enter to continue...");
24:     }
25:     return 0;
26:  }
```

```
27:
28:   void pause(char *message)
29:   {
30:       printf("\n%s", message);
31:       while ((getchar()) != '\n') { }
32:       fflush(stdin);
33:   }
```

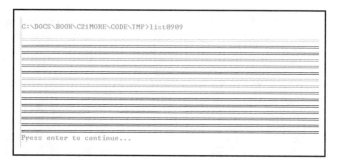

Note: The output will be in color; however, it isn't shown here.

This program is fun because you are working with color. As you can see, Listing 9.10 does a little more than print a bunch of double lines. As usual, line 8 includes the TYAC.H header file. The TYAC.H header file should contain all the function prototypes for the new functions that you are creating. In addition, the TYAC.LIB file should contain all the functions. If you get a link error for cursor(), it could be that you didn't add this function to your library on Day 8.

This program does a lot for the small amount of code presented. It presents the available color combinations by using two for loops to cycle through the foreground and background colors. In addition, double lines are drawn across the screen. Line 21 draws the double lines by repeating character 205, which is a double line. If you wanted single lines instead, you could have used character 196. For fun, try using character 179. This presents vertical, multicolored lines.

The pause() function is used in line 23 to provide a momentary break between each background color. Each time you press the enter key, the screen is redrawn with the next background color. The code for the pause function is in lines 28 to 33. It will be covered at the end of today.

Writing a String in Color

Writing a string in color can be accomplished in several different ways. The simplest way is to break it down into individual characters and print each one. There is an alternate way that won't be shown in this book. It involves using an extended set of registers that aren't always available. Using the write_char() function makes writing a string in color much easier. Listing 9.11 presents the write_string() function.

 Listing 9.11. WRITESTR.C writing a string in color.

```
1:  /* Program: WRITESTR.C
2:   * Authors: Bradley L. Jones
3:   *          Gregory L. Guntle
4:   * Purpose: Write string to the screen
5:   *          Uses   write_char
6:   *=========================================================*/
7:
8:  #include <string.h>   /* for strlen() */
9:  #include "tyac.h"
10:
11: void write_string(char *string, int fcolor, int bcolor, int row,
                      int col)
12: {
13:     int len = strlen(string);
14:     int i;
15:
16:     for (i=0; i < len; i++)
17:     {
18:         cursor(row, col+i);                 /* Position cursor */
19:         write_char( (char)*(string+i), fcolor, bcolor);
20:     }
21: }
```

 This isn't a perfect listing, but it is effective. As you can see, a for loop in lines 16 to 20 enables you to loop through each character of the string. For each iteration of the string, the cursor is placed and a character is written. This is done in line 19 with the write_char() function. The character passed is:

```
(char)*(string+i)
```

Don't let this confuse you. This is just the character at the i offset in string.

The write_string() function is a powerful function. It can write a string at any position on the screen. In addition, write_string() can write it in color. You may find this to be one of your most useful functions. Where write_string() has its flaw is in escape characters. In printf(), certain sequences of characters perform special functions. An exercise at the end of today asks you to update write_string() so some

of the escape sequences are implemented. You should do this exercise. If you don't, you should at least update your write_string() function with the answer provided for the exercise.

Drawing a Box

Setting the cursor, writing characters, and manipulating color give you a lot of power in manipulating the screen. These three capabilities are what have enabled you to draw lines and write colored text. These functions also work together to help you create a box and, on later days, an entire entry screen for an application.

A box is a simple construct that can have several uses when working with output to the screen. A box can be used to create menus, screens, messages, and more. Boxes begin to get more complex when you choose to add borders to them. In addition, there can be an additional level of complexity added when you choose to have filled or unfilled boxes. Figure 9.2 presents different styles of boxes.

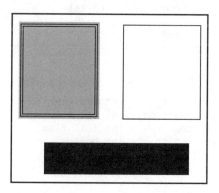

Figure 9.2. *A few examples of boxes.*

Listing 9.12 presents a function that enables you to create all of the boxes in Figure 9.2 using text graphics. Several of the added defined constants in the TYAC.H header file presented in Listing 9.1 were made specifically for the box() function. You should verify that these defined constants are in your TYAC.H header file. You should also add the function prototype for the box function. The defined constants that were added specifically for the box function are:

```
25:  /*  Types of Boxes   */
26:  #define DOUBLE_BOX        1
27:  #define SINGLE_BOX        2
28:  #define BLANK_BOX         3
29:
```

```
30:   /*  Box fill flags  */
31:   #define BORDER_ONLY      0
32:   #define FILL_BOX         1
```

You'll see these constants used within the box() function's listing. In addition, you may choose to use them when you use the box() function in your programs. Listing 9.13 is a small listing that uses the box() function along with several of the defined constants.

Type   **Listing 9.12. BOX.C. The box() function.**

```
 1:    /* -----------------------------------------
 2:     * Program: BOX.C
 3:     * Authors: Bradley L. Jones
 4:     *          Gregory L. Guntle
 5:     * Purpose: Draws a box on the screen using other BIOS
 6:     *          functions.
 7:     *
 8:     * Enter with: start_row    (0-24)
 9:     *             end_row      (0-24)
10:     *             start_col    (0-79)
11:     *             end_col      (0-79)
12:     *=======================================================*/
13:
14:    #include "tyac.h"
15:
16:    void box(int start_row, int end_row,
17:             int start_col, int end_col,
18:             int box_type,  int fill_flag,
19:             int fcolor,    int bcolor )
20:    {
21:        int row;
22:
23:        /* BOX CHARACTERS */
24:        static unsigned char DBL_BOX[6] = " ╔ ║ ╚ " ; /* Double-sided box
                                                            characters */
25:        static unsigned char SGL_BOX[6] = " ┌ │ └ " ; /* Single-sided box
                                                            characters */
26:        static unsigned char BLK_BOX[6] = "         " ; /* Spaces for
                                                            erasing a box */
27:        static unsigned char *USE_BOX;                  /* Set this vari
                                                            able to the
                                                            appropriate box
                                                            characters to
                                                            use */
28:
29:        /* Determine BOX Type to Draw */
30:        switch (box_type)
31:        {
32:          case DOUBLE_BOX:    USE_BOX = DBL_BOX;
33:                              break;
```

```
34:         case SINGLE_BOX:    USE_BOX = SGL_BOX;
35:                             break;
36:         case BLANK_BOX:     USE_BOX = BLK_BOX;
37:                             break;
38:         default:            USE_BOX = DBL_BOX;
39:                             break;
40:      }
41:
42:      /* Draw the top two corner characters */
43:      cursor(start_row, start_col);
44:      write_char(USE_BOX[0], fcolor,bcolor);
45:      cursor(start_row, end_col);
46:      write_char(USE_BOX[2], fcolor,bcolor);
47:
48:      /* Draw the top line */
49:      cursor(start_row, start_col+1);
50:      repeat_char(USE_BOX[1],end_col-start_col-1,fcolor,bcolor);
51:
52:      /* Draw the bottom line */
53:      cursor(end_row,start_col+1);
54:      repeat_char(USE_BOX[1],end_col-start_col-1,fcolor,bcolor);
55:
56:      /* Draw the sides */
57:      for (row=start_row+1; row < end_row; row++ )
58:      {
59:        cursor(row,start_col);
60:        write_char(USE_BOX[3],fcolor,bcolor);
61:        cursor(row,end_col);
62:        write_char(USE_BOX[3],fcolor,bcolor);
63:      }
64:
65:      /* Draw the bottom corner pieces */
66:      cursor(end_row, start_col);
67:      write_char(USE_BOX[4],fcolor,bcolor);
68:      cursor(end_row,end_col);
69:      write_char(USE_BOX[5],fcolor,bcolor);
70:
71:      /* fill box */
72:
73:      if(fill_flag != BORDER_ONLY)
74:      {
75:         for( row= start_row+1; row < end_row; row++ )
76:         {
77:            cursor( row, start_col+1 );
78:            repeat_char( ' ', ((end_col-start_col)-1), fcolor,
                           bcolor);
79:         }
80:      }
81: }  /* end of BOX */
```

Listing 9.13. DRAWBOX.C. Using the box() function to draw boxes.

```
 1:  /* Program: DRAWBOX.C
 2:   * Authors: Bradley L. Jones
 3:   *          Gregory L. Guntle
 4:   * Purpose: Draws boxes on the screen using BIOS
 5:   *=======================================================*/
 6:
 7:  #include "tyac.h"
 8:
 9:  int main()
10:  {
11:     int start_row = 5;
12:     int start_col = 20;
13:     int end_row = 13;
14:     int end_col = 60;
15:
16:     box(start_row, end_row, start_col, end_col,
17:         SINGLE_BOX, FILL_BOX, RED, CYAN );
18:
19:     box( 18, 23, 1, 10, DOUBLE_BOX, BORDER_ONLY, YELLOW, BLUE );
20:
21:     return 0;
22:  }
```

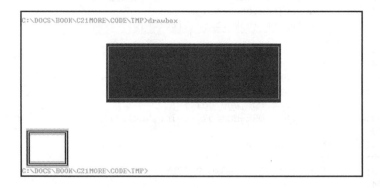

 This output is from Listing 9.12. As you can see, two different boxes are created on the screen. In addition, these boxes are in color. The first box is a filled cyan box with a red border. The red border is a single solid line. The second box is not filled and has a yellow border on a blue background. In looking at Listing 9.13, this follows the two calls to box() in lines 16 and 19.

As you can see, the box() function takes eight parameters. While this may seem like a lot, by having eight parameters, the box() function becomes very useful. Listing 9.13

contains the box function itself. Line 16 starts the function. Here you can see the eight parameters that are received. The first two parameters are the starting row and the ending row for the box. The third and fourth parameters are the starting and ending columns. By setting these four parameters, you define the size of the box. The four variables, start_row, end_row, start_col, and end_col will be used throughout the box() function.

The next parameter, box_type, determines the type of border on the box. One of three possible borders are available in the box, DOUBLE_BOX, SINGLE_BOX, or BLANK_BOX. These are defined constants that are in the TYAC.H header file. Their corresponding values, two, one, or zero, could also be used. This parameter is used in line 30 to determine which borders are going to be used in the box.

The fifth parameter, fill_flag, also uses defined constants from the TYAC.H header file. fill_flag can be set to BORDER_ONLY or FILL_BOX. This variable determines whether the inside of the box will be filled. If the fill_flag contains BORDER_ONLY, the box won't be filled.

The last two parameters, fcolor and bcolor, are the colors. These are used to set the foreground and background colors of the individual box characters.

This listing needs more explanation than those previously presented. Line 16 contains the function parameters, which have already been discussed. Lines 24 to 26 contain character arrays that contain the characters used to create the border on the box. Line 27 contains a character pointer, USE_BOX, that is set to point at one of these three sets of border types. Lines 30 to 40 use the box_type parameter to set the appropriate array to the USE_BOX pointer. Notice that if an inappropriate value is received in box_type, then the default sets DBL_BOX, the double-lined border.

The box is drawn in lines 42 to 69. Line 43 places the cursor at the location of the top-left corner of the box. The write_char() function is then used to write the top-left corner character from the array that USE_BOX points to. The top-right character is drawn in lines 45 and 46, the bottom two corners are drawn in lines 65 to 69. The corners are connected with the edge lines in lines 52 to 63. The repeat_char() function is used to draw the horizontal lines. A for loop in lines 57 to 63 is used to draw the vertical lines. In each case, the appropriate character is used from the array being pointed at by USE_BOX.

Lines 73 to 80 fill the box by printing spaces inside the box border. The spaces effectively place the background color in the box. Only the inside of the box is filled because the border has already been drawn.

This function makes the assumption that the row and column values passed in are correct. If you pass a `start_row` that is greater than an `end_row`, or a `start_col` that is greater than an `end_col`, then you won't get a box, but the function will still work. Another flaw that can cause problems is a result of the row and column values. There is no check to ensure that the values are appropriate for the screen. If you pass 1000 for a row value, you'll get unpredictable results. Both of these problems could be avoided with coding additions; however, the coding additions can cause limitations in the function. As long as you are aware of the possible problems, they can be avoided easily.

Note: Writing foolproof code can be costly in the amount of time required to handle every situation. It's best to handle the problems that are most likely to occur or that will cause serious problems. The amount of time needed to add the code must be weighed against the value added by the code.

A Pausing Function

One last function is going to be presented as an added bonus. This function isn't really a text graphics function; however, it's one that you may find useful. This is the `pause()` function. It was used in Listing 9.13. It enables you to stop what is being displayed and wait for the user to press the enter key. This is a good addition to your TYAC library.

Listing 9.14. PAUSE.C. A pausing function.

```
 1:  /* Program: PAUSE.C
 2:   * Authors: Bradley L. Jones
 3:   *          Gregory L. Guntle
 4:   * Purpose: Causes the program to PAUSE until the ENTER
 5:   *          key is pressed.
 6:   * Note:    This program requires the calling routine
 7:   *          to pass a message to display.
 8:   *=======================================================*/
 9:  #include <stdio.h>
10:
11:  void pause(char *message)
12:  {
13:     printf("\n%s", message);
```

```
14:    while ((getchar()) != '\n') { }
15:    fflush(stdin);
16: }
```

This short function receives a message that is displayed using the `printf()` function. It then uses `getchar()` to get characters until it reads a new line (enter). Once it reads an enter key, it flushes the keyboard and returns.

Updating Your TYAC Library and Header File

At this point you should ensure that your TYAC.H header file and your TYAC.LIB are both up-to-date. Exercise 1 asks you to update your library with all of today's functions. In addition, you should verify that your TYAC.H header file is similar to Listing 9.15.

Listing 9.15. LIST0914.H. A new version of TYAC.H.

```
 1: /* Program: TYAC.H
 2:  *          (Teach Yourself Advanced C)
 3:  * Authors: Bradley L. Jones
 4:  *          Gregory L. Guntle
 5:  * Purpose: Header file for TYAC library functions
 6:  *=======================================================*/
 7:
 8: #ifndef _TYAC_H_
 9: #define _TYAC_H_
10:
11: /* DOS and BIOS Interrupts */
12: #define BIOS_VIDEO        0x10
13: #define DOS_FUNCTION      0x21
14:
15: /* BIOS function calls */
16: #define SET_VIDEO         0x00
17: #define SET_CURSOR_SIZE   0x01
18: #define SET_CURSOR_POS    0x02
19: #define GET_CURSOR_INFO   0x03
20: #define WRITE_CHAR        0x09
21: #define SET_COLOR         0x0B
22: #define GET_VIDEO         0x0F
23: #define WRITE_STRING      0x13
24:
25: /*  Types of Boxes  */
```

continues

Listing 9.15. continued

```
26:  #define DOUBLE_BOX      1
27:  #define SINGLE_BOX      2
28:  #define BLANK_BOX       3
29:
30:  /*  Box fill flags  */
31:  #define BORDER_ONLY     0
32:  #define FILL_BOX        1
33:
34:  /* Colors */
35:  #define    BLACK          0
36:  #define    BLUE           1
37:  #define    GREEN          2
38:  #define    CYAN           3
39:  #define    RED            4
40:  #define    MAGENTA        5
41:  #define    BROWN          6
42:  #define    WHITE          7
43:  #define    GRAY           8
44:  #define    LIGHTBLUE      9
45:  #define    LIGHTGREEN     10
46:  #define    LIGHTCYAN      11
47:  #define    LIGHTRED       12
48:  #define    LIGHTMAGENTA   13
49:  #define    YELLOW         14
50:  #define    BRIGHTWHITE    15
51:
52:  /* used to set scrolling direction */
53:  #define SCROLL_UP    0x07
54:  #define SCROLL_DOWN  0x06
55:
56:  /*----------------------*
57:       Function Prototypes
58:   *----------------------*/
59:
60:       /* Gets the current date */
61:  void current_date(int *, int *, int *);
62:
63:       /* Positions the cursor to row/col */
64:  void cursor(int, int);
65:       /* Returns info about cursor */
66:  void get_cursor(int *, int *, int *, int *, int *);
67:       /* Sets the size of the cursor */
68:  void set_cursor_size(int, int);
69:
70:       /* clear the keyboard buffer */
71:  void kbclear( void );
72:       /* determine keyboard hit */
73:  int  kbhit( void );
74:
```

```
75:        /* sroll the screen */
76:   void scroll( int row,   int col,
77:                int width, int height,
78:                int nbr,   int direction);
79:
80:        /* pause until ENTER pressed */
81:   void pause(char *);
82:
83:        /* Video mode functions */
84:   void set_video(int);
85:   void get_video(int *, int *, int *);
86:
87:        /* Text Graphics functions */
88:   void write_char(char, int, int);
89:   void repeat_char(char, int, int, int);
90:   void write_string(char *, int, int, int, int);
91:   void box(int, int, int, int, int, int, int, int);
92:   void set_border_color(int);
93:
94:   #endif
```

DO   DON'T

DO enter all of today's functions and add them to your library.

DON'T over code your functions. If you spend an excessive amount of time coding edits to prevent problems, you may never be able to use the function.

DO code enough edits into your functions to avoid as many problems as is reasonable.

Summary

Today, you covered a multitude of additional functions that work with text graphics. Before jumping into these functions, you were given an overview of the different types of screen graphics. You also moved right into creating new functions. The day focused on functions that put text graphics on the screen; this included colored characters, repeating a character, drawing text lines, and creating boxes. With the functions presented in today's material, you have the beginning building blocks for creating an application's screens.

Q&A

Q What is the benefit of using text graphics instead of pixel graphics?

A Text graphics are much more portable and can be displayed on monitors of varying resolutions, including some monochrome monitors. In addition, text graphics are much easier to work with because you are working with a limited number of characters.

Q Can you write text graphics programs that will be portable to C++ or Windows?

A This is really two different questions. Windows programs use pixel graphics. Windows can run text graphics programs in DOS windows. In regard to portability to C++, all C constructs are portable to C++. This means that you can write text graphics characters in C++ also.

Workshop

The Workshop provides quiz questions to help you solidify your understanding of the material covered and exercises to provide you with experience in using what you've learned.

Quiz

1. What is meant by monochrome?

2. What are text graphics?

3. How many characters are in the ASCII character set?

4. What are considered to be the extended ASCII characters?

5. When you change a library function, what must you do?

6. When you change a header file, what should you do?

7. What is a reason for using defined constant?

8. What are the colors that can be used?

Exercises

1. Add all of the functions that you have created today to your TYAC.LIB library. These functions should be:

```
cursor()      (updated)
get_cursor() (updated)
get_video()
set_video()
set_border_color()
write_char()
repeat_char()
write_string()
box()
pause()
```

2. Write a program that uses the `get_video()` functions. Once the program gets the mode, it should display the values that are set.

3. Modify the program from Exercise 2 to also set the video mode to 40 columns.

4. Change the character in Listing 9.9 to character 177. What does this character do?

5. **ON YOUR OWN:** Use the functions presented today to write a program that displays information on the screen in color. Use your imagination to determine what you should display.

The *getline()*
Function

Up to this point you have learned about a multitude of functions, most of which have been relatively small in size. Today you'll concentrate on a single function to add to your library: the getline() function. In the process, you'll gain the use of a few more functions. Today you will:

☐ See what is needed to get formatted data from the display screen.

☐ Become familiar with the getline() function.

☐ Learn what the getline() function can do.

☐ Learn how to use the getline() function.

Why Is an Entire Day Dedicated to a Single Function?

You have seen a number of functions up to this point. Many of them expand functions that you had in your basic compiler. For example, write_char() expanded functions such as putch() by giving you the ability to write a character in color. In addition, you gained the ability to place the cursor anywhere on the screen. With the functions that you have learned up to this point, you can design a text graphics screen to look any way you want.

What hasn't been covered is retrieving data off the text graphic screen. There are functions such as gets() and scanf() that can get data; however, they aren't suited for data entry within text graphic applications. The getline() function is being presented as a replacement for these functions.

This still doesn't explain why an entire day is needed to cover getline(). As you will see, getting data from the screen can become complex depending on the amount of functionality you build into your applications. The getline() function has been developed with as much functionality as possible. With the getline() function you will be able to do the following:

☐ Get a string or a number. If a number is being entered, characters won't be accepted.

☐ Use the right and left arrow keys to move within the entered field.

☐ Use the backspace key to erase the preceding character.

☐ Set up keys to be used to exit the entry. You'll also be able to know which key was used to exit.

☐ Insert characters in the middle of the string.

☐ Set up colors for the information being entered.

☐ And more.

To accomplish all of the capabilities listed requires a powerful and large function. In fact, the amount of code in the getline() function may be more than in some of the programs you've written up to this point.

An Overview of the *getline()* Function

The getline() function is best understood in steps. Figure 10.1 presents a breakdown of the getline() function.

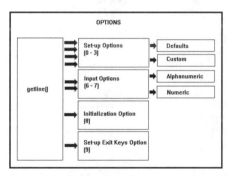

Figure 10.1. *The breakdown of the* getline() *function.*

As you can see, getline() breaks down into several groups of options. In using getline(), you'll need to use at least one of the set up options in order to set up the colors that will be used. In addition, you'll need to use the option to set up the exit keys. Once you have executed getline() with these options, you'll be ready to use the input options which allows either numerics or alphanumerics to be entered.

A New TYAC.H Header File

Before getting into the code and the individual parts of the getline() function, a new TYAC.H header file needs to be introduced. The getline() function needs several

new constants. It also needs a prototype for it and several of the sub-functions that it uses. Listing 10.1 presents a new TYAC.H header file which includes everything needed for getline().

Type Listing 10.1. A new TYAC.H header file.

```
 1: /* Program: TYAC.H
 2:  *              (Teach Yourself Advanced C)
 3:  * Authors: Bradle y L. Jones
 4:  *              Gregory L. Guntle
 5:  * Purpose: Header file for TYAC library functions
 6:  *========================================================*/
 7:
 8:  #ifndef _TYAC_H_
 9:  #define _TYAC_H_
10:
11:  /* DOS and BIOS Interrupts */
12:  #define BIOS_VIDEO       0x10
13:  #define BIOS_KEY         0x16
14:  #define DOS_FUNCTION     0x21
15:
16:  /* BIOS function calls */
17:  #define SET_VIDEO        0x00
18:  #define SET_CURSOR_SIZE  0x01
19:  #define SET_CURSOR_POS   0x02
20:  #define GET_CURSOR_INFO  0x03
21:  #define WRITE_CHAR       0x09
22:  #define SET_COLOR        0x0B
23:  #define GET_VIDEO        0x0F
24:  #define WRITE_STRING     0x13
25:
26:  /* BIOS used to set scrolling direction */
27:  #define SCROLL_UP        0x07
28:  #define SCROLL_DOWN      0x06
29:
30:  /* DOS functions calls */
31:  #define GET_DATE         0x2A
32:
33:
34:  /*  Types of Boxes   */
35:  #define DOUBLE_BOX       1
36:  #define SINGLE_BOX       2
37:  #define BLANK_BOX        3
38:
39:  /*  Box fill flags   */
40:  #define BORDER_ONLY      0
41:  #define FILL_BOX         1
42:
43:  /* Colors */
44:  #define BLACK            0
```

```
45:   #define BLUE               1
46:   #define GREEN              2
47:   #define CYAN               3
48:   #define RED                4
49:   #define MAGENTA            5
50:   #define BROWN              6
51:   #define WHITE              7
52:   #define GRAY               8
53:   #define LIGHTBLUE          9
54:   #define LIGHTGREEN         10
55:   #define LIGHTCYAN          11
56:   #define LIGHTRED           12
57:   #define LIGHTMAGENTA       13
58:   #define YELLOW             14
59:   #define BRIGHTWHITE        15
60:
61:   #define BLANK              ' '
62:   #define SPACE              ' '
63:   #define NEWLINE            '\n'
64:   #define TAB                '\t'
65:   #ifndef NULL
66:      #define NULL            '\0'
67:   #endif
68:
69:   #define EOS                0
70:   #define YES                1
71:   #define NO                 0
72:   #define TRUE               1
73:   #define FALSE              0
74:
75:   #define CR                 13
76:   #define LF                 10
77:   #define EOL                13
78:
79:   #define CLR_INS            1          /* Clear Inside Box Flag */
80:   #define NO_CLR             0          /* Don't Clear Inside the Box */
81:
82:   #define CTR_STR            1          /* Centering a string on the
                                               screen */
83:   #define NO_CTR_STR         0          /* Don't center the string */
84:
85:
86:   /* ------------------------------- *
87:    *        New Type Definitions     *
88:    * ------------------------------- */
89:
90:   typedef int BOOLEAN;
91:   typedef unsigned short PTR;       /*          0 -          65535 */
```

continues

299

Listing 10.1. continued

```
92: typedef char CHAR;                 /*          -128 -   127 */
93: typedef unsigned char EXTCHAR;     /*             0 -   255 */
94: typedef short NUM32K;              /*         -32768 - 32767 */
95: typedef unsigned short NUM64K;     /*             0 - 65535 */
96: typedef long NUM2GIGA;             /*-2,147,483,648 - 2,147,483,647 */
97: typedef unsigned long NUM4GIGA;    /*             0 - 4,294,967,295 */
98: typedef unsigned char ARRAY;       /* Used for creating an array */
99:
100:
101: /* --------------------------- *
102:  *              KEYS           *
103:  * --------------------------- */
104:
105: /* Numeric keypad scan codes    */
106: #define   HOME        71          /*   home key    */
107: #define   UP_ARROW    72          /*   up arrow    */
108: #define   PAGE_UP     73          /*   page up     */
109: #define   LT_ARROW    75          /*   left arrow  */
110: #define   RT_ARROW    77          /*   right arrow */
111: #define   END         79          /*   end key     */
112: #define   DN_ARROW    80          /*   down arrow  */
113: #define   PAGE_DN     81          /*   page down   */
114: #define   INS         82          /*   insert      */
115: #define   DEL         83          /*   delete      */
116: #define   SHIFT_TAB   15          /*   shift tab   */
117: #define   ENTER_KEY   28
118:
119: /* Function key scan codes */
120: #define   F1          59          /*    F1 KEY   */
121: #define   F2          60          /*    F2 KEY   */
122: #define   F3          61          /*    F3 KEY   */
123: #define   F4          62          /*    F4 KEY   */
124: #define   F5          63          /*    F5 KEY   */
125: #define   F6          64          /*    F6 KEY   */
126: #define   F7          65          /*    F7 KEY   */
127: #define   F8          66          /*    F8 KEY   */
128: #define   F9          67          /*    F9 KEY   */
129: #define   F10         68          /*    F10 KEY  */
130:
131: /*  Other non scan keys as ASCII   */
132:
133: #define   BK_SP_KEY   8
134: #define   ESC_KEY     27
135: #define   CR_KEY      13
136: #define   TAB_KEY     9
137: #define   SPACE_BAR   32
138:
```

```
139: /* ---------------------------------- *
140: *              Getline Options          *
141: * ---------------------------------- */
142: #define SET_DEFAULTS  0
143: #define SET_NORMAL    1
144: #define SET_UNDERLINE 2
145: #define SET_INS       3
146: #define GET_ALPHA     6
147: #define GET_NUM       7
148: #define CLEAR_FIELD   8
149: #define SET_EXIT_KEYS 9
150:
151: /*----------------------*
152:      Function Prototypes
153:    *----------------------*/
154:      /* Gets the current date */
155: void current_date(int *, int *, int *);
156:
157:      /* Positions the cursor to row/col */
158: void cursor(int, int);
159:      /* Returns info about cursor */
160: void get_cursor(int *, int *, int *, int *, int *);
161:      /* Sets the size of the cursor */
162: void set_cursor_size(int, int);
163:
164:      /* clear the keyboard buffer */
165: void kbclear( void );
166:      /* determine keyboard hit */
167: int  kbhit( void );
168:
169:      /* scroll the screen */
170: void scroll( int row,    int col,
171:              int width, int hieght,
172:              int nbr,    int direction);
173:
174:      /* pause until ENTER pressed */
175: void pause(char *);
176:
177:      /* Video mode functions */
178: void set_video(int);
179: void get_video(int *, int *, int *);
180:
181:      /* Text Graphics functions */
182: void write_char(char, int, int);
183: void repeat_char(char, int, int, int);
184: void write_string(char *, int, int, int, int);
185: void box(int, int, int, int, int, int, int, int);
186: void set_border_color(int);
187: char getline(int, char, int, int, int, int, char * );
188:
```

continues

The *getline( )* Function

Listing 10.1. continued

```
189:     /* misc functions */
190: void boop( void );
191: void waitsec( double );
192: long get_timer_ticks( void );
193:
194: #endif
```

You should review this header file to ensure that you are familiar with everything it contains. Lines 8, 9, and 194 used defined constants to prevent you from including the header file more than once. This is a common practice used by many programmers. If the constant _TYAC_H_ isn't defined, then the header file hasn't been included before. You know this because line 9 defines this constant. If _TYAC_H_ has been defined, the file skips to line 194.

Lines 11 through 83 define several different groups of constants. Lines 11 through 31 contain the defined constants for the BIOS functions that you worked with on previous days. Lines 27 and 28 contain the constants used with the scroll function from Day 8. Lines 35 to 41 contain constants used with the box() function that you created on Day 9. The colors are defined in lines 44 to 59. Various additional values are defined in lines 61 to 83. These are values that can be used by other functions that you create. This includes values for TRUE, FALSE, YES, NO, EOS (end of string), and more.

Lines 90 to 98 contain type definitions. Several new types have been declared that will be useful in your programs. Lines 106 to 137 declare type definitions for the keyboard keys. These values will be used when setting the exit keys for getline() which is covered later. Lines 142 to 149 contain the last of the defined constants. These constants can be used instead of numbers when calling getline(). The rest of the TYAC.H header file contains prototypes for the functions that should be in your TYAC.LIB library after you complete today's material.

Understanding the Use of *getline( )*

Before presenting the code for the getline() function, the use of getline() needs to be explained. By covering the usage first, you'll find it much easier to understand the actual code.

The prototype for getline() is:

```
char getline( int option, char cParm1, int iParm1, int iParm2,
              int iParm3, int iParm4, char *char_ptr);
```

As you can see, the getline() function has several parameters. The most important parameter is the first, option. The *option* parameter determines exactly what getline() is going to do. getline() gains its functionality through the option parameter. Based on the option, the other parameters may or may not contain values. Because of the multiple uses of the rest of the parameters, they have been given generic names.

Note: When a getline() parameter isn't used, it's filled with 0.

The Option Parameter

There are eight different options that can be used when calling the getline() function. These options are based on a numeric value passed in option.

Options 0, 1, 2, and 3

If a value of 0, 1, 2, or 3 is passed to getline(), then different color values will be set. The colors that can be set in getline() are as follows:

norm_color_fg	The normal foreground color
norm_color_bg	The normal background color

The normal colors are used for the color of the text that is being entered. If you enter "BRADLEY", it will appear in the normal colors.

high_color_fg	The highlighted character's foreground color
high_color_bg	The highlighted character's background color

The highlighted character is the character that is currently being entered when the insert key is on. If the insert key is off, there won't be a highlighted character.

undr_color_fg	The underline character's foreground color
undr_color_bg	The underline character's background color

The getline() function has been written to display the extent of an enterable field. For example, if a string was to be entered that was 20 characters long, getline() would display 20 underline characters on the screen. The underline colors define the color of these underlines.

303

| ins_color_fg | The "INS" message's foreground color |
| ins_color_bg | The "INS" message's background color |

The getline() displays the characters "INS" in the lower-right corner of the screen. This insert message is toggled on and off with the insert key. The colors for this message are determined by the insert colors.

Each of the first four options set up different values. If you use option 1, you will set all of the colors to default values along with several other default values. Option 1 enables the normal and highlight colors to be set. Option 2 enables the underline colors to be set. Option 3 enables the insert message color, along with its position, to be set.

Options 4 and 5

The values 4 and 5 are not used as options. These two values are left open for future expansion of the getline() function.

Options 6 and 7

Options 6 and 7 are the options that allow getline() to get data. Option 6 accepts the input of alphanumeric values. Option 7 accepts the input of numeric values. Along with these options, you'll also need to specify screen coordinates for the input and the length of the value to be entered. These options will be detailed later.

Option 8

Using getline() with option 8 provides you with an alternative way to clear a string to nulls. By calling getline() with option 8 before calling it with option 6 or 7, you can ensure that no bad data is remaining in a variable that should be empty.

Option 9

This is the final option used with the getline() function. Option 9 enables you to set up the exit keys for getline(). An exit key is a key that enables you to leave the entry field. For example, the exit key for gets() is the enter key. The exit key returns control back to the program. Option 9 enables you to set up the keys that you want to exit the entry of a single field. Example of keys that are generally used for exiting are tab, enter, shift+tab, F1, and F3.

Other *getline()* Parameters

The values passed in the other parameters are dependent upon which option is called. The specific details of each parameter will be covered when getline() is analyzed in the next section. Generally, the first parameter, cParm1, is rarely used. The next four parameters, iParm1, iParm2, iParm3, and iParm4 are used to pass in numeric values. For the options that set colors, the iParm# parmeters contain color values. For options 6, 7, and 8, these variables contain the starting location and the length for the information to be entered. For option 9, the parameters contain the number of exit keys that are defined.

The last parameter in the prototype is str_ptr. This is used in options 6, 7, 8, and 9. In options 6 and 7, str_ptr contains the address of a character pointer. This address is where the information retrieved will be placed. For option 8, it should also be the location where data will be placed. Option 8 uses this pointer as the starting location to be cleared to nulls.

Option 9 uses the str_ptr differently. Option 9 will use the str_ptr as the pointer to the first exit_key in an array. These exit keys should be listed one after the other in a character array. The values used for the exit keys are those defined in the TYAC.H header file.

The Return Value of *getline()*

The return value of getline() is a character value. This value is the ASCII value of the last key pressed before exiting getline(). This value is one of the keys defined as a valid exit key with option 9.

The Code Behind *getline()*

Having an understanding of the options for getline() and the parameters prepares you for the function itself. Following is the complete getline() listing. It contains four different functions: getline(), get_it(), check_list(), and setup_exit_keys(). The getline() function uses get_it() with options 6 and 7 (getting data). The setup_exit_keys() function is used with option 9.

Note: The getline() function uses several of the functions presented earlier in this book. By keeping the getline() function in your TYAC.LIB library, you'll have access to these other functions. Additionally, you'll need a few more functions that you previously didn't have. The getline() function uses a function called boop() to make the computer beep. The boop() function in turn requires two other functions.

Listing 10.2. GETLINE.C. The getline() function.

```
 1:   /* Name    : getline.c
 2:    * Authors: Bradley L. Jones
 3:    *          Gregory L. Guntle
 4:    *
 5:    * Purpose: Receive string inputs from the user through
 6:    *          the keyboard.  This routine replaces SCANF for
 7:    *          reading keyboard responses from the user.
 8:    *
 9:    * Function  : getline(opt,ch1,int1,int2,int3,int4,str_ptr)
10:    *
11:    * Enter with: opt = One of the following:
12:    *
13:    *          0 - Set default parameters
14:    *              norm_color_fg = WHITE
15:    *              norm_color_bg = BLACK
16:    *              high_color_fg = BRIGHTWHITE
17:    *              high_color_bg = BLACK
18:    *              undr_color_fg = GREEN
19:    *              undr_color_bg = BLACK
20:    *              ins_color_fg  = YELLOW
21:    *              ins_color_bg  = BLACK
22:    *              ins_row       = 24
23:    *              ins_col       = 70
24:    *              stop_key      = CR_KEY
25:    *
26:    *          1 - Set highlight/normal colors for string
27:    *              int1 - foreground normal color
28:    *              int2 - background normal color
29:    *              int3 - foreground highlighted color
30:    *              int4 - background highlighted color
31:    *
32:    *          2 - Setup underline colors
33:    *              int1 - foreground color for underline character
34:    *              int2 - background color for underline character
35:    *              int3 - foreground color highlighting underline
36:    *              int4 - background color highlighting underline
37:    *
38:    *          3 - Setup INS message colors & row/col positioning
39:    *              int1 - foreground color for INS message
40:    *              int2 - background color for INS message
41:    *              int3 - Row where to display INS message
42:    *              int4 - Col where to display INS message
43:    *
44:    *          4 -
45:    *
46:    *          5 -
47:    *
48:    *          6 - Get alphanumeric input
```

SAMS
SAMS
PUBLISHING
Sams
Learning
Center

10

```
49:    *              int1 - Upper left corner - row #
50:    *              int2 - Upper left corner - col #
51:    *              int4 - Max length of input
52:    *              str_ptr - Address for placing the chars
53:    *
54:    *        7 - Get numeric input
55:    *              int1 - Upper left corner - row #
56:    *              int2 - Upper left corner - col #
57:    *              int4 - Max length of input
58:    *              str_ptr - Address to store chars
59:    *
60:    *        8 - Clear char field value to NULLS
61:    *              int1 - Length of string for clearing
62:    *              str_ptr - Address of string to clear
63:    *
64:    *        9 - Clear and load valid exit keys
65:    *              The array is static and will remain
66:    *              until changed.
67:    *              There is no default value.
68:    *              int1 - # of keys in array
69:    *              str_ptr - Address of array (array name)
70:    *
71:    * Returns   : (applies to options 6,7 only )
72:    *              Char type of ascii value of the last
73:    *              key pressed that is within VALID_EXIT_KEYS.
74:    *
75:    * -----------------------------------------------------------*/
76:
77:   #include <string.h>
78:   #include <conio.h>
79:   #include "tyac.h"
80:
81:   #define MAX_KEYS 17
82:
83:   /*--------------------------------*
84:    *    Global static variables     *
85:    *--------------------------------*/
86:
87:   static int  norm_color_fg;      /* foreground - normal color */
88:   static int  norm_color_bg;      /* background - normal color */
89:   static int  high_color_fg;      /* foreground - highlight */
90:   static int  high_color_bg;      /* background - highlight */
91:   static int  undr_color_fg;      /* foreground - underlines */
92:   static int  undr_color_bg;      /* background - underlines */
93:   static int  ins_color_fg;       /* foreground - INS message */
94:   static int  ins_color_bg;       /* background - INS message */
95:   static int  st_col, end_col;    /* constants     */
96:   static int  length;             /* string length */
97:   static int  row, col;
98:   static int  st_row;             /* constants     */
```

continues

Listing 10.2. continued

```
 99: static int   ins_row;              /* Row for INS message */
100: static int   ins_col;              /* Col for INS message */
101: static char  stop_key;             /* key to stop accepting input */
102:
103:      /* valid exit keys loaded here */
104: static char VALID_EXIT_KEYS[MAX_KEYS];
105:
106: /*--------------------------------*
107:  *     Subroutines               *
108:  *--------------------------------*/
109:
110:  char getline(int, char, int, int, int, int, char *);
111:  char get_it(int, char *);
112:  int  check_list( char );
113:  void setup_exit_keys( char *, int);
114:
115: /*-------------------------------------------*
116:  *                Start of Function          *
117:  *-------------------------------------------*/
118:
119: char getline(int option, char cParm1, int iParm1, int iParm2,
120:                int iParm3, int iParm4, char *char_ptr)
121: {
122:    int     ctr;        /* misc counter */
123:    char    last_key;   /* Holds last key pressed & returns it */
124:
125:    VALID_EXIT_KEYS[16] = '\0';    /* keep last key a null */
126:
127:    switch ( option )
128:    {
129:      case 0:  /* set default parameters */
130:              norm_color_fg=WHITE;
131:              norm_color_bg=BLACK;
132:              high_color_fg=BRIGHTWHITE;
133:              high_color_bg=BLACK;
134:              stop_key=CR_KEY;
135:              undr_color_fg=GREEN;
136:              undr_color_bg=BLACK;
137:              ins_color_fg= YELLOW;
138:              ins_color_bg= BLACK;
139:              ins_row = 24;
140:              ins_col = 70;
141:              break;
142:
143:      case 1:  /* set colors */
144:              norm_color_fg=iParm1;
145:              norm_color_bg=iParm2;
146:              high_color_fg=iParm3;
147:              high_color_bg=iParm4;
```

```
148:              break;
149:
150:      case 2:  /* insert normal and high colors */
151:              undr_color_fg=iParm1;
152:              undr_color_bg=iParm2;
153:              break;
154:
155:      case 3:  ins_color_fg = iParm1;
156:              ins_color_bg = iParm2;
157:              ins_row = iParm3;
158:              ins_col = iParm4;
159:              break;
160:
161:      case 4:  break;
162:
163:      case 5:  break;
164:
165:      case 6:  row = st_row = iParm1;
166:              col = st_col = iParm2;
167:              end_col = st_col + iParm4;
168:              length = iParm4;
169:              last_key = get_it(option,char_ptr);
170:              break;
171:
172:      case 7:  row = st_row = iParm1;
173:              col = st_col = iParm2;
174:              end_col=st_col + iParm4;
175:              length=iParm4;
176:              last_key = get_it(option,char_ptr);
177:              break;
178:
179:      case 8:  for (ctr=0; ctr < iParm1; ctr++)
180:                   char_ptr[ctr] = '\0';
181:              break;
182:
183:      case 9:  setup_exit_keys(char_ptr,iParm1);
184:              break;
185:
186:    }      /* end of switch */
187:
188:    return(last_key);
189:
190: }    /* end of subroutine */
191:
192:
193:
194: /*---------------------------------------*
195:  *  subroutine:   get_it()              *
196:  *                                       *
197:  *  this actually gets the data once    *
```

continues

Listing 10.2. continued

```
198:  *    everything has been setup           *
199:  *------------------------------------*/
200:
201: char get_it(int option, char *str_ptr)
202: {
203:     int ins_pos;
204:     int ch;
205:     int str_ctr=0;        /* tracks current character position */
206:     int ins_on=FALSE;     /* tracks INS key being pressed */
207:     int prn_switch=FALSE;/* determines if char should be accepted */
208:     int loop_exit=FALSE;
209:     int test;
210:
211: /* --------------------------------------------------- */
212:
213:     cursor(st_row,st_col);
214:     repeat_char('_', length, undr_color_fg, undr_color_bg);
215:     write_string(str_ptr, norm_color_fg, norm_color_bg,
216:                                         st_row, st_col);
217:
218:     while (loop_exit == FALSE)
219:     {
220:       if ( ( ch=getch() ) == 0 )    /* if scan code read next byte */
221:       {
222:         ch = getch();
223:         switch ( ch )
224:           {
225:               case HOME: /* goto to begining of string */
226:                       col = st_col;
227:                       cursor(row, col);
228:                       if (ins_on == TRUE)
229:                           write_string(str_ptr, norm_color_fg,
230:                                           norm_color_bg, st_row,
231:                                           st_col);
232:                       break;
233:
234:               case END:  /*  end key  - pos cursor at end */
235:                       col = strlen(str_ptr) + st_col;
236:                       cursor(row, col);
237:                       if (ins_on == TRUE)
238:                           write_string(str_ptr, norm_color_fg,
239:                                           norm_color_bg, st_row,
240:                                           st_col);
241:                       break;
242:
243:               case DEL:  /* 1 past end of string ? */
244:                       if ( col != strlen(str_ptr) + st_col)
245:                       {
246:                               /* save current position  */
```

```
247:                        str_ctr = col;
248:                            /* if nxt pos is != null move it */
249:                        while (str_ptr[col-st_col+1] != '\0')
250:                        {
251:                                /* the value is moved over */
252:                            str_ptr[col-st_col] = str_ptr
                                [col-st_col+1];
253:                            col++;          /* next position  */
254:                        }
255:                            /* terminate end of string */
256:                        str_ptr[col-st_col] = '\0';
257:                            /* reprint string */
258:                        write_string(str_ptr, norm_color_fg,
259:                                    norm_color_bg, st_row,
260:                                    st_col);
261:                            /* Go to end of line  */
262:                        cursor(row, st_col+strlen(str_ptr));
263:                            /* Rewrite underline char */
264:                        write_char('_', undr_color_fg,
                            undr_color_bg);
265:                            /* restore cursor pos */
266:                        col = str_ctr;
267:                            /* Restore cursor position */
268:                        cursor(row,col);
269:                    }
270:                    if (ins_on == TRUE)
271:                        write_string(str_ptr,norm_color_fg,
272:                                    norm_color_bg, st_row,
273:                                    st_col);
274:                    break;
275:
276:        case INS:   if (ins_on == FALSE )
277:                    {
278:                        write_string("INS", ins_color_fg,
279:                                    ins_color_bg, ins_row,
280:                                    ins_col);
281:                        ins_on=TRUE;
282:                    }
283:                    else
284:                    {
285:                        write_string("   ", ins_color_fg,
286:                                    ins_color_bg, ins_row,
287:                                    ins_col);
288:                        write_string(str_ptr, norm_color_fg,
289:                                    norm_color_bg, st_row,
290:                                    st_col);
291:                        ins_on=FALSE;
292:                    }
293:                    break;
294:
```

continues

Listing 10.2. continued

```
295:                case LT_ARROW: if (col > st_col )
296:                               {
297:                                 cursor(row, --col);
298:                                 if (ins_on == TRUE)
299:                                   write_string(str_ptr, norm_color_fg,
300:                                               norm_color_bg, st_row,
301:                                               st_col);
302:                               }
303:                               break;
304:
305:             case RT_ARROW: if ( col < end_col &&
306:                            ((col-st_col) < strlen(str_ptr)) )
307:                            {
308:                              cursor(row, ++col);
309:                              if (ins_on == TRUE)
310:                                write_string(str_ptr, norm_color_fg,
311:                                            norm_color_bg, st_row,
312:                                            st_col);
313:                            }
314:                            break;
315:
316:          default:   loop_exit = check_list(ch);
317:                     if (ins_on == TRUE)
318:                        write_string(str_ptr, norm_color_fg,
319:                                    norm_color_bg, st_row,
320:                                    st_col);
321:                     /* key a valid exit key ?*/
322:                     if ( loop_exit == FALSE )
323:                        boop();
324:                     break;
325:
326:      }        /* end of switch  */
327:   }       /* end of if  */
328:   else
329:   {
330:      switch ( ch )         /* test for other special keys  */
331:      {
332:         case BK_SP_KEY:
333:                    if (col > st_col )
334:                    {
335:                        /* move cursor left 1 */
336:                      cursor(row, --col);
337:                        /* save cur curs pos, len determ ltr */
338:                     str_ctr = col;
339:                        /* if next pos != null move it ovr */
340:                     while (str_ptr[col-st_col+1] != '\0')
341:                     {
342:                         /* move next char over  */
```

```
343:                              str_ptr[col-st_col] = str_ptr
                                    [col-st_col+1];
344:                                  /* next position  */
345:                              col++;
346:                          }
347:                              /* End string with a null */
348:                          str_ptr[col-st_col] = '\0';
349:                          write_string(str_ptr, norm_color_fg,
350:                                        norm_color_bg, st_row,
351:                                        st_col);
352:                              /* Move cursor to end of line */
353:                          cursor(row, st_col+strlen(str_ptr));
354:                              /* Rewrite underline char */
355:                          write_char('_', undr_color_fg,
                                undr_color_bg);
356:                              /* restore current cusor pos */
357:                          col = str_ctr;
358:                              /* Restore cursor position */
359:                          cursor(row,col);
360:                      }
361:                  break;
362:
363:          default:  if (col < end_col )
364:                    {
365:                          /* get numeric input */
366:                      if ( option == 7  &&  (ch >= 48 &&
                            ch <= 57))
367:                        {
368:                          prn_switch=TRUE;
369:                        }
370:                          /* greater than space */
371:                      if ( option == 6  && ch > 31 )
372:                        {
373:                          /* get alphanumeric input */
374:                          prn_switch=TRUE;
375:                        }
376:                      if ( prn_switch==TRUE )
377:                        {
378:                          /* field not full = shift */
379:                        if(ins_on==TRUE && strlen(str_ptr)
                              <length)
380:                          {
381:                              /* assign str_ctr to the cur
                                    location */
382:                            str_ctr=strlen(str_ptr);
383:                            while (str_ctr !=col-st_col)
384:                            {
385:                              str_ptr[str_ctr] = str_ptr
                                    [str_ctr-1];
```

continues

Listing 10.2. continued

```
386:                               /* point to previous position  */
387:                          str_ctr--;
388:                      }
389:                          /* add character into string */
390:                      str_ptr[col-st_col]=ch;
391:                      write_string(str_ptr, norm_color_fg,
392:                                      norm_color_bg, st_row,
393:                                      st_col);
394:                      write_char((char)ch, high_color_fg,
395:                                           high_color_bg);
396:                      cursor(row, ++col);
397:                      prn_switch=FALSE;
398:                  }     /* end of ins_on and strlen test */
399:                  else
400:                  {
401:                      /* INS off put a char */
402:                      if (ins_on==FALSE )
403:                      {
404:                          /* add character into string */
405:                          str_ptr[col-st_col]=ch;
406:                          write_string(str_ptr, norm_color_fg,
407:                                          norm_color_bg,
408:                                          st_col);
409:                          cursor(row, ++col);
410:                          prn_switch=FALSE;
411:                      }
412:                      else
413:                      {
414:                          /* ins_on is TRUE and trying */
415:                          /* to put a char past end    */
416:                          boop();
417:                      }
418:                  }
419:              }     /* end of prn == TRUE test */
420:              else
421:              {
422:                  /* exit key? */
423:                  if((loop_exit = check_list(ch)) == FALSE)
424:                  {
425:                      /* not a valid exit key */
426:                      boop();
427:                  }
428:                  else
429:                  {
430:                      write_string(str_ptr, norm_color_fg,
431:                                      norm_color_bg, st_row,
432:                                      st_col);
433:                  }
```

```
434:                                }
435:                           }       /* end of if from (col < end_col )  */
436:                      else      /* from ( col < end_col ) */
437:                      {
438:                           /* exit key? */
439:                         if ( (loop_exit = check_list(ch)) == FALSE )
440:                         {
441:                             /* not a valid exit key */
442:                             boop();
443:                         }
444:                         else
445:                         {
446:                             write_string(str_ptr, norm_color_fg,
447:                                             norm_color_bg, st_row,
448:                                             st_col);
449:                         }
450:                      }
451:                      break;
452:
453:           }    /* end of switch */
454:         }     /* end of else */
455:      }        /* end of while loop */
456:
457:     return(ch);
458:
459: }  /* end of subroutine getline  */
460:
461: /* --------------------------------------------- *
462:  * function: check_list()                        *
463:  *                                               *
464:  * This subroutine checks the key pressed against *
465:  * a list of keys that can end the procedure.    *
466:  * It receives the key pressed and returns TRUE  *
467:  * if key is in the list, else FALSE if not in   *
468:  * list.                                         *
469:  * --------------------------------------------- */
470:
471: int check_list(char key_pressed)
472: {
473:         /* return a true or false to return_code */
474:     int return_code=FALSE;
475:     int loop_ctr = 0;
476:
477:     while ( loop_ctr <= MAX_KEYS && !return_code)
478:       if ( key_pressed == VALID_EXIT_KEYS[loop_ctr++])
479:          return_code=TRUE;
480:
481:     return(return_code);
```

continues

Listing 10.2. continued

```
482: }
483:
484: /* ----------------------------------------------- *
485:  * function: setup_exit_keys(keys_array,num)       *
486:  *                                                 *
487:  * Sets up valid exit keys in the VALID_EXIT_KEYS  *
488:  * array.                                          *
489:  *                                                 *
490:  * Enter with: - keys_array                        *
491:  *                   char array of ASCII key values *
492:  *             - num                               *
493:  *                   nbr of elements to processed  *
494:  * Returns:     Nothing                            *
495:  * ----------------------------------------------- */
496:
497: void setup_exit_keys(char *keys_array, int num)
498: {
499:    int ctr;                        /* misc counter */
500:
501:    for (ctr=0; ctr < num; ctr++)
502:    {
503:        /* load valid keys */
504:      VALID_EXIT_KEYS[ctr] = *(keys_array + ctr);
505:    }
506:
507:    while (ctr < MAX_KEYS)
508:    {
509:        /* clear unused portion */
510:      VALID_EXIT_KEYS[ctr++] = '\0';
511:    }
512: }
```

Analysis   As you can see, this is an extremely long function. Having read the material presented earlier today, you should be able to follow some of this listing. To help in your understanding of getline(), the function contains many comments. In fact, the first 75 lines of the function are dedicated to a detailed description of the parameters. If you haven't already, then you should read these comments. They include a description of what each of the parameters that is passed to getline() should be.

Lines 87 to 104 contain variables that will be used by getline(). These variables are all defined as static. This is so their values will be retained for subsequent calls to getline(). The comments within the code state what each variable is used for.

> **Note:** If you want the default values automatically set in `getline()`, you should assign the default values to the variables as they are declared. For example, line 87 would become:
>
> ```
> static int norm_color_fg = WHITE;
> ```

Lines 110 to 113 are the last of the set-up before starting the `getline()` function. These lines declare the prototypes to the subroutines used by `getline()`. As you can see, the `getline()` function has three subroutines or functions that it uses.

Lines 119 to 190 contain `getline()`. This portion of the `getline()` process is straightforward. Line 125 ensures that the array that contains the exit keys (or will contain them if they aren't yet set up) ends with a null value. Line 127 then calls a switch statement. The program switches based on the option that was passed.

If the option was zero, the defaults will be set. The defaults include all of the colors, an exit key (line 134), and a position for the "INS" message (lines 139 and 140). The colors that have been set here—and that are stated in the comments in lines 14 to 24— are the defaults that I have choosen. The values you choose for your default values should be those that you will use most often. You can always change these values using `getline()`'s other options.

Options 1, 2, and 3 are set in lines 143 to 159. These options set different sets of the variables. By looking at each of these options, you'll see which parameters are translated to which variables.

Options 4 and 5 in lines 161 and 163 don't exist. These are left for future growth. If you later decide to expand on `getline()`, these two values are available for options.

Options 6 and 7 in lines 165 to 170 and 172 to 177 are identical. These functions each set a row and column value to the `iParm1` and `iParm2` parameters. Also set are `st_row` and `st_col` which are static constants used to retain the initial row and column positions. Lines 167 and 174 calcuate the ending column, `end_col`, of the information being input. Each of these two cases ends with a call to `get_it()` which does the work of retrieving the input information for `getline()`.

Option 8 is covered in lines 179 to 181. This case is easy to follow. A `for` loop is used to set each position of the passed string, `char_ptr`, to null values.

Option 9 in lines 183 and 184 is the final option. This option simply calls the `setup_exit_keys()` subroutine which is covered later today.

The *get_it()* Subroutine

The get_it() function is used to get both numeric and alphanumeric values. This function continues from line 201 through line 459. Although this function is very long, it's easy to follow because it's broken into segments by case statements.

Before starting into its main loop, the get_it() function sets up a few keys. In addition, line 213 sets the cursor to the starting position that was set in the getline() function. Line 214 then sets the underscore on the screen using the repeat_char() function. Line 215 writes the value in the string that may have been initially passed to getline() and forwarded to get_it(). Line 218 then begins a large while loop.

The while loop in line 218 begins the process of getting each character one at a time. Line 220 checks to see if the first character retrieved with getch() is a 0. If it is, the key entered is a scan code. A *scan code* is part of an extended key such as the home key, the end key, or the delete key. If a scan code is read, a second key is read to get the second half of the scan code. The second character contains a key value that is used in a switch statement in lines 225 to 326. The functions for each of the different keys is detailed later today.

If the initial character read in line 222 was not equal to 0, then the else statement in line 328 is executed. In this case, the character is a normal ASCII character. Included with the ASCII characters are characters such as the backspace key. Any ASCII characters that need special processing are checked first. For getline(), only the backspace character, BK_SP_KEY, needs to be handled specially. (All the other special exit keys are scan codes handled by the if in line 220.)

Line 363 is the default case for ASCII characters. It's here that getline() will determine whether the appropriate key has been entered.

Getting the Characters (Lines 363 to 451)

In lines 366 to 375, the character entered is compared with ASCII values to determine if it is valid based on the getline() option. For option 7, the character must be an ASCII value from 48 to 57 (line 366). For option 6, the character entered must be greater than 31. If the character read fits either of these options, then the prn_switch is set to TRUE.

If the character passed (the prn_switch was set to TRUE), then lines 364 to 435 are executed. Line 379 then checks to see if the insert key is on. If it is, and if the length of the string is less than the total length of the field being entered, then the character is added to the string. Because the character could be in the middle of the string, the

rest of the string is adjusted to the right (lines 383 to 388). Line 391 then redisplays the updated string to ensure that it's displayed on the screen properly. Because the insert key is on, the added character should be highlighted. This is done in line 394 before the cursor is adjusted. If the insert key was off, or if the character is being set in a field that is already full, then the else in lines 399 to 417 is executed. If the insert key is off, then the character is added to the string at the current position (line 405), the string is rewritten to ensure that it is displayed properly (line 406), and the cursor is repositioned (line 409). If the insert key is on and the string is full, then the computer beeps with the boop() function, which is covered later today.

If the character entered didn't meet the valid characters for options 6 or 7, then the else statement in line 420 is executed. In this else, the character entered is checked to see if it is actually an exit key. This is accomplished by using the check_list() function. The check_list() function in lines 461 to 482 simply loops through the exit key array to see if a match is found. If a match is found, a code of TRUE is returned in line 481. If the key isn't a valid exit key, the value of FALSE is returned. This value of FALSE causes the get_it() function in line 426 to execute boop(), which beeps the computer. This is done because the character entered wasn't valid for the option, nor was it an exit key. If the key was a valid exit key, then line 430 reprints the string to the screen, and the loop_exit causes the looping to end along with getline().

The Backspace Character (Lines 332 to 361)

The backspace character is a special case that is handled in lines 332 to 361. If the current position isn't the first position, then the code for the backspace character is entered in lines 335 to 359. The code in these lines starts by moving the cursor to the left one column (line 336). It then shifts each character one space to the left to effectively delete the character that was backspaced over. Line 349 then rewrites the string to the screen to ensure that it is displayed correctly. Because this moving of the characters to the left will mess up the underlines that mark the end of the field, lines 353 to 356 redraw them.

The Delete Key (Lines 243 to 274)

The delete key (DEL) works nearly identically to the backspace character. The main difference is the cursor isn't moved to the left like the backspace. Instead, the function shifts the characters starting to the right of the cursor. Each is shifted one space to the left. The string is then rewritten, and the underscores for the field redrawn.

The Home Key (Lines 225 to 232)

The home key (HOME) is much easier to follow than the delete or backspace key. The home key simply adjusts the cursor position to the starting column. If the insert character is on, the string is redrawn to ensure it is displayed correctly.

The End Key (Lines 234 to 241)

The end key (END) works just like the home key. Instead of moving the cursor to the beginning of the string, it is moved to the end of the entered characters.

The Insert Key (Lines 276 to 293)

The insert key (INS) is different from the others. If the insert key wasn't already on, ins_on is equal to FALSE, then the "INS" string is written in the lower-right corner of the string and ins_on is set to TRUE. If the insert key was on, then a blank string is written over the "INS" that is in the lower-right corner and the flag is set to FALSE. This flag was used when entering a key earlier.

The Left Arrow (Lines 295 to 303)

If the cursor isn't already at the beginning of the field being entered, the left arrow key (LT_ARROW) executes lines 297 to 302. The left arrow key adjusts the cursor by subtracting one from the column, and then redisplaying it. This, in effect, moves the cursor one space to the left. If the insert key was on, then the string is redisplayed to ensure that it is correct on the screen.

The Right Arrow (Lines 305 to 314)

The right arrow (RT_ARROW) does just the opposite of the left arrow. In line 305, it first checks to see if the cursor is already at the end of the string. If it isn't, then one is added to the column, and the cursor is redisplayed. This has the effect of moving the cursor one space to the right.

The Default Scan Key

If the scan key entered wasn't one of the designated keys, then the default case is executed in lines 316 to 324. The default case checks to see if the entered key is an exit key (line 316). If it is, then the loop_exit flag is set. After this test, the string is redisplayed in line 318 to ensure that it is properly presented on the screen. If an exit key wasn't entered in this default case, then boop() beeps the computer in line 323 to signal that a bad key was entered.

The *setup_exit_keys()* Subroutine

The setup_exit_keys() function is all that is left to the getline() function. This function initializes the VALID_EXIT_KEYS array to the keys provided by the calling program. Each key in the array passed by the calling program is placed in the array. Any array positions that aren't used are then filled with null values (lines 507 to 511).

The *boop()* Function

The boop() function is used by getline() to cause the computer's speaker to beep. This function, which is presented in Listing 10.3, is also useful at other times, and therefore, makes a good addition to your TYAC.LIB library.

 Listing 10.3 BOOP.C. The boop() function.

```
1:    * Program: boop.c
2:    * Authors: Bradley L. Jones
3:    *          Gregory L. Guntle
4:    *
5:    * Purpose: Toggles the speaker to produce a sound.  This
6:    *          sound is used for notifying the user of an
7:    *          invalid key pressed.
8:    *
9:    * Note:    This is not an ANSI compatible function. When
10:   *          compiled, you may receive warnings. The value
11:   *          of result is not used; however, it is needed
12:   *          in order to compiler on some computers.
13:   *------------------------------------------------------------*/
14:
15:   #include <conio.h>
16:   #include "tyac.h"
17:
18:   #define CLOCKFREQ    1193180L              /* Timer frequency */
19:   #define SPKRMODE     0xB6                  /* Set timer for speaker */
20:   #define T_MODEPORT   0x43                  /* Timer-mode port */
21:   #define FREQPORT     0x42                  /* Frequency control port */
22:   #define FREQ0        0x12c                 /* A frequency */
23:   #define DIV0         CLOCKFREQ / FREQ0 /* Set frequency to use */
24:   #define CLICK        .15                   /* Tone duration */
25:
26:   #define SPKRPORT     0x61                  /* Speaker port */
27:   #define SPKRON       0x03                  /* On bits for speaker */
28:
29:
30:   void boop()
```

continues

Listing 10.3. continued

```
31: {
32:     unsigned char port0;
33:     unsigned int div0  = DIV0*2;
34:     float delay = CLICK;
35:     int result;
36:
37:     result = outp(T_MODEPORT, SPKRMODE);   /* setup timer */
38:     port0 = inp(SPKRPORT);                  /* get old port setting */
39:
40:     result = outp(FREQPORT, (div0 & 0xFF));    /* send low byte */
41:     result = outp(FREQPORT, (div0 >> 8));      /* send high byte */
42:     result = outp(SPKRPORT, (port0 ¦ SPKRON)); /* turn on speaker */
43:
44:     waitsec(delay);                            /* wait */
45:
46:     result = outp(SPKRPORT, port0);   /* restore original setting */
47: }
```

 This function uses the `outp()` and `inp()` functions to send information to the speaker port. These aren't ANSI-compatible functions. Because of this, the listing may not be compatible with all compilers.

Lines 18 to 27 define several constants that are then used in the actual code. The `boop()` function creates a beep by writing information directly to the speaker port. Before doing so, line 38 saves the original port setting. Line 46 then restores the settings.

Lines 41 and 42 send the values to the port. Line 42 then turns on the speaker. The speaker will then remain on until turned off. The speaker is turned off when the original setting is restored. To allow the beep to last long enough to be heard, the program is paused using the `waitsec()` function in line 44. The `waitsec()` function is a new function that is covered next.

The *waitsec()* Function

The `waitsec()` function causes the computer to pause for a specified period of time, which is defined in seconds. Most people choose to use a looping function to pause the computer. This may be coded as follows:

```
for( ctr = 0; ctr < 10000; ctr++ ) { /* pausing */ };
```

This will cause the computer to pause for different lengths of time depending on how fast the computer can process the `for` loop. This can cause a problem because you can never be sure how long the loop will last. The waitsec() function gets around this problem. Listing 10.4 presents the waitsec() function.

Listing 10.4. WAITSEC.C. The waitsec() function.

```
1:  /* Program:   waitsec.c
2:   * Authors:   Bradley L. Jones
3:   *            Gregory L. Guntle
4:   *
5:   * Purpose:   Causes the program to wait a number of seconds.
6:   *
7:   * Enter with: seconds - Number of seconds to pause program.
8:   *
9:   * Returns    : N/A
10:  * ------------------------------------------------------- */
11:
12: void waitsec( double secs )
13: {
14:     unsigned long count0, count;
15:
16:     count0 = get_timer_ticks();
17:     count = count0 + secs * 18.2;
18:     while ( get_timer_ticks() < count );
19:
20: }
```

The waitsec() function uses the computer's timer to determine exactly how much time has passed. The function starts by getting the number of timer ticks using the get_timer_ticks() function. Listing 10.5 will present the get_timer_ticks() function. Once the timer tick count is obtained, it is used as a base to determine at what number the time will be up. In a second, 18.2 ticks will occur. By taking 18.2 times the number of seconds requested to wait, you determine the total number of ticks that must occur. This calculated number is added to the original number that was received by the call to get_timer_ticks() (line 17). The program is then put into a while loop that continuously calls the get_timer_ticks() function until the returned value is a number greater than the number that was calculated. Once the appropriate number of ticks has passed, the function returns.

The *get_timer_ticks()* Function

The get_timer_ticks() function is a new BIOS function. As stated in the analysis of the waitsec() function, the get_timer_ticks() function simply returns the computer's current tick counter value. Listing 10.5 presents this function.

Listing 10.5. GETTICKS.C. The `get_timer_ticks()` function.

```
 1: /* Program : getticks.c
 2:  * Authors : Bradley L. Jones
 3:  *           Gregory L. Guntle
 4:  *
 5:  * Purpose   : Returns the number of clock ticks.
 6:  *
 7:  * Function  : get_time_ticks()
 8:  *
 9:  * Enter with: N/A
10:  *
11:  * Returns   : Number of clock ticks that has elapsed.
12:  *             This is a long value.
13:  * -------------------------------------------------------- */
14:
15: #include <dos.h>
16:
17: #define INT_TIME  0x1A
18:
19: long get_timer_ticks()
20: {
21:    union REGS inregs;
22:    long tc;
23:
24:    inregs.h.ah = 0;
25:    int86(INT_TIME, &inregs, &inregs);
26:    tc = ((long) inregs.x.cx) << 16;  /* get high bytes */
27:    tc += inregs.x.dx;                /* add low bytes */
28:    return(tc);
29: }
```

 There isn't a lot to analyze about this listing. Interrupt 0x1Ah is used to get the current clock tick count. The values returned in the x.cx and x.dx registers are used to determine the exact number of ticks. Line 28 then returns this value.

 Note: The new functions that you have created today should be added to your TYAC.LIB library. This library will be used in creating the programs throughout the rest of this book.

Using *getline()*

Now, you are ready to use getline() in a program. Listing 10.6 presents a very simple program that uses the getline() function. This program in Listing 10.6 will allow a string to be entered.

 Listing 10.6. GL_TEST.C using the getline() function.

```
1:  /* Program:  gl_test.c
2:   * Author:   Bradley L. Jones
3:   *           Gregory L. Guntle
4:   * Purpose:  Demonstrate the getline function.
5:   *=========================================================*/
6:
7:  #include <stdio.h>
8:  #include "tyac.h"
9:
10: int main()
11: {
12:     char ch;
13:     char strng[40];
14:     int i;
15:     char exit_keys[] = {ESC_KEY, F1, F10, CR_KEY};
16:
17:             /* Initialize getline w/defaults */
18:     ch = getline(0,0,0,0,0,0,0);
19:             /* Clear the array to hold input */
20:     ch = getline(8,0,40,0,0,0,strng);
21:             /* Load valid exit keys */
22:     ch = getline(9,0,4,0,0,0,exit_keys);
23:
24:     write_string("Enter string:", LIGHTBLUE, BLACK, 10, 5 );
25:     ch = getline(6,0,10,20,0,20,strng);  /* Get line */
26:
27:     printf("\n\nThe string that was entered = %s\n",strng);
28:     printf("The key used to exit getline is: ");
29:     switch( ch )
30:     {
31:         case ESC_KEY:  printf("Esc key\n");
32:                        break;
33:         case F1:       printf("F1 key \n");
34:                        break;
35:         case F10:      printf("F10 key\n");
36:                        break;
37:         case CR_KEY:   printf("CR key\n");
38:                        break;
39:         default:       printf("Unknown\n");
40:                        break;
```

continues

Listing 10.6. continued

```
41:         }
42:
43:         return 0;
44: }
```

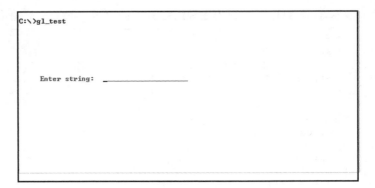

```
C:\>gl_test



       Enter string:  _____
```

This is a short program that does a lot of work by using the getline() function. It's a good program for showing just how the getline() function and its options should be used. Lines 7 and 8 include the appropriate header files. The TYAC.H header file should be the same as the one presented in Listing 10.1.

The main part of the program starts in line 10 where several variables are declared. In line 15, the character array, exit_keys is declared and initialized to four keys. The constants defined in the TYAC.H header file are used as the values for the exit keys. In your programs, you should create a similar character array that contains the keys that will stop entry of information. From line 15, you can see that the escape key, the F1 function key, the F10 function key, and the carriage-return (or enter) key will all stop entry of information.

Line 18 presents the first call to getline(). The first parameter is the option parameter. In the case of line 18, option 0 is being called. Option 0 sets the default colors and values for getline(). Line 20 calls getline() a second time. In Line 20, option 8 is used. Option 8 clears the field passed in the last parameter to null values. In this case, the strng character array is being set to nulls to ensure that there is no bad data in it. It's a good practice to always initialize your data fields so that you are sure what is in them.

Line 22 calls the getline() function a third time. With this call, option 9 is used. This sets up the option keys that were defined in the last parameter, exit_keys. Once this call is made, you have set up `getline()` for the rest of the program. In this case, that is only one more call to `getline()`; however, generally, you will be calling `getline()` with options 6 or 7 several times after these initial setup calls.

Line 24 prints a prompt on the screen so that the user will know what to enter. This prompt can be seen in the output. Line 25 then calls `getline()` with option 6. Option 6 enables the user to enter a string. In this case, the string will be displayed at row 10 and column 20. The string can be up to 20 characters long. It will be stored in `strng`. All this was stated in the call to `getline()` on line 25.

With the call in line 25, `getline()` does its job of enabling the user to input data. If the insert key is pressed, then the "INS" message will be toggled on and off. In addition, if insert is on, then the inserted character will be highlighted. Once the user presses one of the exit keys, `getline()` returns control to the key pressed. The rest of this program prints what was entered. In addition, lines 29 to 41 display which exit key was used to exit.

You should take time to play with this program and the other `getline()` options. Practice setting up different colors and different exit keys. The `getline()` function will be a critical function in creating the applications later in this book.

DO	**DON'T**

DO understand the `getline()` function. It will be used intensively on Day 13.

DO initialize data fields if you are unsure what is in them. This way you can be certain.

DON'T forget to set up your exit keys when using the `getline()` function. You need to define what values can be used to exit the function.

Summary

Today's materials present a function that will replace `gets()` and `scanf()` in getting data from the screen. This function, called `getline()`, will provide you with much more functionality than the functions generally provided. The `getline()` function will allow text or numeric information to be entered. In addition it will allow for color and cursor placement. In addition to the `getline()` function, several other functions

are presented. These functions are boop(), waitsec(), and get_timer_ticks(). These functions are used by getline() and can also be used by your other functions.

Q&A

Q Why can't gets() be used instead of getline() for reading character strings?

A gets() does not enable you to have control over the color or position of the text being entered. You could use a function such as cursor() to place the prompt in the correct location before reading; however, you'll still have problems. The additional problem is that gets() won't limit the length of the string that you are reading. If you have a last name field that is only 15 characters, getline() will enable you to read only 15 characters. This is not true with gets().

Q Why can't scanf() be used instead of getline() for reading character strings?

A scanf() is another good function to use; however, like gets(), it isn't as full-featured as getline(). (See the answer to the previous question.)

Workshop

The Workshop provides quiz questions to help you solidify your understanding of the material covered and exercises to provide you with experience in using what you've learned.

Quiz

1. What is the purpose of getline()?

2. What does boop() do?

3. What is a reason for using boop()?

4. What is the advantage of waitsec() over the pause() function that you learned on Day 9?

5. How do you set the getline() input text color to yellow on red?

6. What are the default colors for `getline()`?

7. What is the difference between `getline()`'s option 6 and option 7?

Exercises

1. Add the functions that you created today to your TYAC.LIB if you have not done so already. The functions from today are:

   `getline()`

   `boop()`

   `waitsec()`

   `get_timer_ticks()`

Note: `get_it()` and `setup_exit_keys()` are a part of `getline()` so they don't need to be added on their own.

2. **BUG BUSTER:** What, if anything, is wrong with the following:

```
#include <stdio.h>
#include "tyac.h"

int main()
{
    char ch;
    char strng[40];

    ch = getline(0,0,0,0,0,0,0);
    ch = getline(8,0,40,0,0,0,strng);
    write_string("Last name:", LIGHTBLUE, BLACK, 10, 8 );
    ch = getline(6,0,10,20,0,20,strng);  /* Get line */

    return 0;
}
```

3. Use the functions that you have learned to create a box on the screen. In the box, display a message and ask the user to enter Y or N. Use the `getline()` function to get the Y or N.

4. Modify Exercise 3 to beep if a wrong character is entered.

5. **ON YOUR OWN:** Use the `getline()` function to create a data entry screen. Use the functions that you have used in the previous chapters also.

Note: Day 13 does just this! It uses `getline()` and most of the other functions presented so far to create an entry and edit screen.

Building a
Routine Library

WEEK
2

On Day 10, you were presented with a bunch of new functions. You'll use many of these throughout the rest of the book. In addition to the functions presented on Day 10, you'll also need to have several other functions available. Today you will:

☐ Learn about several functions that are important when creating applications.

☐ Create several functions, among them:

    ☐ Hide the cursor

    ☐ Clear the screen (in color)

    ☐ Display a grid (great for shadows)

☐ Learn how to overwrite and restore a screen.

Some Important Issues

When you are creating applications, there are several functions that are often not thought of. Many of these functions can be easy to create. Today, you'll be presented with a few of these functions so that you can add them to your TYAC.LIB library. The first two files presented are cursor_on() and cursor_off().

The *cursor_off()* Function

The cursor_off() function enables you to hide the cursor. There are several times in running an application when the user is not entering data. During these times, the cursor can become a nuisance. The cursor_off() function does just what its name implies. It turns the cursor off.

Listing 11.1. CURSOFF.C. The cursor_off() function.

```
 1:  /* -------------------------------------------------------
 2:   * Program: CURSOFF.C
 3:   * Authors: Bradley L. Jones
 4:   *          Gregory L. Guntle
 5:   *
 6:   * Purpose: Turns the cursor off.
 7:   *
 8:   * Enter with: N/A
 9:   *
10:   * Returns:
11:   *
12:   * ------------------------------------------------------- */
13:
```

```
14:   #include <dos.h>
15:   #include "tyac.h"
16:
17:
18:   void cursor_off()
19:   {
20:      union REGS inreg, outreg;          /* Assembly Registers */
21:      inreg.h.ah = 1;                    /* int 10h function 1 */
22:      inreg.x.cx = 0x0F00;               /* Wrap cursor around to
23:                                             turn it off */
24:      int86(BIOS_VIDEO, &inreg, &outreg);  /* BIOS Call */
25:   }
```

As you can see, Listing 11.1 presents the cursor_off() function, which is very short. This is a BIOS function similar to those that you have seen before. In this function, the ah register is set to function 1 (line 21). The BIOS video interrupt is then called. The BIOS interrupt is interrupt 0x10h, which is defined in the TYAC.H header file.

The *cursor_on()* Function

Once you turn the cursor off, it remains off until you turn it on again. You'll need the cursor back on when you are ready to have the user input data. You'll also want to make sure that if the cursor is turned off, you turn in back on before you exit your program. Listing 11.2 presents cursor_on(), which is a counter function to the cursor_off() function.

Warning: If you turn the cursor off and then exit the program, the cursor may remain off.

Listing 11.2. CURSON.C. The cursor_on() function.

```
1:   /* -------------------------------------------------------
2:    * Program: CURSON.C
3:    * Authors: Bradley L. Jones
4:    *          Gregory L. Guntle
5:    *
6:    * Purpose: Turns the cursor on.
7:    *
8:    * Enter with:
```

continues

Listing 11.2. continued

```
 9:     *
10:     * Returns:
11:     *
12:     * -------------------------------------------------------*/
13:
14:    #include <dos.h>
15:    #include "tyac.h"
16:
17:
18:    void cursor_on()
19:    {
20:       union REGS inreg, outreg;
21:       inreg.h.ah = 1;                /* int 10h function 1 */
22:       inreg.x.cx = 0x0607;           /* Cursor size for CGA/VGA */
23:       int86(BIOS_VIDEO, &inreg, &outreg);  /* BIOS call */
24:    }
```

This function is almost identical to the `cursor_off()` function. The difference is that the value in the `x.cx` register is set to 0x0607. This turns on a cursor that is appropriate for most monitors.

Now that you have functions that can turn a cursor off and on, you are probably interested in seeing them in action. Listing 11.3 presents a small program that uses the TYAC.LIB library. You should go ahead and compile the cursor functions and add them to your library. You should also include prototypes in the TYAC.H header file.

Type **Listing 11.3. LIST1103.C. Using the cursor functions.**

```
 1:    /*=========================================================
 2:     * Filename: LIST1103.c
 3:     *
 4:     * Author:    Bradley L. Jones
 5:     *            Gregory L. Guntle
 6:     *
 7:     * Purpose:  Demonstrate the cursor on and off functions.
 8:     *=========================================================*/
 9:
10:    #include <stdio.h>
11:    #include <conio.h>              /* not an ANSI header, for getch() */
12:    #include "tyac.h"
13:
14:    void main(void)
```

```
15:  {
16:      cursor_off();
17:
18:      box(12, 14, 20, 60, SINGLE_BOX, FILL_BOX, YELLOW, BLUE );
19:
20:      write_string( "Press any key to continue...",
21:                    YELLOW, BLUE, 13, 23 );
22:
23:      getch();
24:      cursor_on();
25:  }
```

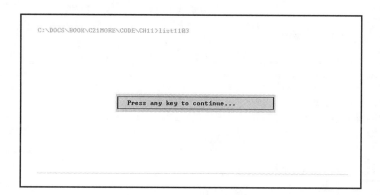

Output

```
C:\DOCS\BOOK\C21MORE\CODE\CH11>list1103




                            Press any key to continue...

```

11

Analysis

This program displays a box on the screen with a message in it. Line 18 uses the box() function followed in line 20 by the write_string() function. Before setting up this box, line 16 calls the cursor_off() function. This function could have been called at any time before line 23. In line 23, the program pauses with a call to getch(), which waits for any character to be entered. When a key is pressed, the cursor_on() function returns the cursor.

If the cursor had not been turned off, it would be seen flashing on the screen when this box is displayed. You can see this by commenting out line 16. Another good experiment to try is to uncomment line 16 and then comment out line 24. This will cause the cursor to not be turned back on when the program exits. By observing each of these scenarios, you should begin to understand the importance of making sure you know the condition of the cursor—either on or off.

Clearing the Screen

Clearing the screen can be very important. Most programs that work with the screen will start by clearing the screen. You can never be sure about what is on the screen when

you first start a program. Listing 11.4 presents a function that will effectively clear the screen. In addition to removing everything on the screen, this function enables you to state what colors the screen should be cleared to.

Listing 11.4. CLEARSCN.C. The `clear_screen()` function.

```
1:  /* Program: CLRSCRN.C
2:   * Author:  Bradley L. Jones
3:   *          Gregory L. Guntle
4:   * Purpose: Function to clear the entire screen
5:   *          Borland offers a clrscr() function.
6:   *-------------------------------------------------------
7:   * Parameters:
8:   *          fcolor,
9:   *          bcolor          colors for clearing screen
10:  *=======================================================*/
11:
12: #include <dos.h>
13: #include "tyac.h"
14:
15: void clear_screen(int fcolor, int bcolor)
16: {
17:     union REGS irreg;
18:
19:     ireg.h.ah = SCROLL_UP;
20:     ireg.h.al = 0;          /* Clear entire screen area */
21:     ireg.h.ch = 0;
22:     ireg.h.cl = 0;
23:     ireg.h.dh = 24;
24:     ireg.h.dl = 79;
25:     ireg.h.bh = (bcolor <<4) ¦ fcolor;
26:
27:     int86( BIOS_VIDEO, &ireg, &ireg );
28: }
```

This function provides a means to clear the screen. This is done by scrolling the information off of the screen; this is a common practice. As you can see, this function enables you to set the foreground and background colors.

If you are using the Borland compiler, you have the option of using a different function. Borland provides a function called `clrscr()`, which clears the screen

without the option of setting the colors. You should remember that this is a Borland-specific function and, as a result, may not be portable.

Listing 11.5 demonstrates clearing the screen. This listing enables you to clear the screen several times before exiting.

 Listing 11.5. TESTCLR.C. Test the `clear_screen()` function.

```
 1:  /* Program:   testclr.c
 2:   * Author:    Bradley L. Jones
 3:   *            Gregory L. Guntle
 4:   * Purpose:   Demonstrate the clear_screen function.
 5:   *=========================================================*/
 6:
 7:  #include <stdio.h>
 8:  #include <conio.h>          /* not an ANSI header, for getch() */
 9:  #include "tyac.h"
10:
11:  void main(void)
12:  {
13:     int  ctr = 0;
14:     char buffer[40];
15:
16:     cursor_off();
17:
18:     for( ctr = 0; ctr < 16; ctr++ )
19:     {
20:        clear_screen( GREEN, ctr );
21:
22:        box(11, 14, 20, 60, SINGLE_BOX, FILL_BOX, YELLOW, BLUE);
23:
24:        sprintf( buffer, "Trying background number %d of 16",
25:                                                    ctr+1);
26:        write_string( buffer, YELLOW, BLUE, 12, 23 );
27:        write_string( "Press any key to continue...",
28:                              YELLOW, BLUE, 13, 23 );
29:
30:        getch();
31:     }
32:
33:     clear_screen( GREEN, BLACK );
34:     cursor_on();
35:  }
```

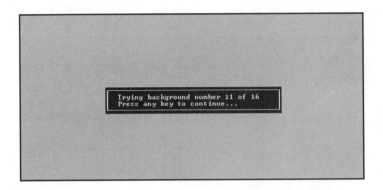

This program enables you to see the different colors that the background can be cleared to. As you can see, the cursor_on() and cursor_off() functions are used to turn the cursor off at the beginning of the listing and then back on at the end of the listing.

The for loop, which makes up the bulk of this program (lines 18 to 31), displays the counter number, ctr, in a message box. Line 24 formats this counter number into a descriptive message using sprintf(). The sprintf() function is a standard ANSI function that enables you to format information into a string. Before formatting buffer, line 22 displays a box similar to the box in Listing 11.3. Once the box is displayed with its message, the program pauses and waits for the user to enter a key. When a character is pressed, the for loop cycles through to the next counter value. This continues for 16 iterations. Line 33 clears the screen one last time before restoring the cursor and exiting.

The *grid()* Function

There are times when you'll want to clear the screen to a textured background. There are also times when you'll want to create a shadow that is somewhat different than just a box. Listing 11.6 presents a function called grid() that enables you to display a box created with one of the ASCII grid characters.

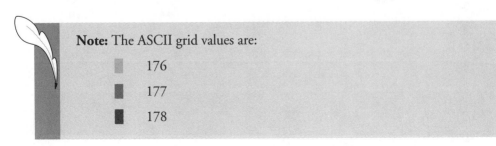

Note: The ASCII grid values are:

176

177

178

Listing 11.6. GRID.C. The `grid()` function.

```
 1:  /* Program: GRID.C
 2:   * Authors: Bradley L. Jones
 3:   *          Gregory L. Guntle
 4:   *
 5:   * Purpose: When passed the parameter list it displays
 6:   *          a grid background using BIOS.
 7:   *
 8:   * Enter with: start_row, end_row (0-24)
 9:   *             start_col, end_col (0-79)
10:   *             fcolor, bcolor
11:   *             gtype
12:   * ------------------------------------------------------*/
13:
14:  #include <dos.h>
15:  #include "tyac.h"
16:
17:  void grid( int start_row, int end_row,
18:             int start_col, int end_col,
19:             int fcolor,    int bcolor, int gtype)
20:  {
21:     int row, col;
22:
23:     /*   grid types  */
24:     static unsigned char GRID_1[1] = "▒"; /* ASCII value 176 */
25:     static unsigned char GRID_2[1] = "▓"; /* ASCII value 177 */
26:     static unsigned char GRID_3[1] = "█"; /* ASCII value 178 */
27:     static unsigned char *GRID;
28:
29:     switch (gtype)
30:     {
31:       case 1:   GRID = GRID_1;
32:                 break;
33:
34:       case 2:   GRID = GRID_2;
35:                 break;
36:
37:       case 3:   GRID = GRID_3;
38:                 break;
39:     }
40:
41:     for (row=start_row; row < end_row+1; row++)
42:     {
43:         for ( col=start_col; col < end_col+1; col++)
44:         {
45:             cursor(row,col);
46:             write_char( (char)*GRID, fcolor, bcolor );
47:         }
48:     }
49:  }
```

The grid function can be added to your TYAC.LIB library along with all the other functions. In addition, you should add an appropriate prototype to your TYAC.H header file.

Line 17 begins the grid() function. As you can see, there are several parameters being passed. The starting row and column, along with the ending row and column, are passed in the same manner as they were in the box() function. The foreground and background colors are also passed so that the color of the grid is able to be customized. The final parameter, gtype, is used to determine which ASCII grid character is used.

Line 21 declares two temporary variables, row and col, that will be used later in the function to display the grid characters. Lines 24 to 27 set up the three different grid characters. Line 28 contains a pointer that will be used in lines 29 to 39 to point to the appropriate character based on the value passed in gtype. If gtype contains a 1, then the GRID_1 character will be used. If gtype contains a 2 or 3, then GRID_2 or GRID_3 will be used. The pointer from line 28 will be set to point at the appropriate character.

Lines 41 to 49 contain two nested for loops that draw the grid character on the screen. Using the for loops, the row and column values are incremented and a character is written using write_char(). When the for loops are completed, the grid is drawn.

Listing 11.3 uses each of the three grid types. The grid() function is called three times displaying boxes with each of the different grids.

 Listing 11.7. TESTGRID.C. Testing the grid() function.

```
1:  /* Program:   testgrid.c
2:   * Author:    Bradley L. Jones
3:   *            Gregory L. Guntle
4:   * Purpose:   Demonstrate the grid function.
5:   *=========================================================*/
6:
7:  #include "tyac.h"
8:
9:  int main( void )
10: {
11:     grid(4,10,3,20,RED,GREEN,1);
12:     grid(10,20,20,40,WHITE, BLUE,2);
13:     grid(15,20,15,25,BRIGHTWHITE,CYAN,3);
14:
15:     return 0;
16: }
```

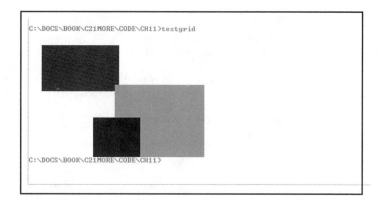

 This listing is as straightforward as they can come. The grid() function is called three times. You should notice that different parameters are passed that modify the grids displayed. In addition to different grid styles, the location, size, and colors also vary in each of the three calls.

Saving and Restoring the Screen

It's quite useful when you can place items on the screen and then remove them without overwriting the underlying information. For example, if you use the box() function to place a box with a message on the screen, you overwrite what was underneath. You must redraw the screen to restore the lost information. By saving off a copy of the screen, or a copy of the portion of the screen that will be overwritten, you can then simply restore it when you are done.

To help you understand this, an example will be presented in Listing 11.10, but you first need to see the save_screen_area() function in Listing 11.8 and the restore_screen_area() function in Listing 11.9.

Type **Listing 11.8. SAVESCRN.C. Saving a portion of the screen.**

```
1:  /* Program: SAVESCRN.C
2:   *
3:   * Authors: Bradley L. Jones
4:   *          Gregory L. Guntle
5:   *
```

continues

Listing 11.8. continued

```
 6:    * Purpose: Saves the information that is on the screen
 7:    *           which is defined within a row/col area.
 8:    *
 9:    * Function: save_screen_area(int start_row, int end_row,
10:    *                            int start_col, int end_col)
11:    *
12:    * Enter with: start_row  (0-24)
13:    *             end_row    (0-24)
14:    *             start_col  (0-79)
15:    *             end_col    (0-79)
16:    *
17:    * Returns:  Address to the memory location where screen info
18:    *           has been saved
19:    * ------------------------------------------------------------ */
20:
21:    #include <dos.h>
22:    #include "tyac.h"
23:    #include <stdlib.h>
24:    #include <stdio.h>
25:
26:    #define READ_CHAR_ATTR   0x08
27:
28:    char *save_screen_area(int start_row, int end_row,
29:                           int start_col, int end_col)
30:    {
31:        char *screen_buffer;
32:        union REGS inregs, outregs;
33:
34:        int total_space;        /* Holds space requirements */
35:        int row = start_row;  /* Used to loop through row/cols */
36:        int col;
37:        int ctr;                /* offset ctr for info in buffer */
38:        int trow, tcol, page, cur_st, cur_end;  /* Hold curs info */
39:
40:            /* Page is critical */
41:        get_cursor( &trow, &tcol, &page, &cur_st, &cur_end);
42:
43:            /* Determine amount of space for holding the area */
44:        total_space =
45:            (((end_row-start_row+1)*(end_col-start_col+1)) * 2);
46:
47:        total_space+=5;   /* Hold row/col/page info at beginning */
48:
49:        screen_buffer = (char *)malloc(total_space);
50:        if (!screen_buffer)
51:        {
52:          printf("Unable to allocate memory!\n");
53:          exit(1);
54:        }
```

```
55:
56:        /* Save screen area position */
57:        *(screen_buffer+0) = (char) start_row;
58:        *(screen_buffer+1) = (char) end_row;
59:        *(screen_buffer+2) = (char) start_col;
60:        *(screen_buffer+3) = (char) end_col;
61:        *(screen_buffer+4) = (char) page;
62:
63:        /* Save the current info row by row */
64:        ctr = 5;
65:
66:        while (row <= end_row)
67:        {
68:          col = start_col;              /* Reset col pos */
69:          while (col <= end_col)
70:          {
71:              /* Position cursor */
72:              cursor( row, col );
73:              inregs.h.ah = READ_CHAR_ATTR;
74:              inregs.h.bh = page;
75:              int86(BIOS_VIDEO, &inregs, &outregs);
76:
77:                  /* Save character */
78:              *(screen_buffer+ctr++) = (char )outregs.h.al;
79:                  /* Save attribute */
80:              *(screen_buffer+ctr++) = (char )outregs.h.ah;
81:
82:              col++;  /* next col */
83:          }
84:          row++;    /* Next row */
85:        }
86:
87:        /* Address where screen area saved */
88:        return(screen_buffer);
89:    }
```

Analysis   The first thing you should notice about this function is the comments, which describe what is going to happen in the save_screen_area(). The parameters that are received in line 28 are discussed in lines 12 to 15 of the comments. These parameters are the starting row, start_row, the ending row, end_row, the starting column, start_col, and the ending column, end_col. These define a rectangular area on the screen that will be saved. This can be the entire screen or any portion of it.

Just as important as the parameters is the return value, which returns a character pointer. This pointer will be the address of the buffer used to save the screen information. This returned pointer will be needed to restore the screen information.

> **Warning:** If you choose not to restore a saved portion of the screen, you'll need to use the `free()` function on the returned character pointer. This will free the memory that the `save_screen_area()` function allocated.

Before the function starts working to save the screen area, information on the cursor is retrieved with the `get_cursor()` function to determine the video page. When saving the screen area, you'll need to know the current page.

The `save_screen_area()` function saves the area of screen into a buffer. The first five bytes of this buffer are set aside to hold information on the area that is being saved. Figure 11.1 is a representation of this buffer.

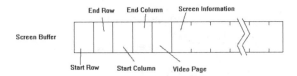

Figure 11.1. *Representation of the saved screen buffer.*

Line 44 determines the amount of space that will be needed to save the screen area. This is done by determining the difference between the starting and ending rows and columns and then multiplying them together. This is then multiplied by two because two bytes will be needed for each position on the screen. One for the actual character displayed, the other for the attributes or color of the character. Line 47 then adds five to this calculated number for the overhead bytes presented in Figure 11.1.

Lines 49 to 54 work to allocate the amount of space that was calculated. If the space is not allocated, an error message is printed and the program ends. This isn't the cleanest exit for a memory allocation error; however, it is acceptable.

Lines 57 to 61 fill in the first five bytes of the screen buffer with the rows, columns, and page of the screen area being saved. While this is done by dereferencing offsets, it could also have been done by using the following:

```
screen_buffer[0] = (char) start_row;
```

>
>
> **Tip:** Because the `screen_buffer` is a pointer, it is more consistent to use dereferencing.

In line 64, the ctr variable, the offset into the screen_buffer, is set to five. It is from this point that you are ready to begin saving screen information. Line 66 begins a while loop that cycles through each column. Line 69 begins a second while loop that cycles through each row. The result is that each row is read within each column until the entire block is read.

For each position read in the while loops, several things occur. In line 72, the cursor() function is used to set the cursor to the current row and column position within the block. Line 73 sets the ah register to the appropriate BIOS function number for reading a character and its attribute. The bh register also needs to be set to the page number that was determined by using the get_cursor() function earlier. Once the registers are set, line 75 calls the BIOS_VIDEO function. This function returns the character in the al register and the attributes in the ah register. These values are placed in the screen_buffer. At the time the values are placed in the buffer, the offset pointer, ctr, is incremented to the next position.

This process cycles through the entire area to be saved. Once the entire screen area is saved, line 88 returns the pointer to the screen_buffer to the calling program. The calling program will use this pointer to restore the screen with the restore_screen_area() function. This function is presented in Listing 11.9.

11

Listing 11.9. RESSCRN.C. Restoring the saved portion of the screen.

```
1:  /* Program: RESSCRN.C
2:   *
3:   * Authors: Bradley L. Jones
4:   *          Gregory L. Guntle
5:   *
6:   * Purpose: Restores information from the screen_buffer area
7:   *          that was saved using the  save_screen_area
8:   *          function.
9:   *
10:  * Function: restore_screen_area()
11:  *
12:  * Enter with: Address of area containing data from last
13:  *             save_screen_area call.
14:  *-------------------------------------------------------*/
15:
16: #include <dos.h>
17: #include <stdlib.h>
18: #include "tyac.h"
19:
20: void restore_screen_area(char *screen_buffer)
```

continues

345

Listing 11.9. continued

```
21:  {
22:      union REGS inregs, outregs;
23:      int   start_row, start_col, end_row, end_col, video_page;
24:      int   ctr=5;
25:      int   row;
26:      int   col;
27:
28:      start_row  = (int)*(screen_buffer+0);
29:      end_row    = (int)*(screen_buffer+1);
30:      start_col  = (int)*(screen_buffer+2);
31:      end_col    = (int)*(screen_buffer+3);
32:      video_page = (int)*(screen_buffer+4);
33:      row        = start_row;
34:
35:      while (row <= end_row)
36:      {
37:        col = start_col;              /* Start col at beginning */
38:        while (col <= end_col)
39:        {
40:          /* Position cursor */
41:          cursor( row, col );
42:
43:          inregs.h.ah = WRITE_CHAR;
44:          inregs.h.bh = video_page;
45:
46:          /* Get character */
47:          inregs.h.al = *(screen_buffer+ctr++);
48:          /* Get attribute */
49:          inregs.h.bl = *(screen_buffer+ctr++);
50:          inregs.x.cx = 1;
51:
52:          int86(BIOS_VIDEO, &inregs, &outregs);
53:
54:          col++;   /* next col */
55:        }
56:        row++;     /* Next row */
57:      }
58:
59:      free(screen_buffer);          /* Free memory */
60:  }
```

Analysis After seeing the save_screen_area() function, you should be able to follow this listing. This listing works almost backwards from the way the save_screen_area() function worked. In lines 28 to 33, the values that had been saved off for the rows, columns, and page are taken out of the screen buffer and placed in variables.

Note: Because the values for the buffer location were included in the saved buffer, there was no need to tell the restore_screen_area() anything more than where the screen_buffer array was.

Lines 35 to 57 include the two while statements that are used to loop through the screen buffer. Like the save_screen_area() function, the cursor is placed in the appropriate location, the BIOS registers are set up, a BIOS function is called, values are incremented, and the offset into the buffer is incremented. While the process is nearly identical, characters are being written instead of read. In line 43, you see that the WRITE_CHAR value is placed in the ah register. In lines 47 and 49, the character and attributes are taken from the screen_buffer array and placed in the al and bl registers before calling the BIOS_VIDEO interrupt.

The last code line of this function is very important. Line 59 frees the screen_buffer. Once freed, this buffer can no longer be used. If you don't free the buffer, the memory will still be allocated.

Saving and Restoring in Practice

You can now save and restore areas of the screen. Listing 11.10 is a program that shows save_screen_area() and restore_screen_area() in action.

Listing 11.10. LIST1110.C. Demonstration of saving and restoring the screen.

```
1:  /* Program:  LIST1110.C
2:   * Author:   Bradley L. Jones
3:   *           Gregory L. Guntle
4:   * Purpose:  Use the screen saving/restoring functions.
5:   *=========================================================*/
6:
7:  #include <stdio.h>
8:  #include <conio.h>       /* for getch() prototype */
9:  #include "tyac.h"
10:
11: int main(void)
12: {
13:     int crow, ccol, cpage, c_st, c_end; /* for cursor */
14:     char *screen_buffer;
15:
```

continues

Listing 11.10. continued

```
16:        screen_buffer = save_screen_area(0,24,0,79);
17:        get_cursor( &crow, &ccol, &cpage, &c_st, &c_end);
18:
19:        clear_screen( LIGHTBLUE, RED );
20:
21:        write_string("The screen is cleared....",
22:                          LIGHTBLUE, RED, 10, 28);
23:        write_string("Press any key to continue",
24:                          LIGHTBLUE, RED, 12, 28);
25:
26:        getch();
27:
28:        restore_screen_area(screen_buffer);
29:        cursor( crow, ccol );
30:
31:        return 0;
32:   }
```

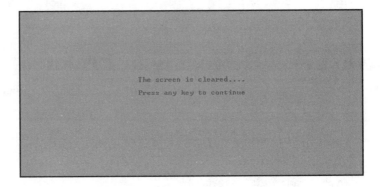

The screen is cleared....
Press any key to continue

This listing should be enlightening if you have ever run a program that causes the screen to look like it was before you started. This program saves the screen when it starts and then restores it when it is complete. The save_screen_area() function and the get_cursor() function are called when the program starts. The save_screen_area() is used to save the entire screen by passing the standard height and widths. The get_cursor() function saves the cursor information.

Once the information is saved, no matter what the program does, you can return the screen to its original look at the end of the listing. In this program, the screen is cleared and a message is displayed. Even though all the information on the screen has been wiped out, you have retained a copy in screen_buffer. Line 28 restores the screen with restore_screen_area(). The cursor is then placed back to its location before the program ends.

DO	**DON'T**

DON'T forget to turn the cursor back on before exiting your program if you turned it off.

DO hide the cursor if there aren't any entry fields on your screen (such as when you ask the user to press any key to continue).

DO call `restore_screen_area()` or `free()` if you call `save_screen_area()` so that you release the memory allocated to save the screen.

Summary

This chapter contained several functions that you will find useful. The first functions presented are used to hide and show the cursor. These functions are valuable when you are displaying screens that don't have any enterable fields. While some compilers have functions to clear the screen, not all do. A function was presented that enables you to clear the screen. This `clear_screen()` function includes the capability to state what colors you want the screen cleared to. A grid function was also presented, which enables you to place grid boxes in your applications. The final functions presented are used to save and restore areas of the screen. These functions help you create overlapping items on your screens without loosing the underlying information.

Q&A

Q What are some uses for the `grid()` function?

A There are two main uses that you will see in the remainder of this book. One use is to give an application a textured background screen. The second is to give texture to shadows on boxes.

Q What will happen if I use the `save_screen_area()` function, but never call the `restore_screen_area()` function?

A The `save_screen_area()` function allocates memory dynamically. This memory must be freed at some point. The `restore_screen_area()` function does the freeing when it redraws the screen area. You may need the memory elsewhere; however, it will remain unavailable until it is freed. If you decide you don't want to restore the screen area, you can use the `free()` function to free the screen buffer area that was allocated.

Workshop

The Workshop provides quiz questions to help you solidify your understanding of the material covered and exercises to provide you with experience in using what you've learned.

Quiz

1. Why would you want to hide the cursor?

2. What happens if you call the `cursor_off()` function and then exit your program? Will the cursor automatically come back on?

3. Why do you need a `clear_screen()` function?

4. What is the difference between Borland's `clrscr()` function and your `clear_screen()` function?

5. How many different ASCII grid patterns are there?

6. What are the numerical values of the ASCII grid characters?

7. What is the benefit of saving the screen?

8. What happens if you don't restore a saved screen?

9. Why are the row and column positions stored in the `screen_buffer` along with the screen data in the `save_screen_area()` function?

10. Why are two bytes allocated for each position on the screen instead of just one?

Exercises

1. Add the new functions that you created today to your TYAC.LIB library. In addition, add the prototypes for these functions to the TYAC.H header. The new functions from today are as follows:

```
cursor_off()
cursor_on()
clear_screen()
grid()
save_screen_area()
restore_screen_area()
```

2. In the analysis of Listing 11.3, you were asked to comment out various lines of the listing. Try commenting out the lines presented in each of the following scenarios to see what happens.

   a. Comment out the `cursor_on()` line.

   b. Comment out the `cursor_off()` line.

   c. Comment out both the `cursor_on()` and `cursor_off()` lines.

3. Use the save and restore screen area functions in a program.

4. What happens if you keep calling the save screen function and then never restore the screen? Write a program that calls the `save_screen_area()` function over and over without restoring or freeing the allocated area.

5. **ON YOUR OWN:** Write a function that takes a character string as a parameter. Display this message in a box in the center of the screen. The box should have a grid shadow. In addition, the user should be asked to press a key. Once the key is pressed, the box should be removed and the screen should appear as it was before the message and box were displayed.

12

Systems Analysis
and Design

Many programmers try to sit down and write a program without any preplanning. Programmers who write successful programs tend to follow a more structured approach. Today you will learn:

☐ Several approaches to creating a complete program.

☐ Why you should follow a structured approach when creating a program.

☐ What is meant by structured systems analysis and design.

☐ About prototyping.

☐ How to apply some of the systems analysis and design concepts to an actual application.

Creating a Computer System

Many programmers believe that the way you create a computer program is at the keyboard. You get the idea, you think about it for a few minutes (or longer), and then you start keying in the code. For many programmers, this works for awhile; however, it poses several problems.

The most common problem with this method of programming is maintainability. Typically, programs that have been written without first thinking through what is being developed are disorganized. They may appear structured and clean to the user, but the underlying code is generally tangled and patched.

Most—if not all—successful corporations or programming development shops won't allow programs to be written without forethought. Successful companies generally follow a methodology when developing programs. A methodology is a highly glorified term that has a simple meaning. A *methodology* is a set of procedures that are followed to accomplish a task. Methodologies for creating computer programs generally follow a set of systems analysis and design procedures. These procedures cover what should be done from the time an idea for a program or system is thought of until the time it is complete and turned over for use.

Note: A computer system differs from a computer program. A *computer system* may include programs, procedures, hardware, and more. A *computer program* is simply software.

There are several methodologies that are used within the development of computer programs. Three will be briefly covered today. The first is structured systems analysis and design. This is a methodology that is equipped to handle the biggest or even the smallest of computer programs or systems. The second methodology covered is a form of rapid or accelerated systems development. This is a scaled-down version of structured systems analysis and design that is intended to enable you to develop a system quicker, yet still follow the structured approach. The third methodology covered is prototyping. This is the methodology that a large number of PC programmers choose to follow.

Understanding these three methodologies will help you in your approach of the development of a computer system of any size. After these three methodologies are covered, you will be introduced to a fourth approach. This fourth method uses parts of the other three. It is aimed more directly at smaller PC-developed systems. This fourth methodology is what has been applied to the application that will be developed throughout the rest of this book. As you develop your own systems, you'll need to decide which methodology best suits your needs.

The Traditional Approach: Structured Systems Analysis and Design

The traditional approach is the most commonly used in businesses. It is broken down into five stages. Each of these stages has specific procedures that need to be completed. In addition, each stage follows the preceding stage. If a step is missed in a preceding stage, then you should go back and redo everything from that point. The five stages are:

Stage 1: Preliminary Analysis
Stage 2: Systems Analysis (Logical Design)
Stage 3: Systems Design (Physical Design)
Stage 4: Construction
Stage 5: Wrap Up (Testing and Implementation)

Each of these stages is also broken down into specific steps that should be followed. It's the structure of the stages and steps, along with the specific order, that gives this approach its name.

In addition to the specific steps, structured systems analysis and design has several documents that get produced. The documentation that is produced through this methodology won't be covered in this book. There are complete books and several college courses available on this methodology.

Stage 1: Preliminary Analysis

The first stage of structured systems analysis and design is the preliminary analysis. In this stage, the problem is defined and the overall direction is set. This stage generally starts with someone presenting an idea. To help formulate the idea, a preliminary study is done. This study is used to determine if the system (or program) is feasible. The following steps are performed in the preliminary study:

Step 1: Overview the problem/objective
Step 2: Set the objectives/capabilities
Step 3: Determine the scope of the project
Step 4: Determine the business rules/assumptions/constraints
Step 5: Do preliminary estimates
Step 6: Scheduling

Step 1: Overview the Problem/Objective

A statement of what is intended to be accomplished or what problem needs to be solved should be made. This should be composed in a few sentences to a couple of paragraphs. This should be a very high-level description of what the system will do.

Step 2: Set the Objectives/Capabilities

The overall goals and capabilities of the system should be listed. These should be presented in a bulleted list that describe not what the system is, but what the system should be. By listing the capabilities and objectives, you begin to define what the system will need to do. If you are developing a system similar to something that already exists, then you should state what your system will do differently. Examples of objectives include:

☐ System should help save time.

☐ System should provide information so that decisions can be made faster.

☐ System should help provide more accurate information.

☐ System should be easy to use so that learning time is short.

Note: The objectives should state what your system or program will offer that other programs don't already offer.

Step 3: Determine the Scope of the Project

The scope of the project refers to the size of the project. It's the scope of a project that prevents it from getting too large. If a project doesn't have a scope, then there is nothing to prevent it from growing forever. For example, consider a program that lists a text file. The only objective of the program is to be able to list the program to the screen or to the printer. Without a scope, there are several solutions to solve just such a problem. The simplest solution would involve simply printing a listing as it appears to either the printer or the screen; however, there are a variety of solutions that would be much more interesting. You could create a system that displays the file on the screen and enables you to view it before selecting a menuing option to print it. The printing could enable you to select only a portion of the text or all of it. In addition, the system could enable you to edit the program before printing. The possibilities can grow until they get out of hand. In addition, what could have been a simple command at the operating system level may become a system that requires several programmers many months to create.

With scope, you determine the limits of the program. You can set what information is needed, what equipment may—or may not—be used, what the budget is, and the amount of time that is available. Anything that can cause limitations on the final system should be included.

Step 4: Determine the Business Rules/Assumptions/Constraints

In addition to scope factors, there are also business rules and other rules that can constrain a system. Such rules may include company policies and practices, equipment limitations, or cost factors. For example, you can't effectively develop a UNIX system if you don't have UNIX. In addition, you can't develop a virtual reality operating system if you don't have the hardware to work with virtual reality.

Step 5: Do Preliminary Estimates

Once you have an idea of the objectives and limitations, you can make a first attempt at determining the costs and benefits of the system or program. Costs come in several forms such as the software and licensing that may be required, and the time to develop and program.

These costs should be compared to the benefits that will be achieved to determine if it's worth proceeding with the system. Many of the possible benefits can be seen in the objectives listed earlier. An example of cost versus benefits can be seen in the development of a calculator program for Microsoft Windows. Because Windows comes with a calculator built in, people aren't going to spend money to buy a new one unless it offers something extra. If the cost of developing the new calculator is more than what you think you can make selling it, then it may be a bad project—unless there are other benefits that the user will receive.

Step 6: Scheduling

Like the functionality of a system or program, the amount of time can also get out of hand. To let others know when they can expect the new program or system, a schedule needs to be set. This schedule should include time frames for the rest of the Structured Systems Analysis and Design steps.

Generally, Project Management Tools are used to schedule large systems. Such tools include Project Workbench, Super Project, Project Scheduler, and more. These programs enable you to make estimates on when tasks should be accomplished. They then chart your progress to show when you are on time and when you are behind. They can also chart the relationships between tasks—which tasks must be accomplished before others. Such tools help make managing your time and the project much easier.

Stage 2: Systems Analysis (Logical Design)

The steps in the preliminary study should be done at a very high level and in a relatively quick time frame. Their purpose is simply to set the stage for the detailed research that will be performed on the system. In addition, they should provide enough information so that a decision on continuing the system can be made.

In the second stage, systems analysis, the level of detail becomes much more detailed. This involves the following four steps:

Step 1: Refine the problem/create team
Step 2: Determine the facts
Step 3: Provide alternatives
Step 4: Determine the next step

Step 1: Refine the Problem/Create Team

Refining the problem means you need to ensure that what was stated in the Preliminary Design was accurate. The information gathered should be reviewed to ensure that it sets the proper direction.

If the direction is accurate, then a team must be pulled together to analyze and construct the system. The team may be you alone or with more people. If there are several people working on the project, then the roles that these people are going to serve should be defined.

Step 2: Determine the Facts

Once you determine who is on the project, it's time to begin the detailed analysis by gathering the facts. The facts are any information that is related to what needs to be accomplished by the system. In addition, this includes the details of what must be accomplished. Specifics are determined. These specifics fall into three areas: what comes into the system, what leaves the system, and what does the system do in between receiving information and providing it. In addition to these three areas, the volume of information that will be used by the system needs to be determined. You may find that what you are attempting to do is impossible.

For example, if you are creating a database to track your contacts, then you could have several inputs and outputs. The inputs may include photographs, demographic information, a history of contacts, and more. The outputs may include a number of different types of inquiries into the information. You should estimate how much room it will take to store the information for each contact. In addition, you should estimate the number of contacts that will be tracked. If each contract is expected to take 1MB of storage space (with a photo and history information this is possible), and if you are expecting 1,000 contacts, then you have a system that requires a gigabyte of data storage. Your business rules may state that this is not possible.

Consider Logical, Not Physical

In doing the systems analysis, you should consider the logical nature of the system, not the physical. Physical considerations are those that assume specific computer programs, specific computer hardware, specific storage mediums, specific display

mediums, or any other physical items that will be used. You should only consider the logical information by concentrating on what needs to be done and why. For example, if a system such as the one mentioned previously is to capture contact information, then you consider the logical aspects. What information needs to be captured, not how it needs to be captured. What information needs to be accessed, not whether it's displayed on a report or on the screen. The physical characteristics will be designed in the next stage of structured systems analysis and design.

Consider Available Tools

There are several tools that have been developed to help pull together the facts and to help document them. The tools include flow charts and CASE tools. Flow charting, data flow diagrams, structure charts, action diagrams, input/output models, context diagrams, and entity-relationship models are all different methods for documenting different parts of a system. Books have been written on most of these forms of documentation.

Pull the Facts Together

A systems analysis document should be created when all the facts have been gathered. This document should contain detailed information on the logical flow and design of the system. It should contain all of the charting that may have been done with analysis tools along with descriptions of the data that comes into and leaves the system. It also should contain the process that acts on the data.

Step 3: Provide Alternatives

Once the detailed analysis has been performed, you should consider your alternatives. Most people assume they need to develop a new system on their own; however, this is a poor assumption. There may be a number of systems already out there doing the same thing you are attempting to do. It may also be that what you are attempting to do is not feasible. In this case, your only option may be to kill the project. Alternatives should be determined. Generally, the alternatives fall into the following four areas:

1. Use an off-the-shelf package.

2. Modify an off-the-shelf package.

3. Create your own new system.

4. Cancel the system and do nothing.

Expert Tip: Determining if an off-the-shelf package is the right solution is not always easy. You may need to talk to software dealers, visit local software stores, and consult trade publications. You should look for packages that come close to meeting the needs that you have detailed.

Step 4: Determine the Next Step

Before you can continue to the next stage, you must make a decision. You must pick one of the alternatives that you stated in the previous step. In corporations, the user(s) of the system would pick the alternative. If the alternative is to modify a package or to create your own system, then you would continue on to the next stage of structured systems analysis and design.

Stage 3: Systems Design (Physical Design)

At this point, you know what needs to be done and you now have to design the physical aspects of the system. This includes the way information will be stored, accessed, and processed.

Note: A *prototype* is a mock-up of what a screen or report will look like.

This is all done with tools similar to those used in the systems analysis stage. Most of the outputs from systems analysis should be used as the starting point of the design. This stage involves creating file layouts, screen prototypes, and more. The physical nature of the system also is detailed. In addition, decisions on the hardware to be used in the system will need to be made. These include decisions such as whether reports appear on paper, the screen, or both. The specific information that will appear in the reports should be detailed; and screen prototypes should also be developed.

Stage 4: Construction

This is most people's favorite stage. Most people think of construction as the coding stage. While it is the coding, construction also includes tasks that help in coding.

These tasks include creating structure charts, writing pseudo-code, and flowcharting. These again are tasks that help organize and identify problems before the coding starts. Books have been written on methods and rules for accomplishing these tasks.

When this stage is done, the programs should be coded and ready for use; however, the project is not done. Before the project is done, the fifth stage (Wrap Up) should be completed.

Stage 5: Wrap Up (Testing and Implementation)

This is the most overlooked stage of structured systems analysis and design. This stage contains the following steps that can make or break a software program or system:

> **Step 1:** Testing
> **Step 2:** Documenting
> **Step 3:** Implementing

Step 1: Testing

Testing is often neglected by most software developers. Once the program is completed and appears to work, it is passed on. Programs stand a better chance of success if they are tested. The two levels of testing that are generally performed are unit testing and integration testing.

Unit testing means testing individual programs. A word processing package may be composed of several programs—a spell checker, a thesaurus, an entry program, a printing program, and more. The users of the word processing package may not be aware that several programs are running. To them, it is a single, complete system. In unit testing, each of these pieces is tested on its own to ensure that it is complete.

Integration testing tests the system as a whole. Integration testing ensures that all the individual pieces work together. In addition, integration testing ensures that the programs work with the operating system and other programs that may be running.

By doing both integration and unit testing, you help ensure that a program is error free. In addition, by setting up these tests, you can ensure that the system works properly. If there is a problem, once it is fixed, not every test needs to be rechecked. You need to rerun only the unit test for the changed code. You should also rerun the integration tests to ensure that no interactions have been affected.

Step 2: Documenting

Any user manuals or other documentation should be created at this point. Because structured systems analysis and design was used, there should be a large amount of documentation already created. In this stage of the project, the documentation should be reformatted, and user manuals and other documents can be created.

Step 3: Implementing

When testing is done, a system is ready to be implemented. Implementation may involve preparing the software to be sold, setting up a system, uploading the software to a bulletin board as shareware, or installing it on your own computer. The documentation should also be provided.

All the steps of structured systems analysis and design should enable you to implement a system that works almost exactly as needed. There should be no surprises. By following all of the steps, you should have completed the best system based on the objectives and restrictions.

> **Note:** This has been a very high-level discussion of structured analysis and design. The main purpose of this discussion is to make you aware of the complexity that can be involved in developing large computer systems or programs. If you were attempting to create a software package similar to one of the larger packages on the market (for example, Paradox, WordPerfect, Excel, etc.), you would want to use a methodology such as structured systems analysis and design to control the size. For smaller systems, other methodologies may be better.

12

DO / DON'T

DO understand the overall idea of structured systems analysis and design.

DON'T confuse logical design with physical design.

DO consider other books if you are interested in more information on structured systems analysis and design.

Rapid or Accelerated Systems Analysis and Design

Rapid or accelerated systems analysis and design was developed to help create a system quicker. This methodology follows what was presented in structured systems analysis and design; however, there are a few subtle twists.

The first is that prototyping is done as early as possible. As soon as you have an idea of what is going to be created, you create prototypes. These prototypes are dynamic throughout the analysis and design. As new information is learned, new iterations, or new versions, of the prototypes are created. In addition, alternatives are eliminated. You make the assumption that you are creating a new system. As soon as there is a high comfort level with the prototypes, construction begins.

Expert Tip: There is no set number of versions that the prototypes will go through. You should continue updating the prototypes until there is a high comfort level.

This methodology has a greater chance for failure than the structured approach. Because prototypes are created early on, there is a tendency to lock into designs early on. In addition, while most of the steps in the structured method are followed, there is a tendency to leave out as many as possible. Because of this and the accelerated nature of this methodology, objectives or business rules may be overlooked.

Prototyping

Most at-home PC developers use prototyping if they use any methodology at all. Prototyping ignores most, if not all, of the analysis and design. Screen prototypes and report prototypes are developed. Once developed, construction begins. While this methodology isn't much better than no methodology at all, it does provide some chance for thinking a system through before coding begins.

Several tools are available for prototyping. One of the more popular screen prototyping tools is Demo II. Some editors will also enable you to prototype screens. For prototyping reports, text editors generally will work fine.

A Program Specification

In developing smaller PC systems, I use a methodology that is different from all of those presented so far. It is also similar to that used by several of the companies that I have worked in. This methodology involves developing a single document—a program specification—that serves as an overview for the system, or part of a system, to be developed. In developing this specification, concepts presented in the structured systems analysis and design are used. In addition, a large portion of the specification revolves around the prototypes.

A program specification should have the following parts:

☐ An overview/purpose

☐ Capabilities/objectives

☐ Business rules/assumptions/limitations

☐ Processing components

☐ Prototypes

☐ Input/output requirements

Most of the remaining days that you spend reading this book revolve around developing a single application. A specification for this application has been created. This specification follows today's material. You should use it as a template for creating your own specifications. This specification doesn't contain information on the entire system that will be developed. The reporting sections of the application will be contained in their own specification later in the book.

Although most of the specification follows what is presented in structured analysis and design, a few comments bear mentioning. You should complete the first three sections before creating a prototype. These sections help layout an overview of the program(s).

When the first three sections are completed, the prototype can be developed. The prototype can then be used to fill in the processing components. The processing components detail the actions that are available on each screen. Each key is detailed.

In addition, data matrixes may be used. These can detail descriptions of the fields on entry screens. They can include information on the data types, the field sizes, and the edits that should be performed. If there are special edits, they may need to be detailed in the processing components section of the specification, rather than the data matrix.

The input/output requirements detail the database access that the program is going to require. This helps you to later determine the appropriate structure for your program's files.

Tracking Questions

One addition that you may choose to add to your specification is a question and answer section. If you are working with others in the system that you are creating, it's often important to track questions. It's not uncommon for users to change their mind on what they want. As you ask questions, or as users change their minds, you may wish to track this. A good place to place these questions and answers is after the business rules and before the processing components.

DO	DON'T

DO review the specification following today's lessons. It details the program that will be developed throughout this book.

DO track questions and answers if you are working with users who change their minds a lot.

Summary

Today's material covered a very important advanced programming topic. Methodologies for developing computer systems were presented. By using a methodology, you have a better chance of developing a system that will be truly useful. Four different approaches were covered. The first, structured systems analysis and design, is the most detailed. Rapid or accelerated systems analysis and design is a similar approach that works at a faster pace by using prototypes. Prototyping, the third methodology presented, enables you to create mock-ups of your program's screens and reports before coding begins. Program specification was the fourth approach presented. A program specification has been created that details the entry portion of the application that will be developed in the rest of this book. You should review this specification.

Q&A

Q What percentage of structured systems analysis and design is spent coding programs?

A If done correctly, only a small portion of time will be spent actually coding a system. Generally, 20 to 30 percent of the time spent on the project should be in coding. This may seem strange, however, because of the pre-thinking provided by the methodology, the time spent coding will be extremely focused on the correct tasks.

Q Why is following a methodology important?

A In following a methodology—even a scaled down version of a methodology—you are pre-planning. It's easier to make corrections before you start coding than after. Once you start coding a system, a change can be harder to make. Generally, a change requires much more work if it is made after coding has started. Changes caught before programming beings are easier to implement. If a large number of changes occur after contraction begins, the code can be come convoluted.

Q What is the difference between logical design and physical design?

A Logical design should come first. Logical design evaluates what a system should do. Physical design evaluates how a system should do the what. Physical design deals with the hardware and software that may be needed, where as the logical design will only deal with information.

Q What is object-oriented design?

A Where as structured systems analysis and design starts with an overview and focuses later on the detail; object-oriented design starts with the data and builds out toward the entire systems. This is an extremely high-level definition. For more information, consider reading a book on systems analysis and design or a book specifically on object-oriented design.

Workshop

The Workshop provides quiz questions to help you solidify your understanding of the material covered and exercises to provide you with experience in using what you've learned.

Quiz

1. What is a methodology?

2. What is meant by scope?

3. What is a prototype?

4. Should a methodology be followed?

5. What is a reason for not following a methodology?

Exercises

1. Review the program specification in the following section. Look at each section to see what information is presented.

2. After looking at the following specification, create your own. Create a specification for a similar type of application that allows for the entry of information. You can use this specification to create your own application during the following days.

Specification for
Record of Records!
Version 1.00

Purpose

This application allows information about a person's musical collection to be stored. It can store information about individual tapes, records, CDs, and so forth. In addition, it allows information to be stored on the musical groups contained within the music collection.

Objectives/Capabilities

1. Be capable of storing information on which storage medium a particular musical item is contained, including cassettes, albums, CDs, and DATs. In addition, the system should allow for other types of mediums to be used.

2. Be capable of storing information concerning the cost and value of each musical item. In addition, the system should provide a means for storing other identifiable information. See data matrix later in specification.

3. Be capable of reporting the information that has been provided. These reports are defined in their own specification.

4. Be capable of tracking information about the musical groups contained within the musical items. This information should include the members of the group, along with the albums they have produced. See data matrix later in specification for specific information about musical groups that can be tracked.

5. Individual songs on an album should be tracked along with their duration. The number of songs for a single album should be unlimited. (Actual maximum of 250 songs.) This information is detailed in the data matrix later in this specification.

6. There should be the capability to add new musical items, change information on existing musical items, or delete musical items.

7. There must be the capability to add, change, or delete storage medium types.

8. There must be the capability to add, change, or delete musical group information.

9. The capability to see the information on a musical group should be available when entering musical items.

Rules/Assumptions

1. Data will be stored on Groups, Musical Items, and storage mediums separately.

2. If a musical item is added that does not have a corresponding musical group, a warning should be given.

3. If a musical group is deleted that has any corresponding musical items, a warning should be presented.

4. The capability to automatically go from one album to another should exist.

5. Musical items should be sorted by title when going from one musical item to the next.

6. (Technical) Will need to be able to rebuild the databases in case of corruption.

7. The word *album* may be used to signify any musical item.

Processing Components

```
SCREEN:  MUSICAL ITEMS
Prototype:
                           Musical Items                00/00/00
   File    Edit    Search   Help


      Title:  ---------------------------
      Group:  -----------------------

   Medium:  --

   Date Purchased:  99/99/99     Cost:  $---.--      Value:  $---.--

        Track   Song Title                                    Time

        01:     -------------------------------------         --:--
        02:     -------------------------------------         --:--
        03:     -------------------------------------         --:--
        04:     -------------------------------------         --:--
        05:     -------------------------------------         --:--
        06:     -------------------------------------         --:--
        07:     -------------------------------------         --:--

                               Total Album Time:  --:--:--


   <PgDn=More Titles>                          <F10=Action Bar>
```

Keys/Functions

Initial Entry

Upon initial entry to the screen, all fields will be blank. The cursor will be on the Title field.

\<Enter\>

\<Tab\>

Move the cursor from one field to the next. If the cursor is on the last field, it should move to the first field.

\<Shift\>\<Tab\>

Move the cursor from one field to the previous field. If the cursor is on the first field, it should be moved to the last field.

\<PgUp\>

Place the cursor on the first field on the screen.

\<PgDn\>

Place the cursor on the last field on the screen.

\<F1\>

Display box containing information on using the current screen.

\<Esc\>

\<F3\>

Enable the users to leave the screen. Before leaving, the users will be prompted to see if they are sure.

\<F4\>

Before adding the record, all edits within the data matrix must be passed. The edits should be evaluated starting with the first field on the screen and working to the last field. If an edit does not pass, then an error message should be displayed and the cursor should be returned to the field in error.

If all the edits pass, prompt the user to add the record to the file. If the user agrees, add the record, and display a message. After the user responds to the message, the screen should be re-initialized.

<F5>

If the user is adding a new record, display an error stating the record must be added.

Before updating the record, all edits within the data matrix must be passed. The edits should be evaluated starting with the first field on the screen and working to the last field. If an edit does not pass, then an error message should be displayed and the cursor should be returned to the field in error.

If all the edits pass, prompt the user to update the record in the file. If the user agrees, update the record, and display a message. After the user responds to the message, the screen should be re-initialized.

<F6>

If the user is adding a new record, display an error stating the record cannot be deleted because it has not been added.

Prompt the user to make sure he wants to delete the record. If the user agrees, delete the record, and display a message. After the user responds to the message, the screen should be re-initialized.

<F7>

Display a message briefly that states that the previous record will be displayed. The previous record in the database should then be displayed. If there is not a previous record, display an error message.

<F8>

Display a message briefly that states that the next record will be displayed. The next record in the database should then be displayed. If there is not a next record, display an error message.

<F10>

If the cursor is on the entry screen, place it on the first item on the action bar.

<ALT><S>

Prompt the user with the search dialog box described later in the specificaiton.

Action Bar Items

<FILE>

<Exit>
Same function as <F3>.

<EDIT>

<Add>
Same function as <F4> except that user should not be prompted to add.

<Change>
Same function as <F5> except that user should not be prompted to update.

<Delete>
Same functions as <F6>. User should be prompted to delete.

<SEARCH>

<Find>
A dialog box should be displayed prompting the user for a Title. The first record found with a matching title should be displayed.

<Next Record>
Same function as <F7>.

<Previous Record>
Same function as <F8>.

<HELP>

<Help>
Same function as <F1>.

<About>
Display a dialog box with information on the program.

Special Musical Item Functions

<Alt><G>

Pop up a box that dispays the description field from the group file. If a matching group does not exist, display an error.

Total Time

This field should keep a running total of the times entered in each Song Title. It should originally default to 00:00:00.

```
SCREEN:  GROUPS
Prototype:
                                    Groups                    00/00/@00
    File    Edit    Search   Help


    Group:  -------------------------

    Date formed:  99/99/99

    Type of Music:  XXXXXXXXXXXXXXXX

    Members:

        ----------------------------------------------------------
        ----------------------------------------------------------
        ----------------------------------------------------------

    Description:

        ----------------------------------------------------------
        ----------------------------------------------------------
        ----------------------------------------------------------



    <F1=Help>    <F3=Exit>                        <F10=Action Bar>
```

Keys/Functions

This screen should operate in the same manner as the Musical Items screen with the following exceptions:

\<Alt>\<S>

Instead of searching for a Title, prompt and search for a group.

```
SCREEN:  MEDIUM TYPES
Prototype:
                                    Medium                    00/00/00
      File    Edit    Search   Help


      Medium Code:    - - -

      Medium Description:   - - - - - - - - - - - - - - - - - - - - - - - - - -
```

```
     <F1=Help>    <F3=Exit>                        <F10=Action Bar>
```

Database Access Requirements

Musical Items—sorted A to Z by title

☐ Need to be able to add new title.

☐ Need to be able to randomly read existing title information.

☐ Need to be able to sequentially read existing title information.

☐ Need to be able to delete an existing title.

☐ Need to be able to update information on a specific title.

Groups—sorted A to Z by group name

☐ Need to be able to add new groups.

☐ Need to be able to randomly read existing groups.

☐ Need to be able to sequentially read groups.

☐ Need to be able to delete a given group.

☐ Need to be able to update information on a given group.

Medium Types

☐ Need to be able to add new medium type.

☐ Need to be able to randomly read existing medium type.

☐ Need to be able to delete a given medium type.

☐ Need to be able to update information on a given medium type.

Table Specifications 1.1. ALBUMS Matrix.

Field	Type	Size	Edits
Title	Alphanumeric	30	Cannot be blank.
Group	Alphanumeric	25	Cannot be blank; Give warning if not in Group file.
Cost	Alpha	5.2	Must be positive number or blank (999.99).
Value	Alphanumeric	5.2	Must be a positive number or blank (999.99).
Date purchased	Alphanumeric	8	Must be a valid date or blank. If filled, must be before today.
Medium type	Alphanumeric	2	Must be a code in the Medium file or blank.
Number of songs	Alpha	3	Cannot be greater than 250.
Total time	Numeric	No edits	Protected.

continues

Table Specifications 1.1. continued

The following fields occur multple times depending on the value of "Number of songs."			
Song title	Alphanumeric	40	Cannot be blank if length filled in.
Song length (minutes)	Numeric	2	Cannot be negative.
Song length (seconds)	Numeric	2	Must be from 0 to 59 if not blank.

Table Specifications 1.2. Medium Types Matrix.

Field	Type	Size	Edits
Medium code	Alphanumeric	2	Cannot be blank; Must be unique.
Medium description	Alphanumeric	35	Cannot be blank.

Table Specifications 1.3. Groups Matrix.

Field	Type	Size	Edits
Group Name	Alphanumeric	25	Cannot be blank.
Date formed	Date	8	Must be valid date or blank; If filled, must be before today's date.
Description of group	Alphanumeric	???	No edits.
Type of Music	Alphanumeric	20	Must be one of a set list to be determined later.
Members[6]	Alphanumeric	30	No edits.

Technical/Implementation Notes

1. Complete prototypes have been developed in a Demo II file called ALBUMS.DBD.

The User Interface:
Screen Design

Now that you have a specification, your direction is set. You are ready to begin constructing your application. When developing a large-scale application, you should develop in steps. The specification should be your first step. Today, you'll begin the second step. Today you will:

☐ Learn about creating entry and edit screens.

☐ Learn some of the standards for screen design.

☐ Create entry and edit screens for the application presented on Day 12's specification.

☐ Create a screen for the musical items (albums).

☐ Create a screen for the medium codes.

☐ Create a screen for the groups.

User Interfaces

The most fun that you'll have when developing an application is creating the user interfaces. The *user interface* is the part of an application that the user sees. These interfaces are generally screens that allow the entry and editing of information; however, they may also include menus, pop-up dialog boxes, message boxes, and more. Figures 13.1 through 13.4 show several different user interfaces.

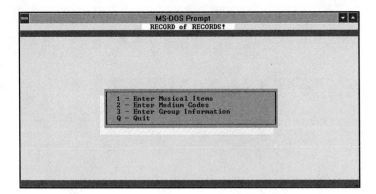

Figure 13.1. *A menu interface from a DOS application.*

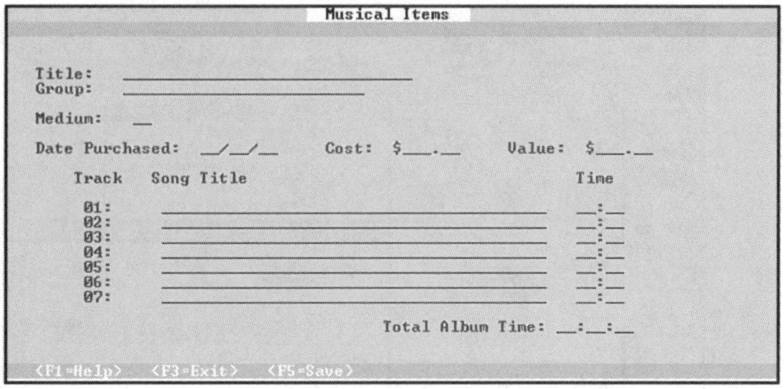

Figure 13.2. *An entry and edit screen.*

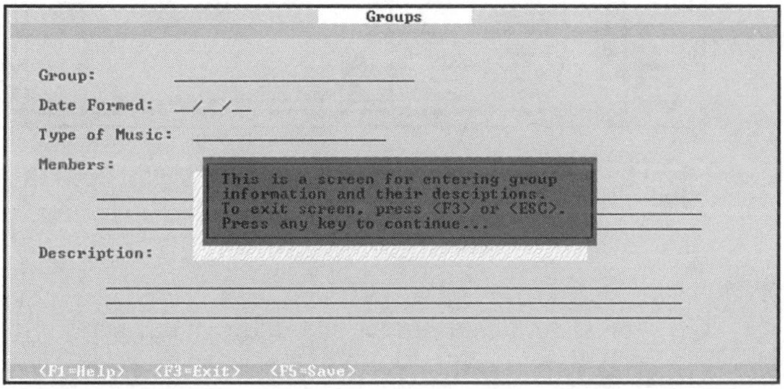

Figure 13.3. *An informational interface.*

All of these interfaces use the text graphics that were discussed on Day 8. There are also Graphical User Interfaces (GUIs), which take advantage of pixel graphics. Programs such as Microsoft's Windows (see Figure 13.4), IBM's OS/2, and Geoworks all use graphical user interfaces.

Today, you will learn about entry and edit screens such as the one in Figure 13.2. Before presenting the code, you'll be introduced to the standards on creating entry and edit screens. On Day 14, you'll learn how to create menuing interfaces such as the one in Figure 13.1. On Day 14, you'll also cover action bar items. The days following will help to build the internal functions and reports.

13

Figure 13.4. *A graphical user interface (Microsoft Windows 3.1).*

 Tip: You should concentrate on building your application one day at a time. Today, you should concentrate on creating the entry and edit portion of your application.

Creating a User Interface

Many new programmers have a tendency to create screens based solely on what they believe looks neat. To them, the screen actually may look neat; however, they may not have considered the audience that will be using the screen. If you are developing a system that will be given to others, you should consider some standards in screen design. While there are few published standards, there are informal standards that have been accepted by most developers.

Note: Standards are usually operating-system specific. For example, DOS applications follow one set of standards, but OS/2 applications have a different set of standards. Several of the standards may cross operating systems.

The Benefit of Following Standards

There are several possible benefits that can be gained by following a few standards when developing your applications. These benefits include:

- ☐ Lower learning curve for people using the application.
- ☐ Higher comfort level for users in regard to the application.
- ☐ Consistency among your applications.
- ☐ Reduced cost in developing.
- ☐ Increased productivity for you.

The most commonly touted benefit is a consistency in look and feel. Because your application will be designed similar to other programs, users won't feel lost when they use it (look at it). Because parts of your application will look familiar, users will be able to concentrate on learning what the heart of the application does, and not the little things that make the application work. This will help your users increase their productivity with the application.

Additionally, because many functions are predetermined, you won't spend time re-thinking how to accomplish a lot of tasks. This cuts the time you spend on developing applications, which in turn can increase your productivity and reduce your cost of development.

The benefits of standards can also be seen with an experiment. If you have several applications, try running them. In each application, press the F1 function key. In most of your applications, this should provide you with help information.

13

Creating a Common User Interface

You should work to create your entry and edit screens similar to others that are available. To do this, you should understand the parts of a screen. Figures 13.5 and 13.6 present the different parts of an entry and edit screen. You'll see each of these parts as you develop an application over the next few days.

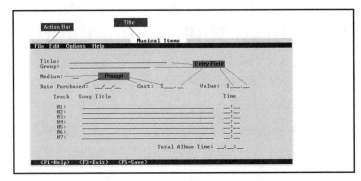

Figure 13.5. *Some of the parts of an entry and edit screen.*

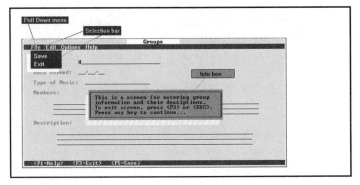

Figure 13.6. *Additional parts of an entry and edit screen.*

These figures present an entry and edit screen. There are also standards for working with menus and function keys.

The Entry and Edit Standards

In the entry and edit portions of an application, there are several areas that you should concentrate on providing standards. These areas include the interface itself and its navigation, the function or special keys, and the feedback to the user.

The feedback to the user is the most straightforward area. An application should provide predictable, consistent feedback. If the user does something that is wrong, either a warning message should be displayed or the computer should beep. A beep should not be used to signal that something was done right. Additionally, if a user does something drastically wrong, a message should be displayed explaining what the error is. Errors can be displayed in message boxes that are red with yellow text to stand out. In addition, the color red is associated with stopping.

The navigation in an entry and edit window should also follow some standards. When entering fields on a screen, the user should start at the top left and work toward the bottom right. When possible, the fields should be presented in the same order as they would be read on a book page. In addition to this navigation, the keys used should follow the functionality presented in Table 13.1.

Table 13.1. Standards for navigating an entry and edit window.

Key	Function
Enter	Accept information on-screen and process. Move to next entry field.
Page Up	Scroll the screen to the previous page, or to the previous set of information. Go to the first field on the screen.
Page Down	Scroll the screen to the next page, or to the next set of information. Go to the last field on a screen.
up arrow	Move the cursor to the previous field. If you reach the top of the screen, go to the bottom. Move the cursor to the field directly above the cursor's current location. If you reach the top of the screen, go to the bottom.
down arrow	Move the cursor to the next field. If you reach the bottom of the screen, go back to the top. Move the cursor to the field directly below the cursor's current position. If you reach the bottom of the screen, go back to the top.
right arrow	Move the cursor to the next position on the current field.
left arrow	Move the cursor to the previous position on the current field.
Tab	Move the cursor to the next field on the screen. If on the last field, go to the first field.

continues

Table 13.1. continued

Key	Function
Shift+Tab	Move the cursor to the previous field on the screen. If on the first field, go to the last field.
Home	Put the cursor on the first position of a field. Put the cursor on the first field on the screen.
End	Put the cursor on the last filled position of a field. Put the cursor on the last field on the screen.
Ctrl+Home	Move the cursor to the first field on the screen.
Ctrl+End	Move the cursor to the last field on the screen.
Ctrl+Page Down	Move the cursor to the last page.
Ctrl+Page Up	Move the cursor to the first page.
Alt	Access the action bar if it exists.
Backspace	Move the cursor one position to the left if in a field. Remove the character. Move the cursor to the previous field.
Delete	Delete the character at the current cursor position.
Insert	Toggle whether characters are inserted or overwritten in an entry field.
Ctrl+left arrow	Show the page or screen to the left.
Ctrl+right arrow	Show the page or screen to the right.

Note: These are informal standards. In some cases, more than one usage is given. This is due to the informality of these uses. You should use these as guidelines.

The Function Key Standards

The standards for the function keys are probably more important than those for navigation in Table 13.1. Many people get used to the functionality generally

provided by the function keys and other special keys. Table 13.2 presents the functionality usually associated with these keys. Additionally, the table shows which keys should not be used for other functions.

Table 13.2. The function keys and other special keys.

Key	Reusable	Function
F1	No	Help (context sensitive)
F2	**	Extended Help
F3	No	Exit
F4		
F5		
F6		
F7		Previous
F8		Next
F9		Help on key assignments
F10	**	Access action bar
F11		Provide alphabetical listing of help topics
F12		
Escape	No	Cancel current task

No means you should not reuse the key.

** Means you can reuse it, but it is not advised.

Note: You should avoid the F11 and F12 keys because not all computers have them.

Warning: Do not change the function of the keys in Table 13.2 that are marked. Keys such as F1 and F3 have been used in too many applications to be given different functions unless you have no choice. Most people will assume F1 will provide help and F3 will provide a way of exiting.

Note: While standards for menuing exist, they won't be covered here. Day 14 covers menuing in detail.

Creating an Entry and Edit Screen

The three entry and edit screens that make up the *Record of Records!* application specified on Day 12 will be created today. These entry and edit screens include the Medium Codes screen, the Group Information screen, and the Musical Items screen. Each screen will be modeled after the screens in the prototypes of Day 12's specification. Day 14 will present a menuing program that will tie all three of these entry and edit screens together into a single application.

Because menuing won't be covered until Day 14, you'll need a temporary way of accessing the entry and edit screens. In addition to providing a cryptic menu, Listing 13.1—the RECOFREC.C listing—provides several functions. Most importantly, Listing 13.1 contains a `main()` function. The rest of the listings will be linked with RECOFREC.C to create a single executable program. Because of this, they won't contain `main()` functions. RECOFREC.C also contains several functions that will be used in the other listings presented today.

Listing 13.2 contains the header file called RECOFREC.H. This header file contains the prototypes for the functions in Listing 13.1, RECOFREC.C. Listing 13.3 contains RECORDS.H. This file contains the structures that will be used in the *Record of Records!* application.

Note: Today's listings are very long; however, they should be easy to follow. The analyses following each listing describes them. Now may be a good time to consider using the diskette that accompanies this book.

Listing 13.1. RECOFREC.C. A temporary *Record of Records!* menu.

```
 1:   /*===========================================================
 2:    * Filename: RECofREC.c
 3:    *           RECORD OF RECORDS - Version 1.0
 4:    *
 5:    * Author:   Bradley L. Jones
 6:    *           Gregory L. Guntle
 7:    *
 8:    * Purpose:  Allow entry and edit of medium codes.
 9:    *
10:    * Note:     Assumes 80 columns by 25 columns for screen.
11:    *===========================================================*/
12:
13:   #include <stdio.h>
14:   #include <conio.h>          /* not an ANSI header, used for getch()
*/
15:   #include <string.h>         /* for strlen() */
16:   #include <ctype.h>
17:   #include "tyac.h"
18:   #include "records.h"
19:
20:   /*-------------------*
21:    *     prototypes    *
22:    *-------------------*/
23:   #include "recofrec.h"
24:
25:   int  do_main_menu(void);
26:   void initialize_color_table( void );
27:
28:   /*------------------------*
29:    * define global variables *
30:    *------------------------*/
31:
32:   struct color_table ct;           /* color table */
33:
34:   /*=========================================================*
35:    *                      main()                             *
36:    *=========================================================*/
37:
38:   main()
39:   {
40:     int rv = 0;
41:
42:     initialize_color_table();
43:
44:     while( rv != 4 )                   /* loop in temp menu */
45:     {
46:       rv = do_main_menu();
```

13

continues

Listing 13.1. continued

```
47:      switch( rv )
48:      {
49:          case '1':  /* Menu option 1 */
50:  //                  do_albums_screen();
51:                      break;
52:
53:          case '2':  /* Menu option 2 */
54:  //                  do_medium_screen();
55:                      break;
56:
57:          case '3':  /* Menu option 3 */
58:  //                  do_groups_screen();
59:                      break;
60:
61:          case 'q':  /* exit */
62:          case 'Q':  rv = 4;
63:                      break;
64:
65:          default:   /* continue looping */
66:                      boop();
67:                      break;
68:      }
69:      }
70:
71:      /* clean up screen for exit */
72:      clear_screen( BRIGHTWHITE, BLACK );
73:      cursor(0,0);
74:      repeat_char(' ', 80, YELLOW, BLUE );
75:      write_string( "Thank you for using RECORD OF RECORDS!",
76:                      YELLOW, BLUE, 0, 21 );
77:      return 0;
78:  }
79:
80:  /*--------------------------------------------------------*
81:   *   do_main_menu                                         *
82:   *--------------------------------------------------------*/
83:  int do_main_menu(void)
84:  {
85:      int rv;
86:
87:      draw_borders("  RECORD of RECORDS!  " );
88:
89:      grid( 11, 16, 19, 59, ct.shdw_fcol, ct.bg_bcol, 3 );
90:      box(10, 15, 20, 60, SINGLE_BOX, FILL_BOX, ct.help_fcol,
             ct.help_bcol);
91:
92:      write_string( "1 - Enter Musical Items", YELLOW, GREEN, 11, 23 );
93:      write_string( "2 - Enter Medium Codes", YELLOW, GREEN, 12, 23 );
94:      write_string( "3 - Enter Group Information", YELLOW, GREEN, 13, 23
                     );
```

```
 95:     write_string( "Q - Quit", YELLOW, GREEN, 14, 23 );
 96:
 97:     cursor(24,79);
 98:     rv = getch();
 99:
100:     return( rv );
101: }
102:
103: /*--------------------------------------------------------*
104:  *    draw_borders()                                      *
105:  *--------------------------------------------------------*/
106: void draw_borders(char *title)
107: {
108:     int col=0;     /* used to center title */
109:
110:     clear_screen( ct.bg_fcol, ct.bg_bcol );
111:
112:     col = (( 80 - strlen(title)) / 2 );
113:
114:     write_string( title, ct.ttl_fcol, ct.ttl_bcol, 0, col );
115:
116:     cursor(1,0);
117:     repeat_char(' ', 80, ct.abar_fcol, ct.abar_bcol );
118:     cursor(24,0);
119:     repeat_char(' ', 80, ct.abar_fcol, ct.abar_bcol );
120: }
121:
122: /*--------------------------------------------------------*
123:  *    display_msg_box()                                   *
124:  *--------------------------------------------------------*/
125: void display_msg_box(char *msg, int fcol, int bcol )
126: {
127:     char *scrn_buffer = NULL;
128:     scrn_buffer = save_screen_area( 11, 15, 19, 60 );
129:
130:     grid( 12, 15, 19, 59, ct.shdw_fcol, ct.bg_bcol, 3 );
131:     box(11, 14, 20, 60, SINGLE_BOX, FILL_BOX, fcol, bcol);
132:
133:     write_string( msg, fcol, bcol, 12, 23 );
134:     write_string( "Press any key to continue...",
135:                    fcol, bcol, 13, 23 );
136:
137:     cursor(24, 79);
138:     getch();
139:
140:     restore_screen_area( scrn_buffer );
141: }
142:
143: /*--------------------------------------------------------*
```

13

continues

Listing 13.1. continued

```
144:  *   yes_no_box()                                          *
145:  *-------------------------------------------------------*/
146: char yes_no_box(char *msg, int fcol, int bcol )
147: {
148:    char ch;
149:    char *scrn_buffer = NULL;
150:    scrn_buffer = save_screen_area( 11, 15, 19, 60 );
151:
152:    grid( 12, 15, 19, 59, ct.shdw_fcol, ct.bg_bcol, 3 );
153:    box(11, 14, 20, 60, SINGLE_BOX, FILL_BOX, fcol, bcol);
154:
155:    write_string( msg, fcol, bcol, 12, 23 );
156:    write_string( "Enter (Y) or (N)", fcol, bcol, 13, 23 );
157:
158:    ch = getch();
159:    ch = toupper(ch);
160:
161:    cursor(24, 79);
162:    while( ch != 'Y' && ch != 'N' )
163:    {
164:       ch = toupper( getch() );
165:    }
166:
167:    restore_screen_area( scrn_buffer );
168:    return(ch);
169: }
170:
171: /*-------------------------------------------------------*
172:  *   Function: zero_fill_field();                        *
173:  *   Purpose:  Right justifies a character array and then*
174:  *             pads the left side with zeros. (Assumes   *
175:  *             that the field is NOT null terminated.)   *
176:  *   Returns:  # of zeros used to pad field              *
177:  *             -1 if field too large (longer than 20 )   *
178:  *             0  if field is blank (not padded)         *
179:  *-------------------------------------------------------*/
180:
181: int zero_fill_field( char *field, int size )
182: {
183:    int  ctr,
184:         pads = 0;
185:
186:    char tmp[20];
187:
188:    if( size > 20 )
189:    {
190:       pads = -1;    /* field too long */
191:    }
192:    else
193:    if( strlen(field) == 0 )
```

```
194:    {
195:        pads = 0;     /* leave blank fields blank. */
196:    }
197:    else
198:    {
199:        pads = size - (strlen(field));    /* How many 0s? */
200:
201:        for( ctr = 0; ctr < pads; ctr++ ) /* pad tmp field */
202:            tmp[ctr] = '0';
203:
204:            /* copy original info to end of tmp field */
205:        strncpy( tmp+pads, field, strlen(field));
206:            /* replace original field with padded tmp */
207:        strncpy(field, tmp, size);
208:    }
209:
210:    return(pads);
211: }
212:
213: /*-------------------------------------------------------*
214:  * initialize_color_table()                             *
215:  *                                                      *
216:  * Set up global color table for rest of application    *
217:  *-------------------------------------------------------*/
218:
219: void initialize_color_table( void )
220: {
221:    ct.bg_fcol = YELLOW;
222:    ct.bg_bcol = BLUE;
223:
224:    ct.fld_prmpt_fcol = CYAN;
225:    ct.fld_prmpt_bcol = BLUE;
226:
227:    ct.fld_fcol = BRIGHTWHITE;
228:    ct.fld_bcol = BLUE;
229:
230:    ct.fld_high_fcol = YELLOW;
231:    ct.fld_high_bcol = BLUE;
232:
233:    ct.ttl_fcol = BRIGHTWHITE;
234:    ct.ttl_bcol = BLACK;
235:
236:    ct.abar_fcol = BLACK;
237:    ct.abar_bcol = WHITE;
238:
239:    ct.err_fcol = YELLOW;
240:    ct.err_bcol = RED;
241:
242:    ct.db_fcol = WHITE;
243:    ct.db_bcol = BROWN;
```

continues

Listing 13.1. continued

```
244:
245:    ct.help_fcol = YELLOW;
246:    ct.help_bcol = GREEN;
247:
248:    ct.shdw_fcol = BLACK;
249: }
250:
251: /*========================================================*
252:  *                    end of listing                     *
253:  *========================================================*/
```

Note: Lines 50, 54, and 58 have been commented out. These lines should be uncommented when the listings presented later in this chapter have been included. You'll be told when each line should be uncommented.

Listing 13.2. RECOFREC.H. The *Record of Records!* program header.

```
1:    /*============================================================
2:     * Filename: RECofREC.H
3:     *
4:     * Author:    Bradley L. Jones & Gregory L. Guntle
5:     *
6:     * Purpose:   Header file for RECORD of RECORDS! application
7:     *            This contains the function prototypes needed
8:     *            by more than one source file.
9:     *============================================================*/
10:
11:   #ifndef __RECOFREC_H
12:   #define __RECOFREC_H
13:
14:   /*---------------------------*
15:    * Prototypes from recofrec.c *
16:    *---------------------------*/
17:
18:   void draw_borders(char *);
19:
20:   int  do_medium_screen(void);
21:   int  do_albums_screen(void);
22:   int  do_groups_screen(void);
23:   void display_msg_box( char *, int, int );
24:   char yes_no_box( char *, int, int );
```

```
25:  int  zero_fill_field( char *, int );
26:
27:  #endif
28:  /*=========================================================*
29:   *                   end of header                         *
30:   *=========================================================*/
```

**Listing 13.3. RECORDS.H. The *Record of Records!*
program header containing the structures for the
record layouts.**

```
1:  /*===========================================================
2:   * Filename: RECORDS.H
3:   *
4:   * Author:   Bradley L. Jones & Gregory L. Guntle
5:   *
6:   * Purpose:  Header file for RECORD of RECORDS! application
7:   *===========================================================*/
8:
9:  #ifndef __RECORDS_H
10: #define __RECORDS_H
11:
12: /*---------------------------*
13:  * File structures definitions*
14:  *---------------------------*/
15:
16: typedef struct
17: {
18:    char year[2];
19:    char month[2];
20:    char day[2];
21:
22: } DATE;
23:
24: typedef struct
25: {
26:    char title[ 30+1 ];
27:    char group[ 25+1];
28:    char medium_code[2+1];
29:    DATE date_purch;
30:    char cost[ 5+1 ];
31:    char value[ 5+1 ];
32:    int  nbr_songs;
33:
34: } ALBUM_REC;
35:
36: typedef struct
37: {
```

13

continues

Listing 13.3. continued

```
38:      char title[40+1];
39:      char minutes[2+1];
40:      char seconds[2+1];
41:
42:  } SONG_REC;
43:
44:  typedef struct
45:  {
46:      char code[2+1];
47:      char desc[35+1];
48:
49:  } MEDIUM_REC;
50:
51:  typedef struct
52:  {
53:      char group[25+1];
54:      DATE date_formed;
55:      char music_type[20+1];
56:      char member[6][30+1];
57:      char info[3][60+1];
58:
59:  } GROUP_REC;
60:
61:  /*-------------------*
62:   * color table       *
63:   *-------------------*/
64:
65:  struct color_table
66:  {
67:      int  bg_fcol;            /* background */
68:      int  bg_bcol;
69:
70:      int  fld_prmpt_fcol;     /* field prompt */
71:      int  fld_prmpt_bcol;
72:
73:      int  fld_fcol;           /* input field */
74:      int  fld_bcol;
75:
76:      int  fld_high_fcol;      /* highlight character */
77:      int  fld_high_fcol;
78:
79:      int  ttl_fcol;           /* screen title */
80:      int  ttl_bcol;
81:
82:      int  abar_fcol;          /* action bar & bottom */
83:      int  abar_bcol;
84:
85:      int  err_fcol;           /* error */
86:      int  err_bcol;
```

```
87:
88:    int  db_fcol;                 /* dialog box & msg box */
89:    int  db_bcol;
90:
91:    int  help_fcol;               /* help box colors */
92:    int  help_bcol;
93:
94:    int  shdw_fcol;               /* shadow color */
95: };
96:
97: /*-------------------------------------------*
98:  * extern declarations for global variables *
99:  *-------------------------------------------*/
100:
101: extern struct color_table ct;
102:
103: #endif
104: /*===========================================================*
105:  *                      end of header                        *
106:  *===========================================================*/
```

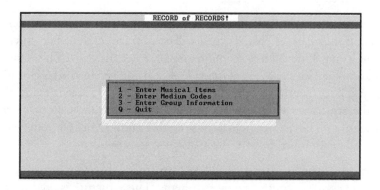

Listing 13.1 presents a shadowed box on a colorful screen with a simple menu. This can be seen in the output previously presented. In addition to this menu, there are several functions that will be used by the rest of the application. On Day 14, this menu will be replaced with a full functioning menu.

In lines 13 to 23, several header files are included. All of these header files, except for CONIO.H, are ANSI-compatible. While CONIO.H is not defined by the ANSI standards, it should not limit the portability of the program. Lines 17, 18, and 23 include header files that you have created. The TYAC.H header file is used with your TYAC.LIB library, which needs to be linked with these listings. Line 18 contains the header file that is in Listing 13.3. The RECOFREC.H header file is in Listing 13.2.

13

The RECOFREC.H header file is a small listing. It contains function prototypes for the functions that are used in more than one of the source files in the *Record of Records!* application. You will see this file included in each of the screen files presented later today.

Expert Tip: Many programmers consolidate prototypes for all the functions in an application into a single header file. This consolidated header file is then included in all of the source files for the given application.

The RECORDS.H header file, which is included in line 18 of RECOFREC.C, is in Listing 13.3. This header file contains all of the record structures that are used in the *Record of Records!* application. The typedef command has been used to create constant data types with each of these structures. Later, in the screen source files, these constants will be used to declare records.

Lines 16 to 22 of RECOFREC.H begin the structure declarations with a date structure called DATE. This structure will become part of the other structures in the rest of the listing. Lines 24 to 34 contain the ALBUM_REC structure. This is the structure that will be used with the Musical Items screen. If you review the specification from Day 12, you'll see that the information presented in the data matrix matches the members in the structure. The SONG_REC structure follows the ALBUM_REC structure. This structure will be used to hold each song title on the Musical Items screen. This will be used in conjunction with the ALBUM_REC structure.

Lines 44 to 49 contain the MEDIUM_REC structure. This is a much simpler structure to follow because it contains only two items. This structure is used in the first screen presented. Lines 51 to 59 contain the GROUP_REC structure, which is used to hold and save the group information.

The final structure in this header is the color_table structure. Because only a single color table will be created, there is no reason to create a type defined constant. Instead, a color table structure is declared in line 32 of the RECOFREC.C source file. Looking down the color table, you can see that there are variables defined for each of the different type of colors that could be used in your application (lines 67 to 94). As you review the source code presented over the next few days, you'll see that these structure members are used instead of the color constants presented in the TYAC.H header file.

A color_table structure is actually declared and initialized in RECOFREC.C (Listing 13.1). This structure is declared in line 32 as ct. This structure is then filled

with values when the `initialize_color_table()` function (lines 213 to 249) is called in line 42 of `main()`. This function is simple to follow. Each member of the color table that will be used in the application is initialized to an appropriate value. Because this function is called at the beginning of the application and because the color table, `ct`, is declared global, the color table can be used by the entire application.

The `main()` function in RECOFREC.C is easy to follow. A `while` loop in lines 44 to 69 puts the program into a loop that displays a menu and then waits for the user to enter a menu option of 1, 2, 3, or Q. The program continues to loop until the letter Q is entered. Once the user enters Q, the program performs some cleanup, displays a message, and then exits. While the program is looping, only three other values are valid, 1, 2, and 3. If the user enters any value other than these, the `boop()` function will cause the program to beep (line 66). If 1, 2, or 3 is called, then the function for the appropriate entry and edit screen is called. Each of these functions is presented in listings later today. Until you create these listings, you should leave these functions commented out.

As was stated, the main menu is displayed with a function call in line 46, `do_main_menu()`. This function is declared in lines 80 to 101. As you will see, this function doesn't present any features that you haven't already seen on earlier days. The `write_string()`, `grid()`, and `box()` functions should all be familiar now. The `draw_borders()` function, which is called in line 87, is defined in lines 103 to 120. This function is broken out from the `do_main_menu()` because the screen entry and edit applications will also use it. Again, the functions shouldn't present anything new.

You should note that in the `do_main_menu()` and the `draw_borders()` functions, color constants aren't used. Instead, the `ct` structure members are used. While this may seem a little cryptic at first, you'll find that using a structure like this will make your program more functional in the long run.

This leaves three final functions in RECOFREC.C. These are `display_msg_box()`, `yes_no_box()`, and `zero_fill_field()`. They are application-specific functions that are used in multiple source files. Because they are used in multiple places, they have been declared in the RECOFREC.C listing along with the `main()` function. Each of these has its own purpose. The `display_msg_box()` function displays a one line message on the screen in a shadowed box. It also displays a "Press any key to continue..." message before waiting for a key to be pressed by the user. You'll see this function used throughout the application. The `yes_no_box()` function in lines 143 to 165 is nearly identical to the `display_msg_box()`. It also displays a message; however, instead of waiting for any key to be pressed, it waits for a Y or an N to be pressed. This value, Y or N, is then passed back to the calling program. The final function, `zero_fill_field()`, may seem a little confusing. This function pads a field with zeros.

13

It pads the zeros on the left. For example, if a date of 1/1/94 were to be entered, you would use this function to add zeros to the day and month, thus making the date 01/01/94. This function contains a limitation in that it cannot pad a field that is larger than 20 characters in size. This limitation can be changed by modifying line 189. If the size is increased, the temporary character array, tmp, would also need to be increased in size (line 186). The comments in the listing should help you understand the rest of this function.

Overview of Creating Entry and Edit Screens

Now that you have a temporary menu and a table full of colors, you are ready to create your first full-fledged entry and edit screen. The next three listings contain each of the three entry and edit screens for the *Record of Records!* application. Each of these three listings is presented in the same format. In fact, the Medium Codes screen's code was used as a template to create the other two listings. You'll find that this listing makes a good template for creating your own entry and edit screens.

Figure 13.7 presents a pseudo-flow chart of the flow used by an entry and edit screen. This is a simplistic representation of what will occur in the entry and edit screen; however, it should help you understand the overall flow.

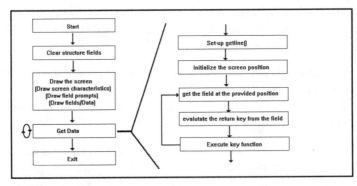

Figure 13.7. *The flow of an entry and edit screen.*

The analysis of the medium screen will follow the same order as in this figure.

The Medium Code
Entry and Edit Screen

The medium screen is used to capture the medium code and a description of what the code represents. For example, the code "CD" could be used to represent a compact disc. On a later day, you'll use the medium codes entered in this screen to validate the medium codes entered on the Musical Items screen.

The Code Behind the Medium Screen

Most of the code for the medium screen is presented all at once in Listing 13.4. This will help you more easily understand the code. The analysis for this listing will be covered in the next few sections. This listing should be compiled along with Listing 13.1, RECOFREC.C. In addition, it will need to be linked with your TYAC.LIB library.

Note: Don't forget to uncomment line 54 of RECOFREC.C (Listing 13.1).

Listing 13.4. MEDIUMS.C. The medium screen.

```
 1:  /*==========================================================
 2:   * Filename: medium.c
 3:   *
 4:   * Author:   Bradley L. Jones
 5:   *           Gregory L. Guntle
 6:   *
 7:   * Purpose:  Allow entry and edit of medium codes.
 8:   *
 9:   * Note:     This listing is linked with RECofREC.c
10:   *           (There isn't a main() in this listing!)
11:   *==========================================================*/
12:
13:  #include <stdio.h>
14:  #include <string.h>
15:  #include <conio.h>          /* for getch() */
16:  #include "tyac.h"
17:  #include "records.h"
18:
19:  /*-------------------*
20:   *     prototypes    *
21:   *-------------------*/
```

continues

Listing 13.4. continued

```
22:   #include "recofrec.h"
23:
24:   void draw_medium_screen( void );
25:   void draw_medium_prompts( void );
26:   void display_medium_fields( void );
27:
28:   int  clear_medium_fields(void);
29:   int  get_medium_data( int row );
30:   int  get_medium_input_data( void );
31:   void display_medium_help(void);
32:   int  add_medium_data( void );
33:
34:   /*------------------*
35:    * Defined constants *
36:    *------------------*/
37:
38:   #define MEDIUM_DBF    "MEDIUMS.DBF"
39:
40:   /*----------------------*
41:    * structure declarations *
42:    *----------------------*/
43:
44:   MEDIUM_REC medium;
45:   MEDIUM_REC *p_medium = &medium;
46:
47:   /*=======================================================*
48:    *    do_medium_screen()                                 *
49:    *=======================================================*/
50:
51:   int do_medium_screen(void)
52:   {
53:       clear_medium_fields();
54:       draw_medium_screen();
55:       get_medium_input_data();
56:       return 0;
57:   }
58:
59:   /*----------------------*
60:    *    draw_medium_screen()  *
61:    *----------------------*/
62:
63:   void draw_medium_screen( void )
64:   {
65:       draw_borders("     MEDIUM       ");  /* draw screen bckgrnd */
66:
67:       write_string( "<F1=Help>   <F3=Exit>   <F4=Save>",
68:             ct.abar_fcol, ct.abar_bcol, 24, 3);
69:
70:       draw_medium_prompts();
71:       display_medium_fields();
```

```
72:     }
73:
74:     /*------------------------*
75:      *    draw_medium_prompts() *
76:      *------------------------*/
77:
78:     void draw_medium_prompts( void )
79:     {
80:         write_string("Medium Code:",
81:                 ct.fld_prmpt_fcol, ct.fld_prmpt_bcol, 4, 3 );
82:         write_string("Medium Description:",
83:                 ct.fld_prmpt_fcol, ct.fld_prmpt_bcol, 6, 3 );
84:     }
85:
86:     /*------------------------*
87:      *    draw_medium_fields()  *
88:      *------------------------*/
89:
90:     void display_medium_fields( void )
91:     {
92:         write_string("__", ct.fld_fcol, ct.fld_bcol, 4, 17 );
93:         write_string("_____",
94:                 ct.fld_fcol, ct.fld_bcol, 6, 24 );
95:
96:         /* display data, if exists */
97:
98:         write_string(medium.code, ct.fld_fcol, ct.fld_bcol, 4, 17 );
99:         write_string(medium.desc, ct.fld_fcol, ct.fld_bcol, 6, 24 );
100: }
101:
102: /*---------------------------------------------------------*
103:  *    get_medium_input_data()                              *
104:  *---------------------------------------------------------*/
105: int get_medium_input_data( void )
106: {
107:     int    position,
108:        rv,
109:        loop = TRUE;
110:
111:     /*  Set up exit keys.  */
112:     static char fexit_keys[ 13 ] = { F1, F3, F4, ESC_KEY,
113:                     PAGE_DN, PAGE_UP, CR_KEY,
114:                     TAB_KEY, ENTER_KEY, SHIFT_TAB,
115:                     DN_ARROW, UP_ARROW, NULL };
116:
117:     static char *exit_keys = fexit_keys;
118:     getline( SET_EXIT_KEYS, 0, 12, 0, 0, 0, exit_keys );
119:
120:     /*** setup colors and default keys ***/
121:     getline( SET_DEFAULTS, 0, 0, 0, 0, 0, 0 );
```

continues

Listing 13.4. continued

```
122:        getline( SET_NORMAL, 0, ct.fld_fcol, ct.fld_bcol,
123:                    ct.fld_high_fcol, ct.fld_high_bcol, 0 );
124:        getline( SET_UNDERLINE, 0, ct.fld_fcol, ct.fld_bcol,
125:                    ct.fld_high_fcol, ct.fld_high_bcol, 0 );
126:        getline( SET_INS, 0, ct.abar_fcol, ct.abar_bcol, 24, 76, 0 );
127:
128:
129:
130:
131:
132:        position = 0;
133:
134:        while( loop == TRUE )        /** get data for top fields **/
135:        {
136:           switch( (rv = get_medium_data( position )) )
137:             {
138:               case CR_KEY    :
139:               case TAB_KEY   :
140:               case ENTER_KEY :
141:               case DN_ARROW  : /* go down a field */
142:                               ( position == 1 ) ? ( position = 0 ) :
143:                                 position++;
                                  break;
144:
145:               case SHIFT_TAB :
146:               case UP_ARROW  : /* go up a field */
147:                               ( position == 0 ) ? ( position = 1 ) :
148:                                 position--;
                                  break;
149:
150:               case ESC_KEY :
151:               case F3        :   /* exit back to main menu */
152:                               if( (yes_no_box( "Do you want to exit?",
153:                                       ct.db_fcol, ct.db_bcol )) =='Y')
154:                               {
155:                                   loop = FALSE;
156:                               }
157:
158:                               break;
159:
160:               case F4  :       /* add data */
161:
162:                               if( strlen( medium.code ) == 0 )
163:                               {
164:                                   display_msg_box("Must enter a medium
                                                   code",
165:                                       ct.err_fcol, ct.err_bcol);
166:
```

```
167:                                }
168:                                else
169:                                if( strlen( medium.desc ) == 0 )
170:                                {
171:                                    display_msg_box("Must enter a"
                                                        "description",
172:                                            ct.err_fcol, ct.err_bcol);
173:                                }
174:                                else /* all okay, so add data */
175:                                {
176:                                    add_medium_data();
177:
178:                                    clear_medium_fields();
179:                                    draw_medium_screen();
180:                                    position = 0;
181:                                }
182:
183:                                break;
184:
185:            case PAGE_DN :   /* go to last data entry field */
186:                             position = 1;
187:                             break;
188:
189:            case PAGE_UP :   /* go to first data entry field */
190:                             position = 0;
191:                             break;
192:
193:            case F1:         /* help */
194:                             display_medium_help();
195:                             draw_medium_screen();
196:                             break;
197:
198:            default:         /* error */
199:                             display_msg_box( " Error ",
200:                                     ct.err_fcol, ct.err_bcol );
201:                             break;
202:
203:         }      /* end of switch */
204:      }          /* end of while  */
205:
206:      return( rv );
207: }
208:
209: /*------------------------------------------------------------*
210:  *    get_medium_data()                                       *
211:  *------------------------------------------------------------*/
212:
213: int get_medium_data( int row )
214: {
215:     int rv;
```

continues

Listing 13.4. continued

```
216:
217:     switch( row )
218:     {
219:       case 0 :
220:           rv = getline( GET_ALPHA, 0,  4, 17, 0,  2, medium.code);
221:           break;
222:       case 1 :
223:           rv = getline( GET_ALPHA, 0,  6, 24, 0, 35, medium.desc);
224:           break;
225:     }
226:     return( rv );
227: }
228:
229: /*-------------------------------------------------------*
230:  *   clear_medium_fields()                               *
231:  *-------------------------------------------------------*/
232:
233: int clear_medium_fields(void)
234: {
235:   getline( CLEAR_FIELD, 0,  3, 0, 0, 0, medium.code );
236:   getline( CLEAR_FIELD, 0, 36, 0, 0, 0, medium.desc );
237:
238:   return(0);
239: }
240:
241: /*-------------------------------------------------------*
242:  *   display_medium_help()                               *
243:  *-------------------------------------------------------*/
244:
245: void display_medium_help(void)
246: {
247:   grid( 11, 16, 19, 59, ct.shdw_fcol, ct.bg_bcol, 3 );
248:   box(10, 15, 20, 60, SINGLE_BOX, FILL_BOX,
249:                       ct.help_fcol, ct.help_bcol);
250:
251:   write_string( "This is a screen for entering medium",
252:                 ct.help_fcol, ct.help_bcol, 11, 22 );
253:   write_string( "codes and their descriptions. To exit",
254:                 ct.help_fcol, ct.help_bcol, 12, 22 );
255:
256:   write_string( "this screen, press <F3> or <ESC>.",
257:       ct.help_fcol, ct.help_bcol, 13, 22 );
258:   write_string( "Press any key to continue...",
259:                 ct.help_fcol, ct.help_bcol, 14, 22 );
260:
261:   cursor(24, 79);
262:   getch();
263: }
264:
```

```
265:  /*------------------------------------------------------------*
266:   *   add_medium_data();                                      *
267:   *   Returns:  1 - if all okay                               *
268:   *             0 - if not all okay                           *
269:   *------------------------------------------------------------*/
270:
271:  int add_medium_data( void )
272:  {
273:     int    rv = 0;
274:     FILE *fp;
275:
276:     if( (fp = fopen( MEDIUM_DBF, "a" )) == NULL )
277:     {
278:           display_msg_box("Error opening file...",
279:                          ct.err_fcol, ct.err_bcol );
280:     }
281:     else
282:     {
283:        if( (fwrite( p_medium, sizeof( medium ), 1, fp )) == 0 )
284:        {
285:           display_msg_box("Error writing data...",
286:                          ct.err_fcol, ct.err_bcol );
287:        }
288:        else
289:        {
290:           display_msg_box("Record added", ct.db_fcol, ct.db_bcol);
291:           rv = 1;
292:        }
293:
294:        fclose( fp );
295:     }
296:     return( rv );
297:  }
298:  /*============================================================*
299:   *                   end of listing                          *
300:   *============================================================*/
```

13

```
                              MEDIUM

   Medium Code:  __
   Medium Description:  _____


    <F1=Help>   <F3=Exit>   <F5=Save>
```

 This is a long listing; however, the results are worth all the code. Throughout this listing, you can see many of the functions that you created in the previous chapters. One thing you won't find is a main() function. This is because the medium screen will be called by the menu presented in Listing 13.1, RECOFREC.C.

The *do_medium_screen()* Function

The do_medium_screen() function is called from line 54 of the RECOFREC.C source file. This function calls three other functions and then returns back to the menu. These three functions follow the flow presented in Figure 13.5. First a function is called to clear the fields, then the screen is drawn, and finally the data is retrieved.

Before MEDIUM.C begins the do_medium_screen() function, several things occur. In lines 13 to 17, various header files are included. In lines 22 through 32, function prototypes are declared. The RECOFREC.H header file is then included. RECOFREC.H is included in the prototype section because it contains mostly prototypes. Line 38 contains a defined constant, MEDIUM_DBF. This contains the name of the disk file that will be used to store the medium file. By using a defined constant, it will be easy for you to change the name of the database file. Lines 44 and 45 declare a MEDIUM_REC structure called medium and a pointer to the structure called p_medium. This structure is declared globally so that it is easy to use.

Clearing the Structure Fields

Line 53 in do_medium_screen() calls the function clear_medium_fields(), which clears the fields in the structure declared in line 44. The clear_medium_fields() function in lines 229 to 239 uses getline() to clear each structure member to Nulls. In the case of the medium structure, this is the code and the desc fields. By clearing the fields in this manner, you can be assured that they do not contain any erroneous data.

Setting Up the Screen

The next step presented in Figure 13.5 was drawing or setting up the screen. The do_medium_screen() calls the draw_medium_screen() function in line 54. The draw_medium_screen() function is declared in lines 59 to 72. Line 65 of this function calls the draw_borders() function that was defined in RECOFREC.C (Listing 13.1). The keys that are valid for special functions are then written on the bottom line of the screen (line 67). The next line, line 70, then calls the draw_medium_prompts(), which is presented in lines 74 to 84. This function draws each of the field prompts on the screen.

Line 71 of draw_medium_screen() calls the display_medium_fields() function. This function is important. It draws underlines on the screen in the locations where

getline() will retrieve data. If you leave this function out, getline() will draw the underlines one field at a time. It looks better to draw all the underlines on the screen up front. The second half of display_medium_fields() writes the actual field values on top of the underscores. Although they will be blank the first time into the screen, later functionality may require that the data be displayed too. Once the underlines and data have been drawn, the screen is complete and data entry is ready to begin.

Capturing the Data

Capturing the data takes up most of the listing. This capturing of the data starts when the do_medium_screen() function calls the get_medium_input_data() in line 55. The get_medium_input_data() function is presented in lines 102 to 207. This function starts by setting up the getline() function. Line 112 sets up the exit keys. As you can see, several exit keys are being set up. If you review the specification on Day 12, you will find that not all of the exit keys have been declared. The rest of the keys will be declared as they are needed on later days. Line 117 sets up a static character array pointing to the exit keys. Line 118 then sets up the exit keys. Lines 121 to 126 use the getline() function to set up the default colors. You should notice that the color table values are being used. These color table values were set up in the RECOFREC.C listing.

> **Tip:** If the getline() commands seem unfamiliar, you should review Day 10.

Once set up, the screen position is initialized to 0 in line 132. The first field on the screen is given position 0. Each field on the screen should then be given a sequential number following this one. The order in which the fields will be retrieved is based on their respective position numbers. For the Medium Codes screen, the Medium Codes field is considered position 0 and the description field is considered position 1.

Line 134 begins the loop for getting the data. This loop continues until a key action causes the looping flag, loop, to be chained to FALSE. For each iteration of the loop, a single data item is retrieved. This is done in line 136 using the get_medium_data() function. The current position is passed to the get_medium_data() function so that it knows which field on the screen to retrieve.

Once a field is retrieved, the key returned is evaluated within a switch statement. This return value will be one of the exit keys set up in line 112. Looking at lines 138 to 201, you can see what each exit key does. If the CR_KEY (carriage-return key), TAB_KEY (tab key), ENTER_KEY (enter key), or DN_ARROW (down arrow key) is pressed, then the position is incremented so that the next field is retrieved. If the field is the last field on the screen (in this case, field number 1), then the position is reset to the first field, 0. The SHIFT_TAB (shift+tab) and the UP_ARROW (up arrow key) do just the opposite. They decrement the position. If the position is the first position on the screen, then the position is reset to the last position on the screen, 1.

The ESC_KEY and the F3 keys function in the same manner. This functionality is presented in lines 151 to 158. Both keys offer the user a way of leaving the entry and edit screen. This follows the standards mentioned previously. The yes_no_box() function provided in the RECOFREC.C listing is used to ask the user if he is sure he wishes to exit. If he is not, then the program returns control to the entry screen and the user is left on the field he was previously on. If the user is sure, then loop is set to FALSE so that it will end.

The F4 key, lines 160 to 183, is used to add data. Before adding the data, edits may be performed. In this case, the user cannot add the data until he has entered a medium code (lines 162 to 167). If a medium code has not been entered, then a message is displayed explaining the situation to the user. If the code is okay, then the add_medium_data() function is called. This function, presented in lines 265 to 297 opens a file, writes the structure, displays a message, and returns. Line 178 then clears the structure fields and redraws the medium screen. This effectively clears the data entry screen for the next record. The position is then reset to 0 and the program resumes accepting data. On Day 15, the add_medium_data() function will be replaced as better file handling capabilities are added to the application.

The PAGE_DN and PAGE_UP keys operate in similar ways. PAGE_DN puts the cursor on the last field on the entry screen by changing the value of the position. This is done in line 186 by setting the position to 1. PAGE_UP sets the position to the first field on the screen. This will invariably be the value of 0.

> **Note:** There are times when you don't want to set the page down and page up values to the first or last field. This will be seen in the group screen presented later today.

The last key worked with is the F1 key. This key has been defined as the help key. Line 194 calls a function called draw_medium_screen(), which is presented in lines 241 to 263. This function creates a box that contains a little bit of help information. On Day 16, you'll see how to create context-sensitive help in your application.

The `default` case in lines 198 to 201 is a safety feature. The `getline()` function should only return those values set up in the exit keys; however, it's always a good programming tactic to include a `default` case in all of your `switch` calls. This can help catch potential problems.

Getting Individual Data Fields

The `get_medium_input_data()` function called the `get_medium_data()` function in line 136. In doing so, the position of the field that should be retrieved is passed. The `get_medium_data()` function is defined in lines 209 to 227. This function is basically a single `switch` statement that has a case for each field on the screen. Each case has a call to `getline()` that gets the individual field. The return value from `getline()` is captured in `rv` and then returned back to the `get_medium_input_data()` function. This returned value will only be one of the valid exit keys that were set up for `getline()`.

> **Note:** Edits on fields can be incorporated in this area of the program. If you want an edit on a field as it is being entered, it could be placed right after the call to `getline()`. In the analysis for the group screen, you will see an example of this.

> **Tip:** Review the Medium Codes screen before trying to understand the Group Screen's code. Each of these screens is progressively harder than the previous.

13

Everything Else

This is everything in the medium screen! As you should have noticed, this doesn't contain all the features that were mentioned in the specification. In addition, it doesn't have very good file control. Each record is written to a file; however, they can never be accessed. Over the next few days, these holes in the medium screen's functionality will be filled so that your application is complete.

The Group Information Screen

The Group screen is presented in Listing 13.5. As you will see, this listing is a little more complex than the Medium Codes screen. Some of the differences are caused by the additional number of fields in the group structure; however, there are a few other differences. Following is Listing 13.5, which contains the code for the Group Information screen.

> **Note:** This listing should be compiled and linked along with Listing 13.1 (RECOFREC.C), Listing 13.4 (MEDIUM.C), and your TYAC.LIB library. You should uncomment line 58 in Listing 13.1 before compiling and linking.

 Listing 13.5. The Group Information screen.

```
 1:  /*============================================================
 2:   * Filename: groups.c
 3:   *
 4:   * Author:   Bradley L. Jones
 5:   *
 6:   *
 7:   * Purpose:  Allow entry and edit of group information.
 8:   *
 9:   * Note:     This listing is linked with RECofREC.c
10:   *           (There isn't a main() in this listing!)
11:   *============================================================*/
12:
13:  #include <stdio.h>
14:  #include <string.h>
15:  #include <conio.h>          /* for getch() */
16:  #include "tyac.h"
17:  #include "records.h"
18:
19:  /*-------------------*
20:   *     prototypes    *
21:   *-------------------*/
22:  #include "recofrec.h"
23:
24:  void draw_groups_screen( void );
25:  void draw_groups_prompts( void );
26:  void display_groups_fields( void );
27:
28:  int  clear_groups_fields(void);
29:  int  get_groups_data( int row );
30:  int  get_groups_input_data( void );
31:  void display_groups_help(void);
```

```
32:    int  add_groups_data( void );
33:
34:    /*------------------*
35:     * Defined constants*
36:     *------------------*/
37:
38:    #define GROUPS_DBF    "GROUPS.DBF"
39:
40:    /*----------------------*
41:     * structure declarations *
42:     *----------------------*/
43:
44:    GROUP_REC groups;
45:    GROUP_REC *p_groups = &groups;
46:
47:    /*=======================================================*
48:     *    do_groups_screen()                                 *
49:     *=======================================================*/
50:
51:    int do_groups_screen(void)
52:    {
53:        clear_groups_fields();
54:        draw_groups_screen();
55:        get_groups_input_data();
56:        return 0;
57:    }
58:
59:    /*-----------------------*
60:     *    draw_groups_screen() *
61:     *-----------------------*/
62:
63:    void draw_groups_screen( void )
64:    {
65:        draw_borders("     Groups       ");  /* draw screen bckgrnd */
66:
67:        write_string( "<F1=Help>   <F3=Exit>   <F4=Save>",
68:                      ct.abar_fcol, ct.abar_bcol, 24, 3);
69:
70:        draw_groups_prompts();
71:        display_groups_fields();
72:    }
73:
74:    /*-----------------------*
75:     *    draw_groups_prompts()*
76:     *-----------------------*/
77:
78:    void draw_groups_prompts( void )
79:    {
80:        write_string("Group:",
81:                     ct.fld_prmpt_fcol, ct.fld_prmpt_bcol, 4, 3 );
```

continues

13

Listing 13.5. continued

```
82:      write_string("Date Formed:     /   /",
83:                      ct.fld_prmpt_fcol, ct.fld_prmpt_bcol, 6, 3 );
84:      write_string("Type of Music:",
85:                      ct.fld_prmpt_fcol, ct.fld_prmpt_bcol, 8, 3 );
86:      write_string("Members:",
87:                      ct.fld_prmpt_fcol, ct.fld_prmpt_bcol, 10, 3 );
88:      write_string("Description:",
89:                      ct.fld_prmpt_fcol, ct.fld_prmpt_bcol, 16, 3 );
90:  }
91:
92:  /*------------------------*
93:   *   draw_groups_fields() *
94:   *------------------------*/
95:
96:  void display_groups_fields( void )
97:  {
98:      char tmp[3] = { 0, 0, 0 };   /* initialize to null values */
99:      char under_30[31] = {"_____"};
100:
101:     write_string(under_30+5, /* 25 underlines */
102:            ct.fld_fcol, ct.fld_bcol, 4, 17 );
103:     write_string("__", ct.fld_fcol, ct.fld_bcol, 6, 17 );
104:     write_string("__", ct.fld_fcol, ct.fld_bcol, 6, 20 );
105:     write_string("__", ct.fld_fcol, ct.fld_bcol, 6, 23 );
106:     write_string(under_30+10, /* 20 underlines */
107:            ct.fld_fcol, ct.fld_bcol, 8, 19 );
108:     write_string(under_30, ct.fld_fcol, ct.fld_bcol, 12,  9 );
109:     write_string(under_30, ct.fld_fcol, ct.fld_bcol, 12, 42 );
110:     write_string(under_30, ct.fld_fcol, ct.fld_bcol, 13,  9 );
111:     write_string(under_30, ct.fld_fcol, ct.fld_bcol, 13, 42 );
112:     write_string(under_30, ct.fld_fcol, ct.fld_bcol, 14,  9 );
113:     write_string(under_30, ct.fld_fcol, ct.fld_bcol, 14, 42 );
114:     /* write the groups.info underlines in two parts */
115:     write_string(under_30, ct.fld_fcol, ct.fld_bcol, 18, 10 );
116:     write_string(under_30, ct.fld_fcol, ct.fld_bcol, 18, 40 );
117:     write_string(under_30, ct.fld_fcol, ct.fld_bcol, 19, 10 );
118:     write_string(under_30, ct.fld_fcol, ct.fld_bcol, 19, 40 );
119:     write_string(under_30, ct.fld_fcol, ct.fld_bcol, 20, 10 );
120:     write_string(under_30, ct.fld_fcol, ct.fld_bcol, 20, 40 );
121:
122:     /* display data, if exists */
123:
124:     write_string(groups.group,
125:                     ct.fld_fcol, ct.fld_bcol, 4, 17 );
126:     write_string(groups.music_type,
127:                     ct.fld_fcol, ct.fld_bcol, 8, 19 );
128:     write_string(groups.member[0],
129:                     ct.fld_fcol, ct.fld_bcol, 12,  9 );
130:     write_string(groups.member[1],
131:                     ct.fld_fcol, ct.fld_bcol, 12, 42 );
```

```
132:    write_string(groups.member[2],
133:              ct.fld_fcol, ct.fld_bcol, 13,  9 );
134:    write_string(groups.member[3],
135:              ct.fld_fcol, ct.fld_bcol, 13, 42 );
136:    write_string(groups.member[4],
137:              ct.fld_fcol, ct.fld_bcol, 14,  9 );
138:    write_string(groups.member[5],
139:              ct.fld_fcol, ct.fld_bcol, 14, 42 );
140:    write_string(groups.info[0],
141:              ct.fld_fcol, ct.fld_bcol, 18, 10 );
142:    write_string(groups.info[1],
143:              ct.fld_fcol, ct.fld_bcol, 19, 10 );
144:    write_string(groups.info[2],
145:              ct.fld_fcol, ct.fld_bcol, 20, 10 );
146:
147:    strncpy( tmp, groups.date_formed.month, 2 );
148:    write_string(tmp, ct.fld_fcol, ct.fld_bcol, 6, 17 );
149:    strncpy( tmp+4, groups.date_formed.day, 2 );
150:    write_string(tmp, ct.fld_fcol, ct.fld_bcol, 6, 20 );
151:    strncpy( tmp, groups.date_formed.year, 2 );
152:    write_string(tmp, ct.fld_fcol, ct.fld_bcol, 6, 23 );
153: }
154:
155: /*-----------------------------------------------------*
156:  *    get_groups_input_data()                          *
157:  *-----------------------------------------------------*/
158: int get_groups_input_data( void )
159: {
160:    int    position,
161:           rv,
162:           okay,                  /* used with edits */
163:           loop = TRUE;
164:
165:    /*  Set up exit keys.  */
166:    static char fexit_keys[ 13 ] = { F1, F3, F4, ESC_KEY, PAGE_DN,
                                         PAGE_UP, CR_KEY, TAB_KEY,
167:                                     ENTER_KEY, SHIFT_TAB, DN_ARROW,
                                         UP_ARROW, NULL };
168:
169:    static char *exit_keys = fexit_keys;
170:    getline( SET_EXIT_KEYS, 0, 12, 0, 0, 0, exit_keys );
171:
172:    /*** setup colors and default keys ***/
173:    getline( SET_DEFAULTS, 0, 0, 0, 0, 0, 0 );
174:    getline( SET_NORMAL, 0, ct.fld_fcol, ct.fld_bcol,
175:                            ct.fld_high_fcol, ct.fld_high_bcol, 0 );
176:    getline( SET_UNDERLINE, 0, ct.fld_fcol, ct.fld_bcol,
177:                            ct.fld_high_fcol, ct.fld_high_bcol, 0 );
178:    getline( SET_INS, 0, ct.abar_fcol, ct.abar_bcol, 24, 76, 0 );
179:
```

continues

Listing 13.5. continued

```
180:      position = 0;
181:
182:      while( loop == TRUE )        /**  get data for top fields  **/
183:      {
184:        switch( (rv = get_groups_data( position )) )
185:        {
186:      case CR_KEY    :
187:      case TAB_KEY   :
188:      case ENTER_KEY :
189:      case DN_ARROW  : /* go down a field */
190:              ( position == 13 ) ? ( position = 0 ) : position++;
191:              break;
192:
193:      case SHIFT_TAB :
194:      case UP_ARROW  : /* go up a field */
195:              ( position == 0 ) ? ( position = 13 ) : position--;
196:              break;
197:
198:      case ESC_KEY :
199:      case F3      :    /* exit back to main menu */
200:              if( (yes_no_box( "Do you want to exit?",
201:                   ct.db_fcol, ct.db_bcol )) == 'Y' )
202:              {
203:                  loop = FALSE;
204:              }
205:              break;
206:
207:      case F4 :        /* add data */
208:
209:              okay = TRUE;
210:
211:              if( strlen( groups.group ) == 0 )
212:              {
213:                  display_msg_box("Must enter a group name",
214:                     ct.err_fcol, ct.err_bcol);
215:                  position = 0;
216:                  okay = FALSE;
217:              }
218:              else
219:              {
220:                  /* rest of edits. (i.e. edit date) */
221:              }
222:
223:              if( okay == TRUE )
224:              {
225:                  add_groups_data();
226:
227:                  clear_groups_fields();
228:                  draw_groups_screen();
229:                  position = 0;
```

```
230:                    }
231:
232:                    break;
233:
234:         case PAGE_DN :    /* go to last data entry field */
235:                    position = 11;
236:                    break;
237:
238:         case PAGE_UP :    /* go to first data entry field */
239:                    position = 0;
240:                    break;
241:
242:         case F1:          /* help */
243:                    display_groups_help();
244:                    draw_groups_screen();
245:                    break;
246:
247:         default:          /* error */
248:                    display_msg_box( " Error ",
249:                       ct.err_fcol, ct.err_bcol );
250:                    break;
251:
252:         }      /* end of switch */
253:      }         /* end of while  */
254:
255:      return( rv );
256: }
257:
258: /*--------------------------------------------------------*
259:  *    get_groups_data()                                   *
260:  *--------------------------------------------------------*/
261:
262: int get_groups_data( int row )
263: {
264:      int  rv;
265:      char tmp[3] = { 0, 0, 0 }; /* initialize to null values */
266:
267:      switch( row )
268:      {
269:         case 0 :
270:            rv = getline( GET_ALPHA, 0,  4, 17, 0, 25, groups.group);
271:            break;
272:         case 1 :
273:            strncpy( tmp, groups.date_formed.month, 2 );
274:            rv = getline( GET_NUM,  0, 6, 17, 0,  2, tmp );
275:            zero_fill_field(tmp, 2);
276:            write_string(tmp, ct.fld_fcol, ct.fld_bcol, 6, 17);
277:            strncpy( groups.date_formed.month, tmp, 2);
278:            break;
```

continues

Listing 13.5. continued

```
279:            case 2 :
280:                strncpy( tmp, groups.date_formed.day, 2 );
281:                rv = getline( GET_NUM,    0,  6, 20, 0,  2, tmp );
282:                zero_fill_field(tmp, 2);
283:                write_string(tmp, ct.fld_fcol, ct.fld_bcol, 6, 20);
284:                strncpy( groups.date_formed.day, tmp, 2 );
285:                break;
286:            case 3 :
287:                strncpy( tmp, groups.date_formed.year, 2 );
288:                rv = getline( GET_NUM,    0,  6, 23, 0,  2, tmp );
289:                zero_fill_field(tmp, 2);
290:                write_string(tmp, ct.fld_fcol, ct.fld_bcol, 6, 23);
291:                strncpy( groups.date_formed.year, tmp, 2 );
292:                break;
293:            case 4 :
294:                rv = getline( GET_ALPHA, 0,  8, 19, 0, 20,
295:                                    groups.music_type);
295:                break;
296:            case 5 :
297:                rv = getline( GET_ALPHA, 0, 12,  9, 0, 30,
                                    groups.member[0]);
298:                break;
299:            case 6 :
300:                rv = getline( GET_ALPHA, 0, 12, 42, 0, 30,
                                    groups.member[1]);
301:                break;
302:            case 7 :
303:                rv = getline( GET_ALPHA, 0, 13,  9, 0, 30,
                                    groups.member[2]);
304:                break;
305:            case 8 :
306:                rv = getline( GET_ALPHA, 0, 13, 42, 0, 30,
                                    groups.member[3]);
307:                break;
308:            case 9 :
309:                rv = getline( GET_ALPHA, 0, 14,  9, 0, 30,
                                    groups.member[4]);
310:                break;
311:            case 10 :
312:                rv = getline( GET_ALPHA, 0, 14, 42, 0, 30,
                                    groups.member[5]);
313:                break;
314:            case 11 :
315:                rv = getline( GET_ALPHA, 0, 18, 10, 0, 60,
                                    groups.info[0]);
316:                break;
317:            case 12 :
318:                rv = getline( GET_ALPHA, 0, 19, 10, 0, 60,
                                    groups.info[1]);
```

```
319:              break;
320:          case 13 :
321:              rv = getline( GET_ALPHA, 0, 20, 10, 0, 60,
                                    groups.info[2]);
322:              break;
323:      }
324:      return( rv );
325: }
326:
327: /*-------------------------------------------------------*
328:  *   clear_groups_fields()                              *
329:  *-------------------------------------------------------*/
330:
331: int clear_groups_fields(void)
332: {
333:   getline( CLEAR_FIELD, 0, 26, 0, 0, 0, groups.group );
334:   getline( CLEAR_FIELD, 0,  2, 0, 0, 0, groups.date_formed.year );
335:   getline( CLEAR_FIELD, 0,  2, 0, 0, 0, groups.date_formed.month );
336:   getline( CLEAR_FIELD, 0,  2, 0, 0, 0, groups.date_formed.day );
337:   getline( CLEAR_FIELD, 0, 21, 0, 0, 0, groups.music_type );
338:   getline( CLEAR_FIELD, 0, 31, 0, 0, 0, groups.member[0] );
339:   getline( CLEAR_FIELD, 0, 31, 0, 0, 0, groups.member[1] );
340:   getline( CLEAR_FIELD, 0, 31, 0, 0, 0, groups.member[2] );
341:   getline( CLEAR_FIELD, 0, 31, 0, 0, 0, groups.member[3] );
342:   getline( CLEAR_FIELD, 0, 31, 0, 0, 0, groups.member[4] );
343:   getline( CLEAR_FIELD, 0, 31, 0, 0, 0, groups.member[5] );
344:   getline( CLEAR_FIELD, 0, 61, 0, 0, 0, groups.info[0] );
345:   getline( CLEAR_FIELD, 0, 61, 0, 0, 0, groups.info[1] );
346:   getline( CLEAR_FIELD, 0, 61, 0, 0, 0, groups.info[2] );
347:
348:   return(0);
349: }
350:
351: /*-------------------------------------------------------*
352:  *   display_groups_help()                              *
353:  *-------------------------------------------------------*/
354:
355: void display_groups_help(void)
356: {
357:   grid( 11, 16, 19, 59, ct.shdw_fcol, ct.bg_bcol, 3 );
358:   box(10, 15, 20, 60, SINGLE_BOX, FILL_BOX,
359:                         ct.help_fcol, ct.help_bcol);
360:
361:   write_string( "This is a screen for entering group",
362:                 ct.help_fcol, ct.help_bcol, 11, 22 );
363:   write_string( "information and their descriptions.",
364:                 ct.help_fcol, ct.help_bcol, 12, 22 );
365:
366:   write_string( "To exit screen, press <F3> or <ESC>.",
367:                 ct.help_fcol, ct.help_bcol, 13, 22 );
```

continues

421

Listing 13.5. continued

```
368:   write_string( "Press any key to continue...",
369:                 ct.help_fcol, ct.help_bcol, 14, 22 );
370:
371:   cursor(24, 79);
372:   getch();
373: }
374:
375: /*----------------------------------------------------------*
376:  *  add_groups_data();                                     *
377:  *  Returns:  1 - if all okay                              *
378:  *            0 - if not all okay                          *
379:  *----------------------------------------------------------*/
380:
381: int add_groups_data( void )
382: {
383:    int    rv = 0;
384:    FILE *fp;
385:
386:    if( (fp = fopen( GROUPS_DBF, "a" )) == NULL )
387:    {
388:         display_msg_box("Error opening file...",
389:                         ct.err_fcol, ct.err_bcol );
390:    }
391:    else
392:    {
393:       if( (fwrite( p_groups, sizeof( groups ), 1, fp )) == 0 )
394:       {
395:          display_msg_box("Error writing data...",
396:                          ct.err_fcol, ct.err_bcol );
397:       }
398:       else
399:       {
400:          display_msg_box("Record added", ct.db_fcol, ct.db_bcol);
401:          rv = 1;
402:       }
403:
404:       fclose( fp );
405:    }
406:    return( rv );
407: }
408: /*========================================================*
409:  *                    end of listing                     *
410:  *========================================================*/
```

At first glance, this listing may not seen too different from the MEDIUM.C listing (Listing 13.4). The MEDIUM.C listing was actually used as a template to create this listing. All of the medium-specific information was then changed to the corresponding group information. Because a detailed analysis was made on the medium screen, only the major differences need to be covered.

The first change can be seen in line 38. The name of the file being used is more appropriately named GROUPS.DBF. Lines 44 and 45 declare a group structure and a pointer using the type-defined constants from the RECORDS.H structure. This structure and the corresponding pointer are used throughout the rest of the listing to hold the data being entered by the user.

Several changes have been made in setting up the screen. In line 65, the draw_borders() function is called using the header for groups. In the draw_groups_prompts() function in lines 74 to 90, different prompts are displayed. These prompts are more appropriate for the group's information. In line 82, a prompt for a date is displayed. Because only the numeric part of the date will be retrieved, the separators are displayed along with the prompts.

The function to display the fields, display_groups_fields(), has some subtle changes also. To conserve on a little bit of storage area, a character array of 30 underlines has been created. This array is used to write several of the field underlines. Line 101 might be a little confusing at first. This is writing the field underlines for the group name. At first glance, the under_30 character array may seem too long. To get around this, only the last 25 characters are printed. This is accomplished by printing the character array starting at the sixth position—by adding five to its starting address. Line 106 prints 20 underlines in the same manner.

An additional difference in display_groups_fields() is the use of the tmp character array. This is a temporary character array used to display the individual date members—month, day, year. Because the date fields are stored without null terminators,

they can't be displayed like the other null terminated character arrays. To get around this, the date fields are copied into the temporary, `tmp`, field and then the `tmp` field is displayed (lines 147 to 152). When the data is retrieved using `getline()` in the `get_groups_data()` function, this same approach is used. An example of this can be seen in lines 284 to 287.

Getting the Group Data:
The *get_groups_input_data()* Function

Getting data is nearly identical to what was presented in the MEDIUM.C listing. Lines 190 and 195 are changed to reflect that the group's screen has 14 fields. In addition to the other cursor movement functions, the page down function is also modified to set the screen's last position to 13.

The case for the F4 key in lines 207 to 233 is modified only slightly. This is the function to add the groups record. Before adding the record, the entered data should be verified to ensure that it is accurate. In this listing, the only edit performed is a check on the group name, `group.group`. This name can't be blank. Additional edits, such as an edit on the date, could be added in the `else` statement. A flag called `okay` is used to see if all the edits passed. If they did, the record is added and data entry continues. If the edits didn't pass, a descriptive message is displayed and control is returned to the screen.

The `get_groups_data()` has the actual `getline()` cases for retrieving each field. You should notice that both numbers and characters are retrieved using either `GET_NUM` or `GET_ALPHA` with `getline()`. Several of the `getline()` cases could be expanded to include edits. For example, if the user enters a `month` of 13 in case 1 (lines 272 to 278), then there is an error. You could capture this error at this time, rather than waiting for the user to add the record. One of today's exercises will ask you to add this edit to the group's listing.

> **Note:** You can add edits to the `getline()` functions; however, you shouldn't make them mandatory. If the escape key or the F3 key (for exiting) are pressed, then the user should still be able to leave the screen. It would be up to you to determine if the other keys would enable them to continue.

One last function needs to be reviewed. This is the `zero_fill_field()` function, which is used in several of the `case` statements for getting data. After the call to `getline()`, the field is padded on the left with zeros with this function. The next line

uses write_string() to rewrite the field on the screen with the zeros. The
zero_fill_field() was a part of the RECOFREC.C listing (Listing 13.1).

DO	**DON'T**

DO use edits in your programs to ensure the data entered is valid.

DON'T forget to initialize the data elements in your structures. This way
you can be assured that they don't contain garbage.

DO use Listing 13.4, MEDIUMS.C, as a template for creating your own
data entry screens. "Real" programmers only write one program of any given
type. They then copy it for a starting point of the next program.

The Musical Items
Entry and Edit Screen

Having created the Medium Codes and the Group Information screens, you now only
need the Musical Items screen. Listing 13.6 presents the first cut of this screen. The
functionality is not complete; however, the frame work is. Several of the advanced
features of this listing will be covered on Days 15 through 19. Today, we concentrate
solely on the basic data entry functions.

Note: This listing should be compiled and linked along with Listings
13.1, 13.2, 13.3, and your TYAC.LIB library. You should uncomment
line 58 in Listing 13.1 before compiling and linking.

13

**Listing 13.6. ALBUMS.C. The Musical Items entry and
edit screen.**

```
1:    /*==========================================================
2:     * Filename: albums.c
3:     *
4:     * Author:   Bradley L. Jones
5:     *           Gregory L. Guntle
6:     *
```

continues

Listing 13.6. continued

```
 7:    * Purpose:   Allow entry and edit of information on musical
 8:    *            items.
 9:    *
10:    * Note:      This listing is linked with RECofREC.c
11:    *            (There isn't a main() in this listing!)
12:    *=========================================================*/
13:
14:   #include <stdio.h>
15:   #include <string.h>
16:   #include <conio.h>          /* for getch() */
17:   #include "tyac.h"
18:   #include "records.h"
19:
20:   /*-------------------*
21:    *     prototypes    *
22:    *-------------------*/
23:   #include "recofrec.h"
24:
25:   void draw_albums_screen( void );
26:   void draw_albums_prompts( void );
27:   void display_albums_fields( void );
28:
29:   int  clear_albums_fields(void);
30:   int  get_albums_data( int row );
31:   int  get_albums_input_data( void );
32:   void display_albums_help(void);
33:   int  add_albums_data( void );
34:
35:   /*-----------------*
36:    * Defined constants*
37:    *-----------------*/
38:
39:   #define ALBUMS_DBF    "ALBUMS.DBF"
40:
41:   /*----------------------*
42:    * structure declarations *
43:    *----------------------*/
44:
45:   ALBUM_REC albums;
46:   ALBUM_REC *p_albums = &albums;
47:   SONG_REC  songs[7];
48:
49:   /*=======================================================*
50:    *    do_albums_screen()                                 *
51:    *=======================================================*/
52:
53:   int do_albums_screen(void)
54:   {
55:       clear_albums_fields();
```

```
56:        draw_albums_screen();
57:        get_albums_input_data();
58:        return 0;
59:    }
60:
61:    /*-----------------------*
62:     *   draw_albums_screen() *
63:     *-----------------------*/
64:
65:    void draw_albums_screen( void )
66:    {
67:        draw_borders("  Musical Items  ");  /* draw screen bckgrnd */
68:
69:        write_string( "<F1=Help>    <F3=Exit>    <F4=Save>",
70:                       ct.abar_fcol, ct.abar_bcol, 24, 3);
71:
72:        draw_albums_prompts();
73:        display_albums_fields();
74:    }
75:
76:    /*-----------------------*
77:     *   draw_albums_prompts()*
78:     *-----------------------*/
79:
80:    void draw_albums_prompts( void )
81:    {
82:        int  ctr;
83:        char tmp[10];
84:
85:        write_string("Title:",
86:                       ct.fld_prmpt_fcol, ct.fld_prmpt_bcol, 4, 3 );
87:        write_string("Group:",
88:                       ct.fld_prmpt_fcol, ct.fld_prmpt_bcol, 5, 3 );
89:        write_string("Medium:",
90:                       ct.fld_prmpt_fcol, ct.fld_prmpt_bcol, 7, 3 );
91:        write_string("Date Purchased:    /  /",
92:                       ct.fld_prmpt_fcol, ct.fld_prmpt_bcol, 9, 3 );
93:        write_string("Cost:  $   .",
94:                       ct.fld_prmpt_fcol, ct.fld_prmpt_bcol, 9, 33 );
95:        write_string("Value: $   .",
96:                       ct.fld_prmpt_fcol, ct.fld_prmpt_bcol, 9, 52 );
97:        write_string("Track    Song Title",
98:                       ct.fld_prmpt_fcol, ct.fld_prmpt_bcol, 11, 7 );
99:        write_string("Time",
100:                       ct.fld_prmpt_fcol, ct.fld_prmpt_bcol, 11, 59 );
101:        for( ctr = 0; ctr < 7; ctr++ )
102:        {
103:            sprintf(tmp, "%02d:",ctr+1);
104:            write_string( tmp,
105:                    ct.fld_prmpt_fcol, ct.fld_prmpt_bcol, 13+ctr, 8 );
```

13

continues

Listing 13.6. continued

```
106:            write_string(":",
107:                ct.fld_prmpt_fcol, ct.fld_prmpt_bcol, 13+ctr, 61 );
108:        }
109:
110:    write_string("Total Album Time:    :   :",
111:                ct.fld_prmpt_fcol, ct.fld_prmpt_bcol, 21, 39 );
112:
113:    /* Track information */
114:
115: }
116:
117: /*-----------------------*
118:  *   draw_albums_fields() *
119:  *-----------------------*/
120:
121: void display_albums_fields( void )
122: {
123:    int ctr;
124:    char tmp[4] = { 0, 0, 0, 0 };    /* set to null values */
125:    char under_40[41] =
126:            {"_____"};
127:
128:    write_string(under_40+10,    /* 30 underscores */
129:                ct.fld_fcol, ct.fld_bcol, 4, 12 );
130:    write_string(under_40+15,      /* 25 underlines */
131:                ct.fld_fcol, ct.fld_bcol, 5, 12 );
132:    write_string("__", ct.fld_fcol, ct.fld_bcol, 7, 13 );
133:    write_string("__", ct.fld_fcol, ct.fld_bcol, 9, 20 );
134:    write_string("__", ct.fld_fcol, ct.fld_bcol, 9, 23 );
135:    write_string("__", ct.fld_fcol, ct.fld_bcol, 9, 26 );
136:
137:    write_string("__", ct.fld_fcol, ct.fld_bcol, 9, 41 );
138:    write_string("__",  ct.fld_fcol, ct.fld_bcol, 9, 45 );
139:
140:    write_string("__", ct.fld_fcol, ct.fld_bcol, 9, 61 );
141:    write_string("__",  ct.fld_fcol, ct.fld_bcol, 9, 65 );
142:
143:    for( ctr = 0; ctr < 7; ctr++)
144:    {
145:       write_string(under_40,
146:                ct.fld_fcol, ct.fld_bcol, 13+ctr, 16 );
147:       write_string("__",
148:                ct.fld_fcol, ct.fld_bcol, 13+ctr, 59 );
149:       write_string("__",
150:                ct.fld_fcol, ct.fld_bcol, 13+ctr, 62 );
151:    }
152:
153:    write_string("__", ct.fld_fcol, ct.fld_bcol, 21, 57);
154:    write_string("__", ct.fld_fcol, ct.fld_bcol, 21, 60);
```

```
155:        write_string("__", ct.fld_fcol, ct.fld_bcol, 21, 63);
156:
157:        /*** display data, if exists ***/
158:
159:        write_string(albums.title, ct.fld_fcol, ct.fld_bcol, 4, 12);
160:        write_string(albums.group, ct.fld_fcol, ct.fld_bcol, 5, 12);
161:        write_string(albums.medium_code,
162:                     ct.fld_fcol, ct.fld_bcol, 7, 13 );
163:
164:        strncpy( tmp, albums.date_purch.month, 2 );
165:        write_string(tmp, ct.fld_fcol, ct.fld_bcol, 9, 20 );
166:        strncpy( tmp+4, albums.date_purch.day, 2 );
167:        write_string(tmp, ct.fld_fcol, ct.fld_bcol, 9, 23 );
168:        strncpy( tmp, albums.date_purch.year, 2 );
169:        write_string(tmp, ct.fld_fcol, ct.fld_bcol, 9, 26 );
170:
171:        strncpy(tmp, albums.cost, 3);
172:        write_string(tmp, ct.fld_fcol, ct.fld_bcol, 9, 41 );
173:        strncpy(tmp, albums.cost+3, 2 );
174:        tmp[3] = NULL;
175:        write_string(tmp, ct.fld_fcol, ct.fld_bcol, 9, 45 );
176:
177:        strncpy(tmp, albums.value, 3);
178:        write_string(tmp, ct.fld_fcol, ct.fld_bcol, 9, 61 );
179:        strncpy(tmp, albums.value+3, 2 );
180:        tmp[3] = NULL;
181:        write_string(tmp, ct.fld_fcol, ct.fld_bcol, 9, 65 );
182:
183:        /* song title information */
184:        for( ctr = 0; ctr < 7; ctr++ )
185:        {
186:           write_string(songs[ctr].title,
187:               ct.fld_fcol, ct.fld_bcol, 13+ctr, 16 );
188:           write_string(songs[ctr].minutes,
189:               ct.fld_fcol, ct.fld_bcol, 13+ctr, 69 );
190:           write_string(songs[ctr].seconds,
191:               ct.fld_fcol, ct.fld_bcol, 13+ctr, 62 );
192:         /* calc total here. */
193:        }
194:        /* finish total count and print here */
195: }
196:
197: /*----------------------------------------------------------*
198:  *    get_albums_input_data()                               *
199:  *----------------------------------------------------------*/
200: int get_albums_input_data( void )
201: {
202:     int    position,
203:            rv,
204:            okay,                   /* used with edits */
```

continues

Listing 13.6. continued

```
205:            loop = TRUE;
206:
207:       /*  Set up exit keys.  */
208:       static char fexit_keys[ 13 ] = { F1, F3, F4, ESC_KEY, PAGE_DN,
                                             PAGE_UP, CR_KEY, TAB_KEY,
209:                                          ENTER_KEY, SHIFT_TAB,
                                             DN_ARROW, UP_ARROW, NULL };
210:
211:       static char *exit_keys = fexit_keys;
212:       getline( SET_EXIT_KEYS, 0, 12, 0, 0, 0, exit_keys );
213:
214:       /*** setup colors and default keys ***/
215:       getline( SET_DEFAULTS, 0, 0, 0, 0, 0, 0 );
216:       getline( SET_NORMAL, 0, ct.fld_fcol, ct.fld_bcol,
217:                               ct.fld_high_fcol, ct.fld_high_bcol, 0 );
218:       getline( SET_UNDERLINE, 0, ct.fld_fcol, ct.fld_bcol,
219:                               ct.fld_high_fcol, ct.fld_high_bcol, 0 );
220:       getline( SET_INS, 0, ct.abar_fcol, ct.abar_bcol, 24, 76, 0 );
221:
222:       position = 0;
223:
224:       while( loop == TRUE )        /**  get data for top fields  **/
225:       {
226:         switch( (rv = get_albums_data( position )) )
227:           {
228:         case CR_KEY    :
229:         case TAB_KEY   :
230:         case ENTER_KEY :
231:         case DN_ARROW  : /* go down a field */
232:                 ( position == 30 ) ? ( position = 0 ) : position++;
233:                 break;
234:
235:         case SHIFT_TAB :
236:         case UP_ARROW  : /* go up a field */
237:                 ( position == 0 ) ? ( position = 30 ) : position--;
238:                 break;
239:
240:         case ESC_KEY :
241:         case F3      :  /* exit back to main menu */
242:                 if( (yes_no_box( "Do you want to exit?",
243:                     ct.db_fcol, ct.db_bcol )) == 'Y' )
244:                 {
245:                     loop = FALSE;
246:                 }
247:                 break;
248:
249:         case F4 :   /* add data */
250:
251:                 okay = TRUE;
252:
```

```
253:                    if( strlen( albums.title ) == 0 )
254:                    {
255:                        display_msg_box("Must enter a Title",
256:                            ct.err_fcol, ct.err_bcol);
257:                        position = 0;
258:                        okay = FALSE;
259:                    }
260:                    else
261:                    {
262:                        /* edit date */
263:
264:                    }
265:
266:                    if( okay == TRUE )
267:                    {
268:                        add_albums_data();
269:
270:                        clear_albums_fields();
271:                        draw_albums_screen();
272:                        position = 0;
273:                    }
274:
275:                    break;
276:
277:          case PAGE_DN :   /* go to last data entry field */
278:                    position = 30;
279:                    break;
280:
281:          case PAGE_UP :   /* go to first data entry field */
282:                    position = 0;
283:                    break;
284:
285:          case F1:          /* help */
286:                    display_albums_help();
287:                    draw_albums_screen();
288:                    break;
289:
290:          default:          /* error */
291:                    display_msg_box( " Error ",
292:                        ct.err_fcol, ct.err_bcol );
293:                    break;
294:
295:          }      /* end of switch */
296:      }          /* end of while  */
297:
298:      return( rv );
299: }
300:
```

continues

Listing 13.6. continued

```
301: /*--------------------------------------------------------*
302:  *   get_albums_data()                                    *
303:  *--------------------------------------------------------*/
304:
305: int get_albums_data( int row )
306: {
307:     int  rv;
308:     char tmp[4] = { 0, 0, 0, 0 }; /* set to null values */
309:
310:     switch( row )
311:     {
312:        case 0 :
313:            rv = getline( GET_ALPHA, 0,  4, 12, 0, 30, albums.title);
314:            break;
315:        case 1 :
316:            rv = getline( GET_ALPHA, 0,  5, 12, 0, 25, albums.group);
317:            break;
318:        case 2 :
319:            rv = getline( GET_ALPHA, 0,  7, 13, 0,  2,
320:                              albums.medium_code);
320:            break;
321:        case 3 :
322:            strncpy( tmp, albums.date_purch.month, 2 );
323:            rv = getline( GET_NUM,   0,  9, 20, 0,  2, tmp );
324:            zero_fill_field(tmp, 2);
325:            write_string(tmp, ct.fld_fcol, ct.fld_bcol, 9, 20);
326:            strncpy( albums.date_purch.month, tmp, 2);
327:            break;
328:        case 4 :
329:            strncpy( tmp, albums.date_purch.day, 2 );
330:            rv = getline( GET_NUM,   0,  9, 23, 0,  2, tmp );
331:            zero_fill_field(tmp, 2);
332:            write_string(tmp, ct.fld_fcol, ct.fld_bcol, 9, 23);
333:            strncpy( albums.date_purch.day, tmp, 2 );
334:            break;
335:        case 5 :
336:            strncpy( tmp, albums.date_purch.year, 2 );
337:            rv = getline( GET_NUM,   0,  9, 26, 0,  2, tmp );
338:            zero_fill_field(tmp, 2);
339:            write_string(tmp, ct.fld_fcol, ct.fld_bcol, 9, 26);
340:            strncpy( albums.date_purch.year, tmp, 2 );
341:            break;
342:        case 6 :
343:            strncpy( tmp, albums.cost, 3 );
344:            rv = getline( GET_NUM,   0,  9, 41, 0,  3, tmp );
345:            zero_fill_field(tmp, 3);
346:            write_string(tmp, ct.fld_fcol, ct.fld_bcol, 9, 41);
347:            strncpy( albums.cost, tmp, 3 );
348:            break;
```

```
349:        case 7 :
350:            strncpy( tmp, albums.cost+3, 2 );
351:            rv = getline( GET_NUM,   0,  9, 45, 0,  2, tmp );
352:            zero_fill_field(tmp, 2);
353:            write_string(tmp, ct.fld_fcol, ct.fld_bcol, 9, 45);
354:            strncpy( albums.cost+3, tmp, 2 );
355:            break;
356:        case 8 :
357:            strncpy( tmp, albums.value, 3 );
358:            rv = getline( GET_NUM,   0,  9, 61, 0,  3, tmp );
359:            zero_fill_field(tmp, 3);
360:            write_string(tmp, ct.fld_fcol, ct.fld_bcol, 9, 61);
361:            strncpy( albums.value, tmp, 3 );
362:            break;
363:        case 9 :
364:            strncpy( tmp, albums.value+3, 2 );
365:            rv = getline( GET_NUM,   0,  9, 65, 0,  2, tmp );
366:            zero_fill_field(tmp, 2);
367:            write_string(tmp, ct.fld_fcol, ct.fld_bcol, 9, 65);
368:            strncpy( albums.value+3, tmp, 2 );
369:            break;
370:        case 10 :
371:            rv = getline( GET_ALPHA, 0,  13, 16, 0, 40,
372:                                              songs[0].title);
373:            break;
374:        case 11 :
375:            rv = getline( GET_NUM, 0, 13, 59, 0, 2,
376:                                              songs[0].minutes);
377:            zero_fill_field(songs[0].minutes, 2);
378:            write_string(songs[0].minutes,
379:                    ct.fld_fcol, ct.fld_bcol, 13, 59);
380:            break;
381:        case 12 :
382:            rv = getline( GET_NUM, 0, 13, 62, 0, 2,
383:                                              songs[0].seconds);
384:            zero_fill_field(songs[0].seconds, 2);
385:            write_string(songs[0].seconds,
386:                    ct.fld_fcol, ct.fld_bcol, 13, 62);
387:            break;
388:        case 13 :
389:            rv = getline( GET_ALPHA, 0, 14, 16, 0, 40,
390:                                              songs[1].title);
391:            break;
392:        case 14 :
393:            rv = getline( GET_NUM, 0, 14, 59, 0, 2,
394:                                              songs[1].minutes);
395:            zero_fill_field(songs[1].minutes, 2);
396:            write_string(songs[1].minutes,
397:                    ct.fld_fcol, ct.fld_bcol, 14, 59);
398:            break;
```

continues

Listing 13.6. continued

```
399:        case 15 :
400:            rv = getline( GET_NUM, 0, 14, 62, 0, 2,
401:                                        songs[1].seconds);
402:            zero_fill_field(songs[1].seconds, 2);
403:            write_string(songs[1].seconds,
404:                        ct.fld_fcol, ct.fld_bcol, 14, 62);
405:            break;
406:        case 16 :
407:            rv = getline( GET_ALPHA, 0, 15, 16, 0, 40,
408:                                        songs[2].title);
409:            break;
410:        case 17 :
411:            rv = getline( GET_NUM, 0, 15, 59, 0, 2,
412:                                        songs[2].minutes);
413:            zero_fill_field(songs[2].minutes, 2);
414:            write_string(songs[2].minutes,
415:                        ct.fld_fcol, ct.fld_bcol, 15, 59);
416:            break;
417:        case 18 :
418:            rv = getline( GET_NUM, 0, 15, 62, 0, 2,
419:                                        songs[2].seconds);
420:            zero_fill_field(songs[2].seconds, 2);
421:            write_string(songs[2].seconds,
422:                        ct.fld_fcol, ct.fld_bcol, 15, 62);
423:            break;
424:        case 19 :
425:            rv = getline( GET_ALPHA, 0, 16, 16, 0, 40,
426:                                        songs[3].title);
427:            break;
428:        case 20 :
429:            rv = getline( GET_NUM, 0, 16, 59, 0, 2,
430:                                        songs[3].minutes);
431:            zero_fill_field(songs[3].minutes, 2);
432:            write_string(songs[3].minutes,
433:                        ct.fld_fcol, ct.fld_bcol, 16, 59);
434:            break;
435:        case 21 :
436:            rv = getline( GET_NUM, 0, 16, 62, 0, 2,
437:                                        songs[3].seconds);
438:            zero_fill_field(songs[3].seconds, 2);
439:            write_string(songs[3].seconds,
440:                        ct.fld_fcol, ct.fld_bcol, 16, 62);
441:            break;
442:        case 22 :
443:            rv = getline( GET_ALPHA, 0, 17, 16, 0, 40,
444:                                        songs[4].title);
445:            break;
446:        case 23 :
447:            rv = getline( GET_NUM, 0, 17, 59, 0, 2,
448:                                        songs[4].minutes);
```

```
449:            zero_fill_field(songs[4].minutes, 2);
450:            write_string(songs[4].minutes,
451:                        ct.fld_fcol, ct.fld_bcol, 17, 59);
452:            break;
453:        case 24 :
454:            rv = getline( GET_NUM, 0, 17, 62, 0, 2,
455:                                             songs[4].seconds);
456:            zero_fill_field(songs[4].seconds, 2);
457:            write_string(songs[4].seconds,
458:                        ct.fld_fcol, ct.fld_bcol, 17, 62);
459:            break;
460:        case 25 :
461:            rv = getline( GET_ALPHA, 0, 18, 16, 0, 40,
462:                                             songs[5].title);
463:            break;
464:        case 26 :
465:            rv = getline( GET_NUM, 0, 18, 59, 0, 2,
466:                                             songs[5].minutes);
467:            zero_fill_field(songs[5].minutes, 2);
468:            write_string(songs[5].minutes,
469:                        ct.fld_fcol, ct.fld_bcol, 18, 59);
470:            break;
471:        case 27 :
472:            rv = getline( GET_NUM, 0, 18, 62, 0, 2,
473:                                             songs[5].seconds);
474:            zero_fill_field(songs[5].seconds, 2);
475:            write_string(songs[5].seconds,
476:                        ct.fld_fcol, ct.fld_bcol, 18, 62);
477:            break;
478:        case 28 :
479:            rv = getline( GET_ALPHA, 0, 19, 16, 0, 40,
480:                                             songs[6].title);
481:            break;
482:        case 29 :
483:            rv = getline( GET_NUM, 0, 19, 59, 0, 2,
484:                                             songs[6].minutes);
485:            zero_fill_field(songs[6].minutes, 2);
486:            write_string(songs[6].minutes,
487:                        ct.fld_fcol, ct.fld_bcol, 19, 59);
488:            break;
489:        case 30 :
490:            rv = getline( GET_NUM, 0, 19, 62, 0, 2,
491:                                             songs[6].seconds);
492:            zero_fill_field(songs[6].seconds, 2);
493:            write_string(songs[6].seconds,
494:                        ct.fld_fcol, ct.fld_bcol, 19, 62);
495:            break;
496:    }
497:    return( rv );
```

13

continues

435

Listing 13.6. continued

```
498: }
499:
500: /*----------------------------------------------------------*
501:  *    clear_albums_fields()                               *
502:  *----------------------------------------------------------*/
503:
504: int clear_albums_fields(void)
505: {
506:    int ctr;
507:
508:    getline( CLEAR_FIELD, 0, 31, 0, 0, 0, albums.title );
509:    getline( CLEAR_FIELD, 0, 26, 0, 0, 0, albums.group );
510:    getline( CLEAR_FIELD, 0,  3, 0, 0, 0, albums.medium_code );
511:    getline( CLEAR_FIELD, 0,  2, 0, 0, 0, albums.date_purch.month );
512:    getline( CLEAR_FIELD, 0,  2, 0, 0, 0, albums.date_purch.day );
513:    getline( CLEAR_FIELD, 0,  2, 0, 0, 0, albums.date_purch.year );
514:    getline( CLEAR_FIELD, 0,  6, 0, 0, 0, albums.cost );
515:    getline( CLEAR_FIELD, 0,  6, 0, 0, 0, albums.value );
516:    albums.nbr_songs = 0;
517:    for( ctr = 0; ctr < 7; ctr++ )
518:    {
519:       getline( CLEAR_FIELD, 0, 41, 0, 0, 0, songs[ctr].title );
520:       getline( CLEAR_FIELD, 0,  3, 0, 0, 0, songs[ctr].minutes );
521:       getline( CLEAR_FIELD, 0,  3, 0, 0, 0, songs[ctr].seconds );
522:    }
523:    return(0);
524: }
525:
526: /*----------------------------------------------------------*
527:  *    display_albums_help()                    *
528:  *----------------------------------------------------------*/
529:
530: void display_albums_help(void)
531: {
532:    grid( 11, 16, 19, 59, ct.shdw_fcol, ct.bg_bcol, 3 );
533:    box(10, 15, 20, 60, SINGLE_BOX, FILL_BOX,
534:                       ct.help_fcol, ct.help_bcol);
535:
536:    write_string( "This is a screen for entering musical",
537:                  ct.help_fcol, ct.help_bcol, 11, 22 );
538:    write_string( "items such as albums.",
539:                  ct.help_fcol, ct.help_bcol, 12, 22 );
540:
541:    write_string( "To exit screen, press <F3> or <ESC>.",
542:                  ct.help_fcol, ct.help_bcol, 13, 22 );
543:    write_string( "Press any key to continue...",
544:                  ct.help_fcol, ct.help_bcol, 14, 22 );
545:
```

SAMS
Sams
Learning
Center
SAMS
PUBLISHING

```
546:    cursor(24, 79);
547:    getch();
548: }
549:
550: /*-----------------------------------------------------*
551:  *   add_albums_data();                                *
552:  *   Returns:   1 - if all okay                        *
553:  *             0 - if not all okay                     *
554:  *   Note:     Titles are not written to file. These   *
555:  *             will be covered on a later day.         *
556:  *-----------------------------------------------------*/
557:
558: int add_albums_data( void )
559: {
560:    int   rv = 0;
561:    FILE *fp;
562:
563:    if( (fp = fopen( ALBUMS_DBF, "a" )) == NULL )
564:    {
565:          display_msg_box("Error opening file...",
566:                          ct.err_fcol, ct.err_bcol );
567:    }
568:    else
569:    {
570:       if( (fwrite( p_albums, sizeof( albums ), 1, fp )) == 0 )
571:       {
572:          display_msg_box("Error writing data...",
573:                          ct.err_fcol, ct.err_bcol );
574:       }
575:       else
576:       {
577:          display_msg_box("Record added", ct.db_fcol, ct.db_bcol);
578:          rv = 1;
579:       }
580:
581:       fclose( fp );
582:    }
583:    return( rv );
584: }
585:
586: /*=====================================================*
587:  *                    end of listing                  *
588:  *=====================================================*/
```

13

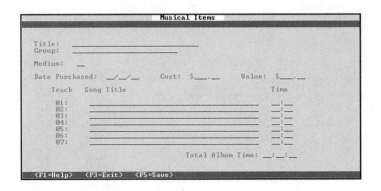

This listing is almost identical in functionality to the Group Information listing. There is only one subtle difference in the display of the title fields. When the file access controls are covered on Day 19, this listing will be equipped with the capability to add a variable number of record titles. In this version of the listing, only seven titles can be entered. When adding the data with the F4 key, only the album information is added; the individual titles are not. Again, this will be rectified on Day 19 when file access is covered.

You should note each of the areas that are affected by the titles. The first area is the additional structure in line 47. Because only seven titles are worked with at this time, an array is created that will hold only seven. In lines 101 to 108, the prompts for the titles are displayed on the screen. Rather than display each individually, a loop is used. Similar loops are used in lines 143 to 151 to display the field underlines and in lines 184 to 193 to display the field values.

In lines 342 to 354, cases are presented to retrieve the cost of the album. Because the cost can be a decimal number, the input is retrieved in two pieces. First, the numbers to the left of the decimal are retrieved. This is followed by retrieving the numbers to the right. While this works, it isn't an optimal solution. You should consider modifying your getline() function to accept decimal numbers using one of the unused option numbers.

Synopsis: Where Do You Go from Here?

Today, you have covered a great deal of code. While your application is beginning to do quite a bit, it isn't complete. In fact, you have just begun. On Day 14, you will cover menuing, which will help complete your application's user interface. Day 15 will give your application the capability to work with the data files. On this day your application will be almost fully functional; there will still be more to do. Days 16 and 17 will help bring the application to near completion. Day 16 will aid you in adding help to your program. This will include an easy way of providing context sensitive help. Day 17 will add the little features that were mentioned in the specification. In addition, Day 17 will help you create a screen that will enable the user of a program to change the application's colors. When you complete Day 17, you will have completed your application with the exception of testing and reporting.

Summary

Today is what can be considered an exciting day. Using all of the functions that you have created on the previous days, along with the specification from Day 12, you began your application. Before starting, some of the standards for creating an entry and edit screen were covered. With these in mind, the code was then presented. First, a simplistic menu was presented, which will be replaced on Day 14. After this, you were presented with three listings that perform each of the entry and edit windows in the specification from Day 12. Detailed analysis helped you understand exactly what is going on.

Q&A

Q Are there different kinds of edits?

A Yes, three different types of edits are generally performed: pre-edits, post-edits, and process edits.

Q What are the differences among pre-edits, post-edits, and process edits?

A The pre-edits occur when a field is first entered. A post-edit occurs when leaving a field. A process edit occurs when the user is ready to process the information on the entire screen. Common pre-edits involve initializations and calculations. Post-edits are a more popular edit. They generally validate information entered into a field. Process edits ensure all the necessary fields are entered in addition to performing edits involving more than one field.

Q Should I use my creativity to reuse the available function keys?

A You should not try to make up your own uses for the keys on the keyboard. At the beginning of today's material, some of the standard uses for keys— and the benefits of using them—were presented. If you were to use the F1 key to delete a record, many people would inadvertently delete records when they tried to get help. (F1 is generally used for help.)

Q Are there published standards for creating applications?

A IBM has created standards for creating applications. These standards are referred to in its Systems Application Architecture (SAA) documents. IBM's standards for screen interfaces are referred to as Common User Access (CUA) standards. Microsoft has also developed standards for developing Windows applications.

Workshop

The Workshop provides quiz questions to help you solidify your understanding of the material covered and exercises to provide you with experience in using what you've learned.

Quiz

1. What are some of the benefits that can be gained by following standards— even if the standards are informal?

2. What should the F1 function key do?

3. What should the F3 function key do?

4. What should the F5 function key do?

5. If you were given a message box that was red with yellow letters, should you be concerned?

6. True or false: A beep can serve several purposes in an application. You can have it beep when the application starts, when a record is added, when an error occurs, and when the user exits.

7. What is an easy approach to creating your own entry and edit screens?

Exercises

1. Add an edit to the Group Information screen. This should be a post-edit for the month field. If a value is entered, it should be from 1 to 12. Any other value should receive an error message. (Keep in mind, if a key such as the Escape key or F3 is entered, it should still be processed.)

2. **ON YOUR OWN:** Add additional edits to the preceding listings. Use your own judgment on what edits should be added. Edits can include edits on cost, dates, times, and more.

3. **ON YOUR OWN:** Create an application of your own. Create a contact system that contains an entry screen for entering the names, addresses, and phone numbers of each person.

Note: Because Exercise 3 will take you some time, only three exercises are presented. On following days, you will only be presented with a few exercises. Some of these exercises will ask you to expand on the application you developed today. This application is from Exercise 3.

13

Enhancing the User Interface: Menuing

On Day 13, you created a temporary menu that was somewhat cryptic in regard to functionality. While the menu worked, it was prone to having the user enter information that was not valid. Today, you'll learn how to create and use a much better menu. Today you will:

☐ Learn about adding menus to your application.

☐ Learn some suggestions for creating menus.

☐ Add menus to your application's front end.

☐ Add a menu to the entry and edit portion of your application.

What Is Considered a Menu?

A menu is a list of choices available for selection. These choices can usually be made in one of several ways. Figure 14.1 presents a menu along with tags showing various ways to select an item.

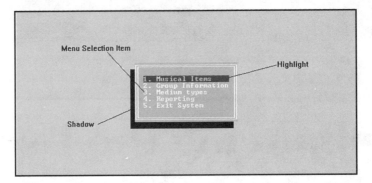

Figure 14.1. *A menu.*

The menu in Figure 14.1 is a menu that you will actually create today. This menu is like many menus in that it offers several ways of selecting an item. The most obvious way of selection is to use the cursor keys to scroll the highlight bar up and down. Additionally, the Home and End keys place the cursor on the first or last menu item. Each row of the menu, or each selection item, has several other ways that it can be selected. The numeric value to the left of each option can be used. For example, if you press 4, the Exit program option will be highlighted. In addition to the obvious numeric value, a mnemonic character can be used. For example, you can type E or e to also select Exit program. The mnemonic key used is generally the first letter, or the

most descriptive letter of the selection item. The actual selection of an item is made by pressing Enter. Additionally, other keys may apply when you are on a menu. In the menu presented in Figure 14.1, if the Escape key is pressed, it may act in the same manner as if menu selection 4 were selected.

Expert Tip: In most cases, the mnemonic key is the first letter of the menu item. Although it starts with E, when Exit is a menu item, it is a common practice to use X as the mnemonic.

Displaying a Menu

To display a menu is not a quick process; however, taken in stride, it isn't too difficult. Listing 14.1 presents a function called `display_menu()`. In this listing, you'll notice a lot of similarities to the `getline()` function that was presented on Day 10. This listing will be explained throughout the sections immediately following it.

Listing 14.1. MENU.C. The `display_menu()` routine.

```
 1:   /* -----------------------------------------------------------
 2:    * Program: MENU.C
 3:    * Authors: Bradley L. Jones
 4:    *          Gregory L. Guntle
 5:    * Purpose: Manages a menu on the screen
 6:    *
 7:    * Enter with: * row, col - for positioning menu
 8:    *             * box_type - SINGLE_BOX, DOUBLE_BOX or NOBOX
 9:    *             * array of ptrs to the menu items to display
10:    *                 array is setup this way:
11:    *                     char *array_name[10] = { "menu item",
12:    *                                                "keys" };  etc.
13:    *             * nbr_items - number of menu items (incl keys)
14:    *             * exit_keys - special keys for exit menu
15:    *                     (F3, etc)
16:    *             * address to return menu item selected in
17:    *             * arrow flag - should R/L arrows be used
18:    *             * do_shadow  - should shadow be displayed?
19:    *
20:    * Returns: The exit key and modifies one parm to hold the
21:    *          selected item.
22:    *
23:    * Note(s): The cursor is turned off. Calling function
```

continues

445

Listing 14.1. continued

```
24:    *            must turn it back on if it is needed.
25:    *=========================================================*/
26:
27:   #include <string.h>
28:   #include <conio.h>
29:   #include "tyac.h"
30:   #include "colortbl.h"
31:
32:   /* =============================================== *
33:    * External Global variables defined in MAIN       *
34:    * =============================================== */
35:
36:   extern struct color_table ct;
37:
38:   /* =============================================== *
39:    * Global variables for other functions in this file *
40:    * =============================================== */
41:
42:   int  row, col;
43:   int  nbr;
44:   char **menu_ptr;
45:   char *EXIT_KEYS;
46:   int  nbr_exit_keys;
47:
48:   /* =============================================== *
49:    * Function declarations used in this file         *
50:    * =============================================== */
51:
52:   int display_menu(int, int,    int,    char **,
53:                    int, char *, int *, int, int );
54:
55:   void rewrite_menu_items(int, int);
56:   int check_menu_keys(char);
57:
58:   /* ------------------------------------------------- *
59:    * DISPLAY_MENU:                                     *
60:    *                                                   *
61:    * This function does the real chore in handling     *
62:    * menus.                                            *
63:    * ------------------------------------------------- */
64:
65:   int display_menu(int   srow,    int  scol,      int  box_type,
66:                    char **menu, int nbr_items, char *exit_keys,
67:                    int *sel,    int arr_flg,   int  do_shadow )
68:   {
69:     int  i=0;
70:     int  menu_pos;            /* Maintaining menu selections */
71:     int  old_menu_pos;
72:     int  loop_exit = FALSE;
```

```
73:    int  ch;                /* Character pressed */
74:    int  max_len = 0;       /* max string length in array */
75:    int  temp_len = 0;
76:    int  key_found;         /* Indicate if key is exit keys */
77:    char *ptr_to_key;       /* Holds comp val for matching keys */
78:
79:    /*--------------------------------------------------*
80:     * Set up global variables - other functions to use *
81:     *--------------------------------------------------*/
82:
83:        /* Set Global ptr to menu items */
84:    menu_ptr = menu;
85:    row = srow;
86:    col = scol;
87:    EXIT_KEYS = exit_keys;
88:    nbr = nbr_items;
89:        /* number of exit keys */
90:    nbr_exit_keys = strlen(EXIT_KEYS);
91:
92: /* --------------------------- */
93: /*   Calculate string lengths   */
94: /* --------------------------- */
95:
96:    while( i < (nbr/2) )
97:    {
98:       temp_len = strlen( *(menu+(i*2)) );
99:       if(temp_len > max_len )
100:      {
101:          max_len = temp_len;
102:      }
103:      i++;
104:   }
105:
106:   nbr = nbr_items/2;          /* Exclude keys of selection */
107:
108: /* --------------------------- */
109: /*   If Box is needed Draw now   */
110: /* --------------------------- */
111:
112:   if (box_type != 0)
113:   {
114:      if( do_shadow == SHADOW )
115:      {
116:         grid(row, row+nbr+1, col-3, col+max_len,
117:              ct.shdw_fcol, ct.bg_bcol, 2);
118:      }
119:
120:      box( row-1, row+nbr, col-2, col+max_len+1,
121:           box_type, FILL_BOX, ct.abar_fcol, ct.abar_bcol);
122:   }
```

continues

Listing 14.1. continued

```
123:
124: /* --------------------------- */
125: /*           Display Menu           */
126: /* --------------------------- */
127:
128:   /* Display menu */
129:   for (i=0; i<nbr; i++)
130:   {
131:     write_string( *(menu+(i*2)),
132:                   ct.menu_fcol, ct.menu_bcol, row+i, col);
133:   }
134:
135:   /*  Highlight first menu item */
136:   write_string( *(menu), ct.menu_high_fcol,
137:                          ct.menu_high_bcol, row, col);
138:
139: /* ------------------------------------------------- */
140:
141:     cursor_off();          /* Turn off cursor */
142:     old_menu_pos = 1;      /* Track selection prior */
143:     menu_pos = 1;          /* Track current sel */
144:
145:     while (loop_exit == FALSE)
146:     {
147:       if ( ( ch=getch() ) == 0 )
148:       {
149:         /* Scan code so read next byte */
150:         ch = getch();
151:         switch ( ch )
152:         {
153:           case HOME: /* goto to TOP of menu */
154:                      menu_pos = 1;
155:                      rewrite_menu_items(menu_pos,
156:                                             old_menu_pos);
157:                      old_menu_pos = menu_pos;
158:                      break;
159:
160:           case END:  /*  goto LAST menu item */
161:                      menu_pos = nbr;
162:                      rewrite_menu_items(menu_pos,
163:                                             old_menu_pos);
164:                      old_menu_pos = menu_pos;
165:                      break;
166:
167:           case RT_ARROW: /* Is LR Arrow movement allowed ?*/
168:                      if ( arr_flg == NO_LR_ARROW)
169:                      {
170:                          /* No - treat like DN_ARROW */
171:                          menu_pos++;
```

```
172:                                 if (menu_pos > nbr)
173:                                     menu_pos = 1;
174:                                 rewrite_menu_items(menu_pos,
175:                                                 old_menu_pos);
176:                                 old_menu_pos = menu_pos;
177:                             }
178:                             else
179:                             {
180:                                 /* LR movement allowed */
181:                                 loop_exit = TRUE;
182:                             }
183:                             break;
184:
185:         case LT_ARROW: /* Is LR Arrow movement allowed ?*/
186:                             if ( arr_flg == NO_LR_ARROW)
187:                             {
188:                                 menu_pos--;
189:                                 if (menu_pos < 1)    /* At end ? */
190:                                     menu_pos = nbr;
191:                                 rewrite_menu_items(menu_pos,
192:                                                 old_menu_pos);
193:                                 old_menu_pos = menu_pos;
194:                             }
195:                             else
196:                             {
197:                                 /* LR movement allowed */
198:                                 loop_exit = TRUE;
199:                             }
200:                             break;
201:
202:         case DN_ARROW: /* Move DOWN one menu selection */
203:                             menu_pos++;
204:                             if (menu_pos > nbr)
205:                                 menu_pos = 1;
206:                             rewrite_menu_items(menu_pos,
207:                                             old_menu_pos);
208:                             old_menu_pos = menu_pos;
209:                             break;
210:
211:         case UP_ARROW:  /* Move UP one menu selection */
212:                             menu_pos--;
213:                             if (menu_pos < 1)    /* At end ? */
214:                                 menu_pos = nbr;
215:                             rewrite_menu_items(menu_pos,
216:                                             old_menu_pos);
217:                             old_menu_pos = menu_pos;
218:                             break;
219:
220:         default:    loop_exit = check_menu_keys(ch);
221:                     if ( loop_exit == FALSE )
```

continues

449

Listing 14.1. continued

```
222:                        {
223:                          /* key a valid exit key ?*/
224:                            boop();
225:                        }
226:                    break;
227:      }   /* end of switch  */
228:    }    /* end of if  */
229:    else
230:    {
231:       switch ( ch )   /* test for other special keys */
232:       {
233:          case CR_KEY:  loop_exit = TRUE;
234:                        break;
235:
236:          case ESC_KEY: /* is ESC_KEY an exit key? */
237:
238:                        i = 0;
239:                        while(i < nbr_exit_keys && !loop_exit)
240:                        {
241:                          if ( ch == EXIT_KEYS[i++])
242:                          {
243:                              loop_exit=TRUE;
244:                          }
245:                        }
246:
247:                        if( !loop_exit )
248:                        {
249:                           boop();
250:                        }
251:
252:                        break;
253:
254:          default: /* Search thru valid keys on Menu items */
255:                   i=0;
256:                   key_found = FALSE;
257:                   while (i<nbr && !key_found)
258:                   {
259:                       ptr_to_key = strchr( *(menu+(i*2)+1), ch );
260:                       if (!ptr_to_key)
261:                       {
262:                          /* Not found - look at next one */
263:                          i++;
264:                       }
265:                       else
266:                       {
267:                          /* found key - exit */
268:                          key_found=TRUE;
269:                       }
270:                   }
```

```
271:
272:                        if (!key_found)
273:                        {
274:                            boop();
275:                        }
276:                        else
277:                        {
278:                            /* Found letter - position menu sel */
279:                            menu_pos = i+1;
280:                            rewrite_menu_items(menu_pos,
281:                                               old_menu_pos);
282:                            old_menu_pos = menu_pos;
283:                        }
284:                        break;
285:
286:            }    /* end of switch */
287:        }        /* end of else */
288:
289:    }            /* end of while loop */
290:
291:    *sel = menu_pos;
292:    return(ch);
293:
294: }  /* end of subroutine display_menu */
295:
296:
297: /* --------------------------------------------- *
298:  * function: rewrite_menu_items()               *
299:  *                                              *
300:  * This subroutine redisplays the menu items.   *
301:  * The previous selection in NORMAL colors      *
302:  * and the new selections in HIGHLIGHTED colors. *
303:  * --------------------------------------------- */
304:
305: void rewrite_menu_items( int new_pos, int old_pos )
306: {
307:    /* rewrite last selection - normal colors */
308:    write_string( *(menu_ptr+((old_pos-1)*2)),
309:                    ct.menu_fcol, ct.menu_bcol,
310:                    row+old_pos-1, col);
311:
312:    /* Now rewrite new one w/selections color */
313:    write_string( *(menu_ptr+((new_pos-1)*2)),
314:                    ct.menu_high_fcol, ct.menu_high_bcol,
315:                    row+new_pos-1, col);
316: }
317:
318: /* --------------------------------------------- *
319:  * function: check_menu_keys()                  *
320:  *                                              *
```

continues

Listing 14.1. continued

```
321:      * This subroutine checks the key pressed against *
322:      * a list of keys that can end the procedure.      *
323:      * It receives the key pressed and returns TRUE     *
324:      * if key is in the list, else FALSE if not in       *
325:      * list.                                            *
326:      * ------------------------------------------------- */
327:
328:  int check_menu_keys(char key_pressed)
329:  {
330:        /* return a true or false to return_code */
331:     int return_code=FALSE;
332:     int loop_ctr = 0;
333:
334:     while ( loop_ctr < nbr_exit_keys && !return_code)
335:     {
336:       if ( key_pressed == EXIT_KEYS[loop_ctr++])
337:       {
338:          return_code=TRUE;
339:       }
340:     }
341:
342:     return(return_code);
343:  }
```

Analysis   The display_menu() function includes several headers. You should notice that two local header files are included in the listing rather than just the TYAC.H header that you have seen in most of the functions presented so far. The new header is COLORTBL.H. This is a header file that contains a color table structure that is almost identical to the structure in RECORD.H from Day 13. Listing 14.2 presents the COLORTBL.H header file.

Type   **Listing 14.2. COLORTBL.H. The color table.**

```
1:   /*============================================================
2:    * Filename: COLORTBL.H
3:    *
4:    * Author:   Bradley L. Jones & Gregory L. Guntle
5:    *
6:    * Purpose:  Header file for color table definition
7:    *============================================================*/
8:
9:   #ifndef __COLORTBL
10:  #define __COLORTBL
11:
12:  /*--------------------*
```

```
13:    * color table          *
14:    *------------------*/
15:
16:   struct color_table
17:   {
18:       int  bg_fcol;           /* background */
19:       int  bg_bcol;
20:
21:       int  fld_prmpt_fcol;    /* field prompt */
22:       int  fld_prmpt_bcol;
23:
24:       int  fld_fcol;          /* input field */
25:       int  fld_bcol;
26:
27:       int  fld_high_fcol;     /* highlight character */
28:       int  fld_high_bcol;
29:
30:       int  ttl_fcol;          /* screen title */
31:       int  ttl_bcol;
32:
33:       int  abar_fcol;         /* action bar & bottom */
34:       int  abar_bcol;
35:
36:       int  menu_fcol;         /* menu text */
37:       int  menu_bcol;
38:
39:       int  menu_high_fcol;    /* Highlighted menu line */
40:       int  menu_high_bcol;
41:
42:       int  err_fcol;          /* error */
43:       int  err_bcol;
44:
45:       int  db_fcol;           /* dialog box & msg box */
46:       int  db_bcol;
47:
48:       int  help_fcol;         /* help box colors */
49:       int  help_bcol;
50:
51:       int  shdw_fcol;         /* shadow color */
52:   };
53:
54:   /*------------------------------------------------*
55:    * extern declarations for global variables *
56:    *------------------------------------------------*/
57:
58:   extern struct color_table ct;
59:
60:   #endif
61:   /*================================================*
62:    *                      end of header             *
63:    *================================================*/
```

14

As you can see, this listing is just the color table. The inclusion of four more color variables has been made to the color table. These are in lines 36 to 40. The values stored in these variables will be used in drawing the menu (`menu_fcol` and `menu_bcol`) and highlighting the currently selected menu item (`menu_high_fcol` and `menu_high_bcol`).

You may wonder why the RECORD.H header file was not included instead of the new COLORTBL.H header file. While the RECORD.H header file already had a color table structure, it also contains structures that are specific to the *Record of Records!* application. The `display_menu()` function will be added to the library. In any applications that use the `display_menu()` function, the color table will need to be included. The other structures that are included in the RECORD.H header file will not be needed by other applications; however, the color table will. By moving the color table into its own file, it can be included wherever needed.

> **Tip:** Remove the color table structure from your RECORD.H file and include the COLORTBL.H header instead. You can include the color table header file in the RECORD.H header file.

The Parameters for the *display_menu()* Function

The `display_menu()` function can be reviewed starting at the top. Like most of the functions presented in this book, the `display_menu()` function's listing starts with several lines of comments. You should pay special attention to lines 7 to 18, which display information on each of the parameters that will be received by the function.

The first two values that will be received by the `display_menu()` function compose the position for the menu. As you will see later, these are the coordinates where the text in the first menu selection item will be positioned. The surrounding box will be offset from this position. The box types have already been defined in your TYAC.H header file with the exception of `NOBOX`. You should add a type definition for `NOBOX`. Set it to a value other than those already used by the other box type definitions.

The fourth parameter is a pointer to a pointer called `menu`. You can cross-reference this variable to the beginning of the function in line 65. The `menu` pointer is used to point to an array of strings. These strings should contain the selection items that will be presented in the menu. Every other item in the array should contain a string with the

escape keys. Following is an example of an array that has been created to be passed in the menu parameter:

```
char *menu[10] = {
        "1. Musical Items    ", "1Mm",
        "2. Group Information", "2Gg",
        "3. Medium types     ", "3Tt",
        "4. Reporting        ", "4Rr",
        "5. Exit System      ", "5Ee"  };
```

As you can see, the first item is a menu selection item option. The second is the selection keys, or mnemonics, that will place the highlight on the given option. In this example, the menu will have five different options, each with its own set of mnemonics.

The fifth option contains a number stating how many items are in the menu array. In the previous example, there were 10 items in the array—five menu items and five sets of selection mnemonics. This number is needed by the menu program to know how large the menu array is. If the menu program didn't receive this number, it wouldn't know where the end of the menu array is.

DO / DON'T

DON'T forget the mnemonic strings.

DO remember to pass the total of both the menu selection items and the mnemonic strings in parameter five.

The next item is a character array similar to one seen in the getline() function. This is the exit_keys array that contains the keys that will cause the menu program to end. An example of an exit key array would be:

```
char MENU_EXIT_KEYS[MAX_KEYS] = {F3, F10, ESC_KEY};
```

For the menu that uses this array, the F3 key, F10 key, and Escape keys will all cause the menu to return to the calling program. In addition, the Enter key will also work. In fact, the Enter key is defaulted to always work.

The next parameter is a pointer to an integer. This integer, called sel in line 67, will be used to store the number of the final menu selection. Each selection item is given a number starting with one for the top item. When a selection is made or when an exit key is pressed, the value of sel will be filled with the currently highlighted item.

The last two parameters are flags. First is the arrow flag, arr_flg, which informs the display_menu() program whether the left and right arrows are to be used as exit keys.

14

When working with action bars on Day 15, you'll find that it is advantageous to treat the arrow keys as special exit keys. If a single menu is being used, then this flag should be turned off so that the arrow keys won't exit the menu. Defined constants should be added to your TYAC.H header file to be used for this parameter:

```
#define NO_LR_ARROW      0    /* Are Left/Right allowed to exit menu */
#define LR_ARROW         1
```

The last parameter, do_shadow, takes a similar value. It, however, is used to determine whether a shadow should be placed on the box containing the menu. Again, defined constants can be added to your TYAC.H header that can be used for this parameter:

```
/* Menu shadow options */
#define SHADOW           1
#define NO_SHADOW        0
```

Warning: The listings presented later assume that you have added the previous type definitions to your TYAC.H header file.

In addition to these parameters, there are several other values that are declared globally for the display_menu() function to use. Line 36 has a definition for the external color table. You will need to set up a color table in any program that is going to use the display menu function. Lines 42 to 46 declare global variables that will be used to hold copies of some of the parameters to avoid losing their values while processing the menu. In addition, these global variables will give all the functions in the listing access to necessary information.

Warning: You must set up a global color table structure called ct in any programs that call display_menu().

Several local variables are also declared within the display_menu() function in lines 69 to 77. The comments included in the code detail what these do. If no comment is included, then they will be covered as they are used in the function.

The *display_menu()* Function

The actual display_menu() function begins in line 65 of Listing 14.1. The function's processes begin in lines 84 to 90 with some of the parameter variables being copied

to local variables. Lines 96 through 104 determine the length of the longest menu selection item. This number, which will be stored in max_len, will be used to determine how wide to draw the menu box. In line 98, the length of a menu selection item is determined. The menu selection items are retrieved using the parameter menu. Don't forget that menu is a pointer to an array of strings. This means that dereferencing the value of menu produces a string. If you add 0 to menu and then dereference it, you get the first string in the array. If you add 1 to menu and dereference, you get the second string. Because menu contains both selection items for the menu and mnemonic strings, you will only want to check the length of every other item. The multiplication of i by 2 does just this.

Line 106 resets the value stored in nbr to the number of selection items on the menu instead of the number of items in the menu array that was passed in. The nbr variable will be used throughout the rest of the listing.

Lines 108 though 138 draw the menu on the screen. Line 112 checks to see if a box is to be drawn. If so, then line 114 determines if a shadow should also be drawn. If a shadow is to be drawn, then the grid() function is used. Line 120 then draws the box with the appropriate boarder. The menu box is drawn in the same color as the action bar. You should note that the row and column values passed to display_menu() are used to position the text. Because of this, the box is drawn outside of this position. In line 120, you should be able to see that the box is drawn with one row above and below the selection items. In addition, the box is drawn two columns to the left of the position provided. This gives sufficient border room within the menu. Lines 128 to 133 display each of the menu selection items that were provided in the menu array. Again, notice that every other element of the menu array is printed by adding an offset times two to menu. The final step to drawing the initial menu is to highlight the first item on the menu. This is done in line 136 by rewriting the first item in the menu highlight colors.

Note: You'll need to compensate for the box position when passing row and column values to the display_menu() function if you are displaying a box. If you opt not to display a box, then the text will be in the row and column position.

14

Now that the menu is drawn, you are almost ready to give control to the user just as you did with getline() on Day 10. Because a cursor is not needed for menuing, line 141 turns the cursor off. Line 142 saves the current menu position and the prior menu position. Because the menu has not been used yet, both values are set to the first menu item, 1. With this completed, a while loop is started that will process until the user exits the menu.

Line 147 gets a key hit from the user with the getch() function. If the value retrieved is equal to 0, then a scan code was entered. Lines 148 to 228 process the scan codes. If a non-scan code key was entered, then the else in lines 229 to 287 is called.

Processing the Menu Scan Codes

If a scan code was entered, then getch() must be called a second time to see what the scan code is. This is done in line 150. A switch statement is then used to determine the appropriate processing for the scan code (lines 151 to 227). Several scan keys have special processing. If one of the special scan keys is not pressed, then a default case, in lines 220 to 226, is called that checks to see if the scan key is a valid exit key. This is done using the check_menu_keys() function in lines 318 to 343. This function is virtually identical to the exit key function that was in getline().

The Menu and the Home Key

The Home key positions the highlight on the first menu item. This is done by setting menu_pos to 1, then calling the rewrite_menu_items() function, and finally setting the old menu position, old_menu_pos, to the current menu position, which is 1.

The rewrite_menu_items() is used by many of the scan codes. This function is presented in lines 297 to 316. The rewrite_menu_items() function takes the new position, new_pos, and the old position, old_pos. The purpose of this function is to remove the highlight from the old position and highlight the new position. This is done by calling write_string() for each. Line 308 calls write_string() to remove the highlight from the old option. The old option is rewritten on the menu in the normal menu colors, menu_fcol and menu_bcol. Don't be confused by the string that is passed to write_string() as the first parameter. This is the same information that you have seen previously in drawing the menu:

```
*(menu_ptr+((old_pos-1) * 2))
```

This is simply an offset into the menu items array that was mentioned earlier. menu_ptr is a global variable set to point to the array of strings. Starting from the middle, this code is easy to follow. The old menu position is converted to a 0 offset by subtracting 1. This is then multiplied by 2 because only every other item in the menu array is a menu selection item—don't forget you need to skip the mnemonics. This determines the offset that needs to be added to menu_ptr and then dereferenced to get the appropriate menu selection item string.

The second `write_string()` in line 313 works in the same manner. Instead of writing the selection item in the normal menu colors, the highlight colors are used.

The Menu and the End Key

The End key works just the opposite of the Home key. The new menu position is set to the last menu item, which is now stored in `nbr` because it was divided by 2 in line 106. This new position is then passed along with the old menu position to the `rewrite_menu_items()` function to update the menu. The old position is set to the new position, and the menu processing continues.

The Menu and the Arrow Keys

The right and left arrow keys may either exit the menu program or work in the same manner as the up and down arrow keys. This is based on the `arr_flg` argument that was passed to the `display_menu()` function. In line 168, the `arr_flg` is checked to determine if the arrows are supposed to exit the program. If the arrows are disabled in regard to exiting, then the `if` is executed. If the right arrow is used, the menu position will be incremented by one. The new position will be checked to ensure that it has not scrolled off the bottom of the menu. If the new position is off the menu, then the position will be reset to the first menu item (lines 171 and 173). For the left arrow key, the menu position is decremented and set to the last position if needed (lines 188 to 190). The process is completed by calling the `rewrite_menu_items()` function and updating the old menu position.

If the right and left arrow keys are set to exit, then the `else` statements are executed in lines 178 to 182 for the right arrow, or lines 195 to 199 for the left arrow. In these cases, the flag to exit the loop, `loop_exit`, is set to TRUE so that the `while` statement processing the menu will end.

The up and down arrows work in a manner identical to what was described for the right and left arrow keys. The only difference is that the up and down arrows do not have the exit options. They simply increment or decrement the current menu position, check to see that the new position is still on the menu, call `rewrite_menu_items()`, save the old menu position, and exit back to the menu.

Processing the Non-Scan Code Menu Keys

A non-scan key can be one of only a few keys. Either the key will be the Enter key, the Escape key, or an alphanumeric character. If the Enter key was pressed, then line 233 will set the looping flag, `loop_exit`, to TRUE so that the `while` loop will end.

14

If the key pressed was the Escape key, then a check is done to see if it is an exit key (lines 238 to 244). If the Escape key is an exit key, then the loop_exit flag is set to TRUE. If the Escape key is not an exit key, then the loop_exit key will still be FALSE. This will cause line 248 to execute the boop() function.

In the case of any other non-scan code value, the default case in line 254 is executed. Lines 256 to 270 are similar to the search done for an exit key. The difference is that instead of searching the exit key array, the mnemonic strings in the menu selection items array are searched. Each string of mnemonic characters is checked using the ANSI strchr() function. This function checks to see if the character the user entered, ch, is in the mnemonics string for each menu selection item. If it isn't, strchr() returns a NULL value. Line 260 checks to see if the character was found. If it wasn't, the next mnemonic string is checked. If it was, then the while loop is ended by setting a flag, key_found, to TRUE.

Once all the mnemonic strings are checked, or when the entered character is found, the program continues on. If the character wasn't found, then line 274 beeps the computer using the boop() function. If the character was found, then the menu position is set and the menu items are rewritten using rewrite_menu_items(). Control is then returned to the menu.

Final Notes on *display_menu()*

Once the user ends the menu, lines 291 and 292 are performed. Line 291 sets the value in the display_menu() selection parameter to the current menu position. Line 292 then returns the last key that was pressed to the calling program.

Using the *display_menu()* Function

With all of the previous description, you should be raring to use the display_menu() function. Before adding it to the *Record of Records!* program, you should look at it being used in a simpler program. Following in Listing 14.3 is a program showing exactly how to use the display_menu() function.

Listing 14.3. TESTMENU.C. A test program for display_menu().

```
1:    /* Program:   testmenu.c
2:     * Author:    Bradley L. Jones
3:     *            Gregory L. Guntle
4:     * Purpose:   Demonstrate the menu function.
5:     *=======================================================*/
6:
```

```
7:     #include <stdio.h>
8:     #include "tyac.h"
9:     #include "colortbl.h"
10:
11:    char *main_menu[10] = {
12:                "1. Musical Items     ", "1Mm",
13:                "2. Group Information", "2Gg",
14:                "3. Medium types      ", "3Tt",
15:                "4. Reporting         ", "4Rr",
16:                "5. Exit System       ", "5Ee"  };
17:
18:    char MENU_EXIT_KEYS[MAX_KEYS] = {F3, F10, ESC_KEY};
19:
20:    struct color_table ct;
21:
22:    void initialize_color_table(void);
23:
24:    int main()
25:    {
26:        int rv;
27:        int menu_sel=0;
28:
29:        initialize_color_table();
30:        clear_screen( ct.bg_fcol, ct.bg_bcol );
31:
32:        rv = display_menu(10, 30, DOUBLE_BOX, main_menu, 10,
33:                        MENU_EXIT_KEYS, &menu_sel, NO_LR_ARROW,
34:                        SHADOW);
35:
36:        cursor( 20, 0 );
37:        printf("\nSelection = %d \n", menu_sel);
38:        printf("Char to exit = %x (hex)\n", rv);
39:        cursor_on();
40:        return(0);
41:    }
42:
43:    /*-------------------------------------------------------*
44:     * initialize_color_table()                             *
45:     *                                                      *
46:     * Set up global color table for rest of application    *
47:     *-------------------------------------------------------*/
48:
49:    void initialize_color_table( void )
50:    {
51:        ct.bg_fcol = YELLOW;
52:        ct.bg_bcol = BLUE;
53:
54:        ct.fld_prmpt_fcol = CYAN;
55:        ct.fld_prmpt_bcol = BLUE;
56:
```

continues

Listing 14.3. continued

```
57:        ct.fld_fcol = BRIGHTWHITE;
58:        ct.fld_bcol = BLUE;
59:
60:        ct.fld_high_fcol = YELLOW;
61:        ct.fld_high_bcol = BLUE;
62:
63:        ct.ttl_fcol = BRIGHTWHITE;
64:        ct.ttl_bcol = BLACK;
65:
66:        ct.abar_fcol = BLACK;
67:        ct.abar_bcol = WHITE;
68:
69:        ct.menu_fcol = BLACK;
70:        ct.menu_bcol = WHITE;
71:
72:        ct.menu_high_fcol = BLUE;
73:        ct.menu_high_bcol = CYAN;
74:
75:        ct.err_fcol = YELLOW;
76:        ct.err_bcol = RED;
77:
78:        ct.db_fcol = WHITE;
79:        ct.db_bcol = BROWN;
80:
81:        ct.help_fcol = YELLOW;
82:        ct.help_bcol = GREEN;
83:
84:        ct.shdw_fcol = BLACK;
85:  }
```

While the display_menu() function was complex and long, using it isn't too difficult. As you can see, half of the TESTMENU.C listing is used to set up the color table with the colors to be used. This is done in a function called

`initialize_color_table()` in lines 43 to 85. This function is almost identical to the function presented on Day 13 in the RECOFREC.C listing.

> **Expert Tip:** You should notice that the menu foreground color, `menu_fcol`, and the menu background color, `menu_bcol`, are set to the same colors as the action bar. This is a common practice.

In lines 8 and 9, you see the TYAC.H header file being included for your library functions, and you see the COLORTBL.H header file being included for the color table structure. Lines 11 to 16 contain the menu structure with the mnemonic keys. This structure will be passed to the display menu function. Line 18 sets up the exit keys for the menu. The last couple of lines before the program start declare a color table, `ct`, and provide a prototype for the function that will be used to initialize the color table.

The `main()` function begins in line 24. This function sets up the color table, calls the menu, prints a couple of lines, restores the cursor, and ends. This is a small amount of code when you consider all the program does. The reason for the small amount of code is because of the power of the `display_menu()` function that you have created.

You should review the call to the `display_menu()` function in line 32. As you can see, this menu will be placed with the text starting in row 10 and column 20 (the first two parameters). The menu will be in a box with a double-lined border (third parameter). The `main_menu` pointer, declared in lines 11 to 16, will be passed in the fourth parameter. Because this array has 10 elements, the number 10 is the fifth parameter. This is followed by the name of the exit key array, which was declared in line 19. The selection that is chosen will be filled into the next parameter, which is the local integer, `menu_sel`. Notice that the address of the `menu_sel` variable is passed because `display_menu()` is expecting an address. The last two parameters are `NO_LR_ARROW` and `SHADOW`. These tell `display_menu()` that the left and right arrows shouldn't exit the menu. Additionally, the menu should have a shadow. When you run the program, you should use the left and right arrow keys to see what they do.

14

> **Tip:** Change the `NO_LR_ARROW` parameter to `LR_ARROW` and rerun the program to see the effect. Change `SHADOW` to `NO_SHADOW` and see what effect that has.

Lines 37 and 38 print information that can be determined after a call to display_menu().
Line 38 prints the returned value from the function. This is printed in hexadecimal;
however, you may choose to print it in decimal by changing the x to a d in the printf().
You will find that this value should match one of the exit keys that you set up or the
value of Enter. Line 37 prints the value that display_menu() placed into the seventh
parameter, menu_sel. This will be the number of the option that was highlighted when
the user exited the menu.

Adding a Menu to *Record of Records!*

Now that you have seen a menu in use, you should be ready to use them in your
applications. The *Record of Records!* application would be a good place to begin.
Following is Listing 14.4. This is a replacement for the RECOFREC.C listing
presented in Day 13. Instead of the cryptic menu provided on Day 13, this listing uses
the display_menu() function.

Note: You should replace your RECOFREC.C listing with
Listing 14.4.

**Listing 14.4. LIST1404.C. A new *Record of Records!*
listing.**

```
1:   /*===========================================================
2:    * Filename: RECofREC.c
3:    *           RECORD OF RECORDS - Version 1.0
4:    *
5:    * Author:   Bradley L. Jones
6:    *           Gregory L. Guntle
7:    *
8:    * Purpose:  Allow entry and edit of medium codes.
9:    *
10:   * Note:     Assumes 80 columns by 25 columns for screen.
11:   *===========================================================*/
12:
13:  #include <stdio.h>
14:  #include <conio.h>            /* not an ANSI header, used for getch() */
15:  #include <string.h>           /* for strlen() */
16:  #include <ctype.h>
17:  #include "tyac.h"
18:  #include "records.h"
19:
20:  /*-------------------*
```

```
21:    *        prototypes      *
22:    *-------------------*/
23:   #include "recofrec.h"
24:
25:   void initialize_color_table( void );
26:
27:   /*------------------------*
28:    * define global variables  *
29:    *------------------------*/
30:
31:   struct color_table ct;           /* color table */
32:
33:   /*=======================================================*
34:    *                          main()                       *
35:    *=======================================================*/
36:
37:   main()
38:   {
39:     int rv        = 0;
40:     int cont      = TRUE;
41:     int menu_sel = 0;
42:
43:     char *main_menu[10] = {
44:             "1. Enter Musical Items      ", "1Mm",
45:             "2. Enter Medium Codes       ", "2Cc",
46:             "3. Enter Group Information ", "3Gg",
47:             "4. Reporting                ", "4Rr",
48:             "5. Exit System             ", "5EeQqXx"  };
49:
50:     char MENU_EXIT_KEYS[MAX_KEYS] = {F3, F10, ESC_KEY};
51:
52:     initialize_color_table();
53:
54:     while( cont == TRUE )                    /* loop in temp menu */
55:     {
56:
57:       draw_borders("  RECORD of RECORDS!  " );
58:       write_string( "Help", ct.abar_fcol, ct.abar_bcol, 1, 3);
59:
60:
61:       rv = display_menu(10, 27, DOUBLE_BOX, main_menu, 10,
62:                         MENU_EXIT_KEYS, &menu_sel, NO_LR_ARROW,
63:                         SHADOW);
64:
65:       switch( rv )
66:       {
67:         case ENTER_KEY: /* accept selection */
68:         case CR:
69:                     switch( menu_sel )
70:                     {
```

14

continues

Listing 14.4. continued

```
 71:                                    case 1:  /* Menu option 1 */
 72:                                             cursor_on();
 73:                                             do_albums_screen();
 74:                                             break;
 75:
 76:                                    case 2:  /* Menu option 2 */
 77:                                             cursor_on();
 78:                                             do_medium_screen();
 79:                                             break;
 80:
 81:                                    case 3:  /* Menu option 3 */
 82:                                             cursor_on();
 83:                                             do_groups_screen();
 84:                                             break;
 85:
 86:                                    case 4:  /* Reporting */
 87:                                             boop();
 88:                                             boop();
 89:                                             break;
 90:
 91:                                    case 5:  /* exit */
 92:                                             cont = FALSE;
 93:                                             break;
 94:
 95:                                    default: /* continue looping */
 96:                                             boop();
 97:                                             break;
 98:                            }
 99:                    break;
100:
101:        case F3:        /* exiting */
102:        case ESC_KEY:   /* could display 'Are you sure message' */
103:                        cont = FALSE;
104:                        break;
105:
106:        case F10:       /* action bar */
107: //                     rv = do_main_actionbar();
108:
109: //                     if( rv == F3 )
110: //                         cont = FALSE;
111:
112:                        break;
113:
114:        default:        boop();
115:                        break;
116:    }
117: }
118:
119:    /* clean up screen for exit */
```

```
120:    clear_screen( BRIGHTWHITE, BLACK );
121:    cursor_on();
122:    cursor(0,0);
123:    repeat_char(' ', 80, YELLOW, BLUE );
124:    write_string( "Thank you for using RECORD OF RECORDS!",
125:                    YELLOW, BLUE, 0, 21 );
126:    return 0;
127: }
128:
129: /*----------------------------------------------------------*
130:  *   draw_borders()                                        *
131:  *----------------------------------------------------------*/
132: void draw_borders(char *title)
133: {
134:    int col=0;    /* used to center title */
135:
136:    clear_screen( ct.bg_fcol, ct.bg_bcol );
137:
138:    col = (( 80 - strlen(title)) / 2 );
139:
140:    write_string( title, ct.ttl_fcol, ct.ttl_bcol, 0, col );
141:
142:    cursor(1,0);
143:    repeat_char(' ', 80, ct.abar_fcol, ct.abar_bcol );
144:    cursor(24,0);
145:    repeat_char(' ', 80, ct.abar_fcol, ct.abar_bcol );
146: }
147:
148: /*----------------------------------------------------------*
149:  *   display_msg_box()                                     *
150:  *----------------------------------------------------------*/
151: void display_msg_box(char *msg, int fcol, int bcol )
152: {
153:    char *saved_screen = NULL;
154:    saved_screen = save_screen_area( 11, 15, 19, 60 );
155:
156:    grid( 12, 15, 19, 59, ct.shdw_fcol, ct.bg_bcol, 3 );
157:    box(11, 14, 20, 60, SINGLE_BOX, FILL_BOX, fcol, bcol);
158:
159:    write_string( msg, fcol, bcol, 12, 23 );
160:    write_string( "Press any key to continue...",
161:                    fcol, bcol, 13, 23 );
162:
163:    cursor_off();
164:    getch();
165:    cursor_on();
166:
167:    restore_screen_area(saved_screen);
168: }
169:
```

continues

Listing 14.4. continued

```
170: /*-------------------------------------------------------*
171:  *    yes_no_box()                                       *
172:  *-----------------------------------------------------*/
173: char yes_no_box(char *msg, int fcol, int bcol )
174: {
175:    char ch;
176:    char *saved_screen = NULL;
177:    saved_screen = save_screen_area( 11, 15, 19, 60 );
178:
179:    grid( 12, 15, 19, 59, ct.shdw_fcol, ct.bg_bcol, 3 );
180:    box(11, 14, 20, 60, SINGLE_BOX, FILL_BOX, fcol, bcol);
181:
182:    write_string( msg, fcol, bcol, 12, 23 );
183:    write_string( "Enter (Y) or (N)", fcol, bcol, 13, 23 );
184:
185:    cursor_off();
186:    ch = getch();
187:    ch = toupper(ch);
188:
189:    while( ch != 'Y' && ch != 'N' )
190:    {
191:       ch = toupper( getch() );
192:    }
193:
194:    cursor_on();
195:    restore_screen_area(saved_screen);
196:    return(ch);
197: }
198:
199: /*-------------------------------------------------------*
200:  *    Function: zero_fill_field();                       *
201:  *    Purpose:  Right justifies a character array and then*
202:  *              pads the left side with zeros. (Assumes   *
203:  *              that the field is NOT null terminated.)   *
204:  *    Returns:  # of zeros used to pad field             *
205:  *              -1 if field too large (longer than 20 )  *
206:  *              0  if field is blank (not padded)        *
207:  *-----------------------------------------------------*/
208:
209: int zero_fill_field( char *field, int size )
210: {
211:    int  ctr,
212:         pads = 0;
213:
214:    char tmp[20];
215:
216:    if( size > 20 )
217:    {
218:       pads = -1;   /* field too long */
```

```
219:    }
220:    else
221:    if( strlen(field) == 0 )
222:    {
223:        pads = 0;    /* leave blank fields blank. */
224:    }
225:    else
226:    {
227:        pads = size - (strlen(field));    /* How many 0s? */
228:
229:        for( ctr = 0; ctr < pads; ctr++ ) /* pad tmp field */
230:            tmp[ctr] = '0';
231:
232:            /* copy original info to end of tmp field */
233:        strncpy( tmp+pads, field, strlen(field));
234:            /* replace original field with padded tmp */
235:        strncpy(field, tmp, size);
236:    }
237:
238:    return(pads);
239: }
240:
241: /*-------------------------------------------------------*
242:  * initialize_color_table()                             *
243:  *                                                      *
244:  * Set up global color table for rest of application    *
245:  *-------------------------------------------------------*/
246:
247: void initialize_color_table( void )
248: {
249:    ct.bg_fcol = YELLOW;
250:    ct.bg_bcol = BLUE;
251:
252:    ct.fld_prmpt_fcol = CYAN;
253:    ct.fld_prmpt_bcol = BLUE;
254:
255:    ct.fld_fcol = BRIGHTWHITE;
256:    ct.fld_bcol = BLUE;
257:
258:    ct.fld_high_fcol = YELLOW;
259:    ct.fld_high_bcol = BLUE;
260:
261:    ct.ttl_fcol = BRIGHTWHITE;
262:    ct.ttl_bcol = BLACK;
263:
264:    ct.abar_fcol = BLACK;
265:    ct.abar_bcol = WHITE;
266:
267:    ct.menu_fcol = BLACK;
268:    ct.menu_bcol = WHITE;
```

14

continues

Listing 14.4. continued

```
269:
270:     ct.menu_high_fcol = BLUE;
271:     ct.menu_high_bcol = CYAN;
272:
273:     ct.err_fcol = YELLOW;
274:     ct.err_bcol = RED;
275:
276:     ct.db_fcol = WHITE;
277:     ct.db_bcol = BROWN;
278:
279:     ct.help_fcol = YELLOW;
280:     ct.help_bcol = GREEN;
281:
282:     ct.shdw_fcol = BLACK;
283: }
284:
285:
286: /*=======================================================*
287:  *                     end of listing                    *
288:  *=======================================================*/
```

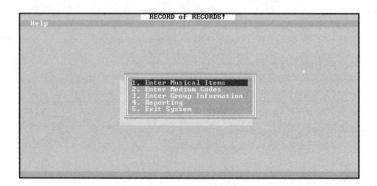

Much of this listing is the same as the original RECOFREC.C listing. The changes start in the `main()` function. Line 41 sets up a `menu_sel` variable to accept the return value from the menu that will be displayed. Lines 43 to 48 set up the menu items that will be displayed along with their mnemonic values. Line 50 sets up the exit keys. For this main menu, the F3, F10, and Escape keys will all cause the menu to exit. By default, the Enter key will also cause the menu to exit.

Line 52 calls the `initialize_color_table()` function that is presented in lines 241 to 285. As you can see, lines 262 to 266 include the color variables for the menu.

Lines 54 to 114 contain a `while` loop that will keep the menu displayed until the user signals to exit. The screen is drawn in line 57 with a call to `draw_borders()`. The `draw_borders()` function has not changed.

Line 61 begins the actual menu process with a call to `display_menu()`. The menu is set up to be in a box with a shadow. In addition, the box will have a double-lined border. The left and right arrow keys have been turned off because you don't want this menu to end if they are pressed. The menu will be displayed until a user presses one of the exit keys or makes a selection.

Lines 65 to 117 react to the result of the call to `display_menu()`. A `switch` statement routes control based on what key was returned from the menu. If F3 or the Escape key was pressed, then the `cont` flag will be set to `FALSE` so that the loop will end. If the F10 key is pressed, then the action bar function will be called. Because this function will be presented on Day 15, it should be commented out for now.

> **Warning:** The action bar function, `do_main_actionbar()`, is included in the listing because the F10 key is an exit key for the menu. This function will be filled in on Day 15.

If Enter was pressed to exit the menu, then the user made a selection. A `switch` statement, in lines 69 to 98, routes the appropriate action based on the value of `menu_sel`. Remember that `menu_sel` contains the number of the selection made. For selections 1 through 3, the processing is almost identical to what it was before adding the new menu. Each of the corresponding screen functions is called. The only change is that the `cursor_on()` function is called first. Because the menu turned the cursor off, you need to turn it back on.

The other cases are different. Case 4 calls the `boop()` function twice. This is done because reporting won't be covered until Day 20. If the menu selection was 5, then the user selected to exit. The `cont` flag is set to `FALSE` so that the program will exit. A `default` case is also included even though there should never be a value in `menu_sel` other than 1 through 5. It's good programming practice to include a `default` case in every `switch`.

The last few lines of `main()` are almost identical to what was presented before. The big change is the addition of the `cursor_on()` function in line 121. Without this, the cursor would remain off even after you exit the program. The rest of the listing is the same as it was before.

14

Using a Menu with Entry and Edit

On Day 13, you allowed the user to enter data into entry and edit screens. To retrieve the data from the user, you used the `getline()` function. There are times when only a certain number of choices are valid and these choices will never change. For example, on the Groups screen, you may decide that there are only a certain number of Types of Music that the user will be able to enter into the system. In this situation, you can choose to let the user select a value from a menu instead of typing the value.

You already have all the information you need to accept the type of music from a menu instead of having the user enter the information. In the GROUPS.C listing (originally presented on Day 13 in Listing 13.5), you included a case for each field on the screen. Each case did a call to `getline()` along with any edits that may have been required. The case for the Type of Music field was as follows:

```
293:        case 4 :
294:            rv = getline( GET_ALPHA, 0,  8, 19, 0, 20,
                                groups.music_type);
295:            break;
```

Instead of calling `getline()`, this case will now set up to use a menu. To make it easier to add the menu to the GROUPS.C listing, it will be created in a separate function that the case will call. Replace the `getline()` function with the following:

```
        case 4 :
          rv = do_type_of_music_menu( groups.music_type);
          write_string( groups.music_type,
                        ct.fld_fcol, ct.fld_bcol, 8, 19);
          break;
```

You will need to add a new prototype at the top of the GROUPS.C file for this function. The prototype will be as follows:

```
int do_type_of_music_menu( char * );
```

Once you have made these changes, you are ready to create the menu in the `do_type_of_music_menu()` function. The code for this function is presented in Listing 14.5. You will want to add this to the end of your GROUPS.C listing.

 Listing 14.5. The Type of Music entry and edit menu.

```
1:    /*============================================================
2:     * Filename: LIST1405.c
3:     *
4:     * Author:    Bradley L. Jones
5:     *            Gregory L. Guntle
6:     *
```

```
 7:    * Purpose:  Information to be added to GROUPS.C. This allows
 8:    *                for a menu to be created for the TYPE OF MUSIC
 9:    *                field.
10:    *=========================================================*/
11:
12:
13:   /*----------------------------------------------------------*
14:    *  do_type_of_music_menu();                                *
15:    *  Returns:  key used to exit menu                         *
16:    *----------------------------------------------------------*/
17:
18:   int do_type_of_music_menu( char *field )
19:   {
20:      char *saved_screen = NULL;
21:      int  menu_sel = 0;
22:      int  rv;
23:
24:      char *menu_data[22] = {
25:            "Alternative ", "1Aa",
26:            "cLassic rock", "2Ll",
27:            "classical(X)", "3Xx",
28:            "Country     ", "4Cc",
29:            "Disco       ", "5Dd",
30:            "Instrumental", "6Ii",
31:            "New age     ", "7Nn",
32:            "Speed metal ", "8Ss",
33:            "Rock        ", "9Rr",
34:            "Pop rock    ", "Pp",
35:            "sofT rock   ", "Tt"  };
36:
37:      char exit_keys[MAX_KEYS] = { F3, F10, ESC_KEY, SHIFT_TAB };
38:
39:
40:      saved_screen = save_screen_area( 6, 20, 27, 60 );
41:
42:      rv = display_menu( 8, 30, SINGLE_BOX, menu_data, 22,
43:                         exit_keys, &menu_sel, LR_ARROW,
44:                         SHADOW);
45:      cursor_on();
46:
47:      switch( rv )
48:      {
49:         case F3:
50:         case F10:
51:         case ESC_KEY:
52:         case SHIFT_TAB: break;
53:
54:         case LT_ARROW:  rv = SHIFT_TAB;
55:                         break;
56:
```

continues

473

Listing 14.5. continued

```
57:        case RT_ARROW:  rv = TAB;
58:                        break;
59:
60:        default:  /* item selected */
61:                   strcpy( field, *(menu_data+((menu_sel-1)*2)));
62:                   break;
63:    }
64:
65:    restore_screen_area( saved_screen );
66:
67:    return( rv );
68: }
69:
70: /*========================================================*
71:  *                    end of listing                     *
72:  *========================================================*/
```

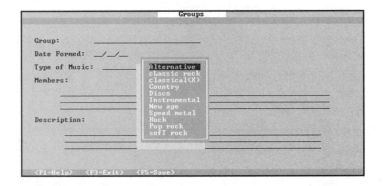

Analysis Once you add this to the GROUP.C listing, you will be prompted with the menu presented in the output whenever you enter the Type of Music field. In looking at the listing, you should see that the menu is done in the same manner as the menus presented earlier today. Line 21 declares the integer variable to hold the menu selection. Lines 24 to 35 contain the menu_data array. This is the values that will be displayed in the menu along with their mnemonics. Line 37 declares the exit keys that the menu will use.

> **Tip:** You should notice that in lines 25 to 35 one letter in each of the menu items is capitalized. This is the mnemonic letter that will move the highlight. You should also notice that even though numbers are

not presented on the menu, numeric mnemonics are still used. This is
to give the menu added flexibility.

Before displaying the menu, the `saved_screen` pointer declared in line 20 is used to save off the area of the screen where the menu will be positioned. Line 40 then saves the screen using the `save_screen_area()` function from Day 11. The screen is restored before the function returns control to the entry and edit screen.

The menu is displaced in line 43. As you can see, a single-bordered box is used along with a shadow. In addition, the left and right arrows are enabled. Once the menu has been displayed and returns controls, line 45 turns the cursor back on. (Remember the menu turns it off.)

Lines 47 to 63 react to the returned value from the call to `display_menu()` in line 42. If the F3 key, F10 key, Escape key, or Shift+Tab is pressed, then the key value is returned to the calling screen to process. If the left or right arrow key is pressed, then they are translated to `SHIFT_TAB` and `TAB` values and returned to the screen to process. This causes the left and right arrows to place the cursor on the next or previous field.

If the return value is anything else, then the data should be accepted. The corresponding menu item is copied into the screen field (line 61). Don't let the math in this line confuse you. You are copying an element from the `menu_data` array. The value of `menu_sel` is from 1 to 11, depending on which menu item was selected. The offset into the `menu_data` array will be 2 times the result of the `menu_item` selected minus 1 (so the offsets begin with 0). The reason you multiply by 2 is because only every other item in the `menu_data` array is a menu item. You want to skip the mnemonic key strings.

DO   DON'T

DON'T forget to turn the cursor back on after using the menu.

DO remember to set up the exit keys before calling `display_menu()`.

DO compare `display_menu()` to the `getline()` function so that you can understand the similarities.

14

Summary

Today, you covered the topic of menus. You were presented with a function called `display_menu()`, which enables you to display menus in your applications. Once you create the `display_menu()` function, you have the ability to add menus to your applications with very little work. You are able to display menus at virtually any location on the screen. In addition, you are able to state which keys you want to work within the menu. These keys include mnemonics that will take the highlight within the menu to a specific menu item. Your menus can be displayed in a box, with shadows, with single- or double-sided borders, and more. Today's information will be followed with action bars tomorrow.

Q&A

Q Can menus call other menus?

A Yes, you can have menus call other menus. In fact, action bars on Day 15 will do just that.

Q Is there a maximum number of menu items that can be listed in a menu?

A Yes. Common sense should tell you not to list more items in your menu than what will fit on the screen.

Q What changes should be made to the TYAC.H header file after creating today's programs?

A The following information should be added to the TYAC.H header file to accommodate the `display_menu()` function:

```
/* Menu shadow options */
#define SHADOW          1
#define NO_SHADOW       0


/* ---------------------------------- *
 *          Menu Items                *
 * ---------------------------------- */
#define NOBOX           0
#define MAX_MENU_NBR    10
#define MAX_MENU_LEN    30
#define MAX_KEYS        17
#define NO_LR_ARROW      0   /* Are Left/Right allowed to exit
```

```
menu */
#define LR_ARROW        1

int  display_menu(int,   int, int, char **, int, char*,
                     int *, int, int );
```

Workshop

The Workshop provides quiz questions to help you solidify your understanding of the material covered and exercises to provide you with experience in using what you've learned.

Quiz

1. What are mnemonic characters used for?

2. Why is it best to keep the color table structure in its own listing?

3. What does the Home key do within a menu?

4. What does the Page Down key do within a menu?

5. What is the most selection items that you can have on a menu?

Exercises

1. **ON YOUR OWN:** Add the display_menu() function to your TYAC.LIB library.

2. **ON YOUR OWN:** Be sure to create the COLORTBL.H listing presented today. Modify your RECORDS.H header to include this listing instead of containing the color table structure.

3. Write a program that displays a menu with the following options:

    1. RED

    2. YELLOW

    3. BLUE

    4. GREEN

   Include mnemonics.

4. **ON YOUR OWN:** Experiment with the NO_LR_ARROW, LR_ARROW, SHADOW, and NO_SHADOW menu parameters.

5. **ON YOUR OWN:** Create menus in your own applications.

6. What would be appropriate mnemonic keys for the menu selection item, "5. Exit"?

At this point, you should have created the foundation of the *Record of Records!* application. The entry and edit portion of your application has been created along with the menus. This is just the beginning of your application. In this third week, you will continue to build on your application.

Day 15 continues where Day 14 left off. Menus are applied to creating action bars in your application. Not only are the concepts behind action bars discussed, but so are the steps for creating them.

Day 16 helps you to understand the different types of help that can be added to your application. In addition to describing the different types of help, you are guided in adding context-sensitive help, extended help, and an about box to your application.

On Days 17 and 18, you will add file access routines to a portion of your application. These routines will include the capability to add records to the file, update records, and delete records. In addition, you will incorporate the capability for your entry and edit screens to display each record in the database one after another. The access to these routines will be via the function keys and the action bar that was created on Day 15.

On the nineteenth day, you will be presented with reporting. In addition to adding a reporting menu to your application, you will also add a couple of reports. You will be presented with ideas on helping your users to get the reports they need.

Although Day 19 completes the coding, it will not complete the application. On Day 20, you will be presented with the finishing touches of application development. This is testing, debugging, maintaining, and upgrading. In addition to this, you will be presented with tips on rectifying the problems you may find (debugging).

The book is concluded with Day 21. Although the main part of the book ends after Day 21, you will not feel lost. On the final day, you will be presented with the most common directions that C programmers follow. You are also presented with additional information on libraries and types of libraries that are available.

This is where you're headed. For now, you should continue on with Day 15.

The User Interface:
Action Bars

On Day 14, you added menus to your application. This helped you produce a front end to your application. In addition, it helped to provide boxes that listed selections instead of requiring data entry. Today, you'll expand on your menus by moving into action bars. Today you will:

☐ Learn what action bars are.

☐ See how action bars work in conjunction with accelerator keys.

☐ See how to add an action bar to your main menu.

☐ See how to add an action bar to your entry and edit screens.

What Are Action Bars?

Action bars are menus containing options for various actions that your program can perform. An action bar is generally placed at the top of the screen on the line just below the title. Figure 15.1 presents an action bar menu.

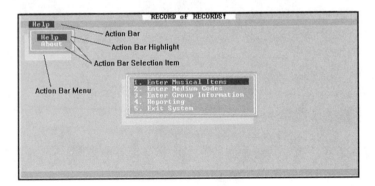

Figure 15.1. *An action bar.*

As you can see, the File action bar item has a single option called Exit. When this option is selected, the exiting routine will be called.

Many action bar items also have accelerator keys. An *accelerator key* is a keyboard key that automatically causes an action to occur. If an action bar option has an accelerator key, it's usually listed in the action bar menu. In Figure 15.1, you can see that the Exit action has an accelerator key of F3.

Standards in Action Bars

Most people choose to follow the same format and naming conventions in their action bars. This provides a consistency for the user between applications. The naming of action bar selections can even cross application types. For instance, a word processor may have an action bar with a selection called File that allows files to be opened, closed, printed, and more. A database program could also have a File action bar item with these same options even though the file types are completely different. The actions that these applications are performing are the same.

There are several action bar items that are prevalent in applications. File, Edit, View, Options, and Help are a few action bar items; however, they aren't the only ones that can be used. For example, a word processor may also include action bar items such as Insert, Format, Tools, and Table. However, keep in mind that File, Edit, View, Options, and Help are common in many different types of applications. Each of these action bar menu items has certain types of actions that should be categorized in their action bar menus. You should create a new action bar item only when an item won't fit into one of these.

The File Action Bar Item

The File option should be used for actions that apply to an entire file. If your application is going to enable the user to choose which file they are working with, then possible options would be those listed in Table 15.1.

Table 15.1. Possible selection items for the File action bar item's menu.

Item	Purpose
New	Open a new file
Open...	Open an existing file
Close	Close the current file, but do not exit
Save	Save the current file
Save as...	Save the current file as a new name
Print	Print the current files information
Exit	Exit the current file

If any of these actions apply to your application, you should use the item name presented in the table. This will help your application be consistent with other applications.

> **Note:** In the *Record of Records!* application, a default file is being used. The only File option that will be used is Exit.

> **Tip:** On an entry and edit screen with an action bar, you should always provide a File action bar option with at least the option to Exit.

The Edit Action Bar Item

The Edit option contains actions that modify the current information that is being presented. The options that are presented here may vary depending on the type of application. In working with a document in a word processor, the Edit options may involve moving textual information around. This would be selection items such as Copy, Cut, and Paste. In a database application, the Edit options may involve manipulations to the current record. This could include Clear, Add, and Delete. Table 15.2 presents many common selection items for an Edit action bar menu.

Table 15.2. Possible selection items for the Edit action bar item's menu.

Item	Purpose
Undo	Counteract the last action
Cut	Remove a portion of the current screen
Copy	Copy a portion of the current screen
Paste	Insert the last Cut or Copied portion of the screen
Clear	Remove a portion or all of the screen
Add	(Database) Add the current information to the database as a new record

Item	Purpose
Update	(Database) Update the corresponding database record with the current screen information
Delete	(Database) Delete the database record that corresponds to the current screen record
	(Non-database) Remove a portion of the screen

As you can see from Table 15.2, different selection items may be presented based on the type of application; however, the overriding functionality is the same. For example, deleting is always removing something. You should remember that the wording of the options in your action bar menu should correspond to those presented in the table if they are the same actions.

The View Action Bar Item

The View action bar item contains selections that enable you to look in different ways at information from the current file. Again, different applications are going to provide different view options. A word processor may have selection items such as Normal and Page layout. A database application may have items such as Next and Previous.

In addition to options that display data, there may also be options that customize the interface of your application. The View action bar menu may include options as setting the tab stops in a word processing application, customizing the colors used in the screen interface, and setting up accelerator keys. Table 15.3 contains the View options that you will use in the *Record of Records!* application.

Table 15.3. Selection items for the View action bar item's menu for *Record of Records!*

Item	Purpose
Find...	Find a specific record and display
Next	Find the next record and display
Previous	Find the previous record and display

As you can see, each of the items in Table 15.3 presents a different record for viewing. You may be wondering why these options aren't in the File action bar menu because

they manipulate information in the file. The reason is because they are working at a record level not a file level.

The Options Action Bar Item

The Options action bar item is used to present selection items that customize the user interface. These are options that change what is or isn't displayed to the user. An example of an Option selection item would be an option to turn the command line at the bottom of the screen on and off. This option doesn't change what the application does, it only changes what the user sees. Actions that customize the use of the application fall under the View option.

An example of an Option action versus a View option is in order:

If there is an option to customize the accelerator keys that are displayed at the bottom of the screen, then it falls in the View options because it is a customization of functionality.

If there is an option to display or not display the accelerator keys, then it falls under Options because this is a customization to what the user sees, not how to do it.

Warning: Most programs confuse the use of View and Option.

The Help Action Bar Item

The Help option contains actions that are informational. Although you may think that Help is as simple as just presenting some information, there is actually more to it. The Help option will generally contain several options. Table 15.4 presents the selection items commonly included on the Help action bar menu.

Table 15.4. Possible selection items for the Help action bar item's menu.

Item	Purpose
Help for help...	Presents information on using help
Extended help...	Presents general information about the current screen

Item	Purpose
Keys help...	Presents information on accelerator keys
Help index...	Presents an index for the help information
Tutorial...	Presents a connection to a tutorial program
About...	Presents general information about the application

Note: Detailed information on each of these selections is presented on Day 16 when the use of Help is covered in detail.

Other Action Bar Items

While the action bar items presented are the most common, they aren't the only options. All applications that have action bars should have a Help option. A File option should also be included in most cases because it can provide a means of exiting the application. Other options may include those that were mentioned earlier or application-specific options.

Expert Tip: Always use the action bar items previously listed instead of making up your own names. This will provide consistency with other applications.

DO   DON'T

DO follow the standard names presented here when creating your action bars.

DON'T make up your own names for standard functions. This may confuse the user of your application.

A Simple Action Bar in Action

In the *Record of Records!* application that you've been developing, there are several action bars. On the main menu is a simple action bar that contains only a single selection item, Help. In most cases, there will be more than a single item; however, by having only a single item, it makes for a good introductory demonstration.

The *Record of Records!* application has followed the standard of setting the F10 key to access the action bar. When you set up the new main menu on Day 14, the F10 key was included as an exit key. If fact, in line 104 of Listing 14.4, a function call was included in the case for F10. At that time, you were told to comment the line out. The action bar functionality is like any other selected functionality in that once a key is pressed, the action bar processes can be performed separately. The do_main_actionbar() function can be created in a separate source file that is linked with the rest of the *Record of Records!* files, or it can be added to the end of the RECOFREC.C listing.

Listing 15.1 presents the main menu's action bar function in a separate listing. In addition to incorporating this listing, you need to also make a few other subtle changes. First, you need to uncomment the action bar lines in the RECORREC.C listing (approximately lines 104 to 107). You should also include a do_main_actionbar() prototype in the RECOFREC.H header file.

Type

Listing 15.1. MMNUABAR.C. The main menu's action bar functions.

```
 1:  /*==========================================================
 2:   * Filename: mmnuabar.c
 3:   *           RECORD OF RECORDS - Version 1.0
 4:   *
 5:   * Author:   Bradley L. Jones
 6:   *
 7:   * Purpose:  Action bar for main menu.  This is a single
 8:   *           menu. Functions for selections will need to
 9:   *           be added later.
10:   *
11:   * Return:   Return value is either key used to exit menu
12:   *           with the exception of F10 which is returned
13:   *           as Enter to re-display main menu.
14:   *==========================================================*/
15:
16:  #include <stdio.h>
17:  #include "tyac.h"
18:  #include "records.h"
19:
```

```
20:   /*-------------------*
21:    *       prototypes      *
22:    *-------------------*/
23:   #include "recofrec.h"
24:
25:   static void do_something(char *msg);
26:
27:   /*--------------------------------------------*/
28:
29:   int do_main_actionbar( void )
30:   {
31:      int    rv        = 0;
32:      int    menu_sel = 0;
33:
34:      char *help_menu[4] = {
35:              " Help  ", "1Hh",
36:              " About ", "2Aa" };
37:
38:      char MENU_EXIT_KEYS[MAX_KEYS] = {F3, F10, ESC_KEY};
39:
40:      write_string( " Help ",
41:                     ct.menu_high_fcol, ct.menu_high_bcol, 1, 2);
42:      rv = display_menu( 3, 4, SINGLE_BOX, help_menu, 4,
43:                     MENU_EXIT_KEYS, &menu_sel, NO_LR_ARROW,
44:                     SHADOW);
45:
46:      switch( rv )
47:      {
48:         case ENTER_KEY: /* accept selection */
49:         case CR:
50:                        switch( menu_sel )
51:                        {
52:                           case 1:   /* Menu option 1 */
53:                                     do_something(
54:                                         "Main Menu Help...");
55:
56:                                     break;
57:
58:                           case 2:   /* Menu option 2 */
59:                                     do_something(
60:                                         "An about box...");
61:
62:                                     break;
63:
64:                           default: /* continue looping */
65:                                     boop();
66:                                     break;
67:                        }
68:
```

continues

Listing 15.1. continued

```
69:                       rv = ENTER_KEY;
70:                       break;
71:
72:         case F3:      /* exiting */
73:         case ESC_KEY:
74:                       break;
75:
76:         case F10:     /* action bar */
77:                       rv = ENTER_KEY;
78:                       break;
79:
80:         default:      boop();
81:                       break;
82:     }
83:     cursor_on();
84:     return(rv);
85: }
86:
87: /*------------------------------------------------------*
88:  *   Generic function - temporary                       *
89:  *------------------------------------------------------*/
90: static void do_something(char *msg)
91: {
92:   display_msg_box( msg, ct.help_fcol, ct.help_bcol );
93: }
```

This code should look similar to the code in the menus that you created on Day 14. In essence, an action bar with only one item is simply a menu that is displayed near the top of the screen.

Because the action bar is being created before all the actions are developed, a generic function will be used to fill the holes. For example, Help is not covered until Day 16.

Instead of calling a function to do help, a generic function called `do_something()` has been created. The `do_something()` function is prototyped in line 31 as a `static void` function. Because the `static` modifier is used, only this listing will be able to use the `do_something()` function that is included in lines 87 to 93. Other listings can have their own versions of the `do_something()` function. In this listing, the `do_something()` function simply displays a message that it receives as a parameter.

> **Tip:** While not done in this book, if a function isn't going to be used by any source files other than the current one, you should add the `static` modifier. This prevents any other source files from accessing the function.

The main function begins in line 29. A variable is declared for the return value and also for the action bar menu selection. In lines 34 to 44, you should notice that a menu is being created in almost the same manner as those shown on Day 14. The one exception is in line 40. The action bar word, " Help " is highlighted by using the `write_string()` function and the highlight colors.

Line 46 reacts to the returned value from the menu. The returned value should be one of the exit keys or Enter. Because this is a single menu action bar, the left and right arrows are turned off. The `switch` statement in line 46 causes the appropriate action to occur. If the Enter key was pressed, then the user made a selection. A second `switch` statement routes the processing based on which action bar item the user selected (lines 48 to 70). In lines 53 and 59, the `do_something()` function is called. When you learn about adding help to your application on Day 16, you'll want to replace these function calls with calls to appropriate routines.

If F3 or Esc was pressed, you want to pass the key's value back to the main menu. When the main menu's F10 case receives the values back, you'll want to check for the F3 key. It is assumed that if the F3 key is pressed on the main menu's action bar, the user is ready to exit the program. Following is the F10 case in the main menu (RECOFREC.C):

```
case F10:      /* action bar */
               rv = do_main_actionbar();

               if( rv == F3 )
                   cont = FALSE;

               break;
```

The User Interface: Action Bars

The F10 case, in lines 76 of Listing 15.1, is also unique. If the user presses F10 on the action bar, then line 77 changes it to the Enter key. Because of this translation, there will be no need to worry about the main menu reacting to the F10 key, which it originally used to display the action bar. The final result of this is that the F10 key will toggle between the main menu and the action bar.

The last two lines of the function are straightforward. The cursor is turned back on with the `cursor_on()` function because the previous menu turned it off. Because control is going to another menu, it isn't necessary to turn the cursor back on; however, not all action bars return to menus. Line 84 returns the value in `rv`, which is either the exit key from the action bar or the Enter key.

> **Note:** The functions called by the action bar will be the same functions that could be accessed via accelerator keys. For example, selecting Exit off of the main menu's File action bar is the same as pressing F3. To ensure that the functionality is the same, you should place it in a function of its own. This function should then be called from both the F3 case in the main menu and the F3 case in the File action bar. This becomes more important in the entry and edit screen action bars.

A Multi-Menu Action Bar

The action bar presented in Listing 15.1 is an exception in that only one action bar option existed. Most action bars will have at least two options. If you have two items, the functionality becomes a little more complicated; however, the functionality is still not too complex.

Two major differences exist in a multi-option action bar from that of the single-option action bar already presented. The first difference is in the use of the left and right arrows. In a multi-option action bar, the left and right arrows should move the cursor from one action bar menu to the next. Consider an action bar with a File option followed by an Edit option. If the File option menu is currently displayed and the user presses the right arrow key, then the File option menu should be closed and the Edit options menu opened. Each press of the right arrow key should move one action bar menu to the right. If you are on the last menu, then you should circle back around to the first menu. The left key should do the same, except it should move one menu to the left for each press.

The second change from the single menu should already be obvious from the discussion on the right and left arrow keys. With a multi-option action bar, you need to keep track of which Action bar option is current. Listing 15.3 presents the code for the action bar in the Medium Codes screen of the *Record of Records!* application. Because most of the functions that the action bar calls have not yet been developed, a generic do_something() function has been used. The days following will begin to fill in these functions with Help routines, File routines, and more.

Before entering Listing 15.3, you need to make a few minor changes to some of your other listings. You should include the prototype for the Medium Code screen's action bar function in the RECOFREC.H header file. Listing 15.2 contains a RECOFREC.H header file with prototypes for all three entry and edit screens action bars.

Type

Listing 15.2. RECOFREC.H with the action bar function prototypes.

```
 1:   /*===========================================================
 2:    * Filename: RECofREC.H
 3:    *
 4:    * Author:    Bradley L. Jones & Gregory L. Guntle
 5:    *
 6:    * Purpose:   Header file for RECORD of RECORDS! application
 7:    *            This contains the function prototypes needed
 8:    *            by more than one source file.
 9:    *===========================================================*/
10:
11:   #ifndef __RECOFREC_H
12:   #define __RECOFREC_H
13:
14:   /*--------------------------*
15:    * Prototypes from recofrec.c  *
16:    *--------------------------*/
17:
18:   void draw_borders(char *);
19:
20:   int  do_medium_screen(void);
21:   int  do_albums_screen(void);
22:   int  do_groups_screen(void);
23:   void display_msg_box( char *, int, int );
24:   char yes_no_box( char *, int, int );
25:   int  zero_fill_field( char *, int );
26:
27:   int  do_main_actionbar(void);
28:
29:
```

continues

Listing 15.2. continued

```
30:  /*-----------------------------*
31:   * Prototypes for medium screen *
32:   *-----------------------------*/
33:
34:  int  do_medium_actionbar(void);
35:  void display_medium_help(void);
36:
37:
38:  /*-----------------------------*
39:   * Prototypes for groups screen *
40:   *-----------------------------*/
41:
42:  int  do_groups_actionbar(void);
43:  void display_groups_help(void);
44:
45:  /*-----------------------------*
46:   * Prototypes for albums screen *
47:   *-----------------------------*/
48:
49:  int  do_albums_actionbar(void);
50:  void display_albums_help(void);
51:
52:
53:  #endif
54:  /*===========================================================*
55:   *                      end of header                       *
56:   *===========================================================*/
```

As you can see, the action bar function for the Medium Code screen will be called
`do_medium_actionbar()`. A call to this function needs to be added to the Medium
Code screen's listing, MEDIUM.C. You also need to add F10 as an exit key in the
`get_medium_input_data()` function. Following is the new set-up lines for `getline()`
followed by the new F10 case that should be added to MEDIUM.C:

```
/* Set up exit keys. */
static char fexit_keys[ 14 ] = { F1, F3, F4, F10,
                ESC_KEY, PAGE_DN, PAGE_UP, CR_KEY,
                TAB_KEY, ENTER_KEY, SHIFT_TAB,
                DN_ARROW, UP_ARROW, NULL };

static char *exit_keys = fexit_keys;
getline( SET_EXIT_KEYS, 0, 13, 0, 0, 0, exit_keys );
```

The new F10 case:

```
  case F10:          /* action bar */
                     rv = do_medium_actionbar();
```

```
               if( rv == F3 )
               {
                   if( (yes_no_box( "Do you want to exit?",
                          ct.db_fcol, ct.db_bcol )) == 'Y' )
                   {
                       loop = FALSE;
                   }
               }

               position = 0;
               break;
```

One other modification also needs to be made. In the function that draws the screen, `draw_medium_screen()`, the addition of drawing the action bar options needs to be made. This is a simple call to `write_string` as follows:

```
    write_string( " File    Edit    Search    Help",
        ct.abar_fcol, ct.abar_bcol, 1, 2);
```

Once these modifications have been made, you're ready to create the Medium Code screen's action bar. Listing 15.3 contains all you need. It is followed by the Screen prints of each of the four menus.

 Listing 15.3. MEDMABAR.C. The action bar for the Medium Code screen.

```
1:   /*=============================================================
2:    * Filename: medmabar.c
3:    *
                  RECORD OF RECORDS - Version 1.0
4:    *
5:    * Author:   Bradley L. Jones
6:    *
7:    * Purpose:  Action bar for medium screen.  This will
8:    *           contain multiple menus. The functions called
9:    *           by the menu selections may not be available
10:   *           until later days.
11:   *
12:   * Return:   Return value is either key used to exit a menu
13:   *           with the exception of F10 which is returned
14:   *           as Enter to re-display main menu.  In each menu
15:   *           the left and right keys will exit and move
16:   *           control to the right or left menu.
17:   *=============================================================*/
18:
19:
20:  #include <stdio.h>
21:
```

continues

Listing 15.3. continued

```
22:   #include "tyac.h"
23:   #include "records.h"
24:
25:   /*-------------------*
26:    *     prototypes    *
27:    *-------------------*/
28:
29:   #include "recofrec.h"
30:
31:   int do_medium_menu1( void );
32:   int do_medium_menu2( void );
33:   int do_medium_menu3( void );
34:   int do_medium_menu4( void );
35:
36:   static void do_something( char * );
37:
38:   /*--------------------------*
39:    *  medium screen action bar  *
40:    *--------------------------*/
41:
42:   int do_medium_actionbar( void )
43:   {
44:     int  menu  = 1;
45:     int  cont  = TRUE;
46:     int  rv    = 0;
47:     char *abar_text ={" File    Edit    Search    Help "};
48:
49:
50:     while( cont == TRUE )
51:     {
52:        write_string(abar_text, ct.abar_fcol, ct.abar_bcol, 1, 2);
53:
54:        switch( menu )
55:        {
56:
57:           case 1:  /* file menu */
58:                    write_string( " File ", ct.menu_high_fcol,
59:                         ct.menu_high_bcol, 1, 2);
60:
61:                    rv = do_medium_menu1();
62:                    break;
63:
64:           case 2:  /* edit menu */
65:                    write_string( " Edit ", ct.menu_high_fcol,
66:                         ct.menu_high_bcol, 1, 9);
67:
68:                    rv = do_medium_menu2();
69:                    break;
70:
```

```
71:          case 3:   /* search menu */
72:                  write_string( " Search ", ct.menu_high_fcol,
73:                       ct.menu_high_bcol, 1, 16);
74:
75:                  rv = do_medium_menu3();
76:                  break;
77:
78:          case 4:   /* Help menu */
79:                  write_string( " Help ", ct.menu_high_fcol,
80:                       ct.menu_high_bcol, 1, 25);
81:
82:                  rv = do_medium_menu4();
83:                  break;
84:
85:          default: /* error */
86:                  cont = FALSE;
87:                  break;
88:      }
89:
90:      switch( rv )
91:      {
92:          case LT_ARROW:  menu--;
93:                          if( menu < 1 )
94:                              menu = 4;
95:                          break;
96:
97:          case RT_ARROW:  menu++;
98:                          if( menu > 4 )
99:                              menu = 1;
100:                          break;
101:
102:          default:        cont = FALSE;
103:                          break;
104:      }
105:  }
106:  write_string(abar_text, ct.abar_fcol, ct.abar_bcol, 1, 2);
107:  cursor_on();
108:  return(rv);
109: }
110:
111:
112:
113: /*-------------------*
114:  *  do_menu 1  (File)  *
115:  *-------------------*/
116:
117: int do_medium_menu1( void )
118: {
119:  int   rv       = 0;
120:  int   menu_sel = 0;
```

continues

Listing 15.3. continued

```
121:   char *saved_screen = NULL;
122:
123:   char *file_menu[2] = { " Exit   <F3> ", "1Ee" };
124:   char exit_keys[MAX_KEYS] = {F3, F10, ESC_KEY};
125:
126:   saved_screen = save_screen_area( 0, 10, 0, 40 );
127:
128:   rv = display_menu( 3, 4, SINGLE_BOX, file_menu, 2,
129:                      exit_keys, &menu_sel, LR_ARROW, SHADOW);
130:
131:   switch( rv )
132:   {
133:      case ENTER_KEY: /* accept selection */
134:      case CR:
135:                      rv = F3;
136:                      break;
137:
138:      case F3:        /* exiting */
139:      case ESC_KEY:
140:      case LT_ARROW:  /* arrow keys */
141:      case RT_ARROW:
142:                      break;
143:
144:      case F10:       /* exit action bar */
145:                      rv = ENTER_KEY;
146:                      break;
147:
148:      default:        boop();
149:                      break;
150:   }
151:   restore_screen_area( saved_screen );
152:
153:   return(rv);
154: }
155:
156: /*-------------------*
157:  *  do_menu 2  (Edit)  *
158:  *-------------------*/
159:
160: int do_medium_menu2( void )
161: {
162:   int   rv       = 0;
163:   int   menu_sel = 0;
164:   char *saved_screen = NULL;
165:
166:   char *edit_menu[8] = {
167:          " New           ", "1Nn",
168:          " Add     <F4> ", "2Aa",
169:          " Change  <F5> ", "3Cc",
```

```
170:             " Delete  <F6> ", "4Dd" };
171:
172:    char exit_keys[MAX_KEYS] = {F3, F10, ESC_KEY};
173:
174:    saved_screen = save_screen_area( 1, 10, 8, 40 );
175:
176:    rv = display_menu( 3, 11, SINGLE_BOX, edit_menu, 8,
177:                       exit_keys, &menu_sel, LR_ARROW, SHADOW);
178:
179:    switch( rv )
180:    {
181:       case ENTER_KEY: /* accept selection */
182:       case CR:
183:                    switch( menu_sel )
184:                    {
185:                        case 1:  /* Clear the screen */
186:                                 do_something( "CLEARING..." );
187:                                 break;
188:
189:
190:                        case 2:  /* Add a record */
191:                                 do_something( "Adding..." );
192:
193:                                 break;
194:
195:                        case 3:  /* Update the current record */
196:                                 do_something( "Updating..." );
197:
198:                                 break;
199:
200:                        case 4:  /* Deleting the current record */
201:                                 do_something( "Deleting..." );
202:
203:                                 break;
204:
205:                        default: /* continue looping */
206:                                 boop();
207:                                 break;
208:                    }
209:
210:                    rv = ENTER_KEY;
211:                    break;
212:
213:       case F3:      /* exiting */
214:       case ESC_KEY:
215:       case LT_ARROW: /* arrow keys */
216:       case RT_ARROW:
217:                    break;
218:
```

continues

499

Listing 15.3. continued

```
219:        case F10:        /* action bar */
220:                         rv = ENTER_KEY;
221:                         break;
222:
223:        default:         boop();
224:                         break;
225:    }
226:    restore_screen_area( saved_screen );
227:
228:    return(rv);
229: }
230:
231: /*--------------------*
232:  *  do menu 3  (Search)  *
233:  *--------------------*/
234:
235: int do_medium_menu3( void )
236: {
237:    int    rv       = 0;
238:    int    menu_sel = 0;
239:    char *saved_screen = NULL;
240:
241:    char *search_menu[6] = {
242:            " Find...        ", "1Ff",
243:            " Next     <F7> ", "2Nn",
244:            " Previous <F8> ", "3Pp" };
245:
246:    char exit_keys[MAX_KEYS] = {F3, F10, ESC_KEY};
247:
248:    saved_screen = save_screen_area( 1, 10, 0, 60 );
249:
250:    rv = display_menu( 3, 18, SINGLE_BOX, search_menu, 6,
251:                       exit_keys, &menu_sel, LR_ARROW, SHADOW);
252:
253:    switch( rv )
254:    {
255:       case ENTER_KEY: /* accept selection */
256:       case CR:
257:                       switch( menu_sel )
258:                       {
259:                          case 1:  /* Do find dialog */
260:                                   do_something( "Find...");
261:
262:                                   break;
263:
264:                          case 2:  /* Next Record */
265:                                   do_something( "Next...");
266:
```

```
267:                              break;
268:
269:                    case 3:  /* Previous Record */
270:                             do_something( "Previous..." );
271:
272:                             break;
273:
274:                    default: /* shouldn't happen */
275:                             boop();
276:                             break;
277:                 }
278:
279:                 rv = ENTER_KEY;
280:                 break;
281:
282:     case F3:        /* exiting */
283:     case ESC_KEY:
284:     case LT_ARROW:  /* arrow keys */
285:     case RT_ARROW:
286:                 break;
287:
288:     case F10:       /* action bar */
289:                 rv = ENTER_KEY;
290:                 break;
291:
292:     default:        boop();
293:                 break;
294:   }
295:   restore_screen_area( saved_screen );
296:
297:   return(rv);
298: }
299:
300: /*--------------------*
301:  *  do menu 4  (Help) *
302:  *--------------------*/
303:
304: int do_medium_menu4( void )
305: {
306:   int   rv       = 0;
307:   int   menu_sel = 0;
308:   char *saved_screen = NULL;
309:
310:   char *help_menu[4] = {
311:         " Help   <F2> ", "1Hh",
312:         " About       ", "2Ee" };
313:
314:   char exit_keys[MAX_KEYS] = {F3, F10, ESC_KEY};
315:
```

continues

Listing 15.3. continued

```
316:    saved_screen = save_screen_area( 1, 10, 0, 60 );
317:
318:    rv = display_menu( 3, 27, SINGLE_BOX, help_menu, 4,
319:                       exit_keys, &menu_sel, LR_ARROW, SHADOW);
320:
321:    switch( rv )
322:    {
323:       case ENTER_KEY: /* accept selection */
324:       case CR:
325:                       switch( menu_sel )
326:                       {
327:                          case 1:  /* Extended Help */
328:                                   display_medium_help();
329:
330:                                   break;
331:
332:                          case 2:  /* About box */
333:                                   do_something( "About box..." );
334:
335:                                   break;
336:
337:                          default: /* continue looping */
338:                                   boop();
339:                                   break;
340:                       }
341:
342:                       break;
343:
344:       case F3:        /* exiting */
345:       case ESC_KEY:
346:       case LT_ARROW: /* arrow keys */
347:       case RT_ARROW:
348:                       break;
349:
350:       case F10:       /* action bar */
351:                       rv = ENTER_KEY;
352:                       break;
353:
354:       default:        boop();
355:                       break;
356:    }
357:    restore_screen_area( saved_screen );
358:
359:    return(rv);
360: }
361:
362:
363: /*------------------------------------------------------*
364:  *    Generic function - temporary                      *
```

```
365:  *------------------------------------------------------*/
366: static void do_something(char *msg)
367: {
368:   display_msg_box( msg, ct.help_fcol, ct.help_bcol );
369: }
```

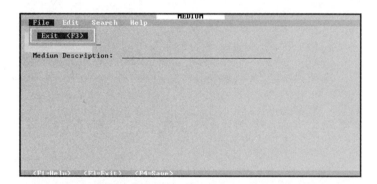

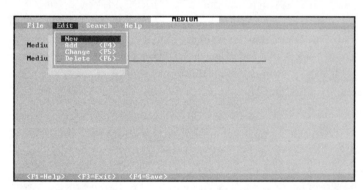

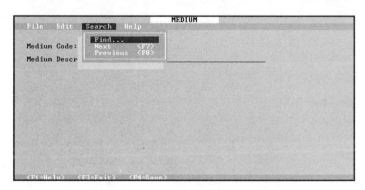

While this is a long listing, don't be intimidated by it. Most of it is identical to Listing 15.1. You'll see this as the listing is explained.

Listing 15.3 starts out like most other listings. Lines 20 to 23 include the appropriate headers. Line 29 includes the RECOFREC.H header file, which contains the prototypes for the do_medium_actionbar() function (see Listing 15.2). Lines 31 to 34 contain four additional prototypes. These prototypes are for each of the action bar options for the Medium Code screen. While I choose to use numbers, it may be better to use descriptive names. For example, do_medium_menu1() will present the File action bar menu. This could be named do_medium_abar_file(). You can choose whatever name you feel most comfortable with.

Line 36 contains a prototype for the do_something() function. Again, the static modifier was used so that this source file's function would be separate from all the other source file's do_something() functions. When you complete the functionality of the action bar on later days, you will want to remove the do_something() function.

Line 42 begins the do_medium_actionbar() function. Four variables are set up to be used with the action bar. The first is menu. This variable keeps track of which menu is currently being used. Figure 15.2 presents how the numbers relate to the Medium Code screen's action bar.

As you can see, File is 1, Edit is 2, Search is 3, and Help is 4. Because the File menu is highlighted when you first use the action bar, the default value for menu is 1.

The remaining variables are easier to understand. A flag, cont, is needed to know when to exit the action bar. The variable rv is declared to hold a return value. The last variable is a string called abar_text. Because the text for the action bar will be written several times, it has been consolidated into a single string.

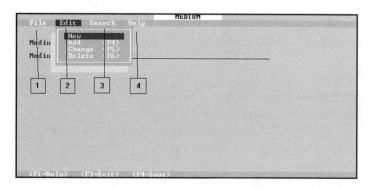

Figure 15.2. *The value of* menu *for the Medium Code Screen's action bar.*

Lines 50 to 105 contain a while statement that keeps processing the action bar as long as the flag, cont, is TRUE. The first step is to redraw the action bar across the top of the screen. The first time into the action bar this is redundant; however, each iteration of the while following needs the action bar redrawn to overwrite the previous high-lighted option. A switch beginning in line 54 routes the processing to the current menu. This will be a value from 1 to 4. As you can see by the cases, the processing for each menu is nearly identical. The first step is to highlight the corresponding action bar item by rewriting it in the highlight colors. For menu 1, File is rewritten, for menu 2, Edit, for menu 3, Search, and for menu 4, Help.

Once the action bar item is highlighted, then the corresponding action bar selection items menu is displayed. Each action bar items menu is in a separate function because of its customized options. Each of these functions is formatted in the same manner as the menu in Listing 15.1. The only major difference is that the left and right arrows are enabled. If either of these arrow keys is pressed, they are returned to the calling case in lines 57 to 83.

Each menu handles the selection from the user. When completed, control returns to the do_medium_actionbar() case. A switch statement, in lines 90 to 104, evaluates the exit key that was used by each menu. If the left arrow is used, then the current menu is decremented (line 92). If the previous menu was 1, then the last menu will be made current. The right arrow key works the same way except that, instead of decrementing the current menu, it is incremented. If the last menu had been current, then the first menu is made current. With the current menu reset, the next iteration of the while loop is called.

If any other key had been used to exit the menu, then processing is done. The continue flag, cont, is set to FALSE so that the while loop will end. Before returning to the calling program, the action bar is redrawn without any highlights and the cursor is turned on. Once completed, the last key used is returned to the calling function in MEDIUMS.C.

> **Expert Tip:** In *Record of Records!*, after an action bar selection item is executed, control is returned to the main screen. You could return control to the action bar by removing the default case in lines 85 to 87—or at least line 86.

The rest of this listing contains the four action bar menus, each in its own function. Each of these menus is similar to Listing 15.1 presented earlier with the exceptions already noted.

Summary

Today's material expanded upon yesterday's. Once you understand menus, you're ready to add action bars to your applications. An action bar is the menu across the top of a screen that contains several menus with actions that can be performed. Today, you were presented with several standard action bar options and the standard selection items that fall within them. Common action bar options include File, Edit, View, Options, and Help. When naming your action bar items, you should try to use standard names rather than make up your own. After covering the action bar naming standards, examples of action bars were created. First, a single menu action bar was developed. This was followed by an action bar for the Medium Code screen.

Q&A

Q Is it okay to make up your own names for action bar items?

A While many people believe that making up their own names for action bar items is better than using the standard names, this isn't really true. You may believe that you are creating names that are more descriptive, and you may be correct. However, by using names consistent with most other applications, your users will be more comfortable with the application. In addition, they may actually have a better indication of the action than your seemingly more descriptive name.

Q **Are all the standard action bar names presented in today's tables?**

A Absolutely not. There are a multitude of standard names. I would suggest looking at several other applications to get an understanding of many of the standard action bar item names. In addition, you can contact companies such as Microsoft Corporation and IBM in regard to standards that they suggest.

Q **Does the order of action bar items matter?**

A It's best to follow an order when presenting action bar items. The order that the items were presented in this chapter is the standard order. This is File, Edit, View, Options, and then Help. If you need to add additional items, they should be placed between Options and Help. The Help option should always be on the far right.

Workshop

The Workshop provides quiz questions to help you solidify your understanding of the material covered and exercises to provide you with experience in using what you've learned.

Quiz

1. What is an action bar?

2. What are the most common action bar items?

3. What types of selections should be allowed in a File action bar menu?

4. What types of selections should be allowed in an Edit action bar menu?

5. What types of selections should be allowed in a View action bar menu?

6. What types of selections should be allowed in an Options action bar menu?

7. What types of selections should be allowed in a Help action bar menu?

8. Is a Help option necessary?

9. What do the left and right arrows do on an action bar?

10. Why are action bars called action bars rather than menu bars?

Exercises

1. **ON YOUR OWN:** Review several commercial applications to see what names they use in their action bars. If possible, look at different operating environments or systems also. Many of the action bar names cross over from DOS, OS/2, and Windows applications.

2. Create an action bar function for the Group Information screen.

3. **ON YOUR OWN:** Create an action bar function for the Musical Items screens.

16

Help!

At one time or another, everybody needs help. When building an application, there are several features that you can add to aid your users in their times of need. This aid is what today's information focuses on. Today you will learn:

- [ ] About adding help to your application.
- [ ] What the different types of help are.
- [ ] Which types of help are more important than others.
- [ ] How to add the different types of help to your applications.

Who Needs Help?

Everyone needs help at one time or another. In applications, users don't always understand what is being displayed or what they are expected to do. By adding help to your applications, you provide a means for the users to get aid.

There are specific types of information that should be provided in help. This help should focus on the application being used. In addition, help is not meant to teach a user how to use the application. Help is intended to provide assistance to the user.

What Are the Different Types of Help?

The types of assistance to be provided can vary. Each type of assistance, or form of help, has a specific intent. Following is a list of the different help types commonly found in applications:

- [ ] Startup help
- [ ] General help
    - [ ] Help for help
    - [ ] Extended help
    - [ ] Help for keys
    - [ ] Help index
- [ ] About... help
- [ ] Context-sensitive help
- [ ] Tutorials

Startup Help

Startup help is provided when an application is first started. It can be provided in one of two ways, either automatically or when the user requests it.

Startup help is most common in applications that require command line parameters. Consider the DOS TYPE command. If you enter TYPE at the command without the name of a file to be listed, you get the following response:

```
C>TYPE
Required parameter missing
```

This information is provided because you didn't start the program correctly. The information is intended to assist you in beginning the program correctly.

The TYPE command's help was provided automatically. Some programs provide startup help that has to be requested. This request is made when you start the program. To receive the aid, an additional parameter is passed. This parameter is generally a special character such as a dash (-) or a slash (/), followed by the letter H or the word help. An example of a program that uses this form of help is the shareware utility, PKZIP by PKWARE Inc. When running PKZIP, you can include a -h on the command line for help information. The following illustrates what is presented when you type PKZIP -h and press enter:

```
PKZIP (R)   FAST!   Create/Update Utility   Version 2.04g   02-01-93
Copr. 1989-1993 PKWARE Inc.  All Rights Reserved.  Shareware Version
PKZIP Reg. U.S. Pat. and Tm. Off.   Patent No. 5,051,745


PKZIP /h[1] for basic help   PKZIP /h[2¦3¦4] for other help screens.


Usage:  PKZIP [options] zipfile [@list] [files...]


        Simple Usage:   PKZIP zipfile file(s)...
                          ¦        ¦       ¦
Program --------------- '        ¦       ¦
                                 ¦       ¦
New zipfile to create --------- '       ¦
                                        ¦
File(s) you wish to compress --------- '
```

The above usage is only a very basic example of PKZIP's capability.

```
Press 2 for more options (including spanning & formatting), press 3 for
advanced options, 4 for trouble shooting options, any other key to quit
help.
```

As you can see, the information provided by PKZIP is helpful in showing you how to use the program. This information aids you in the operation of PKZIP. If you don't know this information, you will be unable to operate the program.

Note: Startup information is provided to help the user start an application.

If your program requires command line parameters, you should provide startup help if the user doesn't include the appropriate command line parameters. At a minimum, you should tell the user what is needed to run the program. Listing 16.1 provides a program called PRINTIT.C. This program types a listing with line numbers. This listing provides startup help if command line parameters aren't entered.

 Listing 16.1. PRINTIT.C. Listing using startup help.

```
1:   /*   Program: PRINTIT.C
2:    *   Author:  Bradley L. Jones
3:    *   Purpose: This program prints out a listing with
4:    *   line numbers!
5:    *=========================================================*/
6:
7:   #include <stdio.h>
8:   #include <stdlib.h>
9:
10:  void do_heading(char *filename);
11:
12:  int line, page;
13:
14:  main( int argv, char *argc[] )
15:  {
16:     char buffer[256];
17:     FILE *fp;
18:
19:     if( argv < 2 )
20:     {
21:        fprintf(stderr, "\nProper Usage is: " );
22:        fprintf(stderr, "\n\nPRINTIT filename.ext\n" );
23:        exit(1);
24:     }
25:
26:     if (( fp = fopen( argc[1], "r" )) == NULL )
27:     {
28:         fprintf( stderr, "Error opening file, %s!", argc[1] );
29:         exit(1);
30:     }
```

```
31:
32:     page = 0;
33:     line = 1;
34:     do_heading( argc[1]);
35:
36:     while( fgets( buffer, 256, fp ) != NULL )
37:     {
38:         if( line % 55 == 0 )
39:             do_heading( argc[1] );
40:
41:         fprintf( stdprn, "%4d:\t%s", line++, buffer );
42:     }
43:
44:     fprintf( stdprn, "\f" );
45:     fclose(fp);
46:     return 0;
47: }
48:
49: void do_heading( char *filename )
50: {
51:     page++;
52:
53:     if ( page > 1 )
54:         fprintf( stdprn, "\f" );
55:
56:     fprintf( stdprn, "Page: %d, %s\n\n", page, filename );
57: }
```

16

C:\PROG\DAY16> Printit

Proper Usage is:

PRINTIT filename.ext

The output displayed is the result of running PRINTIT without any command line parameters. As you can see from the output, the user is informed of how to run the program. This is just enough information to help the user try again.

This startup help was easy to add in the listing. By adding the argc and argv parameters to your main() function, you can capture command line parameters. The argv parameter contains the number of separate commands that were on the command line. For PRINTIT, two arguments are needed, the PRINTIT program and the file to be printed. Line 19 uses an if to determine if less than two parameters were entered. If true, then the user is provided with the startup help (lines 20 to 24). If two or more parameters were entered, then the program runs. If additional commands or filenames are passed, they are ignored.

DO	**DON'T**

DO use startup help when your application doesn't have any screens (for example, in command line utilities).

General Help

General help is provided in the application. Each of the types of general help are usually available in two different ways. The first is via the Help pull-down menu on the action bar. The second is by using an accelerator key. Table 16.1 presents each of the types of general help along with its corresponding accelerator key.

Table 16.1. General help.

Action Bar Text	Accelerator Key
Help for help	Shift+F10
Extended help	F2
Keys help	F9
Help index	F11

Note: Graphical applications will also contain a Help button that can be clicked on with a mouse to access help.

Although there are accelerator keys for each of the types of general help, it isn't mandatory that the accelerator keys be used. They are just suggestions. Each of these keys can be used for other purposes in your application, even if you include the general help options.

Expert Tip: The F2 accelerator key for Extended help is used quite often. The other accelerator keys in Table 16.1 aren't used as often. I suggest that you set up F2 for extended help and leave the other accelerator keys off if they are needed for other functions. It is suggested that you don't use F2 for other tasks. The other accelerator keys in Table 16.1 can be used for other tasks.

What Is Help for Help?

Help for help may seem somewhat rhetorical, but it may well be needed. In some systems, the help that is provided can be more complicated than the system itself. This aid informs the user on how to use the help provided with the application.

Note: Many applications do not provide help for help.

What Is Extended Help?

Extended help is provided in virtually all applications that provide help. It provides information for the portion of the application currently being used.

Extended help should provide an overview of using the current screen. This information can include the purpose of the current screen, specific values for fields presented, and how to accomplish special tasks on the screen. This help should be available via the action bar. In addition, you should allow this information to be available through a function key. If the F1 key isn't being used for context-sensitive help (covered later today), then it should be used for extended help. If the F1 key is unavailable, the F2 function key should be used for extended help.

Expert Tip: You should make it easy for users to access help in your applications.

Expert Tip: Whenever possible, you should include both context-sensitive help and extended help in your applications.

In an application such as *Record of Records!*, there would be different extended help for each of the entry screens. In addition, the menus would have separate extended help. Because each of the screens is functionally different, it should make sense that each extended help would be separate.

The help boxes that were provided in the *Record of Records!* application would be considered scaled-down versions of extended help. Because the *Record of Records!* application doesn't have context-sensitive help—yet—the F1 function key is used for extended help. At this time, you should modify the *Record of Records!* application to provide better extended help. A replacement for the `display_medium_help()` function for the medium code screen is in Listing 16.2. You'll notice that this version of the function provides much more descriptive help.

 Listing 16.2. LIST1602.C. A new `display_medium_help()` function.

```
 1:   /*-----------------------------------------------*
 2:    *    display_medium_help()                       *
 3:    *-----------------------------------------------*/
 4:
 5:   void display_medium_help(void)
 6:   {
 7:     int  ctr;
 8:     char *scrnbuffer;
 9:
10:     char helptext[19][45] = {
11:       "                Medium Codes",
12:       "-----------------------------------------",
13:       "",
14:       "The medium code screen allows you to track",
15:       "the different types of storage mediums that",
16:       "your music collection may be stored on. A",
17:       "two character code will be used in the",
18:       "Musical Items Screen to verify that the",
19:       "medium type is valid. The code entered will",
20:       "need to match a code entered on this screen.",
21:       "Additionally, the codes will be used in",
22:       "reporting on your musical items.",
23:       "",
24:       "An example of a musical code might be:",
25:       "",
```

```
26:          "          CD - Compact Disk",
27:          "          CS - Cassette",
28:          "          VD - Video",
29:          "------------------------------------------" };
30:
31:      scrnbuffer = save_screen_area(2, 23, 28, 78 );
32:
33:
34:      grid( 3, 23, 28, 77, ct.shdw_fcol, ct.bg_bcol, 3 );
35:      box(2, 22, 29, 78, SINGLE_BOX, FILL_BOX,
36:                              ct.help_fcol, ct.help_bcol);
37:
38:      for( ctr = 0; ctr < 19; ctr++ )
39:      {
40:        write_string( helptext[ctr],
41:                       ct.help_fcol, ct.help_bcol, 3+ctr, 32 );
42:      }
43:
44:      cursor(24, 79);
45:      getch();
46:      restore_screen_area(scrnbuffer);
47:  }
```

16

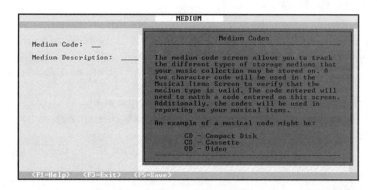

 You'll notice that the help information has been coded into an array. This is not necessarily the best way of adding help because this uses a lot of data space. You may find that it is better to create a separate disk file that you can read into your application. This is similar to what will be done later when you add context-sensitive help to your application.

517

Note: By using a separate file, you'll be able to change the help information without recompiling your application.

What Is Keys Help?

Keys help is relevant to an application that uses a lot of accelerator keys. Keys help should provide information on what accelerator keys or function keys do. This information is generally presented in a format similar to the following:

F1	Help
F3	Exit program
F5	Add a record to the database
F10	Access action bar
<Esc>	Cancel current function
<Enter>	Next field

What Is Index Help?

In some applications, the extended help can become very detailed and very long. The help may be broken down into sections similar to the sections in this book. To help users get the specific help that they need, an index may be provided. This index for the extended help provides a means for users to quickly find exactly what they need.

The Index help should provide a list of the topics available. The user should be able to select an item from the list. Upon selection, the corresponding extended help should be presented.

Note: Index help, which may also be referred to as the Help index, is only provided in applications with a large amount of help.

Using an About Box

An about box is the most commonly used help screen. It can also be the least helpful. An about box serves a slightly different purpose from the other types of help. Instead of providing help directly aimed at using the application, an about box provides high-level information. The information included will be the application's name, its

version number, the company that produced/owns the software, and any copyright information. As you can see, this is identifying information rather than help information.

Other information that may be included in an about box would be the registration number, if one exists, a company logo, the software's logo, or some system information. System information that may be included would be the available memory and the total memory.

As you should see, all the information is helpful to you in addition to the user. If a user calls for support, the information in the about box helps you identify which program and which version of the program the user is running. In addition, it helps the user to know who to contact because the company name should be in the about box.

Following is Listing 16.3. This listing contains the code for the *Record of Records!* about box. This code can be linked to the function calls in the *Record of Records!* about boxes.

Type

Listing 16.3. ABOUT.C. The *Record of Records!* about box code.

```
 1:   /*============================================================
 2:    * Filename: ABOUT.C
 3:    *           About box for RECORD OF RECORDS
 4:    *
 5:    * Author:   Bradley L. Jones
 6:    *
 7:    * Purpose:  Dispays about box for Record of Records!
 8:    *
 9:    * Note:     This listing can either be linked with other
10:    *           listing in the Rec of Rec app, or it can be
11:    *           added to the bottom of the RECOFREC.C listing
12:    *
13:    *           Prototype should be added to recofrec.h
14:    *============================================================*/
15:
16:   #include <stdio.h>
17:   #include <conio.h>        /* not an ANSI header, used for getch() */
18:   #include <string.h>       /* for strlen() */
19:   #include <ctype.h>
20:   #include "tyac.h"
21:   #include "records.h"
22:   #include "recofrec.h"
23:
24:
25:   void display_about_box(void);
```

continues

Listing 16.3. continued

```
26:
27:    void display_about_box( void )
28:    {
29:        char *scrn_buffer = NULL;
30:
31:        scrn_buffer = save_screen_area( 6, 17, 19, 64);
32:
33:        grid( 7, 17, 19, 63, ct.shdw_fcol, ct.bg_bcol, 3 );
34:        box( 6, 16, 20, 64, DOUBLE_BOX, FILL_BOX,
35:            ct.help_fcol, ct.help_bcol);
36:
37:        /* draw graphic boxes on box */
38:        box( 7, 12, 24, 34, SINGLE_BOX, BORDER_ONLY,
39:                    ct.help_fcol, ct.help_bcol);
40:        box( 8, 13, 22, 32, SINGLE_BOX, FILL_BOX,
41:                    ct.help_fcol, ct.help_bcol);
42:
43:
44:        box(  9, 12, 46, 59, SINGLE_BOX, BORDER_ONLY,
45:                    ct.help_fcol, ct.help_bcol);
46:        box( 10, 13, 47, 60, SINGLE_BOX, FILL_BOX,
47:                    ct.help_fcol, ct.help_bcol);
48:
49:
50:        /* Fill in text */
51:        write_string( "*** RECORD OF RECORDS ***",
52:                    ct.help_fcol, ct.help_bcol, 7, 37 );
53:        write_string( "albums",
54:                    ct.help_fcol, ct.help_bcol, 9, 24 );
55:        write_string( "cassettes",
56:                    ct.help_fcol, ct.help_bcol, 11, 49 );
57:        write_string( "Version 1.00",
58:                    ct.help_fcol, ct.help_bcol, 8, 43 );
59:        write_string( "(c)1994, RTSoftware - All Rights Reserved",
60:                    ct.help_fcol, ct.help_bcol, 15, 22 );
61:
62:        cursor(24, 79);
63:        getch();
64:
65:        restore_screen_area(scrn_buffer);
66:    }
67:
68:    /*=======================================================*
69:     *                    end of listing                     *
70:     *=======================================================*/
```

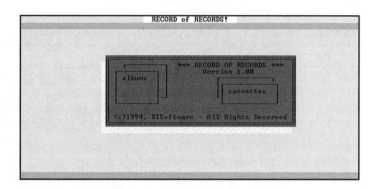

This function will need to be linked with the other programs for the *Record of Records!* application. You can choose to add it to the RECOFREC.C listing, or you can keep it in its own separate listing. You'll need to add the prototype to the RECOFREC.H header file because you will be calling this function from each of the different areas. In fact, you'll want to call this from each of the three entry and edit screens along with the main menu. Each of these should have the display_about_box() function called from the About... option on the Help pull-down menu.

This function shouldn't offer any surprises. The function saves the screen area that will hold the about box (line 31). A grid and a box are then displayed to hold the about information. Lines 38 to 47 draw the graphic boxes that are to appear in the about box. Lines 51 to 60 display the textual information. In your applications, you can draw and write any textual information you want. In the case of *Record of Records!*, the application name, some graphics that give an idea of what the application does, a version number, and, finally, a copyright with a company name and date are presented. Line 65 restores the screen when the user presses a key. The function then ends and control returns to the calling program.

Context-Sensitive Help

Context-sensitive help is generally the most valuable to a user. It is help that provides information on the task that is currently being executed. For example, if a user is on the Medium Code field in the medium screen, then the context-sensitive help would provide information on what a medium code is or on what values are valid for medium codes.

In Listing 16.4, a function that provides context-sensitive help has been created. This function should be added to the medium code screen that was originally presented on Day 13. A few changes need to be made to integrate this function into the medium code listing. These changes are detailed after Listing 16.4.

Type

Listing 16.4. LIST1604.C. The context-sensitive help.

```
 1:  #include <stdlib.h>
 2:  /*********************************************************
 3:   *    NOTE:     Prototypes for following two functions are   *
 4:   *              in the recofrec.h header file.  These same   *
 5:   *              functions are usable in other screens.       *
 6:   *********************************************************/
 7:
 8:  /*-----------------------------------------------------*
 9:   * Function: display_context_help()                    *
10:   * Purpose:  Display help that is relative to a specific *
11:   *           field on a specific screen.               *
12:   * Notes:    The first parameter needs to be the       *
13:   *           name of the help file.                    *
14:   *           Each screen should have its own help file *
15:   *           since offsets in the file are based on    *
16:   *           field position.                           *
17:   *           Each position should have 3 lines in its  *
18:   *           help file. Max line length 64 characters. *
19:   *-----------------------------------------------------*/
20:  void display_context_help( char *file, int position )
21:  {
22:      FILE *fp;
23:      int   ctr;
24:      char *rv = NULL;
25:
26:      char *buffer1 = NULL;
27:      char *buffer2 = NULL;
28:      char *buffer3 = NULL;
29:
30:      /* allocate buffers */
31:      buffer1 = (char *) malloc(65 * sizeof(char));
32:      buffer2 = (char *) malloc(65 * sizeof(char));
33:      buffer3 = (char *) malloc(65 * sizeof(char));
34:
35:      /* make sure all the allocations worked */
36:      if( buffer1 == NULL ¦¦ buffer2 == NULL ¦¦ buffer3 == NULL)
37:      {
38:          display_msg_box("Error allocating memory...",
39:                          ct.err_fcol, ct.err_bcol );
40:          if( buffer1 != NULL )
41:              free(buffer1);
42:          if( buffer2 != NULL )
43:              free(buffer2);
44:          if( buffer3 != NULL )
45:              free(buffer3);
46:
47:          return;
48:      }
```

```
49:
50:
51:        fp = fopen( file, "r");
52:
53:        if( fp == NULL )   /* make sure the file was opened */
54:        {
55:            display_msg_box("Error opening help file...",
56:                               ct.err_fcol, ct.err_bcol );
57:        }
58:        else
59:        {
60:            /* spin through to appropriate record */
61:            for( ctr = 0; (ctr < (position * 3)) ; ctr++ )
62:            {
63:                rv = fgets( buffer1, 65, fp );
64:                if( rv == NULL)
65:                    break;
66:            }
67:
68:            /* ready to read three lines */
69:            if( rv != NULL || position == 0 )
70:            {
71:                rv = fgets( buffer1, 65, fp );
72:                if( rv != NULL )
73:                {
74:                    rv = fgets( buffer2, 65, fp );
75:                    if( rv != NULL )
76:                        rv = fgets( buffer3, 65, fp );
77:                }
78:
79:                display_cntxt_help_msg( buffer1, buffer2, buffer3 );
80:            }
81:            else   /* hit end of file too soon */
82:            {
83:                display_msg_box( "Error in message file...",
84:                                   ct.err_fcol, ct.err_bcol );
85:            }
86:
87:            fclose( fp );
88:        }
89:
90:        free( buffer1 );
91:        free( buffer2 );
92:        free( buffer3 );
93:    }
94:
95:    /*-------------------------------------------------------*
96:     *    display_context_help()                             *
97:     *-------------------------------------------------------*/
```

continues

Listing 16.4. continued

```
 98:  void display_cntxt_help_msg( char *string1,
 99:                                char *string2,
100:                                char *string3 )
101:  {
102:     char *scrn_buffer = NULL;
103:     scrn_buffer = save_screen_area( 10, 16, 10, 70 );
104:
105:     grid( 11, 16, 10, 69, ct.shdw_fcol, ct.bg_bcol, 3 );
106:     box(10, 15, 11, 70, SINGLE_BOX, FILL_BOX,
107:                      ct.help_fcol, ct.help_bcol);
108:
109:     write_string( string1, ct.help_fcol, ct.help_bcol, 11, 14 );
110:     write_string( string2, ct.help_fcol, ct.help_bcol, 12, 14 );
111:     write_string( string3, ct.help_fcol, ct.help_bcol, 13, 14 );
112:
113:     write_string( "Press any key to continue...",
114:                   ct.help_fcol, ct.help_bcol, 14, 14 );
115:
116:     cursor(24, 79);
117:     getch();
118:
119:     restore_screen_area(scrn_buffer);
120:  }
121:
122:  /*=======================================================*
123:   *                     end of listing                    *
124:   *=======================================================*/
```

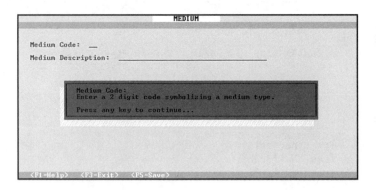

This function can be added to the end of the medium code screen's listing. A few changes need to be made to the medium code screen listing. The F1 case within the get_medium_input_data() function (lines 193 to 196 in Listing 13.4) should be modified. The call in the F1 case was used to access extended help. This should now be moved to an F2 function. The resulting code for the F1 and F2 function keys should be similar to the following listing. This code should replace lines 193 to 196 in Listing 13.4.

Listing 16.5. LIST1605.C. Replacement F1 case and new F2 case.

```
case F1:            /* context sensitive help */
                    display_context_help( HELP_DBF, position );
                    break;

case F2:            /* extended help */
                    display_medium_help();
                    break;
```

16

In addition to replacing your F1 case with the preceding code, you should also modify the getline() calls that set up the exit keys. You need to add the F2 key to the list. This requires that you increase the number of exit keys by one from 12 to 13 keys. The following lines should replace lines 111 to 118 in Day 13's Listing 13.4.

```
/*  Set up exit keys.  */
static char fexit_keys[ 14 ] = { F1, F2, F3, F4, ESC_KEY,
                PAGE_DN, PAGE_UP, CR_KEY,
                TAB_KEY, ENTER_KEY, SHIFT_TAB,
                DN_ARROW, UP_ARROW, NULL };

static char *exit_keys = fexit_keys;
getline( SET_EXIT_KEYS, 0, 13, 0, 0, 0, exit_keys );
```

The output of Listing 16.4 presented the context-sensitive help that is received when F1 is pressed and the cursor is on the Medium Code field. To get the medium code to work, you need to incorporate all of the changes mentioned so far. In addition, you need to create a help file called MEDIUM.HLP. This file needs to contain the context-sensitive help. The following unnumbered listing contains the text in the MEDIUM.HLP help file.

Listing 16.6. MEDIUM.HLP. The context-sensitive help for the medium code screen.

```
Medium Code:
Enter a 2 digit code symbolizing a medium type.

Medium Description:
Enter a description for the Medium Code.
```

The MEDIUM.HLP listing contains the contextual help. You should note that the file contains six lines. The last line is blank.

Looking back at Listing 16.4, you can see how the context-sensitive help works. When F1 is pressed, the context-sensitive help function, `display_context_help()`, is called. The `display_context_help()` function was presented in Listing 16.4 (line 2). The `display_context_help()` function starts by declaring three character buffers and allocating them with the `malloc` function (lines 26 to 33). Line 36 then verifies that all three character buffers were allocated. If one of them was not allocated, then an error message is displayed. Lines 40 to 45 then perform cleanup to ensure that any memory that was allocated is freed before returning to the calling program. Notice that the program reports the problem and keeps going. As long as users are doing functions that don't require allocating more memory, they will be able to continue with the program.

If the allocation was okay, then the function continues in line 51. Here, the function attempts to open the filename that was passed. In this case, the file is MEDIUM.HLP. Because a file name wasn't hard coded, this function will be usable in the other entry and edit screens.

If the open isn't successful, then once again an error message is displayed in line 55. If the file is opened, then the appropriate information needs to be found. The help files should be set up so that there are three lines for each position on the screen. The first three lines of the help file should contain the information that will be displayed for the field in position one. The second set of three lines should contain the information for the second position on the screen, and so on. If a field doesn't have three lines of help, then blank lines should be included in the file.

The `for` statement, in lines 61 to 66, spins through the file to the appropriate set of help lines by doing reads in the file. The `fgets()` function is used because the lines of text are variable length. If the lines were all a set length, then `fseek()` could be used along with `fread()`. Using the `fseek()` and `fread()` functions would be more efficient; however, they require that the help file contain lines that are all the same length. Each line of the file is read from the beginning. What is in the lines is ignored until the offset is reached based on the field position.

Line 69 begins the read for the three lines of information that will be displayed on the screen. If the end of the file has been reached, then you don't want to continue reading the help file. The signal for the end of the file is when `fgets()` returns the value of NULL. Line 69 checks to see if the end of the file has been reached. If the position is 0, then the file hasn't been read. Lines 71 to 76 then do three additional reads to obtain the

appropriate help information. With each read, a check is done to ensure that everything went okay. Once completed, line 79 calls a function to actually display the three lines on the screen. This function, `display_cntxt_help_msg()`, is similar to the `display_msg_box()` function. Instead of a single line, three lines of information are displayed (see lines 95 to 120).

After displaying the context help, the program waits for the user to press a key. The help file is then closed (line 87) and the allocated memory is released back to the system (lines 90 to 93). Control is then returned to the calling function.

This function could be sped up a little bit. Instead of opening and closing the file each time the help is needed, you could open it at the beginning of the program and close it when the program ends.

Note: The exercises at the end of today will ask you to create context-sensitive help for the other screens in the *Record of Records!* application.

Tutorials

Tutorials are different from Help. Whereas help provides aid in using an application, tutorials provide training. A tutorial walks the user through the steps of using the applications. These instructions can be presented in several forms. These forms can be either online, in paper documentation, or both.

Online tutorials can either be interactive or non-interactive. An *interactive tutorial* enables the user to interact with what is being presented. For example, a data-entry screen within the tutorial may require the user to actually enter data.

A *non-interactive tutorial* presents the information, but doesn't enable the user to actually perform any of the application's functions. Most non-interactive tutorials are presented in slide show format. One slide containing information is presented with textual information for the user to read. Included are pictures of screens, messages, dialog boxes, and more.

Note: Interactive tutorials are more effective than non-interactive tutorials; however, they can be more difficult to develop.

Tutorials that aren't online are easier to produce. These paper tutorials are generally interactive. They walk the user through using each portion of the application. Included in the tutorial are the same constructs that are included in the non-interactive tutorials. In addition, steps are presented that tell the user how to get into the application and actually perform the different processes.

 Note: Tutorials and Help are not the same. A tutorial is not a replacement for help. Help should not be written to be a tutorial.

Documentation and Manuals

An entire book could be written on preparing documentation for computer applications. Documentation comes in several forms and serves several purposes. The main goal of documentation should be to help the users in their utilization of the application.

Documentation can come in the form of several different types of manuals. There are installation or set-up manuals, user guides, reference guides, and tutorials. In addition, several application specific manuals may be provided.

Each of the different manuals has a different purpose. The installation or set-up manuals help the user install and set up the software. Once the software is running, these manuals are generally put aside. The user guide is provided as an overview to the application. It should contain sections on each portion of the application. A reference guide may contain information similar to the user guide, but it will differ in the way it's organized. In addition, the level of detail in a reference will generally be greater than that of a user guide. A reference manual should be designed so that information is easy to access. A user manual will be set up in the order that a user is most likely to use the application.

Tutorials, which were described earlier, provide the user with step-by-step instructions in actually using the application. These instructions have the users actually enter information into the application so that they get hands-on experience.

 Note: Tutorials that are provided in manuals are generally hands-on in nature, which means that they have the user actually enter information into the application. Online tutorials may or may not be hands-on.

DO	**DON'T**

DO include help in your applications.

DON'T confuse tutorials with help.

DO include documentation with your applications if you plan to sell them.

Summary

Today's chapter provides help. Actually, it provides information on adding help to your application. There are several different forms of help that can be added to your applications. Context-sensitive help is the most helpful. It provides information on the action that is being performed at the time help is requested. Extended help is more common. Extended help provides information relative to the current screen being used. Several other types of help are also available. These include help for help, index help, keys help, and about boxes. In addition to help, some applications provide tutorials. To supplement help, documentation may be provided in the form of startup or installation manuals, user guides, or reference manuals.

Q&A

Q Do you have to add help to your applications?

A No, you don't have to add help to your applications; however, most times you should. Virtually all applications that are available for sale have some form of help. At a minimum, they contain an about box. Most include context-sensitive help or extended help.

Q Is the F1 key always used for context-sensitive help?

A No, some applications don't provide context-sensitive help, but do provide extended help. In these applications, the F1 key is used for the extended help. The reason behind this is because most people expect the F1 key to provide some form of help.

Q Should a tutorial be a part of the application?

A No, a tutorial should be a separate application. You can provide access to the tutorial through the Help pull-down menu; however, you shouldn't include the tutorial as a part of the application. The application should be written to serve a function. A tutorial is written to teach the user that function. Your prime objective should be to write the application, not the tutorial.

Workshop

The Workshop provides quiz questions to help you solidify your understanding of the material covered and exercises to provide you with experience in using what you've learned.

Quiz

1. Is help necessary in a computer application?

2. What are the different types of help?

3. Are tutorials considered help?

4. When should startup help be used?

5. If you are only providing extended help in your application, what accelerator key should be assigned to it?

6. If you are providing extended help and context-sensitive help, what accelerator keys should be used?

Exercises

Today's exercises are all on your own. You should model your answers after the material presented today.

1. **ON YOUR OWN:** You were shown code for adding extended help to the medium code screen. Add extended help to the Group Information screen and the Musical Items screen.

2. **ON YOUR OWN:** Create context-sensitive help for the Group Information screen and the Musical Items screen.

3. **ON YOUR OWN:** Add help to the application that you are creating on your own. (See "ON YOUR OWN" exercises from previous days.)

File Routines:
The First Step

On Days 14 and 15, you added menus and action bars to your application. This helped the user to navigate effectively through your application. To make your application truly useful, you need to be able to work with data. Until today, your application has only been able to write data to a file. Today, you will expand on this. Today you will:

☐ Look at the different ways that you will want to access a file.

☐ Learn different file formats.

☐ Learn about indexing a file.

☐ Look at the functions that will enable you to work with the Medium Code file.

Storing Data in a Disk File

As you begin accepting data in your application, you'll want to be able to save it so that you can access it later. To do this, you use disk files. By storing information on a disk drive, you'll be able to access it at a later time.

Note: Many beginning C books cover disk files. In addition to covering such concepts as naming them, they also cover the basics of opening, reading, writing, and seeking within them. Much of this will be covered in today's material; however, many of the basics will be skimmed over. If you find the amount of information isn't adequate, then you should reference a beginning C book such as *Teach Yourself C in 21 Days*.

A Review of the Terminology Used with Files

Before examining the concepts involved in using data in a disk file, a few terms should be reviewed to ensure that you understand them. Many of these terms have been used throughout this book. The terms that you should be familiar with are I/O, fields, records, data files, and databases. Figure 17.1 helps to show the relationship of these terms.

I/O is an abbreviation for Input/Output. Many programmers use the term *I/O* to stand for any action that results in information flowing into, or out of, a computer program. Input is information flowing in; output is information flowing out. Information will flow into the *Record of Records!* application in two different ways. One is by being entered into the entry and edit screens. The other is by retrieving a record from the data file. Information is output in two ways also. It is output to the disk file when it is saved. It is also output to the reports that will be presented on Day 19.

A *field* is an individual piece of data. Because data is simply information, a field is simply a piece of information. In the *Record of Records!* application, there are a multitude of fields. Examples of some of the fields are medium code, group name, song title, and type of music.

A *record* is a group of related fields. In the *Record of Records!* application, there are several different records used. The smallest record used is the medium code record, which contains two fields, a medium code, and a medium description.

A *data file* is a group of related records that are stored on a secondary medium such as a disk drive. When you save records, they create files. In the *Record of Records!* application, you have three different data files. They are the Mediums, Groups, and Albums.

A *database* is a group of related data files. Often, the files in a database can be related to each other. For example, in the *Record of Records!* application, the Mediums file can be related to the Albums file via the medium code field. This Groups file can be related to the Albums file via the group name field. In both the examples, an identical field appears in both files. It is these fields that cause the files to be related.

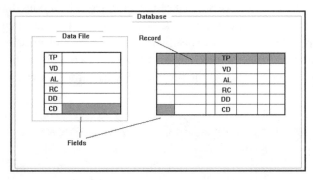

Figure 17.1. *The relationship between the file terms.*

File Formats

As stated before, files are stored on disks. In working with these disk files, there are two things that you must be aware of. The first is the mode of the file. The second is the format.

File Modes

There are two different modes for disk files. These are binary mode and text mode. When you initially open a file for use, you specify which of these two modes you will be using. Because the two modes operate differently, you should understand them.

If you are using text mode, then several translations will occur automatically as you work with the data. Because of this, the text mode is sometimes referred to as translated mode. Following are the translations:

☐ Carriage-return-line-feeds (CR-LF) are translated into a single line feed (LF) on input.

☐ A line-feed character (LF) is translated to a carriage-return-line-feed (CR-LF) on output.

☐ A Control+Z is translated as the end of the file. On input, the Control+Z character is removed (if possible).

A file opened in binary mode doesn't do the translations of a text mode file. In fact, a binary file doesn't do any translations. This means that data is stored exactly as it is.

When you open a file, you specify which mode you want to use, binary or text. In addition, you must specify the type of access that you will need with the file. There are several different accesses that can be specified. The modes that can be used are read (r), write (w), and append (a). If a file is opened to be read, then it cannot be written to or appended to. A file can be opened to both read and write by including a plus sign after the read (r) or write (w). If you open as w+ (write plus), then it will allow reading of and writing to a file. If the file already exists, it will be truncated to a zero length.

Note: Using the standard C file functions is covered in most beginning C books. File functions will be used and explained in some detail later. If you find that you need to know more, then you should consult either your compiler manuals or a beginning C book.

File Formats

In addition to different modes, files can also have different formats. The format of a file is how it is stored on the disk drive. Many C programmers learn to work with flat files; however, this is only one of many different formats of files. Today, you will be presented with three different formats; flat files, comma delimited files, and custom file formats.

Flat Files

With a flat file, information is written straight to the disk one record at a time. The text isn't provided with any special format. If you use an operating system command to list the file (such as the DOS TYPE command), you will see the raw data in the file.

In the *Record of Records!* application, each of the three entry and edit screens wrote the structures to the disk drive. These structures were creating a flat file on your disk. Each time you pressed the function key to add a record, a new record was added to the end of the flat file associated with that screen. You can list this information out. In doing so, you'll find that it is almost always readable. You'll also notice that each record takes the same amount of space. Following is an example of what a flat file might look like:

```
DDD12/25/98DIME DINNER DRINKS      000.10
SAK02/14/92SMILING APPLE KINGS     002.95
BEJ10/23/93BIG EAGLE JIGS          010.99
JMS03/13/93JAR MACARONI SALAD      004.95
```

> **Note:** Numbers in a flat file may be stored as characters or as numbers. If they are stored as numbers, then they will appear differently than what was previously shown. For example, if you write a numeric value that was stored in an integer to a disk file, it would take the same space as an integer. If you wrote the number 65, it would be stored as "A"—the character representation (ASCII) of the number.

Comma Delimited Files

Comma delimited files are most often seen with older spreadsheet applications. Many commercial database applications will read in and write out comma delimited files. A comma delimited file writes a record to the file field-by-field. Each field is separated by a comma—hence the name. In addition, text fields are enclosed in quotes. Numeric fields are typically written as characters. This means that if you type a comma delimited file, you'll know exactly what is in the file. Following is an example of what a portion of a listed comma delimited file may look like:

```
"DEANNA",35,"01/01/92","Body Building",
"CONNIE",21,"12/25/93","Square Dancing",
"JOE",54,"01/14/91","Knitting",
```

Custom File Formats

There are a multitude of custom file formats. Many of these formats have standards surrounding them. Among these standards are C-tree, Btrieve, dBase, and Vsam. These are just a few of the many different file formats.

There are several reasons to have a custom file format. The main reason is to protect your data from other programs. An additional reason for the creation of custom files is based on usage. Depending on how your application works, you may need to create special features in your data.

One common feature that is incorporated into many—but not all—file systems is indexing. Files can either contain built-in indexes or separate files can be created that index other files. The files that you add to the *Record of Records!* application will be a combination of flat files and index files.

Working with an Indexed File

Using an index allows quick access to a large data file. An index file is a separate file from the data file. Because an index contains a smaller amount of information, more of it can be read and manipulated quicker than the data file itself.

An index file generally contains the key field and a pointer. The key field is the field that will be used to sort the file. The pointer will contain the offset into the data file for the corresponding data record. Figure 17.2 illustrates a basic index and data file.

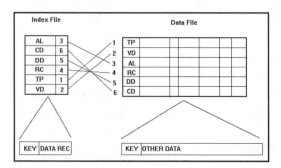

Figure 17.2. *An index file and a data file.*

Not all index files are the same. Index files can be created in two ways. They can be sorted or they can be linked. A sorted index file requires that every time you write a record to the index file, it is written in the correct order on the disk. This means that several records may need to be moved around each time a new index record is added. The index shown in Figure 17.2 was sorted.

Tip: If the index file will be small enough that you can read it into memory in its entirety, then using a sorted index can be time saving.

A linked index requires more work; however, it doesn't require that you do as much rewriting and moving of data records on the disk drive. A linked index works like a linked list. Using pointers, you keep track of the next index record. This is in addition to the key field and the pointer to the data record. If you will only be accessing your records in a single order, such as alphabetically, then you only need one additional pointer. If you will be navigating forward and backward through your data, then you'll need two pointers. Figure 17.3 illustrates a linked index that has the capability to navigate forward and backward.

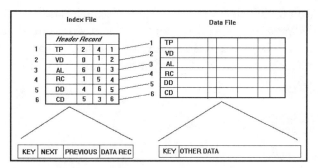

Figure 17.3. *A linked index.*

You should have noticed by now that the data file is stored independent of the indexed file. As new data file records are created, you simply add them to the end of the data file. The index file is then manipulated depending on whether you are using a sorted or linked index. In a linked index, you can also simply add the new index record to the end and then adjust the pointers accordingly. In the *Record of Records!* application, you will use a linked index containing the key field, a pointer to the corresponding data record, a pointer to the next record, and a pointer to the previous record.

Using a File

With the *Record of Records!* application, you'll need to be able to perform several file I/O functions. These I/O functions will use a data file and a linked index. The functions that you need are the following:

- ☐ Opening the file.
- ☐ Closing the file.
- ☐ Adding a record.
- ☐ Updating or changing a record.
- ☐ Deleting a record.
- ☐ Finding the next record.
- ☐ Finding the previous record.
- ☐ Finding a specific record.

Using the indexed file and the data file, you'll be able to do all of these tasks. Before detailing each of these, you first need to be aware of the structures that will be needed.

The medium file will have both an index file and a data file. When working with the *Record of Records!* application, you'll read and write directly from structures. The index file will be kept in one structure and the data will be kept in another structure. The data file's structure will be the same structure that you have been using all along:

```
typedef struct
{
    char code[2+1];
    char desc[35+1];

} MEDIUM_REC;
```

The index file will be a new structure that needs to be added to the RECORDS.H header file that contains all the structures. The index structure for the medium code screen should be:

```
typedef struct
{
    char code[2+1];
    unsigned short prev;
    unsigned short next;
    unsigned short data;

} MEDIUM_INDEX;
```

As you can see, this structure contains a field, code, for the key field. In addition, it contains three variables that will be used to hold record numbers. The record numbers will be for the previous index record, the next index record, and the address of the data in the data file. You will see each of these record numbers used as the file is manipulated.

There will be one additional piece of information needed. This is a header record for the index file. This header record was shown in Figure 17.3. This record will contain the address of the first sorted records in the index file so that you will know where to begin reading the index records. The header will also contain the number of records in the file. For the *Record of Records!* application, the header information will be read and written without the use of a structure. You will see this later.

Preparation for the New I/O Functions

Before jumping into the I/O functions, you should make some modifications to your TYAC.H header file. This header file should be modified to include several defined constants that will be used with the I/O functions. In the next sections, you will create several functions that will be added to your TYAC.LIB library. These functions will be generic I/O functions that will be used by the specific screens to work with the indexed data files.

Several defined constants will be used in the file I/O routines. These defined constants will be used to describe errors that may occur as you are doing file routines. You should add the following to your TYAC.H header file.

```
/* ------------------------------ *
 *      FILE I/O Errors/Flags       *
 * ------------------------------ */

#define NO_ERROR            00
#define OPEN_ERROR          01
#define CREATE_ERROR        02
#define USER_CREATE_ERR     03
#define SEEK_ERROR          04
#define WRITE_ERROR         05
#define READ_ERROR          06
#define CLOSE_ERROR         07
#define NOT_FOUND           08

#define PREVIOUS_REC        01
#define NEXT_REC            00

/* ------------------------------ *
 *    Numeric Conversion Flags      *
 * ------------------------------ */
```

```
#define PACK_ZERO        01    /* For packing numerals */
#define NO_PACK          00    /* w/ zeros at the front */
```

As you can see, most of these constants define errors. The PREVIOUS_REC and NEXT_REC will be used for moving through the database. The PACK_ZERO and NO_PACK constants are conversion flags that will be detailed later.

Before jumping into the specific changes for the *Record of Record!* application screens, the following are prototypes for functions that will be created and described.

```
int open_files(char *, char *);
int close_files(void);
int update_header(void);
int get_rec(int, FILE *, int, int, char * );
int put_rec(int, FILE *, int, int, char * );
```

You should add these prototypes to the TYAC.H header file. The following sections will present each of these functions.

Opening the FILES: *open_files()*

Before being able to work with files, you need to first open them. The open_files() function presented in Listing 17.1 opens both an index and a data file.

Listing 17.1. OPENFILE.C. Opens an index and a data file.

```
 1:  /* -----------------------------------------------------
 2:   * Program: OPENFILE.C
 3:   * Authors: Bradley L. Jones
 4:   *          Gregory L. Guntle
 5:   *
 6:   * Purpose: Opens a file - Sets two global variables
 7:   *          nbr of rec in file and the starting record
 8:   *          in alpha.
 9:   *
10:   * Enter with:
11:   *              idx = Name of index file
12:   *              db  = Name of data file
13:   *
14:   * Returns:
15:   *              0 = No Error
16:   *             >0 = Error - see DEFINES in TYAC.H for FILE I/O
17:   *
18:   *=========================================================*/
19:
20:  #include <stdio.h>
```

```
21:    #include "tyac.h"
22:
23:    /*  Global Variables */
24:    extern FILE *idx_fp;
25:    extern FILE *db_fp;
26:    extern int nbr_records;
27:    extern int start_rec;
28:
29:
30:         /******************
31:          *   OPEN_FILES   *
32:          ******************/
33:    int open_files(char *idx, char *db)
34:    {
35:      int rv = NO_ERROR;
36:      int cr_flg = FALSE;  /* Assume file exist */
37:
38:      /* Open index file first */
39:      if( (idx_fp = fopen(idx, "r+b" )) == NULL )
40:      {
41:        /* Doesn't exist - create it */
42:        if( (idx_fp = fopen(idx, "w+b")) == NULL )
43:          rv = CREATE_ERROR;
44:        else
45:          cr_flg = TRUE;    /*Indicates no hdr exist yet */
46:      }
47:
48:      /* Open Database File - as long as no previous errors */
49:      if ( rv == NO_ERROR )
50:      {
51:        /* Open existing file */
52:        if( (db_fp = fopen(db, "r+b" )) == NULL )
53:        {
54:          /* Create new DB file */
55:          if( (db_fp = fopen(db, "w+b")) == NULL )
56:              rv = CREATE_ERROR;
57:        }
58:      }
59:
60:      /* Only continue if no errors above */
61:      if ( rv==NO_ERROR)
62:      {
63:        /* Get number of records */
64:        if ( !cr_flg ) /* File exist - get hdr record */
65:        {
66:          rv = get_rec(0, idx_fp, sizeof(int), 0,
67:                      (char*)  &nbr_records);
68:          /* Get starting record # */
69:          if (rv == 0)
```

continues

Listing 17.1. continued

```
70:            {
71:               rv = get_rec(0, idx_fp, sizeof(int), sizeof(int),
72:                            (char *) &start_rec);
73:            }
74:        }
75:        else
76:        {
77:            nbr_records = 0;        /* New file - no records yet */
78:            start_rec = 1;
79:        }
80:    }
81:
82:    return(rv);
83: }
```

 The `open_files()` function makes several assumptions. First, it assumes that you will have several external variables defined (lines 23 to 27). These external variables must be declared or else `open_files()` function will fail. Each of these variables is important. The `idx_fp` is a file pointer that will be used with for the index file. The `db_fp` is a file pointer that will be used for the data file. `nbr_records` will be filled with the number of records in the file pointed to be the `db_fp`. The `start_rec` variable will be used to contain the record number for the first sorted record, or the starting record. The starting record's number and the number of records will initially be obtained from the header record when the file is opened.

 Note: Later, you will see that these variables can be set up at the beginning of your applications. All the I/O functions will use these variables.

You call this function with the names of the index file and the data file that you want opened. The function then attempts to open the index file first in line 39. The file is opened using the `fopen()` function. By passing it the value of `"r+b"`, you are attempting to open an existing file for reading and writing in binary mode. If the file does not exist, an error will be returned. Line 42 handles this by then attempting to create the file. If the file can't be created, then `rv` is set to show an error return value of `CREATE_ERROR`. Earlier, you defined `CREATE_ERROR` in your TYAC.H header file. If the file didn't exist and was successfully created, then a flag, `cr_flg`, is set to `TRUE`. This will be used later to indicate that the header information needs to be set up.

Line 49 checks to see if there was an error with the index file. If there wasn't, then the same processes are repeated for opening the data file in lines 52 to 57.

If there hasn't been an error up to this point, then the header information can be set up. Line 61 begins the process of setting up the header file information. Line 64 checks the cr_flg, to see if a new file was created. If a new file wasn't created, then line 66 calls the get_rec() function to read an integer from the index file. This integer is placed in the global variable nbr_records. If the read was successful, then a second read of the index is done to retrieve the address of the starting record, start_rec.

Note: The get_rec() function is a new function that will be covered in the next section.

17

If the index file was created, then lines 77 and 78 set the two global variables, nbr_records and start_rec. The number of records is set to zero because there are no records. The start_rec is set to 1 because there are no records in the file. With this, the header information is set up and the files are ready to use.

Getting a Data Record: *get_rec()*

The get_rec() function enables you to get a record. Listing 17.2 presents this function.

Listing 17.2. GETREC.C. Getting a record—the get_rec() function.

```
 1:   /* ----------------------------------------------------
 2:    * Program: GETREC.C
 3:    * Authors: Bradley L. Jones
 4:    *          Gregory L. Guntle
 5:    *
 6:    * Purpose: Reads a record from a file.
 7:    *
 8:    * Enter with: rec    = record # to retrieve
 9:    *             FILE * = FILE ptr to file
10:    *             rec_size= size of record
11:    *             offset = any offset to adjust to (hdr?)
12:    *             buff = place to put information being read
13:    *
14:    * Returns:  0 = No Error
15:    *           >0 = Error - see DEFINES in TYAC.H for FILE I/O
```

continues

543

Listing 17.2. continued

```
16:     *==============================================================*/
17:
18:   #include <stdio.h>
19:   #include "tyac.h"
20:
21:   int get_rec(int rec, FILE *fp, int rec_size, int offset, char
                  *buff)
22:   {
23:       int rv = NO_ERROR;
24:
25:       if ( rec == 0)   /* Getting Index Header ? */
26:         rec++;         /* Adjust to fit into formula */
27:
28:       /* Seek to position */
29:       if ( fseek(fp, (rec-1)*rec_size+offset,
30:           SEEK_SET) == 0 )
31:       {
32:         /* Read information */
33:         if ( fread(buff, rec_size, 1, fp) != 1 )
34:           rv = READ_ERROR;
35:       }
36:       else
37:         rv = SEEK_ERROR;
38:
39:       return(rv);
40:   }
```

Analysis
The get_rec() function requires several parameters. The first, rec, is the number of the record to retrieve. Each record is numbered sequentially from the beginning to the end of the file. The first record is one, the second is two, and so on. The second parameter, fp, is the file pointer. This will be the opened file that the record is retrieved from. The third parameter, rec_size, is the size of the information or record to be read. The offset, or forth parameter, is the size of the header record in the file if there is one. This offset is needed to adjust for the room taken by the header record. The last parameter, buff, is the area to store the information being read.

The get_rec() function calculates where the record is in the file. This is done by using the record number that tells how many records into the file the record is. The record number is multiplied by the size of each record. Actually, one less than the record number is used so that the value gives the distance into the file that the record is. A final adjustment, by adding the size of the header information, provides the exact location.

This calculation can be seen in line 29 of the get_rec() function. Reviewing the function, you can see how this works. Line 25 checks to see if the record number being retrieved is zero. If a header record or other miscellaneous data is being retrieved, then the record number won't be applicable, so zero will be passed. Because the formula for calculating the position subtracts one, the record number has one added. This allows the final result to be zero.

Line 29 uses the formula for calculating where the record will be located. Using the fseek() command, the position in the file is set to the location that was calculated. If the placement of the position is successful, then line 33 reads the information into the buffer, buff. In the cases of either the seeking or the reading failing, defined error constants are placed in the return value variable, rv. With that, the function ends.

Writing a Data Record: *put_rec()*

While you can retrieve records with a get_rec() function, you can put records back with a put_rec() function. The put_rec() function enables you to write a record at a specific location in the file. This function will look almost identical to the get_rec() function with the exception of the error constants that are used and the use of fwrite() instead of fread(). Listing 17.3 presents the put_rec() function.

 Listing 17.3. PUTREC.C. Writing a record—the put_rec() function.

```
 1:  /* --------------------------------------------------------
 2:   * Program: PUTREC.C
 3:   * Authors: Bradley L. Jones
 4:   *          Gregory L. Guntle
 5:   *
 6:   * Purpose: Writes a record to a file.
 7:   *
 8:   * Enter with: rec    = record # to write
 9:   *             FILE * = FILE ptr to file
10:   *             rec_size= size of record
11:   *             offset = any offset to adjust to (hdr?)
12:   *             buff = place which holds the data to write
13:   *
14:   * Returns:  0 = No Error
15:   *           >0 = Error - see DEFINES in TYAC.H for FILE I/O
16:   *==========================================================*/
17:
18:  #include <stdio.h>
19:  #include "tyac.h"
20:
```

continues

545

Listing 17.3. continued

```
21:  int put_rec(int rec, FILE *fp, int rec_size, int offset, char
                 *buff)
22:  {
23:    int rv = NO_ERROR;
24:
25:    if ( rec == 0)  /* Writing Index Header ? */
26:      rec++;        /* Adjust to fit into formula */
27:
28:    /* Seek to position */
29:    if ( fseek(fp, (rec-1)*rec_size+offset,
30:        SEEK_SET) == 0 )
31:    {
32:      /* Write the information */
33:      if ( fwrite(buff, rec_size, 1, fp) == 1 )
34:        fflush(fp);
35:      else
36:        rv = WRITE_ERROR;
37:    }
38:    else
39:      rv = SEEK_ERROR;
40:
41:    return(rv);
42:  }
```

As stated already, this listing is virtually identical to the get_rec() function described earlier. Line 29 seeks the position that the record is to be written to. If successful, line 33 writes the information that is in the buffer, buff, to the location. If information was already at that particular location, then it will be overwritten. If not, then new information will be added to the file.

Updating the Header Record: *update_header()*

When adding new records to the database, you'll need to update the header information as well. As stated earlier, the index files will have header information. This header information will be the number of records in the file and the record number of the first sorted record. Listing 17.4 includes a function that updates this header information.

Listing 17.4. UPDHDR.C. The update_header() function.

```
1:  /* ---------------------------------------------------------
2:   * Program: UPDHDR.C
```

```
3:    * Authors: Bradley L. Jones
4:    *          Gregory L. Guntle
5:    *
6:    * Purpose: Updates the header info of the Index.
7:    *
8:    * Enter with: All variables are global
9:    *
10:   * Returns:  0 = No Error
11:   *           >0 = Error - see DEFINES in TYAC.H for FILE I/O
12:   *===========================================================*/
13:
14:   #include <stdio.h>
15:   #include "tyac.h"
16:
17:   /*  Global Variables */
18:   extern FILE *idx_fp;
19:   extern FILE *db_fp;
20:   extern int nbr_records;
21:   extern int start_rec;
22:
23:
24:   int update_header()
25:   {
26:      int rv = NO_ERROR;
27:
28:      /* Update number of records */
29:      rv = put_rec(0, idx_fp, sizeof(int), 0,
30:                   &nbr_records);
31:      if (rv == 0)
32:      {
33:         rv = put_rec(0, idx_fp, sizeof(int), sizeof(int),
34:                      &start_rec);
35:      }
36:
37:      return(rv);
38:   }
```

Analysis
You should notice that this function doesn't take any parameters. This is because the function expects global variables to be available. The global variables are the same as those presented in the open_files() listing (Listing 17.1). They are the index file pointer (idx_fp), the data file pointer (db_fp), the number of records (nbr_records), and the starting record number (start_rec). External declarations in lines 18 to 21 help to inform that this function requires these global variables.

Line 29 uses the put_rec() function to write the number of records. From the earlier discussion, you should be able to understand the parameters being passed. The first parameter for record number is set to zero, thus stating that there isn't a record number. The second parameter, idx_fp, shows that the index file is being updated. The third parameter shows that the size of the data being written is an integer. The fourth parameter gives the offset to be added. This is zero because the number of records is first in the file. The last parameter is the address of the nbr_records. This is typecast to a character pointer to avoid a warning when you compile.

If the number of records is written successfully, then the starting record is updated in line 32. This uses a second call to put_rec() with only a slight difference. Instead of the fourth parameter being zero, it is sizeof(int). This allows the start_rec value to be written at an offset of one integer into the file.

Closing the Files: *close_files()*

Just as you opened a file before using it, when you are done with a file, you need to close it. In Listing 17.5, the close_files() function performs the closing functions for the global file pointers that were opened.

Listing 17.5. CLOSFILE.C. Closing a file—the close_files() function.

```
 1:   /* -----------------------------------------------------------
 2:    * Program: CLOSFILE.C
 3:    * Authors: Bradley L. Jones
 4:    *          Gregory L. Guntle
 5:    *
 6:    * Purpose: Closes both the index and DBF file.
 7:    *          Also, updates the hdr information.
 8:    *
 9:    * Enter with:
10:    *
11:    * Returns:  0 = No Error
12:    *          >0 = Error - see DEFINES in TYAC.H for FILE I/O
13:    *=============================================================*/
14:
15:   #include <stdio.h>
16:   #include "tyac.h"
17:
18:   /*  Global Variables */
19:   extern FILE *idx_fp;
20:   extern FILE *db_fp;
21:   extern int nbr_records;
22:   extern int start_rec;
23:
24:
```

```
25:   int close_files()
26:   {
27:       int rv = NO_ERROR;    /* Assume no errors will happen */
28:
29:       /* Close data file first */
30:       if ( fclose(db_fp) == 0 )
31:       {
32:         /* Update hdr record in INDEX file */
33:         rv = update_header();
34:
35:         if (rv == 0)
36:         {
37:
38:            fflush(idx_fp);
39:         }
40:
41:         if ( fclose(idx_fp) != 0 )
42:            rv = CLOSE_ERROR;
43:       }
44:       else
45:          rv = WRITE_ERROR;
46:
47:       return(rv);
48:   }
```

This function again includes the external declarations in lines 19 to 22. In line 30, the function uses the fclose() function to close the data file. If successful, the index will be closed. Before closing the index file, the header information should be updated. This is done in line 33 using the update_header() function that was described earlier. If the update of the header was successful, then line 38 calls fflush() to ensure that the information is actually written to the file and not held in a buffer. Line 41 then closes the index file. Any errors are returned in line 50 to the calling function.

Note: Several C functions were used without explanation. These were fopen(), fclose(), fread(), fwrite(), and fflush(). These are standard functions. If you need more information on these functions, they are in most beginning C books. In addition, they should be covered in your compiler's function reference materials.

Working with the Medium Screen

With the functions presented, you are ready to begin modifying the *Record of Records!* application so that it will be able to work with files. You will start with the medium screen. Before beginning, however, you should add the previous five functions to your TYAC.LIB library. You should have already added the prototypes to the header earlier today.

Before adding the processes of manipulating medium records, you will need to make a few modifications to the RECOFREC.C source file. The global variables needed by many of the functions have to be declared. You should add the following global declarations to the beginning of the RECOFREC.C source file.

```
FILE *idx_fp;            /* Index File Ptr */
FILE *db_fp;             /* Data file */
int nbr_records;         /* Total # of recs */
int start_rec;           /* Starting rec for alpha */
int disp_rec;
```

The first four of these variables will be used in the ways described before. The `disp_rec` variable will be used to hold the record number of any record that is currently being displayed.

The RECOFREC.H header file should receive a few modifications also. To this header file, you should add the prototypes of a few new functions that will be created later today. By adding them now, you will be ready to dive into the medium code's file I/O functions. The following function prototypes should be in the RECOFREC.H header file medium code prototypes.

```
/*----------------------------*
 * Prototypes for medium screen  *
 *----------------------------*/

int  do_medium_actionbar(void);
void display_medium_help(void);

void display_context_help( char *, int );
void display_cntxt_help_msg( char *, char *, char * );

void clear_medium_fields(void);

int  verify_mdata(void);
int  add_mdata(void);
int  add_medium_rec(void);
int  del_med_rec(void);
int  proc_med_rec(int);
```

> **Note:** Earlier today you were asked to modify the RECORDS.H header file. Make sure that you added the medium code's index file structure:
>
> ```
> typedef struct
> {
>     char code[2+1];
>     unsigned short prev;
>     unsigned short next;
>     unsigned short data;
> } MEDIUM_INDEX;
> ```

17

In addition to the RECORDS.H header file, the RECOFREC.C file, and the RECOFREC.H header file, the MEDIUM.C file will also need several changes. Following is an updated MEDIUM.C file.

 Listing 17.6. MEDIUM.C. The medium screen's main file.

```
 1:    /*==========================================================
 2:     * Filename: medium.c
 3:     *
 4:     * Author:   Bradley L. Jones
 5:     *           Gregory L. Guntle
 6:     *
 7:     * Purpose:  Allow entry and edit of medium codes.
 8:     *
 9:     * Note:     This listing is linked with RECofREC.c
10:     *           (There isn't a main() in this listing!)
11:     *==========================================================*/
12:
13:    #include <stdlib.h>
14:    #include <stdio.h>
15:    #include <string.h>
16:    #include <conio.h>          /* for getch() */
17:    #include "tyac.h"
18:    #include "records.h"
19:
20:    /*--------------------*
21:     *      prototypes    *
22:     *--------------------*/
23:
24:    #include "recofrec.h"
25:
26:    void draw_medium_screen( void );
27:    void draw_medium_prompts( void );
```

continues

Listing 17.6. continued

```
28:  void display_medium_fields( void );
29:
30:  int  clear_medium_fields(void);
31:  int  get_medium_data( int row );
32:  int  get_medium_input_data( void );
33:  void display_medium_help(void);
34:
35:  int  add_mdata(void);
36:
37:  /* Global variables */
38:  extern FILE *idx_fp;        /* Main File ptr to data file */
39:  extern FILE *db_fp;         /* Data file */
40:  extern nbr_records;         /* Total # of rec for mediums */
41:  extern int start_rec;
42:  extern int disp_rec;
43:
44:
45:  /*------------------*
46:   * Defined constants *
47:   *------------------*/
48:
49:  #define MEDIUM_IDX    "MEDIUMS.IDX"
50:  #define MEDIUM_DBF    "MEDIUMS.DBF"
51:  #define HELP_DBF      "MEDIUM.HLP"
52:
53:  /*---------------------*
54:   * structure declarations *
55:   *---------------------*/
56:
57:  MEDIUM_REC medium;
58:  MEDIUM_REC *p_medium = &medium;
59:  MEDIUM_REC med_prev;
60:
61:  /*=======================================================*
62:   *    do_medium_screen()                                 *
63:   *=======================================================*/
64:
65:  int do_medium_screen(void)
66:  {
67:    int rv;
68:
69:    /* Open both Index and DBF file */
70:    if ( (rv = open_files(MEDIUM_IDX, MEDIUM_DBF)) == 0 )
71:    {
72:      /* Setup for adding new records at beginning */
73:      memset(&med_prev, '\0', sizeof(med_prev));
74:      disp_rec = 0;              /* Initialize displaying rec # */
75:      clear_medium_fields();
76:      draw_medium_screen();
```

```
77:        get_medium_input_data();
78:        rv = close_files();        /* Close IDX and DBF file */
79:      }
80:      else
81:      {
82:        display_msg_box("Error opening MEDIUM files...",
83:                       ct.err_fcol, ct.err_bcol );
84:      }
85:      return(rv);
86:    }
87:
88:    /*-----------------------*
89:     *   draw_medium_screen()  *
90:     *-----------------------*/
91:
92:    void draw_medium_screen( void )
93:    {
94:
95:
96:        draw_borders("     MEDIUM      ");  /* draw screen bckgrnd */
97:
98:        write_string( " File   Edit   Search   Help",
99:             ct.abar_fcol, ct.abar_bcol, 1, 2);
100:       write_string(
101:        "<F1=Help> <F3=Exit> <F4=Save> <F7=Next> <F8=Prev>"
102:            "<F10=Actions>",
102:             ct.abar_fcol, ct.abar_bcol, 24, 3);
103:
104:       draw_medium_prompts();
105:       display_medium_fields();
106:   }
107:
108:   /*-----------------------*
109:    *   draw_medium_prompts() *
110:    *-----------------------*/
111:
112:   void draw_medium_prompts( void )
113:   {
114:      write_string("Medium Code:",
115:           ct.fld_prmpt_fcol, ct.fld_prmpt_bcol, 4, 3 );
116:      write_string("Medium Description:",
117:           ct.fld_prmpt_fcol, ct.fld_prmpt_bcol, 6, 3 );
118:   }
119:
120:   /*-----------------------*
121:    *   draw_medium_fields()  *
122:    *-----------------------*/
123:
124:   void display_medium_fields( void )
125:   {
```

continues

Listing 17.6. continued

```
126:    write_string("__", ct.fld_fcol, ct.fld_bcol, 4, 17 );
127:    write_string("_____",
128:          ct.fld_fcol, ct.fld_bcol, 6, 24 );
129:
130:    /* display data, if exists */
131:
132:    write_string(medium.code, ct.fld_fcol, ct.fld_bcol, 4, 17 );
133:    write_string(medium.desc, ct.fld_fcol, ct.fld_bcol, 6, 24 );
134: }
135:
136: /*-------------------------------------------------------*
137:  *    get_medium_input_data()                           *
138:  *-------------------------------------------------------*/
139: int get_medium_input_data( void )
140: {
141:    int    position,
142:           rv,
143:           loop = TRUE;
144:
145:    /*  Set up exit keys.  */
146:    static char fexit_keys[ 19 ] = { F1, F2, F3, F4, F5, F6,
147:                    F7, F8, F10,
148:                    ESC_KEY, PAGE_DN, PAGE_UP, CR_KEY,
149:                    TAB_KEY, ENTER_KEY, SHIFT_TAB,
150:                    DN_ARROW, UP_ARROW, NULL };
151:
152:    static char *exit_keys = fexit_keys;
153:    getline( SET_EXIT_KEYS, 0, 18, 0, 0, 0, exit_keys );
154:
155:    /*** setup colors and default keys ***/
156:    getline( SET_DEFAULTS, 0, 0, 0, 0, 0, 0 );
157:    getline( SET_NORMAL, 0, ct.fld_fcol, ct.fld_bcol,
158:                ct.fld_high_fcol, ct.fld_high_bcol, 0 );
159:    getline( SET_UNDERLINE, 0, ct.fld_fcol, ct.fld_bcol,
160:                ct.fld_high_fcol, ct.fld_high_bcol, 0 );
161:    getline( SET_INS, 0, ct.abar_fcol, ct.abar_bcol, 24, 76, 0 );
162:
163:
164:    position = 0;
165:
166:    while( loop == TRUE )          /**  get data for top fields  **/
167:    {
168:       switch( (rv = get_medium_data( position )) )
169:       {
170:          case CR_KEY    :
171:          case TAB_KEY   :
172:          case ENTER_KEY :
173:          case DN_ARROW  : /* go down a field */
174:                  ( position == 1 ) ? ( position = 0 ) : position++;
```

```
175:                         break;
176:
177:         case SHIFT_TAB :
178:         case UP_ARROW  : /* go up a field */
179:              ( position == 0 ) ? ( position = 1 ) : position—;
180:                         break;
181:
182:         case ESC_KEY :
183:         case F3      :    /* exit back to main menu */
184:                         if( (yes_no_box( "Do you want to exit?",
185:                                 ct.db_fcol, ct.db_bcol )) == 'Y' )
186:                         {
187:                             loop = FALSE;
188:                         }
189:                         break;
190:
191:         case F4:  /* add data */
192:                 rv = add_mdata();
193:                 if ( rv == NO_ERROR )
194:                 {
195:                    /* Reset display counter */
196:                    display_msg_box("Added record!",
197:                            ct.db_fcol, ct.db_bcol);
198:                    disp_rec = 0;
199:                    clear_medium_fields();
200:                    draw_medium_screen();
201:                    position = 0;
202:                 }
203:                 else  /* Only do next part if File I/O  */
204:                 if ( rv > NO_ERROR )
205:                 {
206:                    display_msg_box("Fatal Error writing data...",
207:                        ct.err_fcol, ct.err_bcol );
208:                    exit(1);
209:                 }
210:                 break;
211:
212:         case F5:  /* Change Record */
213:
214:                 rv = add_mdata();   /* updates record */
215:
216:                 if ( rv == NO_ERROR )
217:                 {
218:                    /* Reset display counter */
219:
220:                    display_msg_box("Record Updated!",
221:                            ct.db_fcol, ct.db_bcol);
222:                 }
223:                 else
224:                 if ( rv > NO_ERROR )
```

continues

Listing 17.6. continued

```
225:                           {
226:                              display_msg_box("Fatal Error writing
                                               data...",
227:                                 ct.err_fcol, ct.err_bcol );
228:
229:                              exit(1);
230:                           }
231:                        break;
232:
233:          case F6:  /* Delete data */
234:                    /* Make sure rec is on screen */
235:                    if( (yes_no_box( "Delete record ?",
236:                         ct.db_fcol, ct.db_bcol )) == 'Y' )
237:                    {
238:                       rv = del_med_rec();
239:                       if (rv == NO_ERROR)
240:                       {
241:                          disp_rec = 0;
242:                          clear_medium_fields();
243:                          draw_medium_screen();
244:                       }
245:                       else
246:                       {
247:                          display_msg_box("Fatal Error deleting
                                               data...",
248:                             ct.err_fcol, ct.err_bcol );
249:                          exit(1);
250:                       }
251:                    }
252:                    break;
253:
254:          case F7:  /* Next record */
255:                    rv = proc_med_rec(NEXT_REC);
256:                    if ( rv == NO_ERROR )
257:                    {
258:                       draw_medium_screen();
259:                    }
260:                    else
261:                    {
262:                       display_msg_box("Fatal Error processing
                                               data...",
263:                          ct.err_fcol, ct.err_bcol );
264:                       exit(1);
265:                    }
266:                    break;
267:
268:          case F8:  /* Prev record */
269:                    rv = proc_med_rec(PREVIOUS_REC);
```

```
270:                      if ( rv == NO_ERROR )
271:                      {
272:                          draw_medium_screen();
273:                      }
274:                      else
275:                      {
276:                          display_msg_box("Fatal Error
                                          processing data...",
277:                              ct.err_fcol, ct.err_bcol );
278:                          exit(1);
279:                      }
280:                      break;
281:
282:          case F10:       /* action bar */
283:                      rv = do_medium_actionbar();
284:
285:                      if( rv == F3 )
286:                      {
287:                          if( (yes_no_box( "Do you want to exit?",
288:                              ct.db_fcol, ct.db_bcol )) == 'Y' )
289:                          {
290:                              loop = FALSE;
291:                          }
292:                      }
293:
294:                      position = 0;
295:                      break;
296:
297:          case PAGE_DN :  /* go to last data entry field */
298:                      position = 1;
299:                      break;
300:
301:          case PAGE_UP :  /* go to first data entry field */
302:                      position = 0;
303:                      break;
304:
305:          case F1:        /* context sensitive help */
306:                      display_context_help( HELP_DBF, position );
307:                      break;
308:
309:          case F2:        /* extended help */
310:                      display_medium_help();
311:                      break;
312:
313:          default:        /* error */
314:                      display_msg_box( " Error ",
315:                              ct.err_fcol, ct.err_bcol );
316:                      break;
317:
318:      }     /* end of switch */
```

continues

557

Listing 17.6. continued

```
319:    }          /* end of while  */
320:
321:    return( rv );
322: }
323:
324: /*-------------------------------------------------------*
325:  *   get_medium_data()                                   *
326:  *-------------------------------------------------------*/
327:
328: int get_medium_data( int row )
329: {
330:    int rv;
331:
332:    switch( row )
333:    {
334:       case 0 :
335:          rv = getline( GET_ALPHA, 0,  4, 17, 0,  2, medium.code);
336:          break;
337:       case 1 :
338:          rv = getline( GET_ALPHA, 0,  6, 24, 0, 35, medium.desc);
339:          break;
340:    }
341:    return( rv );
342: }
343:
344: /*-------------------------------------------------------*
345:  *   clear_medium_fields()                               *
346:  *-------------------------------------------------------*/
347:
348: int clear_medium_fields(void)
349: {
350:   getline( CLEAR_FIELD, 0,  3, 0, 0, 0, medium.code );
351:   getline( CLEAR_FIELD, 0, 36, 0, 0, 0, medium.desc );
352:
353:   return(0);
354: }
355:
356: /*-------------------------------------------------------*
357:  *   add_mdata()                                         *
358:  *                                                       *
359:  *   Returns  0 - No Errors                              *
360:  *           >0 - File I/O Error                         *
361:  *           <0 - Missing info before can store          *
362:  *-------------------------------------------------------*/
363:
364: int add_mdata()
365: {
366:    int rv = NO_ERROR;
367:
```

```
368:     /* Verify data fields */
369:     rv = verify_mdata();
370:     if ( rv == NO_ERROR )
371:     {
372:       /* Check to see if matches old rec */
373:       /* If match - then update db record only */
374:       if ( stricmp(med_prev.code, medium.code) == 0)
375:         rv = put_rec(disp_rec, db_fp,
376:               sizeof(medium), 0, (char *)&medium);
377:       else
378:         /* Keys no longer match - need to
379:            add this key as a new one */
380:         rv = add_medium_rec();
381:     }
382:
383:     return(rv);
384: }
385:
386: /*--------------------------------------------------------*
387:  *    Verify data fields                                  *
388:  *--------------------------------------------------------*/
389: int verify_mdata()
390: {
391:     int rv = NO_ERROR;
392:
393:     if( strlen( medium.code ) == 0 )
394:     {
395:       display_msg_box("Must enter a medium code",
396:              ct.err_fcol, ct.err_bcol);
397:       rv = -1;
398:     }
399:     else
400:     if( strlen( medium.desc ) == 0 )
401:     {
402:       display_msg_box("Must enter a description",
403:              ct.err_fcol, ct.err_bcol);
404:       rv = -1;
405:     }
406:
407:     return(rv);
408: }
409:
410: /*--------------------------------------------------------*
411:  *    display_medium_help()                               *
412:  *--------------------------------------------------------*/
413:
414: void display_medium_help(void)
415: {
416:    int  ctr;
417:    char *scrnbuffer;
```

continues

Listing 17.6. continued

```
418:
419:    char helptext[19][45] = {
420:        "                    Medium Codes",
421:        "-------------------------------------------",
422:        "",
423:        "The medium code screen allows you to track",
424:        "the different types of storage mediums that",
425:        "your music collection may be stored on. A",
426:        "two character code will be used in the",
427:        "Musical Items Screen to verify that the",
428:        "medium type is valid. The code entered will",
429:        "need to match a code entered on this screen.",
430:        "Additionally, the codes will be used in",
431:        "reporting on your musical items.",
432:        "",
433:        "An example of a musical code might be:",
434:        "",
435:        "          CD - Compact Disk",
436:        "          CS - Cassette",
437:        "          VD - Video",
438:        "-------------------------------------------" };
439:
440:    scrnbuffer = save_screen_area(2, 23, 28, 78 );
441:    cursor_off();
442:
443:    grid( 3, 23, 28, 77, ct.shdw_fcol, ct.bg_bcol, 3 );
444:    box(2, 22, 29, 78, SINGLE_BOX, FILL_BOX,
445:                        ct.help_fcol, ct.help_bcol);
446:
447:    for( ctr = 0; ctr < 19; ctr++ )
448:    {
449:      write_string( helptext[ctr],
450:                ct.help_fcol, ct.help_bcol, 3+ctr, 32 );
451:    }
452:
453:    getch();
454:    cursor_on();
455:    restore_screen_area(scrnbuffer);
456: }
457:
458: /*------------------------------------------------------ *
459:  * Function: display_context_help()                     *
460:  * Purpose:  Display help that is relative to a specific *
461:  *           field on a specific screen.                 *
462:  * Notes:    The first parameter needs to be one of the  *
463:  *           following:                                  *
464:  *               medium - medium screen                  *
465:  *               album  - musical items screen           *
466:  *               group  - groups screen                  *
```

```
467:   *           It is assumed that each screen has its own   *
468:   *           file                                         *
469:   *------------------------------------------------------- */
470: void display_context_help( char *file, int position )
471: {
472:    FILE *fp;
473:    int   ctr;
474:    char *rv = NULL;
475:
476:    char *buffer1 = NULL;
477:    char *buffer2 = NULL;
478:    char *buffer3 = NULL;
479:
480:    /* allocate buffers */
481:    buffer1 = (char *) malloc(65 * sizeof(char));
482:    buffer2 = (char *) malloc(65 * sizeof(char));
483:    buffer3 = (char *) malloc(65 * sizeof(char));
484:
485:    /* make sure all the allocations worked */
486:    if( buffer1 == NULL ¦¦ buffer2 == NULL ¦¦ buffer3 == NULL)
487:    {
488:        display_msg_box("Error allocating memory...",
489:                        ct.err_fcol, ct.err_bcol );
490:        if( buffer1 != NULL )
491:           free(buffer1);
492:        if( buffer2 != NULL )
493:           free(buffer2);
494:        if( buffer3 != NULL )
495:           free(buffer3);
496:
497:        return;
498:    }
499:
500:
501:    fp = fopen( file, "r");
502:
503:    if( fp == NULL )  /* make sure the file was opened */
504:    {
505:        display_msg_box("Error opening help file...",
506:                        ct.err_fcol, ct.err_bcol );
507:    }
508:    else
509:    {
510:        /* spin through to appropriate record */
511:        for( ctr = 0; (ctr < (position * 3)) ; ctr++ )
512:        {
513:           rv = fgets( buffer1, 65, fp );
514:           if( rv == NULL)
515:              break;
516:        }
```

continues

Listing 17.6. continued

```
517:
518:        /* ready to read three lines */
519:        if( rv != NULL || position == 0 )
520:        {
521:           rv = fgets( buffer1, 65, fp );
522:           if( rv != NULL )
523:           {
524:              rv = fgets( buffer2, 65, fp );
525:              if( rv != NULL )
526:                 rv = fgets( buffer3, 65, fp );
527:           }
528:
529:           display_cntxt_help_msg( buffer1, buffer2, buffer3 );
530:        }
531:        else  /* hit end of file too soon */
532:        {
533:           display_msg_box( "Error in message file...",
534:                        ct.err_fcol, ct.err_bcol );
535:        }
536:
537:        fclose( fp );
538:     }
539:
540:     free( buffer1 );
541:     free( buffer2 );
542:     free( buffer3 );
543: }
544:
545: /*-------------------------------------------------------*
546:  *    display_context_help()                            *
547:  *-------------------------------------------------------*/
548: void display_cntxt_help_msg( char *string1,
549:                              char *string2,
550:                              char *string3 )
551: {
552:     char *scrn_buffer = NULL;
553:     scrn_buffer = save_screen_area( 10, 16, 10, 70 );
554:     cursor_off();
555:
556:     grid( 11, 16, 10, 69, ct.shdw_fcol, ct.bg_bcol, 3 );
557:     box(10, 15, 11, 70, SINGLE_BOX, FILL_BOX,
558:                     ct.help_fcol, ct.help_bcol);
559:
560:     write_string( string1, ct.help_fcol, ct.help_bcol, 11, 14 );
561:     write_string( string2, ct.help_fcol, ct.help_bcol, 12, 14 );
562:     write_string( string3, ct.help_fcol, ct.help_bcol, 13, 14 );
563:
564:     write_string( "Press any key to continue...",
565:                    ct.help_fcol, ct.help_bcol, 14, 14 );
```

```
566:
567:    getch();
568:    cursor_on();
569:    restore_screen_area(scrn_buffer);
570: }
571:
572:
573:
574: /*=========================================================*
575:  *                      end of listing                     *
576:  *=========================================================*/
```

Note: The *Record of Records!* application should have several source files, not including the TYAC.LIB library. The files that you should be compiling include the following:

RECOFREC.C   ABOUT.C
ALBMABAR.C   GRPSABAR.C   MEDMABAR.C   MMNUABAR.C
MEDIUM.C   ALBUMS.C   GROUPS.C

To these files, you should link the TYAC.LIB library, which should contain all the functions learned in this book, including those from earlier today.

Warning: If you compile the medium screen with these changes, you will get unresolved externals for del_med_rec(), proc_med_rec(), and add_medium_rec(). These new functions will be covered later today.

Analysis   While the MEDIUM.C listing is getting long, you should already have much of it from previous days. This should be a nearly complete MEDIUM.C source file. You'll still need a few additional files to complete the file I/O functions and eliminate the unresolved externals that you received from the new MEDIUM.C listing.

The changes in this listing start in line 35. The prototype for add_mdata() has been placed here. Following this, several external declarations are present in lines 38 to 42. These are the same external declarations that you have seen before. In lines 49 to 51, you should also notice a change. There is now more than one MEDIUM file. The defined constant MEDIUM_DBF contains the name of the data file. The MEDIUM_IDX contains the name of the index file. The help file has remained the same.

Expert Tip: It's best to give an index and a data file the same name with the exception of the three character extension. For example, both of the Medium Code's files are called MEDIUMS.

Line 59 has also been added. A second Medium Code structure has been declared. This will be used to hold information about a Medium Code record before changes are made. You will see it used later.

The changes up to this point have been outside of the actual medium code functions. Line 72 starts the internal changes. When you first enter the medium code, you will open the files. Line 70 does this using the open_files() function described earlier. The index and data files for the Medium Codes screen are opened. If the open was not successful, then an error message is displayed in line 82. If the open was successful, then the med_prev Medium Code structure is cleared out with memset(). The currently displayed record, disp_rec is set to zero because no records are being displayed. The functions that were present in this function before are then called. When the user is done entering data, then line 78 calls the close_files() function from earlier.

In displaying the screen, only a minor change is made. In line 101, the keys' values that are displayed on the bottom of the screen are updated. The F4, F7, and F8 keys are added to the display. You can choose to display whichever keys you believe are the most important. In the get_medium_input_data() function, a similar change is made in lines 146 to 153. The setup for the getline() function needs to be changed to include the newly-added key functions. The F4, F5, F6, F7, and F8 keys need to be added, bringing the total number of exit keys to 18.

In the following switch statement, cases will need to be added or modified for each of these new function keys. The F4 key in lines 191 to 210 is used to add new data to the data file. This function calls the add_mdata() function. If the add_mdata() function doesn't return an error, then line 196 displays a message box stating that the add was successful. The screen is then cleared for a new record to be added. Line 198

then resets the current display record field, `disp_rec`. The fields and screen are then cleared, followed by the position being reset to zero. If the `add_mdata()` returned a fatal error—a number greater than `NO_ERROR(0)`—then a message is displayed and the program instantly exits.

> **Tip:** You should avoid exiting in the middle of a program, such as shown in line 208. The only time that you should do this is when a fatal error occurs. You should allow the program to continue running whenever possible.

The `add_mdata()` function is in lines 356 to 384. This function does two things. First, it calls a function, `verify_mdata()`, that checks to see that all of the data entered is valid (line 369). It then checks to see if the user is adding a new record, or trying to add a record that was changed. This is done starting in line 374. Using `stricmp()`, the code from the current entry and edit screen, `medium.code`, is compared to the medium code in `med_prev.code`. If the two values match, then line 375 calls `put_rec()` to update the current record, `disp_rec`. In the case of a new record, the `med_prev.code` will be empty so they won't match. The codes also won't match if the user changed the one on the screen. In these cases, line 380 calls the `add_medium_rec()` function to add a new record. The `add_medium_rec()` function will be presented later today. As you should be able to see, the `add_mdata()` function effectively covers both adding and updating records.

> **Warning:** The `add_mdata()` function makes the assumption that the code field is required. This assumes that the `verify_mdata()` will give an error if the `medium.code` field is blank. If this key field is allowed to be blank, then this logic will need to be modified; however, you shouldn't allow the key field to be blank.

Before returning to the new cases in the `get_medium_data()` function, you should first look at the `verify_mdata()` function in lines 386 to 408. This function contains all the edits that need to occur before the record can be added to the data file. By consolidating them in a function such as this, it makes them easy to call from several functions. You'll see that the add functions aren't the only function that verifies the data.

The F5 case in lines 212 to 231 is used to update a record that is currently displayed on the screen. This function is nearly identical to the add function. The difference is that the change function doesn't refresh the screen. The record that was updated remains displayed.

The F6 case in lines 233 to 252 is used to delete or remove a record from the data and index files. Because deleting a record involves permanently removing it from the file, this case starts by prompting the user to ensure that the user really wants to delete. This is done in line 235 using the yes_no_box() function. If the user does want to delete, then the del_med_rec() function is called to actually do the delete. This function is covered later today. If the del_med_rec() function is successful, then the screen is refreshed for a new record (lines 241 to 243); otherwise, a fatal error message is displayed and the program exits.

The F7 function in lines 254 to 266 and the F8 function in lines 268 to 280 are similar. These functions display the next or previous record. They start by calling the proc_med_rec() function, which retrieves a record. One of the two defined constants—NEXT_REC or PREVIOUS_REC—are passed to signal if the next or previous record is retrieved. The proc_med_rec() function will be covered later today. If the proc_med_rec() function is successful, then the medium screen is redrawn to display the new information. If the function wasn't successful, then a fatal error is displayed and the program exits.

With this, you have seen all the changes made to MEDIUM.C. Three new functions were called that need to be created, add_medium_rec(), del_med_rec(), and proc_med_rec(). These are each covered next.

Adding a Record:
The *add_medium_rec()* function

The add_medium_rec() function is used to add a new record to the medium code data file. This function is presented in Listing 17.7.

Type **Listing 17.7. ADDMREC.C. Adding a medium code.**

```
1:  /*===========================================================
2:   * Filename: ADDMREC.C
3:   *
4:   * Author:   Bradley L. Jones
5:   *           Gregory L. Guntle
6:   *
7:   * Purpose: Adds a record to a MEDIUM DB
8:   *
```

```
 9:    *=========================================================*/
10:
11:   #include <stdio.h>
12:   #include <string.h>
13:
14:   #include "records.h"
15:   #include "tyac.h"
16:
17:   /* Global variables */
18:   extern MEDIUM_REC medium;        /* Record structure with data */
19:   extern MEDIUM_REC med_prev;
20:   extern FILE *idx_fp;             /* Main File ptr to data file */
21:   extern FILE *db_fp;              /* Data file */
22:   extern int nbr_records;          /* Total # of recs */
23:   extern int start_rec;            /* Starting rec for alpha */
24:
25:   /*-------------------------------------------------------*
26:    *  add_medium_rec();                                   *
27:    *  Returns:  0 - No Error                              *
28:    *            >0 Error - see defines at top of file     *
29:    *-------------------------------------------------------*/
30:
31:   int add_medium_rec()
32:   {
33:    int result;
34:    MEDIUM_INDEX temp, newrec;
35:    int rv = NO_ERROR;
36:    int found;
37:    int srch_rec;
38:
39:    nbr_records++;
40:    if (nbr_records == 1)     /* Is this first record */
41:    {
42:      temp.prev = 0;
43:      temp.next = 0;
44:      temp.data = 1;           /* First rec in data file */
45:      strcpy(temp.code, medium.code);
46:      /* Write Index record */
47:      rv = put_rec(nbr_records, idx_fp, sizeof(temp),
48:                  sizeof(int)*2, (char *) &temp);
49:      if (rv == NO_ERROR)      /* No Error from prior */
50:      {
51:        /* Store data */
52:        rv = put_rec(nbr_records, db_fp, sizeof(medium),
53:                    0, (char *) &medium);
54:      }
55:
56:      /* Update Alpha starting pointer */
57:      if (rv == NO_ERROR)
58:      {
```

continues

Listing 17.7. continued

```
59:         start_rec = nbr_records; /* Update global starting point */
60:         rv = update_header();
61:     }
62:
63:     fflush(idx_fp);
64:     fflush(db_fp);
65:  }
66:  /* Need to search for appropriate place to hold rec */
67:  else
68:  {
69:     found = FALSE;
70:     srch_rec = start_rec;
71:     while (!found)
72:     {
73:        rv = get_rec(srch_rec, idx_fp, sizeof(temp),
74:                       sizeof(int)*2, (char *)&temp);
75:        /* Proceed only if no errors */
76:        if (rv == NO_ERROR)
77:        {
78:          /* Compare two keys - ignoring CASE of keys */
79:          result = stricmp(medium.code, temp.code);
80:          if (result < 0)    /* New key is < this rec key */
81:          {
82:             /* Found place to put it - store info */
83:             found = TRUE;
84:             /* See if this new rec is < start rec   */
85:             /* If so - need to adjust starting ptr */
86:             if (srch_rec == start_rec)
87:                 start_rec = nbr_records;
88:
89:             /* First build new Index rec & store new rec */
90:             newrec.prev = temp.prev;   /* Previous record */
91:             newrec.next = srch_rec;    /* Point to record just read */
92:             newrec.data = nbr_records;   /* Pt to data */
93:             strcpy(newrec.code, medium.code);
94:             rv = put_rec(nbr_records, idx_fp, sizeof(newrec),
95:                          sizeof(int)*2, (char *)&newrec);
96:             if (rv == NO_ERROR)
97:             {
98:                /* Update previous rec */
99:                temp.prev = nbr_records;
100:               rv = put_rec(srch_rec, idx_fp, sizeof(temp),
101:                            sizeof(int)*2, (char *)&temp);
102:
103:               /* Now write data - only if no errors */
104:               if (rv == NO_ERROR)
105:               {
106:                  /* Now write data */
107:                  rv = put_rec(nbr_records, db_fp, sizeof(medium),
```

```
108:                              0, (char *)&medium);
109:           }
110:
111:          /* Now check on updating Next pointer */
112:          /* Is there a ptr pointing to this new rec ?*/
113:          if (rv == NO_ERROR)
114:          {
115:            if (newrec.prev !=0 )
116:            {
117:              rv = get_rec(newrec.prev, idx_fp, sizeof(temp),
118:                           sizeof(int)*2, (char *)&temp);
119:              if ( rv == NO_ERROR)
120:              {
121:                temp.next = nbr_records;
122:                rv = put_rec(newrec.prev, idx_fp, sizeof(temp),
123:                             sizeof(int)*2, (char *)&temp);
124:              }
125:            }
126:          }
127:
128:        }
129:      }
130:      else    /* new rec >= alpha, adjust ptr */
131:      {
132:        if (temp.next == 0) /* End of chain - add to end */
133:        {
134:          found = TRUE;
135:
136:          /* Build Index record */
137:          /* Point backwards to prev rec */
138:          newrec.prev = srch_rec;
139:          newrec.next = 0;          /* There is no next rec */
140:          newrec.data = nbr_records;
141:          strcpy(newrec.code, medium.code);
142:          rv = put_rec(nbr_records, idx_fp, sizeof(newrec),
143:                       sizeof(int)*2, (char *)&newrec);
144:          if (rv == NO_ERROR)
145:          {
146:            /* Update previous rec */
147:            temp.next = nbr_records;
148:            rv = put_rec(srch_rec, idx_fp, sizeof(temp),
149:                         sizeof(int)*2, (char *)&temp);
150:            if (rv == NO_ERROR)
151:            {
152:              /* Now write data */
153:              rv = put_rec(nbr_records, db_fp, sizeof(medium),
154:                           0, (char *)&medium);
155:            }
156:          }
157:        }
```

continues

Listing 17.7. continued

```
158:              else   /* Not at end - get next rec ptr */
159:                  srch_rec = temp.next;
160:          }
161:      }
162:      else
163:        found = TRUE;   /* Exit because of error */
164:    }   /* End of While */
165:
166:    /* Update starting alpha ptr in hdr */
167:    if (rv == NO_ERROR)
168:    {
169:      rv = update_header();
170:    }
171:
172:    /* Makes sure file gets updated */
173:    fflush(idx_fp);
174:    fflush(db_fp);
175:
176:  }   /* End else */
177:
178:  return(rv);
179: }
```

This function has the overall objective of adding a record. While the process of physically adding the record is simple, you must also update the index file. It is the updating of the index file that gives this function its size.

This function starts out in the same way as most of the other I/O functions. External declarations are provided for the file pointers, the Medium Code structures, and the header information (lines 16 to 22). In the add_medium_rec() function, several additional variables are declared. These include two new MEDIUM_INDEX structures, temp and newrec. In addition to these, a found flag is declared.

Line 38 starts the code off by adding one to the total number of records in the file. Because we are adding a record, this will be accurate. Line 39 then checks to see if this is the first record being added to the file. The first record is a special case. If this is the first record, then the values in the temp index structure are all set. The record number of the prev and next records are zero because neither exists. The data record is one because this will be the first record in the data file. Line 44 copies the medium code into the key field of the temp index's data field. With this, the temp index structure is set up and ready to be written.

Line 46 uses the put_rec() function to write the index record from the temp structure that you just set up. The first parameter, nbr_records will be one because this is the

first record. The `idx_fp` is the pointer to the index file. The third parameter is the size of the data you want to write. In this case, it's the size of the index structure, temp. The fourth parameter is the offset for the header record. You should remember that the header record is two integers. The last parameter is the `temp` structure that you just set up.

If the writing of the index structure was successful, then the data record is written in line 51. Its parameters are similar. The fourth parameter is zero because the data file doesn't have a header.

In line 55, you are still working with the addition of the first record in the file. If the addition of the first record was successful, then the `start_rec` is set to `nbr_records`. This could have been set to one because you know that there is only one record in the file. Line 59 ensures that the header record is updated. The addition of the first record is completed with the flushing of the index and data files with the `fflush()` function. This ensures that the records are written to the disk and not buffered.

If the record isn't the first record to be added to the files, then the processing is different. The `else` statement starting in line 66 works with this. If the record isn't the first in the file, then you need to find the area in the indexes where the record is to be placed. Consider adding the code `GG` to Figure 17.3. While the GG would be added to the end, the NEXT, PREVIOUS, and DATA REC values all need to be determined. Figure 17.4 shows the result of adding GG to the files in Figure 17.3.

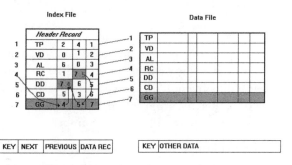

Figure 17.4. *Adding the* `GG` *code.*

As you can see from the figure, the new records are added to the end of both the index and the data file. Before they can be added, the `next` and `prev` record numbers need to be determined. In addition, the `next` and `prev` index records need to be updated with the new record.

The process that will be used to do this is relatively easy to follow. Starting with the first record signified by start_rec (line 69), each index record will be read into a temporary index structure, temp, (line 72) using a while loop, which starts in line 70. If the read is successful, then the code from the read index record is compared to the code from the record that is being added. The if statement in line 79 checks to see if the code from the screen is less than the code that was was just read into temp. If not, then another index record may need to be read unless the end of the index file has been reached.

The else statement to the if in line 79 checks the end of file condition. If the end has been reached, then the index structure for the new record to be added can be set up in lines 137 to 139. The prev record is set to the current srch_rec because it is the last record in the index file. The next record is set to zero because there isn't a next record. The data record is the last record in the data file. You should note that the last record in the data file is the same as the number of records, nbr_records. After copying the code to the new index structure, the record is written to the file in line 141. If the write is successful, then the previous record needs its next record number updated so that it points to the new last number. This is done in lines 146 to 148. If this update is successful, then the index file is up-to-date. All that's left is to write the new data record. This is done in line 152.

If the code was less than the search record read in line and if it was not the last sorted record in the index file, then the while loop starts again. The while loop continues until the new code is either the last code in the sort order, or until it is greater than a code that is already in the file.

If the new code is found to be greater than a code already in the file, then the if in line 79 takes effect. This starts by marking the found flag as TRUE in line 82 because a position has been found. In line 85, a test is done to see if the new code is the first record in sorted order. If so, then the start_rec field is set to the record number of the new code. In any other cases, the starting record number remains what it was.

Lines 89 to 91 set up the new record's index structure, newrec. This is similar to what was explained earlier in adding the index record as the last sorted record. The difference is that the previous record is set to the previous record from the last record read. The next record is then set to the last record read. The data record is set to the last record in the data file, which, as stated earlier, is the same as the number of records. If this sounds confusing, then take it one step at a time and use Figure 17.4 as a reference.

Tip: If you are confused, read the previous paragraph slowly and step through the process while looking at Figure 17.4.

Once these values are set, then the new index record is written to the end of the index file (line 93). If there were no problems, then the last search record that was read has its prev record number changed to point to the new record (line 98). This record is then updated with a call to put_rec(). Line 105 then updates the data record if the previous updates were successful.

This writes or updates all of the records except one. The new record isn't yet a part of the next record pointers. The record that comes before the new record needs to be updated so that its next pointer points to the new number. Lines 114 to 124 do just this. The new records previous record number is used to find the record that needs to be updated. Once found, the record's next record number is set to the last record number and is then updated in line 121.

If the updating is successful, then line 168 updates the header. Lines 172 and 173 force the writes to occur. The function then ends with the return of any error values in line 177.

Deleting a Record:
The *del_med_rec()* function

The del_med_rec() function is used to remove a record from the medium data file. Listing 17.8 presents the DELMREC.C source file, which contains this function.

Listing 17.8. DELMREC.C. Deleting a medium code.

```
 1:   /*=============================================================
 2:    * Filename: DELMREC.C
 3:    *
 4:    * Author:    Bradley L. Jones
 5:    *            Gregory L. Guntle
 6:    *
 7:    * Purpose: Deletes a record from the DB
 8:    *          It adjusts the pointers and takes the last DB
 9:    *          record and overwrites the record being deleted
10:    *
11:    *=============================================================*/
12:
```

continues

Listing 17.8. continued

```
13:   #include <stdio.h>
14:
15:   #include "records.h"
16:   #include "tyac.h"
17:
18:   /* Global variables */
19:   extern MEDIUM_REC medium;        /* Record structure with data */
20:   extern MEDIUM_REC med_prev;
21:   extern FILE *idx_fp;             /* Main File ptr to data file */
22:   extern FILE *db_fp;              /* Data file */
23:   extern int nbr_records;          /* Total # of recs */
24:   extern int start_rec;            /* Starting rec for alpha */
25:   extern int disp_rec;
26:
27:   int del_med_rec()
28:   {
29:     int rv = NO_ERROR;
30:     MEDIUM_INDEX temp, delrec;
31:     MEDIUM_REC hold_data;
32:     int chg;
33:     int srch_rec;
34:
35:     /* Are we trying to delete a blank record */
36:     if (disp_rec != 0)  /* No - then proceed */
37:     {
38:        /* Get the index info for this rec */
39:        rv = get_rec(disp_rec, idx_fp, sizeof(delrec),
40:                     sizeof(int)*2, (char *)&delrec);
41:        if (rv == NO_ERROR)
42:        {
43:          /* Are there any pointers in this rec
44:             If both pointers are 0 - then this must
45:             be the only record in the DB            */
46:          if (delrec.prev == 0 && delrec.next == 0)
47:          {
48:            nbr_records = 0;
49:            disp_rec = 0;
50:            start_rec = 1;
51:          }
52:          else
53:          {
54:            chg = FALSE;
55:            srch_rec = 1;   /* Start at first */
56:
57:            /* Are we deleting the starting alpha record ? */
58:            if (disp_rec == start_rec)
59:            {
60:              start_rec = delrec.next;    /* Reset pointer */
61:            }
```

```
62:
63:              /* Go until all the ptrs have been adjusted */
64:              while ( (srch_rec <= nbr_records) && (rv == NO_ERROR) )
65:              {
66:                /* Get record */
67:                rv = get_rec(srch_rec, idx_fp, sizeof(temp),
68:                        sizeof(int)*2, (char *)&temp);
69:                if (rv == NO_ERROR)
70:                {
71:                  /* Does this rec prev pointer need to
72:                      be adjusted */
73:                  if (temp.prev == disp_rec)
74:                  {
75:                      chg = TRUE;
76:                      temp.prev = delrec.prev;
77:                  }
78:
79:                  /* Since moving last record up - need
80:                      to adjust pointers to last one as well */
81:                  if (temp.prev == nbr_records)
82:                  {
83:                      chg = TRUE;
84:                      temp.prev = disp_rec;
85:                  }
86:
87:                  if (temp.next == disp_rec)
88:                  {
89:                      chg = TRUE;
90:                      temp.next = delrec.next;
91:                  }
92:
93:                  /* Since moving last record up - need
94:                      to adjust pointers to last one as well */
95:                  if (temp.next == nbr_records)
96:                  {
97:                      chg = TRUE;
98:                      temp.next = disp_rec;
99:                  }
100:
101:                  /* Data Ptr - match last nbr */
102:                  if (temp.data == nbr_records)
103:                  {
104:                      chg = TRUE;
105:                      temp.data = delrec.data;
106:                  }
107:
108:                  /* Only update rec if change has been made */
109:                  if (chg)
110:                  {
111:                    /* Is this the rec to overlay ? */
```

continues

Listing 17.8. continued

```
112:                if (srch_rec == nbr_records)
113:                {
114:                   /* Write new index into deleted spot */
115:                   rv = put_rec(disp_rec, idx_fp, sizeof(temp),
116:                       sizeof(int)*2, (char *)&temp);
117:                }
118:                else
119:                {
120:                   /* Rewrite index back to file in same position */
121:                   rv = put_rec(srch_rec, idx_fp, sizeof(temp),
122:                       sizeof(int)*2, (char *)&temp);
123:                }
124:                chg = FALSE;
125:             }
126:
127:             if (rv == NO_ERROR)
128:             {
129:                /* Go to next record */
130:                srch_rec++;
131:             }
132:          }
133:       }
134:
135:       /* DATA    */
136:       /* Delete the data rec - take last rec in data
137:          file and overwrite the rec to be deleted
138:          then search for index pointer that points to
139:          the last rec and update its data pointer.    */
140:       if (rv == 0)
141:       {
142:          /* Only need to adjust if not last rec */
143:          if (nbr_records != disp_rec)
144:          {
145:             /* Get last rec */
146:             rv = get_rec(nbr_records, db_fp, sizeof(medium),
147:                 0, (char *)&hold_data);
148:             if (rv == 0)
149:             {
150:                /* Overwrite data to delete w/Last one */
151:                rv = put_rec(delrec.data, db_fp, sizeof(medium),
152:                    0, (char *)&hold_data);
153:             }
154:          }
155:       }
156:
157:       nbr_records—;   /* Adjust global number of recs */
158:    }
159:    if (rv == NO_ERROR)
160:    {
```

```
161:              rv = update_header();
162:          }
163:
164:          /* Makes sure file gets updated */
165:          fflush(idx_fp);
166:          fflush(db_fp);
167:      }
168:  }
169:  else
170:    boop();  /* Let them know - can't delete blank rec */
171:
172:  return(rv);
173: }
```

 The deleting of records operates differently from the adding of a record. When deleting a record, you need to adjust the index record numbers just as you did when you added a record; however, additional complexity exists. You could simply adjust the index pointers. This would prevent you from being able to access the deleted record; however, this would put holes throughout your files. To prevent these holes, when a record is deleted, the last record in the file is moved forward and placed in the hole that is created. This is exactly what the del_med_rec() function does.

> **Note:** If you wanted to be able to undelete a record, then you shouldn't move the last record to the deleted record. By adding a flag to your record, you could signal whether a record had been deleted or not. Additional functions could then read the flag to determine if the record should be used.

The del_med_rec() starts with the same external declarations as the add_medium_rec() function. In addition, several local variables are declared in lines 29 to 33. The first, rv, is the return value in line 29. Two additional MEDIUM_INDEX structures are declared, temp and delrec. The temp structure will be used to hold a temporary index structure. The delrec index structure will be used to hold the index record for the record that is being deleted. The chg field is used as a flag to signal if a change has been made to a given index record. If a change is made to an index record then it will need to be updated in the file. The srch_rec variable is used to keep track of the index record that is currently being checked. As you will see later, each record in the index is checked to ensure that it doesn't need to be adjusted.

Line 36 starts the processing by ensuring that the user wasn't adding a new record. If a record hasn't been added, then it can't be deleted. Line 170 beeps the computer with the boop() function if the user isn't editing a record. If the user is editing a record, then line 39 retrieves the index record for the currently displayed information. This index record is stored in delrec.

Line 46 checks to see if the record being deleted is the only record in the database. You know a record is the only record if both the prev and next record numbers are zero. If this is the only record, then lines 48 to 50 set the values of nbr_records, disp_rec, and start_rec accordingly. Otherwise, the rest of the function is executed.

If there is more than one record in the file, then processing, starting in line 54, is executed. First, the chg flag is defaulted to FALSE. The srch_rec is initialized to one. Line 58 checks to see if the first record in the file is being deleted. This is done by seeing if the current record, disp_rec, is equal to the starting record number, start_rec. If the first record is the one being deleted, then the start_rec value is adjusted to the delete record's next record. Once this is completed, you are ready to loop through the index file and make all the updates.

The while statement in lines 64 to 133 loops through each record in the index file. It continues to loop until all of the records have been processed or until there is an error. Line 67 retrieves the current record, srch_rec, into the temporary index structure, temp. If there isn't an error, then line 73 checks to see if the current record needs the prev record number updated. If the prev record number is equal to the record that is being deleted, disp_rec, then it needs to be changed. It is changed to the prev record from the deleted record in line 76. Additionally, the chg flag is set to TRUE so that the record will be updated. Because the last record in the file will be moved to fill in the deleted record's position, line 81 is needed. In line 81, the prev value is checked to see if it is equal to the last record. If the prev record is equal to the last record, then it is set to the position of the record being deleted. This is because the last record will be moved to the deleted position.

Lines 87 to 99 are similar to what was just described. Instead of working with the previous record, these lines work with the next record number pointer.

Line 102 checks the index file's data record number. If this number is pointing to the last data record in the file, then it will also need adjusted. The last data record will also be moved to fill in the deleted record's position. While these lines of code don't change the data record's position, they do go ahead and update the data record flag in the index records. Later in this function, the data record will actually be moved.

Line 109 checks the chg flag to see if there was a change to a record. If there was a change, then lines 110 to 123 are executed. If the record that is currently being processed is the last record in the file (`srch_rec` is equal to `nbr_records`), then you will want to write the record in the deleted records position instead of at the end of the file. This is exactly what line 114 does. You should note that `disp_rec` is the position that is written to instead of the `srch_rec` position. If this isn't the last record in the index file, then line 121 writes the record back to its current location. If this is all successfully accomplished, then line 130 increments the `srch_rec` counter and the next iteration of the while loop occurs.

Once you have looped through all of the index records, the delete will be completely processed. All that will be left to do is delete the actual data record. This is a much simpler process, which is accomplished in lines 140 to 155. Line 143 checks to see if the last record is the one being deleted. If the last record is the record being deleted, then no changes need to be made. If the record being deleted isn't the last record, then the last record is read in line 146. This record is then written in line 151 to the location where the deleted record is. This effectively deletes the record.

In line 157, the number of records is adjusted. This is followed by some housekeeping. In line 161, the header record is updated with the `update_header()` function. Lines 165 and 166 prevent any buffering of data by forcing the writes with the `fflush()` function. With this, the job of deleting a record is complete.

Processing a Record (Next/Previous)

The last function needed before you will be able to compile the medium code without external errors is the `proc_med_rec()` function. This function is presented in Listing 17.9, which contains the PROCMREC.C source file.

Listing 17.9. PROCMREC.C. Processing the next and previous records.

```
1:   /*============================================================
2:    * Filename: PROCMREC.C
3:    *
4:    * Author:   Bradley L. Jones
5:    *           Gregory L. Guntle
6:    *
7:    * Purpose: Process the requests for getting next/prev
8:    *          records from the MEDIUM DB
9:    *
10:   *============================================================*/
11:
12:  #include <stdio.h>
13:  #include <string.h>
```

continues

Listing 17.9. continued

```
14:   #include "records.h"
15:   #include "tyac.h"
16:
17:
18:   /* Global variables required */
19:   extern FILE *idx_fp;
20:   extern FILE *db_fp;
21:   extern nbr_records;          /* Total # of rec for mediums */
22:   extern int start_rec;
23:   extern int disp_rec;
24:
25:   extern MEDIUM_REC medium;
26:   extern MEDIUM_REC med_prev;
27:
28:   int proc_med_rec(int);
29:   int get_med_info(void);
30:
31:   /*------------------------------------------------------*
32:    *    proc_med_rec                                      *
33:    *------------------------------------------------------*/
34:
35:   int proc_med_rec(int direct)
36:   {
37:     MEDIUM_INDEX temp;
38:     int rv = NO_ERROR;
39:
40:     /* Only do - if there are records in the file */
41:     if (nbr_records != 0)
42:     {
43:       /* Do we just need to display the very first rec */
44:       if (disp_rec == 0)
45:       {
46:         disp_rec = start_rec;
47:         rv = get_med_info();
48:       }
49:       else
50:       {
51:         /* Get Index ptrs for record on screen */
52:         rv = get_rec(disp_rec, idx_fp, sizeof(temp),
53:                           sizeof(int)*2, (char *)&temp);
54:         if (rv == NO_ERROR)
55:         {
56:           if( direct == NEXT_REC )
57:           {
58:             if (temp.next == 0)      /* There is no other rec */
59:               boop();                /* No more records */
60:             else
61:             {
62:               disp_rec = temp.next;
```

```
63:                      rv = get_med_info();
64:                 }
65:             }
66:           else   /* Need to go backwards */
67:             {
68:               if (temp.prev == 0)      /* There is no other rec */
69:                  boop();                /* No more records */
70:               else
71:                 {
72:                   disp_rec = temp.prev;
73:                   rv = get_med_info();
74:                 }
75:             }
76:         }
77:       }
78:     }
79:   else
80:     boop();
81:
82:   return(rv);
83:
84: }
85:
86: /* ------------------------------------------------ *
87:  *  get_med_info()                                   *
88:  *                                                   *
89:  *  Handles getting the Index rec, getting the       *
90:  *  data pointer from the index and then getting     *
91:  *  the appropriate data rec.  It then updates       *
92:  *  the Global MEDIUM record, as well as updating    *
93:  *  a copy of the medium record for later use.       *
94:  *                                                   *
95:  * ------------------------------------------------ */
96:
97: int get_med_info()
98: {
99:   MEDIUM_INDEX temp;
100:   int rv;
101:
102:   /* Get Index record for this Request */
103:   rv = get_rec(disp_rec, idx_fp, sizeof(temp),
104:                 sizeof(int)*2, (char *)&temp);
105:   if (rv == NO_ERROR)
106:   {
107:     /* Now get the actual data record to display */
108:     rv = get_rec(temp.data, db_fp, sizeof(medium),
109:                 0, (char *)&medium);
110:     if (rv == NO_ERROR)
111:     {
112:       memcpy(&med_prev, &medium, sizeof(medium));
```

continues

Listing 17.9. continued

```
113:     }
114:   }
115:   return(rv);
116: }
```

This listing should be easier to follow than the `add_medium_rec()` and `del_med_rec()` listings. This listing enables you to get a next or previous record from the medium data file. Like all the other functions, this function also starts with the list of external declarations before starting into the function in line 35.

> **Tip:** The external declarations could be put into a header file that is included in each of the source files. This cut the amount of code that would need to be written.

This function is called with a value of either `NEXT_REC` or `PREVIOUS_REC`, which is stored in the direct parameter. This determines which direction the reading should occur. In line 41, a test is performed to see if there are any records in the file. If there aren't any records, then line 80 beeps the computer. If there are, then the processing moves to line 44. Line 44 determines if a record is currently being displayed. If the `disp_rec` is equal to zero, then there isn't a record being displayed. In this case, the first record is set to be the displayed record and the `get_med_info()` function is called.

The `get_med_info()` function is presented in lines 97 to 116. This function gets the record that is in the `disp_rec` variable. Line 103 gets the index record. If successful, then line 108 gets the data record based on the index's data value. Again, if this read is successful, then this new record is copied into the `med_prev` structure to be used elsewhere. With this completed, the new record is stored in the medium code structure, `medium`. All that is left to do is redisplay the record, which must be done by the calling program.

If `disp_rec` didn't equal zero when this function was called, then you must determine the new record before calling `get_med_info()`. Line 52 starts this process by getting the index record for the currently displayed data record. If the direction is `NEXT_REC`, then lines 58 to 65 process, otherwise, lines 66 to 74 process. In both cases, the processing is similar. In the case of `NEXT_REC` being the direction, if the index record's next value is zero, the end of the file has been reached. In this case, the `boop()` function

is called to signal the end of the file. If the next value isn't zero, then it is set to the disp_rec variable and get_med_info() is called to display the record.

Check Point

This completes the functions that are necessary to compile the Medium Screen without any external errors; however, you still have several holes in your entry and edit screen. You haven't added any of the file functions to the action bar. In addition, the action bar contains two additional file functions that haven't been covered, Clear and Find.... Tomorrow, you'll continue with the Medium Code entry and edit screen. You'll update the action bar with the functions you created today. In addition, you'll add the remaining functions. You'll also work with the albums screen, which has some slightly different processing. You should update the group screen's code as a part of today's exercises.

DO | **DON'T**

DO complete Exercise 3, which asks you to update the Group's source files.

Summary

Today was a big day. You began to pull in the most important part of the application—file access. Today, you learned a little background on file I/O and the terms used with it. In addition, you learned about different file modes and different file formats. Using some of what you should have already learned from your C experiences, you were lead in the development of an indexed file. You worked with the Medium Code entry and edit screen to create functions that enabled you to add, update, and delete records from your medium codes file. In addition, you created functions that enabled you to retrieve the next or previous record in alphabetical order from the database. Today's material stops short of completing everything you need to know about indexed files and file I/O in the *Record of Records!* application. Tomorrow will pick up where today left off and complete the topic.

Q&A

Q Why is there a need for text files to translate the CR-LF characters when reading and writing the file?

A The C programming language uses a single character to represent CR-LF. This is the \n character that you use all the time. DOS expects two characters for this process, a carriage return and then a line feed. Because DOS and C are expecting different things, there has to be a translation.

Q Are the file I/O functions presented today the best ones to use in an application?

A Not necessarily. Many applications need to be compatible with other custom formats. In these cases, you will need to use routines that write your data in the custom format. Additionally, if your application doesn't need to worry about quick access to records in order, then the indexing may not be necessary.

Q Is the use of global variables good as shown in today's listings?

A You should avoid using global variables whenever possible. At times, it becomes much easier to use global variables than always passing a variable around. Typically, file pointers are declared globally. Because these variable are small, they don't take up much space. You should avoid declaring variables globally whenever possible.

Workshop

The Workshop provides quiz questions to help you solidify your understanding of the material covered and exercises to provide you with experience in using what you've learned.

Quiz

1. What is the difference between input and output?

2. What is a field?

3. What is a record?

4. What is a file?

5. What is a database?

6. What is an index file?

7. What is the difference between a file opened in text mode and a file opened in binary mode?

8. A preexisting file is opened with the a mode of "w+b". What does this mean?

9. What would Figure 13.3 look like if the "AA" code was added?

10. What would Figure 13.3 look like if the "TP" code was deleted?

Exercises

1. Make sure that you updated your TYAC.LIB library file with today's library functions:

```
put_rec()
get_rec()
open_files()
close_files()
```

2. Create the index structure for the group file and add it to the RECORDS.H header file.

3. **ON YOUR OWN:** Add the file functions such as the ones presented today to the Groups entry and edit screen.

File Routines:
Using Dynamic
Data

On Day 17, you added file routines to the medium code and the group information screens in your *Record of Record!* applications. While you added these functions to the screen, you still need to complete the action bar routines. Additionally, while these routines worked for those screens, they do not work for the Musical Items screen. The number of Titles with each musical item is a variable. Today, you'll use what you learned on Day 17 as a starting point; however, you will do much more. Today you will:

☐ Add the file routines to the action bar.

☐ Create a function to find a specific record.

☐ Understand why the routines from Day 17 won't work for the Musical Items screen.

☐ Look at what the differences are for the file routines needed for the Musical Items screen.

☐ Create file routines for the Musical Items screen.

File Functions and the Action Bar

On Day 17, you added all the functions to the Medium Code screen; however, you didn't add them to the action bar. Each of the file functions needs to be added to the action bar. Listing 18.1 contains the new MEDMABAR.C code.

 Listing 18.1. MEDMABAR.C. The medium action bar function.

```
 1:  /*============================================================
 2:   * Filename: medmabar.c
 3:   *            RECORD OF RECORDS - Version 1.0
 4:   *
 5:   * Author:   Bradley L. Jones
 6:   *
 7:   * Purpose:  Action bar for medium screen.  This will
 8:   *           contain multiple menus. The functions called
 9:   *           by the menu selections may not be available
10:   *           until later days.
11:   *
12:   * Return:   Return value is either key used to exit a menu
13:   *           with the exception of F10 which is returned
14:   *           as Enter to redisplay main menu.  In each menu
15:   *           the left and right keys will exit and move
16:   *           control to the right or left menu.
17:   *============================================================*/
```

```
18:
19:   #include <stdio.h>
20:   #include <stdlib.h>      /* for exit() */
21:   #include <string.h>
22:
23:   #include "tyac.h"
24:   #include "records.h"
25:
26:   /* Global variables/functions for MEDIUM */
27:   extern MEDIUM_REC medium;      /* Record structure with data */
28:   extern MEDIUM_REC prev;
29:   extern FILE *idx_fp;           /* Main File ptr to data file */
30:   extern FILE *db_fp;            /* Data file */
31:   extern int nbr_records;        /* Ttl # of index rec for mediums */
32:   extern int start_rec;
33:   extern int disp_rec;
34:
35:   /*-------------------*
36:    *     prototypes    *
37:    *-------------------*/
38:
39:   #include "recofrec.h"
40:
41:   int do_medium_menu1( void );
42:   int do_medium_menu2( void );
43:   int do_medium_menu3( void );
44:   int do_medium_menu4( void );
45:
46:   void draw_medium_screen( void );
47:   void draw_medium_prompts( void );
48:   void display_medium_fields( void );
49:   int  search_med_rec(char *);
50:
51:
52:
53:   /*--------------------------*
54:    * medium screen action bar *
55:    *--------------------------*/
56:
57:   int do_medium_actionbar( void )
58:   {
59:     int  menu  = 1;
60:     int  cont  = TRUE;
61:     int  rv    = 0;
62:     char *abar_text ={" File   Edit    Search    Help "};
63:
64:
65:     while( cont == TRUE )
66:     {
67:        write_string(abar_text, ct.abar_fcol, ct.abar_bcol, 1, 2);
68:
```

continues

Listing 18.1. continued

```
69:        switch( menu )
70:        {
71:
72:            case 1:   /* file menu */
73:                    write_string( " File ", ct.menu_high_fcol,
74:                        ct.menu_high_bcol, 1, 2);
75:
76:                    rv = do_medium_menu1();
77:                    break;
78:
79:            case 2:   /* edit menu */
80:                    write_string( " Edit ", ct.menu_high_fcol,
81:                        ct.menu_high_bcol, 1, 9);
82:
83:                    rv = do_medium_menu2();
84:                    break;
85:
86:            case 3:   /* search menu */
87:                    write_string( " Search ", ct.menu_high_fcol,
88:                        ct.menu_high_bcol, 1, 16);
89:
90:                    rv = do_medium_menu3();
91:                    break;
92:
93:            case 4:   /* Help menu */
94:                    write_string( " Help ", ct.menu_high_fcol,
95:                        ct.menu_high_bcol, 1, 25);
96:
97:                    rv = do_medium_menu4();
98:                    break;
99:
100:           default: /* error */
101:                    cont = FALSE;
102:                    break;
103:        }
104:
105:        switch( rv )
106:        {
107:            case LT_ARROW:  menu--;
108:                            if( menu < 1 )
109:                                menu = 4;
110:                            break;
111:
112:            case RT_ARROW:  menu++;
113:                            if( menu > 4 )
114:                                menu = 1;
115:                            break;
116:
117:            default:        cont = FALSE;
118:                            break;
```

```
119:        }
120:    }
121:    write_string(abar_text, ct.abar_fcol, ct.abar_bcol, 1, 2);
122:    cursor_on();
123:    return(rv);
124: }
125:
126:
127:
128: /*--------------------*
129:  *  do_menu 1  (File) *
130:  *--------------------*/
131:
132: int do_medium_menu1( void )
133: {
134:    int    rv      = 0;
135:    int    menu_sel = 0;
136:    char *saved_screen = NULL;
137:
138:    char *file_menu[2] = { " Exit  <F3> ", "1Ee" };
139:    char exit_keys[MAX_KEYS] = {F3, F10, ESC_KEY};
140:
141:    saved_screen = save_screen_area( 0, 10, 0, 40 );
142:
143:    rv = display_menu( 3, 4, SINGLE_BOX, file_menu, 2,
144:                       exit_keys, &menu_sel, LR_ARROW, SHADOW);
145:
146:    switch( rv )
147:    {
148:       case ENTER_KEY: /* accept selection */
149:       case CR:
150:                       rv = F3;
151:                       break;
152:
153:       case F3:        /* exiting */
154:       case ESC_KEY:
155:       case LT_ARROW:  /* arrow keys */
156:       case RT_ARROW:
157:                       break;
158:
159:       case F10:       /* exit action bar */
160:                       rv = ENTER_KEY;
161:                       break;
162:
163:       default:        boop();
164:                       break;
165:    }
166:    restore_screen_area( saved_screen );
167:
168:    return(rv);
```

continues

Listing 18.1. continued

```
169: }
170:
171: /*-------------------*
172:  *  do_menu 2  (Edit) *
173:  *-------------------*/
174:
175: int do_medium_menu2( void )
176: {
177:   int   rv      = 0;
178:   int   menu_sel = 0;
179:   char *saved_screen = NULL;
180:
181:   char *edit_menu[8] = {
182:           " New            ", "1Nn",
183:           " Add      <F4> ", "2Aa",
184:           " Change   <F5> ", "3Cc",
185:           " Delete   <F6> ", "4Dd" };
186:
187:   char exit_keys[MAX_KEYS] = {F3, F10, ESC_KEY};
188:
189:   saved_screen = save_screen_area( 1, 10, 8, 40 );
190:
191:   rv = display_menu( 3, 11, SINGLE_BOX, edit_menu, 8,
192:                      exit_keys, &menu_sel, LR_ARROW, SHADOW);
193:
194:   switch( rv )
195:   {
196:     case ENTER_KEY: /* accept selection */
197:     case CR:
198:             switch( menu_sel )
199:             {
200:                case 1:  /* Clear the screen */
201:                         restore_screen_area( saved_screen );
202:                         disp_rec = 0;
203:                         clear_medium_fields();
204:                         draw_medium_screen();
205:                         break;
206:
207:                case 2:  /* Add a record */
208:                         restore_screen_area( saved_screen );
209:                         rv = add_mdata();
210:                         if ( rv == NO_ERROR )
211:                         {
212:                            /* Reset display counter */
213:                            display_msg_box("Added record!",
214:                                    ct.db_fcol, ct.db_bcol);
215:                            disp_rec = 0;
216:                            clear_medium_fields();
217:                            draw_medium_screen();
```

```
218:                              }
219:                              else   /* Only do if File I/O */
220:                              if ( rv > NO_ERROR)
221:                              {
222:                                display_msg_box("Fatal Error writing
                                                   data...",
223:                                    ct.err_fcol, ct.err_bcol );
224:                                exit(1);
225:                              }
226:                              break;
227:
228:             case 3:    /* Update the current record */
229:                        restore_screen_area( saved_screen );
230:                        rv = add_mdata();    /* updates record */
231:
232:                        if ( rv == NO_ERROR )
233:                        {
234:                            /* Reset display counter */
235:
236:                            display_msg_box("Record Updated!",
237:                                    ct.db_fcol, ct.db_bcol);
238:                        }
239:                        else
240:                        if ( rv > NO_ERROR )
241:                        {
242:                          display_msg_box("Fatal Error writing
                                             data...",
243:                              ct.err_fcol, ct.err_bcol );
244:
245:                          exit(1);
246:                        }
247:                        break;
248:
249:             case 4:    /* Deleting the current record */
250:                        restore_screen_area( saved_screen );
251:                        if( (yes_no_box( "Delete record ?",
252:                            ct.db_fcol, ct.db_bcol )) == 'Y' )
253:                        {
254:                          rv = del_med_rec();
255:                          if (rv == NO_ERROR)
256:                          {
257:                            disp_rec = 0;
258:                            clear_medium_fields();
259:                            draw_medium_screen();
260:                          }
261:                          else
262:                          {
263:                            display_msg_box("Fatal Error deleting
                                               data...",
264:                                ct.err_fcol, ct.err_bcol );
```

continues

Listing 18.1. continued

```
265:                              exit(1);
266:                          }
267:                      }
268:                      break;
269:
270:              default: /* continue looping */
271:                      boop();
272:                      break;
273:              }
274:
275:          rv = ENTER_KEY;
276:          break;
277:
278:     case F3:       /* exiting */
279:     case ESC_KEY:
280:     case LT_ARROW: /* arrow keys */
281:     case RT_ARROW:
282:              restore_screen_area( saved_screen );
283:              break;
284:
285:     case F10:      /* action bar */
286:              restore_screen_area( saved_screen );
287:              rv = ENTER_KEY;
288:              break;
289:
290:     default:       boop();
291:              break;
292:   }
293:
294:   return(rv);
295: }
296:
297: /*--------------------*
298:  *  do menu 3  (Search) *
299:  *--------------------*/
300:
301: int do_medium_menu3( void )
302: {
303:   int   rv      = 0;
304:   int   menu_sel = 0;
305:   char *saved_screen = NULL;
306:
307:   char *search_menu[6] = {
308:          " Find...        ", "1Ff",
309:          " Next     <F7> ", "2Nn",
310:          " Previous  <F8> ", "3Pp" };
311:
312:   char exit_keys[MAX_KEYS] = {F3, F10, ESC_KEY};
313:
314:   saved_screen = save_screen_area( 1, 10, 0, 60 );
```

```
315:
316:      rv = display_menu( 3, 18, SINGLE_BOX, search_menu, 6,
317:                      exit_keys, &menu_sel, LR_ARROW, SHADOW);
318:
319:      switch( rv )
320:      {
321:          case ENTER_KEY: /* accept selection */
322:          case CR:
323:                  switch( menu_sel )
324:                  {
325:                    case 1:   /* Do find dialog */
326:                          restore_screen_area( saved_screen );
327:
328:                          rv = search_med_rec(medium.code);
329:
330:                          if( rv == NO_ERROR )
331:                          {
332:                              /* record found */
333:                              draw_medium_screen();
334:                              display_msg_box("Record Found!",
335:                                      ct.db_fcol, ct.db_bcol);
336:                          }
337:                          else
338:                          if( rv < 0 )
339:                          {
340:                              display_msg_box("Record Not Found!",
341:                                      ct.err_fcol, ct.err_bcol);
342:                          }
343:                          else
344:                          {
345:                            display_msg_box("Fatal Error processing
                                                  data...",
346:                                  ct.err_fcol, ct.err_bcol );
347:                            exit(1);
348:                          }
349:                          break;
350:
351:                  case 2:   /* Next Record */
352:                          restore_screen_area( saved_screen );
353:                          rv = proc_med_rec(NEXT_REC);
354:                          if ( rv == NO_ERROR )
355:                          {
356:                              draw_medium_screen();
357:                          }
358:                          else
359:                          {
360:                            display_msg_box("Fatal Error processing
                                                    data...",
361:                                  ct.err_fcol, ct.err_bcol );
362:                            exit(1);
```

continues

Listing 18.1. continued

```
363:                              }
364:                              break;
365:
366:                  case 3:   /* Prev record */
367:                              restore_screen_area( saved_screen );
368:                              rv = proc_med_rec(PREVIOUS_REC);
369:                              if ( rv == NO_ERROR )
370:                              {
371:                                 draw_medium_screen();
372:                              }
373:                              else
374:                              {
375:                                 display_msg_box("Fatal Error processing
                                                      data...",
376:                                    ct.err_fcol, ct.err_bcol );
377:                                 exit(1);
378:                              }
379:                              break;
380:
381:                  default: /* shouldn't happen */
382:                              boop();
383:                              break;
384:                  }
385:
386:                              rv = ENTER_KEY;
387:                              break;
388:
389:       case F3:        /* exiting */
390:       case ESC_KEY:
391:       case LT_ARROW: /* arrow keys */
392:       case RT_ARROW:
393:                              restore_screen_area( saved_screen );
394:                              break;
395:
396:       case F10:       /* action bar */
397:                              rv = ENTER_KEY;
398:                              restore_screen_area( saved_screen );
399:                              break;
400:
401:       default:        boop();
402:                              break;
403:   }
404:
405:    return(rv);
406: }
407:
408: /*-------------------*
409:  *  do menu 4  (Help) *
410:  *-------------------*/
```

```
411:
412: int do_medium_menu4( void )
413: {
414:    int    rv       = 0;
415:    int    menu_sel = 0;
416:    char *saved_screen = NULL;
417:
418:    char *help_menu[4] = {
419:            " Help   <F2> ", "1Hh",
420:            " About       ", "2Ee" };
421:
422:    char exit_keys[MAX_KEYS] = {F3, F10, ESC_KEY};
423:
424:    saved_screen = save_screen_area( 1, 10, 0, 60 );
425:
426:    rv = display_menu( 3, 27, SINGLE_BOX, help_menu, 4,
427:                       exit_keys, &menu_sel, LR_ARROW, SHADOW);
428:
429:    switch( rv )
430:    {
431:       case ENTER_KEY: /* accept selection */
432:       case CR:
433:                    switch( menu_sel )
434:                    {
435:                       case 1:  /* Extended Help */
436:                                display_medium_help();
437:
438:                                break;
439:
440:                       case 2:  /* About box */
441:                                display_about_box();
442:
443:                                break;
444:
445:                       default: /* continue looping */
446:                                boop();
447:                                break;
448:                    }
449:
450:                    break;
451:
452:       case F3:        /* exiting */
453:       case ESC_KEY:
454:       case LT_ARROW:  /* arrow keys */
455:       case RT_ARROW:
456:                    break;
457:
458:       case F10:       /* action bar */
459:                    rv = ENTER_KEY;
460:                    break;
```

18

continues

Listing 18.1. continued

```
461:
462:      default:        boop();
463:                      break;
464:  }
465:  restore_screen_area( saved_screen );
466:
467:  return(rv);
468: }
469:
470: /*==========================================================
471:  * Function: search_med_rec()
472:  *
473:  * Author:   Bradley L. Jones
474:  *           Gregory L. Guntle
475:  *
476:  * Purpose: Searches for the key to locate
477:  *
478:  * Returns:  0 - No errors - key found
479:  *          <0 - Key not found
480:  *          >0 - File I/O Error
481:  *==========================================================*/
482:
483: int search_med_rec(char *key)
484: {
485:   int rv = NO_ERROR;
486:   int done = FALSE;
487:   int srch_rec;
488:   int result;
489:
490:   MEDIUM_INDEX temp;
491:
492:   /* Start at top of chain */
493:   /* Stop when either
494:      1 - The key passed matches   or
495:      2 - The key passed is < rec read
496:      The latter indicates the key is not in the file  */
497:
498:   srch_rec = start_rec;
499:   while (!done)
500:   {
501:     /* Get record */
502:     rv = get_rec(srch_rec, idx_fp, sizeof(temp),
503:           sizeof(int)*2, (char *)&temp);
504:     if (rv == 0)
505:     {
506:       result = stricmp(key, temp.code);
507:       if (result == 0)    /* Found match */
508:       {
509:          /* Now get data */
```

```
510:        done = TRUE;
511:        rv = get_rec(temp.data, db_fp, sizeof(medium),
512:              0, (char *)&medium);
513:      }
514:      else
515:      if (result < 0)
516:      {
517:        /* Key < next rec in DB - key doesn't exist */
518:        done = TRUE;
519:        rv = -1;                 /* Key not found */
520:      }
521:      else
522:      {
523:        srch_rec = temp.next;
524:        if (srch_rec == 0)    /* At end of list ? */
525:        {
526:          done = TRUE;
527:          rv = -1;               /* Key not found */
528:        }
529:      }
530:    }
531:  }
532:
533:  return(rv);
534:
535: }
```

18

 A lot of this code hasn't changed from Day 15 when you initially created the MEDMABAR.C source. The new code begins with the addition of the STRING.H header file in line 21. Line 38 contains a prototype for a new function, search_med_rec(). Additional new code begins in line 26 with the declaration of several external variables. These external variables were all covered on Day 17. The rest of the changes are in the do_medium_menu2() and do_medium_menu3() functions.

The do_medium_menu2() function begins on line 175. This action bar menu contained the EDIT options for creating a new record, adding a new record, changing an existing record, and deleting a record. Creating a new record means to clear the screen so that a new record can be entered. This is a function that wasn't presented on Day 17; however, the logic behind this was. Adding a new record, changing an existing record, and deleting a record were all covered on Day 17. Today, you will see them added to the action bar.

Clearing for a new record is done within case 1 in lines 200 to 205. This case starts by restoring the saved screen area. The current record, disp_rec, is then set to zero because you won't be editing a preexisting record. Line 203 then calls the clear_medium_fields() function to clear any data that may be in the medium code structure. Once the screen is redrawn in line 204, you are ready for a new record.

The second EDIT action bar menu option is to add a record. This is accomplished in case 2 (lines 207 to 226). Again, this starts with the restoring of the screen. Line 209 calls the add_mdata() function that was presented on Day 17. This function adds a record to the files. If this addition of the records was successful, then line 213 displays a message so that users will know they were successful. Lines 215 to 217 then repeat the process of clearing the screen for a new record. If the writing of the record failed, then a fatal error is displayed in line 221 and the program exits.

The third case handles updating or changing a record. This case is presented in lines 228 to 250. This function follows a flow similar to adding a record. As shown on Day 17, the add_mdata() function handles both the updating and the adding of records. If the add_mdata() function successfully updates the current record, then an appropriate message is displayed in line 236. If the addition wasn't successful, then a fatal error message is displayed in line 242 and the program exits.

Deleting a record can be accomplished with the fourth case in lines 249 to 268. The process of deleting should always start with asking the users if they are sure they want to remove a record. This is done in line 251. If the user says yes, then the del_med_rec() function is called (Line 254). If the delete is successful, lines 256 to 258 refresh the screen so a new record can be added. If there is a problem in deleting, then an error message is displayed and the program exits. With this, the functions in the EDIT action bar menu are complete.

The SEARCH menu also contains three functions that work with file I/O. These are handled in the do_medium_menu3(). These are the Find..., the next search, and the previous search.

The Find... case is new. This is presented in lines 325 to 349. This function starts with the restoration of the screen in the same manner as all the other functions. Line 328 then does the actual finding with the search_med_rec() function. This function attempts to find the corresponding record for the value in the code field on the screen. If a matching record is found, then the medium screen is redrawn (line 333) and a message is displayed. Line 338 checks to see if the record wasn't found. If rv is less than zero, then the provided code wasn't found. If rv is greater than zero, then a fatal error is displayed in line 345.

The search_med_rec() function is presented in lines 470 to 535. The search starts at the first alphabetic record in the index and works its way until it finds a record that either matches or is greater than its own value. Line 498 starts the process by

initializing the counter, srch_rec, to the first index record, start_rec. A while loop then begins the processing of each index record in sorted (next) order. Line 502 retrieves the index for the current search number. If there isn't a problem, then line 506 compares the current index's code to the code that is being searched for. If the values are equal, then line 510 sets the done flag to TRUE and the data record is retrieved. Otherwise, if the result is less than zero (line 515), then there isn't a need to continue because the current search code is greater than the code being looked for. Negative one is returned so that the calling program will know that the code was not found—not that there was an error.

If the search code was less than the code being looked for, then lines 523 to 528 are executed. The srch_rec is set to the next index record number, temp.next. If this number is zero, then the end of the index file has been reached without finding the record. This process continues until the done flag is set to TRUE. As you just saw, this happens when either the record is found, the end of the file is reached, or a code greater than the current code is found.

In the do_medium_menu3() function, you can see the next and previous records are found in lines 351 to 379. Finding the next or finding the previous record are completed in the same way with one difference. The proc_med_rec() function is used to get the record. If successful, the screen is redrawn; otherwise, a fatal error message is displayed. The difference in the two cases is that the next record case passes NEXT_REC to proc_med_rec() in line 353 and the previous record case passes PREVIOUS_REC to proc_med_rec() in line 368.

With this, you have completed the action bar routines. The do_something() case that had been added as a filler can be removed because all of the action bar items are complete. In fact, at this point, the entire Medium Codes screen is complete!

Note: At this point the Medium Codes entry and edit screen is complete!

DO   DON'T

DO always ask the users to ensure they want to delete a record.

DO display messages to let the user know when he or she has done something such as adding, deleting, or changing a record.

The Musical Items Screen

At this point, you have completed the Medium Code screen. The Group Information screen has been left for you to do as exercises. This leaves the Musical Items screen.

The Musical Items screen is a little more complex than the Medium Code and the Group Information screens. The complexity stems from the addition of the structure for holding songs. In the following sections, you'll see the code for working with the Musical Items screen. The code presented will show you how to process the medium screen information using the index structure, the data structure for the main medium information, and an array of song structures.

Preliminary Changes for the Albums Screen

Before adding the processes of manipulating the song records, you need to make a few additional modifications to several of your existing files. Changes need to be made to RECOFREC.C, RECOFREC.H, and RECORDS.H.

The RECOFREC.C source file needs several additional global variables. These variables are needed by many of the musical item functions. You should add the following global declarations to the beginning of the RECOFREC.C source file:

```
FILE *song_fp;          /* For tracking songs */
int total_songs;        /* Nbr of songs in the song file */
```

The additional FILE pointer, song_fp, will be used to point to the data file that will hold the song records. The total_songs value will keep track of the total number of songs in the song file. The importance of total_songs will be seen later in the Musical Items screen's code.

As with the Medium Code screen, the RECOFREC.H header file should receive a few modifications also. To this header file you should add the prototypes for the new functions you will be adding. The following are the function prototypes that should be included in RECOFREC.H for the Musical Items screen:

```
/*----------------------------*
 * Prototypes for albums screen *
 *----------------------------*/

int  do_albums_actionbar(void);
void display_albums_help(void);

int  clear_albums_fields(void);
```

```
void draw_albums_screen(void);

int   verify_adata(void);
int   add_adata(void);
int   add_album_rec(void);
int   del_alb_rec(void);
int   proc_alb_rec(int);

int   open_songs(void);
```

Each of these new prototypes will be covered as the listings for the Musical Items
screen are presented. In addition to adding the preceding prototypes to the
RECOFREC.H header file, you should also ensure that you have all the necessary
structures in the RECORDS.H header file. There should be three separate structures
for the albums screen. These are:

```
typedef struct
{
   char title[ 30+1 ];
   char group[ 25+1];
   char medium_code[2+1];
   DATE date_purch;
   char cost[ 5+1 ];
   char value[ 5+1 ];
   int  nbr_songs;
   int  del_flag;

} ALBUM_REC;

typedef struct
{
   int  del_flag;
   char title[40+1];
   char minutes[2+1];
   char seconds[2+1];
   int  next;              /* next song record */

} SONG_REC;

typedef struct
{
   char title[ 30+1 ];
   int  nbr_songs;
   int  del_flag;
   unsigned short prev;
   unsigned short next;
   unsigned short data;
   unsigned short song;

} ALBUM_INDEX;
```

The `ALBUM_REC` structure and the `SONG_REC` structure should be familiar for the most part. The `ALBUM_REC` structure has one additional field called `del_flag` that will be used to signal if the record has been marked as deleted. This will be covered later.

The `ALBUM_INDEX` structure is new. This structure is similar to the index file presented for the Medium Code screen; however, there are three differences. First, you'll notice that this structure also has a deleted flag, `del_flag`. The structure also has a `nbr_songs` field and a song field. The `nbr_songs` field will be used to hold the total number of songs saved with this album. The song field will be used to hold the record number in the song data file where the first song is stored. This is simply an index for the song file. Figure 18.1 presents a representation of these structures. Figure 18.2 shows portions of these structures with data.

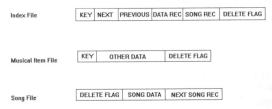

Figure 18.1. *A representation of the musical item structures.*

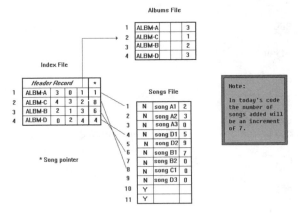

Figure 18.2. *The musical item structures with data.*

The Musical Items Screen

In addition to the RECORDS.H header file, the RECOFREC.C file, and the RECOFREC.H header file, the ALBUMS.C file also will need several changes.

Because you haven't had many listings involving the Musical Items screen, the entire ALBUMS.C listing is presented in Listing 18.2.

Warning: Only the differences from the medium code listing presented on Day 17 will be analyzed in the following listings.

Listing 18.2. ALBUMS.C. The Musical Items screen's main file.

```
1:  /*============================================================
2:   * Filename: albums.c
3:   *
4:   * Author:    Bradley L. Jones
5:   *            Gregory L. Guntle
6:   *
7:   * Purpose:   Allow entry and edit of information on musical
8:   *            items.
9:   *
10:  * Note:      This listing is linked with RECofREC.c
11:  *            (There isn't a main() in this listing!)
12:   *============================================================*/
13:
14:  #include <stdio.h>
15:  #include <stdlib.h>
16:  #include <string.h>
17:  #include <conio.h>          /* for getch() */
18:  #include "tyac.h"
19:  #include "records.h"
20:
21:  /*-------------------*
22:   *    prototypes     *
23:   *-------------------*/
24:  #include "recofrec.h"
25:
26:  void draw_albums_screen( void );
27:  void draw_albums_prompts( void );
28:  void display_albums_fields( void );
29:
30:  int  clear_albums_fields(void);
31:  int  get_albums_data( int row );
32:  int  get_albums_input_data( void );
33:  void display_albums_help(void);
34:
35:  /*-----------------*
36:   * Global Variables *
```

continues

Listing 18.2. continued

```
37:    *-----------------*/
38:
39:  extern FILE *idx_fp;        /* Main File ptr to data file */
40:  extern FILE *db_fp;         /* Data file */
41:  extern FILE *song_fp;       /* Pointer for songs */
42:  extern nbr_records;         /* Total # of rec for albums */
43:  extern int start_rec;
44:  extern int disp_rec;
45:  extern int total_songs;
46:
47:  /*-----------------*
48:   * Defined constants*
49:   *-----------------*/
50:
51:  #define ALBUMS_DBF    "ALBUMS.DBF"
52:  #define ALBUMS_IDX    "ALBUMS.IDX"
53:  #define SONGS_DBF     "SONGS.DBF"
54:  #define HELP_DBF      "ALBUMS.HLP"
55:
56:  /*---------------------*
57:   * structure declarations *
58:   *---------------------*/
59:
60:  ALBUM_REC albums;
61:  ALBUM_REC *p_albums = &albums;
62:  ALBUM_REC alb_prev;
63:  SONG_REC  songs[7];
64:
65:  int song_pg;         /* Tracks page of songs being displayed */
66:  int max_song_pg;     /* Max number of pages allocated to    */
67:                       /*    hold the songs                    */
68:  char *song_ptr;      /* Ptr to dynamic mem where songs are   */
69:  char *temp_ptr;      /* Used for reallocating memory */
70:
71:  #define ONE_SONG     sizeof(songs[0])
72:  #define SEVEN_SONGS  sizeof(songs)
73:
74:  /*=======================================================*
75:   *    do_albums_screen()                                 *
76:   *=======================================================*/
77:
78:  int do_albums_screen(void)
79:  {
80:    int rv;
81:
82:    /* Open both Index and DBF file */
83:    if ( (rv = open_files(ALBUMS_IDX, ALBUMS_DBF)) == 0 )
84:    {
85:      if ( (rv = open_songs()) == NO_ERROR)
86:      {
```

```
87:           /* Try and get enough mem for
88:              holding 7 songs (1 screen) */
89:           song_ptr = (char *)malloc(SEVEN_SONGS);
90:           /* Check for mem error */
91:           if (song_ptr != NULL)    /* No error - continue */
92:           {
93:             /* Setup for adding new records at beginning */
94:             memset(&alb_prev, '\0', sizeof(alb_prev));
95:             max_song_pg = 1;        /* Only one pg of mem */
96:             song_pg = 1;            /* Displaying 1 pg of songs */
97:
98:             disp_rec = 0;           /* Initialize displaying rec # */
99:
100:            clear_albums_fields();
101:            draw_albums_screen();
102:
103:            get_albums_input_data();
104:
105:            fclose(song_fp);        /* Close song DBF */
106:            rv = close_files();     /* Close IDX and DBF file */
107:            free(song_ptr);         /* Release memory */
108:          }
109:        else
110:          {
111:            display_msg_box(
112:                "Fatal Error - Unable to allocate memory!",
113:                ct.err_fcol, ct.err_bcol );
114:
115:            fclose(song_fp);         /* Close song DBF */
116:            rv = close_files();      /* Close IDX and DBF file */
117:            exit(1);
118:          }
119:      }
120:    }
121:  else
122:    {
123:      display_msg_box("Error opening ALBUMS files...",
124:                      ct.err_fcol, ct.err_bcol );
125:    }
126:    return(rv);
127: }
128:
129: /*-----------------------*
130:  *   draw_albums_screen() *
131:  *-----------------------*/
132:
133: void draw_albums_screen( void )
134: {
135:    char rec_disp[6];
136:
```

continues

Listing 18.2. continued

```
137:    draw_borders("  Musical Items  ");  /* draw screen background */
138:
139:    write_string("<F1=Help>    <F3=Exit>    <PgUp/PgDn=More Songs>",
140:                    ct.abar_fcol, ct.abar_bcol, 24, 3);
141:
142:    write_string( " File    Edit    Search    Help",
143:        ct.abar_fcol, ct.abar_bcol, 1, 2);
144:
145:    draw_albums_prompts();
146:    display_albums_fields();
147: }
148:
149: /*------------------------*
150:  *   draw_albums_prompts()*
151:  *------------------------*/
152:
153: void draw_albums_prompts( void )
154: {
155:    int  ctr;
156:    char tmp[10];
157:
158:    write_string("Title:",
159:                    ct.fld_prmpt_fcol, ct.fld_prmpt_bcol, 4, 3 );
160:    write_string("Group:",
161:                    ct.fld_prmpt_fcol, ct.fld_prmpt_bcol, 5, 3 );
162:    write_string("Medium:",
163:                    ct.fld_prmpt_fcol, ct.fld_prmpt_bcol, 7, 3 );
164:    write_string("Date Purchased:    /  /",
165:                    ct.fld_prmpt_fcol, ct.fld_prmpt_bcol, 9, 3 );
166:    write_string("Cost: $   .",
167:                    ct.fld_prmpt_fcol, ct.fld_prmpt_bcol, 9, 33 );
168:    write_string("Value: $   .",
169:                    ct.fld_prmpt_fcol, ct.fld_prmpt_bcol, 9, 52 );
170:    write_string("Track   Song Title",
171:                    ct.fld_prmpt_fcol, ct.fld_prmpt_bcol, 11, 7 );
172:    write_string("Time",
173:                    ct.fld_prmpt_fcol, ct.fld_prmpt_bcol, 11, 59 );
174:    for( ctr = 0; ctr < 7; ctr++ )
175:    {
176:        sprintf(tmp, "%02d:",((song_pg-1)*7+ctr+1) );
177:        write_string( tmp,
178:            ct.fld_prmpt_fcol, ct.fld_prmpt_bcol, 13+ctr, 8 );
179:        write_string(":",
180:            ct.fld_prmpt_fcol, ct.fld_prmpt_bcol, 13+ctr, 61 );
181:    }
182:
183:    write_string("Total Album Time:    :  :",
184:                    ct.fld_prmpt_fcol, ct.fld_prmpt_bcol, 21, 39 );
185:
186:    /* Track information */
```

```
187:
188: }
189:
190: /*-----------------------*
191:  *   draw_albums_fields() *
192:  *-----------------------*/
193:
194: void display_albums_fields( void )
195: {
196:    int ctr;
197:    char tmp[7] = { 0, 0, 0, 0, 0, 0, 0 }; /* set to nulls */
198:    char under_40[41] =
199:              {"_____"};
200:
201:    write_string(under_40+10,    /* 30 underscores */
202:                 ct.fld_fcol, ct.fld_bcol, 4, 12 );
203:    write_string(under_40+15,    /* 25 underlines */
204:                 ct.fld_fcol, ct.fld_bcol, 5, 12 );
205:    write_string("__", ct.fld_fcol, ct.fld_bcol, 7, 13 );
206:    write_string("__", ct.fld_fcol, ct.fld_bcol, 9, 20 );
207:    write_string("__", ct.fld_fcol, ct.fld_bcol, 9, 23 );
208:    write_string("__", ct.fld_fcol, ct.fld_bcol, 9, 26 );
209:
210:    write_string("___", ct.fld_fcol, ct.fld_bcol, 9, 41 );
211:    write_string("__",  ct.fld_fcol, ct.fld_bcol, 9, 45 );
212:
213:    write_string("___", ct.fld_fcol, ct.fld_bcol, 9, 61 );
214:    write_string("__",  ct.fld_fcol, ct.fld_bcol, 9, 65 );
215:
216:    for( ctr = 0; ctr < 7; ctr++)
217:    {
218:       write_string(under_40,
219:                    ct.fld_fcol, ct.fld_bcol, 13+ctr, 16 );
220:       write_string("__",
221:                    ct.fld_fcol, ct.fld_bcol, 13+ctr, 59 );
222:       write_string("__",
223:                    ct.fld_fcol, ct.fld_bcol, 13+ctr, 62 );
224:    }
225:
226:    write_string("__", ct.fld_fcol, ct.fld_bcol, 21, 57);
227:    write_string("__", ct.fld_fcol, ct.fld_bcol, 21, 60);
228:    write_string("__", ct.fld_fcol, ct.fld_bcol, 21, 63);
229:
230:    /*** display data, if exists ***/
231:
232:    write_string(albums.title, ct.fld_fcol, ct.fld_bcol, 4, 12);
233:    write_string(albums.group, ct.fld_fcol, ct.fld_bcol, 5, 12);
234:    write_string(albums.medium_code,
235:                 ct.fld_fcol, ct.fld_bcol, 7, 13 );
236:
```

continues

Listing 18.2. continued

```
237:      strncpy( tmp, albums.date_purch.month, 2 );
238:      write_string(tmp, ct.fld_fcol, ct.fld_bcol, 9, 20 );
239:      strncpy( tmp+4, albums.date_purch.day, 2 );
240:      write_string(tmp, ct.fld_fcol, ct.fld_bcol, 9, 23 );
241:      strncpy( tmp, albums.date_purch.year, 2 );
242:      write_string(tmp, ct.fld_fcol, ct.fld_bcol, 9, 26 );
243:
244:      strncpy(tmp, albums.cost, 3);
245:      write_string(tmp, ct.fld_fcol, ct.fld_bcol, 9, 41 );
246:      strncpy(tmp, albums.cost+3, 2 );
247:      tmp[2] = NULL;
248:      write_string(tmp, ct.fld_fcol, ct.fld_bcol, 9, 45 );
249:
250:      strncpy(tmp, albums.value, 3);
251:      write_string(tmp, ct.fld_fcol, ct.fld_bcol, 9, 61 );
252:      strncpy(tmp, albums.value+3, 2 );
253:      tmp[2] = NULL;
254:      write_string(tmp, ct.fld_fcol, ct.fld_bcol, 9, 65 );
255:
256:      /* Get songs from appropriate memory location and */
257:      /*    move into the structured array */
258:      memcpy(&songs,
259:              song_ptr+((song_pg-1)*SEVEN_SONGS), SEVEN_SONGS);
260:
261:      /* song title information */
262:      for( ctr = 0; ctr < 7; ctr++ )
263:      {
264:        write_string(songs[ctr].title,
265:             ct.fld_fcol, ct.fld_bcol, 13+ctr, 16 );
266:        write_string(songs[ctr].minutes,
267:             ct.fld_fcol, ct.fld_bcol, 13+ctr, 59 );
268:        write_string(songs[ctr].seconds,
269:             ct.fld_fcol, ct.fld_bcol, 13+ctr, 62 );
270:       /* calc total here. */
271:      }
272:      /* finish total count and print here */
273: }
274:
275: /*-------------------------------------------------------------*
276:  *   get_albums_input_data()                                  *
277:  *-------------------------------------------------------------*/
278: int get_albums_input_data( void )
279: {
280:     int   position,
281:           rv,
282:           okay,                    /* used with edits */
283:           loop = TRUE;
284:
285:     /*  Set up exit keys.  */
286:      static char fexit_keys[ 19 ] = { F1, F2, F3, F4, F5, F6,
```

```
287:                         F7, F8, F10,
288:                         ESC_KEY, PAGE_DN, PAGE_UP, CR_KEY,
289:                         TAB_KEY, ENTER_KEY, SHIFT_TAB,
290:                         DN_ARROW, UP_ARROW, NULL };
291:
292:     static char *exit_keys = fexit_keys;
293:     getline( SET_EXIT_KEYS, 0, 18, 0, 0, 0, exit_keys );
294:
295:     /*** setup colors and default keys ***/
296:     getline( SET_DEFAULTS, 0, 0, 0, 0, 0, 0 );
297:     getline( SET_NORMAL, 0, ct.fld_fcol, ct.fld_bcol,
298:                             ct.fld_high_fcol, ct.fld_high_bcol, 0 );
299:     getline( SET_UNDERLINE, 0, ct.fld_fcol, ct.fld_bcol,
300:                             ct.fld_high_fcol, ct.fld_high_bcol, 0 );
301:     getline( SET_INS, 0, ct.abar_fcol, ct.abar_bcol, 24, 76, 0 );
302:
303:     position = 0;
304:
305:     while( loop == TRUE )        /**  get data for top fields  **/
306:     {
307:         switch( (rv = get_albums_data( position )) )
308:         {
309:            case CR_KEY    :
310:            case TAB_KEY   :
311:            case ENTER_KEY :
312:            case DN_ARROW  : /* go down a field */
313:                             ( position == 30 ) ?
314:                                     (position = 0 ) : position++;
315:                             break;
316:
317:            case SHIFT_TAB :
318:            case UP_ARROW  : /* go up a field */
319:                             ( position == 0 ) ?
320:                                     ( position = 30 ) : position--;
321:                             break;
322:
323:            case ESC_KEY :
324:            case F3      :   /* exit back to main menu */
325:                         if( (yes_no_box( "Do you want to exit?",
326:                             ct.db_fcol, ct.db_bcol )) == 'Y' )
327:                         {
328:                             loop = FALSE;
329:                         }
330:                         break;
331:
332:            case F4: /* add data */
333:                         /* Save songs back into memory location */
334:                         memcpy(song_ptr+((song_pg-1)*SEVEN_SONGS),
```

continues

Listing 18.2. continued

```
335:                          &songs, SEVEN_SONGS);
336:                  rv = add_adata();
337:                  if ( rv == NO_ERROR )
338:                  {
339:                    disp_rec = 0;
340:                    reset_memory();
341:                    clear_albums_fields();
342:                    draw_albums_screen();
343:                    position = 0;
344:                  }
345:                  else  /* Only do next part if File I/O  */
346:                  if ( rv > NO_ERROR )
347:                  {
348:                    display_msg_box(
349:                        "Fatal Error writing data...",
350:                        ct.err_fcol, ct.err_bcol );
351:                    exit(1);
352:                  }
353:                  break;
354:
355:          case F5: /* Change Record */
356:                  /* Save songs back into memory location */
357:                  memcpy(song_ptr+((song_pg-1)*SEVEN_SONGS),
358:                          &songs, SEVEN_SONGS);
359:                  rv = add_adata();
360:                  if ( rv == NO_ERROR )
361:                  {
362:                    disp_rec = 0;
363:                    reset_memory();
364:                    clear_albums_fields();
365:                    draw_albums_screen();
366:                    position = 0;
367:                  }
368:                  else  /* Only do next part if File I/O  */
369:                  if ( rv > NO_ERROR )
370:                  {
371:                    display_msg_box(
372:                        "Fatal Error changing data...",
373:                        ct.err_fcol, ct.err_bcol );
374:                    exit(1);
375:                  }
376:                  break;
377:
378:          case F6: /* Delete data */
379:                  /* Make sure rec is on screen */
380:                  if( (yes_no_box( "Delete record ?",
381:                        ct.db_fcol, ct.db_bcol )) == 'Y' )
382:                  {
383:                    rv = del_alb_rec();
384:                    if (rv == NO_ERROR)
```

```
385:                         {
386:                            disp_rec = 0;
387:                            clear_albums_fields();
388:                            draw_albums_screen();
389:                            position = 0;
390:                         }
391:                         else
392:                         {
393:                            display_msg_box(
394:                                "Fatal Error deleting data...",
395:                                ct.err_fcol, ct.err_bcol );
396:                            exit(1);
397:                         }
398:                      }
399:                      break;
400:
401:          case F7: /* Next record */
402:                      rv = proc_alb_rec(NEXT_REC);
403:                      if ( rv == NO_ERROR )
404:                      {
405:                         draw_albums_screen();
406:                         position = 0;
407:                      }
408:                      else
409:                      {
410:                         display_msg_box(
411:                             "Fatal Error processing data...",
412:                             ct.err_fcol, ct.err_bcol );
413:                         exit(1);
414:                      }
415:                      break;
416:
417:          case F8: /* Prev record */
418:                      rv = proc_alb_rec(PREVIOUS_REC);
419:                      if ( rv == NO_ERROR )
420:                      {
421:                         draw_albums_screen();
422:                         position = 0;
423:                      }
424:                      else
425:                      {
426:                         display_msg_box(
427:                             "Fatal Error processing data...",
428:                             ct.err_fcol, ct.err_bcol );
429:                         exit(1);
430:                      }
431:                      break;
432:
433:      case F10: /* action bar */
434:                  rv = do_albums_actionbar();
```

continues

Listing 18.2. continued

```
435:
436:                    if( rv == F3 )
437:                    {
438:                        if( (yes_no_box( "Do you want to exit?",
439:                             ct.db_fcol, ct.db_bcol )) == 'Y' )
440:                        {
441:                            loop = FALSE;
442:                        }
443:                    }
444:
445:                    position = 0;
446:                    break;
447:
448:        case PAGE_DN :   /* Used for display 7 songs @ time */
449:                    /* First resave - structure to memory */
450:                    memcpy(song_ptr+((song_pg-1)*SEVEN_SONGS),
451:                           &songs, SEVEN_SONGS);
452:                    song_pg++;     /* Get next page  */
453:                    /* Only allow 13 pages (91 songs) */
454:                    /* because displaying only 2 digit track # */
455:                    if (song_pg > 13)
456:                    {
457:                      boop();
458:                      song_pg--;
459:                    }
460:                    else
461:                    {
462:                        /* Do we need to allocate more memory */
463:                        if (song_pg > max_song_pg )
464:                        {
465:                          temp_ptr = song_ptr;   /* Save original */
466:                          song_ptr = (char *)realloc(song_ptr,
467:                                     song_pg*SEVEN_SONGS);
468:
469:                          /* check to see if memory was obtained. */
470:                          if (song_ptr == NULL)
471:                          {
472:                            display_msg_box("Memory not available!",
473:                                    ct.db_fcol, ct.db_bcol);
474:                            song_ptr = temp_ptr; /* restore orig. */
475:                            song_pg--;
476:                          }
477:                          else
478:                          {
479:                            memset(song_ptr+((song_pg-1)*SEVEN_SONGS),
480:                                   '\0', SEVEN_SONGS);
481:                            max_song_pg++;          /* Up the pages */
482:                          }
483:                        }
484:                    }
```

```
485:
486:                    position = 10;   /* Start at top of song */
487:                    draw_albums_screen();   /* Redraw screen */
488:                    break;
489:
490:        case PAGE_UP :    /* Go up a page of songs */
491:                    /* First resave - structure to memory */
492:                    memcpy(song_ptr+((song_pg-1)*SEVEN_SONGS),
493:                            &songs, SEVEN_SONGS);
494:                  song_pg--;
495:                  if (song_pg < 1)
496:                  {
497:                    boop();
498:                    song_pg++;
499:                  }
500:                  else
501:                  {
502:                    position = 10;   /* Start at top of song */
503:                    draw_albums_screen();   /* Redraw screen */
504:                  }
505:                  break;
506:
507:        case F1:   /* context sensitive help */
508:                  display_context_help( HELP_DBF, position );
509:                  break;
510:
511:        case F2:   /* extended help */
512:                  display_medium_help();
513:                  break;
514:
515:        default:   /* error */
516:                  display_msg_box( " Error ",
517:                     ct.err_fcol, ct.err_bcol );
518:                  break;
519:
520:        }      /* end of switch */
521:    }          /* end of while  */
522:
523:    return( rv );
524: }
525:
526: /*-------------------------------------------------------*
527:  *    get_albums_data()                                  *
528:  *-------------------------------------------------------*/
529:
530: int get_albums_data( int row )
531: {
532:    int  rv;
533:    char tmp[4] = { 0, 0, 0, 0 }; /* set to null values */
534:
```

continues

615

Listing 18.2. continued

```
535:      switch( row )
536:      {
537:          case 0 :
538:              rv = getline( GET_ALPHA, 0,   4, 12, 0, 30,
539:                                  albums.title);
540:              break;
541:          case 1 :
542:              rv = getline( GET_ALPHA, 0,   5, 12, 0, 25,
543:                                  albums.group);
544:              break;
545:          case 2 :
546:              rv = getline( GET_ALPHA, 0,   7, 13, 0,  2,
547:                                  albums.medium_code);
548:              break;
549:          case 3 :
550:              strncpy( tmp, albums.date_purch.month, 2 );
551:              rv = getline( GET_NUM,   0,  9, 20, 0,  2, tmp );
552:              zero_fill_field(tmp, 2);
553:              write_string(tmp, ct.fld_fcol, ct.fld_bcol, 9, 20);
554:              strncpy( albums.date_purch.month, tmp, 2);
555:              break;
556:          case 4 :
557:              strncpy( tmp, albums.date_purch.day, 2 );
558:              rv = getline( GET_NUM,   0,  9, 23, 0,  2, tmp );
559:              zero_fill_field(tmp, 2);
560:              write_string(tmp, ct.fld_fcol, ct.fld_bcol, 9, 23);
561:              strncpy( albums.date_purch.day, tmp, 2 );
562:              break;
563:          case 5 :
564:              strncpy( tmp, albums.date_purch.year, 2 );
565:              rv = getline( GET_NUM,   0,  9, 26, 0,  2, tmp );
566:              zero_fill_field(tmp, 2);
567:              write_string(tmp, ct.fld_fcol, ct.fld_bcol, 9, 26);
568:              strncpy( albums.date_purch.year, tmp, 2 );
569:              break;
570:          case 6 :
571:              strncpy( tmp, albums.cost, 3 );
572:              rv = getline( GET_NUM,   0,  9, 41, 0,  3, tmp );
573:              zero_fill_field(tmp, 3);
574:              write_string(tmp, ct.fld_fcol, ct.fld_bcol, 9, 41);
575:              strncpy( albums.cost, tmp, 3 );
576:              break;
577:          case 7 :
578:              strncpy( tmp, albums.cost+3, 2 );
579:              rv = getline( GET_NUM,   0,  9, 45, 0,  2, tmp );
580:              zero_fill_field(tmp, 2);
581:              write_string(tmp, ct.fld_fcol, ct.fld_bcol, 9, 45);
582:              strncpy( albums.cost+3, tmp, 2 );
583:              break;
```

```
584:        case 8 :
585:            strncpy( tmp, albums.value, 3 );
586:            rv = getline( GET_NUM,   0,  9, 61, 0,  3, tmp );
587:            zero_fill_field(tmp, 3);
588:            write_string(tmp, ct.fld_fcol, ct.fld_bcol, 9, 61);
589:            strncpy( albums.value, tmp, 3 );
590:            break;
591:        case 9 :
592:            strncpy( tmp, albums.value+3, 2 );
593:            rv = getline( GET_NUM,   0,  9, 65, 0,  2, tmp );
594:            zero_fill_field(tmp, 2);
595:            write_string(tmp, ct.fld_fcol, ct.fld_bcol, 9, 65);
596:            strncpy( albums.value+3, tmp, 2 );
597:            break;
598:        case 10 :
599:            rv = getline( GET_ALPHA, 0,  13, 16, 0, 40,
600:                                               songs[0].title);
601:            break;
602:        case 11 :
603:            rv = getline( GET_NUM, 0, 13, 59, 0, 2,
604:                                               songs[0].minutes);
605:            zero_fill_field(songs[0].minutes, 2);
606:            write_string(songs[0].minutes,
607:                        ct.fld_fcol, ct.fld_bcol, 13, 59);
608:            break;
609:        case 12 :
610:            rv = getline( GET_NUM, 0, 13, 62, 0, 2,
611:                                               songs[0].seconds);
612:            zero_fill_field(songs[0].seconds, 2);
613:            write_string(songs[0].seconds,
614:                        ct.fld_fcol, ct.fld_bcol, 13, 62);
615:            break;
616:        case 13 :
617:            rv = getline( GET_ALPHA, 0, 14, 16, 0, 40,
618:                                               songs[1].title);
619:            break;
620:        case 14 :
621:            rv = getline( GET_NUM, 0, 14, 59, 0, 2,
622:                                               songs[1].minutes);
623:            zero_fill_field(songs[1].minutes, 2);
624:            write_string(songs[1].minutes,
625:                        ct.fld_fcol, ct.fld_bcol, 14, 59);
626:            break;
627:        case 15 :
628:            rv = getline( GET_NUM, 0, 14, 62, 0, 2,
629:                                               songs[1].seconds);
630:            zero_fill_field(songs[1].seconds, 2);
631:            write_string(songs[1].seconds,
632:                        ct.fld_fcol, ct.fld_bcol, 14, 62);
633:            break;
```

continues

Listing 18.2. continued

```
634:        case 16 :
635:          rv = getline( GET_ALPHA, 0, 15, 16, 0, 40,
636:                                      songs[2].title);
637:          break;
638:        case 17 :
639:          rv = getline( GET_NUM, 0, 15, 59, 0, 2,
640:                                      songs[2].minutes);
641:          zero_fill_field(songs[2].minutes, 2);
642:          write_string(songs[2].minutes,
643:                       ct.fld_fcol, ct.fld_bcol, 15, 59);
644:          break;
645:        case 18 :
646:          rv = getline( GET_NUM, 0, 15, 62, 0, 2,
647:                                      songs[2].seconds);
648:          zero_fill_field(songs[2].seconds, 2);
649:          write_string(songs[2].seconds,
650:                       ct.fld_fcol, ct.fld_bcol, 15, 62);
651:          break;
652:        case 19 :
653:          rv = getline( GET_ALPHA, 0, 16, 16, 0, 40,
654:                                      songs[3].title);
655:          break;
656:        case 20 :
657:          rv = getline( GET_NUM, 0, 16, 59, 0, 2,
658:                                      songs[3].minutes);
659:          zero_fill_field(songs[3].minutes, 2);
660:          write_string(songs[3].minutes,
661:                       ct.fld_fcol, ct.fld_bcol, 16, 59);
662:          break;
663:        case 21 :
664:          rv = getline( GET_NUM, 0, 16, 62, 0, 2,
665:                                      songs[3].seconds);
666:          zero_fill_field(songs[3].seconds, 2);
667:          write_string(songs[3].seconds,
668:                       ct.fld_fcol, ct.fld_bcol, 16, 62);
669:          break;
670:        case 22 :
671:          rv = getline( GET_ALPHA, 0, 17, 16, 0, 40,
672:                                      songs[4].title);
673:          break;
674:        case 23 :
675:          rv = getline( GET_NUM, 0, 17, 59, 0, 2,
676:                                      songs[4].minutes);
677:          zero_fill_field(songs[4].minutes, 2);
678:          write_string(songs[4].minutes,
679:                       ct.fld_fcol, ct.fld_bcol, 17, 59);
680:          break;
681:        case 24 :
682:          rv = getline( GET_NUM, 0, 17, 62, 0, 2,
683:                                      songs[4].seconds);
```

```
684:          zero_fill_field(songs[4].seconds, 2);
685:          write_string(songs[4].seconds,
686:                     ct.fld_fcol, ct.fld_bcol, 17, 62);
687:          break;
688:       case 25 :
689:          rv = getline( GET_ALPHA, 0, 18, 16, 0, 40,
690:                                          songs[5].title);
691:          break;
692:       case 26 :
693:          rv = getline( GET_NUM, 0, 18, 59, 0, 2,
694:                                          songs[5].minutes);
695:          zero_fill_field(songs[5].minutes, 2);
696:          write_string(songs[5].minutes,
697:                     ct.fld_fcol, ct.fld_bcol, 18, 59);
698:          break;
699:       case 27 :
700:          rv = getline( GET_NUM, 0, 18, 62, 0, 2,
701:                                          songs[5].seconds);
702:          zero_fill_field(songs[5].seconds, 2);
703:          write_string(songs[5].seconds,
704:                     ct.fld_fcol, ct.fld_bcol, 18, 62);
705:          break;
706:       case 28 :
707:          rv = getline( GET_ALPHA, 0, 19, 16, 0, 40,
708:                                          songs[6].title);
709:          break;
710:       case 29 :
711:          rv = getline( GET_NUM, 0, 19, 59, 0, 2,
712:                                          songs[6].minutes);
713:          zero_fill_field(songs[6].minutes, 2);
714:          write_string(songs[6].minutes,
715:                     ct.fld_fcol, ct.fld_bcol, 19, 59);
716:          break;
717:       case 30 :
718:          rv = getline( GET_NUM, 0, 19, 62, 0, 2,
719:                                          songs[6].seconds);
720:          zero_fill_field(songs[6].seconds, 2);
721:          write_string(songs[6].seconds,
722:                     ct.fld_fcol, ct.fld_bcol, 19, 62);
723:          break;
724:    }
725:    return( rv );
726: }
727:
728: /*-------------------------------------------------------*
729:  *    clear_albums_fields()                              *
730:  *-------------------------------------------------------*/
731:
732: int clear_albums_fields(void)
733: {
```

18

continues

Listing 18.2. continued

```
734:    int ctr;
735:
736:    getline(CLEAR_FIELD, 0, 31, 0, 0, 0, albums.title);
737:    getline(CLEAR_FIELD, 0, 26, 0, 0, 0, albums.group);
738:    getline(CLEAR_FIELD, 0,  3, 0, 0, 0, albums.medium_code);
739:    getline(CLEAR_FIELD, 0,  2, 0, 0, 0, albums.date_purch.month);
740:    getline(CLEAR_FIELD, 0,  2, 0, 0, 0, albums.date_purch.day);
741:    getline(CLEAR_FIELD, 0,  2, 0, 0, 0, albums.date_purch.year);
742:    getline(CLEAR_FIELD, 0,  6, 0, 0, 0, albums.cost);
743:    getline(CLEAR_FIELD, 0,  6, 0, 0, 0, albums.value);
744:
745:    for( ctr = 0; ctr < 7; ctr++ )
746:    {
747:       getline(CLEAR_FIELD, 0, 41, 0, 0, 0, songs[ctr].title);
748:       getline(CLEAR_FIELD, 0,  3, 0, 0, 0, songs[ctr].minutes);
749:       getline(CLEAR_FIELD, 0,  3, 0, 0, 0, songs[ctr].seconds);
750:       songs[ctr].del_flag = FALSE;
751:       songs[ctr].next = 0;
752:    }
753:    /* Save to memory location */
754:    memcpy(song_ptr+((song_pg-1)*SEVEN_SONGS),
755:           &songs, SEVEN_SONGS);
756:    return(0);
757: }
758:
759: /*-------------------------------------------------------*
760:  *    add_adata()                                        *
761:  *                                                       *
762:  *    Returns  0 - No Errors                             *
763:  *            >0 - File I/O Error                        *
764:  *            <0 - Missing info before can store         *
765:  *-------------------------------------------------------*/
766:
767: int add_adata()
768: {
769:    int rv = NO_ERROR;
770:
771:    /* Verify data fields */
772:    rv = verify_adata();
773:    if ( rv == NO_ERROR )
774:    {
775:       /* Check to see if matches old rec */
776:       /* If match - then update db record only */
777:       if ( stricmp(alb_prev.title, albums.title) == 0)
778:       {
779:          /* Rewrite ALBUMS DATA */
780:          rv = put_rec(disp_rec, db_fp,
781:              sizeof(albums), 0, (char *)&albums);
782:
783:          /* Now Update SONGS */
```

```
784:            if (rv == NO_ERROR)
785:                rv = update_songs();
786:
787:            display_msg_box("Record updated!",
788:                ct.db_fcol, ct.db_bcol);
789:        }
790:        else
791:        {
792:            /* Keys no longer match - need to
793:               add this key as a new one */
794:            rv = add_album_rec();
795:            display_msg_box("Record added!",
796:                ct.db_fcol, ct.db_bcol);
797:        }
798:    }
799:
800:    return(rv);
801: }
802:
803: /*-----------------------------------------------------*
804:  *    Verify data fields                               *
805:  *-----------------------------------------------------*/
806: int verify_adata()
807: {
808:    int rv = NO_ERROR;
809:
810:    if( strlen( albums.title ) == 0 )
811:    {
812:        display_msg_box("Must enter a Title",
813:            ct.err_fcol, ct.err_bcol);
814:        rv = -1;
815:    }
816:    else
817:    {
818:        /* edit date and any other fields */
819:
820:    }
821:
822:    return(rv);
823: }
824:
825: /*-----------------------------------------------------*
826:  *    Opens SONGS DBF                                  *
827:  *-----------------------------------------------------*/
828: int open_songs()
829: {
830:
831:    int rv = NO_ERROR;
832:
833:    if( (song_fp = fopen(SONGS_DBF, "r+b" )) == NULL )
```

continues

621

Listing 18.2. continued

```
834:    {
835:      /* Doesn't exist - create it */
836:      if( (song_fp = fopen(SONGS_DBF, "w+b")) == NULL )
837:      {
838:        rv = CREATE_ERROR;
839:      }
840:      else
841:      {
842:        total_songs = 0;  /* First time file opened */
843:      }
844:    }
845:    else    /* Get total songs from song file */
846:    {
847:      rv = get_rec(0, song_fp, sizeof(int), 0,
848:                 (char *)&total_songs);
849:    }
850:
851:    return(rv);
852: }
853:
854: /*-----------------------------------------------------*
855:  *    display_albums_help()                            *
856:  *-----------------------------------------------------*/
857:
858: void display_albums_help(void)
859: {
860:    int  ctr;
861:    char *scrnbuffer;
862:
863:    char helptext[19][45] = {
864:        "              Musical Items",
865:        "-----------------------------------------",
866:        "",
867:        "",
868:        "This is a screen for entering musical",
869:        "items such as albums.          ",
870:        "To exit screen, press <F3> or <ESC>. ",
871:        "",
872:        "",
873:        "Up to 91 songs can be entered for each",
874:        "album.  Songs are entered 7 per page. Use",
875:        "The Page Up and Page Down keys to add or",
876:        "view additional songs.",
877:        "",
878:        "",
879:        "",
880:        "   ***  Press any key to continue ***",
881:        "",
882:        "-----------------------------------------" };
```

```
883:
884:     scrnbuffer = save_screen_area(2, 23, 28, 78 );
885:     cursor_off();
886:
887:     grid( 3, 23, 28, 77, ct.shdw_fcol, ct.bg_bcol, 3 );
888:     box(2, 22, 29, 78, SINGLE_BOX, FILL_BOX,
889:                        ct.help_fcol, ct.help_bcol);
890:
891:     for( ctr = 0; ctr < 19; ctr++ )
892:     {
893:       write_string( helptext[ctr],
894:                   ct.help_fcol, ct.help_bcol, 3+ctr, 32 );
895:     }
896:
897:     getch();
898:     cursor_on();
899:     restore_screen_area(scrnbuffer);
900: }
901:
902: /*=========================================================*
903:  *                    end of listing                       *
904:  *=========================================================*/
```

18

Note: The *Record of Records!* application should have several source files not including the TYAC.LIB library. The files that you should be compiling include:

RECOFREC.C	ABOUT.C	
ALBMABAR.C	GRPSABAR.C	MEDMABAR.C
MMNUABAR.C		
MEDIUM.C	ALBUMS.C	GROUPS.C
ADDMREC.C	DELMREC.C	PROCMREC.C
ADDGREC.C	DELGREC.C	PROCGREC.C

To these files, you should link the TYAC.LIB library, which should contain all the functions learned in this book including those from earlier today. Following, you will be presented with four more files that will need to be compiled and linked with these. These are:

ADDAREC.C   DELAREC.C   PROCAREC.C   SONGS.C

> **Warning:** If you compile the *Record of Records!* application with the preceding ALBUMS.C listing, you may get unresolved externals for `del_alb_rec()`, `proc_alb_rec()`, `add_album_rec()`, `reset_memory()`, `update_songs()`, `add_new_songs()`, and `calc_nbr_songs()`. These new functions will all be covered later today.

 While the ALBUMS.C listing is much longer than the other screen listings, this is mainly a result of the number of fields on the screen. Listing 18.2 presents a nearly complete source file. You'll still need to create the musical item I/O functions to eliminate the unresolved externals. In addition, you'll need to update the action bar to also contain the I/O functions. Because the functionality of adding songs is unique, you'll also need to create several additional functions specifically for them.

The beginning of this listing is nearly identical to the medium code and the group information listings. The first real difference comes in line 53. A second data file is defined for holding the songs. Lines 60 to 63 also offer some differences. Line 60 declares an album structure, `ALBUM_REC`. Line 61 declares a pointer to this structure. Line 62 declares a second album structure, `alb_prev`. This is similar to what you have seen before.

Starting in line 63 are several new statements that will be used for holding songs. Line 63 declares an array of `SONG_REC` structures that will be used to hold seven songs. This is the number of songs that are presented on the screen. Two variables, `song_pg` and `max_song_pg`, are declared in lines 65 and 66 to keep track of song pages. Because seven songs can be displayed on the screen at a time, they are grouped together as a page. If the screen is displaying song tracks one to seven, then the first page is displayed. Song tracks eight to 14 make up the second page, 15 to 21 make up the third page, and so on. The `song_pg` variable keeps track of which page is currently displayed. The `max_song_pg` variable keeps track of what the highest page for the current musical item record is.

Because you don't know how many songs there will be, you'll need to dynamically allocate storage space for them. Lines 68 and 69 declare two pointers, `song_ptr` and `temp_ptr`, that will be used for setting up the storage areas. To help in allocating the appropriate amount of memory, lines 71 and 72 contain two defined constants, `ONE_SONG` and `SEVEN_SONGS`. These will be used in allocating the appropriate amounts of memory later in the listing.

The processing of the Musical Items screen begins in the same manner as the other entry and edit program. Line 83 calls the open_files() function to open the main data and index files. This is followed in line 85 by a call to open_songs(). Because open_files() only opens one data file and one index file, the song file must be opened separately.

The open_songs() function is presented in lines 825 to 852. This function uses the open() function to open the file for reading. If the file doesn't exist, then it is created in line 836. If the file is created, then the total number of songs, total_songs, is set to zero in line 842. If the file already existed, then line 847 gets the number of songs from the beginning of the file.

Once all the files are opened, memory is allocated to hold the first song page (line 89). If the allocation was successful, then processing continues. In line 94, memset() is used to clear the alb_prev structure to NULL values. Lines 95 and 96 set the max_song_pg and song_pg variables to one because a new record only has one page. Because a record is not yet displayed, disp_rec is set to zero in line 98. At this point, processing begins to follow the same flow as the other screens.

When the files are closed, the song data file must be closed separately because the close_files() function only closes the main data file and index file. Line 105 uses fclose() to close the song file. In addition to closing the song file, you need to free the dynamic memory that was allocated to hold the song. This is accomplished in line 107.

18

> **Expert Tip:** When using dynamic memory allocation functions such as malloc(), always verify that memory was allocated.

Most of the other functions in the listing operate like their counterparts in the medium code screen. The clear_albums_fields() function in lines 728 to 757 uses getline() to clear the fields. The clear_albums_fields() function also clears out the dynamic memory by copying the cleared song structure to the dynamic memory area (lines 754 to 755). The draw_albums_screen() function in lines 129 to 147 also operates in a familiar manner.

The *get_albums_input_data()* Function

The get_albums_input_data() function is presented in lines 275 to 524. The overall structure of this function is the same as the Medium Code screen. A few of the cases have differences that should be reviewed one at a time. The switch statement in line 307 calls the get_albums_data() function. The get_albums_data() is presented in lines 526 to 726. It doesn't offer anything that hasn't already been presented.

The first real difference can be seen in the F4 case, which is used for adding a record. In line 334, the songs that are currently displayed on the screen are copied to the memory area that has been dynamically allocated. This is followed by line 336, which calls the add_adata() function to do the actual adding. If the add is successful, then lines 339 to 353 are executed. Line 339 resets the display record to zero, and line 340 calls reset_memory() to free the dynamic memory that had been allocated. The reset_memory() function is presented in the SONGS.C listing later today. The fields are then cleared and the screen is redrawn.

The F5 case in lines 355 to 376 is used for updating information. This code follows the same flow as the add case. The only difference is that the fatal error message in line 372 is more specific to changing data instead of writing data.

The next few cases aren't really different from the Medium Code screens. The delete case is activated by F6. This function calls del_alb_rec() in line 383. The del_alb_rec() function will be covered later today. The F7 and F8 cases call proc_alb_rec(), which will also be covered later. Both of these functions will have similarities to their medium code screen counterparts.

The Page Up and Page Down Functions

The page up and page down functions are different for the Musical Items screen than they are for the Medium Code or Group Information screens. The page down function displays the next seven songs. The page up function displays the previous seven. If there isn't a previous page, or if the maximum number of pages has been reached, then the system will beep.

Note: Line 455 sets the maximum number of pages that can be displayed to 13.

A structure was declared earlier called songs. This structure holds seven songs because that is the number of songs displayed on the screen. The user of the application can enter more than seven songs by pressing page down. Each time page down is pressed, an additional area of dynamic memory is allocated. Each of these areas can be referred to as a page. Each page is declared a size that can hold seven songs. Figure 18.3 illustrates the structure and the dynamic area for pages.

Figure 18.3. *The song structure and the dynamic song pages.*

As you page down, additional pages may be added to the end of the dynamic memory area. The information for the current page is copied to the songs structure. As you page up and page down, information is swapped to and from the songs structure. The song information that is currently displayed on the screen is kept in the structure.

> **Note:** You could work directly from the dynamic memory and not with the songs structure; however, the code becomes more complicated.

Page down is presented in lines 448 to 488. The first step is to copy the current song structure information to the dynamic memory. This is done in line 450 with the memcpy() function. Line 452 then increments the current page, song_pg, to the next page.

> **Review Tip:** The memcpy() function is an ANSI C function that copies from one memory location to another.

In line 455, a check is done to see if more than 13 pages have been allocated. The limit of 13 pages is subjective. You can raise or lower this limit. If they were already on the 13th page, then the computer beeps in line 457 and the song_pg is reset to 13.

If song_pg is less than 13, then the next page can be displayed. This is handled in lines 461 to 483. In line 463, a check is done to see if the current song page is within the pages that have already been allocated. This is done by checking the max_song_pg value. If the new song_pg is greater, then a new page must be allocated. This is done in line 466 using the realloc() function to increase the overall size of the allocated memory. If the realloc() fails, then line 472 displays an error message, the pointer to the song pages is reset to its original value (line 474), and the song page, song_pg, is set back to the original page.

If the allocation was successful, then line 479 is called. This line uses the memset() function to clear out the newly-allocated page of memory. Once done, the maximum page counter, max_song_pg, is incremented to include the new page.

Review Tip: The memset() is an ANSI function that fills a specified memory location with a character value.

The page down logic ends with resetting the screen with the field position being set to 10, the first song field. The Musical Items screen is then redrawn. With this, the page down functionality is complete.

The page up functionality is much simpler. With page up, you don't have to worry about allocating additional pages. Line 492 starts by copying the current song information back to the dynamic memory area. The song page, song_pg, is then decremented (line 494). If the line number is less than one, then you are at the beginning of the dynamic memory area. The computer beeps (line 497) and the song page is set back to the original page (line 498). If a previous page is available, then the screen position is set to 10 and the screen is redrawn.

Supportive Functions: The SONGS.C Listing

Due to some of the extra complexity in the Musical Items screen, several additional functions are needed. These are functions that were not present with the medium code listings. Listing 18.3 contains the SONGS.C file. This file contains four functions that are called by other portions of the musical items code. These are add_new_songs(), update_songs(), calc_nbr_songs(), and reset_memory().

Listing 18.3. SONGS.C. Functions needed for the Musical Items screen.

```
 1:   /*========================================================
 2:    * Filename: SONGS.C
 3:    *
 4:    * Author:    Bradley L. Jones
 5:    *            Gregory L. Guntle
 6:    *
 7:    * Purpose: Routines for add/changing and calculating
 8:    *          songs for working with I/O.
 9:    *
10:    *========================================================*/
```

```
11:
12:   #include <stdio.h>
13:   #include <stdlib.h>
14:   #include <string.h>
15:   #include "records.h"
16:   #include "tyac.h"
17:
18:   /*------------------*
19:    * Global Variables *
20:    *------------------*/
21:
22:   extern FILE *idx_fp;        /* Main File ptr to data file */
23:   extern FILE *db_fp;         /* Data file */
24:   extern FILE *song_fp;       /* Points to Songs */
25:   extern nbr_records;         /* Total # of rec for albums */
26:   extern int start_rec;
27:   extern int disp_rec;
28:   extern int total_songs;     /* Total songs in the song file */
29:
30:   extern ALBUM_REC albums;
31:   extern ALBUM_REC alb_prev;
32:   extern SONG_REC songs[7];
33:
34:   extern int song_pg;         /* Tracks pg of songs being displayed */
35:   extern int max_song_pg;     /* Max number of pages allocated */
36:                               /*      to hold the songs        */
37:   extern char *song_ptr;      /* Ptr to dynamic mem where songs are */
38:
39:   #define ONE_SONG           sizeof(songs[0])
40:   #define SEVEN_SONGS        sizeof(songs)
41:
42:   /*-------------------*
43:    *     prototypes    *
44:    *-------------------*/
45:
46:   #include "recofrec.h"
47:
48:   /*----------------------------------------------------------*
49:    *  add_new_songs();                                        *
50:    *  Returns:  0 - No Error                                  *
51:    *            >0 Error - see defines at top of file         *
52:    *----------------------------------------------------------*/
53:   int add_new_songs()
54:   {
55:     int rv = NO_ERROR;
56:     int recnbr;
57:     int pgs, sngs;
58:     int hold_start;
59:
60:     /* Starting point to add record */
61:     hold_start = total_songs+1;
```

continues

Listing 18.3. continued

```
62:    recnbr = hold_start;
63:
64:    /* Loop through the all the pages */
65:    /* Start at first page of songs - 1 page = 7 songs*/
66:    pgs = 0;
67:    while ( pgs < max_song_pg && rv == NO_ERROR )
68:    {
69:      sngs = 0;  /* Reset songs to start at top */
70:      /* Load structure with appropriate memory location */
71:      memcpy(&songs, song_ptr + (pgs*SEVEN_SONGS),
72:              SEVEN_SONGS);
73:
74:      /* Now loop through individual songs */
75:      while ( sngs < 7 && rv == NO_ERROR )
76:      {
77:        /* Set the next pointer to point to the next
78:           possible record */
79:        /* Are we writing last record ? */
80:        if (sngs == 6 && pgs == max_song_pg-1)
81:          songs[sngs].next = 0;
82:        else
83:          songs[sngs].next = recnbr+1;
84:        rv = put_rec(recnbr, song_fp, ONE_SONG, sizeof(int),
85:                     (char *)&songs[sngs]);
86:        sngs++;        /* Next song in structure */
87:        recnbr++;      /* Next record location */
88:      }
89:      pgs++;     /* Next page in memory */
90:    }
91:
92:    if (rv == NO_ERROR)
93:    {
94:      total_songs += (recnbr-hold_start); /* Update # of songs */
95:      /* Save the total to the file */
96:      rv = put_rec(0, song_fp, sizeof(int), 0,
97:              (char *)&total_songs);
98:    }
99:
100:   return(rv);
101: }
102:
103:
104: /*------------------------------------------------------*
105:  *  update_songs();                                     *
106:  *  Returns:  0 - No Error                              *
107:  *               >0 Error - see defines at top of file  *
108:  *------------------------------------------------------*/
109: int update_songs()
110: {
111:   int rv=NO_ERROR;
112:   int recnbr;
```

```
113:    SONG_REC one_song;       /* For holding one song */
114:    int pgs, sngs;
115:    ALBUM_INDEX alb_idx;
116:    int next_rec;            /* Holds ptr to next song rec */
117:    int new_nbr_songs;
118:    int adding_new = FALSE;      /* Flag for adding new recs */
119:
120:    /* Calc nbr songs - mostly needed to eliminate
121:       any blank pages - resets max_song_pg to be accurate */
122:    new_nbr_songs = calc_nbr_songs();
123:
124:    /* Get starting record number */
125:    rv = get_rec(disp_rec, idx_fp, sizeof(alb_idx),
126:                 sizeof(int)*2, (char *)&alb_idx);
127:    if (rv == NO_ERROR)
128:    {
129:      recnbr = alb_idx.song;     /* Get first record from index */
130:
131:      /* Loop through all the pages */
132:      /* Start at first page of songs - 1 page = 7 songs*/
133:      pgs = 0;
134:      while ( pgs < max_song_pg && rv == NO_ERROR )
135:      {
136:        sngs = 0;   /* Reset songs to start at top */
137:        /* Load structure with appropriate memory location */
138:        memcpy(&songs, song_ptr + (pgs*SEVEN_SONGS),
139:               SEVEN_SONGS);
140:
141:        /* Now loop through individual songs - skip last one */
142:        while ( sngs < 7 && rv == NO_ERROR)
143:        {
144:          if (!adding_new)
145:          {
146:            rv = get_rec(recnbr, song_fp, ONE_SONG,
147:                  sizeof(int), (char *)&one_song);
148:            next_rec = one_song.next;
149:          }
150:
151:          /* Are we at end of chain & there is still more
152:             to come - another page                    */
153:          if (next_rec == 0 && pgs+1<max_song_pg)
154:          {
155:            adding_new = TRUE;
156:          }
157:
158:          if (adding_new)
159:          {
160:            total_songs++;           /* Increase global counter */
161:            next_rec = total_songs;     /* Next rec to put */
162:            /* Ck to see if at end of records to store */
163:            if (pgs+1 == max_song_pg && sngs == 6)
```

continues

Listing 18.3. continued

```
164:              {
165:                 next_rec = 0;       /* Mark as end of song */
166:              }
167:           }
168:
169:          if (rv == NO_ERROR)
170:          {
171:             songs[sngs].next = next_rec;
172:             rv = put_rec(recnbr, song_fp, ONE_SONG, sizeof(int),
173:                      (char *)&songs[sngs]);
174:             sngs++;  /* Next song in structure */
175:             recnbr = next_rec;       /* Follow chain */
176:          }
177:        }
178:      pgs++;      /* Next page in memory */
179:     }
180:
181:     /* Have we added new records ? */
182:     /* If so - let's adjust total records */
183:     if (adding_new)
184:     {
185:        total_songs--;     /* Adjust for true number */
186:     }
187:
188:     /* Are we adding more records than previously there ? */
189:     /* If so update index record as well */
190:     if (new_nbr_songs > alb_idx.nbr_songs)
191:     {
192:       alb_idx.nbr_songs = new_nbr_songs;
193:        /* Resave index */
194:       rv = put_rec(disp_rec, idx_fp, sizeof(alb_idx),
195:              sizeof(int)*2, (char *)&alb_idx);
196:     }
197:
198:     /* Resave total number of songs in file */
199:     if (rv == NO_ERROR)
200:     {
201:        rv = put_rec(0, song_fp, sizeof(int), 0,
202:              (char *)&total_songs);
203:     }
204:
205:    fflush(song_fp);
206:   }
207:
208:   return(rv);
209: }
210:
211: /*------------------------------------------------------*
212: *  calc_nbr_songs();                                    *
213: *                                                       *
```

```
214:   *   This calculates the number of songs.  It will        *
215:   *   return a multiple of 7.  It is mostly used to          *
216:   *   determine the true number of pages - so a lot of       *
217:   *   blank song records don't get written to disk.          *
218:   *                                                          *
219:   *   Returns: number of songs (multiple of 7)               *
220:   *-------------------------------------------------------*/
221: int calc_nbr_songs()
222: {
223:   int fnd;
224:   int pgs, sngs;
225:   int nbrsongs = 0;
226:
227:   pgs = 0;
228:   while (pgs < max_song_pg)
229:   {
230:     sngs=0;
231:     fnd = FALSE;
232:     /* Load structure with proper mem location */
233:     memcpy(&songs, song_ptr + (pgs*SEVEN_SONGS), SEVEN_SONGS);
234:
235:     while (sngs<7 && !fnd)
236:     {
237:       /* Is there anything in title - if find one
238:          skip rest - use entire block of 7         */
239:       if ( strlen(songs[sngs].title) > 0 )
240:         fnd = TRUE;
241:       else
242:         sngs++;
243:     }
244:
245:     if (fnd)
246:     {
247:       nbrsongs+=7;
248:     }
249:     pgs++;       /* Next page in memory */
250:   }
251:
252:   /* Adjust true number of pages */
253:   /* Make sure at least writing first seven songs */
254:   if (nbrsongs == 0)
255:   {
256:     nbrsongs = 7;
257:   }
258:   max_song_pg = nbrsongs/7;
259:   /* Readjust memory locations as well */
260:   song_ptr = (char *)realloc(song_ptr, max_song_pg*SEVEN_SONGS);
261:   if (song_ptr == NULL)
262:   {
263:     display_msg_box("Memory error !",
264:             ct.err_fcol, ct.err_bcol);
```

continues

Listing 18.3. continued

```
265:    exit(1);
266:   }
267:
268:   return(nbrsongs);
269: }
270:
271: /*----------------------------------------------------------*
272:  *  reset_memory();                                        *
273:  *                                                         *
274:  *  Resets memory - clears it out, adjusts it back to     *
275:  *  a single page, etc.                                    *
276:  *----------------------------------------------------------*/
277: void reset_memory()
278: {
279:   /* Null out current memory block */
280:   memset(song_ptr, '\0', max_song_pg*SEVEN_SONGS);
281:
282:   /* Adjust global numbers */
283:   max_song_pg = 1;
284:   song_pg = 1;
285:
286:   /* reduce memory to hold one page - 7 songs */
287:   song_ptr = (char *)realloc(song_ptr, SEVEN_SONGS);
288:   if (song_ptr == NULL)
289:   {
290:     display_msg_box("Memory error - resizing !",
291:             ct.err_fcol, ct.err_bcol);
292:     exit(1);
293:   }
294:
295: }
```

Analysis   The add_new_songs() function is presented in lines 48 to 101. This
function is used to add songs when a musical item record is being added.
This function adds songs to the song data file. Songs are added in groups
of seven. Remember, each group of seven is considered a page. For each page, the songs
are added one at a time. The while statement starting in line 67 controls the looping
of the pages.

A second while statement in line 75 controls the adding of each of the seven records
on each page. As each song is added, it is provided with a pointer to the next song. If
the song being added is the last song, then the pointer to the next record is set to zero
to signal the end of the song linked list (line 81). If it isn't the last song, then the pointer
to the next record is set to the next record number (line 83). Once the next pointer
is set, line 84 adds the record using the put_rec() function. After adding the record,

the song counter, sngs, and the record counter, recnbr, are both incremented for the next song.

Once all the songs on each page are added, the processing continues to line 92. It is here that a check is done to ensure that there hasn't been an error. If there hasn't been an error, then the total number of songs is updated. Line 96 updates the first position of the song file with the new total number of songs.

Updating song records is more complicated than adding songs. When you add songs, you are always working from the end of the file. Updating requires reading each record already in the database. Once you reach the last song record, you may need to add new songs to the end. The update_songs() function in lines 104 to 209 does just this.

The update function starts off with a call to the calc_nbr_songs() function. This function is presented in lines 211 to 269. The calc_nbr_songs() loops through each page to see if a song has been entered. This function uses a flag, fnd, to signal if there is a record on a page. If a record is found on a page, then the page must be added, so the number of songs, nbrsongs, is incremented by seven.

After checking each page for songs, line 254 checks to see if there were any songs. If there weren't any songs, then line 256 sets the number of songs to seven so that at least one page of songs is added. Line 258 determines how many pages of songs there are. This is done by dividing the number of songs by seven. The global variable, max_song_pg, is then reset to this number. The allocated memory is then adjusted accordingly in line 260. The final result for the number of songs is returned to the calling function in line 268.

The final function in this listing is the reset_memory() function in lines 271 to 295. This function frees the memory above the first page. When you are ready to start a new record, you need to reset the amount of memory that is being used. This function starts by clearing out the first page of memory. Lines 283 and 284 reset the maximum song page to 1 and the current song page to 1. The final step to resetting the memory is to reset the allocated amount down to a single page. This is done with the realloc() function in line 287. As should always be done, a check is performed to ensure that the allocation was competed without an error.

Adding a Record: The *add_album()_rec* Function

The add_album_rec() function is used to add a new record to the Musical Items screen's data files. This function is presented in Listing 18.4.

Type Listing 18.4. ADDAREC.C. Adding a medium code.

```
 1:  /*=========================================================
 2:   * Filename: ADDAREC.C
 3:   *
 4:   * Author:    Bradley L. Jones
 5:   *            Gregory L. Guntle
 6:   *
 7:   * Purpose: Adds a record to the ALBUMS DBF
 8:   *
 9:   *=========================================================*/
10:
11:  #include <stdio.h>
12:  #include <string.h>
13:  #include "records.h"
14:  #include "tyac.h"
15:
16:  /*------------------*
17:   * Global Variables *
18:   *------------------*/
19:
20:  extern FILE *idx_fp;        /* Main File ptr to data file */
21:  extern FILE *db_fp;         /* Data file */
22:  extern FILE *song_fp;       /* Points to Songs */
23:  extern nbr_records;         /* Total # of rec for albums */
24:  extern int start_rec;
25:  extern int disp_rec;
26:  extern int total_songs;     /* Total songs in the song file */
27:
28:  extern ALBUM_REC albums;
29:  extern ALBUM_REC alb_prev;
30:  extern SONG_REC songs[7];
31:
32:  /*--------------------*
33:   *     prototypes     *
34:   *--------------------*/
35:
36:  #include "recofrec.h"
37:  int add_album_rec(void);
38:
39:  /*----------------------------------------------------------*
40:   * add_album_rec();                                         *
41:   * Returns:  0 - No Error                                   *
42:   *           >0 Error - see defines at top of file          *
43:   *----------------------------------------------------------*/
44:
45:  int add_album_rec()
46:  {
47:   int result;
48:   ALBUM_INDEX temp, newrec;
49:   int rv = NO_ERROR;
```

```
50:    int found;
51:    int srch_rec;
52:
53:    nbr_records++;
54:    if (nbr_records == 1)      /* Is this first record */
55:    {
56:      temp.prev = 0;
57:      temp.next = 0;
58:      temp.data = 1;              /* First rec in data file */
59:      temp.song = total_songs+1;
60:      temp.del_flag = FALSE;
61:      temp.nbr_songs = calc_nbr_songs();
62:      strcpy(temp.title, albums.title);
63:
64:      /* Write Index record */
65:      rv = put_rec(nbr_records, idx_fp, sizeof(temp),
66:                    sizeof(int)*2, (char *) &temp);
67:      if (rv == NO_ERROR)       /* No Error from prior */
68:      {
69:        /* Store Album data */
70:        rv = put_rec(nbr_records, db_fp, sizeof(albums),
71:                      0, (char *) &albums);
72:
73:        /* Store songs */
74:        if (rv == NO_ERROR)
75:          rv = add_new_songs();
76:      }
77:
78:      /* Update Alpha starting pointer */
79:      if (rv == NO_ERROR)
80:      {
81:        start_rec = nbr_records; /* Update global starting point */
82:        rv = update_header();
83:        fflush(song_fp);
84:      }
85:
86:    }
87:    /* Need to search for appropriate place to hold rec */
88:    else
89:    {
90:      found = FALSE;
91:      srch_rec = start_rec;
92:      while (!found)
93:      {
94:        rv = get_rec(srch_rec, idx_fp, sizeof(temp),
95:                      sizeof(int)*2, (char *)&temp);
96:        /* Proceed only if no errors */
97:        if (rv == NO_ERROR)
98:        {
99:          /* Compare two keys - ignoring CASE of keys */
```

continues

Listing 18.4. continued

```
100:        result = stricmp(albums.title, temp.title);
101:        if (result < 0)    /* New key is < this rec key */
102:        {
103:          /* Found place to put it - store info */
104:          found = TRUE;
105:          /* See if this new rec is < start rec  */
106:          /* If so - need to adjust starting ptr */
107:          if (srch_rec == start_rec)
108:            start_rec = nbr_records;
109:
110:          /* First build new Index rec & store new rec */
111:          newrec.prev = temp.prev;  /* Previous rec     */
112:          newrec.next = srch_rec;    /* Point to rec just read */
113:          newrec.data = nbr_records;  /* Pt to data */
114:          newrec.song = total_songs+1;
115:          newrec.del_flag = FALSE;
116:          newrec.nbr_songs = calc_nbr_songs();
117:          strcpy(newrec.title, albums.title);
118:
119:          rv = put_rec(nbr_records, idx_fp, sizeof(newrec),
120:                       sizeof(int)*2, (char *)&newrec);
121:          if (rv == NO_ERROR)
122:          {
123:            /* Update previous rec */
124:            temp.prev = nbr_records;
125:            rv = put_rec(srch_rec, idx_fp, sizeof(temp),
126:                         sizeof(int)*2, (char *)&temp);
127:
128:            /* Now write data - only if no errors */
129:            if (rv == NO_ERROR)
130:            {
131:              /* Now write Album data */
132:              rv = put_rec(nbr_records, db_fp, sizeof(albums),
133:                           0, (char *)&albums);
134:
135:              /* Now write Songs */
136:              if (rv == NO_ERROR)
137:                rv = add_new_songs();
138:            }
139:
140:            /* Now check on updating Next pointer */
141:            /* Is there a ptr pointing to this new rec ?*/
142:            if (rv == NO_ERROR)
143:            {
144:              if (newrec.prev !=0 )
145:              {
146:                rv = get_rec(newrec.prev, idx_fp, sizeof(temp),
147:                             sizeof(int)*2, (char *)&temp);
148:                if ( rv == NO_ERROR)
```

```
149:                   {
150:                       temp.next = nbr_records;
151:                       rv = put_rec(newrec.prev, idx_fp, sizeof(temp),
152:                                    sizeof(int)*2, (char *)&temp);
153:                   }
154:               }
155:           }
156:
157:        }
158:     }
159:     else    /* new rec >= alpha, adjust ptr */
160:     {
161:       if (temp.next == 0) /* End of chain - add to end */
162:       {
163:         found = TRUE;
164:
165:         /* Build Index record */
166:         /* Point backwards to prev rec */
167:         newrec.prev = srch_rec;
168:         newrec.next = 0;          /* There is no next rec */
169:         newrec.data = nbr_records;
170:         newrec.song = total_songs+1;
171:         newrec.del_flag = FALSE;
172:         newrec.nbr_songs = calc_nbr_songs();
173:         strcpy(newrec.title, albums.title);
174:
175:         rv = put_rec(nbr_records, idx_fp, sizeof(newrec),
176:                      sizeof(int)*2, (char *)&newrec);
177:         if (rv == NO_ERROR)
178:         {
179:           /* Update previous rec */
180:           temp.next = nbr_records;
181:           rv = put_rec(srch_rec, idx_fp, sizeof(temp),
182:                        sizeof(int)*2, (char *)&temp);
183:           if (rv == NO_ERROR)
184:           {
185:             /* Now write data */
186:             rv = put_rec(nbr_records, db_fp, sizeof(albums),
187:                          0, (char *)&albums);
188:             if (rv == NO_ERROR)
189:             {
190:               /* Store songs */
191:               rv = add_new_songs();
192:             }
193:           }
194:         }
195:       }
196:       else  /* Not at end - get next rec ptr */
197:         srch_rec = temp.next;
198:     }
```

continues

Listing 18.4. continued

```
199:      }
200:      else
201:        found = TRUE;  /* Exit because of error */
202:    }   /* End of While */
203:
204:    /* Update starting alpha ptr in hdr */
205:    if (rv == NO_ERROR)
206:    {
207:      rv = update_header();
208:    }
209:
210:    /* Makes sure file gets updated */
211:    fflush(idx_fp);
212:    fflush(db_fp);
213:    fflush(song_fp);
214:
215:  }  /* End else */
216:
217:  return(rv);
218: }
```

Analysis This function is very similar to the add_medium_rec() function presented on Day 17. The main difference is that after adding to the album data file and the album index file, you must also add the individual songs to the song file. You were already presented with a function that does the adding, add_new_songs().

There is a second difference that needs to be covered. This is the use of a delete flag. Rather than actually deleting records from the files, a delete flag is used. A delete flag is used to state whether a record is active or not. Instead of physically removing a record from the database, it is simply removed from the indexes. By removing the record from the indexes, you cause it to be inaccessible.

There are reasons for using a delete flag. It is used in the musical instrument files to make the logic easier. You don't have to move around the records in the same way that you did for the medium screen. Additionally, if you use a delete flag, it gives you the ability to undelete an item. The functionality to undelete isn't presented in this book. Undeleting is just a matter of switching the delete flag from TRUE back to FALSE. You'll see in the delete code that deleting is just a matter of setting all the delete flags to TRUE.

Deleting a Record:
The *del_alb_rec()* Function

The del_alb_rec() function is used to delete musical items. Listing 18.5 presents the DELAREC.C source file, which contains this function. Deleting records in the musical items file is done differently than the medium code and group files.

 Listing 18.5. DELAREC.C. Deleting a musical item.

```
 1:    /*============================================================
 2:     * Filename: DELAREC.C
 3:     *
 4:     * Author:    Bradley L. Jones
 5:     *            Gregory L. Guntle
 6:     *
 7:     * Purpose: Deletes a record from the DB
 8:     *            For albums - this simply marks the record
 9:     *            as being deleted.  It also marks the data record
10:     *            as being deleted.  Then it spins through all the
11:     *            songs marking them as deleted.  It leaves
12:     *            all pointers alone.  This allows the reader the
13:     *            ability to write an undelete function.
14:     *
15:     *============================================================*/
16:
17:    #include <stdio.h>
18:
19:    #include "records.h"
20:    #include "tyac.h"
21:
22:    /*-------------------*
23:     *  Global Variables  *
24:     *-------------------*/
25:
26:    extern FILE *idx_fp;        /* Main File ptr to data file */
27:    extern FILE *db_fp;         /* Data file */
28:    extern FILE *song_fp;       /* Pointer for songs */
29:    extern nbr_records;         /* Total # of rec for mediums */
30:    extern int start_rec;
31:    extern int disp_rec;
32:    extern int total_songs;
33:
34:    /*-----------------*
35:     * Defined constants*
36:     *-----------------*/
37:
38:    #define ALBUMS_DBF    "ALBUMS.DBF"
39:    #define ALBUMS_IDX    "ALBUMS.IDX"
```

continues

Listing 18.5. continued

```
40:    #define SONGS_DBF      "SONGS.DBF"
41:    #define HELP_DBF       "ALBUMS.HLP"
42:
43:    /*-----------------------*
44:     * structure declarations *
45:     *-----------------------*/
46:    extern ALBUM_REC albums;
47:    extern ALBUM_REC alb_prev;
48:    extern SONG_REC songs[7];
49:
50:    extern int song_pg;       /* Tracks pg of songs being displayed */
51:    extern int max_song_pg; /* Max number of pages allocated to   */
52:                             /* hold the songs                     */
53:    extern char *song_ptr;  /* Ptr to dynamic mem where songs are */
54:
55:    #define ONE_SONG          sizeof(songs[0])
56:    #define SEVEN_SONGS       sizeof(songs)
57:
58:
59:    int del_alb_rec()
60:    {
61:      int rv = NO_ERROR;
62:      ALBUM_INDEX temp, delrec;
63:      ALBUM_REC hold_data;
64:      SONG_REC hold_song;
65:      int chg;
66:      int srch_rec;
67:      long fpos;
68:      int true_rec;  /* Includes deleted records as well */
69:      int rec;
70:
71:      /* Are we trying to delete a blank record */
72:      if (disp_rec != 0)  /* No - then proceed */
73:      {
74:        /* Get the index info for this rec */
75:        rv = get_rec(disp_rec, idx_fp, sizeof(delrec),
76:              sizeof(int)*2, (char *)&delrec);
77:        if (rv == NO_ERROR)
78:        {
79:          /* Are there any pointers in this rec
80:             If both pointers are 0 - then this must
81:             be the only record in the DB            */
82:          if (delrec.prev == 0 && delrec.next == 0)
83:          {
84:            nbr_records = 0;
85:            disp_rec = 0;
86:            start_rec = 1;
87:            total_songs = 0;
88:          }
89:          else
```

```
90:              {
91:                  chg = FALSE;
92:                  srch_rec = 1;      /* Start at first */
93:                  fseek(idx_fp, 0, SEEK_END); /* Go to end of Index file */
94:                  fpos = ftell(idx_fp);           /* Get nbr of bytes in file*/
95:                  fpos -= sizeof(int)*2;          /* Adjust for header info  */
96:                  true_rec = fpos/(sizeof(temp)); /* Gets number of recs */
97:
98:                  /* Are we deleting the starting alpha record ? */
99:                  if (disp_rec == start_rec)
100:                     start_rec = delrec.next;         /* Reset pointer */
101:
102:                  /* Go until all the ptrs have been adjusted */
103:                  while ( (srch_rec <= true_rec) && (rv == NO_ERROR) )
104:                  {
105:                    rv = get_rec(srch_rec, idx_fp, sizeof(temp),
106:                            sizeof(int)*2, (char *)&temp);
107:                    if (rv == NO_ERROR)
108:                    {
109:                      /* Only do it - rec read has not been deleted */
110:                      if (!temp.del_flag)
111:                      {
112:                        /* There is no need to update pointers for
113:                           the record being deleted - so only do the
114:                           logic below if they don't match          */
115:                        if (srch_rec != disp_rec)
116:                        {
117:
118:                          /* Get record */
119:                          rv = get_rec(srch_rec, idx_fp, sizeof(temp),
120:                                  sizeof(int)*2, (char *)&temp);
121:                          if (rv == NO_ERROR)
122:                          {
123:                            /* Does this rec prev pointer need to
124:                               be adjusted */
125:                            if (temp.prev == disp_rec)
126:                            {
127:                              chg = TRUE;
128:                              temp.prev = delrec.prev;
129:                            }
130:
131:                            if (temp.next == disp_rec)
132:                            {
133:                              chg = TRUE;
134:                              temp.next = delrec.next;
135:                            }
136:
137:                            /* Since not moving last record up -
138:                               the code to do this is not necessary
139:                               for the previous and next pointers    */
```

continues

Listing 18.5. continued

```
140:
141:                          /* Not moving data - so don't adjust
142:                              pointer to data - will leave so
143:                              reader can write an undelete routine */
144:
145:                          /* Only update rec if change has been made */
146:                          if (chg)
147:                          {
148:                              /* Rewrite index back to file in same pos */
149:                              rv = put_rec(srch_rec, idx_fp, sizeof(temp),
150:                                      sizeof(int)*2, (char *)&temp);
151:                              chg = FALSE;
152:                          }
153:
154:                          if (rv == NO_ERROR)
155:                          {
156:                              /* Go to next record */
157:                              srch_rec++;
158:                          }
159:                      }    /* If NO_ERROR  */
160:                  }        /* If SRCH != DISP_REC */
161:              else
162:                      srch_rec++;
163:          }            /* checking for DEL record */
164:          else
165:              srch_rec++;
166:      }                /* NO ERROR  */
167:  }                    /* WHILE */
168:
169:      /* Clean out NEXT/PREV Ptrs in the deleted rec
170:          Index - but leave rec there  and leave data ptrs
171:          alone - they can be used for purging the old recs */
172:      if (rv == NO_ERROR)
173:      {
174:          delrec.prev = 0;
175:          delrec.next = 0;
176:          delrec.nbr_songs = 0;
177:          delrec.del_flag = TRUE;
178:          /* Overwrite data to delete w/Last one */
179:          rv = put_rec(disp_rec, idx_fp, sizeof(delrec),
180:                  sizeof(int)*2, (char *)&delrec);
181:      }
182:
183:      /* DATA     - ALBUMS */
184:      /* Mark the del_flag component of the record    */
185:      /* leave data alone.                            */
```

```
186:            rv = get_rec(delrec.data, db_fp, sizeof(hold_data),
187:                    0, (char *)&hold_data);
188:          if (rv == NO_ERROR)
189:          {
190:            /* Mark flag and rewrite data */
191:            hold_data.del_flag = TRUE;
192:            rv = put_rec(delrec.data, db_fp, sizeof(hold_data),
193:                    0, (char *)&hold_data);
194:          }
195:
196:          /* DATA      - SONGS */
197:          /* Spin through all songs - mark them as deleted */
198:          rec = delrec.song;      /* Starting point */
199:          while (rec !=0 && rv == NO_ERROR)
200:          {
201:            rv = get_rec(rec, song_fp, sizeof(hold_song),
202:                    sizeof(int), (char *)&hold_song);
203:            if (rv == NO_ERROR)
204:            {
205:              hold_song.del_flag = TRUE;
206:              rv = put_rec(rec, song_fp, sizeof(hold_song),
207:                      sizeof(int), (char *)&hold_song);
208:              if (rv == NO_ERROR)
209:                rec = hold_song.next;
210:            }
211:          }
212:        }                        /* end of ELSE  */
213:
214:        if (rv == NO_ERROR)
215:        {
216:          rv = update_header();  /* Update header info */
217:          if (rv == NO_ERROR)
218:            rv = put_rec(0, song_fp, sizeof(int), 0,
219:                (char *)&total_songs);
220:        }
221:
222:        fflush(idx_fp);    /* Make sure all items written to disk*/
223:        fflush(db_fp);
224:        fflush(song_fp);   /* Update song DB as well */
225:
226:      }    /* If NO_ERROR from 1st time */
227:    }      /* If disp_rec != 0  */
228:    else
229:      boop();  /* Let them know - can't delete blank rec */
230:
231:    return(rv);
232: }
```

As stated earlier, the deleting of records in the `del_alb_rec()` operates differently than the `del_med_rec()` function. Rather than physically removing the records from the databases, the `del_flag` field in each structure is set to TRUE. This will give you the ability to undelete. As you can see by the listing, there are several comments that point out the differences between this listing and the `del_med_rec()` listing that was detailed on Day 17.

Processing a Record (Next/Previous)

The last function needed before you'll be able to compile the musical items code without external errors is the `proc_alb_rec()` function. This function is presented in Listing 18.6, which contains the PROCAREC.C source file.

 Listing 18.6. PROCAREC.C. Processing the next and previous records.

```
1:  /*===========================================================
2:   * Filename: PROCAREC.C
3:   *
4:   * Author:   Bradley L. Jones
5:   *           Gregory L. Guntle
6:   *
7:   * Purpose: Process the requests for getting next/prev
8:   *           records from the ALBUMS DBF
9:   *
10:  *=========================================================*/
11:
12: #include <stdio.h>
13: #include <stdlib.h>
14: #include <string.h>
15: #include "records.h"
16: #include "tyac.h"
17:
18: #include "recofrec.h"
19:
20: /*------------------*
21:  * Global Variables *
22:  *------------------*/
23:
24: extern FILE *idx_fp;        /* Main File ptr to data file */
25: extern FILE *db_fp;         /* Data file */
26: extern FILE *song_fp;       /* Pointer for songs */
27: extern nbr_records;         /* Total # of rec for albums */
28: extern int start_rec;
29: extern int disp_rec;
30: extern int total_songs;
31:
```

```
32:   extern ALBUM_REC albums;
33:   extern ALBUM_REC alb_prev;
34:   extern SONG_REC songs[7];
35:
36:   extern int song_pg;      /* Tracks page of songs displayed */
37:   extern int max_song_pg;  /* Max number of pages allocated  */
38:                            /*  to allocated to hold the songs */
39:   extern char *song_ptr;   /* Ptr to dynamic mem where songs are */
40:
41:   #define ONE_SONG         sizeof(songs[0])
42:   #define SEVEN_SONGS      sizeof(songs)
43:
44:
45:   int proc_alb_rec(int);
46:   int get_alb_info(void);
47:
48:   /*-------------------------------------------------------*
49:    *    proc_alb_rec                                       *
50:    *-------------------------------------------------------*/
51:
52:   int proc_alb_rec(int direct)
53:   {
54:     ALBUM_INDEX temp;
55:     int rv = NO_ERROR;
56:
57:     /* Only do - if there are records in the file */
58:     if (nbr_records != 0)
59:     {
60:       /* Do we just need to display the very first rec */
61:       if (disp_rec == 0)
62:       {
63:         disp_rec = start_rec;
64:         rv = get_alb_info();
65:       }
66:       else
67:       {
68:         /* Get Index ptrs for record on screen */
69:         rv = get_rec(disp_rec, idx_fp, sizeof(temp),
70:                 sizeof(int)*2, (char *)&temp);
71:         if (rv == NO_ERROR)
72:         {
73:           if( direct == NEXT_REC )
74:           {
75:             if (temp.next == 0)      /* There is no other rec */
76:             {
77:               boop();                /* No more records */
78:             }
79:             else
80:             {
81:               disp_rec = temp.next;
```

continues

Listing 18.6. continued

```
 82:                 rv = get_alb_info();
 83:             }
 84:         }
 85:         else  /* Need to go backwards */
 86:         {
 87:             if (temp.prev == 0)       /* There is no other rec */
 88:             {
 89:                 boop();                    /* No more records */
 90:             }
 91:             else
 92:             {
 93:                 disp_rec = temp.prev;
 94:                 rv = get_alb_info();
 95:             }
 96:         }
 97:     }
 98:     }
 99:     }
100:     else
101:     {
102:       boop();
103:     }
104:
105:     return(rv);
106: }
107:
108: /* --------------------------------------------- *
109:  *  get_alb_info()                               *
110:  *                                               *
111:  *  Handles getting the Index rec, getting the   *
112:  *  data pointer from the index and then getting *
113:  *  the appropriate data rec.  It also gets the  *
114:  *  songs from the SONGS.DBF file.               *
115:  *                                               *
116:  * --------------------------------------------- */
117:
118: int get_alb_info()
119: {
120:     ALBUM_INDEX temp;
121:     int rv;
122:     int recnbr;
123:     int pgs, sngs;
124:
125:     /* Get Index record for this Request */
126:     rv = get_rec(disp_rec, idx_fp, sizeof(temp),
127:                  sizeof(int)*2, (char *)&temp);
128:     if (rv == NO_ERROR)
129:     {
130:
131:       /* Now get the actual data record to display */
```

```
132:        rv = get_rec(temp.data, db_fp, sizeof(albums),
133:                    0, (char *)&albums);
134:        if (rv == NO_ERROR)
135:        {
136:          /* Setup previous record */
137:          memcpy(&alb_prev, &albums, sizeof(albums));
138:
139:          /* Clear out any items from memory location */
140:          reset_memory();
141:
142:          /* Adjust new max song pages to meet the needs */
143:          /* of the title */
144:          max_song_pg = temp.nbr_songs/7;
145:
146:          /* Does it need more than 1 page ?  */
147:          if (max_song_pg > 1)
148:          {
149:             song_ptr = (char *)realloc(song_ptr,
150:                          max_song_pg*SEVEN_SONGS);
151:             if (song_ptr == NULL)  /* Not able to get mem */
152:             {
153:               display_msg_box("Memory not available!",
154:                          ct.err_fcol, ct.err_bcol );
155:               exit(1);
156:             }
157:          }
158:
159:          /* Get all the songs */
160:          recnbr = temp.song;  /* Starting point */
161:
162:          /* Loop through all the pages */
163:          /* Start at first page of songs - 1 page = 7 songs*/
164:          pgs = 0;
165:          while ( pgs < max_song_pg && rv == NO_ERROR )
166:          {
167:            sngs = 0;
168:            /* Now loop through individual songs */
169:            while ( sngs < 7 && rv == NO_ERROR )
170:            {
171:              /* Get the record and place into memory */
172:              rv = get_rec(recnbr, song_fp, ONE_SONG,
173:                   sizeof(int),(char *)&songs[sngs]);
174:              if ( rv == NO_ERROR )
175:              {
176:                recnbr = songs[sngs].next;
177:                sngs++;
178:              }
179:            }
180:
181:            /* Move the information into memory */
```

continues

Listing 18.6. continued

```
182:            if (rv == NO_ERROR)
183:            {
184:              memcpy(song_ptr+(pgs*SEVEN_SONGS),
185:                      &songs, SEVEN_SONGS);
186:            }
187:            pgs++;    /* Get Next page worth of songs */
188:          }
189:        }
190:      }
191:    return(rv);
192: }
```

 The `proc_alb_rec()` function is called with a value of either `NEXT_REC` or `PREVIOUS_REC`, which is stored in the direct parameter. As with the medium code function, this determines in which direction the reading should occur. Most of this function follows what was presented in `proc_med_rec()` on Day 17.

The one difference that deserves mentioning is in lines 164 to 188 in the `get_alb_info()` function. These lines operate similarly to the code seen earlier today. Line 165 uses a `while` loop to read a page of songs. In each page, seven songs are read using the `while` loop that begins in line 169. After each page of records is read into the songs structure, it is copied into the dynamic memory area. This is done in line 184. The rest of the code presented in this listing doesn't present anything you haven't already seen earlier today.

The Musical Items Screen's Action Bar

To help complete the Musical Item code, Listing 18.7 is included. This contains the action bar routines for the Musical Items screen. With the addition of this listing, your Musical Items screen should be complete.

 Listing 18.7. ALBMABAR.C. The Musical Items screen action bar.

```
1:  /*=============================================================
2:   * Filename: albmabar.c
3:   *           RECORD OF RECORDS - Version 1.0
4:   *
5:   * Author:   Bradley L. Jones
```

```
 6:    *
 7:    * Purpose:   Action bar for musical items screen.  This will
 8:    *            contain multiple menus. The functions called
 9:    *            by the menu selections may not be available
10:    *            until later days.
11:    *
12:    * Return:    Return value is either key used to exit a menu
13:    *            with the exception of F10 which is returned
14:    *            as Enter to redisplay main menu.  In each menu
15:    *            the left and right keys will exit and move
16:    *            control to the right or left menu.
17:    *===========================================================*/
18:
19:   #include <string.h>
20:   #include <stdio.h>
21:   #include <stdlib.h>
22:   #include "tyac.h"
23:   #include "records.h"
24:
25:
26:   /*-------------------*
27:    *     prototypes    *
28:    *-------------------*/
29:
30:   #include "recofrec.h"
31:
32:   int do_albums_menu1( void );
33:   int do_albums_menu2( void );
34:   int do_albums_menu3( void );
35:   int do_albums_menu4( void );
36:
37:   static void do_something( char * );
38:
39:   /*-------------------*
40:    *  Global Variables *
41:    *-------------------*/
42:
43:   extern FILE *idx_fp;        /* Main File ptr to data file */
44:   extern FILE *db_fp;         /* Data file */
45:   extern FILE *song_fp;       /* Pointer for songs */
46:   extern nbr_records;         /* Total # of rec for mediums */
47:   extern int start_rec;
48:   extern int disp_rec;
49:   extern int total_songs;
50:
51:   /*-----------------*
52:    * Defined constants*
53:    *-----------------*/
54:
55:   #define ALBUMS_DBF    "ALBUMS.DBF"
```

18

continues

Listing 18.7. continued

```
56:  #define ALBUMS_IDX      "ALBUMS.IDX"
57:  #define SONGS_DBF       "SONGS.DBF"
58:  #define HELP_DBF        "ALBUMS.HLP"
59:
60:  /*----------------------*
61:   * structure declarations *
62:   *----------------------*/
63:  extern ALBUM_REC albums;
64:  extern ALBUM_REC alb_prev;
65:  extern SONG_REC songs[7];
66:
67:  extern int song_pg;         /* Tracks page of songs being displayed */
68:  extern int max_song_pg;     /* Max number of pages allocated to
69:                                 hold the songs */
70:  extern char *song_ptr;      /* Ptr to dynamic mem where songs are
                                    kept */
71:
72:  #define ONE_SONG        sizeof(songs[0])
73:  #define SEVEN_SONGS     sizeof(songs)
74:
75:  /*--------------------------*
76:   *  albums screen action bar  *
77:   *--------------------------*/
78:
79:  int do_albums_actionbar( void )
80:  {
81:    int  menu  = 1;
82:    int  cont  = TRUE;
83:    int  rv    = 0;
84:    char *abar_text ={" File    Edit    Search   Help "};
85:
86:
87:    while( cont == TRUE )
88:    {
89:       write_string(abar_text, ct.abar_fcol, ct.abar_bcol, 1, 2);
90:
91:       switch( menu )
92:       {
93:
94:          case 1:  /* file menu */
95:                   write_string( " File ", ct.menu_high_fcol,
96:                       ct.menu_high_bcol, 1, 2);
97:
98:                   rv = do_albums_menu1();
99:                   break;
100:
101:         case 2:  /* edit menu */
102:                  write_string( " Edit ", ct.menu_high_fcol,
```

```
103:                        ct.menu_high_bcol, 1, 9);
104:
105:                rv = do_albums_menu2();
106:                break;
107:
108:        case 3:   /* search menu */
109:                write_string( " Search ", ct.menu_high_fcol,
110:                        ct.menu_high_bcol, 1, 16);
111:
112:                rv = do_albums_menu3();
113:                break;
114:
115:        case 4:   /* Help menu */
116:                write_string( " Help ", ct.menu_high_fcol,
117:                        ct.menu_high_bcol, 1, 25);
118:
119:                rv = do_albums_menu4();
120:                break;
121:
122:        default: /* error */
123:                cont = FALSE;
124:                break;
125:        }
126:
127:        switch( rv )
128:        {
129:           case LT_ARROW:  menu--;
130:                           if( menu < 1 )
131:                               menu = 4;
132:                           break;
133:
134:           case RT_ARROW:  menu++;
135:                           if( menu > 4 )
136:                               menu = 1;
137:                           break;
138:
139:           default:        cont = FALSE;
140:                           break;
141:        }
142:    }
143:    write_string(abar_text, ct.abar_fcol, ct.abar_bcol, 1, 2);
144:    cursor_on();
145:    return(rv);
146: }
147:
148:
149: /*--------------------*
150:  *  do_menu 1  (File) *
151:  *--------------------*/
152:
```

Listing 18.7. continued

```c
153: int do_albums_menu1( void )
154: {
155:   int   rv      = 0;
156:   int   menu_sel = 0;
157:   char *saved_screen = NULL;
158:
159:   char *file_menu[2] = { " Exit  <F3> ", "1Ee" };
160:   char exit_keys[MAX_KEYS] = {F3, F10, ESC_KEY};
161:
162:   saved_screen = save_screen_area( 0, 10, 0, 40 );
163:
164:   rv = display_menu( 3, 4, SINGLE_BOX, file_menu, 2,
165:                      exit_keys, &menu_sel, LR_ARROW, SHADOW);
166:
167:   restore_screen_area( saved_screen );
168:
169:   switch( rv )
170:   {
171:     case ENTER_KEY: /* accept selection */
172:     case CR:
173:               rv = F3;
174:               break;
175:
176:     case F3:       /* exiting */
177:     case ESC_KEY:
178:     case LT_ARROW: /* arrow keys */
179:     case RT_ARROW:
180:               break;
181:
182:     case F10:      /* exit action bar */
183:               rv = ENTER_KEY;
184:               break;
185:
186:     default:       boop();
187:               break;
188:   }
189:   return(rv);
190: }
191:
192: /*--------------------*
193:  *  do_menu 2  (Edit) *
194:  *--------------------*/
195:
196: int do_albums_menu2( void )
197: {
198:   int   rv      = 0;
199:   int   menu_sel = 0;
200:   char *saved_screen = NULL;
201:
202:   char *edit_menu[8] = {
```

```
203:                " New          ", "1Nn",
204:                " Add     <F4> ", "2Aa",
205:                " Change  <F5> ", "3Cc",
206:                " Delete  <F6> " };
207:
208:     char exit_keys[MAX_KEYS] = {F3, F10, ESC_KEY};
209:
210:     saved_screen = save_screen_area( 1, 10, 8, 40 );
211:
212:     rv = display_menu( 3, 11, SINGLE_BOX, edit_menu, 8,
213:                        exit_keys, &menu_sel, LR_ARROW, SHADOW);
214:
215:     restore_screen_area( saved_screen );
216:
217:     switch( rv )
218:     {
219:         case ENTER_KEY: /* accept selection */
220:         case CR:
221:                 switch( menu_sel )
222:                 {
223:                     case 1: /* Clear the screen */
224:                             disp_rec = 0;
225:                             reset_memory();
226:                             clear_albums_fields();
227:                             draw_albums_screen();
228:                             break;
229:
230:                     case 2:  /* Add a record */
231:                             /* Save songs back into memory location */
232:                             memcpy(song_ptr+((song_pg-1)*SEVEN_SONGS),
233:                                     &songs, SEVEN_SONGS);
234:                             rv = add_adata();
235:                             if ( rv == NO_ERROR )
236:                             {
237:                               disp_rec = 0;
238:                               reset_memory();
239:                               clear_albums_fields();
240:                               draw_albums_screen();
241:                             }
242:                             else  /* Only do next part if File I/O  */
243:                             if ( rv > NO_ERROR )
244:                             {
245:                               display_msg_box("Fatal Error adding...",
246:                                   ct.err_fcol, ct.err_bcol );
247:                               exit(1);
248:                             }
249:                             break;
250:
251:                     case 3:  /* Update the current record */
252:                             /* Save songs back into memory location */
```

continues

Listing 18.7. continued

```
253:                         memcpy(song_ptr+((song_pg-1)*SEVEN_SONGS),
254:                             &songs, SEVEN_SONGS);
255:                         rv = add_adata();
256:                         if ( rv == NO_ERROR )
257:                         {
258:                           disp_rec = 0;
259:                           reset_memory();
260:                           clear_albums_fields();
261:                           draw_albums_screen();
262:                         }
263:                         else   /* Only do next part if File I/O  */
264:                         if ( rv > NO_ERROR )
265:                         {
266:                           display_msg_box("Fatal Error updating...",
267:                               ct.err_fcol, ct.err_bcol );
268:                           exit(1);
269:                         }
270:                         break;
271:
272:                 case 4:  /* Deleting the current record */
273:                         if( (yes_no_box( "Delete record ?",
274:                             ct.db_fcol, ct.db_bcol )) == 'Y' )
275:                         {
276:                           rv = del_alb_rec();
277:                           if (rv == NO_ERROR)
278:                           {
279:                             disp_rec = 0;
280:                             clear_albums_fields();
281:                             draw_albums_screen();
282:                           }
283:                           else
284:                           {
285:                             display_msg_box("Fatal Error
                                            deleting...",
286:                                 ct.err_fcol, ct.err_bcol );
287:                             exit(1);
288:                           }
289:                         }
290:                         break;
291:
292:                 default: /* continue looping */
293:                         boop();
294:                         break;
295:             }
296:
297:             rv = ENTER_KEY;
298:             break;
299:
300:     case F3:        /* exiting */
```

```
301:         case ESC_KEY:
302:         case LT_ARROW: /* arrow keys */
303:         case RT_ARROW:
304:                     break;
305:
306:         case F10:      /* action bar */
307:                     rv = ENTER_KEY;
308:                     break;
309:
310:         default:       boop();
311:                     break;
312:     }
313:    return(rv);
314: }
315:
316: /*--------------------*
317:  *  do menu 3  (Search) *
318:  *--------------------*/
319:
320: int do_albums_menu3( void )
321: {
322:    int   rv       = 0;
323:    int   menu_sel = 0;
324:    char *saved_screen = NULL;
325:
326:    char *search_menu[6] = {
327:         " Find...         ", "1Ff",
328:         " Next      <F7> ", "2Nn",
329:         " Previous  <F8> ", "3Pp" };
330:
331:    char exit_keys[MAX_KEYS] = {F3, F10, ESC_KEY};
332:
333:    saved_screen = save_screen_area( 1, 10, 0, 60 );
334:
335:    rv = display_menu( 3, 18, SINGLE_BOX, search_menu, 6,
336:                        exit_keys, &menu_sel, LR_ARROW, SHADOW);
337:
338:    restore_screen_area( saved_screen );
339:
340:    switch( rv )
341:    {
342:       case ENTER_KEY: /* accept selection */
343:       case CR:
344:                   switch( menu_sel )
345:                   {
346:                      case 1:  /* Do find dialog */
347:                           rv = search_alb_rec(albums.title);
348:
349:                           if( rv == NO_ERROR )
350:                           {
```

continues

Listing 18.7. continued

```
351:                          /* record found */
352:                          draw_albums_screen();
353:                          display_msg_box("Record Found!",
354:                                      ct.db_fcol, ct.db_bcol);
355:                  }
356:                  else
357:                  if( rv < 0 )
358:                  {
359:                      display_msg_box("Record Not Found!",
360:                                  ct.err_fcol, ct.err_bcol);
361:                  }
362:                  else
363:                  {
364:                    display_msg_box(
365:                          "Fatal Error processing data...",
366:                          ct.err_fcol, ct.err_bcol );
367:                    exit(1);
368:                  }
369:                  break;
370:
371:          case 2:  /* Next Record */
372:                rv = proc_alb_rec(NEXT_REC);
373:                if ( rv == NO_ERROR )
374:                    draw_albums_screen();
375:                else
376:                {
377:                    display_msg_box("Fatal Error processing
                                    data...",
378:                        ct.err_fcol, ct.err_bcol );
379:                    exit(1);
380:                }
381:                break;
382:
383:          case 3:  /* Previous Record */
384:                rv = proc_alb_rec(PREVIOUS_REC);
385:                if ( rv == NO_ERROR )
386:                {
387:                    draw_albums_screen();
388:                }
389:                else
390:                {
391:                    display_msg_box("Fatal Error processing
                                    data...",
392:                        ct.err_fcol, ct.err_bcol );
393:                    exit(1);
394:                }
395:                break;
396:
397:          default: /* shouldn't happen */
398:                  boop();
```

```
399:                          break;
400:                  }
401:                  rv = ENTER_KEY;
402:                      break;
403:
404:      case F3:        /* exiting */
405:      case ESC_KEY:
406:      case LT_ARROW:  /* arrow keys */
407:      case RT_ARROW:
408:                      break;
409:
410:      case F10:       /* action bar */
411:                      rv = ENTER_KEY;
412:                      break;
413:
414:      default:        boop();
415:                      break;
416:   }
417:   return(rv);
418: }
419:
420: /*-------------------*
421:  *  do menu 4  (Help) *
422:  *-------------------*/
423:
424: int do_albums_menu4( void )
425: {
426:    int   rv       = 0;
427:    int   menu_sel = 0;
428:    char *saved_screen = NULL;
429:
430:    char *help_menu[4] = {
431:            " Help   <F2> ", "1Hh",
432:            " About       ", "2Ee" };
433:
434:    char exit_keys[MAX_KEYS] = {F3, F10, ESC_KEY};
435:
436:    saved_screen = save_screen_area( 1, 10, 0, 60 );
437:
438:    rv = display_menu( 3, 27, SINGLE_BOX, help_menu, 4,
439:                       exit_keys, &menu_sel, LR_ARROW, SHADOW);
440:
441:    restore_screen_area( saved_screen );
442:
443:    switch( rv )
444:    {
445:       case ENTER_KEY: /* accept selection */
446:       case CR:
447:                      switch( menu_sel )
448:                      {
```

continues

Listing 18.7. continued

```
449:                        case 1:  /* Extended Help */
450:                                 display_albums_help();
451:
452:                                 break;
453:
454:                        case 2:  /* About box */
455:                                 display_about_box();
456:
457:                                 break;
458:
459:                        default: /* continue looping */
460:                                 boop();
461:                                 break;
462:                    }
463:
464:                    break;
465:
466:        case F3:        /* exiting */
467:        case ESC_KEY:
468:        case LT_ARROW:  /* arrow keys */
469:        case RT_ARROW:
470:                        break;
471:
472:        case F10:       /* action bar */
473:                        rv = ENTER_KEY;
474:                        break;
475:
476:        default:        boop();
477:                        break;
478:    }
479:    return(rv);
480: }
481:
482: /*===========================================================
483:  * Function: search_alb_rec()
484:  *
485:  * Author:   Bradley L. Jones
486:  *           Gregory L. Guntle
487:  *
488:  * Purpose: Searches for the key to locate
489:  *
490:  * Returns:  0 - No errors - key found
491:  *          <0 - Key not found
492:  *          >0 - File I/O Error
493:  *===========================================================*/
494:
495: int search_alb_rec(char *key)
496: {
497:    int rv = NO_ERROR;
498:    int done = FALSE;
```

```
499:    int srch_rec;
500:    int result;
501:
502:    ALBUM_INDEX temp;
503:
504:    /* Start at top of chain */
505:    /* Stop when either
506:        1 - The key passed matches    or
507:        2 - The key passed is < rec read
508:        The latter indicates the key is not in the file   */
509:
510:    srch_rec = start_rec;
511:    while (!done)
512:    {
513:      /* Get record */
514:      rv = get_rec(srch_rec, idx_fp, sizeof(temp),
515:            sizeof(int)*2, (char *)&temp);
516:      if (rv == 0)
517:      {
518:        result = stricmp(key, temp.title);
519:        if (result == 0)    /* Found match */
520:        {
521:          /* Now get data */
522:          done = TRUE;
523:          rv = get_rec(temp.data, db_fp, sizeof(albums),
524:                0, (char *)&albums);
525:        }
526:        else
527:        if (result < 0)
528:        {
529:          /* Key < next rec in DBF - key doesn't exist */
530:          done = TRUE;
531:          rv = -1;                /* Key not found */
532:        }
533:        else
534:        {
535:          srch_rec = temp.next;
536:          if (srch_rec == 0)    /* At end of list ? */
537:          {
538:            done = TRUE;
539:            rv = -1;              /* Key not found */
540:          }
541:        }
542:      }
543:    }
544:
545:    return(rv);
546:
547: }
```

Summary

Today, you were presented with a multitude of code. The day started by completing the code necessary for the Medium Code screen. You were presented with the completed action bar routines. Once everything for the Medium Code screen was presented, the chapter moved into the Musical Items screen. The Musical Items screen offers a higher degree of complexity due to the variable number of songs that can be entered. Whereas most of the Musical Items screen was presented with little analysis, all of the major differences were detailed. This includes the page up and page down functions that are used to display multiple sets of song records.

Q&A

Q Is it better to use an undelete flag or to physically remove records?

A The answer to this question is dependent upon the application. If storage needs to be kept at a minimum, then you should physically remove data from the file. If there is a chance that the user will want to restore a deleted record, then you should use a delete flag.

Q What can be done if the musical items' song file gets too big?

A You can physically remove the records that are marked for deletion. With the functions you have created, it should be easy to write a program that reads each record and writes them to new files. Because only nondeleted records will be read, the new file won't include these. Once you have created all of the records in the album files, you can delete them. The temporary files that you created can then be renamed to the album file names.

Q Can records marked as deleted be reused when adding new records?

A If you don't plan to undelete, then records marked as deleted could be filled with new records. You could change the logic of the add function to read each record in the file in physical order. If the record read is marked as deleted, then the record being added could use the space. If the record isn't marked as deleted, then it would be skipped.

Workshop

The Workshop provides quiz questions to help you solidify your understanding of the material covered and exercises to provide you with experience in using what you've learned.

Quiz

1. What two file functions on the action bar are not accessible with a function key?

2. What do each of the functions from Question 1 do?

3. What should you always do before deleting a record?

4. What is a delete flag used for?

5. What do page up and page down do in the Medium Code screen?

6. What do page up and page down do in the Musical Items screen?

7. What is the most songs that can be stored in the Musical Items screen?

Exercises

1. Complete the *Record of Records!* entry and edit screens. You should now have everything you need to complete all three screens. Tomorrow, you'll add the reporting features.

2. Write a program that prints the information in the Musical Items screen's index file, ALBUMS.IDX. A file such as this can be used for debugging purposes.

3. **ON YOUR OWN:** Write a program that uses a file with a variable number of records such as the songs in the album screen. An example of such a file could include a contact database. You could store the addresses in a separate file and include a billing address, a shipping address, and a home address.

Reporting

An application that tracks data is great. Being able to view information on the screen makes the application useful; however, most applications require the capability to access the information in a printed format. Today you will:

- [ ] Add additional menus to the *Record of Records!* program to support reporting.
- [ ] Discuss the concept behind reporting.
- [ ] Do prototypes for a few reports.
- [ ] Add reports that access a single file.
- [ ] Work with reports that access multiple files.
- [ ] Work with a report that only prints selected records.
- [ ] Understand the importance of providing flexibility for reporting.

Is Reporting Important?

On the entry and edit windows, you can only see records one at a time. Many times this is inadequate. Additionally, there are times when you will want to share the information that is stored in your database with others. Reporting enables you to view or print your data in forms different from the form that you see it in on the entry and edit screen.

Before you start creating reports, you should do a bit of preplanning just as you did with the entry and edit screens. With the entry and edit screens, you created a specification. With reporting, you could also create a specification. On simpler reports, a specification may not be needed. What is almost always needed before coding a report is a prototype.

Prototyping Reports

While specifications aren't always required, a prototype is almost always required. If you are developing an application for others, you will be able to present them with a prototype. If they suggest changes, you can change the prototype. You wouldn't have to change the code because you would not have started it yet. Changing the prototype is much easier than changing the code.

The *Record of Records!* application will have several reports. There will be three different reports listing data from each file. These will be followed by a single report that will be accessible in multiple ways.

Simple List Reports

Three of the four reports will simply list specific information out of each database. These lists are good for verifying that each database contains the information that you expect. In addition, lists can serve many other uses. For example, by printing a list of medium codes and their descriptions, you can use it when entering Musical Items. You could print a list from the Group file to show others what groups you listen to. A list of your musical items would be good to place in a safe place for insurance purposes. Lists are a common type of report.

> **Note:** A list is a report that simply lists fields from a file. Lists generally follow the format of one record per line. You will see this in the proto-types presented later.

Before being able to create these reports, you should look at the prototypes. Following will be the prototypes for the Medium Code List and the Group Information Code List. Creating a prototype for the Musical Items List will be left for you to do in an exercise at the end of today.

The List of Medium Codes Prototype

The first prototype presented is the List of Medium Codes prototype.

```
              List of Medium Codes
                   99/99/99


     Code   Description
     ----   ----------

     XX     XXXXXXXXXXXXXXXXXXXXXXXXXXXXXXXXXXX
     XX     XXXXXXXXXXXXXXXXXXXXXXXXXXXXXXXXXXX
     AL     Album
     CD     Compact Disc

            *** End of Report ***
```

There are several features about this prototype you should be aware of. First is the date that is present under the heading. It is always good to include the current date on a report. This enables the person using the report to know when the information was printed. If an old date is on the report, then there is a good chance the information is out-of-date.

This prototype shows a great deal more. The title and column headings are presented exactly as they will appear, which includes their line spacing. The data is then presented. First, several Xs are presented followed by two examples of "real" data. The purpose of the Xs is to show exactly where the data will be. This includes the size of the data.

One final comment should be made about the prototype. The date is displayed with 9s instead of Xs. This is because the date is composed of numbers. The code and description is composed of Xs because they are alphanumeric fields. In creating your prototypes, you should use 9s for numeric fields and Xs for alphanumerics.

> **Tip:** Not all reports will print every field. In addition, some longer fields may be truncated (that is, chopped off). The number of Xs should signify how may digits or characters should be printed.

The Group Information List's Prototype

The Group file contains more information than will fit on a single line. Because of this, you must be a little more creative in creating the prototype.

```
                      List of Group Information
                            99/99/99


                             Date
   Group                     Formed     Type of Music
   ----------------------    --------   --------------------

   XXXXXXXXXXXXXXXXXXXXXXX   99/99/99   XXXXXXXXXXXXXXXXXXXX

               Members:      XXXXXXXXXXXXXXXXXXXXXXXXXXXXXXX
                             XXXXXXXXXXXXXXXXXXXXXXXXXXXXXXX
                             XXXXXXXXXXXXXXXXXXXXXXXXXXXXXXX
                             XXXXXXXXXXXXXXXXXXXXXXXXXXXXXXX
                             XXXXXXXXXXXXXXXXXXXXXXXXXXXXXXX
                             XXXXXXXXXXXXXXXXXXXXXXXXXXXXXXX


   XXXXXXXXXXXXXXXXXXXXXXX   99/99/99   XXXXXXXXXXXXXXXXXXXX

               Members:      XXXXXXXXXXXXXXXXXXXXXXXXXXXXXXX
                             XXXXXXXXXXXXXXXXXXXXXXXXXXXXXXX
                             XXXXXXXXXXXXXXXXXXXXXXXXXXXXXXX
```

```
                    XXXXXXXXXXXXXXXXXXXXXXXXXXXXXX
                    XXXXXXXXXXXXXXXXXXXXXXXXXXXXXX
                    XXXXXXXXXXXXXXXXXXXXXXXXXXXXXX


   COWBOY JUNKIES              01/01/87     Alternative

                    Members:  Alan Anton
                              Margo Timmins
                              Michael Timmins
                              Peter Timmins


   Violent Femmes              01/01/83     Alternative

                    Members:  Gordon Gano
                              Brian Ritchie
                              Victor DeLorenzo


                    *** End of Report ***
```

This prototype follows the same constructs as the previous prototpye. Xs and 9s mark the location of the fields. Because all the fields don't fit on a single line, part of the data falls on the following lines. You should notice that the additional lines are indented several spaces so that it is easy to follow where new records start.

Expert Tip: By including a couple of "real" records on the prototype, it is often easier to get a better idea of how the report will really look.

19

Note: The Musical Items List will be prototyped in an exercise at the end of the day. There will also be an exercise asking you to create this report.

Complex Reports

In addition to the three list reports that will be added to the application, a fourth report will also be added. This report will be much more complex. The complexity of the report will make it much more useful.

```
XXXXXXXXXXXXXXXXXXXXXXXXXXXXXX                    Today: 99/99/99

Group:      XXXXXXXXXXXXXXXXXXXXXXXX

Group Desc:  XXXXXXXXXXXXXXXXXXXXXXXXXXXXXXXXXXXXXXXXXXXXXXXXXXXXXXXXXX
             XXXXXXXXXXXXXXXXXXXXXXXXXXXXXXXXXXXXXXXXXXXXXXXXXXXXXXXXXX
             XXXXXXXXXXXXXXXXXXXXXXXXXXXXXXXXXXXXXXXXXXXXXXXXXXXXXXXXXX

Type of Music:  XXXXXXXXXXXXXXXXXXX

Medium:  XXXXXXXXXXXXXXXXXXXXXXXXXXXXXXXXXXX

Date Purchased: 99/99/99

Cost:   $999.99
Value:  $999.99

SONGS:

Track    Song Title                                      Time
----     ----------------------------------------        ----
99       XXXXXXXXXXXXXXXXXXXXXXXXXXXXXXXXXXXXXXXXXX       99:99
99       XXXXXXXXXXXXXXXXXXXXXXXXXXXXXXXXXXXXXXXXXX       99:99
99       XXXXXXXXXXXXXXXXXXXXXXXXXXXXXXXXXXXXXXXXXX       99:99
99       XXXXXXXXXXXXXXXXXXXXXXXXXXXXXXXXXXXXXXXXXX       99:99
99       XXXXXXXXXXXXXXXXXXXXXXXXXXXXXXXXXXXXXXXXXX       99:99
99       XXXXXXXXXXXXXXXXXXXXXXXXXXXXXXXXXXXXXXXXXX       99:99
99       XXXXXXXXXXXXXXXXXXXXXXXXXXXXXXXXXXXXXXXXXX       99:99
99       XXXXXXXXXXXXXXXXXXXXXXXXXXXXXXXXXXXXXXXXXX       99:99
99       XXXXXXXXXXXXXXXXXXXXXXXXXXXXXXXXXXXXXXXXXX       99:99
99       XXXXXXXXXXXXXXXXXXXXXXXXXXXXXXXXXXXXXXXXXX       99:99
99       XXXXXXXXXXXXXXXXXXXXXXXXXXXXXXXXXXXXXXXXXX       99:99
99       XXXXXXXXXXXXXXXXXXXXXXXXXXXXXXXXXXXXXXXXXX       99:99
99       XXXXXXXXXXXXXXXXXXXXXXXXXXXXXXXXXXXXXXXXXX       99:99


- - - - - - - - - - - - - - - - - - - - PAGE BREAK - - - - - - - - - - - - - - - - - - - - - - - - - -


Walking on the Moon                              Today: 99/99/99

Group:      Philippe Kahn

Group Desc:  Jazz Music by the Owner of Borland International. Features
             several famous people


Type of Music:  Jazz
```

```
Medium:  Compact Disc

Date Purchased: 12/13/92

Cost:   $ 14.95
Value:  $342.00

SONGS:

Track      Song Title                                   Time
----       ----------------------------------------     ----
 01        OOPs!                                        05:06
 02        Interlude                                    00:00
 03        Walkin' on the Moon                          07:28
 04        Interlude                                    00:00
 05        Epistrophy                                   04:35
 06        Interlude                                    00:00
 07        S, E and L                                   04:10
 08        All's Well That Ends                         08:12
 09        Interlude                                    00:00
 10        This Masquerade                              05:48
 11        Interlude                                    00:00
 12        Ralph's Piano Waltz                          05:45
 13        Interlude                                    00:00
 14        Calor                                        08:07
 15        Interlude                                    00:00
 16        Better Days                                  03:49
 17        Interlude                                    00:00
 18        Mopti                                        05:46
 19        Interlude                                    00:00
 20        Silence                                      05:52
```

19

As you can see, this report is formatted differently from that of the previous lists. In addition, this report contains information from not only the Musical Items file, but also the Group file and the Medium Code file. The formatting of this report has been changed so that only one musical item will be printed per page. The complexity of this report will require a slightly different approach to produce than the lists.

If you printed this layout for every record that could possibly be in your database, you could use a great deal of paper. Because of this, you will want to add selection criteria. Later today, you will add an option that will allow this report to be printed for either all of the records in the file or for only a single musical item.

There are some other issues involved with this report that were not present in the previously prototyped lists. What do you do if you print a musical item that does not have a corresponding medium code or group? In these cases, you may be missing some information that is expected based on the prototype. This is a situation that should be addressed at the time you do the prototypes. In the case of the Musical Items report,

you will print UNKNOWN in the medium code description, and you will leave the group information blank. In addition, if you don't print the group information, you should suppress the blank lines from the report. Sound complicated? Later today, you will see the code necessary to complete this report.

> **Expert Tip:** Because of the complexity of the Musical Items Information report, you may want to create a specification. The specification would contain information such as the selection criteria and what to do if some of the data is missing.

Creating the Reports

Before creating the reports, you will first need to set up the main application to receive them. Based on what was presented earlier, you should have an idea of what will need to be added to the *Record of Records!* application. There already was a reporting menu option included in the Main menu. Because you know what reports need to be added, you should be able to include a reporting menu. A menu should be created to contain the following options:

1. Detailed Information

2. List of Musical Items

3. List of Groups

4. List of Medium Codes

These options are listed in the order that they are most likely to be used. The users of the application are expected to use the Detailed Information Report (on Musical Items) the most. They are expected to use the List of Medium Codes the least. Listing 19.1 is the code necessary to create this menu.

As stated earlier, the Detailed Report will have an option. The users will be able to print all of the musical items, or they will be able to select a specific musical item to print. To provide your users with this option, a third menu will be included accessible from the Detailed Information option. This menu will contain two reporting options, All Items and One Item. Additionally, it will contain a Return option, which will remove the menu. The code for this menu is also included in Listing 19.1.

Type Listing 19.1. REC_RPTG.C. The reporting menu code.

```c
1:   /*=============================================================
2:    * Filename: REC_RPTG.c
3:    *           RECORD OF RECORDS - Version 1.0
4:    *
5:    * Author:   Bradley L. Jones
6:    *           Gregory L. Guntle
7:    *
8:    * Purpose:  The Reporting menus.
9:    *
10:   * Note:     Assumes 80 columns by 25 columns for screen.
11:   *=============================================================*/
12:  #include <string.h>
13:  #include <stdio.h>
14:  #include <ctype.h>
15:  #include "tyac.h"
16:  #include "records.h"
17:
18:  /*-------------------*
19:   *     prototypes    *
20:   *-------------------*/
21:  #include "recofrec.h"
22:
23:  int do_detail_album_menu(void);
24:
25:  /*=============================================================*
26:   *                         main()                             *
27:   *=============================================================*/
28:
29:  int do_reporting(void)
30:  {
31:    int  rv       = 0;
32:    int  cont     = TRUE;
33:    int  menu_sel = 0;
34:    char *saved_screen = NULL;
35:
36:
37:    char *rpt_menu[10] = {
38:            "1. Detailed Information", "1Dd",
39:            "2. List of Musical Item", "2Mm",
40:            "3. List of Groups      ", "3Gg",
41:            "4. List of Medium Codes", "4Mm",
42:            "5. Return to Main Menu ", "5RrEeQq" };
43:
44:    char MENU_EXIT_KEYS[MAX_KEYS] = {F3, F10, ESC_KEY};
45:
46:    while( cont == TRUE )                 /* loop in temp menu */
47:    {
```

continues

Listing 19.1. continued

```
48:        saved_screen = save_screen_area(10, 21, 28, 58 );
49:
50:        rv = display_menu(12, 30, DOUBLE_BOX, rpt_menu, 10,
51:                        MENU_EXIT_KEYS, &menu_sel, NO_LR_ARROW,
52:                        SHADOW);
53:
54:        switch( rv )
55:        {
56:            case ENTER_KEY: /* accept selection */
57:            case CR:
58:                    switch( menu_sel )
59:                    {
60:                        case 1:   /* Menu option 1 */
61:                                cursor_on();
62:                                do_detail_album_menu();
63:                                break;
64:
65:                        case 2:   /* Menu option 2 */
66:                                cursor_on();
67: //                             list_musical_items();
68:                                display_msg_box("Report 2...",
69:                                    ct.help_fcol, ct.help_bcol );
70:                                break;
71:
72:                        case 3:   /* Menu option 3 */
73:                                cursor_on();
74: //                             list_groups();
75:                                display_msg_box("Report 3...",
76:                                    ct.help_fcol, ct.help_bcol );
77:                                break;
78:
79:                        case 4:   /* Reporting */
80:                                cursor_on();
81: //                             list_medium_codes();
82:                                display_msg_box("Report 4...",
83:                                    ct.help_fcol, ct.help_bcol );
84:                                break;
85:
86:                        case 5:   /* exit */
87:                                cont = FALSE;
88:                                break;
89:
90:                        default: /* continue looping */
91:                                boop();
92:                                break;
93:                    }
94:                break;
95:
96:            case ESC_KEY: rv = ENTER_KEY;   /* don't exit totally */
```

```
 97:                        cont = FALSE;     /* exit */
 98:                        break;
 99:
100:        case F3:        /* exiting */
101:                        cont = FALSE;
102:                        break;
103:
104:        case F10:       /* action bar */
105:                        rv = do_main_actionbar();
106:
107:                        if( rv == F3 )
108:                            cont = FALSE;
109:
110:                        break;
111:
112:        default:        boop();
113:                        break;
114:      }
115:    }
116:    restore_screen_area(saved_screen);
117:
118:    return(rv);
119: }
120:
121: /*------------------------------------------------*
122:  * Detailed Musical Item Report                  *
123:  *------------------------------------------------*/
124:
125: int do_detail_album_menu(void)
126: {
127:    int  rv       = 0;
128:    int  cont     = TRUE;
129:    int  menu_sel = 0;
130:    char *saved_screen = NULL;
131:
132:
133:    char *album_menu[6] = {
134:            "1. All Items", "1Aa",
135:            "2. One Item ", "2Oo",
136:            "3. Return   ", "3RrEeQq" };
137:
138:    char MENU_EXIT_KEYS[MAX_KEYS] = {F3, F10, ESC_KEY};
139:
140:    while( cont == TRUE )                  /* loop in temp menu */
141:    {
142:      saved_screen = save_screen_area(13, 19, 35, 55 );
143:
144:      rv = display_menu(14, 40, DOUBLE_BOX, album_menu, 6,
145:                        MENU_EXIT_KEYS, &menu_sel, NO_LR_ARROW,
146:                        SHADOW);
```

19

continues

Listing 19.1. continued

```
147:
148:      switch( rv )
149:      {
150:         case ENTER_KEY: /* accept selection */
151:         case CR:
152:               switch( menu_sel )
153:                 {
154:                    case 1:  /* Menu option 1 */
155:                            cursor_on();
156: //                        music_rpt(0);
157:                            display_msg_box("Do All of em....",
158:                                ct.help_fcol, ct.help_bcol );
159:                            break;
160:
161:                    case 2:  /* Menu option 2 */
162:                            cursor_on();
163: //                        music_rpt(1);
164:                            display_msg_box("Do only one...",
165:                                ct.help_fcol, ct.help_bcol );
166:                            break;
167:
168:                    case 3:  /* Exit menu */
169:                            cont = FALSE;
170:                            break;
171:
172:                    default: /* continue looping */
173:                            boop();
174:                            break;
175:                 }
176:               break;
177:
178:         case ESC_KEY: rv = ENTER_KEY;  /* so don't exit clear out */
179:                       cont = FALSE;    /* exit */
180:                       break;
181:
182:         case F3:      /* exiting */
183:                       cont = FALSE;
184:                       break;
185:
186:         case F10:     /* action bar */
187:                       rv = do_main_actionbar();
188:
189:                       if( rv == F3 )
190:                           cont = FALSE;
191:
192:                       break;
193:
194:         default:      boop();
195:                       break;
```

```
196:     }
197:   }
198:   restore_screen_area(saved_screen);
199:
200:   return(rv);
201: }
202:
203: /*=========================================================*
204:  *                    end of listing                      *
205:  *=========================================================*/
```

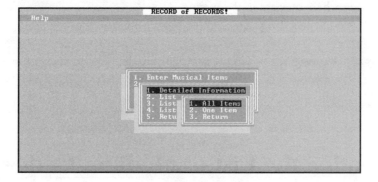

In order for the *Record of Records!* application to access these new menus, you will also need to make some changes to RECOFREC.C and RECOFREC.H. The following prototypes should be added to RECOFREC.H.

```
/*------------------------------*
 * Prototypes for Reporting     *
 *------------------------------*/

int  do_reporting(void);
```

```
void list_medium_codes(void);
void list_groups(void);
void list_musical_items(void);
void music_rpt(int);
void setup_today(void);          /* in listmed.c */
```

The changes to RECOFREC.C involve changing case 4 in the main() function to the following:

```
case 4:   /* Reporting */
          do_reporting();
          break;
```

Once you have changed these files, you can recompile. Listing 19.1 has been set up so that comments are printed when the reporting options are selected. You can see this in lines 68, 75, 82, 157, and 164. The actual reports will each be created in its own source file. The call to the functions are included in both Listing 19.1 and the RECOFREC.H file if you made all the changes mentioned. As you create the reports, you will be able to remove the comments from the call and delete the message.

The rest of this listing should not need explanation. The Reporting menu operates like the other menus you have seen. You should notice that this menu was called by the Main menu. In addition, option one in lines 60 to 63 calls a third menu. From the output, you can see that the menus do not completely cover each other. This helps the users see where they are in the menus.

Expert Tip: When presenting more than one menu on the screen at the same time, you should avoid completely covering a lower menu. This helps the users see where they are.

Creating the List of Medium Codes

The list of medium codes will be created in a function called list_medium_codes(), which will be created in a file called LISTMED.C. This is presented in Listing 19.2.

Type **Listing 19.2. LISTMED.C. The list of medium codes.**

```
1:   /*===========================================================
2:    * Filename: listmed.c
3:    *
4:    * Author:   Bradley L. Jones
5:    *           Gregory L. Guntle
```

```
 6:      *
 7:      * Purpose:   Lists the information in the medium DB.
 8:      *
 9:      *=========================================================*/
10:
11: #include <stdio.h>
12: #include <string.h>
13: #include "tyac.h"
14: #include "records.h"
15:
16: /*-------------------*
17:  *  Global Variables  *
18:  *-------------------*/
19: extern FILE *idx_fp;        /* Main File ptr to data file */
20: extern FILE *db_fp;         /* Data file */
21: extern nbr_records;         /* Total # of rec for mediums */
22: extern int start_rec;
23: extern int disp_rec;
24:
25:
26: /*-----------------*
27:  * Defined constants*
28:  *-----------------*/
29:
30: #define MEDIUM_IDX    "MEDIUMS.IDX"
31: #define MEDIUM_DBF    "MEDIUMS.DBF"
32:
33: /*----------------------*
34:  * structure declarations *
35:  *----------------------*/
36:
37: extern MEDIUM_REC medium;
38:
39: /*------------------*
40:  *  Prototypes       *
41:  *------------------*/
42:
43: #include "recofrec.h"
44:
45: void setup_today(void);
46: void print_med_hdr(void);
47: int process_med_list(void);
48:
49: char today[8];
50:
51: /*=========================================================*
52:  *    list_medium_codes()                                  *
53:  *=========================================================*/
54:
55: int list_medium_codes(void)
```

continues

Listing 19.2. continued

```
56:  {
57:    int rv=NO_ERROR;
58:
59:    /* Open both Index and DBF file */
60:    if ( (rv = open_files(MEDIUM_IDX, MEDIUM_DBF)) == 0 )
61:    {
62:      /* Are there any records to process ? */
63:      if (nbr_records == 0)
64:      {
65:        display_msg_box("No medium records to process",
66:            ct.err_fcol, ct.err_bcol);
67:      }
68:      else
69:      {
70:        setup_today();
71:        print_med_hdr();
72:        rv = process_med_list();
73:      }                    /* End ELSE - records to process */
74:
75:      rv = close_files();
76:    }                    /* End No Errors on Opening Files */
77:    return(rv);
78:  }
79:
80:  /*=======================================================*
81:   *    setup_today()                                      *
82:   *=======================================================*/
83:  void setup_today()
84:  {
85:    int year, month, day;
86:    char hold_date[6];
87:
88:    current_date(&month, &day, &year);
89:    convert_str(hold_date, month, PACK_ZERO);
90:    strncpy(today, hold_date+3, 2);
91:    today[2] = '/';
92:    convert_str(hold_date, day, PACK_ZERO);
93:    strncpy(today+3, hold_date+3, 2);
94:    today[5] = '/';
95:    if (year >1900)
96:       year-=1900;
97:    convert_str(hold_date, year, PACK_ZERO);
98:    strncpy(today+6, hold_date+3, 2);
99:    today[8] = '\0';
100:
101: }
102:
103: /*=======================================================*
```

```
104:  *    print_med_hdr()                                          *
105:  *==========================================================*/
106: void print_med_hdr()
107: {
108:   fprintf(stdprn,"\n\r\t\tList of Medium Codes\n\r");
109:   fprintf(stdprn,"\t\t    %s\n\r\n\r", today);
110:
111:   fprintf(stdprn,"\tCode\tDescription\n\r");
112:   fprintf(stdprn,"\t----\t-----------\n\r");
113: }
114:
115: /*==========================================================*
116:  *    process_med_list()                                    *
117:  *==========================================================*/
118: int process_med_list()
119: {
120:   int rv = NO_ERROR;
121:   int done = FALSE;
122:   int srch_rec = start_rec;
123:   MEDIUM_INDEX temp;
124:
125:   while (rv == NO_ERROR && !done)
126:   {
127:     /* Get INDEX */
128:     rv = get_rec(srch_rec, idx_fp, sizeof(temp),
129:         sizeof(int)*2, (char *)&temp);
130:     if (rv == NO_ERROR)
131:     {
132:       /* Get the data record */
133:       rv = get_rec(temp.data, db_fp, sizeof(medium),
134:             0, (char *)&medium);
135:       if (rv == NO_ERROR)
136:       {
137:         /* Print the data */
138:         fprintf(stdprn, "\t%-2s\t%-35s\n\r",
139:             medium.code, medium.desc);
140:         srch_rec = temp.next;
141:         /* Check for end of list */
142:         if (srch_rec == 0)
143:         {
144:            done = TRUE;
145:            fprintf(stdprn, "\f");
146:         }
147:       }        /* End of NO_ERROR - from DBF */
148:     }        /* End of NO_ERROR - from INDEX */
149:   }        /* End WHILE */
150:   return(rv);
151: }
```

Note: The current_date() function was taken from Listing 8.2 in Day 8. This function should be added to your TYAC.H library if it isn't already there.

 Output

```
List of Medium Codes
        02/20/94

Code    Description
----    -----------
cd      Compact Disc
cs      Cassette Tape
```

Note: Your output will look like the prototype. The specific data printed will be dependent upon the data in your files.

Analysis

This listing starts in the same manner as most of the listings in the *Record of Records!* application. In lines 1 to 9, comments are included giving information on the listing. In lines 11 to 14, the necessary header files are included. The TYAC.H header is included so that your library routines are available. The RECORDS.H header is included for the record layouts that will be needed to hold the medium information. Lines 19 to 23 include the external declarations that you should be very familiar with by now. These are the declarations that are needed to access the databases.

Lines 30 and 31 create the same defined constants that you saw in the Medium Code listing for the entry and edit screen. These constants, MEDIUM_IDX and MEDIUM_DBF, contain the name of the medium code index file and data file. Line 37 contains an external declaration for a medium code structure. Lines 43 to 47 contain prototypes for the functions included later in the listing.

Expert Tip: The defined constants for the Medium Code files are included in more than one file. Because of this, it would be better to place the constants in a header file. This header file could then be included where needed. In addition, if the file names defined in the constants change, then only one area of the code needs to be modified instead of several.

The first line of unfamiliar code should be line 49. A character array called today is declared in line 49. This global array will be used to hold the current date.

Line 55 begins the list_medium_code() function, which is the purpose of this listing. Before printing the report, you need to open the file. Line 60 calls the open_file() function to open the medium code files. If there wasn't an error, then line 63 checks the global variable, nbr_records, that was filled when the file was opened. If there aren't any records in the file, then a message is displayed in line 65; otherwise the report is processed. Line 70 calls a function to set up the current date, line 71 prints the first header on the report, and then line 72 processes the detailed information. Once the processing is done, or if there weren't any records, the files are then closed (line 75). Line 77 ends the function by returning the value in rv.

Setting up the current date occurs in lines 80 to 101 in the setup_today() function. The current_date() function, which was presented on Day 8, is used to get the current month, day, and year.

One other function is used that has not been covered. This is the convert_str() function. This function is used to modify a number into a string. The code for this function is presented in Listing 19.3.

Lines 103 to 113 contain the function, print_med_hdr(). It is a common practice to create a function that prints only the header to a report. This function can then be called whenever needed by the function that prints the detailed information. Lines 108 to 112 contain several fprintf() statements that display information to stdprn.

19

Review Tip: The fprintf() function is just like printf() except that it has an additional parameter. The first parameter of fprintf() is a pointer to where you want the printed information to go. This can be a file such as the medium file or one of the standard I/O streams. The most common standard I/O streams are stdout, stdprn, and stderr. The stdout stream is for standard output. This is almost always the screen. The stdprn stream is for standard print. This is almost always a printer. The stderr stream is for standard errors. This is also almost always the screen.

The processing of the detail information in the report starts on line 118 with the process_med_list() function. A while loop in lines 125 to 149 will execute as long as all the records are not processed and as long as no errors occur.

Line 128 will read an index record from the index file. This will initially be the starting record. If the read is successful, then the corresponding data record will be read in line 133. If this read is successful, then line 138 prints the detail line containing the medium code and description. Line 140 sets the srch_rec to the next sorted record in the index file by using the next pointer. If the next index record to be read is zero, then the end of the file has been reached. In this case, line 144 sets the done flag to TRUE so that the printing loop will end. Additionally, line 145 does a form feed on the report.

> **Note:** This report does not take page size into consideration. It assumes that the number of records that will be printed will not go over one page. In the next listing, this assumption is not made.

The convert_str() function was used in Listing 19.2. This function is presented in Listing 19.3. You should add this function to your TYAC.LIB library.

 Listing 19.3. The convert_str() function.

```
1:    /* ---------------------------------------------------------
2:     * Program: CONVSTR.C
3:     * Authors: Bradley L. Jones
4:     *          Gregory L. Guntle
5:     *
6:     * Purpose: Converts an integer variable to a string
7:     *
8:     * Enter with: rec_disp - char * to place new string
9:     *             rec_nbr  - integer to convert
10:    *             flag   - Whether to front-end it with 0's
11:    *
12:    * Returns: N/A
13:    *=========================================================*/
14:
15:   #include <stdlib.h>   /* Required by itoa */
16:   #include <string.h>
17:   #include <mem.h>
18:
19:   #define PACK_ZERO    1
20:   #define NOPACK       0
21:
22:   void convert_str(char *disp_buff, int nbr, int pack_flag)
23:   {
24:      char hold_convert[18];             /* Required by itoa */
25:
26:      /* Null out area to store new string */
```

```
27:        memset(disp_buff, '\0', sizeof(disp_buff));
28:
29:        /* Convert integer to string */
30:        itoa(nbr, hold_convert, 10);
31:
32:        /* Should the nbr be front-packed with 0's */
33:        if ( pack_flag == PACK_ZERO )      /* Front pack # with 0's ? */
34:        {
35:          memset(disp_buff, '0', 5-strlen(hold_convert));
36:          disp_buff[5-strlen(hold_convert)] = '\0';
37:        }
38:
39:        /* Place convert number in passed parm */
40:        strcat(disp_buff, hold_convert);
41:
42:    }
```

This function simply converts an integer to a string. Using a defined constant, the string may or may not be packed with zeros. These defined constants, PACK_ZERO and NOPACK, should already be in your TYAC.H header file.

Creating the List of Group Codes

The List of Groups is similar to the List of Medium Codes. The list_groups() function is presented in the RPT_GRPS.C file. This is presented in Listing 19.4.

19

Listing 19.4. RPT_GRPS.C. The List of Groups.

```
1:    /*===========================================================
2:     * Filename: listgrps.c
3:     *
4:     * Author:    Bradley L. Jones
5:     *            Gregory L. Guntle
6:     *
7:     * Purpose:   Lists the information in the groups DB.
8:     *
9:     *===========================================================*/
10:
11:   #include <stdio.h>
12:   #include <string.h>
13:   #include "tyac.h"
14:   #include "records.h"
15:
16:   /*-------------------*
17:    *  Global Variables  *
18:    *-------------------*/
```

continues

Listing 19.4. continued

```
19:   extern FILE *idx_fp;        /* Main File ptr to data file */
20:   extern FILE *db_fp;         /* Data file */
21:   extern nbr_records;         /* Total # of rec for mediums */
22:   extern int start_rec;
23:   extern int disp_rec;
24:
25:   int line_ctr;               /* Line ctr */
26:   int page_ctr;               /* Page ctr */
27:
28:   /*------------------*
29:    * Defined constants*
30:    *------------------*/
31:   #define GROUPS_IDX    "GROUPS.IDX"
32:   #define GROUPS_DBF    "GROUPS.DBF"
33:
34:   /*----------------------*
35:    * structure declarations *
36:    *----------------------*/
37:   extern GROUP_REC groups;
38:
39:   /*------------------*
40:    *  Prototypes      *
41:    *------------------*/
42:   #include "recofrec.h"
43:
44:   int  list_groups(void);
45:   void print_grp_hdr(void);
46:   int  process_groups(void);
47:   void print_group(void);
48:
49:   void setup_date(void);
50:   extern char today[8];
51:
52:   /*========================================================*
53:    *   list_groups()                                        *
54:    *========================================================*/
55:
56:   int list_groups(void)
57:   {
58:      int rv=NO_ERROR;
59:
60:      /* Open both Index and DBF file */
61:      if ( (rv = open_files(GROUPS_IDX, GROUPS_DBF)) == 0 )
62:      {
63:         /* Are there any records to process ? */
64:         if (nbr_records == 0)
65:         {
66:            display_msg_box("No groups records to process",
67:               ct.err_fcol, ct.err_bcol);
```

```
68:        }
69:        else
70:        {
71:          setup_today();
72:          print_grp_hdr();
73:          rv = process_groups();
74:        }              /* End ELSE - records to process */
75:
76:        rv = close_files();
77:    }              /* End No Errors on Opening Files */
78:    return(rv);
79: }
80:
81: /*=========================================================*
82:  *    print_grp_hdr()                                      *
83:  *=========================================================*/
84: void print_grp_hdr()
85: {
86:    fprintf(stdprn,"\n\r\t\tList of Groups\n\r");
87:    fprintf(stdprn,"\t\t   %s\n\r\n\r", today);
88:
89:    fprintf(stdprn,"                                    Date\n\r");
90:    fprintf(stdprn,"Group                               ");
91:    fprintf(stdprn,"Formed      Type of Music\n\r");
92:
93:    fprintf(stdprn,"----------------------      ");
94:    fprintf(stdprn,"--------      ------------\n\r");
95: }
96:
97: /*=========================================================*
98:  *    process_groups()                                     *
99:  *=========================================================*/
100: int process_groups()
101: {
102:    int rv = NO_ERROR;
103:    static int done = FALSE;
104:    static int srch_rec;
105:    static GROUP_INDEX temp;
106:
107:    line_ctr = 0;
108:    page_ctr = 1;
109:
110:    srch_rec = start_rec;
111:    while (rv == NO_ERROR && !done)
112:    {
113:      /* Get INDEX */
114:      rv = get_rec(srch_rec, idx_fp, sizeof(temp),
115:          sizeof(int)*2, (char *)&temp);
116:      if (rv == NO_ERROR)
117:      {
```

continues

Listing 19.4. continued

```
118:        /* Get the data record */
119:        rv = get_rec(temp.data, db_fp, sizeof(groups),
120:              0, (char *)&groups);
121:        if (rv == NO_ERROR)
122:        {
123:          print_group();
124:          srch_rec = temp.next;
125:          /* Check for end of list */
126:          if (srch_rec == 0)
127:          {
128:             done = TRUE;
129:             fprintf(stdprn, "\f");
130:          }
131:          else
132:             done = FALSE;
133:        }          /* End of NO_ERROR - from DBF */
134:      }            /* End of NO_ERROR - from INDEX */
135:   }               /* End WHILE */
136:   return(rv);
137: }
138:
139: /*=========================================================*
140:  *    print_group()                                        *
141:  *=========================================================*/
142: void print_group()
143: {
144:    int i;
145:    char hold_date[8];
146:
147:    if (line_ctr+9 > 55)
148:    {
149:       fprintf(stdprn,"\f");      /* New page */
150:       print_grp_hdr();           /* Reprint header */
151:       fprintf(stdprn,"%-25s",groups.group);
152:       fprintf(stdprn,"   %-8s    %-20s\n\r",
153:              hold_date, groups.music_type);
154:       line_ctr = 6;
155:       page_ctr++;
156:    }
157:    else
158:       line_ctr+=9;
159:
160:    /* Build the date first */
161:    strncpy(hold_date, groups.date_formed.month, 2);
162:    hold_date[2] = '/';
163:    strncpy(hold_date+3, groups.date_formed.day, 2);
164:    hold_date[5] = '/';
165:    strncpy(hold_date+6, groups.date_formed.year, 2);
```

```
166:    hold_date[8] ='\0';
167:
168:    fprintf(stdprn,"%-25s",groups.group);
169:    fprintf(stdprn,"   %-8s    %-20s\n\r",
170:        hold_date, groups.music_type);
171:
172:    fprintf(stdprn,"\n\r\t\t   Members:  %-30s\n\r",
173:      groups.member[0]);
174:
175:    for (i=1; i<=5; i++)
176:    {
177:      fprintf(stdprn,"\t\t               %-30s\n\r",
178:        groups.member[i]);
179:    }
180:
181:    fprintf(stdprn,"\n\r");
182: }
```

Output

```
                        List of Groups
                          02/20/94


                               Date
Group                          Formed      Type of Music
-----------------------        --------    ------------
Violent Femmes                 01/01/87    Alternative

                    Members:   Gordon Gano
                               Brian Ritchie
                               Victor DeLorenzo




Yanni                          09/11/93    Instrumental

                    Members:   Yanni
                               two
                               three
                               four
                               five
                               six
```

Note: Your output will look like the prototype. The specific data printed will be dependent upon the data in your files.

This listing should look similar to the Listing 19.2. Because these two listings are so similar, only the differences need an explanation. You should have expected some of the differences. For example, lines 31 and 32 contain defined constants for the group file names instead of the medium files.

The main function, list_groups(), in lines 52 to 79 is almost identical to the list_medium_codes() function presented earlier. The only difference is that functions related to groups, instead of medium codes, are called.

The List of Groups header information is different from that used by the List of Medium Codes report. Lines 81 to 95 contain the print_grp_header() function. This function simply prints several lines of information exactly as it was presented in the prototype.

Processing the group records is also very similar to processing the medium code records. There are two main differences. The first is that the detail information is printed in a separate function called print_group(). The information printed for each group is much more complex than what was printed for the medium code. To help keep the code easy to follow, the printing of the detail information was placed in its own function.

The second difference is that the report will perform page breaks. In lines 107 and 108, two additional variables have are used, line_ctr and page_ctr. In line 147, an if statement checks to see if there is room on the page to print another record. If there is not, then line 149 does a form feed using fprintf(). Line 150 then calls print_grp_hdr() to print the header information on the new page. The line_ctr is then reset to six in line 154, and the page counter is incremented by one in line 155.

If there was enough room to print the header, then line 158 increments the line counter by nine. This is the number of lines that are printed for an individual group. With the header check completed, the detail information is formatted and printed. The report cycles through each record until all the records have been printed.

Note: The line_ctr was set to six instead of zero because of the header information that was printed.

Note: Most reports contain from 55 to 60 lines on a page.

Creating the Detailed Information Report

The Detailed Information Report will differ from the list reports in several ways. The main difference will be that the Detailed Information Report will use all three databases instead of just one. Listing 19.5 presents the Detailed Information Report.

Listing 19.5. RPT_DETL.C. The detailed Musical Item Report.

```
1:  /*===========================================================
2:   * Filename: listdalb.c
3:   *
4:   * Author:    Bradley L. Jones
5:   *            Gregory L. Guntle
6:   *
7:   * Purpose:   Lists detailed information from the Albums area.
8:   *
9:   * Returns:  0 = No Errors
10:  *           <0 = No records in DB
11:  *           >0 = File I/O Error
12:  *
13:  *==========================================================*/
14:
15: #include <stdio.h>
16: #include <string.h>
17: #include "tyac.h"
18: #include "records.h"
19:
20: /*-----------------*
21:  * Global Variables *
22:  *-----------------*/
23:
24: extern FILE *idx_fp;        /* Main File ptr to data file */
25: extern FILE *db_fp;        /* Data file */
26: extern FILE *song_fp;      /* Pointer for songs */
27: extern nbr_records;        /* Total # of rec for albums */
28: extern int start_rec;
29: extern int disp_rec;
30:
31: extern ALBUM_REC albums;
32: extern SONG_REC songs[7];
33: extern MEDIUM_REC medium;
34: extern GROUP_REC groups;
35:
36: FILE *alb_idx_fp;          /* Needed when opening multiple DB */
37: FILE *alb_db_fp;
```

continues

Listing 19.5. continued

```
38:   FILE *alb_songs_fp;
39:   FILE *med_idx_fp;
40:   FILE *med_db_fp;
41:   FILE *grp_idx_fp;
42:   FILE *grp_db_fp;
43:
44:   int alb_nbr_recs;
45:   int alb_start_rec;
46:   int grp_nbr_recs;
47:   int grp_start_rec;
48:   int med_nbr_recs;
49:   int med_start_rec;
50:   int med_fnd;
51:   int grp_fnd;
52:
53:   /*------------------*
54:    * Defined constants*
55:    *------------------*/
56:
57:   #define ALBUMS_DBF    "ALBUMS.DBF"
58:   #define ALBUMS_IDX    "ALBUMS.IDX"
59:   #define SONGS_DBF     "SONGS.DBF"
60:
61:   #define GROUPS_IDX    "GROUPS.IDX"
62:   #define GROUPS_DBF    "GROUPS.DBF"
63:
64:   #define MEDIUM_IDX    "MEDIUMS.IDX"
65:   #define MEDIUM_DBF    "MEDIUMS.DBF"
66:
67:
68:   #define ALBUMS        00
69:   #define GROUPS        01
70:   #define MEDIUM        02
71:
72:   #define TO_GLOBAL     00
73:   #define FROM_GLOBAL   01
74:
75:   /*----------------------*
76:    * structure declarations *
77:    *----------------------*/
78:
79:   GROUP_INDEX  grp_idx;
80:   GROUP_REC    grp_dbf;
81:   MEDIUM_INDEX med_idx;
82:   MEDIUM_REC   med_dbf;
83:   ALBUM_INDEX  alb_idx;
84:   ALBUM_REC    alb_dbf;
85:   SONG_REC     alb_songs[7];
86:
```

```
87:  /*-------------------*
88:   *  Prototypes        *
89:   *-------------------*/
90:
91:  #include "recofrec.h"
92:
93:  int  open_all_files(void);
94:  void print_song_hdr(void);
95:  int  process_details(char *);
96:  void print_album_details(void);
97:  void switch_globals(int, int);
98:
99:  void setup_date(void);
100: extern char today[8];
101:
102: int get_info(void);
103:
104: /*=========================================================*
105:  *   list_albums()                                         *
106:  *=========================================================*/
107:
108: int music_rpt(char *title)
109: {
110:    int rv=NO_ERROR;
111:
112:    setup_today();
113:    rv = open_all_files();
114:
115:    if (rv == NO_ERROR)
116:    {
117:      rv = process_details(title);
118:
119:      /* Closing ALBUMS */
120:      switch_globals(ALBUMS, TO_GLOBAL);
121:      rv = close_files();
122:
123:      /* Closing GROUPS */
124:      switch_globals(GROUPS, TO_GLOBAL);
125:      rv = close_files();
126:
127:      /* Closing MEDIUM */
128:      switch_globals(MEDIUM, TO_GLOBAL);
129:      rv = close_files();
130:
131:    }
132:    else
133:    if (rv < 0)
134:    {
135:      display_msg_box("No albums records to process",
136:            ct.err_fcol, ct.err_bcol);
```

continues

Listing 19.5. continued

```
137:    }
138:    return(rv);
139: }
140:
141: /*========================================================*
142:  *    open_all_files()                                    *
143:  *========================================================*/
144:
145: int open_all_files()
146: {
147:    int rv = NO_ERROR;
148:
149:    /* Open ALBUMS Index and DBF file */
150:    if ( (rv = open_files(ALBUMS_IDX, ALBUMS_DBF)) == 0 )
151:    {
152:      /* Are there any records to process ? */
153:      if (nbr_records == 0)
154:      {
155:        rv = -1;
156:      }
157:      else
158:      {
159:        switch_globals(ALBUMS, FROM_GLOBAL);
160:        if( (alb_songs_fp = fopen(SONGS_DBF, "r+b" )) == NULL )
161:        {
162:           rv = READ_ERROR;
163:        }
164:      }
165:
166:
167:      if (rv == NO_ERROR)
168:      {
169:        /* Now Open GROUPS Index and DBF file */
170:        if ( (rv = open_files(GROUPS_IDX, GROUPS_DBF)) == 0 )
171:        {
172:          switch_globals(GROUPS, FROM_GLOBAL);
173:        }
174:      }
175:
176:
177:      if (rv == NO_ERROR)
178:      {
179:        /* Open MEDIUM Index and DBF file */
180:        if ( (rv = open_files(MEDIUM_IDX, MEDIUM_DBF)) == 0 )
181:        {
182:          switch_globals(MEDIUM, FROM_GLOBAL);
183:        }
184:      }
185:    }
```

```
186:
187:    return(rv);
188: }
189:
190: /*========================================================*
191:  *    print_song_hdr()                                    *
192:  *========================================================*/
193: void print_song_hdr()
194: {
195:    fprintf(stdprn,"SONGS:\n\r\n\r");
196:    fprintf(stdprn,"Track     Song Title");
197:    fprintf(stdprn,"                                        Time\n\r");
198:    fprintf(stdprn,"----     ");
199:    fprintf(stdprn,"----------------------------------------");
200:    fprintf(stdprn,"    ----\n\r");
201: }
202:
203: /*========================================================*
204:  *    process_details()                                   *
205:  *========================================================*/
206: int process_details(char *title)
207: {
208:    static int rv = NO_ERROR;
209:    static int done = FALSE;
210:    static int srch_rec;
211:
212:    if(strlen(title) == 0)       /* Do all of them */
213:    {
214:      /* Albums Idx will drive report */
215:      srch_rec = alb_start_rec;
216:
217:      while (rv == NO_ERROR && !done)
218:      {
219:        /* GET ALBUM INFORMATION */
220:        rv = get_rec(srch_rec, alb_idx_fp, sizeof(alb_idx),
221:             sizeof(int)*2, (char *)&alb_idx);
222:
223:        if (rv == NO_ERROR)
224:        {
225:          /* Get the Albums data record */
226:          rv = get_rec(alb_idx.data, alb_db_fp, sizeof(alb_dbf),
227:               0, (char *)&alb_dbf);
228:
229:          if (rv == NO_ERROR)
230:          {
231:            rv = get_info();
232:            if (rv == NO_ERROR)
233:            {
234:              srch_rec = alb_idx.next;
235:              print_album_details();
```

continues

Listing 19.5. continued

```
236:                    /* Check for end of list */
237:                if (srch_rec == 0)
238:                {
239:                    done = TRUE;
240:                }
241:            }           /* End of NO_ERROR - from DBF */
242:        }
243:        }               /* End of NO_ERROR - from INDEX */
244:    }                   /* End WHILE */
245: }
246: else     /* Do search for specific record */
247: {
248:     switch_globals(ALBUMS, TO_GLOBAL);
249:
250:     rv = search_alb_rec(title);
251:
252:     if (rv <=0 )   /* No error or Did not find rec */
253:     {
254:       if (rv == NO_ERROR)      /* Found it */
255:       {
256:         /* Transfer into working area */
257:         memcpy(&alb_dbf, &albums, sizeof(albums) );
258:
259:         rv = get_info();
260:
261:         if (rv == NO_ERROR)
262:         {
263:             print_album_details();
264:         }
265:       }
266:       else   /* Must not have found rec */
267:       {
268:         rv = 0;                /* Reset - not really an error */
269:         fprintf(stdprn,"Title:  %s   not found!\f",
270:                 title);
271:       }
272:     }
273:   }
274:   return(rv);
275: }
276:
277: /*=========================================================*
278:  *   get_info()                                            *
279:  *                                                         *
280:  *   Loads all the relevant information from the other     *
281:  *   files.                                                *
282:  *=========================================================*/
283: int get_info()
284: {
```

```
285:    int rv = NO_ERROR;
286:
287:    /* Get Songs */
288:    rv = get_rec(alb_idx.song, alb_songs_fp,
289:              sizeof(alb_songs), 0,
290:              (char *)&alb_songs);
291:
292:    if (rv == NO_ERROR)
293:    {
294:      /* Search for GROUP information */
295:      switch_globals(GROUPS, TO_GLOBAL);
296:
297:      rv = search_grp_rec(alb_dbf.group);
298:
299:      if (rv <=0 )   /* No error or Did not find rec */
300:      {
301:        if (rv == NO_ERROR)
302:        {
303:          /* Transfer into working area */
304:          memcpy(&grp_dbf, &groups, sizeof(groups) );
305:          grp_fnd = TRUE;
306:        }
307:        else   /* Must not have found rec */
308:        {
309:          grp_fnd = FALSE;     /* Set flag */
310:          rv = NO_ERROR;       /* Reset - not really an error */
311:        }
312:      }
313:
314:      /* Search for MEDIUM information */
315:      switch_globals(MEDIUM, TO_GLOBAL);
316:      rv = search_med_rec(alb_dbf.medium_code);
317:
318:      if (rv <=0 )   /* No error or Did not find rec */
319:      {
320:        if (rv == NO_ERROR)
321:        {
322:          /* Transfer into working area */
323:          memcpy(&med_dbf, &medium, sizeof(medium) );
324:          med_fnd = TRUE;
325:        }
326:        else   /* Must not have found rec */
327:        {
328:          med_fnd = FALSE;     /* Set flag */
329:          rv = NO_ERROR;       /* Reset - not really an error */
330:        }
331:      }
332:    }
333:    return(rv);
334: }
```

continues

Listing 19.5. continued

```
335:
336: /*=========================================================*
337:  *    print_album_details()                                *
338:  *=========================================================*/
339: void print_album_details()
340: {
341:   int i;
342:   char hold_items[8];
343:
344: /* ---------------------------------------------*/
345:
346:   /* Display ALBUM TITLE */
347:   fprintf(stdprn,"%-30s",alb_dbf.title);
348:   fprintf(stdprn,"\t\t\t\t\t%8s\n\r\n\r", today);
349:
350: /* ---------------------------------------------*/
351:
352:   /* Display GROUP-related Information */
353:   fprintf(stdprn,"Group:        %-25s\n\r\n\r",
354:        alb_dbf.group);
355:
356:   fprintf(stdprn,"Group Desc:  ");
357:   if (grp_fnd)
358:   {
359:     fprintf(stdprn,"%-60s\n\r",grp_dbf.info[0]);
360:     for (i = 1; i<3; i++)
361:     {
362:       fprintf(stdprn,"                 %-60s\n\r",
363:               grp_dbf.info[i]);
364:     }
365:     fprintf(stdprn,"\n\r");
366:
367:   }
368:   else
369:   {
370:     fprintf(stdprn, "Unknown\n\r\n\r\n\r\n\r");
371:   }
372:
373: /* ---------------------------------------------*/
374:
375:   /* Display Types of Music */
376:   fprintf(stdprn, "Type of Music:  ");
377:   if (grp_fnd)
378:   {
379:     fprintf(stdprn,"%-20s\n\r\n\r",grp_dbf.music_type);
380:   }
381:   else
382:   {
383:     fprintf(stdprn,"Unknown\n\r\n\r");
```

```
384:    }
385:
386: /* ---------------------------------------------*/
387:
388:    /* MEDIUM Information */
389:    fprintf(stdprn, "Medium:   ");
390:    if (med_fnd)
391:    {
392:      fprintf(stdprn,"%-35s\n\r\n\r",med_dbf.desc);
393:    }
394:    else
395:    {
396:      fprintf(stdprn,"Unknown\n\r\n\r");
397:    }
398:
399: /* ---------------------------------------------*/
400:
401:    /* ALBUM Information */
402:
403:    /* Setup date purchased */
404:    strncpy(hold_items, alb_dbf.date_purch.month, 2);
405:    hold_items[2] = '/';
406:    strncpy(hold_items+3, alb_dbf.date_purch.day, 2);
407:    hold_items[5] = '/';
408:    strncpy(hold_items+6, alb_dbf.date_purch.year, 2);
409:    hold_items[8] ='\0';
410:    fprintf(stdprn,"Date Purchased:   %-8s\n\r\n\r", hold_items);
411:
412:    /* Setup formatting for COST */
413:    strncpy(hold_items, alb_dbf.cost, 3);
414:    hold_items[3]='.';
415:    strncpy(hold_items+4, alb_dbf.cost+3, 2);
416:    hold_items[6] = '\0';
417:    fprintf(stdprn,"Cost:   $%6s\n\r", hold_items);
418:
419:    /* Setup formatting for VALUE */
420:    strncpy(hold_items, alb_dbf.value, 3);
421:    hold_items[3]='.';
422:    strncpy(hold_items+4, alb_dbf.value+3, 2);
423:    hold_items[6] = '\0';
424:    fprintf(stdprn,"Value:  $%6s\n\r\n\r", hold_items);
425:
426: /* ---------------------------------------------*/
427:
428:    /* SONGS Information */
429:
430:    print_song_hdr();
431:
432:    for (i=0; i<7; i++)
433:    {
```

19

continues

Listing 19.5. continued

```
434:     fprintf(stdprn," %2d       %-40s    %2s:%2s\n\r",
435:             i+1, alb_songs[i].title,
436:             alb_songs[i].minutes,
437:             alb_songs[i].seconds);
438:    }
439:
440:   fprintf(stdprn,"\n\r");
441:   fprintf(stdprn,"\f");
442: }
443:
444:
445: /*=======================================================*
446:  *    switch_globals()                                   *
447:  *=======================================================*/
448: void switch_globals(int whichone, int whichway)
449: {
450:
451:  switch(whichone)
452:  {
453:    case ALBUMS:
454:               if (whichway == TO_GLOBAL)
455:               {
456:                  idx_fp = alb_idx_fp;
457:                  db_fp  = alb_db_fp;
458:                  nbr_records = alb_nbr_recs;
459:                  start_rec   = alb_start_rec;
460:               }
461:               else    /* Take FROM_GLOBAL */
462:               {
463:                  alb_idx_fp = idx_fp;
464:                  alb_db_fp  = db_fp;
465:                  alb_nbr_recs = nbr_records;
466:                  alb_start_rec = start_rec;
467:               }
468:               break;
469:
470:
471:    case GROUPS: if (whichway == TO_GLOBAL)
472:               {
473:                   idx_fp = grp_idx_fp;
474:                   db_fp  = grp_db_fp;
475:                   nbr_records = grp_nbr_recs;
476:                   start_rec   = grp_start_rec;
477:               }
478:               else    /* Take FROM_GLOBAL */
479:               {
480:                   grp_idx_fp = idx_fp;
481:                   grp_db_fp  = db_fp;
482:                   grp_nbr_recs = nbr_records;
```

```
483:                      grp_start_rec = start_rec;
484:                 }
485:                 break;
486:
487:    case MEDIUM: if (whichway == TO_GLOBAL)
488:                 {
489:                   idx_fp = med_idx_fp;
490:                   db_fp  = med_db_fp;
491:                   nbr_records = med_nbr_recs;
492:                   start_rec  = med_start_rec;
493:                 }
494:                 else    /* Take FROM_GLOBAL */
495:                 {
496:                   med_idx_fp = idx_fp;
497:                   med_db_fp  = db_fp;
498:                   med_nbr_recs  = nbr_records;
499:                   med_start_rec = start_rec;
500:                 }
501:                 break;
502: }
503: }
```

Walking on the Moon   Today: 02/20/94

Group: Philippe Kahn

Group Desc: Jazz Music by the Owner of Borland International.
             Features several famous people

Type of Music: Jazz

Medium: Compact Disc

Date Purchased: 12/13/92

Cost: $ 14.95
Value: $342.00

SONGS:

Track	Song Title	Time
01	OOPs!	05:06
02	Interlude	00:00
03	Walkin' on the Moon	07:28
04	Interlude	00:00
05	Epistrophy	04:35
06	Interlude	00:00
07	S, E and L	04:10

```
08       All's Well That Ends              08:12
09       Interlude                         00:00
10       This Masquerade                   05:48
11       Interlude                         00:00
12       Ralph's Piano Waltz               05:45
13       Interlude                         00:00
14       Calor                             08:07
15       Interlude                         00:00
16       Better Days                       03:49
17       Interlude                         00:00
18       Mopti                             05:46
19       Interlude                         00:00
20       Silence                           05:52
```

Note: Your output will look like the prototype. The specific data printed will be dependent upon the data in your files.

As you can see, a detailed report has the potential of requiring as much code as an entry and edit screen. The outcome of this listing is a detailed report that contains information out of all three data files in the *Record of Records!* system. With the coding that you have already done in this book, you should be able to follow a majority of this listing on your own. There are just a few areas that may need explanation.

Because the I/O functions used a single set of global variables, there is some complexity in the listing. In fact, a function was necessary to swap the global I/O variables between files. This function, called switch_globals(), is presented in lines 445 to 503. Variables are set up to hold each database's global information (see lines 36 to 51). When each of the files is opened, it will call the switch_globals() function to copy the generic global values to the file specific areas. As each file is needed, the file-specific variables will be copied back to the global areas.

To call this report, you pass music_rpt() a string. If the string is of zero length, then all of the records in the albums database are printed. If you pass a string value, then only that particular title is printed. To give the user the ability to enter a specific string, you need to modify the REC_RPTG.C listing.

Two changes need to be made. The first change is to the case statement for printing an individual title with the detail report. This was lines 161 to 166 of Listing 19.1. You should replace this case with the following:

```
case 2:  /* Menu option 2 */
         cursor_on();
```

```
                    rv = get_alb_selection(alb_ttl);
                    if( rv == NO_ERROR )
                    {
                      if( strlen(alb_ttl) != 0 )
                      {
                         music_rpt(alb_ttl);
                      }
                      else
                      {
                         display_msg_box("No title entered.",
                            ct.err_fcol, ct.err_bcol );
                      }
                    }
                    break;
```

As you can see, you will call a function called get_alb_selection() to determine which title should be printed. The parameter being passed is a character array of 31 characters that needs to be declared at the beginning of the do_detail_album_menu() function. If the return value from the get_alb_selection() function is not an error, then a string may have been entered. The next line uses strlen() to ensure that a string has been entered. If you pass a zero length string to music_rpt(), you would get a listing of all the musical items. Because that is a separate menu option, you want to print an error here.

The second change to the REC_RPTG.C listing is the addition of the new get_alb_selection() function. Listing 19.6 presents an updated REC_RPTG.C listing with the new changes and function added. You should also notice that the prototype for this function was added to the beginning of the listing.

Listing 19.6. REC_RPTG.C with the get_alb_selection() function.

```
 1:  /*============================================================
 2:   * Filename: REC_RPTG.c
 3:   *           RECORD OF RECORDS - Version 1.0
 4:   *
 5:   * Author:   Bradley L. Jones
 6:   *           Gregory L. Guntle
 7:   *
 8:   * Purpose:  The Reporting menus.
 9:   *
10:   * Note:     Assumes 80 columns by 25 columns for screen.
11:   *============================================================*/
12:
13:  #include <stdio.h>
14:  #include <string.h>
15:  #include <ctype.h>
```

continues

Listing 19.6. continued

```
16:    #include "tyac.h"
17:    #include "records.h"
18:
19:    /*--------------------*
20:     *      prototypes    *
21:     *--------------------*/
22:    #include "recofrec.h"
23:
24:    int do_detail_album_menu(void);
25:    int get_alb_selection(char *);
26:
27:    /*=======================================================*
28:     *                      main()                           *
29:     *=======================================================*/
30:
31:    int do_reporting(void)
32:    {
33:      int  rv      = 0;
34:      int  cont    = TRUE;
35:      int  menu_sel = 0;
36:      char *saved_screen = NULL;
37:
38:
39:      char *rpt_menu[10] = {
40:              "1. Detailed Information", "1Dd",
41:              "2. List of Musical Item", "2Mm",
42:              "3. List of Groups       ", "3Gg",
43:              "4. List of Medium Codes", "4Mm",
44:              "5. Return to Main Menu ", "5RrEeQq" };
45:
46:      char MENU_EXIT_KEYS[MAX_KEYS] = {F3, F10, ESC_KEY};
47:
48:      while( cont == TRUE )                /* loop in temp menu */
49:      {
50:        saved_screen = save_screen_area(10, 21, 28, 58 );
51:
52:        rv = display_menu(12, 30, DOUBLE_BOX, rpt_menu, 10,
53:                          MENU_EXIT_KEYS, &menu_sel, NO_LR_ARROW,
54:                          SHADOW);
55:
56:        switch( rv )
57:        {
58:          case ENTER_KEY: /* accept selection */
59:          case CR:
60:                switch( menu_sel )
61:                {
62:                    case 1:  /* Menu option 1 */
63:                            cursor_on();
64:                            do_detail_album_menu();
```

```
65:                           break;
66:
67:                case 2:   /* Menu option 2 */
68:                          cursor_on();
69:                          list_musical_items();
70:                          break;
71:
72:                case 3:   /* Menu option 3 */
73:                          cursor_on();
74:                          list_groups();
75:                          break;
76:
77:                case 4:   /* Reporting */
78:                          cursor_on();
79:                          list_medium_codes();
80:                          break;
81:
82:                case 5:   /* exit */
83:                          cont = FALSE;
84:                          break;
85:
86:                default: /* continue looping */
87:                          boop();
88:                          break;
89:              }
90:            break;
91:
92:      case ESC_KEY: rv = ENTER_KEY;   /* so don't exit clear out */
93:                    cont = FALSE;     /* exit */
94:                    break;
95:
96:      case F3:      /* exiting */
97:                    cont = FALSE;
98:                    break;
99:
100:     case F10:     /* action bar */
101:                   rv = do_main_actionbar();
102:
103:                   if( rv == F3 )
104:                       cont = FALSE;
105:
106:                   break;
107:
108:     default:      boop();
109:                   break;
110:        }
111:    }
112:    restore_screen_area(saved_screen);
113:
114:    return(rv);
```

19

continues

Listing 19.6. continued

```
115: }
116:
117: /*-----------------------------------------------*
118:  * Detailed Musical Item Report                  *
119:  *-----------------------------------------------*/
120:
121: int do_detail_album_menu(void)
122: {
123:    int  rv      = 0;
124:    int  cont    = TRUE;
125:    int  menu_sel = 0;
126:    char *saved_screen = NULL;
127:    char alb_ttl[31];
128:
129:
130:    char *album_menu[6] = {
131:            "1. All Items", "1Aa",
132:            "2. One Item ", "2Oo",
133:            "3. Return   ", "3RrEeQq" };
134:
135:    char MENU_EXIT_KEYS[MAX_KEYS] = {F3, F10, ESC_KEY};
136:
137:    while( cont == TRUE )                   /* loop in temp menu */
138:    {
139:       saved_screen = save_screen_area(13, 19, 35, 55 );
140:
141:       rv = display_menu(14, 40, DOUBLE_BOX, album_menu, 6,
142:                         MENU_EXIT_KEYS, &menu_sel, NO_LR_ARROW,
143:                         SHADOW);
144:
145:       switch( rv )
146:       {
147:          case ENTER_KEY: /* accept selection */
148:          case CR:
149:                switch( menu_sel )
150:                {
151:                   case 1:  /* Menu option 1 */
152:                           cursor_on();
153:                           music_rpt(""); /* empty string for all*/
154:                           break;
155:
156:                   case 2:  /* Menu option 2 */
157:                           cursor_on();
158:                           rv = get_alb_selection(alb_ttl);
159:                           if( rv == NO_ERROR )
160:                           {
161:                              if( strlen(alb_ttl) != 0 )
162:                              {
163:                                 music_rpt(alb_ttl);
```

```
164:                                    }
165:                                else
166:                                {
167:                                    display_msg_box("No title entered.",
168:                                        ct.err_fcol, ct.err_bcol );
169:                                }
170:                            }
171:                            break;
172:
173:                    case 3:  /* Exit menu */
174:                            cont = FALSE;
175:                            break;
176:
177:                    default: /* continue looping */
178:                            boop();
179:                            break;
180:                }
181:            break;
182:
183:        case ESC_KEY: rv = ENTER_KEY;  /* so don't exit clear out */
184:                    cont = FALSE;    /* exit */
185:                    break;
186:
187:        case F3:      /* exiting */
188:                    cont = FALSE;
189:                    break;
190:
191:        case F10:     /* action bar */
192:                    rv = do_main_actionbar();
193:
194:                    if( rv == F3 )
195:                        cont = FALSE;
196:
197:                    break;
198:
199:        default:      boop();
200:                    break;
201:    }
202:  }
203:  restore_screen_area(saved_screen);
204:
205:  return(rv);
206: }
207:
208: /*------------------------------------------------*
209:  * Get title for reporting.                       *
210:  *------------------------------------------------*/
211:
212: int get_alb_selection(char *title)
213: {
```

19

continues

Listing 19.6. continued

```
214:        int  rv = NO_ERROR;
215:        char *saved_screen = NULL;
216:
217:        static char fexit_keys[ 5 ] = { F3, ESC_KEY, CR_KEY,
218:                                        ENTER_KEY, NULL };
219:        static char *exit_keys = fexit_keys;
220:        getline( SET_EXIT_KEYS, 0, 4, 0, 0, 0, exit_keys );
221:
222:        /*** setup colors and default keys ***/
223:        getline( SET_DEFAULTS, 0, 0, 0, 0, 0, 0 );
224:        getline( SET_NORMAL, 0, ct.fld_fcol, ct.fld_bcol,
225:                    ct.fld_high_fcol, ct.fld_high_bcol, 0 );
226:        getline( SET_UNDERLINE, 0, ct.fld_fcol, ct.fld_bcol,
227:                    ct.fld_high_fcol, ct.fld_high_bcol, 0 );
228:        getline( SET_INS, 0, ct.abar_fcol, ct.abar_bcol, 24, 76, 0 );
229:
230:
231:        saved_screen = save_screen_area(8, 22, 10, 70 );
232:
233:        box(8, 22, 10, 70, BLANK_BOX, FILL_BOX,
234:                        ct.bg_fcol, ct.bg_bcol);
235:
236:        getline( CLEAR_FIELD, 0, 31, 0, 0, 0, title );
237:
238:        write_string("Enter Album Title:",
239:                    ct.fld_prmpt_fcol, ct.fld_prmpt_bcol, 10, 10 );
240:
241:        rv = getline( GET_ALPHA, 0, 10, 30, 0, 30, title);
242:
243:        if( rv == ESC_KEY |¦ rv == F3 )
244:        {
245:           getline( CLEAR_FIELD, 0, 31, 0, 0, 0, title );
246:           rv = 1;
247:        }
248:        else
249:        {
250:           rv = 0;
251:        }
252:
253:        restore_screen_area(saved_screen);
254:        return( rv );
255: }
256:
257: /*========================================================*
258:  *                  end of listing                        *
259:  *========================================================*/
```

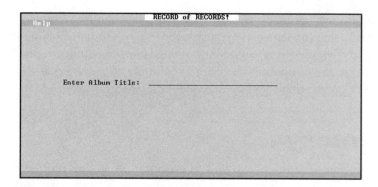

The `get_alb_selection()` function uses the same code that you used to create an entry and edit screen. Lines 217 to 228 set up the `getline()` function. The only exit keys that are used are the Escape key, the Enter or Carriage Return key, and the F3 key. In line 231, the familiar `save_screen_area()` function is used to save off the menus that are displayed on the screen. Line 233 then erases the menus from the screen using the `box()` function to clear with the background colors.

Line 236 begins the process of getting the title. The field that the title will be placed in is cleared. Line 238 displays the prompt to the user. Line 241 calls `getline()` to retrieve that actual data. If the user exits the field with the escape key or the F3 key, then line 245 clears the field and sets the return value to an error. In any other circumstance, the return value is set to zero. Once complete, the screen is restored to the menus and control is returned to the calling function.

Building Flexibility into the Reporting

You have created several reports. In the Detailed Information Report, you used a single report to print either all or a single musical item. Being able to limit the scope of what prints in a report is often a requirement. Many times the scope is limited by using a box similar to the one presented to obtain the musical item title. While this box contained only a single field, it could have contained several.

In addition to limiting the scope of what prints, you may also choose to change whether the report prints to paper or the screen. Based on this choice, you will need to do additional formatting. You will also need to add control for the screen because only 25 lines can be displayed.

Most printers will enable you to format reports with different fonts. These fonts may be as simple as condensed and regular-sized text. In addition, bolding and underlining are also often used in reports. Many of these features require specific information to be sent to the computer. There are a multitude of features that could be added to reports; however, many of them require printer-specific controls.

Summary

Today, you were presented with information on adding printed reports to your applications. Several list reports were presented along with a detailed report. The list reports simply list information from a single file, whereas the detailed report was much more complex. Before beginning the coding on a report, you should create a prototype. A prototype gives you the ability to see what the report will look like before you take the time to code it. It is easier to change a prototype than it is to modify the code.

Q&A

Q How important is reporting in an application?

A Most people prefer to obtain data from a report rather than try to view it from the entry and edit. Most entry and edit screens will only allow one record to be viewed at a time. A report allows multiple records to be seen at the same time.

Q How many reports should be provided?

A You should provide your users with whatever reports are needed. Often, by adding a few selection criteria—such as all or one—you can provide fewer reports and still meet the needs of the users.

Workshop

The Workshop provides quiz questions to help you solidify your understanding of the material covered and exercises to provide you with experience in using what you've learned.

Quiz

1. What is a benefit of prototyping a report?

2. What is a list?

3. What are some of the benefits to listing information from a file?

4. Why are 9s used on a prototype?

5. Why are Xs used on a prototype?

6. Why is it good to include the current date on a report?

7. Why is it good to include "real" data on a report prototype?

8. How many lines can generally print on a page?

9. Using the name data presented below, what would be printed using the following prototype?

   The prototype:

   ```
   Last name   First name   Middle Initial
   XXXXXXX, XXXXX X.
   ```

   The name data:

Last name	First name	Middle name
Foster	MaryBeth	Elizabeth
Bell	Mike	James
Livenstone	Angela	

Exercises

1. Modify the List of Groups Report. Don't print lines that contain blank members.

2. Create a prototype for a Musical Item List. This list should contain the title and the group name.

3. Write the code to create the Musical Item List that was prototyped in Exercise 2.

4. **ON YOUR OWN:** Create additional reports and include them in the *Record of Records!* application.

5. **ON YOUR OWN:** Create your own reports for your own application.

Finishing Touches: Testing, Debugging, Upgrading, and Maintaining

Although your application is finished being coded, you shouldn't consider your job complete. There is still the need to test. In the process of testing (and in constructing) an application, you may encounter problems that need to be resolved. In addition, once others use your software, you'll begin to get feedback of suggested changes or additions. Today you will learn:

☐ Why testing is important.

☐ The different types and stages of testing.

☐ The different categories of problems that may be found in an application.

☐ Approaches to correcting common problems.

☐ When an application is truly complete.

☐ What happens after a program is released to others.

Why Test?

No program is perfectly written. In addition, when programming larger programs, some requirements may have been forgotten or worse, changed. Testing should be done to ensure the accuracy of the application and that all the requirements were included. There are two things to consider about testing. The first is what level of complexity you should incorporate into your testing. Second, you'll need to consider what types of tests will be performed.

The Complexity in Your Testing

The objective of testing is to ensure that there are no problems or errors in your program. In addition, testing should confirm that your program does what was intended. The level of detail involved in testing may determine the likelihood of problems slipping through without being caught.

Expert Tip: Have someone test the application who is not familiar with it. Because you have worked so closely to the application, you'll have a tendency to overlook things. A person unfamiliar with it will lend a new perspective to it.

Many programmers consider testing to be the 15 minutes that they spend running the program right after they code it. Testing can be as informal as this; however, generally, it's better to put in a little more time and effort. Following are some of the different levels of detail that testing can entail. Generally, the greater the detail, the better the chance to find problems. The list starts with the least detailed and increases in detail.

☐ Free-form testing involves just using the application with no direction or guidance. Free-form testing requires no preparation. The objective is to try to cause problems just by using the software.

☐ The next level is testing with an objective list. To give the testing some direction, you should write down what should be accomplished by the test. For example, in the Medium Code screen, the action bar should be tested, along with each item on it, the help functions, the accelerator keys, the entry of each field, the file functions, and so on. The testing is still performed in a free-form manner; however, each objective should be covered in the free-form testing.

☐ Detailed checklist testing involves more work before testing begins. This is an even higher degree of testing. You write out each specific area that should be tested. For example, you can say to test the Exit on the File action bar, the Add on the Edit action bar, the Update on the Edit action bar, and so on. This ensures that every individual portion of the application is tested.

☐ For an even higher degree of confidence in testing, you can script the steps that the tester should follow. This is an expansion on creating the detailed checklist in that the steps the user must take to test each item are included. These steps can begin with starting the application and map each step and each key that the user should enter. In this script testing, you are ensured that everything is tested. (At least everything that is scripted.)

20

Note: When testing, you should enter both valid and invalid information to ensure that the application works as expected. You should ensure that the program can handle erroneous data. For example, a calculator program should be able to handle a "divide by zero" error. This is true regardless of which level of testing you perform.

Different Types of Tests

In addition to the different levels of complexity that can be applied to testing, there are also different categories of testing. There are four general categories of testing:

☐ Unit testing

☐ Integration testing

☐ Alpha testing

☐ Beta testing

> **Warning:** Many programmers don't consider testing worth the time; however, it only takes one serious problem to cause a user to not trust your program. Once the trust in your program is lost, a user will be less inclined to want to use it.

Unit Testing

Unit testing is the first category of testing. A unit is considered an individual part of an application. For example, in the *Record of Records!* application, the main menu is a separate piece of code that is compiled into an object file (.OBJ). You can test the main menu to see that it works as expected. If it does work, you don't need to recompile its source file, RECOFREC.C. If you make a change to the Medium Code screen, you'll need to recompile the MEDIUM.C source file; however, you don't need to recompile RECOFREC.C. You can still use the RECOFREC.OBJ file. Because of this, the main menu, RECOFREC.C, can be considered a separate unit from the Medium Code screen, MEDIUM.C.

> **Expert Tip:** While a unit test could span multiple source files, it's best to keep it at an object file level.

Some people choose to set up unit tests at a screen level. For an application such as the *Record of Records!* application, you could have individual tests for the main menu, the Medium Code screen, the Groups screen, and so on. Setting the unit tests at the screen level is not as good as the object level for one simple reason. If a single source file in the screen changes, then you need to re-unit test the entire screen.

A unit test can be at any of the levels mentioned in the previous section. It is recommended that you don't do free-form unit tests. At a minimum, you should have a set of objectives to test for. A unit test should be performed when all the code for the given unit is complete. There is no need to wait until the entire application is done because other parts of the application shouldn't cause changes to the unit.

If a problem is found when a unit test, or any other test, is performed, then you should fix it. If you make a change to the code, the unit test should be rerun from the beginning to ensure that nothing else changed. While this may seem tedious, it can save you a lot of embarrassment later if you find a problem.

Integration Testing

Integration testing picks up where unit testing leaves off. Unit testing tested each of the individual components of your application. Integration testing should test the integration of the units with each other. Integration testing should be devoted to testing that all the pieces work together. A large part of integration testing will revolve around navigating through different parts of the application.

The *Record of Records!* application can be used for an example of one portion of an integration test. A portion of an integration test for *Record of Records!* may start with the adding of several records, followed by searching for the records, followed by printing a report of the records. This will test to ensure that the report includes any new records that were added. Another test may involve deleting records and then trying to print the report to ensure that they were removed from the report also.

The level of complexity in integration testing is the same as the unit testing. Integration tests can be as loose knit as free-form testing; however, it is again recommended that, at a minimum, you develop a list of testing objectives. For a higher chance of removing all the errors, you can move toward integration tests that are fully scripted.

Note: An integration test should not include tests such as the following:

- [ ] Does the date check to see that the month is from 1 to 12?
- [ ] Is the dollar value greater than 0?
- [ ] Does the Help panel display the correct data?

These are all unit test criteria—they affect only a single unit.

Alpha Testing

Alpha testing is generally done by you or those you are working with. Alpha testing begins where unit and integration testing ends. With alpha testing, you should use the application as it is intended to be used. For an application such as *Record of Records!*, you should enter valid medium codes, musical groups, and musical items. You should also work with the reports, try all the help panels, and navigate through the action bar options. You should store your own real-live data in the application and use it as it was intended.

You may be wondering what the difference is between alpha testing and the preceding unit and integration testing. The difference is how you test. In unit and integration testing, the objective is to try to break the application so that you identify problems before you ship it out. The objective of alpha testing is the opposite. It is to use the application to ensure that it works as intended.

Beta Testing

When you first release your software, you may choose to do a beta test. Whereas you perform an alpha test, beta testing should be done by others. You should find a small number of people who will use the application. Each of these people should be given a copy to use for a predetermined period of time. As these people use the program, they should provide feedback on any problems or suggestions that they may have.

If the beta testers find any substantial changes, then you may need to restart the beta test. This would be done by updating the software and then distributing new copies of the software to each of the beta testers. You should actually release the software to the public only when the beta testers and you are comfortable with the software.

Expert Tip: You should limit the number of beta testers that use your software. You should choose testers that have a high probability of using large portions of your application. The object of beta testing is to have people use actual data in your application. This provides confirmation that your program doesn't have any dormant problems.

Expert Tip: Beta testers are generally given their copies of the pre-release software. In addition, beta testers are also generally given production copies once the software is ready for public release.

Resolving Problems

How many programs have you written that have compiled and run perfectly the first time? If your answer is one or more, then you may be an exceptional programmer. Even when typing in code from a book such as this one, it's not uncommon to introduce mistakes. Before being able to fix problems, you need to be aware of the type of problems that you can encounter.

Types of Problems

A mistake or error in a computer program is called a *bug*. There are two major classifications for computer bugs:

☐ Syntax errors

☐ Logic errors

The Easy Bugs: Syntax Errors

Syntax errors are easy to spot because the compiler tells you about them. *Syntax errors* are errors in the syntax or code that cause the compiler to have problems.

Some syntax problems cause errors, others cause only warnings. If only warnings are caused, the program will still compile and create an executable program. If even one error is caused, then the compiler won't create an executable program. If you compile the following listing, you should get syntax errors similar to those presented in the output.

 Listing 20.1. SYNTAX.C. A program with syntax errors.

```
1:  /* Function: syntax.c
2:   *
3:   * Author:   Bradley L. Jones
4:   *
```

continues

20

Listing 20.1. continued

```
 5:   * Purpose:  A program with syntax errors
 6:   *-----------------------------------------------------*/
 7:
 8:   #include <stdio.h>
 9:
10:   int main( void )
11:   {
12:     char x;
13:
14:
15:     if( x == 1 )
16:     {
17:         printf("Hey! The variable x is equal to 1!!!");
18:     }
19:     else
20:     {
21:         printf("Uh oh! The variable x is equals %d!!!", x )
22:     }
23:
24:     printf("\n\n");
25:
26:     scanf("%d", y);
27:
28:     if( y == 1 );
29:     {
30:         printf("Wow! The variable y is equal to 1!!!");
31:     }
32:     else
33:     {
34:         printf("Bogus! The variable y is equals %d!!!", y );
35:     }
36:   }
```

```
*** COMPILER STUFF ***
Error syntax.c 22: Statement missing ; in function main
Error syntax.c 26: Undefined symbol 'y' in function main
Error syntax.c 32: Misplaced else in function main
Error syntax.c 36: Compound statement missing } in function main
Warning syntax.c 36: Function should return a value in function main
*** 4 errors in Compile ***
```

As you can see, the errors presented tell you roughly what the problems are. Your compiler may present the wording slightly differently than what is presented here; however, it should pick up the same syntax errors.

Review Tip: Fix errors before warnings. A lot of times an error can cause several warnings. Because of this, you could fix multiple problems by starting with the errors.

The Difficult Bugs: Logic Errors

Logic errors are much more difficult to spot and fix. A program can compile without any syntax errors, but still contain several logic errors. A *logic error* is an error in how something is being done. Following are several examples of logic errors:

```
for( x = 1; x < 10; x++ );
{
   printf("%d", x);
}
```

At first glance, you may think that this is a syntax error; however, it is really a logic error. If you didn't spot the problem, the for statement has a semicolon at the end of it. This means the output of this code fragment would be only the number 10 printed once. If that was what the coder intended, then there is not an error here. If the programmer expected 1 through 9 to print, then there is a logic error.

Following is another common logic error:

```
for( x = 1; x < 10; x++ )
{
    do a bunch of stuff...
    x = 2;
    maybe do some more stuff...
}
```

Resetting a variable that is used in a loop can cause the loop to go on forever. This wouldn't cause an syntax error; however, there is a problem.

20

These are simple logic errors that can occur. More complex logic errors can occur as you incorporate code that should do specific functions.

Note: A logic error is any piece of code that doesn't perform as the program specification stated it should, or as the programmer intended.

Finishing Touches

The Oops! Factor: Recursive Errors

Although there are only two types of errors, what seems like a third type is often mentioned. This is the recursive error. A *recursive error* is an error that occurs when another error is fixed. (Oops!) You should work to avoid causing recursive errors by thinking through your changes for syntax and logic errors.

Debugging

Removing bugs in code is called debugging. There are several ways of debugging a program. Generally, the method used will be based on the type of problem. With syntax errors, the compiler informs you of where the problem is. In addition to telling you the problem, it tells you approximately what line the problem is on. By now, you should be familiar with removing these kinds of problems.

For logic errors, debugging becomes much harder. Because the compiler doesn't tell you where the error is, you must find it yourself. There are several methods that you can use to search out logic problems. The most common are the following:

- ☐ Performing a walk-through
- ☐ Using print statements
- ☐ Using compiler functions and preprocessor directives
- ☐ `assert()`
- ☐ `perror()`
- ☐ Using a debugger

To help you understand these methods, each will be covered.

Performing a Walk-Through

For programs that you are going to release either commercially or as shareware, you should always do a complete walk-through. For any other program you create, you should still do a walk-through. Hmmm, sounds like you should always do a walk-through! Better yet, you should have someone else do a walk-through of your code with you. A walk-through is the task of reading each line of code in a program. Generally, the code is read in the order that it would be executed; however, some people choose to read it starting at line one and working through to the end.

Expert Tip: When walking through the code, it is best to walk-through each line in the order that they would be executed.

A walk-through offers many benefits. The main benefit is that you'll have a better chance of understanding all of the code in your program. Secondly, you will be able to identify unused code. You can do this by marking each line that is read. Any lines that are not marked when the walk-through is complete shouldn't be needed. A third benefit is finding code that isn't efficient. If you find that the same lines of code are in several different locations, you'll be able to pull them out into a single function.

A walk-through can also be used to find logic errors. By keeping track of the variables in the code, and by determining what each line does, you can get an idea of what the program is going to do. If you have a logic error you are trying to fix, then you should be able to find it because you are, in essence, running the program.

Note: A walk-through can be automated by using a debugger. Debuggers are covered later.

Using Print Statements

Some programmers choose to use print statements to debug a program. Using print statements is probably the easiest method for debugging; however, it isn't always effective. Using print statements is straightforward. If you are testing to see that a specific function is used, then a `printf()` call at the beginning can be used to signal that you were there. A `printf()` statement can also be used to display the content of any variables.

20

If you decide to use print statements, then you may also want to use preprocessor directives. By including preprocessor directives, you won't need to go through and remove all the print statements when you are ready to create a final version. Consider Listing 20.2.

Listing 20.2. LIST2002.C. A simple listing.

```
1:   /* Function: LIST2002.c
2:    *
3:    * Author:   Bradley L. Jones
```

continues

Listing 20.2. continued

```
4:   *
5:   * Purpose:  A program to print the average and total
6:   *              of 10 numbers.
7:   *-------------------------------------------------------*/
8:
9:   #include <stdio.h>
10:
11:  void main( void )
12:  {
13:    int nbrs[10] = { 1, 2, 3, 4, 5, 6, 7, 8, 9, 10 };
14:    int avg;
15:    int ttl;
16:    int ctr;
17:
18:    for( ctr = 1; ctr <= 10; ctr++ )
19:    {
20:       ttl += nbrs[ctr];
21:    }
22:
23:    avg = ttl/10;
24:
25:    printf("\nThe total of the numbers is:   %d", ttl );
26:    printf("\nThe average of the numbers is: %d", avg );
27:  }
```

```
The total of the numbers is:   960
The average of the numbers is: 96
```

Warning: Your output for this listing and the next may be slightly different.

This listing has a problem. It prints the total and average of 10 numbers. The actual total and average should be 55 and 5.5, not what was shown in the output. This program has a problem that you may be able to easily spot; however, in a more complex program, a similar problem may go undetected. Using print statements, you can easily figure out the problem with this listing. Listing 20.3 contains this same listing with print statements included. This listing also includes preprocessor directives for removing the print statements.

Type

Listing 20.3. LIST2003.C. The simple listing updated.

```c
1:   /* Function: LIST2003.c
2:    *
3:    * Author:    Bradley L. Jones
4:    *
5:    * Purpose:   A program to print the average and total
6:    *            of 10 numbers with print statements.
7:    *------------------------------------------------------*/
8:
9:   #include <stdio.h>
10:
11:  void main( void )
12:  {
13:     int nbrs[10] = { 1, 2, 3, 4, 5, 6, 7, 8, 9, 10 };
14:     int avg;
15:     int ttl;
16:     int ctr;
17:
18:  #ifndef NDEBUG
19:
20:     printf("Starting program....\n");
21:
22:  #endif
23:
24:     for( ctr = 1; ctr <= 10; ctr++ )
25:     {
26:        ttl += nbrs[ctr];
27:
28:  #ifndef NDEBUG
29:
30:     printf("In loop, ttl = %d, ctr = nbrs[%d] = %d.\n",
31:                    ttl, ctr, ctr, nbrs[ctr]);
32:
33:  #endif
34:
35:     }
36:
37:  #ifndef NDEBUG
38:
39:     printf("Done with loop\n");
40:
41:  #endif
42:
43:     avg = ttl/10;
44:
45:     printf("\nThe total of the numbers is:   %d", ttl );
46:     printf("\nThe average of the numbers is: %d", avg );
47:  }
```

20

```
Starting program....
In loop, ttl = 988, ctr = nbrs[1] = 1.
In loop, ttl = 991, ctr = nbrs[2] = 2.
In loop, ttl = 995, ctr = nbrs[3] = 3.
In loop, ttl = 1000, ctr = nbrs[4] = 4.
In loop, ttl = 1006, ctr = nbrs[5] = 5.
In loop, ttl = 1013, ctr = nbrs[6] = 6.
In loop, ttl = 1021, ctr = nbrs[7] = 7.
In loop, ttl = 1030, ctr = nbrs[8] = 8.
In loop, ttl = 1040, ctr = nbrs[9] = 9.
In loop, ttl = 1040, ctr = nbrs[10] = 10.
Done with loop

The total of the numbers is:   1040
The average of the numbers is: 104
```

From the output, you should be able to see two different things. The first is that the value of `ttl` starts out too high. Looking at the code, you will find that it was never initialized. Secondly, you should notice that the subscripts start at 1 and go to 10. They should have started at 0 and gone to 9. Knowing this, you can fix the code and recompile a perfect program.

You should notice that preprocessor directives were used in this listing. If you recompile this listing with NDEBUG defined, the print statements won't be included. NDEBUG can be defined in several ways. The best way to define it is by including a flag when you compile. On the command line, this is done with the /D flag if you are using a Microsoft or Borland compiler. If you compile this with NDEBUG defined, the results are as follows:

```
The total of the numbers is:   960
The average of the numbers is: 96
```

Using Compiler Functions and Macros

The ANSI standard defines functions or macros that can help you in finding some problems. These are `assert()` and `perror()`. Each has a different use that should be examined separately.

Using *assert()*

The `assert()` macro is used to print a message when a predefined condition occurs. If the predefined condition occurs, then the program automatically exits with the following message:

```
Assertion failed: test_condition, file filename, line line_number
```

The test_condition is the condition that has been set up. The filename is the name of the source file that the error occurred in. The line_number is the number of the line in the source file where the error occurred.

The assert() macro is used in program development to determine where logic errors are occurring. The format for using the assert() macro is as follows:

```
assert( condition );
```

When you use the assert() macro, you'll want to make sure that the condition is one that you expect to always remain true. Consider the program in Listing 20.4.

 Listing 20.4. ASSERT.C. Using the assert() macro.

```
 1:  /* Function: Assert.c
 2:   *
 3:   * Author:    Bradley L. Jones
 4:   *
 5:   * Purpose:  Demonstrate assert()
 6:   *-----------------------------------------------*/
 7:
 8:  #include <stdio.h>
 9:  #include <assert.h>
10:
11:  void print_a_string( char * );
12:
13:  int main( void )
14:  {
15:
16:     char *str1 = "test";
17:     char *str3 = "";
18:     char *str2 = NULL;
19:
20:     printf( "\nTest 1:\n" );
21:     print_a_string( str1 );
22:
23:     printf( "\nTest 2:\n" );
24:     print_a_string( str2 );
25:
26:     printf( "\nTest 3:\n" );
27:     print_a_string( str3 );
28:
29:     printf( "\nTest completed\n" );
30:
31:     return 0;
32:  }
33:
34:
```

20

continues

Listing 20.4. continued

```
35:   void print_a_string( char *string )
36:   {
37:     assert( string != NULL );
38:
39:     printf("The value of the string is: %s\n", string);
40:   }
```

```
Test 1:
The value of the string is: test

Test 2:
Assertion failed: string != NULL, file assert.c, line 37
Abnormal program termination
```

This program displays the assert() error the first time the print_a_string() function receives a string that is NULL. Notice that the condition in the assert() in line 37 has the condition of string != NULL. As long as this condition is true, the assertion is ignored. When it evaluates untrue, then the assertion takes over, prints the assert message, and terminates the program. As you can see, the second string that was passed to print_a_string() was NULL. The third string was never passed because the assert() function terminated the program.

You don't need to remove the assert() calls from your program when you are done with them. The assert() macro has been set up in a manner that enables you to turn it off by defining a constant called NDEBUG (no debug). If you compile Listing 20.4 with NDEBUG defined, the assert() macro is ignored. You can define NDEBUG in several ways. You can use the #define preprocessor directive at the beginning of your listing in the following format:

```
#define NDEBUG
```

This requires a coding change and, therefore, isn't the optimal solution. Another solution is to define NDEBUG when you compile the listing. This can be done using the /D in the following manner if you are using the Borland Turbo C compiler:

```
TCC /DNDEBUG ASSERT.C
```

If you are using a Borland compiler or Microsoft compiler, then the /D parameter is used in the same manner. If you are using a different compiler, then you should check its manuals for the proper method of defining a constant when compiling. Following is the output for the ASSERT.C listing with the NDEBUG constant being defined:

```
Test 1:
The value of the string is: test

Test 2:
The value of the string is: (null)

Test 3:
The value of the string is:

Test completed
```

Using *perror()*

The `perror()` function can also be used to help understand problems in your programs. The `perror()` function is used to display a descriptive message for the last system error that occurred. `perror()` prints a message to the `stderr` stream. The `stderr` stream is usually the screen. The prototype for `perror()` is as follows:

```
void perror( const char *s );
```

As you can see, the `perror()` function takes a string as a parameter. When `perror()` is called, this string is used to precede the last system error that occurred.

You may be wondering what kinds of system errors would allow a program to continue executing. The ERRNO.H header file contains the numeric values and symbolic constants for many of the errors that can be set into a behind-the-scenes variable called `errno`. Most of these errors occur because of file I/O. For example, when you open a file, you may not be successful. In the event that the file does not exist, `errno` is set to `ENOENT`, which is the value 2. Consider the following listing. If the `fopen()` fails, then the `errno` variable is set.

 Listing 20.5. PERROR.C. Using the `perror()` function.

```
1:  /* Function: perror.c
2:   *
3:   * Author:    Bradley L. Jones
4:   *
5:   * Purpose:  Demonstrate perror()
6:   *-------------------------------------------------------*/
7:
8:  #include <stdio.h>
9:  #include <errno.h>    /* needed for error numbers */
10:
11:
12:  int main( void )
13:  {
14:    FILE *fp1;
```

continues

Listing 20.5. continued

```
15:    FILE *fp2;
16:
17:
18:    if( (fp1 = fopen( "perror.c", "r")) == NULL )
19:    {
20:        perror("Big Problem Opening 1st File");
21:    }
22:    else
23:    {
24:        fclose(fp1);
25:    }
26:
27:    if( (fp2 = fopen( "abcdefg.hij", "r")) == NULL )
28:    {
29:        perror("Big Problem Opening 2nd File");
30:    }
31:    else
32:    {
33:        fclose(fp2);
34:    }
35:
36:    return 0;
37: }
```

Big Problem Opening 2nd File: No such file or directory

The output displayed shows the program being used with a file that exists and a file that does not exist. As you can see, the perror() function concatenates the system error message to the end of the message passed in the perror() function call. Using the perror() function, you can display descriptive information to the user. You should note, however, that the perror() command doesn't take any corrective action in regard to the error. This is left to you.

DO   DON'T

DO use the NDEBUG constant to remove assert() commands, rather than actually removing them from your listings.

DO use perror() to help display descriptive messages for system errors.

> **DON'T** forget to provide corrective actions if your program has an error.
>
> **DON'T** forget to include the ERRNO.H header file when using the `perror()` function.

Using a Debugger

A debugger is an automated testing tool that is provided with most of the major compilers. Many companies give their compilers names. For example, Borland's debugger is called Turbo Debugger. Microsoft's debugger is called CodeView.

While every debugger is different, most offer similar capabilities. Following is a list of several tasks that a debugger will enable you to do. By looking at the items in this list, you should be able to see why a debugger could help you find coding problems.

Most debuggers can enable you to:

- ☐ View your code as the program runs.

- ☐ View the values stored in variables at any time during the execution of a program.

- ☐ Run a program one line at a time.

- ☐ See the assembler-level code that your program is converted to when compiled.

- ☐ Change the value of variables while the program is running.

- ☐ View or change what is stored in memory.

- ☐ And much more.

In addition to the debugger that comes with your compiler, you can also purchase other debugging tools. In addition to stand-alone debuggers, there are also special-purpose debugging tools. Some tools work to ensure that your system is working with the operating system, others work to ensure that you are using memory properly, some show you what is happening at a machine level. Many of the supportive tools serve a purpose. Depending on the complexity of your programs, these additional tools may be worth the investment.

20

> **Note:** I use a program called Bounds Checker. This program is used to ensure that you are using memory appropriately. Pointers cause a C programmer more problems than anything else. Bounds Checker tracks your use of pointers and memory. Bounds checker will inform you when you use an uninitialized pointer. In addition, it will tell you when you neglect to free memory. Because memory errors can be extremely hard to track down, a tool such as Bounds Checker can help to prevent many serious problems.

When Is an Application Complete?

When you release a program to the public, you will invariably get feedback from some of the users. Some users will make suggestions for improvements for your application. Others will point out even the smallest of problems with your applications. You should welcome these suggestions and comments.

At some point, you may choose to incorporate some of the suggestions and fix the noted errors. In addition to these changes, you may also decide to make your own additions to the application. Updating software with changes and enhancements such as these is a common occurrence.

Three terms are used in making changes to your software. These are updates, patches, and upgrades. A patch and an update are almost the same thing. When your program has a serious problem that needs to be fixed as soon as possible, the change can be distributed as a patch. A patch contains only what is needed to make the fix. An update is similar to a patch in that it is a fix. An update is generally not as critical as a patch. If the use of the software is not inhibited, then an update can be put out.

An upgrade is different. An upgrade may include patches and updates; however, an upgrade will generally include updates to the software's functionality also. Upgrades should include any patches and updates that were already sent out at the initial release or last upgrade to the software. When an upgrade is created, it is often released in the same manner as the initial software. This includes adding a charge. If a charge is added, then the upgrade should add enough functionality to warrant the price of the upgrade.

Generally, with the release of patches, updates, and upgrades, comes the changing of the version number. Patches don't always warrant version number changes; however, updates and upgrades almost always do. By changing the version number, it helps you

to know what changes have been made. There is a pattern to how most version numbers are changed.

Consider the *Record of Records!* application developed in this book. This application was given the version number 1.00. This is the first release of the software, hence the version number is set to 1.00. Each time an update or upgrade is sent out, a new version number should be assigned. The change to the version number is generally reflective of the level of the change. For example, if an update is being incorporated to fix a bug, then the version may be changed to 1.01 to signify that the software has been changed. When a change to the program's functionality is done in an upgrade, then you may consider renumbering the version to 1.1, 1.5, or 2.0, depending on the size of the upgrade. If you are going to change the number to 2.0, then there should be highly notable changes in the software.

Note: Some companies number their beta release of the software with a number less than one.

This section started with the question: When is an application complete? You should have the answer to this question by now. If you offer your software for sale, odds are that your application will never be complete. There will always be upgrades that you can make.

DO	**DON'T**

DON'T send out an upgrade version of your software sooner than six months after the last release. It's best not to update more than once a year.

DO send out a patch if an error can cause problems for the user.

20

Summary

Today, you covered a lot of ground. First, you were presented with information on the importance of testing and the different types of testing. Every application should receive some testing. This testing can be unit testing, which tests only a portion of an application, integration testing, which tests the interaction of an application's parts,

alpha testing, which tests to ensure that the program performs as it was intended, and beta testing, which provides feedback from actual users.

In addition to testing, debugging was also covered. Debugging is the process of removing bugs, or errors, from a program. These can be syntax errors, which are found by the compiler, or logic errors, which require more effort to remove.

Once a program has been coded and tested, it is ready to be released; however, it may not be complete. Once a program is given to users, they will generally provide feedback. From this feedback, patches, updates, or upgrades may need to be made. A patch is a single fix for a critical problem. Updates are fixes for problems or enhancements that are not critical to the application. An upgrade is a larger release of the program that may contain fixes and major updates and enhancements to the program.

Q&A

Q What is the objective of a walk-through?

A The objective of a walk-through is the same as testing—to find any problems and to ensure the software works as specified. Many people do two separate walk-throughs. The first is a code walk-through to ensure the code is accurate, efficient, and, if required, portable. The second is a logic walk-through that checks to ensure the code is doing what is expected based on the initial specification for the program.

Q Is a debugger worth the time it takes to learn?

A Yes. You don't need to know everything about a debugger to get value from it. Most people start by learning how to execute their programs a line at a time. This, along with viewing variable contents, is generally an easy process. You should learn how to use a debugger one process at a time.

Q Should additional debugging tools be purchased?

A Generally, most people don't have the need for tools beyond the debugger that comes with their compiler. If you are developing a large-scale application, then tools such as memory viewers can be worth the investment. You must weigh the cost of the tool with the expected results. For most people doing development at home, the additional cost isn't justified.

Q Do version numbers always follow a sequential numbering?

A No. Some companies choose to skip version numbers for multiple reasons. Generally, this is done when the program has versions on multiple platforms. For example, consider having a program for DOS with a version number of 3.0. If you create a first release of a Windows product, although it should be version 1.0, you may choose to give it version 3.0. If the Windows and the DOS versions provide the same functionality, then you may want the versions to be the same to avoid confusing the user.

Workshop

The Workshop provides quiz questions to help you solidify your understanding of the material covered and exercises to provide you with experience in using what you've learned.

Quiz

1. What is free-form testing?

2. What are the four categories of testing mentioned in this chapter?

3. In what order should the four categories of testing from Question 2 be done?

4. When is testing complete?

5. What is a bug?

6. What is a syntax error?

7. What are the types of errors?

8. What is debugging?

9. What is the difference between a patch and an upgrade?

10. When is a software application complete?

Exercises

1. **ON YOUR OWN:** Consult your compiler to determine what its debugger will do. Try using the debugger to walk through one of the *Record of Records!* listings.

2. **ON YOUR OWN:** Determine the type of testing that should be done with the *Record of Records!* application.

3. **ON YOUR OWN:** Test your own applications.

4. **ON YOUR OWN:** Review the software packages that you have or those in a store or magazine. Do the version numbers seem consistent?

Where To Go from Here?

You have been presented with a multitude of advanced topics ranging from linked lists to dynamic memory allocation, with step-by-step detail on developing your own complete applications from scratch. Today you will learn:

☐ What next steps are available for your use of the C programming language.

☐ What other areas are available for C programming.

☐ What C++ is (an overview).

☐ Why you shouldn't reinvent the wheel.

☐ What canned tools are available that can aid in your C development.

What's Next?

You may now be wondering what you can do with your knowledge of the C language and application development. You may also be wondering what else there is to learn about programming in C. With hundreds of books available on the C language, you may be thinking that there is still a lot to learn.

You should now have a solid foundation for using the C language. Where you go from here is your choice. Most people choose to go in one of three directions:

☐ Specialized programming

☐ Other languages

☐ Other platforms

Specialized Programming

The C language includes constructs that enable you to take advantage of specific machines and specific operating systems. As you incorporate more of its power, you begin to develop applications that may be more machine specific. Many people who do advanced professional programming begin to focus on a specific area. These specific areas can range from graphics programming to writing compilers. Depending on the area of expertise, different constructs are needed. For example, in graphics programming, you may begin working with video memory, advanced math, and more. If you decide to concentrate on programming networks, then graphics are not as important.

You'll find that there are several C books available that cover specialized topics. The most common areas are graphics programming, compilers, and network programming.

Graphics Programming

Graphics programming is an area that many "at home" programmers are interested in. Graphics programs involve working with the video at a pixel-by-pixel level and many functions different than those used by the text graphics presented in this book are needed. In addition, it is often necessary to understand working with dynamic memory and mathematical formulas. It is possible to find books on topics such as graphics, advanced graphics, developing graphical displays, developing games, and more.

Note: The following are just a few books that are available:

Graphics Programming in C by Roger T. Stevens, M&T Books.

High-Performance Graphics in C (Animation and Simulation) by Lee Adams, Wincrest.

Compilers

Some programmers like to understand everything. To understand the full function of the C language, you could attempt to write your own compiler. There are a few books available on writing your own compiler; however, they are very technical in nature. This is an area that you would definitely need to be interested in before attempting to pursue it.

Network Programming

C can be used to create network programs. These can be programs such as the *Record of Records!* program presented throughout this book. You can also write network software using C. In addition, you could even write your own operating system. UNIX is an operating system that was developed with the C language. Again, like writing your own compiler, this is a very technical area to pursue. Books for this area of C development are a little harder to find, but they do exist.

21

> **Note:** The following are just a few books that are available:
>
> *C/C++ For Expert Systems* by David Hu, MIS: Press.
>
> *C Programmer's Guide to NetBIOS* by W. David Schwaderer, Howard W. Sams & Company.

Advanced Application Development

In this book, you created an application with the help of several functions, which you created also. There are several books available that will help you expand your library of functions. In addition, there are several books that offer different approaches to developing applications. Some books are generic; others are extremely specific. Many of these books don't provide you with anything more than what was presented here. Other books, such as Jack Purdum's *C Programmer's Toolkit*, provide you with a multitude of additional useful functions.

> **Note:** The following are just a few books that are available:
>
> *User Interfaces in C* by Mark Goodwin, MIS Press.
>
> *C Programmer's Toolkit* by Jack Purdum, QUE Corporation.
>
> *Advanced C Programming for Displays* by Marc J. Rochkind, Prentice Hall.

Other Languages

In addition to moving into specialized areas, you may also choose to expand into other languages. C programmers will most often move into one of two other languages. These are assembler and C++.

Assembler

Assembler is a language that is much more technical than C. In addition, it is more cryptic. The reason for this is the assembler is one step closer than C to talking to the computer in its own language (ones and zeros). Listing 21.1 is an example of assembler code.

Listing 21.1. Some assembler code.

```
;Assembler code to get a key.
;
waitkey:    move        ah,01h
            int         16h
            jz          waitkey
            mov         ah,0
            int         16h
            or          al,al
            jz          waitkey1
            xor         ah,ah
            jmp         waitkey2
waitkey1    xchg        ah,al
            inc         ah
waitkey2    ret
```

As you can see, this is much harder to follow than a C listing; however, there are benefits to assembler. The main benefit is control. Most C commands break down into several assembler commands. Because of this, the precision of control is greater in assembler. Additionally, because assembler is closer to the ones and zeros that the machine understands, it can be written more efficiently.

The downside of assembler comes from one of the conditions that is also considered a benefit. The downside is that because you are writing so much closer to the machine level, assembler code is not as portable as C code.

If you're going to move into technical programming, then you may need to use assembler. Operating systems or network programming would be considered technical programming. Additionally, if speed is important, you'll be able to write slightly faster code using assembler instead of C.

Expert Tip: Use assembler to write those functions that are speed critical. Use C for the rest of the code.

21

Note: Assembler functions can be linked with C programs.

C++

Many C programmers are moving into C++. C is a subset of C++. This means that a C program could be compiled under C++; however, this would not make the C program a C++ program. C++ is more than just an enhancement to the C language. It is also a different way of developing.

An object-oriented language differs from a hierarchical or procedure language. C++ is an object-oriented language. The C language can be considered a procedural language. A C program is developed by creating functions one after another. Usually the main() function is created and then each of the subsequent functions are created. When the program runs, each function can be called in order. When a function completes, it returns to the previous function. In this manner, you can follow a C program one line at a time. An object-oriented program is developed differently than this.

An object-oriented programming language such as C++ differs from a procedural language such as C because of three concepts that are incorporated. These concepts are encapsulation, polymorphism, and inheritance.

Note: An object-oriented language is identified by its capability to encapsulate, polymorph, and inherit.

Encapsulation

Encapsulation is the concept of making packages that contain everything you need. These packages are called objects. An object contains everything you need to complete a specific function. For example, an object could be created for a square. The square object would do everything that is needed in regard to a square. By encapsulating the square, you create an object that does all the work. All you or any other programmer need to know about the square is how to interact with it.

By encapsulating, you provide a shield to the inner workings of the object. This enables data abstraction. You don't need to worry about how a square works, all you need to concentrate on is how to use it. That is, you only need to worry about what the square can do, not how it does it.

Note: Encapsulation enables you to ignore how an object works and concentrate on what it does.

Polymorphism

Polymorphism means having the capability to assume many forms. Polymorphism can be applied to several different areas of object-oriented programming. It is mainly used in calling a function. A function can be called in many different ways and still provide the same results.

In the example of the square, you may want to call the square object using four points, three points, a single point and a line length, or any of a multitude of other ways. Using any of these sets of parameters, you would expect to get the same results. In a procedural language such as C, you are required to write a different function for each different set of parameters. In addition, each function needs a unique name. In C++, using polymorphism, you may still need to write more than one function; however, you give each of them the same name. Based on the information passed, the correct function is automatically called. Unlike C, in C++ the person using the square function doesn't need to worry about which square function to call—they will all have the same name.

Inheritance

Inheritance is the third identifier of an object-oriented language. Having a square is a beginning, but what if you want a cube? A cube is a special kind of square. It has all the characteristics of a square with a third dimension added. By using a square to create the cube, you can use all of the characteristics of the square. The cube inherits all the characteristics of the square.

Synopsis of C++

As you can see, an object-oriented language has features that are foreign to a procedural language such as C. Because of this, C++ programs cannot be ported to C. The inverse of this, porting C to C++, can occur; however this would not take advantage of C++. In reality, this would be using the C++ compiler to compile your C program. This wouldn't make your C program a C++ program.

> **Warning:** Many C programmers have started using C++ compilers; however, this does not make them C++ programmers. It is when you quit programming procedurally and start using the object-oriented constructs that you become a C++ programmer.

21

By using encapsulation, polymorphism, and inheritance in your program, you can create many benefits to yourself and your users. Because functions are encapsulated,

they are easy to upgrade and replace. As long as the interfaces remain constant, you can change the inner workings. With polymorphism, you can add different ways of calling functions without the need to change any pre-existing code. Because of inheritance, once you create an object, you can use it to build on bigger and better objects. While the learning curve of C++ is a little higher than C, once it's learned, there are benefits to be gained.

> **Note:** Most books that teach C++ assume that you already know C.

Other Platforms

In addition to specializing your C development or moving to other languages to supplement your C programming, you can also move to other platforms. This book has concentrated on developing DOS-based applications. With your understanding of application development, you can either continue to develop DOS applications, or you may choose to move to a different platform. A *different platform* means using a different operating environment or operating system.

The C language can be used on almost every platform. You would need to obtain a C compiler for the given platform. Several of the most commonly used platforms are DOS, UNIX, Windows, OS/2, and System 7 (Macintosh). While the bulk of the C language is the same, some system-level commands are going to differ. In addition, in multitasking operating systems/environments such as Windows and OS/2, you must write your programs to interact with the operating system.

C Utilities

What you've learned in this book should be quite useful. You created a useful library along with several neat applications. In fact, you could market your applications. If you know other programmers, you could give them your TYAC library and header files. Include some documentation on how to use each function, and they will be able to link the TYAC library with their own code. You don't even have to give them the source code if they are using the same compiler as you.

You may now be wondering about other libraries. If you can give your library away, does this mean that you could get other people's libraries? The answer is yes! In fact,

many advanced programmers wouldn't write functions like the ones presented in this book. They would buy a prepackaged library instead.

Note: While you can buy libraries to do everything that was presented in this book, there are a couple of reasons why you wouldn't want to. The main reason is for the sake of learning. By creating these functions as you have done in this book, you learn the background of application development. Additionally, by creating them yourself, you don't have to pay for them! The final reason for creating functions yourself is control. You control exactly what the functions do.

There are a multitude of packages that can be purchased. These packages may be libraries or utilities. When you purchase a library, it may or may not have the source code with it. Most libraries that you can purchase don't automatically come with the source code. Many offer the source code at an additional cost. If you don't plan on ever modifying the functions that are provided in the library, then you shouldn't need the source code. By having the source code, you can modify the functions if they don't meet your exact needs. Some purchased libraries may charge a royalty. This means that if you use the library's functions in your program, you must pay a fee each time you distribute your program. Most purchased libraries don't charge a royalty; however, you should always check.

Following are some of the different libraries and utilities that are available. They are listed here to provide you with an idea of some of the packages that are available. You can find information on packages such as these in several places. You can check your local computer stores, you can talk to local user groups with special interest groups specializing in C/C++, or you can check computer magazines.

Note: The following information is provided to give you an idea of the different types of libraries and utilities available. Their inclusion here is not to be considered an endorsement. You should always research the available utilities before purchasing.

21

Graphics Libraries

Following are several graphics libraries:

Accusoft Image Format Library	By Accusoft Corporation. This set of routines enables you to add the capability to work with TIFF, PCX, DCX, TGA, GIF, BMP, and many other graphics formats. Included are functions that enable you to use several effects including zooming and rotating.
FONT-TOOLS	By Autumn Hill Software. These tools enable you to create, edit, and use fonts within your applications. In addition to providing the functions, a large sample of fonts is also included.
GraphiC	By Scientific Endeavors Corporation. This set of functions can be used to help create scientific and engineering graphics in your applications. This includes the capability to create linear, log, contour, polar, 3D bars, and more.
Graphics-MENU	By Island Systems. This is a set of GUI functions. GUI stands for Graphical User Interface. These routines help you to create several different constructs that are all valuable to an application. These include icons, menus, checklists, entry and edit screens, pop-up messages, and more. The routines also support mouse control.
GX Effects	By Genus Microprogramming. This is a library of special effects. These can be added to your program to display graphics using wipe, split, crush, slide, sand, drip, diagonal, spiral, random, or exploding screens.
PCX ToolKit	By Genus Micro programming. This is a toolkit that enables you to incorporate graphics into your programs. With over 100 routines, you can display, save, scale, and manipulate PCX files into almost any C program you create.
Virt-Win	By TeraTech. This is a set of routines that will help you save and restore the screen. In addition, you'll be able to create screens that are larger then the displayed windows. Using routines provided, you'll be able to pan and zoom different areas.

Communications Libraries

Following are several communications libraries:

C Asynch Manager	By Blaise Computing, Inc. This is a set of library routines that enables you to create asynchronous communications into your applications. This includes several protocols including XMODEM, YMODEM, and ZMODEM. The support is for Hayes-compatible modems.
Essential Communications	By South Mountain Software, Inc. This is a set of asynchronous communications library routines that supports interrupt-driven communications for both receiving and transmitting. Speeds of up to 115,200 baud can be supported along with up to 34 ports. Support for XMODEM, YMODEM, Kermit, and ZMODEM are all provided along with several other protocols.
Greenleaf CommLib	By Greenleaf Software, Inc. This is an asynchronous communications library for both DOS and Windows programs. This library supports several protocols including XMODEM, YMODEM, ZMODEM, and ASCII.
Magna•Comm C	By SoftDesign International, Inc. This is a library that provides full modem support. These fully interrupt-driven routines are for several protocols including ASCII, XMODEM, YMODEM, and ZMODEM.

File Management Libraries

Following are several file management libraries:

AccSys for Paradox	By Copia International. These routines provide an interface between C and Paradox. This includes multi-user capabilities along with routines for working with table files and primary and secondary indexes.

21

AccSys for dBASE   By Copia International. These routines enable you to work with dBASE DBF, MDX, and NDX files. In addition, DBT memo files are also supported. Different levels of support are provided for dBASE II, dBASE III, dBASE III Plus, and dBASE IV.

Btrieve   By Novell, Inc. This is a comprehensive set of routines that will help you incorporate Btrieve file access into your applications. These routines will help in writing applications that will use NetWare Btrieve™.

CodeBase   By Sequiter Software, Inc. This is a set of utilities for accessing dBASE and Clipper files. This includes functions that support multi-user access to the databases. Included are functions for creating pull-down menus, pop-up windows, and data entry and edit screens.

Essential B-Tree   By South Mountain Software, Inc. This set of functions are for creating single- and multiple-key files. In addition, there is support for fixed- and variable-length records.

Memory Management Libraries

"C" EMM Library   By SilverWare, Inc. This is a set of functions that allow for low-level connections between your application and Expanded Memory Manager. Also included are several high-level functions. These high-level functions help you to access and map expanded memory.

E-MEM   By TeraTech. This set of routines will help you to work with both extended and expanded memory.

General Libraries

Following are several general libraries:

C Utility Library   By South Mountain Software, Inc. This is a set of routines for a multitude of functions. This

includes creating pull-down menus, pop-up windows, list boxes, and more. Included with the routines are a menuing system, a screen painter, and a code generator. Using these functions and utilities, you will be able to create entry and edit screens with mouse support.

Greenleaf Functions™   By Greenleaf Software, Inc. This is a large library of varying routines. These include sound functions, graphics functions, directory operation functions, file search functions, and more.

GX Printer   By Genus Microprogramming. This set of functions provides comprehensive graphics printer support.

Hold Everything   By South Mountain Software, Inc. This is a set of routines that enables you to create programs that call other programs. When the called program is complete, you can return to where the original program left off.

/*resident_C*/   By South Mountain Software, Inc. This is a C library that provides functions to help create TSR programs. (TSR stands for Terminate and Stay Resident.)

Vermont Views Plus   By Vermont Creative Software. This is a set of routines that helps create text-based applications such as those presented in this book. This includes the capability to add menus, entry and edit screens, scrolling, help, and more. Mouse support is also included.

Summary

Today, you were presented with material to help set your direction. Now that you have experience in developing full-fledged applications, you are ready to journey into other areas of development. The area you choose can be one of many. You may choose to continue developing entry and edit applications, or you may choose to change your focus. Other areas to concentrate on include graphics programming, using other languages such as C++ or assembler, and using other platforms such as Windows,

UNIX, or OS/2. In today's material, you were presented with some information on each of these different areas that you can choose to focus on.

It isn't necessary to create every routine that you are interested in using. The TYAC.LIB library that you created could be given away. If you create your own libraries, you could sell them, with or without their source code, to others. Several companies offer libraries of routines for sale. Generally, the routines offered center around specific topics. Such topics could include communications routines, graphics routines, file management routines, memory management routines, and more. Several products are listed in today's materials to help you get a feel for what is available.

Q&A

Q Is C going away only to be replaced by C++?

A Probably not. While more and more people are moving to C++, not many of them understand the constructs involved in C++. Most programmers using C++ are using it as a C compiler. There are, however, advantages to using C++ over C.

Q Is it better to create your own libraries or buy them?

A Many of the libraries that can be purchased are royalty free. This means you can include the functions in your application and not worry about owing any money to anyone. Whether a library is worth the cost can be determined in many ways. The easiest way is to figure out how long it would take you to create the functions yourself. Multiply the time by the value you place on your time. The resulting figure compared to the cost of the library should tell you if it is worth the cost.

Workshop

The Workshop provides quiz questions to help you solidify your understanding of the material covered and exercises to provide you with experience in using what you've learned.

Quiz

1. Has this book provided you with a complete knowledge of everything you can do with C?

2. What are three areas where you could increase your C knowledge?

3. What other languages do most C programmers consider learning?

4. What is a benefit of using assembler?

5. What are three characteristics of an object-oriented language?

6. Can a C compiler compile a C++ program?

7. Can a C++ compiler compile a C program?

8. What are some of the platforms that C can be used on?

Exercises

1. **ON YOUR OWN:** Look through a few computer magazines. If you have C programming magazines, they would be even better. Look for adds showing what utilities and libraries are available for C.

2. **ON YOUR OWN:** Take what you have learned in *Teach Yourself Advanced C in 21 Days* and apply it to your own applications.

3. **ON YOUR OWN:** Continue to work with C. Work to improve the functions that were presented in this book. In addition, create your own functions and add them to your library.

21

A

Memory Models

Every C programmer eventually is confronted with memory models. Beginning C programmers tend to avoid the subject. The compiler's default memory model is the one that is used. As programs grow in size, or as writing optimal programs becomes an issue, memory models may become a concern. If your compiler is defaulted to the large memory model, you may never question or worry about memory models. In fact, many programmers who develop at an advanced level don't know the difference between the memory models.

What Are the Memory Models?

There are six different memory models; not all of them are supported by every computer. The six models are:

- ☐ The tiny model
- ☐ The small model
- ☐ The compact model
- ☐ The medium model
- ☐ The large model
- ☐ The huge model

Virtually every computer supports four of these models. These are the small, compact, medium, and large models. The tiny and huge memory models are supported by a large number of compilers, but fewer than the other four.

The Difference Among Memory Models

The preceding memory models apply to the Intel 8086 and other *x*86 microprocessors. The Intel microprocessor uses a *segmented memory architecture.* The *x*86 microprocessors can only address 64K segments of memory at a time. In total, an 8086 can address only a single megabyte of memory. Higher level *x*86 processors have the capability to address more than a single megabyte; however, to be completely compatible with the 8086 microprocessor, only a megabyte of memory can be accessed at a time.

The microprocessor can keep track of more than one segment at a time. Generally, four different segments are tracked. These segments are the code segment, which tracks where the computer—or machine—instructions are, the data segment, which

A

is where the data—or information—is stored, the stack, and an extra segment, which may be used for additional data.

There are several segment registers in the microprocessor. Four of these registers are used to track the segments. The CS register tracks the code segment, the DS register tracks the data segment, the SS register tracks the stack, and ES register tracks the extra segment. Each of these registers contains a 16-bit value. Each of these registers contains a value that is the address of the beginning of a 64K segment. A pointer can then be used to state the offset into this segment.

Note: If you wanted to know where a specific data item is, it would be determined by knowing the offset to the segment along with the offset into the segment. The actual address is determined by taking the segment address, shifting it four bits to the left, and then adding the pointer value containing the offset into the segment.

Note: In a 32-bit compiler, on a 32-bit machine, 32-bit register values may be used.

The segments that are used may or may not overlap. If all four segments completely overlapped with each other, you would only be using 64K at one time. If all four segments didn't overlap at all, then 64K multiplied by four, or 256K, of memory could be used at a time. In the second scenario, each 64K segment must be used for its individual purpose of code, data, stack, and extra.

The Memory Models

Now that the background materials have been presented, you're ready to see the differences among the six memory models. These differences revolve around how the segments are set up.

The Tiny Memory Model

With the tiny memory model, the CS, DS, SS, and ES segments all overlap. Looked at a different way, the CS, DS, SS, and ES registers all point to the same offset.

Additionally, the value in the registers can't be changed. This means only a single 64K segment is used. Figure A.1 illustrates the tiny memory model.

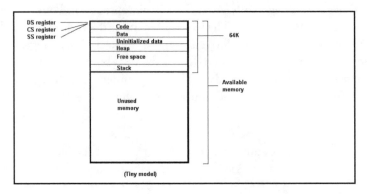

Figure A.1. *The tiny memory model.*

The Small Memory Model

The small memory model enables different values to be placed in the CS and DS registers. This means that the code segment is different than the data segment. In addition, the SS register for the stack contains the same address as the DS register. These values in the registers don't change so only two individual 64K segments are used. Because the addresses of the registers don't change, you only need to worry about the offsets into segments and not their locations. Figure A.2 illustrates the small memory model.

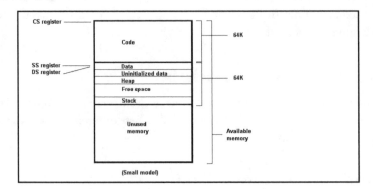

Figure A.2. *The small memory model.*

The Medium Memory Model

Like the small memory model, the medium model allows for two different 64K segments. The use of these segments is the same except the small memory model doesn't allow the address of any of the registers to be changed; the medium model does. In the medium model, the value in the CS register that points to the code segment can be changed, but the value in the DS and SS registers can't. In addition, the DS and SS registers point to the same segment.

By being able to change the CS segment, more than 64K can be used for code. The data and the stack are still limited to a total of 64K because their register values can't be changed, but the code is not—up to a megabyte of code can be used. Figure A.3 illustrates the medium memory model.

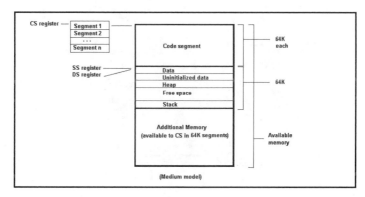

Figure A.3. *The medium memory model.*

The Compact Memory Model

The compact memory model is basically the opposite of the medium model. It enables the value in the DS register to be modified. This allows for a large amount of data within a program. The CS register's value can't be modified, thus limiting the code size.

Whereas the medium model allows for a large amount of code with a limited amount of data, the medium model allows for a maximum of 64K in code and a large amount of data. Figure A.4 illustrates the compact model.

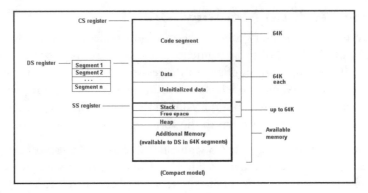

Figure A.4. *The compact memory model.*

The Large Memory Model

Many programmers work with the large memory model. With it, the values in both the DS and CS registers can be modified. This gives you the flexibility of working with up to a megabyte with either the code or the data. Figure A.5 illustrates the large memory model.

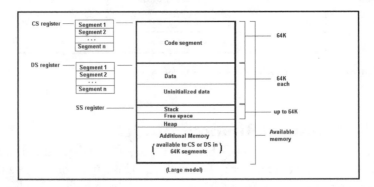

Figure A.5. *The large memory model.*

The Huge Memory Model

The final memory model is the huge model. It may not be supported by every compiler. The huge memory model differs from the large in that the 64K segment size limit on static data isn't applied. This data can occupy the rest of the free memory. Figure A.6 illustrates the huge memory model.

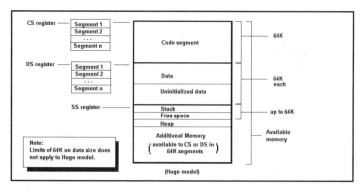

Figure A.6. *The huge memory model.*

Summarizing the Memory Models

Each of the memory models has its place. Depending on the structure of the program you are developing, one memory model may be better than another. The tiny memory model is best when you want to write an extremely small program or when memory is at a premium. The small model is good for most small applications. Most of the applications in this book will compile easily under the small memory model. The medium model is best for larger programs that don't have a lot of data that is used in memory.

Note: We are talking about data in memory, not data stored elsewhere. You can store a great deal of data on a hard drive. If you are only using a few small records at a time, you don't need to worry about a large data segment. It's only when you are loading the data into memory that it's applied to the 64K segments in the data segment.

The compact memory model is most appropriately used with small programs that use a great deal of data in memory. The large program is used for large programs that use a lot of data in memory. The huge memory model is for extremely large programs.

Expert Tip: I use the small memory model for a majority of my programming. The small memory model offers enough room to write utility programs and many other smaller programs. When the small model is no longer big enough to hold the variables or code, the compiler will provide errors. At the time I get these errors, I switch to the large model. If I know the program I am writing will be large, I use the large model.

64K Limits

Although some of the models allow data and code to be larger than 64K, there is a restriction that the code must be broken into segments that are smaller than 64K. If your code is more than 64K, you'll need to break it down into multiple source files. Each source file will need to be compiled separately. Once compiled, they can be linked together.

B

ASCII Chart

Dec X_{10}	Hex X_{16}	Binary X_2	ASCII Character
000	00	0000 0000	null
001	01	0000 0001	☺
002	02	0000 0010	☻
003	03	0000 0011	♥
004	04	0000 0100	◆
005	05	0000 0101	♣
006	06	0000 0110	♠
007	07	0000 0111	●
008	08	0000 1000	■
009	09	0000 1001	○
010	0A	0000 1010	■
011	0B	0000 1011	♂
012	0C	0000 1100	♀
013	0D	0000 1101	♪
014	0E	0000 1110	♪♪
015	0F	0000 1111	☼
016	10	0001 0000	►
017	11	0001 0001	◄
018	12	0001 0010	↕
019	13	0001 0011	‼
020	14	0001 0100	¶
021	15	0001 0101	§
022	16	0001 0110	–
023	17	0001 0111	↨
024	18	0001 1000	↑
025	19	0001 1001	↓
026	1A	0001 1010	→
027	1B	0001 1011	←
028	1C	0001 1100	FS
029	1D	0001 1101	GS
030	1E	0001 1110	RS

Dec X_{10}	Hex X_{16}	Binary X_2	ASCII Character
031	1F	0001 1111	US
032	20	0010 0000	SP
033	21	0010 0001	!
034	22	0010 0010	"
035	23	0010 0011	#
036	24	0010 0100	$
037	25	0010 0101	%
038	26	0010 0110	&
039	27	0010 0111	'
040	28	0010 1000	(
041	29	0010 1001	)
042	2A	0010 1010	*
043	2B	0010 1011	+
044	2C	0010 1100	,
045	2D	0010 1101	-
046	2E	0010 1110	.
047	2F	0010 1111	/
048	30	0011 0000	0
049	31	0011 0001	1
050	32	0011 0010	2
051	33	0011 0011	3
052	34	0011 0100	4
053	35	0011 0101	5
054	36	0011 0110	6
055	37	0011 0111	7
056	38	0011 1000	8
057	39	0011 1001	9
058	3A	0011 1010	:
059	3B	0011 1011	;
060	3C	0011 1100	<
061	3D	0011 1101	=
062	3E	0011 1110	>
063	3F	0011 1111	?
064	40	0100 0000	@

B

continues

Dec X_{10}	Hex X_{16}	Binary X_2	ASCII Character
065	41	0100 0001	A
066	42	0100 0010	B
067	43	0100 0011	C
068	44	0100 0100	D
069	45	0100 0101	E
070	46	0100 0110	F
071	47	0100 0111	G
072	48	0100 1000	H
073	49	0100 1001	I
074	4A	0100 1010	J
075	4B	0100 1011	K
076	4C	0100 1100	L
077	4D	0100 1101	M
078	4E	0100 1110	N
079	4F	0100 1111	O
080	50	0101 0000	P
081	51	0101 0001	Q
082	52	0101 0010	R
083	53	0101 0011	S
084	54	0101 0100	T
085	55	0101 0101	U
086	56	0101 0110	V
087	57	0101 0111	W
088	58	0101 1000	X
089	59	0101 1001	Y
090	5A	0101 1010	Z
091	5B	0101 1011	[
092	5C	0101 1100	\
093	5D	0101 1101	]
094	5E	0101 1110	^
095	5F	0101 1111	–
096	60	0110 0000	`
097	61	0110 0001	a
098	62	0110 0010	b
099	63	0110 0011	c

Dec X_{10}	Hex X_{16}	Binary X_2	ASCII Character
100	64	0110 0100	d
101	65	0110 0101	e
102	66	0110 0110	f
103	67	0110 0111	g
104	68	0110 1000	h
105	69	0110 1001	i
106	6A	0110 1010	j
107	6B	0110 1011	k
108	6C	0110 1100	l
109	6D	0110 1101	m
110	6E	0110 1110	n
111	6F	0110 1111	o
112	70	0111 0000	p
113	71	0111 0001	q
114	72	0111 0010	r
115	73	0111 0011	s
116	74	0111 0100	t
117	75	0111 0101	u
118	76	0111 0110	v
119	77	0111 0111	w
120	78	0111 1000	x
121	79	0111 1001	y
122	7A	0111 1010	z
123	7B	0111 1011	{
124	7C	0111 1100	¦
125	7D	0111 1101	}
126	7E	0111 1110	~
127	7F	0111 1111	DEL
128	80	1000 0000	Ç
129	81	1000 0001	ü
130	82	1000 0010	é
131	83	1000 0011	â
132	84	1000 0100	ä
133	85	1000 0101	à

B

continues

ASCII Chart

Dec X_{10}	Hex X_{16}	Binary X_2	ASCII Character
134	86	1000 0110	å
135	87	1000 0111	ç
136	88	1000 1000	ê
137	89	1000 1001	ë
138	8A	1000 1010	è
139	8B	1000 1011	ï
140	8C	1000 1100	î
141	8D	1000 1101	ì
142	8E	1000 1110	Ä
143	8F	1000 1111	Å
144	90	1001 0000	É
145	91	1001 0001	æ
146	92	1001 0010	Æ
147	93	1001 0011	ô
148	94	1001 0100	ö
149	95	1001 0101	ò
150	96	1001 0110	û
151	97	1001 0111	ù
152	98	1001 1000	ÿ
153	99	1001 1001	Ö
154	9A	1001 1010	Ü
155	9B	1001 1011	¢
156	9C	1001 1100	£
157	9D	1001 1101	¥
158	9E	1001 1110	P$_t$
159	9F	1001 1111	ƒ
160	A0	1010 0000	á
161	A1	1010 0001	í
162	A2	1010 0010	ó
163	A3	1010 0011	ú
164	A4	1010 0100	ñ
165	A5	1010 0101	Ñ
166	A6	1010 0110	ª
167	A7	1010 0111	º
168	A8	1010 1000	¿

Dec X_{10}	Hex X_{16}	Binary X_2	ASCII Character
169	A9	1010 1001	⌐
170	AA	1010 1010	¬
171	AB	1010 1011	½
172	AC	1010 1100	¼
173	AD	1010 1101	¡
174	AE	1010 1110	«
175	AF	1010 1111	»
176	B0	1011 0000	░
177	B1	1011 0001	▒
178	B2	1011 0010	▓
179	B3	1011 0011	│
180	B4	1011 0100	┤
181	B5	1011 0101	╡
182	B6	1011 0110	╢
183	B7	1011 0111	╖
184	B8	1011 1000	╕
185	B9	1011 1001	╣
186	BA	1011 1010	║
187	BB	1011 1011	╗
188	BC	1011 1100	╝
189	BD	1011 1101	╜
190	BE	1011 1110	╛
191	BF	1011 1111	┐
192	C0	1100 0000	└
193	C1	1100 0001	┴
194	C2	1100 0010	┬
195	C3	1100 0011	├
196	C4	1100 0100	─
197	C5	1100 0101	┼
198	C6	1100 0110	╞
199	C7	1100 0111	╟
200	C8	1100 1000	╚
201	C9	1100 1001	╔
202	CA	1100 1010	╩

continues

Dec X_{10}	Hex X_{16}	Binary X_2	ASCII Character
203	CB	1100 1011	╦
204	CC	1100 1100	╠
205	CD	1100 1101	=
206	CE	1100 1110	╬
207	CF	1100 1111	╧
208	D0	1101 0000	╨
209	D1	1101 0001	╤
210	D2	1101 0010	╥
211	D3	1101 0011	╙
212	D4	1101 0100	╘
213	D5	1101 0101	╒
214	D6	1101 0110	╓
215	D7	1101 0111	╫
216	D8	1101 1000	╪
217	D9	1101 1001	┘
218	DA	1101 1010	┌
219	DB	1101 1011	█
220	DC	1101 1100	▄
221	DD	1101 1101	▌
222	DE	1101 1110	▐
223	DF	1101 1111	▀
224	E0	1110 0000	α
225	E1	1110 0001	β
226	E2	1110 0010	Γ
227	E3	1110 0011	π
228	E4	1110 0100	Σ
229	E5	1110 0101	σ
230	E6	1110 0110	μ
231	E7	1110 0111	τ
232	E8	1110 1000	Φ
233	E9	1110 1001	θ
234	EA	1110 1010	Ω
235	EB	1110 1011	δ
236	EC	1110 1100	∞

Dec X_{10}	Hex X_{16}	Binary X_2	ASCII Character
237	ED	1110 1101	ø
238	EE	1110 1110	∈
239	EF	1110 1111	∩
240	F0	1110 0000	≡
241	F1	1111 0001	±
242	F2	1111 0010	≥
243	F3	1111 0011	≤
244	F4	1111 0100	⌠
245	F5	1111 0101	⌡
246	F6	1111 0110	÷
247	F7	1111 0111	≈
248	F8	1111 1000	°
249	F9	1111 1001	•
250	FA	1111 1010	·
251	FB	1111 1011	√
252	FC	1111 1100	η
253	FD	1111 1101	2
254	FE	1111 1110	■
255	FF	1111 1111	

C Keywords

C Keywords

There are several keywords that are reserved as a part of the C programming language. These words shouldn't be used for anything other than their intended uses:

auto   C variable default storage class.

```
auto int x;
```

break   An unconditional exit command. Used to immediately exit a for, while, switch, or do...while statement.

```
while( TRUE )
    {
        commands
        if( done == TRUE )
        {
            break;
        }
    }
```

case   Used in conjunction with the switch statement.

```
switch( x )
    {
        case 'a': commands
                break;
        case 'b': commands
                break;
    }
```

char   The smallest C data type.

```
int char ch = 'A';
```

const   A C data modifier.

```
const float pi = 3.14159;
```

continue   A reset command used to jump to the next instance in a for, while, or do...while statement.

```
for( ctr = 1; ctr <100; ctr++ )
    {
        if( ctr % 2 )
            continue;
        commands;
    }
```

default   A case within a switch that is used when none of the other cases are met.

```
switch( x )
    {
        case 'a': commands
```

```
                        break;
             case 'b': commands
                        break;
             default: commands
                        break;
        }
```

do   Used in conjunction with the `while` statement. This allows looping to occur until the `while` statement evaluates to FALSE. The loop is executed at least one time.

```
do {
     commands;
}while ( condition );
```

double   A data type used to hold double-precision floating point values.

```
double num = 912340000000.123;
```

else   Used to signal commands that should be executed when an `if` statement evaluates to FALSE.

```
if( condition )
{
     commands
}
else
{
     commands
}
```

enum   A data type that can be used to create variables that accept a limited number of predetermined values.

```
enum card_suit = { CLUB, DIAMOND, HEART, SPADE };
```

extern   A data modifier that signals that the variable will be declared in another part of the program.

```
extern global_variable;
```

float   A data type used to hold floating-point values.

```
float num = 123.456;
```

for   An iterative looping command that allows a portion of code to be executed a specific number of times. A `for` statement contains *initialization*, *incrementation*, and *conditional* sections.

```
for( ctr = 1; ctr <= 10; ctr++ )
{
     commands
}
```

C

goto	Transfers program control to a label elsewhere in the program.

```
goto label;
commands
label:
commands
```

if	Allows for branching within program flow. If the expression following the if evaluates to TRUE, then the following command(s) are executed. Also used in conjunction with the else command.

```
if( ctr == 1 )
  {
      commands
  }
  else
  {
      commands
  }
```

int	A C data type used to hold a small integer value. Specific values that can be held are dependent upon CPU's integer size. Generally stores numbers in 2 bytes.

```
int nbr = 150;
```

long	A C data type used to hold larger integer values. Generally stores numbers in 4 bytes.

```
long nbr = 100000;
```

register	A C data modifier used to signal that a C variable should be stored in one of the CPU's registers, if available.

```
register int number;
```

return	A C command that causes a function to end and return to the calling function. The return statement may return a single value to the calling function.

```
function()
  {
      commands;
      return;
  }
```

short	A C data type used to hold a small integer value. Generally stores numbers in 2 bytes.

```
short num = 123;
```

signed   A C data modifier that allows both positive and negative numbers to be stored in a variable.

```
signed int num = -100;
```

sizeof   A C operator (rather than a command) that returns the size of its argument in bytes.

```
sizeof( x );
```

static   A C data modifier that allows a variable to retain its contents.

```
static int ctr = 0;
```

struct   A C construct that allows the grouping of several C data types.

```
struct name {
     char first[15];
     char last[20];
     };
```

switch   A C command that allows program flow to be channeled to various conditions. case statements are used to present the conditions.

```
        switch( x )
   {
     case 'a': commands
             break;
     case 'b': commands
             break;
     default: commands
             break;
   }
```

typedef   A C modifier that allows new names to be created for data types.

```
typedef pos_nbr unsigned int;
pos_nbr x;
x = 100;
```

union   A construct that allows multiple C data types to be stored in the same memory location.

```
union x
   {
     long nmbr;
     char str[4];
   };
```

unsigned   A C modifier that allows a variable to hold only positive numbers.

```
unsigned int nbr = 100;
```

C

void Used to create a generic pointer that can be cast to any type. Can also be used with function declarations to signify that there is not a returned value.

```
void function();
```
or
```
void char *ptr;
```

volatile Opposite of const. A data modifier that allows a variable's contents to be altered.

```
volatile int x = 100;
```

while A looping command that executes until its condition evaluates to TRUE or until a break command causes an exit.

```
while( condition )
  {
      commands
  }
```

Operator
Precedence

Operator Precedence

The C operators are executed in a predetermined order. Parentheses are used to change the order in which operators are executed. The innermost parentheses are given the highest precedence and are, therefore, implemented first.

Several operators can share a level of precedence. In such cases, the operators are generally executed from left to right; however, you should never assume this. If the order of execution for operators at the same level of precedence is important, use parentheses to guarantee the execution order.

Table D.1. Level of precedence for operators.

Highest Precedence

```
          ()(function)    [](array)    ->    .    :>

              ++(postfix)    --(postfix)

++(prefix)    --(prefix)    !    ~    *(indirection)    &(address of)
              +(unary)    -(unary)    sizeof

                      (typecast)

              *(multiplication)    /    %

                        +    -

                        <<    >>

              <    <=    =>    >

                        ==    !=

                   &(bitwise)

                         ^

                         |

                        &&

                        ||

                        ?:

=    +=    -=    *=    /=    %=    &=    ^=    |=    <<=    >>=

                         ,
```

Lowest Precedence

A few examples:

1.  ```
    5 * 3 + 4 * 5
    = 15 + 20
    = 30
    ```

2.  ```
    5 * (3 + 4) * 5
    = 5 * 12 * 5
    = 300
    ```

3.  ```
    x *= 5 + 4 * 3      (assume x = 2)
    x = x * (5 + 4 * 3)
    x = 2 * (5 + 12)
    x = 2 * 17
    x = 34
    ```

D
    ```

ANSI Header Files

E

ANSI Header Files

The American National Standards Institute (ANSI) has set standards on many of the header files that are used in C. The following are header files that fall under the ANSI standard:

ASSERT.H

Contains the assert debugging macro.

CTYPE.H

Character classification and conversion macros that deal with single characters. Examples include:

```
isalnum()
isalpha()
iscntrl()
isdigit()
isgraph()
islower()
isprint()
ispunct()
isspace()
isupper()
isxdigit()
tolower()
toupper()
```

ERRNO.H

Defines constants for the error codes.

FLOAT.H

Defines limits and other constants for floating-point data types. Complements the limits.h header file.

LIMITS.H

Defines limits and other constants for integer variable types. Complements the float.h header file.

LOCALE.H

Defines country- and language-specific information. This includes information on currency format, numeric format, and date format.

math.h

Defines prototypes and constants used with math functions.

setjmp.h

Contains prototypes and other information used in the jump functions—`setjmp()` and `longjmp()`.

signal.h

Defines prototypes and constants that are used with the signaling functions—`signal()` and `raise()`.

stdarg.h

Defines macros and constants for functions that use a variable number of arguments.

stddef.h

Defines several common constants, identifiers, variables, and more.

stdio.h

Defines constants used with standard input and output. This includes the common stream: `stdin`, `stdout`, `stderr`, and `stdprn`.

stdlib.h

Defines prototypes and commonly used declarations for standard functions. This header contains those items that didn't really fit in any of the other ANSI header files.

string.h

Defines constants and prototypes for functions that work with character arrays (strings). This includes functions that work with memory.

time.h

Defines constants, structures, and prototypes for time-related functions.

Additionally...

In addition to these standard header files, your compiler has several of its own. Consult your compiler's reference manuals to see what header files and functions it has in addition to the standard ANSI header files. If you decide to use any of your compiler's non-ANSI header files, you may be limiting the portability of your programs. If you

ANSI Header Files

only use the ANSI header files, then you'll know that your programs will be portable to any other ANSI compatible compiler.

Answers

Day 1 Answers

Following are answers to the quiz and exercises for Chapter 1.

Quiz Answers

1. As you begin to write bigger programs and develop more advanced programs, you will find that memory management is of vital importance. As early as Day 2 you will see several advanced concepts that require memory to be allocated dynamically. These include variable length structures and linked lists.

2. Dynamically allocating memory means that you allocate memory at runtime. In other words, the computer does not reserve room for the variable until a dynamic memory allocation function is executed.

3. You can allocate all the free memory within a computer.

4. You free it. To free dynamically allocated memory, you use one of the free functions. If the memory was allocated with `malloc()`, `calloc()`, or `realloc()`, the ANSI function `free()` is used. For memory allocated with a far function, a far free function should be used.

5. The `calloc()` function has an additional parameter. The `calloc()` function enables you to declare a number of instances of a specific size of memory. This could be done with the `malloc()` function by breaking out the parameter as follows:

```
calloc( 10, 15 );  /* allocates 10 sets of 15 */
malloc( 10*15);    /* allocates 10 * 15 */
```

6. The `malloc()` function is limited to 64K or less of total memory that can be allocated (based on what is not already being used for other data). The far function can allocate beyond this 64K limit.

Exercises Answers

1. The following is one of many possible answers:

```
int *numbers;
numbers = (int *) malloc( 10 * sizeof(int) );
```

2. The following is one of many possible answers:

```
int *numbers;
numbers = (int *) calloc( 10, sizeof(int) );
```

3. This could be considered a trick question. This exercise can be answered
   using either the far version of the malloc() or calloc() functions.

   Borland compiler answers:

```
return_value = (long *) farmalloc( 20000 * sizeof(long) );
return_value = (long *) farcalloc( 20000, sizeof(long) );
```

   Microsoft compiler answers:

```
return_value = (long *) _fmalloc( 20000 * sizeof(long) );
return_value = (long *) _fcalloc( 20000, sizeof(long) );
```

4. This program has two notable problems. The first is that the malloc()
   function needs to be typecast to the type of value it is returning. Because it is
   returning to the variable string, you can assume malloc() is returning a
   character pointer. The second problem is that the variable, string, is not
   declared. The following is a corrected listing.

```
#include <stdlib.h>
#include <stdio.h>
#define MAX   100
void main(void)
{
    char *string;
    string = (char *) malloc( MAX );
    printf( "Enter something: " );
    gets( string );
    puts( string );        /* do something like printing */
    free( string );
}
```

5. This program has the same problem as some of the listings that you saw
   today. This program does not free the memory that it allocates. The following is a corrected listing with the free() function added.

```
/* Day 1: Exercise 5 */
#include <stdlib.h>
#include <stdio.h>
```

```
void main(void)
{
    long *long_array;
    long  total = 0;
    int   ctr;

    long_array = calloc( sizeof(long), 10 );
    printf( "Enter 10 numbers: " );
    for( ctr = 0; ctr < 10; ctr++ )
    {
        scanf( "%ld", long_array+ctr );
        total += *(long_array+ctr);
    }

    printf( "\n\nTotal of numbers is: %ld", total );
    free(long_array);
}
```

Day 2 Answers

Following are answers to the quiz and exercises.

Quiz Answers

1. The basic data types are char, int, short, long, float, and double.

2. The typedef command.

3. DWORD is a type definition of type unsigned long.

4. You can group data in three different ways:

   ☐ With Arrays

   ☐ With Structures

   ☐ With Unions

5. The value of NULL is zero. Displayed as a character, this is '\0'.

6. Word alignment determines how information is stored. If word alignment is on, then there may be gaps between data items. When word alignment is on, all variables are aligned on a word boundary. If word alignment is off,

variables will be packed as close as possible. To know how data is stored, you must know the status of word alignment.

7. A pointer is a special kind of variable. A pointer is a numeric variable that is used to hold a memory address.

8. The "address of" operator—the ampersand (&)—is used to determine the address of a variable.

9. The first is a prototype for a function pointer, the second is a prototype for a function that returns a pointer.

10. One of the main benefits of using a variable length structure is storage space. Only the amount of space needed is used. Using standard structures you may have a large amount of wasted (blank) space, or, your structure may be too small to store everything.

Exercises Answers

1. The following is one example of how this exercise can be solved using a structure:

```
struct ssn_tag {
    int first;
    char breaker1;
    int middle;
    char breaker 2;
    int last;
};
```

The following is an alternate solution:

```
struct ssn_tag {
    char first[3];
    char breaker1;
    char middle[2];
    char breaker 2;
    char last[4];
};
```

2. The following is one example of how this exercise can be solved. To store two different variables at the same memory address, a union is used as follows:

```
union tag {
    long number;
    char string[4];
};
```

3. The following is one possible answer:

```
1:   /* Program:  EXER0203.c
2:    * Author:   Bradley L. Jones
3:    * Purpose:  A program that does not do much. A pointer is
4:    *           assinged its own address as a value.
5:    *=======================================================*/
6:
7:   #include <stdio.h>
8:
9:   void main(void);         /* prototype for main() */
10:
11:  void main(void)
12:  {
13:     long *ptr;
14:
15:     ptr = &ptr;     /* this line may generate a warning */
16:
17:     printf("\nThe value of ptr is:   %ld", ptr);
18:     printf("\nThe address of ptr is: %ld", &ptr);
19:  }
```

```
The value of ptr is:   -720908

The address of ptr is: -720908
```

4. The following is one of many possible answers. This listing includes two different double dimensioned arrays. While not covered in detail in today's material, a double dimensioned array is simply an array of arrays. Notice that the third printing switches the subscripts and causes erroneous information to be printed.

```
1:   /* Program:  EXER0204.c
2:    * Author:   Bradley L. Jones
3:    * Purpose:  Creates a double dimensioned character array
4:    *           and initializes it.  Also creates a double
5:    *           dimensioned integer array and initializes it.
```

```
6:    *            Once declared, both arrays are printed out.
7:    *=======================================================*/
8:
9:   #include <stdio.h>
10:
11:  void main( void );            /* prototype for main() */
12:
13: char checkerboard[8][8] = {'X','O','X','O','X','O','X','O',
14:                            'O','X','O','X','O','X','O','X',
15:                            'X','O','X','O','X','O','X','O',
16:                            'O','X','O','X','O','X','O','X',
17:                            'X','O','X','O','X','O','X','O',
18:                            'O','X','O','X','O','X','O','X',
19:                            'X','O','X','O','X','O','X','O',
20:                            'O','X','O','X','O','X','O','X'};
21:
22:  int number_array[3][4] = { 11, 12, 13, 14,
23:                             21, 22, 23, 24,
24:                             31, 32, 33, 34 };
25:
26:  void main( void )
27:  {
28:     int x, y;              /* counters */
29:
30:     printf( "\n\nPrint Character array...\n");
31:
32:     for (x = 0; x < 8; x++)
33:     {
34:         printf( "\n" );
35:         for ( y = 0; y < 8; y++ )
36:         {
37:             printf( "%c ", checkerboard[x][y] );
38:         }
39:     }
40:
41:     printf( "\n\nPrint numbers with subscripts...\n");
42:
43:     for (x = 0; x < 3; x++)
44:     {
```

F

```
45:        printf( "\n" );
46:        for ( y = 0; y < 4; y++ )
47:        {
48:            printf( "%d ", number_array[x][y] );
49:        }
50:    }
51:
52: printf( "\n\nPrint numbers with switched subscripts..\n");
53:
54:    for (x = 0; x < 4; x++)
55:    {
56:        printf( "\n" );
57:        for ( y = 0; y < 3; y++ )
58:        {
59:            printf( "%d ", number_array[x][y] );
60:        }
61:    }
62: }
63: /*** end of listing ***/
```

Output

```
        Print Character array...
X O X O X O X O
O X O X O X O X
X O X O X O X O
O X O X O X O X
X O X O X O X O
O X O X O X O X
X O X O X O X O
O X O X O X O X

    Print numbers with subscripts...
11 12 13 14
21 22 23 24
31 32 33 34

    Print numbers with switched subscripts...
11 12 13
21 22 23
31 32 33
2570 29264 28265
```

5. You would create an array of the social security number unions:

   ```
   struct ssn_tag SSN[10];
   ```

6. The numeric array can be printed as characters by using `"%c"` and printing each element in a `printf()` statement. The numbers print "BRADLEY".

7. This exercise is "On Your Own."

8. This exercise is "On Your Own."

9. This exercise is "On Your Own."

Day 3 Answers

Following are answers to the quiz and exercises.

Quiz Answers

1. 0

2. The list is empty.

3. A pointer to the same data type as the linked structure is used.

4. A stack is a single-linked list that is always accessed from the top. New elements are added to the top, and removed elements are always taken from the top. A stack has a LIFO (Last In First Out) access order.

5. A queue is a single-linked list that has new elements added to the top. Elements that are removed from the queue are always taken from the bottom (or tail). A queue has a FIFO (First In First Out) access order.

6. A tail pointer is a separate pointer that always points to the last element in a linked list. A top pointer is a separate pointer that always points to the first element in a linked list. If the linked list is empty, then the top and tail pointers will both contain NULL.

7. A tail pointer is generally not needed for a single-linked list. In some cases, they are needed. For example, a queue needs a tail in order to know where to remove elements from.

8. A double-linked list has a pointer to the previous element. This is in addition to the pointer to the next element that both a doubly and single-linked list have. Because there is a pointer to the previous element, a double-linked list can be traversed either forward or backward.

F

9. `calloc()` also initializes the new element to zero. `malloc()` does not initialize.

10. A binary tree has a much quicker access time when looking for specific elements.

Exercises Answers

1. Following is one of many possible solutions:

```
struct character {
    char character_name[25+1];
    int  introduction_year;
    struct character *next_character;
};
```

2. Following is one of many possible solutions:

```
struct food_item {
    char food_name[25+1];
    struct food_item *next_food;
    struct food_item *previous_food;
};
```

3. Following is one of many possible solutions:

```
struct member {
    char name[25+1];
    int age;
    struct member *left_node;
    struct member *right_node;
};
```

4. This is on your own.

5. The structure should contain a pointer to the next customer, not another structure. The corrected structure is:

```
struct customer {
    char lastname[20+1];
    char firstname[15+1];
    char middle_init;
    struct customer *next;
};
```

6. D B E A L I M G N J F K H C

7. A B D E C F G I L M J N H K

8. D E B L M I N J G K H F C A

9. This exercise is on your own.

Day 4 Answers

Following are answers to the quiz and exercises.

Quiz Answers

1. American National Standards Institute

2. Because ANSI sets the standards for many areas. This includes the use of programming languages such as C and C++ along with the use of terminals and more.

3. The ANSI functions are easy to use.

4. The ANSI functions require that the ANSI.SYS driver be loaded on the computer before they will work properly. If this driver is not loaded, then erroneous output will most likely be received.

5. This is a trick question! Red has two values. The foreground color is 31, and the background color is 41.

6. The foreground color is the color applied to the text or graphic being displayed. The background color is the color behind the text or graphic being displayed.

7. When the next ANSI color is applied.

8. It is the fastest method of updating the screen.

9. It is a less compatible means of updating the screen. This is because video memory may be located in different areas of RAM on different machines.

10. Basic Input/Output System

Exercises Answers

1. The escape sequence is an ANSI escape sequence. If the ANSI.SYS driver is loaded, then this will move the cursor up five lines (or as many as possible if there are not five preceding the cursor's original position).

2. Black (30) on White (47)

   White (37) on Black (40)

   Yellow (33) on Blue (44)

   Yellow (33) on Red (41)

3. Yellow on Blue should have been easy. The Bright Yellow may have confused you. Bright Yellow is the same as bold yellow. You gain a bold color by adding a 1 to the escape sequence.

   Yellow on Blue   `"\x1B[33;44m"`

   Bright Yellow on Red `"\x1B[1;33;41m"`

4. The escape sequence uses two foreground colors. The first foreground color will be ignored. Typically you will use a foreground and a background color.

5. This function uses functions provided in today's lessons. This function works just fine if all of the functions used are included. Be careful with screen coordinates. Some programs (and functions) use 0,0 as the starting point, others use 1,1.

6. The following is one possible answer. A `main()` has been added to demonstrate the use of the function. Line numbers have been included. Note that this program must be linked with a_cursor.obj presented in today's chapter.

```
1:    /* Program: EXER0406.c
2:     * Author:  Bradley L. Jones
3:     * Purpose: demonstrate the put_color_string() function
4:     *          This program puts the word "Hello" on the
5:     *          screen in a bunch of colors.
6:     *=========================================================*/
7:
8:    #include <stdio.h>
9:    #include "a_cursor.h"
10:   #include "ansiclrs.h"
11:
```

```
12:   /*---------------------
13:       Function prototypes
14:       ---------------------*/
15:
16:   void put_color_string( int row, int col,
17:                int fcolor, int bcolor,
18:                char *text );
19:   void set_color( int fore, int back );
20:   void main(void);
21:
22:   void main(void)
23:   {
24:      int row, col,
25:          x, y;
26:
27:      set_color( F_WHITE, B_MAGENTA );
28:
29:      clear_screen();
30:
31:      for( y = 40; y <= 47; y++ )
32:      {
33:         col = ( y - 39 ) * 7;
34:
35:         for( x = 30; x <= 37; x++ )
36:         {
37:            row = x - 29;
38:            put_color_string( row, col, x, y, "Hello" );
39:         }
40:      }
41:      set_color(F_WHITE, B_BLACK );   /* your screen color */
42:   }
43:
44:   /*----------------------------------------------------*
45:    * Function:    put_color_string()
46:    *
47:    * Parameters:  row, col      - Screen coordinates.
48:    *              fcolor, bcolor - String colors
49:    *              text          - The string
50:    *
```

```
51:    * Notes:    This function does not verify valid values
52:    *               for the parameters received.
53:    *-------------------------------------------------------*/
54:
55:   void put_color_string( int row,     int col,
56:                                int fcolor, int bcolor, char *text )
57:   {
58:     put_cursor( row, col );
59:     set_color( fcolor, bcolor );
60:     printf( text );
61:   }
62:
63:   void set_color( int fore, int back )
64:   {
65:       printf("\x1B[%d;%dm", fore, back );
66:   }
```

7. The following is one possible answer. Line numbers have also be included.

```
1:    /* Program: EXER0407.C
2:     * Author:  Bradley L. Jones
3:     * Purpose: Re-maps the SHIFTed Function keys to new
4:     *            values.  After this program is ran without
5:     *            any command line parameters, the following
6:     *            are set:
7:     *
8:     *            <shift> F1 = HELP
9:     *            <shift> F2 = DIR
10:    *            <shift> F3 = CLS
11:    *            <shift> F4 = CHKDSK
12:    *            <shift> F5 = CD C:\ID\T7G
13:    *
14:    * Note:    Running the program with an extra command
15:    *            line parameter will reset the keys.
16:    * Note:    The '13' is <enter> - These commands start
17:    *            automatically.
18:    *===========================================================*/
19:
```

```
20:   #include <stdio.h>
21:
22:   #define SHIFT_F1   "0;84"
23:   #define SHIFT_F2   "0;85"
24:   #define SHIFT_F3   "0;86"
25:   #define SHIFT_F4   "0;87"
26:   #define SHIFT_F5   "0;88"
27:
28:   int main(int argc)
29:   {
30:      if( argc < 2 )
31:      {
32:         printf("\x1B[%s;72;69;76;80;13p", SHIFT_F1 );
33:         printf("\x1B[%s;68;73;82;13p", SHIFT_F2 );
34:         printf("\x1B[%s;67;76;83;13p", SHIFT_F3 );
35:         printf("\x1B[%s;67;72;75;68;83;75;13p", SHIFT_F4 );
36:         printf("\x1B[%s;77;69;77;13p", SHIFT_F5 );
37:
38:         printf("\n\nThe Function keys have been set for ");
39:         printf("shift commands.\n\n");
40:      }
41:      else
42:      {
43:         printf("\x1B[%s;%sp",SHIFT_F1, SHIFT_F1);
44:         printf("\x1B[%s;%sp",SHIFT_F2, SHIFT_F2);
45:         printf("\x1B[%s;%sp",SHIFT_F3, SHIFT_F3);
46:         printf("\x1B[%s;%sp",SHIFT_F4, SHIFT_F4);
47:         printf("\x1B[%s;%sp",SHIFT_F5, SHIFT_F5);
48:
49:         printf("\n\nThe Function keys have been reset.\n\n");
50:      }
51:
52:      return;
53:   }
```

Exercises 8 through 10 are on your own.

Day 5 Answers

Following are answers to the quiz and exercises.

Quiz Answers

1. It depends on the overall requirements of the program you are creating. Most times, maintainability will be more important. Efficiency is only important with a program that is time-critical. The most costly part of a program is the time the programmer spends maintaining it.

2. If you are using the ASCII character table, it is 97; however, it could be any other value. A character's numeric value is based on the character set used.

3. The largest unsigned character value will be defined within the numeric constant UCHAR_MAX.

4. American National Standards Institute.

5. Most C compilers are case sensitive. For most compilers, each of the variables would be treated as different. These variable names would not be portable since some compilers don't differentiate case.

6. The isalpha() function is an ANSI function that determines if a character is a letter of the alphabet. It's better to use this function than a function that checks to see if the character is between a and z.

7. The isdigit() function checks to see if a character is a number (0, 1, 2, 3, 4, 5, 6, 7, 8, and 9). This is an ANSI function. It's better to use isdigit() than to check to see if a character is greater than or equal to 0 and less than or equal to 9.

8. As stated in the answers to quiz questions 6 and 7, the functions are ANSI compatible. Using these functions will produce portable code. Because there isn't a proprietary character set for the C language, there is no guarantee what numeric values will represent characters. By using the is...() functions, you gain portability.

9. No. Generally, when working with data files and structures, you must ensure that all things are consistent. Issues such as byte alignment must be known. Because one compiler may have byte alignment on and another may not, portability may be lost.

10. No. The predefined constants are replaced at compile time, not run time. __TIME__ will be replaced with the time the program was compiled.

Exercises Answers

1. This program uses ctr and CTR. These are two separate variables if your compiler is case-sensitive. If you are considering portability, you should rename one of these two variables to allow something other than case to differentiate them.

2. Any listing in this chapter can be used for this exercise. The listing size will shrink; however, the object file and the executable file should remain the same.

   This exercise shows that nothing is added to the program if you add additional spacing. The additional spacing does, however, make the program much more readable.

3. Following is a function that verifies that a character is a vowel.

```
/* Function to verify vowel. All checks are equality, so code will
be portable.*/

int verify_vowel( int ch )
{
    int rv = 0;
    switch ( ch )
    {
        case 'a':
        case 'e':
        case 'i':
        case 'o':
        case 'u':
        case 'A':
        case 'E':
        case 'I':
        case 'O':
        case 'U':    rv = 1;
                     break;
        default:     rv = 0
                     break;
    }
    return( rv );
}
```

F

4. One of many possible answers:

```c
int character_case( int ch )
{
    int rv = 0;
    if ( isalpha( ch ) )
    {
        if( isupper( ch ) )
            rv = 1;
        else
            rv = 2;
    }
    else
        rv = 0;

    return( rv );
}
```

5. This exercise was on your own. This information can be found within your compiler's manuals.

6. No. This program uses `system()`. This function calls an operating specific command—in this case TYPE. This means that your program isn't portable to other operating systems.

7. No. This is quite similar to a program shown in today's materials. The following text would be much more portable:

```c
int to_upper( int x )
{
    if( isalpha( x ) && islower( x ) )
    {
        toupper( x );
    }
    return( x );
}
```

Day 6 Answers

Following are answers to the quiz and exercises.

Quiz Answers

1. Because a computer works with numbers. All characters and symbols are converted to numeric values.

2. For IBM Compatible PCs, the ASCII Standard specifies the conversion values.

3. A decimal value is a base 10 number. Decimal numbers are the numbers that we use to count with every day. Because decimal stands for 10, only 10 numbers are used. These numbers are 0 through 9.

4. The computer stores information in bits. A bit can have one of two states, on or off. Binary numbers are base 2. This means that they can use two digits, 0 and 1, to represent all numbers. These two digits can be used to represent the on and off state of the computer's information.

5. A computer stores information in bytes. A byte is 8 bits. To look at the binary representation of a byte of data means looking at eight digits for a maximum value of 256 (decimal). By using hexadecimal, these 256 possible numbers can be represented in two digits. In addition, the two hexadecimal digits can easily be converted to binary since the first digit represents the left four binary digits and the second hexadecimal digit represents the right four binary digits.

6. While there could be many reasons for wanting to look at the numeric values of data, there is one reason that is most often given. Many characters appear as spaces when viewed as common text. In many cases, the "spaces" may be something quite different. For example, in many of the listings today, you saw the carriage return, line feed. In addition, you saw that spaces were given a decimal 32 value. Other characters such a null (character 0) may also appear as a space when viewed as text; however, 0 and 32 are different.

7. Binary: 0 and 1

8. Decimal: 0, 1, 2, 3, 4, 5, 6, 7, 8, and 9

9. Octal: 0, 1, 2, 3, 4, 5, 6, and 7

10. Hexadecimal: 0, 1, 2, 3, 4, 5, 6, 7, 8, 9, A, B, C, D, E, and F

Exercises Answers

1. Binary: 0100010

   Octal: 102

   Decimal: 66

   Hexadecimal: 42

2. Binary: 10

   Octal: 2

   Decimal: 2

   Hexadecimal: 2

3. a. 88

   b. 32

   c. 120

   d. 49

   e. 3

4. a. A

   b. ? (question mark)

   c. ♣ clover

   d. }

   e. 9

5.
```
/* Program:  Day06E05.c
 * Author:   Bradley L. Jones
 * Purpose:  Print numeric values of an entered character.
 *=======================================================*/

#include <stdio.h>
#include <stdlib.h>

char *char_to_binary( int );
void main(void)
{
```

```c
    int ch;
    char *rv;

    printf("\n\nEnter a number ==>" );
    scanf("%d", &ch);

    printf("\n\n Your number:        %d", ch );
    printf("\n\n Character:          %c", ch );
    printf("\n Octal value:       %o", ch);
    printf("\n Hexidecimal value:  %x", ch );

    rv = char_to_binary(ch);

    printf("\n Binary value:      %s", rv);
    printf("\n\nYour number again:   %d", ch );
}

char *char_to_binary( int ch )
{
  int   ctr;
  char *binary_string;
  int   bitstatus;

  binary_string = (char*) malloc( 9 * sizeof(char) );

  for( ctr = 0; ctr < 8; ctr++)
  {
     switch( ctr )
     {
       case 0:  bitstatus = ch & 128;
                break;
       case 1:  bitstatus = ch & 64;
                break;
       case 2:  bitstatus = ch & 32;
                break;
       case 3:  bitstatus = ch & 16;
                break;
       case 4:  bitstatus = ch & 8;
                break;
```

```
        case 5:  bitstatus = ch & 4;
                 break;
        case 6:  bitstatus = ch & 2;
                 break;
        case 7:  bitstatus = ch & 1;
                 break;
     }

     binary_string[ctr] = (bitstatus) ? '1' : '0';
  }

  binary_string[8] = 0;  /* Null Terminate */

  return( binary_string );
}
```

6. The following is a complete program.

```
/* Program:   Day06E06.c
 * Author:    Bradley L. Jones
 * Purpose:   convert the case of a letter.
 *=======================================================*/

#include <stdio.h>

unsigned char switch_case( unsigned char );

void main(void)
{
   unsigned char letter1 = 'c',
                 letter2 = 'Y',
                 converted1,
                 converted2;

   printf("\n\nThe first letter is %c", letter1);
   converted1 = switch_case(letter1);
   printf("\n\n%c is now %c", letter1, converted1);

   printf("\n\nThe second letter is %c", letter2);
   converted2 = switch_case(letter2);
```

```
        printf("\n\n%c is now %c", letter2, converted2);
    }


    unsigned char switch_case( unsigned char ch )
    {
        /* if lowercase, make uppercase */

        if( ch >= 97 && ch <= 122 )   /* is letter from a to z */
        {
            ch -= 32;           /* change number by subtracting 32 */
        }
        else
        {
            if( ch >= 65 && ch <= 90 )
            {
                ch += 32;           /* change number by adding 32 */
            }
        }

        return(ch);
    }
```

7. **BUG BUSTER:** The letter 'a' has a decimal value of 97 while the letter 'Z'
   has a value of 90. Since the conditional portion of the for statement is to
   print x while it is less than 'Z', nothing will ever print. The uppercase 'Z' is
   less than the lowercase 'a'. Either print only upper- or lowercase letters, or
   print from 'A' to 'z'. If you select to print from 'A' to 'z', then you will get a
   few extra characters printed.

Day 7 Answers

Following are answers to the quiz and exercises.

Quiz Answers

1. A library is a set of functions that have been grouped together. A library
   allows all of the functions to be grouped into a single file.

2. Many libraries will come with a compiler. Additional libraries can be created by you or others. In addition to your own libraries, you can purchase special purpose libraries.

3. The addition operator (+) is used in a manner similar to the following:

```
LIB +objfile
```

4. The subtraction operator (-) is used in a manner similar to the following:

```
LIB -objfile
```

5. You combine the subtraction and addition operators are used in a manner similar to the following:

```
LIB -+objfile
```

or you can do a subtraction followed by an addition:

```
LIB -objfile
```

```
LIB +objfile
```

6. You add a comma followed by the listfile name to the end of the Library command similar to the following:

```
LIB ,listfile.lst
```

7. You use the asterisk in the library command similar to the following:

```
LIB *objname
```

8. You combine the subtraction operator and the asterisk as follows:

```
LIB -*objname
```

or you can do the two operations separately:

```
LIB *objname
```

```
LIB -objname
```

9. How the file is included determines where the compiler looks for the include files. If double quotes are used, the compilers searches the current directory first. If <> brackets are used, then the Library directory is searched first.

10. Source (.C) files should not be included in libraries. Only object (.OBJ) files should be included.

Exercises Answers

Note: Answers may vary for different compilers. For the Microsoft compilers, the answers should end with a semicolon. For Borland's compilers, you will use TLIB instead of LIB.

1. To create the stated library, you would enter the following:

   ```
   LIB STATES +RI +IL +IN
   ```

   (LIB would be replaced by your library program)

2. ```
   LIB STATES ,LISTING.LST
   ```

   (LIB would be replaced by your library program)

3. ```
   LIB STATES +RI +IL +IN ,LISTING.LST
   ```

4. ```
   LIB STATES +KY.OBJ +FL.OBJ
   ```

5. ```
   LIB STATES -KY.OBJ
   ```

6. ```
   LIB STATES -+FL
   ```

7. ```
   LIB STATES *IL
   ```

8. Two listings are included here. First is UPPER.C which contains the edit. Second is a program that uses the upper edit.

   ```
   1:   /* Program:  upper.c
   2:    * Author:   Bradley L. Jones
   3:    * Purpose:  This is an edit to verify that a string
   4:    *           contains all uppercase alpha characters
   5:    *           (A to Z).
   6:    * Returns:  1 = all uppercase characters
   7:    *           0 = not all uppercase
   8:    *=========================================================*/
   9:
   10:  #include <stdio.h>
   11:
   12:  int is_upper_case( char *string)
   13:  {
   14:    int ctr;
   15:    int rv;
   16:
   ```

F

```
17:    for( ctr = 0; string[ctr] != 0; ctr++ )
18:    {
19:       if( string[ctr] < 'A' || string[ctr] > 'Z' )
20:       {
21:          return(0);
22:       }
23:    }
24:
25:    return(1);
26: }
27:
28:
29:
```

```
1:    /* Program:  eday0708.c
2:     * Author:   Bradley L. Jones
3:     * Purpose:  This is the main() for testing the upper edit.
4:     * Returns:  nothing
5:     *=========================================================*/
6:
7:    #include <stdio.h>
8:
9:    int is_upper_case( char *string );
10:
11: void main(void)
12: {
13:    int  rv1,
14:         rv2;
15:    char text1[10] = "BADtext",
16:         text2[10] = "GOODTEXT";
17:
18:    rv1 = is_upper_case(text1);
19:    rv2 = is_upper_case(text2);
20:
21:    printf("\n\nReturn value = %d for text 1, %s", rv1, text1);
22:    printf("\n\nReturn value = %d for text 2, %s", rv2, text2);
23: }
```

9. LIB EDITS +UPPER.OBJ

10. This is on your own!

11. This is on your own; however, your answer will be similar to Exercise 9's answer!

12. Although not covered in the chapter, compilers typically work from left to right. This means that all source files should be listed before the libraries are listed. By having `source2.obj` after the library, you could encounter problems.

Day 8 Answers

Following are answers to the quiz and exercises.

Quiz Answers

1. Basic Input/Output System

2. Two possible reasons follow. First, the BIOS functions do not require the use of an external driver such as ANSI.SYS. Secondly, the BIOS functions provide more functionality than the ANSI functions.

3. An assumption as to the location of the video information in memory has to be made when you access video memory directly. By using the BIOS functions, you go through BIOS to access the video. Because different systems may store the video memory at different locations, the BIOS functions are more portable.

4. An interrupt number is a number passed to BIOS via DOS that activates a certain function or type of function. Table 8.1 lists several of the types of functions implemented by different interrupts.

5. An interrupt function is a specific operation within an interrupt. An interrupt function is designated by a number just as interrupts are. In addition, interrupt functions are used in association with interrupts. Table 8.2 lists many of the interrupt functions available.

6. Some interrupt functions are broken down even further. These smaller breakdowns are subfunctions. Several subfunctions are listed in Table 8.2. For example, interrupt 16 (0x10h) function 15 (0x0Fh) has several subfunctions that work with the video colors.

7. Interrupt 0x33h functions manipulate the mouse.

8. It hides the mouse pointer.

F

9. It reboots the computer.

10. No. BIOS functions are only supported on IBM-compatible machines. In addition, older versions of DOS may not support all of the BIOS functions.

Exercises Answers

1. There is no answer to this exercise. You should end up with a library file that you can use in later chapters of this book. The header file that you create should look like the following:

```
1:  /* Program: TYAC.H
2:   * Authors: Bradley L. Jones
3:   *          Gregory L. Guntle
4:   * Purpose: Header file for TYAC library functions
5:   *=========================================================*/
6:
7:  #ifndef _TYAC_H_
8:  #define _TYAC_H_
9:
10: /* DOS and BIOS Interrupts */
11: #define BIOS_VIDEO       0x10
12:
13: /* BIOS function calls */
14: #define SET_VIDEO        0x00
15:
16: /*----------------------*
17:      Function Prototypes
18:  *----------------------*/
19:
20:      /* Gets the current date */
21: void current_date(int *, int *, int *);
22:
23:      /* Positions the cursor to row/col */
24: void cursor(int, int);
25:      /* Returns info about cursor */
26: void get_cursor(int *, int *, int *, int *, int *);
27:      /* Sets the size of the cursor */
28: void set_cursor_size(int, int);
29:
```

```
30:         /* clear the keyboard buffer */
31:    void kbwait( void );
32:         /* determine keyboard hit */
33:    int  keyhit( void );
34:
35:    #endif
```

2. The program requested is simply a specific version of the function presented in the answer for Exercise 3.

3. The following function enables you to scroll the screen up or down. When the screen scrolls up, the text appears to move down. When the screen scrolls down, the text appears to move up.

```
1:    /* Program: SCROLL.C
2:     * Author:  Bradley L. Jones
3:     *          Gregory L. Guntle
4:     * Purpose: Function to scroll the screen.
5:     *-------------------------------------------------------
6:     * Parameters:
7:     *          row, column    starting position on screen
8:     *                         (0,0)
9:     *          height, width  portion of screen to scroll
10:    *          nbr            number of rows to scroll
11:    *          direction      0x07 is up
12:    *                         0x08 is down
13:    *=======================================================*/
14:
15:    #include "tyac.h"
16:    #include <dos.h>
17:
18:    void scroll( int row,   int col,
19:                 int width, int height,
20:                 int nbr,   int direction)
21:    {
22:        union REGS irreg;
23:
24:        ireg.h.ah = direction;
25:        ireg.h.al = nbr;
26:        ireg.h.ch = row;
27:        ireg.h.cl = col;
```

F

```
28:      ireg.h.dh = row + height;
29:      ireg.h.dl = col + width;
30:      ireg.h.bh = 0;
31:
32:      int86( 0x10, &ireg, &ireg );
33:  }
```

4. The following is a program does not have much functionality. It simply shows the scrolling of the screen in action.

```
1:   /* Program: EXER0804.C
2:    * Author:   Bradley L. Jones
3:    *            Gregory L. Guntle
4:    * Purpose: Demonstrates the use of the  set_control_break()
5:    *            function.
6:    *=========================================================*/
7:
8:   #include "tyac.h"
9:   #include <stdio.h>
10:
11:  #define SCROLL_UP   0x07
12:
13:  void delay(void);
14:  void scroll( int row, int col, int width, int height, int nbr,
                     int direction);
15:
16:  int main(void)
17:  {
18:    int x;
19:
20:    printf( "\n\nStarting program..." );
21:
22:    for( x = 0; x < 10; x++ )
23:    {
24:      printf( "\rScrolling —>%d", x);
25:      delay();
26:      scroll( 0, 0, 80, 25, 2, SCROLL_UP );
27:    }
28:    return 0;
29:  }
```

```
30:
31:   void delay(void)
32:   {
33:       long x;
34:       for( x = 0; x < 1000000; x++ );
35:   }
```

5. See Day 7 if you need help adding the scroll() function to your library. You should also include defined constants in your TYAC.H header file to define SCROLL_UP and SCROLL_DOWN. Don't forget to include the prototype in TYAC.H also.

6. The int86() function is not used properly. You must pass the interrupt registers in and provide for the interrupt registers coming out. The following is how the int86() function should be called:

```
int86(0x21, &inregs, &outregs);
```

Day 9 Answers

Following are answers to the quiz and exercises.

Quiz Answers

1. Monochrome means single colored.

2. Text graphics are graphics created using the characters in a character set such as the ASCII character set.

3. The ASCII characters have numeric values from 0 to 255.

4. The extended ASCII characters are those from 128 to 255.

5. When you change a library function, you must remember to update the library. In addition, you should update any information in header files.

6. If you change a header file, you may need to recompile all the functions and programs that use that header file because the change may affect them too.

7. There are several reasons to use defined constants. The reason presented today was readability.

8. Foreground colors are black, blue, green, cyan, red, magenta, brown, white, gray (light black), light blue, light green, light cyan, light red, light magenta, yellow (light brown), and bright white.

Background colors are black, blue, green, cyan, red, magenta, brown, and white.

Exercises Answers

1. There is no answer to this exercise. You should end up with a library file that you can use in later chapters of this book.

2. See the answer for Exercise 3.

3. The following is one possible answer. The mode is captured, information is displayed, and the program pauses. Once the user presses enter, the mode is changed to 40 columns and the new mode information is displayed. Again the program pauses until the user presses enter. When the user presses enter again, the program resets the mode to its original value.

```
1:   /* Program: EXER0903.c
2:    * Author:  Bradley L. Jones
3:    *          Gregory L. Guntle
4:    * Purpose: Demonstrates the use of the set_video() and
5:    *          get_video() functions.
6:    *=======================================================*/
7:
8:   #include <stdio.h>
9:   #include "tyac.h"
10:
11:  int main(void)
12:  {
13:      int cols, vpage, mode, orig_mode;
14:      char ch;
15:
16:      printf("\n\nGetting video information...");
17:
18:      get_video( &cols, &mode, &vpage );
19:
20:      printf("\n\n   columns = %d", cols );
21:      printf("\n   mode    = %d", mode  );
22:      printf("\n   page    = %d", vpage );
23:
24:      orig_mode = mode;
25:
26:      printf("\n\nPress enter to continue...");
```

```
27:        ch = getchar();
28:
29:        set_video( 1 );
30:
31:        get_video( &cols, &mode, &vpage );
32:
33:        printf("\n\n   columns = %d", cols );
34:        printf("\n   mode    = %d", mode   );
35:        printf("\n   page    = %d", vpage  );
36:
37:        printf("\n\nPress enter to continue...");
38:        ch = getchar();
39:
40:        set_video( orig_mode );
41:
42:        return 0;
43:    }
```

4. This character is a medium grade grid character. It provides a grid on the screen in the different colors.

Day 10 Answers

Following are answers to the quiz and exercises.

Quiz Answers

1. The purpose of `getline()` is to replace `scanf()` on allowing data to be input.

2. `boop()` causes the speaker to beep for a second.

3. `boop()` will enable you to signal when the user makes an error. By having the computer beep, it provides a signal to the user that there is a problem.

4. `pause()` requires the user to press a key, `waitsec()` does not. In addition, `waitsec()` enables you to specify how long you want to pause.

5. The input text color is set by using option 1. To set yellow on red, you use `getline()` as in the following:

```
getline(1, YELLOW, RED, LIGHTYELLOW, RED, 0)
```

This also sets the highlight color to bright yellow on red.

6. The default colors for `getline()` are as follows:

   normal color is WHITE on BLACK

   highlight color is BRIGHTWHITE on BLACK

   underline color is GREEN on BLACK

   "INS" message is YELLOW on BLACK

Exercises Answers

1. There is not an answer to this exercise.

2. The exit keys have not been set up for `getline()`. You should always ensure that you set up the exit keys so that `getline()` knows which keys will exit. Following is a corrected listing:

```
#include <stdio.h>
#include "tyac.h"

int main()
{
    char ch;
    char strng[40];
    char exit_keys[] = {ESC_KEY, TAB, CR_KEY};

    ch = getline(0,0,0,0,0,0,0);
    ch = getline(8,0,40,0,0,0,strng);
    ch = getline(9,0,4,0,0,0,exit_keys);

    write_string("Last name:", LIGHTBLUE, BLACK, 10, 8 );
    ch = getline(6,0,10,20,0,20,strng);  /* Get line */

    return 0;
}
```

3. A single answer is provided in Exercise 4.

4. The following is one of many possible answers for Exercises 3 and 4:

```
/* Program:  EXER1003.c
 * Author:   Bradley L. Jones
 *           Gregory L. Guntle
```

```
 * Purpose:  Exercise to create a function to get yes/no.
 *=========================================================*/

#include <stdio.h>
#include "tyac.h"

int main()
{
    char ch;
    char answer[2];
    int i;
    int done = FALSE;

    char exit_keys[] = {ESC_KEY, F1, CR_KEY};

    /* set up getline() for program's use */
    ch = getline(0,0,0,0,0,0,0);
    ch = getline(1,0,YELLOW,RED,BRIGHTWHITE, RED,0);
    ch = getline(2,0,YELLOW,RED,BRIGHTWHITE, RED,0);
    ch = getline(9,0,4,0,0,0,exit_keys);

    /* clear field */
    ch = getline(8,0,2,0,0,0,answer);

    /* draw message and box */

    while( done == FALSE )
    {
       box( 10, 14, 25, 58, SINGLE_BOX, CLR_INS, YELLOW, RED );
       write_string("Enter (Y)es or (N)o:", YELLOW, RED, 12, 30 );

       ch = getline(6,0,12,52,0,1,answer);

       if( answer[0] == 'Y' || answer[0] == 'N' ||
           answer[0] == 'y' || answer[0] == 'n' ||
           ch == ESC_KEY || ch == F1)
       {
          done = TRUE;
       }
```

F

```
            else
            {
               boop();
            }

        }

        write_string( "You entered " , BRIGHTWHITE, BLACK, 20, 1 );
        write_string( answer, BRIGHTWHITE, BLACK, 20, 13 );

        return 0;
    }
```

5. This exercise is on your own; however, Day 13 presents a solution.

Day 11 Answers

Following are answers to the quiz and exercises.

Quiz Answers

1. There are times when you don't want the cursor displayed on the screen. If a menu is currently being used, or if you are waiting for the user to press any key before continuing, then the cursor is not needed. If you are doing data entry, then the cursor is needed.

2. If you call cursor_off() and then exit your program, your cursor may remain off. You should always turn the cursor back on if you turned it off.

3. Not all compilers provide a clear screen function.

4. Many compilers do not have a function to clear the screen. Borland provides the clrscr() function; however, this function does not give you control over the color that the screen is cleared to.

5. There are three different grid patters in the ASCII table. There are several other graphics characters that could be used, but they aren't grids. Included in the additional characters is a solid block.

6. The ASCII values of the grid characters are 176, 177, and 178. You can see them in Appendix B.

7. The benefit of saving the screen is that you can easily restore it. If you don't save the screen, then you have to attempt to redraw it.

8. Nothing will happen if you don't restore a saved screen; however, you should make sure that you do free the space allocated to hold the screen information.

9. The row and column information is saved so that the restore function doesn't need to know where the saved screen area goes.

10. Two bytes are allocated for each screen position. One is for the actual character that is displayed. The other is for the attributes such as the color.

Exercises Answers

1. There is no answer to this exercise. The following are additions to the TYAC.H header file:

```
#define READ_CHAR_ATTR    0x08

#define SCREEN_ROW    80*2

    /* Hide/show cursor */
void cursor_off(void);
void cursor_on(void);
    /*clear screen */
void clear_screen(int, int);
    /* grid */
void grid(int, int, int, int, int, int, int);
char *save_screen_area(int, int, int, int);
void restore_screen_area( char * );
```

2a. The cursor remains off even when you exit the program.

2b. The cursor remains on when the box is displayed. It should look out of place.

2c. The result of commenting both lines out is equivalent to never turning it off. The cursor remains on when the box is displayed.

3. Following is just one of many possible answers:

```
1:    /* Program:  EXER1103.c
2:     * Author:   Bradley L. Jones
```

```
3:    *            Gregory L. Guntle
4:    * Purpose:  Use the screen saving/restoring functions.
5:    *=========================================================*/
6:
7:    #include <stdio.h>
8:    #include "tyac.h"
9:
10:   int main()
11:   {
12:       char c;
13:       char *screen_buffer;
14:
15:       grid(4,10,3,20,RED,GREEN,1);
16:       write_string("This is a test", LIGHTBLUE, GREEN, 10,20);
17:       write_string("<=  Saving this square area.",
18:                       WHITE, BLACK, 7, 40);
19:       screen_buffer = save_screen_area(4,10,3,20);
20:       write_string("Area has been saved", WHITE, BLACK, 15, 1);
21:       write_string("Press any key to continue",
22:                       WHITE, BLACK,16,1);
23:       c = getch();
24:       clrscr();
25:       grid(10,20,20,40,WHITE, BLUE,2);
26:       grid(15,20,15,25,BRIGHTWHITE,CYAN,3);
27:       printf("\nPress any key to restore screen\n");
28:       c = getch();
29:       restore_screen_area(screen_buffer);
30:       return 0;
31:   }
```

4. If you keep calling save_screen_area() without freeing the screen, then you
    will eventually run out of allocatable memory. At this point the program will
    either end, or your computer will lock up.

Warning: The following program may lock up your computer. This is to
illustrate a point. If it does, just turn your computer off and then back on.

```
1:   /* Program:   EXER1104.c
2:    * Author:    Bradley L. Jones
3:    *            Gregory L. Guntle
4:    * Purpose:   Use the screen save function without restoring.
5:    *
6:    * NOTE:      THIS IS A BAAAAD Program.  It may lock up your
7:    *            computer!  It illustrates what can happen if
8:    *            you don't free or restore your saved screens.
9:    *=========================================================*/
10:
11:  #include <stdio.h>
12:  #include "tyac.h"
13:
14:  void save_screen( void );
15:
16:  int main()
17:  {
18:      char msg[50];
19:      long ctr = 1;
20:
21:      clear_screen( YELLOW, BLUE );
22:
23:      while ( ctr < 1000000 )
24:      {
25:        sprintf( msg, "Saving counter: %ld", ctr );
26:
27:        grid( 11, 13, 28, 54, BLACK, RED, 2);
28:        box( 11, 13, 28, 54, DOUBLE_BOX, FILL_BOX, YELLOW, RED );
29:
30:        write_string(msg, YELLOW, RED, 12, 30);
31:        ctr++;
32:      }
33:
34:      return 0;
35:  }
36:
37:
38:
```

F

```
39:   void save_screen(void)
40:   {
41:       char *screen_buffer;
42:
43:       screen_buffer = save_screen_area( 0, 24, 0, 79 );
44:       /* nothing done with buffer.... */
45:       return;
46:   }
```

5. This exercise is on your own; however, similar functions will be presented on later days.

Day 12 Answers

Following are answers to the quiz and exercises.

Quiz Answers

1. A methodology is a set of procedures that are followed to accomplish a task.

2. Scope is the business rules and objectives that constrain a system. The scope of a project is what limits its size.

3. A prototype is a mock-up of what a screen or report will look like.

4. Yes! Even if you make up your own, the idea is to thoroughly think through a system before you start coding it.

5. You should always follow a methodology. The only time to not follow one is when a program is so small and so straightforward that it doesn't require one. Even then, you generally will think through all the steps.

Exercises Answers

There are no exercise answers for today.

Day 13 Answers

Following are answers to the quiz and exercises.

Quiz Answers

1. Today's chapter lists several different advantages. These include:

   ☐ Lower learning curve for people using the application.

   ☐ Higher comfort level for users in regard to the application.

   ☐ Consistency among your applications.

   ☐ Reduced cost in developing.

   ☐ Increased productivity for you.

2. The F1 function key should provide help information.

3. The F3 function key should exit the program.

4. The F5 function key is available for your use.

5. A well-designed application will only use this combination of colors (yellow on red) when an error has occurred.

6. False, a beep should be used consistently throughout your application. Generally, a beep is used when the user's attention is needed such as when there is an error.

7. An easy approach to creating your own entry and edit screen is to start with an existing screen and then modify it to your purposes.

Exercises Answers

1. The following is one possible solution. This solution requires that you also include the STDLIB.H header file. This code replaced the case 1 that was in the group file.

```
case 1 :
    strncpy( tmp, groups.date_formed.month, 2 );

    while( valid == FALSE )
    {
      rv = getline( GET_NUM, 0,  6, 17, 0,  2, tmp );

      if( rv == ESC_KEY |¦ rv == F3 |¦ rv == F1 )
      {
```

```
      valid = TRUE;   /* exit loop */
   }
   else
   {
      tmp_nbr = atoi(tmp);
      if( tmp_nbr < 0 || tmp_nbr > 12 )
      {
         /* bad month */
         display_msg_box("Month must be from 1 to 12",
                         ct.err_fcol, ct.err_bcol );
      }
      else
      {
         valid = TRUE;
      }
   }
   zero_fill_field(tmp, 2);
   write_string(tmp, ct.fld_fcol, ct.fld_bcol, 6, 17);
}

strncpy( groups.date_formed.month, tmp, 2);
break;
```

2. This exercise is on your own.

3. This exercise is on your own. You should do this exercise because it will be referenced in future days' exercises.

Day 14 Answers

Following are answers to the quiz and exercises.

Quiz Answers

1. Mnemonic characters are used in menus to allow for quick selection of a specific menu item.

2. The color table will be used in a lot of different programs and functions.

3. The Home key moves the highlight to the first menu option.

4. Unless set up as an exit key, the Page Up and Page Down keys have no effect in a menu.

5. If no box and no shadow is placed on a menu, a menu can be as many lines long as there are rows on the screen.

6. Possible mnemonic values would be 5 and E. You may want to consider X instead of E. Many programs use X for exit.

Exercises Answers

Only Exercise 3 has an answer. One possible answer is as follows:

```
 1:    /* Program:   EXER1403.c
 2:     * Author:    Bradley L. Jones
 3:     *            Gregory L. Guntle
 4:     *=========================================================*/
 5:
 6:    #include <stdio.h>
 7:    #include "tyac.h"
 8:    #include "colortbl.h"
 9:
10:    char *main_menu[10] = {
11:                " 1. RED    ", "1Rr",
12:                " 2. YELLOW ", "2Yy",
13:                " 3. BLUE   ", "3Bb",
14:                " 4. GREEN  ", "4Gg",
15:                " 5. Exit   ", "5Ee"  };
16:
17:    char MENU_EXIT_KEYS[MAX_KEYS] = {F3, ESC_KEY};
18:
19:    struct color_table ct;
20:
21:    void initialize_color_table(void);
22:
23:    int main()
24:    {
25:       int rv;
26:       int menu_sel=0;
27:
28:       initialize_color_table();
29:       clear_screen( ct.bg_fcol, ct.bg_bcol );
30:
31:       rv = display_menu(10, 30, DOUBLE_BOX, main_menu, 10,
32:                         MENU_EXIT_KEYS, &menu_sel, NO_LR_ARROW,
```

F

```
33:                        SHADOW);
34:
35:      cursor_on();
36:      return(0);
37:  }
38:
39:  /*----------------------------------------------------------*
40:   * initialize_color_table()                                *
41:   *                                                         *
42:   * Set up global color table for rest of application       *
43:   *----------------------------------------------------------*/
44:
45:  void initialize_color_table( void )
46:  {
47:      ct.bg_fcol = YELLOW;
48:      ct.bg_bcol = BLUE;
49:
50:      ct.fld_prmpt_fcol = CYAN;
51:      ct.fld_prmpt_bcol = BLUE;
52:
53:      ct.fld_fcol = BRIGHTWHITE;
54:      ct.fld_bcol = BLUE;
55:
56:      ct.fld_high_fcol = YELLOW;
57:      ct.fld_high_bcol = BLUE;
58:
59:      ct.ttl_fcol = BRIGHTWHITE;
60:      ct.ttl_bcol = BLACK;
61:
62:      ct.abar_fcol = BLACK;
63:      ct.abar_bcol = WHITE;
64:
65:      ct.menu_fcol = BLACK;
66:      ct.menu_bcol = WHITE;
67:
68:      ct.menu_high_fcol = BLUE;
69:      ct.menu_high_bcol = CYAN;
70:
71:      ct.err_fcol = YELLOW;
72:      ct.err_bcol = RED;
73:
74:      ct.db_fcol = WHITE;
75:      ct.db_bcol = BROWN;
76:
77:      ct.help_fcol = YELLOW;
78:      ct.help_bcol = GREEN;
79:
80:      ct.shdw_fcol = BLACK;
81:  }
```

Day 15 Answers

Following are answers to the quiz and exercises.

Quiz Answers

1. Action bars are menus containing options for various actions that your program can perform.

2. File, Edit, View, Options, and Help.

3. The File option should be used for actions that apply to an entire file.

4. The Edit option contains actions that modify the current information that is being presented.

5. The View action bar item contains selections that enable you to look in different ways at information from the current file.

6. The Options action bar item is used to present selection items that customize the user interface.

7. The Help option contains actions that are informational.

8. Yes, every action bar should contain Help.

9. The left and right arrows should move from one menu to the next, going either left or right depending on which arrow key is used. If the edge of the action bar is reached, then the arrow should scroll to the other end.

10. The options on an action bar are presented in menus; however, each option provides for a different action that can occur. The name comes from the fact that the options are for different actions.

Exercises Answers

1. Exercises 1 and 3 are for you to do on your own.

2. Following is a listing for the Group Information screens action bar. This listing, GRPSABAR.C, provides the same functionality as Listing 15.3. You'll also need to make the appropriate changes to GROUPS.C to call the action bar. These changes, listed in today's material, included adding the action bar when you draw the screen, setting up F10 as an exit key in getline(), and creating an F10 case for when F10 is pressed.

Following is GRPSABAR.C:

```
1:   /*===========================================================
2:    * Filename: grpsabar.c
3:    *           RECORD OF RECORDS - Version 1.0
4:    *
5:    * Author:   Bradley L. Jones
6:    *
7:    * Purpose:  Action bar for groups screen.  This will
8:    *           contain multiple menus. The functions called
9:    *           by the menu selections may not be available
10:   *           until later days.
11:   *
12:   * Return:   Return value is either key used to exit a menu
13:   *           with the exception of F10 which is returned
14:   *           as Enter to re-display main menu.  In each menu
15:   *           the left and right keys will exit and move
16:   *           control to the right or left menu.
17:   *===========================================================*/
18:
19:
20:  #include <stdio.h>
21:
22:  #include "tyac.h"
23:  #include "records.h"
24:
25:
26:  /*--------------------*
27:   *     prototypes     *
28:   *--------------------*/
29:
30:  #include "recofrec.h"
31:
32:  int do_groups_menu1( void );
33:  int do_groups_menu2( void );
34:  int do_groups_menu3( void );
35:  int do_groups_menu4( void );
36:
37:  static void do_something( char * );
38:
39:  /*--------------------------*
40:   *  groups screen action bar  *
41:   *--------------------------*/
42:
43:  int do_groups_actionbar( void )
44:  {
45:     int  menu  = 1;
46:     int  cont  = TRUE;
47:     int  rv    = 0;
48:     char *abar_text ={" File   Edit   Search   Help "};
49:
```

```
50:
51:      while( cont == TRUE )
52:      {
53:          write_string(abar_text, ct.abar_fcol, ct.abar_bcol, 1, 2);
54:
55:          switch( menu )
56:          {
57:
58:              case 1:   /* file menu */
59:                        write_string( " File ", ct.menu_high_fcol,
60:                            ct.menu_high_bcol, 1, 2);
61:
62:                        rv = do_groups_menu1();
63:                        break;
64:
65:              case 2:   /* edit menu */
66:                        write_string( " Edit ", ct.menu_high_fcol,
67:                            ct.menu_high_bcol, 1, 9);
68:
69:                        rv = do_groups_menu2();
70:                        break;
71:
72:              case 3:   /* search menu */
73:                        write_string( " Search ", ct.menu_high_fcol,
74:                            ct.menu_high_bcol, 1, 16);
75:
76:                        rv = do_groups_menu3();
77:                        break;
78:
79:              case 4:   /* Help menu */
80:                        write_string( " Help ", ct.menu_high_fcol,
81:                            ct.menu_high_bcol, 1, 25);
82:
83:                        rv = do_groups_menu4();
84:                        break;
85:
86:          default: /* error */
87:                        cont = FALSE;
88:                        break;
89:          }
90:
91:          switch( rv )
92:          {
93:              case LT_ARROW:  menu--;
94:                              if( menu < 1 )
95:                                  menu = 4;
96:                              break;
97:
98:              case RT_ARROW:  menu++;
99:                              if( menu > 4 )
100:                                 menu = 1;
```

```
101:                          break;
102:
103:        default:          cont = FALSE;
104:                          break;
105:      }
106:   }
107:   write_string(abar_text, ct.abar_fcol, ct.abar_bcol, 1, 2);
108:   cursor_on();
109:   return(rv);
110: }
111:
112:
113:
114: /*--------------------*
115:  *  do_menu 1  (File) *
116:  *--------------------*/
117:
118: int do_groups_menu1( void )
119: {
120:    int    rv       = 0;
121:    int    menu_sel = 0;
122:    char  *saved_screen = NULL;
123:
124:    char *file_menu[2] = { " Exit  <F3> ", "1Ee" };
125:    char  exit_keys[MAX_KEYS] = {F3, F10, ESC_KEY};
126:
127:    saved_screen = save_screen_area( 0, 10, 0, 40 );
128:
129:    rv = display_menu( 3, 4, SINGLE_BOX, file_menu, 2,
130:                       exit_keys, &menu_sel, LR_ARROW, SHADOW);
131:
132:    switch( rv )
133:    {
134:       case ENTER_KEY: /* accept selection */
135:       case CR:
136:                       rv = F3;
137:                       break;
138:
139:       case F3:        /* exiting */
140:       case ESC_KEY:
141:       case LT_ARROW:  /* arrow keys */
142:       case RT_ARROW:
143:                       break;
144:
145:       case F10:       /* exit action bar */
146:                       rv = ENTER_KEY;
147:                       break;
148:
149:       default:        boop();
150:                       break;
151:    }
```

```
152:     restore_screen_area( saved_screen );
153:
154:     return(rv);
155: }
156:
157: /*--------------------*
158:  *  do_menu 2  (Edit) *
159:  *--------------------*/
160:
161: int do_groups_menu2( void )
162: {
163:     int    rv       = 0;
164:     int    menu_sel = 0;
165:     char *saved_screen = NULL;
166:
167:     char *edit_menu[8] = {
168:             " New           ", "1Nn",
169:             " Add      <F4> ", "2Aa",
170:             " Change   <F5> ", "3Cc",
171:             " Delete   <F6> ", "4Dd" };
172:
173:     char exit_keys[MAX_KEYS] = {F3, F10, ESC_KEY};
174:
175:     saved_screen = save_screen_area( 1, 10, 8, 40 );
176:
177:     rv = display_menu( 3, 11, SINGLE_BOX, edit_menu, 8,
178:                        exit_keys, &menu_sel, LR_ARROW, SHADOW);
179:
180:     switch( rv )
181:     {
182:         case ENTER_KEY: /* accept selection */
183:         case CR:
184:                         switch( menu_sel )
185:                         {
186:                             case 1:  /* Clear the screen */
187:                                      do_something( "CLEARING..." );
188:                                      break;
189:
190:
191:                             case 2:  /* Add a record */
192:                                      do_something( "Adding..." );
193:
194:                                      break;
195:
196:                             case 3:  /* Update the current record */
197:                                      do_something( "Updating..." );
198:
199:                                      break;
200:
201:                             case 4:  /* Deleting the current record */
202:                                      do_something( "Deleting..." );
```

F

```
203:
204:                               break;
205:
206:                     default: /* continue looping */
207:                               boop();
208:                               break;
209:                   }
210:
211:                   rv = ENTER_KEY;
212:                   break;
213:
214:      case F3:         /* exiting */
215:      case ESC_KEY:
216:      case LT_ARROW:   /* arrow keys */
217:      case RT_ARROW:
218:                   break;
219:
220:      case F10:        /* action bar */
221:                   rv = ENTER_KEY;
222:                   break;
223:
224:      default:         boop();
225:                   break;
226:    }
227:    restore_screen_area( saved_screen );
228:
229:    return(rv);
230: }
231:
232: /*---------------------*
233:  * do menu 3  (Search) *
234:  *---------------------*/
235:
236: int do_groups_menu3( void )
237: {
238:    int    rv        = 0;
239:    int    menu_sel = 0;
240:    char *saved_screen = NULL;
241:
242:    char *search_menu[6] = {
243:            " Find...          ", "1Ff",
244:            " Next       <F7> ", "2Nn",
245:            " Previous   <F8> ", "3Pp" };
246:
247:    char exit_keys[MAX_KEYS] = {F3, F10, ESC_KEY};
248:
249:    saved_screen = save_screen_area( 1, 10, 0, 60 );
250:
251:    rv = display_menu( 3, 18, SINGLE_BOX, search_menu, 6,
252:                       exit_keys, &menu_sel, LR_ARROW, SHADOW);
253:
```

```
254:    switch( rv )
255:    {
256:        case ENTER_KEY: /* accept selection */
257:        case CR:
258:                        switch( menu_sel )
259:                        {
260:                            case 1:   /* Do find dialog */
261:                                    do_something( "Find..." );
262:
263:                                    break;
264:
265:                            case 2:   /* Next Record */
266:                                    do_something( "Next..." );
267:
268:                                    break;
269:
270:                            case 3:   /* Previous Record */
271:                                    do_something( "Previous..." );
272:
273:                                    break;
274:
275:                            default: /* shouldn't happen */
276:                                    boop();
277:                                    break;
278:                        }
279:
280:                        rv = ENTER_KEY;
281:                        break;
282:
283:        case F3:        /* exiting */
284:        case ESC_KEY:
285:        case LT_ARROW: /* arrow keys */
286:        case RT_ARROW:
287:                        break;
288:
289:        case F10:       /* action bar */
290:                        rv = ENTER_KEY;
291:                        break;
292:
293:        default:        boop();
294:                        break;
295:    }
296:    restore_screen_area( saved_screen );
297:
298:    return(rv);
299: }
300:
301: /*--------------------*
302:  *  do menu 4  (Help) *
303:  *--------------------*/
304:
```

```
305: int do_groups_menu4( void )
306: {
307:    int    rv        = 0;
308:    int    menu_sel = 0;
309:    char *saved_screen = NULL;
310:
311:    char *help_menu[4] = {
312:            " Help   <F2> ", "1Hh",
313:            " About        ", "2Ee" };
314:
315:    char exit_keys[MAX_KEYS] = {F3, F10, ESC_KEY};
316:
317:    saved_screen = save_screen_area( 1, 10, 0, 60 );
318:
319:    rv = display_menu( 3, 27, SINGLE_BOX, help_menu, 4,
320:                        exit_keys, &menu_sel, LR_ARROW, SHADOW);
321:
322:    switch( rv )
323:    {
324:       case ENTER_KEY: /* accept selection */
325:       case CR:
326:                       switch( menu_sel )
327:                       {
328:                          case 1:  /* Extended Help */
329:                                  display_groups_help();
330:
331:                                  break;
332:
333:                          case 2:  /* About box */
334:                                  do_something( "About box..." );
335:
336:                                  break;
337:
338:                          default: /* continue looping */
339:                                  boop();
340:                                  break;
341:                       }
342:
343:                       break;
344:
345:       case F3:        /* exiting */
346:       case ESC_KEY:
347:       case LT_ARROW:  /* arrow keys */
348:       case RT_ARROW:
349:                       break;
350:
351:       case F10:       /* action bar */
352:                       rv = ENTER_KEY;
353:                       break;
354:
355:       default:        boop();
```

```
356:                    break;
357:    }
358:    restore_screen_area( saved_screen );
359:
360:    return(rv);
361: }
362:
363:
364: /*-------------------------------------------------------*
365:  *    Generic function - temporary                      *
366:  *-------------------------------------------------------*/
367: static void do_something(char *msg)
368: {
369:    display_msg_box( msg, ct.help_fcol, ct.help_bcol );
370: }
```

Day 16 Answers

Following are answers to the quiz and exercises.

Quiz Answers

1. If an application requires no explanation, then help isn't necessary. It's doubtful that an application is simple enough that help is not needed.

2. There are several types of help:

   ☐ Startup help

   ☐ General help

   ☐ Help for help

   ☐ Extended help

   ☐ Help for keys

   ☐ Help index

   ☐ About... help

   ☐ Context-sensitive help

3. No, tutorials aren't considered help. They provide the user help in using an application.

4. Startup help should be used by applications that require command line parameters or applications that don't have any screens to present to the user.

F

5. If only extended help is being provided, then F1 should be used.

6. Context-sensitive help should always be assigned to F1. This means that extended help should be assigned to F2.

Exercises Answers

All of today's exercises are on your own. You should refer to today's listings.

Day 17 Answers

Following are answers to the quiz and exercises.

Quiz Answers

1. Many programmers use the term I/O to stand for any action that results in information flowing into or out of a computer program. Input is information flowing in; output is information flowing out.

2. A field is an individual piece of data.

3. A record is a group of related fields.

4. A data file is a group of related records that are stored on a secondary medium such as a disk drive.

5. A database is a group of related data files.

6. An index file is a separate file from the data file. Because an index contains a smaller amount of information, more of it can be read and manipulated quicker than the data file itself. Using an index allows quick access to a large data file.

7. If you are using text mode, then several translations will occur automatically as you work with the data. A file opened in binary mode doesn't do the translations of a text mode file.

8. If a preexisting file is opened with "w+b", then it is being opened for reading and writing in binary mode. Because the "w+" was used, a preexisting file will be cleared. If "r+" had been used instead, then preexisting data would have been retained.

9.

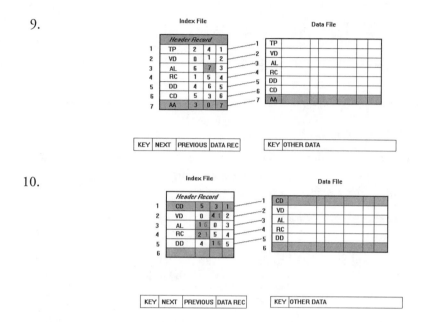

Index File

	Header Record			
1	TP	2	4	1
2	VD	0	1	2
3	AL	6	7	3
4	RC	1	5	4
5	DD	4	6	5
6	CD	5	3	6
7	AA	3	0	7

Data File

TP				
VD				
AL				
RC				
DD				
CD				
AA				

KEY	NEXT	PREVIOUS	DATA REC

KEY	OTHER DATA

10.

Index File

	Header Record			
1	CD	5	3	1
2	VD	0	4	2
3	AL	1	0	3
4	RC	2	5	4
5	DD	4	1	5
6				

Data File

CD				
VD				
AL				
RC				
DD				

KEY	NEXT	PREVIOUS	DATA REC

KEY	OTHER DATA

Exercises Answers

1. There isn't an answer to this exercise.

2. The Group files index should look like the following:

```
typedef struct
{
    char group[25+1];
    unsigned short prev;
    unsigned short next;
    unsigned short data;

} GROUP_INDEX;
```

3. The disk will contain the completed code for the groups entry and edit screen.

F

Day 18 Answers

Following are answers to the quiz and exercises.

Quiz Answers

1. `clear` and `find`...

2. The `clear` function clears the screen so that a new record can be entered. The `find`... function finds a corresponding record for the data in the key field on the screen.

3. You should always ask the users if they are sure they want to delete the record.

4. The delete flag is used to mark a record as deleted. This is used in place of physically deleting a record. It gives you the ability to include an undelete function.

5. On the medium code screen, the page up and page down functions place the cursor on the first or last field on the screen.

6. On the musical items screen, the page up and page down keys display the next or previous set of songs for the given musical item.

7. The code is shown with the capability to hold 13 pages of seven songs for a total of 91 songs. You could modify this to display as many songs as memory would permit.

Exercises Answers

1. There is not an answer to this exercise.

2. The following is one possible answer. This program needs to be linked with the TYAC.LIB library.

```
1:   /*==========================================================
2:    * Filename: DUMPIDX.c
3:    *
4:    * Author:    Bradley L. Jones
5:    *            Gregory L. Guntle
6:    *
7:    * Purpose:  Dump the index information for the album files
8:    *==========================================================*/
9:
10:  #include <stdio.h>
```

```
11:    #include <conio.h>              /* not an ANSI header, used for getch()
*/
12:    #include <string.h>             /* for strlen() */
13:    #include <ctype.h>
14:    #include "tyac.h"
15:    #include "records.h"
16:
17:    /*--------------------*
18:     *      prototypes    *
19:     *--------------------*/
20:    #include "recofrec.h"
21:
22:    /*--------------------*
23:     *   Global Variables *
24:     *--------------------*/
25:    FILE *idx_fp;                    /* Index File Ptr */
26:    FILE *db_fp;                     /* Data file */
27:    FILE *song_fp;                   /* For tracking songs */
28:    int  nbr_records;               /* Total # of recs */
29:    int  start_rec;                 /* Starting rec for alpha */
30:    int  disp_rec;
31:    int  total_songs;               /* Nbr of songs in the song file */
32:
33:    ALBUM_REC albums;
34:    ALBUM_REC *p_albums = &albums;
35:    ALBUM_INDEX alb_idx;
36:
37:    /*------------------------*
38:     * define global variables *
39:     *------------------------*/
40:
41:    #define ONE_SONG    sizeof(songs[0])
42:    #define SEVEN_SONGS sizeof(songs)
43:
44:    #define ALBUMS_DBF   "ALBUMS.DBF"
45:    #define ALBUMS_IDX   "ALBUMS.IDX"
46:
47:    /*========================================================*
48:     *                         main()                         *
49:     *========================================================*/
50:
51:    int main(void)
52:    {
53:       int rv       = 0;
54:       int srch_rec = 0;
55:
56:       /* Open both Index and DBF file */
57:       if ( (rv = open_files(ALBUMS_IDX, ALBUMS_DBF)) == 0 )
58:       {
59:         printf("Nbr records = %2d   Start_rec = %2d\n\n",
60:             nbr_records, start_rec);
```

```
61:        printf(" rv  sr  df  ns   p   n   d   s\n");
62:        printf(" --  --  --  --  --  --  --  --\n");
63:        srch_rec = start_rec;
64:        while (srch_rec !=0)
65:        {
66:          rv = get_rec(srch_rec, idx_fp, sizeof(alb_idx),
67:                    sizeof(int)*2, (char *)&alb_idx);
68:          printf(" %2d  %2d  %2d  %2d  %2d  %2d  %2d  %2d  %s\n",
69:                rv, srch_rec, alb_idx.del_flag, alb_idx.nbr_songs,
70:                alb_idx.prev, alb_idx.next, alb_idx.data,
71:                alb_idx.song, alb_idx.title);
72:          srch_rec = alb_idx.next;
73:        }
74:        rv = close_files();        /* Close IDX and DBF file */
75:    }
76:
77:    return 0;
78: }
79:
80: /*=========================================================*
81:  *                      end of listing                     *
82:  *=========================================================*/
```

Nbr records = 5   Start_rec = 2

Output

```
rv  sr  df  ns   p   n   d   s
--  --  --  --  --  --  --  --
 0   2   0  21   0   1   2  15   10,000 Maniacs: Unplugged
 0   1   0  14   2   4   1   1   Common Thread
 0   4   0   7   1   5   4  43   Violent Femmes
 0   5   0  14   4   0   5  50   White Wedding
```

Analysis

rv = return value

sr = search record

df = delete flag

ns = number of songs

p = previous song record

n = next song record

d = data file record

s = first song record

3. This exercise is on your own.

Day 19 Answers

Following are answers to the quiz and exercises.

Quiz Answers

1. By prototyping a report, you obtain an idea of what the report will look like. It is easier to change a prototype than it is to change code.

2. A list is a report that lists data from a file.

3. Lists are good for verifying that each database contains the information that you expect.

4. 9s are used on prototypes as placeholders for numbers. Where a 9 appears on a prototype, a number field will be.

5. Xs are used on prototypes as placeholders for alphanumeric characters. Where an X appears, an alphanumeric field will be.

6. So that you know when the report was printed. Data could have changed.

7. "Real" data on a prototype presents a view of what the report is really going to look like. Spacing appears different when Xs and 9s are used.

8. Many printers can write up to 60 lines on a page. Many people stop at 55 just to be safe.

9. The following would be printed for the names:

```
Foster , MaryB E.
Bell   , Mike J.
LiVenst, Angela  .
```

You would want to include instructions with the prototype (in a specification) that spaces should be suppressed. Additionally, the period following the middle initial should only be printed if a middle name exists.

Exercises Answers

1.

```
                        List of Albums
                          99/99/99


       Title                         Group
       ----------------------------  ------------------------
       XXXXXXXXXXXXXXXXXXXXXXXXXXXXX  XXXXXXXXXXXXXXXXXXXXXXXX
       XXXXXXXXXXXXXXXXXXXXXXXXXXXXX  XXXXXXXXXXXXXXXXXXXXXXXX
       XXXXXXXXXXXXXXXXXXXXXXXXXXXXX  XXXXXXXXXXXXXXXXXXXXXXXX
       Songs From the Big Chair      Tears for Fears
       Back in Black                 AC/DC
```

2. The following is the List of Musical Items Report based on the specification in Exercise 1.

```
 1:    /*===========================================================
 2:     * Filename: listalb.c
 3:     *
 4:     * Author:    Bradley L. Jones
 5:     *            Gregory L. Guntle
 6:     *
 7:     * Purpose:  Lists the information in the albums DBF.
 8:     *
 9:     *=========================================================*/
10:
11:    #include <stdio.h>
12:    #include <string.h>
13:    #include "tyac.h"
14:    #include "records.h"
15:
16:    /*--------------------*
17:     *  Global Variables  *
18:     *--------------------*/
19:    extern FILE *idx_fp;        /* Main File ptr to data file */
20:    extern FILE *db_fp;         /* Data file */
21:    extern nbr_records;         /* Total # of rec for mediums */
22:    extern int start_rec;
23:    extern int disp_rec;
24:
25:    static int line_ctr;                /* Line ctr */
```

```
26:   static int page_ctr;              /* Page ctr */
27:
28:   /*------------------*
29:    * Defined constants*
30:    *------------------*/
31:   #define ALBUMS_IDX    "ALBUMS.IDX"
32:   #define ALBUMS_DBF    "ALBUMS.DBF"
33:
34:   /*----------------------*
35:    * structure declarations *
36:    *----------------------*/
37:   extern ALBUM_REC albums;
38:
39:   /*------------------*
40:    *  Prototypes      *
41:    *------------------*/
42:   #include "recofrec.h"
43:
44:   void print_alb_hdr(void);
45:   int  process_albums(void);
46:   void print_album(void);
47:
48:   void setup_date(void);
49:   extern char today[8];
50:
51:   /*=======================================================*
52:    *    list_albums()                                      *
53:    *=======================================================*/
54:
55:   int list_musical_items(void)
56:   {
57:     int rv=NO_ERROR;
58:
59:     /* Open both Index and DBF file */
60:     if ( (rv = open_files(ALBUMS_IDX, ALBUMS_DBF)) == 0 )
61:     {
62:        /* Are there any records to process ? */
63:        if (nbr_records == 0)
64:        {
```

F

```
65:          display_msg_box("No album records to process",
66:             ct.err_fcol, ct.err_bcol);
67:       }
68:     else
69:       {
70:       setup_today();
71:       print_alb_hdr();
72:       rv = process_albums();
73:       }               /* End ELSE - records to process */
74:
75:     rv = close_files();
76:   }                   /* End No Errors on Opening Files */
77:   return(rv);
78: }
79:
80: /*=======================================================*
81:  *    print_alb_hdr()                                    *
82:  *=======================================================*/
83: void print_alb_hdr()
84: {
85:   fprintf(stdprn,"\n\r\t\tList of Albums\n\r");
86:   fprintf(stdprn,"\t\t   %s\n\r\n\r", today);
87:
88:   fprintf(stdprn,"Title Group\n");
89:   fprintf(stdprn,"---------------------------");
90:   fprintf(stdprn,"        ----------------------\n\r");
91: }
92:
93: /*=======================================================*
94:  *    process_albums()                                   *
95:  *=======================================================*/
96: int process_albums()
97: {
98:   int rv = NO_ERROR;
99:   static int done = FALSE;
100:   static int srch_rec;
101:   static ALBUM_INDEX temp;
102:
```

```
103:    line_ctr = 0;
104:    page_ctr = 1;
105:
106:    srch_rec = start_rec;
107:    while (rv == NO_ERROR && !done)
108:    {
109:      /* Get INDEX */
110:      rv = get_rec(srch_rec, idx_fp, sizeof(temp),
111:          sizeof(int)*2, (char *)&temp);
112:      if (rv == NO_ERROR)
113:      {
114:        /* Get the data record */
115:        rv = get_rec(temp.data, db_fp, sizeof(albums),
116:              0, (char *)&albums);
117:        if (rv == NO_ERROR)
118:        {
119:          print_album();
120:          srch_rec = temp.next;
121:          /* Check for end of list */
122:          if (srch_rec == 0)
123:          {
124:              done = TRUE;
125:              fprintf(stdprn, "\f");
126:          }
127:          else
128:              done = FALSE;
129:        }         /* End of NO_ERROR - from DBF */
130:      }           /* End of NO_ERROR - from INDEX */
131:    }             /* End WHILE */
132:    return(rv);
133: }
134:
135: /*========================================================*
136:  *    print_album()                                      *
137:  *========================================================*/
138: void print_album()
139: {
140:    int i;
141:    char hold_date[8];
```

```
142:
143:    if (line_ctr+1 > 55)
144:    {
145:        fprintf(stdprn,"\f");      /* New page */
146:        print_alb_hdr();           /* Reprint header */
147:        line_ctr = 6;              /* for heading space */
148:        page_ctr++;
149:    }
150:    else
151:    {
152:        line_ctr++;
153:    }
154:
155:    fprintf(stdprn,"%-30s      %-25s\n\r",
156:                        albums.title, albums.group );
157: }
```

3. Exercise 3 is on your own.

4. Exercise 4 is on your own.

Day 20 Answers

Following are answers to the quiz and exercises.

Quiz Answers

1. Free-form testing does not have any written objectives or requirements. The objective is to "bang on the software and try to break it."

2. The four categories of testing are:

   a. unit testing

   b. integration testing

   c. alpha testing

   d. beta testing

3. In the same order mentioned in Answer 2.

4. When you are confident that the program is as accurate as it can be.

5. A mistake or error in a computer program.

6. Syntax errors are errors in the syntax or code that cause the compiler to have problems.

7. Syntax errors, logic errors, and recursive errors. Recursive errors are actually syntax and logic errors.

8. Removing bugs (errors or problems) from code.

9. A patch is a fix that is sent out because of an error in a program. A patch usually will not be charged for, nor should it cause the version number to change. An upgrade is a release of the software that incorporates patches, updates, and enhancements to the software. It is released with a new version number. In addition, an upgrade may have a fee associated with it.

10. A software package that is released to the public may never be complete. People will always have suggestions for updates and upgrades to the software.

Exercises Answers

All of today's exercises are on your own.

Day 21 Answers

Following are answers to the quiz and exercises.

Quiz Answers

1. No! There is always more to learn in any language.

2. There are several areas in which you can increase your C knowledge. These include graphics programming and advanced applications development. You can also increase your skills in more technical areas such as compiler development and network programming.

3. C++ and assembler.

4. There are several benefits to using assembler. Among them are speed, additional control, and the capability to write more compact programs.

5. An object-oriented language is identified by its capability to encapsulate, polymorph, and inherit.

6. No. C is a subset of C++. Not all C++ constructs are usable in C.

7. Yes. C++ is a superset of C. Everything that can be used in C can be used in C++; however, not everything that can be used in C should be used in C++.

8. The most commonly used platforms are DOS, UNIX, Windows, OS/2, and System 7 (Macintosh). There are C compilers for all of these.

Exercises Answers

All of today's exercises are on your own.

Index

Symbols

A

functions

Add to Your Sams Library Today with the Best Books for Programming, Operating Systems, and New Technologies

The easiest way to order is to pick up the phone and call

1-800-428-5331

between 9:00 a.m. and 5:00 p.m. EST.
For faster service please have your credit card available.

ISBN	Quantity	Description of Item	Unit Cost	Total Cost
0-672-30441-4		Borland C++ 4 Developer's Guide (Book/Disk)	$39.95	
0-672-30279-9		C++ Programming PowerPack (Book/Disk)	$24.95	
0-672-30177-6		Windows Programmer's Guide to Borland C++ Tools (Book/Disk)	$39.95	
0-672-30030-3		Windows Programmer's Guide to Serial Communications (Book/Disk)	$39.95	
0-672-30097-4		Windows Programmer's Guide to Resources (Book/Disk)	$34.95	
0-672-30226-8		Windows Programmer's Guide to OLE/DDE (Book/Disk)	$34.95	
0-672-30364-7		Win32 API Desktop Reference (Book/CD)	$49.95	
0-672-30236-5		Windows Programmer's Guide to DLLs and Memory Management (Book/Disk)	$34.95	
0-672-30295-0		Moving Into Windows NT Programming (Book/Disk)	$39.95	
0-672-30338-8		Inside Windows File Formats (Book/Disk)	$29.95	
0-672-30299-3		Uncharted Windows Programming (Book/Disk)	$34.95	
0-672-30239-X		Window Developer's Guide to Application Design (Book/Disk)	$34.95	
❏ 3 ½" Disk		Shipping and Handling: See information below.		
❏ 5 ¼" Disk		TOTAL		

Shipping and Handling: $4.00 for the first book, and $1.75 for each additional book. Floppy disk: add $1.75 for shipping and handling. If you need to have it NOW, we can ship product to you in 24 hours for an additional charge of approximately $18.00, and you will receive your item overnight or in two days. Overseas shipping and handling adds $2.00 per book and $8.00 for up to three disks. Prices subject to change. Call for availability and pricing information on latest editions.

201 W. 103rd Street, Indianapolis, Indiana 46290

1-800-428-5331 — Orders   1-800-835-3202 — FAX   1-800-858-7674 — Customer Service

Book ISBN 0-672-30471-6

GO AHEAD. PLUG YOURSELF INTO
PRENTICE HALL COMPUTER PUBLISHING.

Introducing the PHCP Forum on CompuServe®

Yes, it's true. Now, you can have CompuServe access to the same professional, friendly folks who have made computers easier for years. On the PHCP Forum, you'll find additional information on the topics covered by every PHCP imprint—including Que, Sams Publishing, New Riders Publishing, Alpha Books, Brady Books, Hayden Books, and Adobe Press. In addition, you'll be able to receive technical support and disk updates for the software produced by Que Software and Paramount Interactive, a division of the Paramount Technology Group. It's a great way to supplement the best information in the business.

WHAT CAN YOU DO ON THE PHCP FORUM?

Play an important role in the publishing process—and make our books better while you make your work easier:

- Leave messages and ask questions about PHCP books and software—you're guaranteed a response within 24 hours

- Download helpful tips and software to help you get the most out of your computer

- Contact authors of your favorite PHCP books through electronic mail

- Present your own book ideas

- Keep up to date on all the latest books available from each of PHCP's exciting imprints

JOIN NOW AND GET A FREE COMPUSERVE STARTER KIT!

To receive your free CompuServe Introductory Membership, call toll-free, **1-800-848-8199** and ask for representative **#597**. The Starter Kit Includes:

- Personal ID number and password

- $15 credit on the system

- Subscription to CompuServe Magazine

HERE'S HOW TO PLUG INTO PHCP:

Once on the CompuServe System, type any of these phrases to access the PHCP Forum:

GO PHCP	**GO BRADY**
GO QUEBOOKS	**GO HAYDEN**
GO SAMS	**GO QUESOFT**
GO NEWRIDERS	**GO PARAMOUNTINTER**
GO ALPHA	

Once you're on the CompuServe Information Service, be sure to take advantage of all of CompuServe's resources. CompuServe is home to more than 1,700 products and services—plus it has over 1.5 million members worldwide. You'll find valuable online reference materials, travel and investor services, electronic mail, weather updates, leisure-time games and hassle-free shopping (no jam-packed parking lots or crowded stores).

Seek out the hundreds of other forums that populate CompuServe. Covering diverse topics such as pet care, rock music, cooking, and political issues, you're sure to find others with the sames concerns as you—and expand your knowledge at the same time.

What's on the Disk

The disk contains the source code, applications, and support files for *Teach Yourself Advanced C in 21 Days*. The programs include the following:

☐ *Record of Records!*, a multifile database system that enables you to track your music collection, including tapes, records, CDs, and DATs. It also enables you to store information about the musical groups in your collection.

☐ **HEX**, a program that displays a file in hexidecimal and text side-by-side.

☐ **DECDUMP**, **HEXDUMP**, **OCTDUMP**, and **BINDUMP**, programs that type a file in decimal, hexidecimal, octal, and binary, respectively.

☐ **PRINTIT**, a program that prints a listing with line numbers to enable you to reference the numbered listings in the book.

☐ A compete C library, which includes functions that handle sound, graphics, character conversion, files, time, cursor manipulation, keyboard input, and much more.

Installing the Floppy Disk

The software included with this book is stored in a compressed form. You cannot use the software without first installing it to your hard drive. The installation program runs from within DOS.

> **NOTE:** To install the files on the disk, you'll need at least 2M of free space on your hard drive.

1. From a DOS prompt, change to the drive that contains the installation disk. For example, if the disk is in drive B:, press B: and press Enter.

2. Type INSTALL <*drive*> (where <*drive*> is the letter of your hard drive) and press Enter. The installation program will begin.

The files will be installed in the \TYAC directory arranged by day in subdirectories.